John L. Mackay's commentary on Jeremiah is a first class explanation of the prophet from a staunchly and well-argued conservative and grammatico-historical perspective. It is certain to become the first 'port of call' in my studies of the book. A thorough and helpful presentation of introductory issues (which includes some fine work on historical context) is followed by an excellent verse-by-verse explanation which does not lose sight of the broader literary canvas. While engaging helpfully and competently with the Hebrew text, the style and format is accessible to the non-specialist. Mackay does not look to major on contemporary application. However, in addition to the various hints offered he has the ability to uncover the significance of the original message in such a way as to leave the application (almost) transparent.

Stephen Dray

Minister, Ferndale Baptist Church, Southend-on-Sea, England

John L. Mackay's commentary on Jeremiah is trebly welcome. First, from his earlier work on Exodus in this series we know that he will take the highest view of Scripture as the Word of God, and do so as one fully conversant with the wide literature on Jeremiah. His workmanlike approach and marvellous attention to detail forbid him to take shortcuts, fudge issues, or misrepresent those who take a different view from his own.

Second, he argues cogently for Jeremiah as author of the whole, contending that the book as we have it represents written records contemporary with the prophet's preaching. He rejects the unsubstantiated idea of an ongoing 'school' of interpreters, adaptors and supplemetarists of a Jeremianic 'core'.

Thirdly, from the start he is unfolding a unified message. Lovers of Hebrew will find a kindred spirit in the author. Those without Hebrew will find a patient teacher leaving no stone unturned to make the Word of God plain.

Alec Motyer

Well known Bible expositor and commentary writer

Poyton, England

This eagerly awaited commentary on one of the longest and most taxing books of the Old Testament fulfills every expectation. Professor Mackay has already demonstrated his erudition and scholarship in previous commentaries, and this work is a landmark in Jeremiah studies as well as in conservative evangelical exposition of the Old Testament text. The message of Jeremiah's forty-year ministry is here firmly rooted in the Old Testament as a message from the Lord to his ancient people; but its abiding relevance is also brought out in Professor Mackay's careful application of the material. This will quickly become an indispensible tool for anyone wishing to study and preach from the Book of Jeremiah.

Iain D. Campbell

Minister, Point Free Church of Scotland, Isle of Lewis

This commentary is refreshing—it actually explains the text of Jeremiah. John L. Mackay knows the critical speculations about the text but doesn't bore us with them. He avoids nothing; he ploughs through every bit of the text and gives a lucid explanation of it. Mackay will not write your sermon for you but gives you what you need to write your sermon – a clear understanding of what the text says.

Dale Ralph Davis

Minister in Residence, First Presbyterian Church, Columbia, South Carolina

JEREMIAH

An Introduction and Commentary

Volume 1: Chapters 1–20

John L. Mackay

Jeremiah Volume 2: Chapters 21–52

ISBN 978-1-85792-938-6

ISBN 978-1-85792 937-9

Published in 2004, reprinted in 2015
in the Mentor imprint
by
Christian Focus Publications
Geanies House,
Fearn, Ross-shire, IV20 1TW, Scotland.

www.christianfocus.com

Cover design by Alister MacInnes

Printed and bound in Great Britain
by the CPI Group (UK Ltd), Croydon, CR0 4YY

CONTENTS
VOLUME 1

INTRODUCTION

COMMENTARY

VOLUME II

PREFACE

Adding another commentary on Jeremiah to the many which have appeared in recent years requires some measure of explanation. While I have frequently and gratefully availed myself of many insights that are to be found in the recent literature on Jeremiah, I have been perplexed by the comparative deficiency of works written from a conservative perspective. There seems to me to be two key components of such an approach. The first is that justice must be done to the prophet's claim that his message is not self-originated but divinely given. This is a subject which is shrouded in mystery, but it is an inadequate response to the claims of the text to pass over it in silence and, at best, treat the prophet as a man of considerable insight and perception who challenged his contemporaries to accept his reading of events during a very troubled period of their history. The second aspect of a conservative approach to the prophecy is surely to take seriously its further claim that the record we now possess originated with the prophet himself. Much contemporary analysis of Jeremiah assumes that the prophet is only indirectly responsible for the present text, and that there has been an assiduous band of later unidentified editors who have shaped, modified and even composed the material that is now presented to us under the name of Jeremiah. The willingness with which modern scholarship has posited the existence of such redactional activity has been a distorting prism which has skewed endeavours to interpret correctly the book as a whole. There can be no doubt that the text of Jeremiah is an edited representation of what the prophet said, but I have written this commentary on the basis that this editing has been done either by the prophet himself or under his direct supervision. If I may be permitted a New Testament analogy, in reading Jeremiah we are as close to the prophet himself as we are to Paul in reading his epistle to the Romans, no matter what role a Tertius played in writing down the letter (Rom. 16:21), or, in certain sections of the prophecy, to the Paul of Acts as portrayed by his friend and companion, Luke. It is the widespread unwillingness of modern scholarship to recognise the prophet as his own editor that has caused much confusion in biblical studies and has undermined confidence in the divine origin of the Scripture. This commentary is therefore presented as an attempt to elucidate the message of Jeremiah on the basis of a commitment to the inspiration and accuracy of the text.

The prophecy of Jeremiah is a book of considerable length, and it is consequently impossible to include within a convenient length all that might reasonably be said about it. The need to be selective is intensified by the vast amount of literature that has been produced in connection with Jeremiah over recent decades. I have written this commentary with a view to exposition and proclamation. There are indeed no ready-prepared sermons within this volume, but there is, I trust, much to stimulate and guide. Though the commentary employs the New International Version as its basic translation, I have in fact worked from the Massoretic Text and have included (generally in footnotes) remarks that may help those who study in the same way. I have not attempted to summarise modern specialist debate regarding Jeremiah. This is done very adequately elsewhere and, because the presuppositions employed are at variance with mine, the relevance of such studies is frequently marginal to the task I have set myself.

Lastly, a preface should include acknowledgment of those who have assisted in the preparation of this work. To do justice to that requirement would almost require a history of my life and so, to keep matters within reasonable bounds, I would simply mention two: the congregation of St. Columba's Free Church, Edinburgh, who during a vacancy some years ago heard an early version of much of the material that is now contained in this book and whose comments were greatly appreciated; and also my wife Mary, whose support and encouragement for this project were invaluable when my stamina and enthusiasm were flagging.

JOHN L. MACKAY,
FREE CHURCH COLLEGE,
EDINBURGH.

ABBREVIATIONS

ABD *Anchor Bible Dictionary.* D. N. Freedman (ed.). 6 volumes. New York: Doubleday, 1992.

ANET *Ancient Near Eastern Texts Relating to the Old Testament.* J. B. Pritchard (ed.) 3rd edition. Princeton: Princeton University Press, 1969.

AV Authorised Version (King James) (1611).

BDB F. Brown, S. R. Driver and C. A. Briggs (eds.), *A Hebrew and English Lexicon of the Old Testament.* Oxford: Clarendon Press, 1907.

BHS *Biblica Hebraica Stuttgartensia.* K. Elliger and W. Rudolph (eds.). Stuttgart: Deutsche Bibelstiftung, 1977.

GKC W. Gesenius, E. Kautzsch and A. E. Cowley, *Gesenius Hebrew Grammar.* Oxford: Clarendon Press, 1910 (second edition). (cited by section.)

GNB Good News Bible (= Today's English Version). Glasgow: Collins/Fontana, 1976.

HALOT *The Hebrew and Aramaic Lexicon of the Old Testament.* L. Koehler, W. Baumgartner and J. J. Stamm. 5 volumes. Brill: Leiden, 1994-1999. (cited by page.)

IBHS *An Introduction to Biblical Hebrew Syntax.* B. K. Waltke and M. O'Connor. Winona Lake, Indiana: Eisenbrauns, 1990. (cited by section.)

ISBE *International Standard Bible Encyclopedia.* G. W. Bromiley (ed.). 4 volumes. Grand Rapids: Eerdmans, 1979-1988.

Joüon Joüon, P. *A Grammar of Biblical Hebrew.* Translated and revised by T. Muraoka. Rome: Editrice Pontificio Istituto Biblico, 1991.

LXX Septuagint, according to *Septuaginta II*, ed. A. Rahlfs. Deutsche Bibelgesellschaft: Stuttgart, 1982.

MT Massoretic Text (as in *BHS* above).

NASB New American Standard Bible. LaHabra, California: The Lockman Foundation, 1995.

NIDOTTE *New International Dictionary of Old Testament Theology and Exegesis.* W. A. VanGemeren (ed.). 5 volumes. Grand Rapids: Zondervan, 1997. (cited by volume and page.)

NIV New International Version. London: Hodder and Stoughton, 1988.

NJPS *Tanakh: The Holy Scriptures: The New JPS Translation according to the Traditional Hebrew Text.* Philadelphia: The Jewish Publication Society, 1985.

NKJV New King James Version. Nashville: Thomas Nelson, 1982.

NLT New Living Translation. Wheaton, Illinois: Tyndale House, 1997.

NRSV New Revised Standard Version. New York and Oxford: Oxford University Press, 1989.

REB Revised English Bible. Oxford University Press and Cambridge University Press, 1989.

RSV Revised Standard Version. London: Oxford University Press, 1963.

TDOT *Theological Dictionary of the Old Testament.* G. J. Botterweck, H. Ringgren and H-J. Fabry (eds.) 11 volumes, continuing. Grand Rapids: Eerdmans, 1974-.

TWOT *Theological Wordbook of the Old Testament.* R. L. Harris and G. L. Archer (eds.). 2 volumes. Chicago: Moody Press, 1980. (cited by entry number.)

Map 1 Syria - Palestine

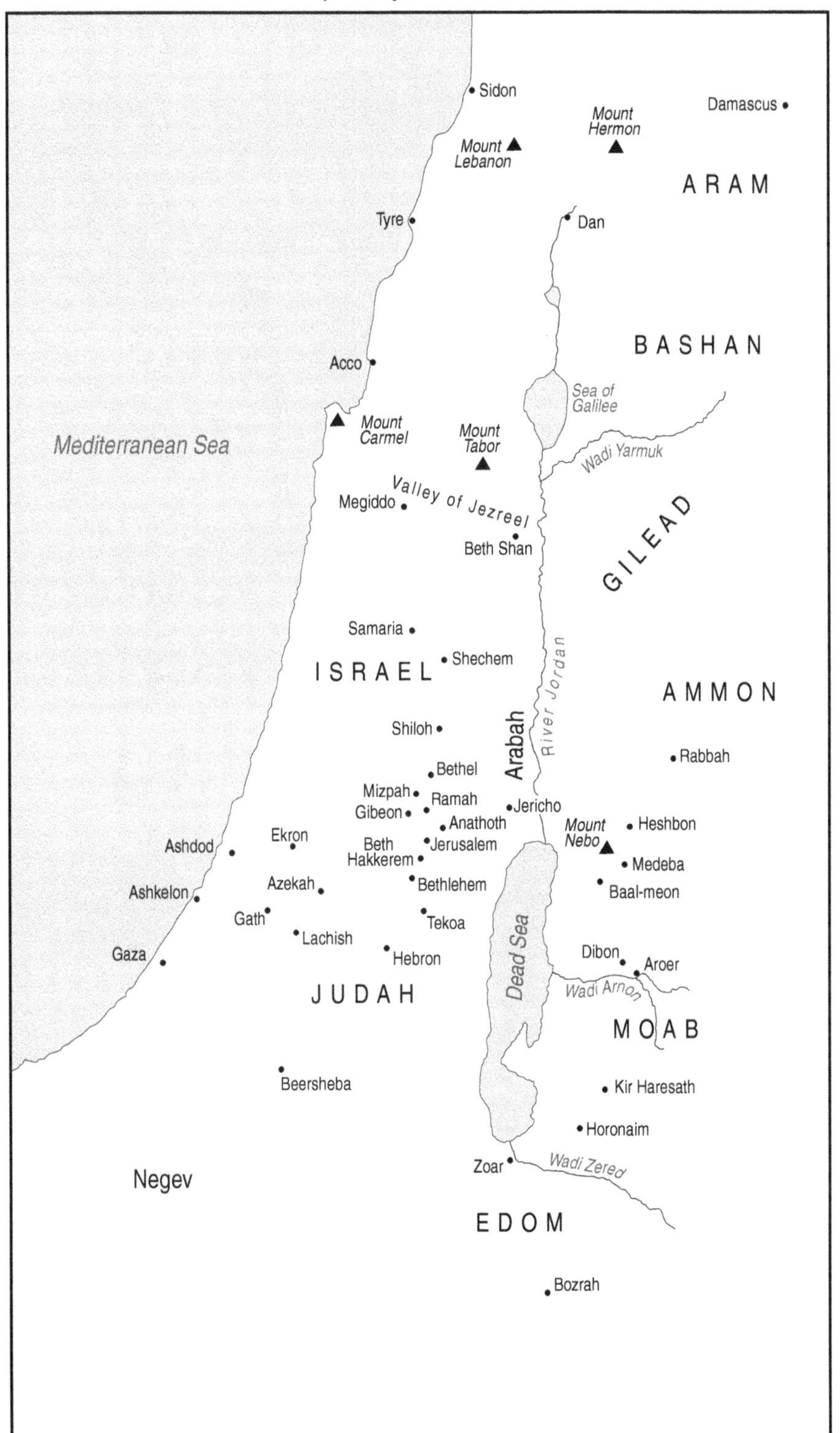

Map 2 The Empire of Nebuchadnezzar around 580 BC

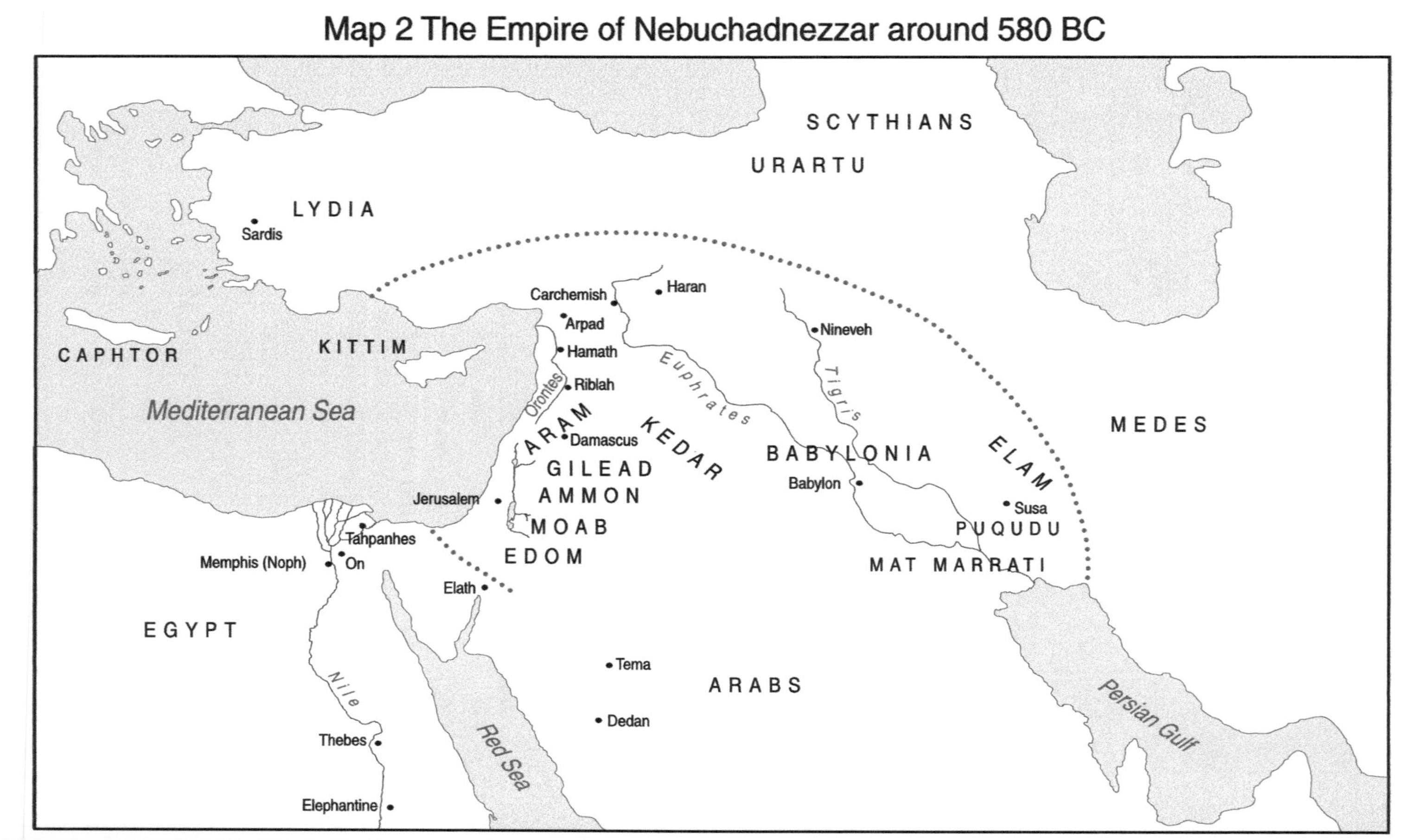

INTRODUCTION

§1. APPROACHING JEREMIAH

The unfolding of divine salvation throughout the centuries of human history has not taken place like the smooth rising of the sun on a clear morning, gradually but steadily dispelling the darkness and spreading its warmth. While the course of events is undoubtedly moving on towards its consummation, there have often been times of darkness which call into question whether God's purposes will ever be achieved. It was at such a period of darkness that Jeremiah served as a prophet of the LORD at the end of the seventh and the beginning of the sixth centuries BC when the expansion of the neo-Babylonian empire under Nebuchadnezzar led to the destruction of Jerusalem in 586 BC.

Centuries earlier the LORD's purpose for his people had involved intervention on their behalf to deliver them from oppression in Egypt. Subsequently they had been divinely brought into the land of promise and given the opportunity to serve God and to enjoy the blessings of the covenant. The land in which Israel dwelt was a precursor of a return to paradise, and designed as a training school for those who would live in obedience to the LORD. But by Jeremiah's day the history of the people was no longer a story of their struggle to realise that potential; instead it had become a tale of failure. At a human level the nation had come to a dead end. The presence of a spiritually insensitive and rebellious people could no longer be tolerated in the land of blessing and promise, and the city of Jerusalem which for centuries had been the focus of the divine presence on earth was to be abandoned by God and captured by her enemies. The people of God would be deported from the land which had been given them in covenant as a token of restored creation, because it was incongruous and unjust that those who had so flagrantly departed from God should occupy and enjoy the land of his blessing. It was a time of turmoil and tragedy that engendered urgent and perplexing questions in the hearts of the faithful remnant among the people. 'Will the LORD reject for ever? Will he never show his favour again? Has his unfailing love vanished for ever? Has his promise failed for all time? Has God forgotten to be merciful? Has he in anger withheld his compassion?' (Ps. 77:7-9; cf. Ps. 79:5). It was at such a time that Jeremiah was called to be a prophet.

Jeremiah's ministry involved the proclamation of impending doom. What was to befall the people would not be a chance occurrence in the flow of human history, nor even the outworking of fundamental, underlying economic and social forces. It was an expression of the sovereign rule of the God who determines the flow of human history and whose covenant had been violated. If the people would not respond in repentance to the situation that had arisen because of their sin, then they would be swept into exile. Over the years repeated calls for repentance were spurned, and so catastrophe became increasingly inevitable for the nation. But even then there were still opportunities for individuals to escape or mitigate the impact of what was happening. What was looked for was faith—a commitment to the LORD and a personal acceptance that his purposes were determinative for life.

However, Jeremiah's ministry was not one of unrelieved gloom. Setting out beforehand an explanation for the trauma that was to befall the people provided a structure for faith to survive through the dark years of divine judgment. Coping with the disaster would not be achieved by an irrational flight of fancy that sprang from a denial of reality, but by accepting the divine perspective on what was happening and why. Even more significantly, Jeremiah was privileged to have revealed to him that restoration would follow judgment. The LORD would not permit sin, even the sin of his people, to have the last word on their destiny. His covenant commitment to them endured even after they had reneged on their obligations to him. So he commissioned Jeremiah to describe the restoration that would take place and to set out the new covenant that would be divinely inaugurated to ensure the permanence of the arrangements which would be instituted after the impact of the catastrophe had been worked through in the nation's life.

That new covenant vision is one aspect of the prophecy that gives it special significance for the church today. While there was a partial fulfilment of the new covenant promises at the expiry of the seventy years of captivity that Jeremiah foretold, that has now been superseded by the consummation inaugurated by the coming of Christ. The age of the new covenant is now revealed as having two principal phases, but already there has been an initial realisation of it in the epochal transformation accomplished by the redeeming work of Christ and in the church's understanding and appropriation of that salvation through the sending of the Spirit. The conceptualisation of that change as 'new covenant' is to be traced to the dark days of Jeremiah's ministry, and in looking back to it, we can come to a more robust grasp of the privileges that are ours.

Alongside the twofold message Jeremiah had to deliver, there was another aspect to his prophetic calling. In a way that had been partially anticipated by Hosea and the marriage he was instructed to enter into (Hos. 1–3), Jeremiah was required to live out his message as well as to proclaim it. The Book of Jeremiah is more than the record of the nation's history; it is a record of the prophet's experience of rejection, hardship, suffering and eventual vindication that parallels that of the people as a whole. Jeremiah lived through a time of personal darkness as well as a time of national catastrophe, so that attention has to be given to the significance of the man himself along with that of the message he proclaimed. This too takes on a deeper meaning in the light of New Testament revelation because it is not difficult to detect the parallels that exist between the reception Jeremiah was accorded and that given to the one who 'came to that which was his own, but his own did not receive him' (John 1:11).

In this Introduction we begin by considering the nature of the evidence that we have in the Book of Jeremiah regarding the life and ministry of the prophet (§2). Then, because the prophet did not speak in detachment from the world of his day, but addressed its circumstances and needs directly, a description is given of the general situation that prevailed in Judah and the surrounding nations in the time of Jeremiah (§3). After that, the course of his career and his personal experience are outlined in terms of contemporary events (§4). Of course, Jeremiah was first and foremost a prophet. It is therefore appropriate to consider what was implied by this, and in particular to ask how he knew what it was he had to say (§5). After an outline of the principal features of the message Jeremiah presented (§6), the final section of the Introduction (§7) brings together various methodological observations about the content of the commentary. Mention should also be made of an Appendix (to be found at the end of Volume 2) in which problems connected with establishing the chronology of this period are looked at in greater detail.

§2. THE FORMATION AND STRUCTURE OF THE BOOK OF JEREMIAH

Before we consider what the Book of Jeremiah tells us about the prophet and his ministry, we must first examine the book itself and account for its origin and form. Traditionally Jeremiah was considered to be written by the prophet himself, or at any rate under his close supervision. Though it was recognised that the material in the book was not ordered in any very easily comprehensible sequence, there was no doubt that the book told us directly about the prophet and was an accurate report of his ministry as he maintained a courageous witness to God's truth in an age of spiritual decline and impending divine judgment. The strength of such an understanding is that it is in accord with a straightforward reading of the text, and, I would contend, nothing has arisen to vitiate such an approach, though it is now generally set aside in favour of taking the book as produced by various redactors over a number of years after Jeremiah's death.

2.1 The Structure of Jeremiah. For the purposes of study it is possible to identify sixteen major divisions in the book of Jeremiah.

(I) *Introduction and Call (1:1-19).* Here we are given basic biographical information about Jeremiah. He was descended from a priestly family that lived in Anathoth near Jerusalem, and at an early age he was called to be a prophet, though not without reluctance on his part because he felt himself unable to cope with the demands of the office. He was assured of divine empowering, and by means of two visions was informed of the LORD's determination to carry out his word and also of the main theme of the message he had to present: that judgment was impending on the nation.

(II) *Jeremiah's Early Ministry (2:1–6:30).* This summary of Jeremiah's initial preaching exposes the persistent apostasy of the people, confronts them with the need for repentance, and warns them of the horrors of enemy invasion that would come as the implementation of God's sentence of judgment on them because they had refused to turn back to him. Although King Josiah had carried through many reforms in the public worship and religious structures of Judah, the thinking of the people was still poisoned by the defection of Manasseh's reign so that they perpetuated the pattern of inner alienation from the LORD and readiness to engage in idol worship. Through the prophet the people were called on to return to faithful observance of their covenant commitment to the LORD.

The prophet's early proclamation also contained themes that would become more significant at later stages in his ministry. The political and religious leaders are held responsible for promoting rebellion against the LORD (2:8; 5:12-13, 30-31; 6:13-15). Even when judgment is seen as coming upon the land, there is a hint that it will not be total (5:10, 19). There is an awareness of future restoration to divine blessing (3:14-18), which even has an international aspect to it (3:17; 4:2). Also, we find that Jeremiah himself is drawn into reacting to the message he conveys, expressing his bewilderment and anguish at what is impending for Judah (4:10, 19-21; 6:11a). At this early stage, though the situation is not irrevocable, the outlook does not look promising.

(III) *Warnings about Worship (7:1–8:3).* This division of the prophecy stands out from the material before and after it by being written in prose rather than poetry. In the Temple Sermon of 7:1-15 we have a record of a key address Jeremiah gave in the early years of King Jehoiakim's reign, challenging the prevailing assumptions of the people that all would be well with them, and setting before them the choice of the covenant: obedience which would lead to divine blessing, or disobedience which would lead to the imposition of the divine curse. Other sections list the corruptions that prevailed in Judah's worship. It was not enough for the LORD's people to mouth religious platitudes and to perform elaborate ceremonies. Holy living had to be practised in every area of life for the covenant ideal to be realised and for the people to be in harmony with the LORD's will.

(IV) *Disobedience and Punishment (8:4–10:25).* This poetic supplement to the foregoing material contains messages probably first proclaimed during Josiah's time but reapplied to the rapidly degenerating situation of later years. The basic themes are those found earlier: that judgment is coming upon the land and that the people should recognise how unnatural and foolish their behaviour was. Jeremiah's grief as he realises how imminent and severe the catastrophe will be is vividly portrayed (8:18–

9:11), and chapter 10, after exposing the futility of idol worship, shows that its consequence will be destruction and exile (10:17-18).

(V) *Rejection of the Covenant (11:1–13:27).*

(VI) *Inescapable Doom (14:1–17:27).*

(VIII) *Jeremiah and the Potter (18:1–20:18).*

In chapters 11–20, material from a variety of backgrounds is presented in prose and poetry to reinforce Jeremiah's message. In 11:1-17 we have a second example of a prose address of Jeremiah setting out the demands of the covenant. There is also the record of a number of symbolic actions he was instructed to perform or witness to bring his message home to the people (13:1-11; 18:1-4; 19:1-13). While from the start of his ministry Jeremiah had been sensitive to the suffering involved in what was revealed to him, these chapters include a number of prayers and dialogues, traditionally known as his Confessions, in which the prophet engages in vehement protest with God (11:18-23; 12:1-6; 15:10-21; 17:14-18; 18:18-23; 20:7-18). We are made aware of how much it cost Jeremiah personally to persevere in his ministry and especially, as the flow of material throughout these chapters increasingly emphasises, to persevere in a ministry that was being rejected. This collection ends with the nation likened to a smashed earthenware jar that cannot be repaired (19:11), and with the prophet flogged and publicly humiliated (20:2), so that he concludes despondently, bemoaning his very existence (20:14-18).

(VIII) *Kings and Prophets Denounced (21:1–24:10).* At the beginning of chapter 21 there is a break in the material presented in the prophecy. The question being examined is no longer whether divine judgment on Judah will be avoided by repentance, but whether Judah, and especially its king, can be brought to see that judgment may be mitigated by accepting the punishment God has sent. The critique given of various kings of Judah does not hold out much hope for an appropriate official response, and the analysis of false prophecy in 23:9-40 shows the absence of spiritual perceptivity among the religious leaders of the day. The doom of the people is certain, and yet the future is not completely black. While the existing representatives of the dynasty of David are to be written off, the LORD will provide a true ruler for his people (23:5-6). Although the exile of the people is not going to be averted, beyond that the LORD will act to provide a new beginning by bringing them back to the land (23:3; 24:4-7). Here are dawning rays of the new day that will be expressed through the new covenant.

(IX) *Judgment on the Nations (25:1-31).* Chapter 25 stands on its own as a significant point of transition in the book. For the part it plays in analysis of the Greek transmission of the text, see below (§2.6). Theologically it is a discussion of the outworking of divine judgment in the light of the emergence of Babylon as the superpower which will be used by the LORD to effect his judgment against Judah. Punishment was inevitable after twenty-three years of ignored warnings (25:1-11), but there is also a divine limit of seventy years on Babylonian dominance before they too are judged (25:12-14). Indeed all nations are shown to come under the sovereign verdict of the LORD against them (25:15-38). This message, which comes from the middle of Jehoiakim's reign, stresses the universality of the LORD's rule and therefore the inescapability of the divine verdict against all. Though Babylon will in turn be overthrown, it is not yet hinted that her downfall has any implications for the restoration of Judah.

(X) *Controversy with False Prophets (26:1–29:32).* This division of the book demonstrates how conditions deteriorated in Jerusalem. Chapter 26 contains another account of Jeremiah's Temple Sermon, but here the emphasis is on the response to it from the religious establishment, leading to a threat against the prophet's life. From a decade later, chapters 27 and 28 set out Jeremiah's opposition to rebellion against Babylon and the response this met with from another prophet, Hananiah. The issue of true and false prophecy is also explored in chapter 29 in terms of the advice that Jeremiah relayed to those taken to Babylon in 597 BC. However, the exiles are shown that the LORD does not intend that Babylon will have the final say on their destiny. He will eventually bring them back (29:10-14).

(XI) *The Restoration of Israel and Judah (30:1–33:26).* These chapters are frequently called the Book of Consolation. In them Jeremiah sets out the programme that was revealed to him while he was imprisoned during the final siege of Jerusalem. To encourage him (and others) during the harsh conditions of those days, the LORD provided greater light on how his purposes would eventually be accomplished. After the terror of invasion and deportation (30:5-7)—that could no longer be averted—there would come a time when the LORD would renew his favour towards the people. These prophecies culminate in the new covenant (31:31-34), which involves restoring the fortunes of the land (31:12, 23-24; 32:15, 44), Zion (30:18; 31:6, 38-40; 33:16), the priests (31:14; 33:18-22) and the king (30:9; 33:15, 17, 20-22). Jeremiah is instructed to buy a field already captured by the enemy as a symbol of this coming restoration (32:6-15).

(XII) *The Need for Faithfulness (34:1–36:32).* In these chapters a set of case studies show the extent of the moral and spiritual deterioration prevalent in the land. This decline justified the LORD's action against the people, and the record also explained to future generations why their national history had developed in the way it did. Chapter 34 shows the leading citizens of Jerusalem going back on a solemn agreement they had entered into before the LORD. Chapter 35 holds up the Rechabites as a group who remained obedient to instructions given by their founder, and in this they provide a decided contrast to Judah's attitude towards the LORD. Then chapter 36 relates how King Jehoiakim burned the scroll that contained the record of Jeremiah's ministry. By this he revealed not only his hostility to the prophet, but also his rejection of the God whom the prophet served.

(XIII) *The Siege and Fall of Jerusalem (37:1–39:18).*

(XIV) *Jeremiah after the Fall of Jerusalem (40:1–45:5).*
Here we have a continuous narrative that centres on the fall of Jerusalem. The first division of the material (chaps. 37–39) focuses on Jeremiah's imprisonment during the siege and on how King Zedekiah in his weakness was unwilling to respond to the prophetic message presented to him. After the city fell, Jeremiah was released from confinement and treated favourably by the Babylonians. However, the new regime that they established in Judah did not last long, and Jeremiah was carried into Egypt by a group of Jews fleeing from anticipated Babylonian reprisals (chaps. 40–41). Though the prophet's long disparaged message had been vindicated, neither this group of refugees nor the wider Jewish émigré community in Egypt were prepared to accept his advice, and the final picture we have of the prophet is of him witnessing faithfully to a still unresponsive audience (chaps. 42–44). Chapter 45 presents an earlier message dealing with the destiny of Baruch, Jeremiah's friend and assistant. Its inclusion here is discussed in §2.2.

(XV) *The LORD's Words against the Nations (46:1–51:64).* The Oracles against the Nations are the last major division of the book, and by the strategic placing of the oracles against Babylon last in sequence they provide a climax to the message. The earlier oracles predict judgment on various nations for offences they have committed, though even in them there occur a number of unexpected glimpses of divine blessing (48:47; 49:6; 49:39). But to Babylon no hope of redemption is extended. Rather her downfall is seen as providing the occasion for the restoration of the LORD's people, who are urged to leave the doomed city and to renew their covenant pledges to the LORD. Thus the vista of hope, which had been becoming clearer throughout the book, is most clearly displayed in the closing section regarding Babylon (chaps. 50–51).

(XVI) *A Supplement: Prophecy Fulfilled (52:1-34).* Chapter 52 is a postscript added by someone other than Jeremiah or Baruch. It draws on material similar to 2 Kgs. 24:18–25:30 to restate various aspects of the fall of Jerusalem and to add additional information about the calamity that came on the land. Like Kings it ends with a note about the release of Jehoiachin from prison, which hints somewhat obscurely about the need for divine intervention to effect a release for the nation from captivity in Babylon.

2.2 The Composition of the Book. The Book of Jeremiah is the record of a prophetic ministry, and much of the material in it therefore originated in the prophet's proclamation to the people. It is, however, improbable that years later he had to rely on his personal recollection of what he had said earlier or on what others could recall. Though the normal mode of communication to one's contemporaries was by speech, ancient

Near Eastern society was insistently literate when it came to recording matters of long-term significance—and there is no doubt that revelation given to a prophet from God would be accorded the highest importance. Thus we find Barstad, who would firmly dissociate himself from 'fundamentalist approaches' to the text, arguing 'because some importance was attached to these words [ancient Near Eastern divinatory texts], it became important to secure the message from the deity in the most accurate way possible, or the message had to be taken down in order that it might be delivered to the correct addressee. ... The same, we should assume, would apply also for ancient Israelite prophetical texts. There is little cause to believe that the ancient Israelites behaved in any way differently from their neighbours in this respect, and, again, there are indications in the biblical material itself suggesting that prophetical texts were written down after they had been delivered' (1993:57).

These records, therefore, formed the basis for the bringing together the record of Jeremiah's preaching, which was supplemented by narratives about his life, written with his knowledge by associates like Baruch who were eyewitnesses of the events they described. Narrative about prophetic action would not have been delivered orally, but would have been written from the start. This collection of material grew in various stages throughout Jeremiah's life, and probably received a substantial major revision shortly before his death. If this was not carried out by the prophet personally, then it was probably effected by Baruch. There is no reason to suppose that the text of Jeremiah as we now have it was not in existence (with the exception of chapter 52) by around 580 BC.

However, even a cursory analysis of the prophecy makes it evident that the material in the book is not ordered chronologically. For instance, the events recorded in chapter 26 took place at some point in the years 609–605 BC and those of chapters 27 and 28 around 594 BC, but chapter 29 moves back to the immediate aftermath of 597 BC. Moreover, chapter 21 has previously dealt with a much later incident from 588 BC, as does chapter 34, but chapter 35 moves back to 598 BC. Chapters 36 and 45 both begin with the date 'in the fourth year of Jehoiakim' (605/04 BC), but chapters 37–44 are an account of incidents in 587 BC and the years immediately following. It is not that when events occurred was unimportant to the writer—after all he has recorded the information that alerts us to these temporal transitions—but that chronology was not the major factor in determining the structure of chapters 21–45. Furthermore, in chapters 1–20 next to no chronological information is given. It is therefore of interest to see to what extent we possess sufficient information to account for the order in which the material in the prophecy has been preserved.

The Two Scrolls. Jeremiah's prophetic activity stretched over a period in excess of forty years, and the record of it was not all prepared simultaneously. The book itself gives significant information about its origin, though unfortunately not as much as we might desire.

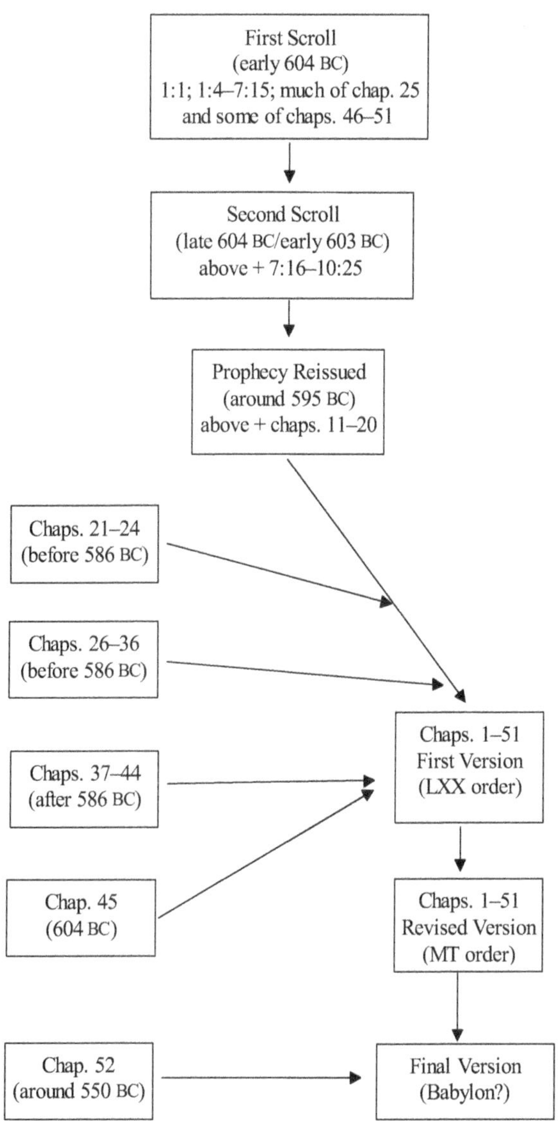

Possible Order of Composition of Jeremiah

Chapter 36 relates how in the momentous fourth year of Jehoiakim (605/4 BC) Jeremiah was commanded by God to prepare a scroll containing 'all the words I have spoken to you concerning Israel, Judah and all the other nations from the time I began speaking to you in the reign of Josiah till now' (36:2). This scroll was prepared with the assistance of Baruch, but it was several months later before it was read in the presence of the king, who then burned it (36:23). However, Jeremiah was subsequently ordered to prepare a Second Scroll with 'all the former words that were in the first scroll, which King Jehoiakim of Judah has burned' (36:28). Verse 32 of the chapter notes that when this was done, 'many similar words were added to them', but it does not make clear if these words were all added at the same time or over a number of years. Also 'added' does not determine whether the additional material of the Second Scroll was an appendix to the First Scroll or whether it was inserted into the existing material, though the former seems more probable. At any rate we know of the existence of the First Scroll from 605/04 BC, and of the Second Scroll from the following year (604/03 BC). The question then inevitably arises as to whether the contents of these scrolls may be traced in the book we now have.

Because of the later setting of chapter 21 and the change in style evident there, the search for the material of the scrolls has generally been confined to the earlier section of the book. However, scholars have been unable to reach an agreed position on the matter. Indeed the variety of views expressed led some to despair altogether of a solution. 'Now it is futile, one thinks, to speculate regarding the precise contents of this scroll; commentators who do so are indulging in guesswork' (Bright 1965:LXI). Subsequent work by Holladay suggests that such a conclusion is overly pessimistic.

Holladay (1980) argues that when Jeremiah composed the First Scroll he would have structured it to make it an effective presentation of the divine message, and that Baruch and other subsequent scribes would have preserved that order. Holladay's work (1976) and other similar rhetorical analyses of Jeremiah identify the verbal techniques that were used to link the various sections of the prophecy, and this gives valuable insight into how the book coheres as a literary unity. When Holladay applies the results of his earlier analysis, while he is prepared to find later insertions into the material, he argues in general terms for the First Scroll as consisting of 1:4-10 and 2:1–7:15, and the Second Scroll as additionally containing 1:11-19, various brief additions in chapters 4–6, and 7:16–11:17 (1980:462-3). However, it must be doubted if our knowledge of the way in which ancient documents were composed is sufficiently comprehensive to warrant the minute discrimination that Holladay practises between the material of the two scrolls, and between the scrolls and even later insertions. The overall result is too elaborate to be totally convincing, but a basic structure of the First Scroll as concluding with 7:15 and the Second

Scroll as extending this to the end of chapter 10 is not without plausibility. This is particularly so in that Holladay brings forward a substantive thematic argument to reinforce the perception of a break at 7:15.

At the beginning of chapter 36 the reason for writing the First Scroll is stated to be that all the people of Judah 'may turn from their evil ways, so that I may forgive their iniquity and their sin' (36:3). Though such repentance is presented as unlikely, it is still possible. This accords with the presentation of 7:1-15. While the gravity of the situation the people are in is not minimised and the potential outcome of their rebellious behaviour is starkly presented, the overall message is a plea for repentance. However, Holladay argues that there is a substantial shift in the situation in chapter 36 after Jehoiakim has burned the scroll. The time for repentance has passed, and the LORD is now presented as having conclusively determined that judgment will fall on the land (1980:458). Holladay is aware that 'extreme expressions of Yahweh's determination to carry out his judgment may still represent only cautionary scenarios' (1980:459), and specifically cites the example of Ezek. 3:18 where the divine verdict of 'You shall surely die' on a wicked man is to be accompanied by a warning so that he may save his life. This means that absolute statements of judgment do not provide a secure criterion for dissection of continuous passages of the prophecy. However, Holladay seems to be on sounder ground when he points to the prohibition of 7:16, 'Do not pray for this people', as marking a substantive change in the message of chapter 7, reflecting the alteration between the beginning and end of chapter 36, and probably pointing to where the Second Scroll takes over and continues the First Scroll in markedly darker tones. It must, however, be observed that this is not an absolute change, but one that reflects the balance of Jeremiah's message.

Oracles Against The Nations. There is, however, one further feature of 36:2 that has to be kept in mind. The First Scroll was not only concerned with Judah and Jerusalem; it also had material about 'all the other nations'. This makes it probable that some matter from chapter 25 and also many of the oracles now found in chapters 46–51 were incorporated in the scroll. It is not easy to determine the extent to which this was so, and the matter is taken up later after considering further evidence.

Subsequent Enlargement of the Scroll. The material incorporated in chapters 11–20 all dates from the period up to the end of Jehoiachin's reign (597 BC). If, as is often supposed, after the burning of the scroll Jeremiah and Baruch were in seclusion and hiding for several years, then most of this material may well have been brought together then, though it includes records of oracles and ministry that took place in earlier years through to the time of Jehoiachin (13:18-19). For this reason some commentators consider these chapters as part of the Second Scroll. However, on balance it seems better to view them separately because they introduce a different type of material generally known as Jeremiah's Confessions, which involve us in the inner life and tensions of the prophet as well as his public ministry.

It is also noteworthy that this block of material ends in chapter 20 on an extremely pessimistic note which seems to correspond with the bleakness that Jeremiah felt at the failure of his ministry and his personal rejection during the closing years of Jehoiakim's reign. There are therefore good grounds for supposing that by the early part of Zedekiah's reign the Jeremiah scroll had grown to include chapters 1–20 and material now to be found in chapters 25 and 46–51.

The beginning of chapter 21 marks a distinct change in the style of the book. This is generally attributed to Baruch (and possibly other scribes) having a more prominent role in the composition of the work, whereas in the previous part of the work Jeremiah had employed them more as amanuenses. This part of the book displays greater interest in the public history of the prophet and in locating his sayings in specific historical settings. It is probable that chapters 21–24 and 26–36 were composed in their present form during the closing stages of the siege of Jerusalem. Chapters 21–24 may have been added to the scroll before the fall of the city, and chapters 26–36 not long after Jeremiah and Baruch arrived in Egypt. Chapters 37–44 along with additional material in chapters 46–51 may come from later in the 580s (cf. 44:1). Along with chapter 44 this material formed the basis for the text that underlies the Septuagintal translation of Jeremiah (see §2.6). The present Hebrew text, reordered and somewhat more extensive, probably originated from Jeremiah in Egypt around the same time. Chapter 52 is clearly marked as separate from the rest of the book and originated later in the exilic period.

Such an approach as that outlined above is viewed as naïve and uncritical by most modern scholars, but it has the enduring merit of listening to the text as it stands. Critical approaches have not been able to arrive at any consensus on the composition and transmission of Jeremiah, and cannot be said to do justice to the record that we possess. Undoubtedly they do point to significant matters that have to be assessed, and a brief review of their stance is necessary to understand modern approaches to Jeremiah and to benefit from the points of substance that they raise. However, the overall conclusions of much contemporary scholarship are deeply unsatisfactory.

2.3 Editors, Scribes and Readers. The earliest surviving documentary evidence for the text of the Old Testament is to be found in the Qumran scrolls, which date from the last few centuries BC. Modern critical study has focused on the immediately preceding period, and made proposals regarding the transmission and consolidation of the text during that time. The most common hypothesis is that the text did not come into its final form until just before the date demanded by the extant manuscripts. During the previous period it is assumed not merely that the text was transmitted, but that it was subject to an ongoing process of refinement and addition. Such a process of editorial rewriting the text is contrary to conservative presuppositions, which distinguish sharply between the activities and intentions of scribes and those of editors.

The historical evidence from the ancient world largely supports the position that the scribal schools which were responsible for the preservation and transmission of texts did so with considerable care. The scrupulous text controls of the Massoretic scribes of later centuries are well known. However, such practices did not represent a new element in eastern scribal traditions, but the consolidation and consistent and detailed application of practices that had grown up over the centuries. Scribes are fallible, and the possibility of scribal errors in surviving manuscripts is not to be discounted. But that is quite a different process from editorial activity where it is envisaged there was deliberate modification of, and addition to, an original core of material. The only substantive evidence that is advanced for the editorial revamping posited by modern scholarship is what is drawn from the text itself in terms of the assumptions and readings of those scholars. There is no external evidence for the existence of such editorial or redactorial groups.

In the case of Jeremiah, when the text is examined in the light of critical presuppositions, three broad schools of thought have emerged. There are those who support the position that Jeremiah as a book is a generally accurate witness to a long and varied ministry (Bright, 1965; Holladay, 1986, 1989). Though the activities of subsequent redactors are discernible in the book, it is to be interpreted as substantially deriving from the prophet's own teaching so that many of his sayings have been preserved for us and much can be said about the historical Jeremiah. Secondly, there are those who express a decided preference for reading the book not as a record of the prophet's ministry, but as a presentation of the prophet as perceived by later generations in the light of their own concerns. Opinions vary as to the extent of the historical core that has been preserved in the transmission of the text. Some, such as Carroll (1986), adopt a minimalist approach in which nothing certain can be attributed to the prophet or said about him; indeed even his existence may be called in question. The person and ministry of the prophet recede into the background, and interest focuses on what may be said about the community that is supposed to have given rise in later times to the text which we now have.

However, Carroll no longer represents the extreme of modern critical approaches to Jeremiah. More recently literary approaches (Diamond et al., 1999) advocate a third style of analysis which abandons any attempt to elucidate the historical reference of the material whether as directly relating to the figure of Jeremiah or to some posited later reconstructed group of editors/community. Such a move away from historical referentiality requires that the book be read on its own terms as literature with its own intrinsic, imaginative world. In fact the book has to be read as an exercise in fiction. But against this the text of the book stoutly, though often tantalisingly, objects. True there is considerable literary skill in the composition of this book, and when that is pointed out, we must be grateful. But the message of Jeremiah possesses abiding validity precisely because it is history: Spirit-inspired and Spirit-interpreted history. To understand and respond to the message that the book brings, the modern reader has not to enter some imagined construct but to be made aware of the actual life situation with which the book grapples and to appreciate the very real parallels with our present individual and collective existence. Mankind has not changed spiritually, nor has the counsel of God altered; and so the teaching of Jeremiah still needs to be heard.

2.4 Jeremiah and Deuteronomy. There are three basic aspects of Jeremiah that criticism has pointed to in elaborating its own hypotheses as to the background and origin of the book: the relationship between Jeremiah and Deuteronomy, the existence of prose and poetry in the book, and the textual variations found in the Septuagint. These are real phenomena, and any approach to Jeremiah must give some account of these features. Let us look at them in turn.

It has long been recognised that Jeremiah contains words and phrases that are characteristic of the style of Deuteronomy. Driver (1895:xciii) noted from earlier research that sixty-six passages in Deuteronomy are echoed no less than eighty-six times in Jeremiah, and gave as significant specimens of this the following instances:

'a distant nation against you … a people whose language you do not know, whose speech you do not understand'—5:15, compare Deut. 28:49;

'the fortified cities in which you trust'—5:17, compare Deut. 28:52;

'walk in all the ways I command you, that it may go well with you'—7:23, compare Deut. 5:30;

'Then the carcases of this people will become food for the birds of the air and the beasts of the earth, and there will be none to frighten them away'—7:33 (cf. 16:4; 19:7), compare Deut. 28:26;

'I will scatter them among nations that neither they nor their fathers have known'—9:16, compare Deut. 28:64;

'when I brought them out of Egypt, out of the iron-smelting furnace'—11:4, compare Deut. 4:20;

'I will make them abhorrent to all the kingdoms of the earth'—15:4 (cf. 24:9; 29:18; 34:17), compare Deut. 28:25;

'into a land neither you nor your fathers have known, and there you will serve other gods day and night'—16:13, compare Deut. 28:36;

'I will make them eat the flesh of their sons and daughters … during the stress of the siege imposed on them by the[ir] enemies'—19:9, compare Deut. 28:53;

'Why has the LORD done such a thing to this great city?'—22:8 (cf.

16:10), compare Deut. 29:23;
'do not follow other gods to serve and worship them'—25:6 (cf. 13:10; 16:11), compare Deut. 8:19;
'you will seek me and find me when you seek me with all your heart'—29:13, compare Deut. 4:49;
'in my name have spoken lies, which I did not tell them to do'—29:23, compare Deut. 18:20;
'with signs and wonders, by a mighty hand and an outstretched arm and with great terror'—32:21, compare Deut. 4:34;
'so that they will always fear me for their own good'—32:39, compare Deut. 4:10;
'I will rejoice in doing them good'—32:41, compare Deut. 28:63.

There are also extended passages in Jeremiah which seem to be based on particular passages in Deuteronomy (e.g. 3:1 as compared with Deut. 24:1-4; or 34:8-14 compared with Deut. 15:2) or which seem to promote the message of Deuteronomy in general terms (e.g. 11:1-14). There is therefore much that is undeniably in Deuteronomic style: distinctive vocabulary, repetition of memorable and sonorous phrases, simple and strong patterns of thought and sermon structure.

The interconnection is obvious: but how is it to be explained? From a conservative point of view there is little problem. Centuries earlier Moses wrote Deuteronomy, and the influence of the founder of the nation and his book on the subsequent thinking and religious vocabulary of the people may be taken for granted. Furthermore, if Deuteronomy constituted part or the whole of the scroll found in the Temple in 622 BC, then it would have been natural for the style of that work to be copied by others. What we are observing is the shared literary style common to authors in that age.

From a critical approach, however, matters are more complicated. Deuteronomy is no longer of Mosaic provenance, and may only have been written just before it was 'discovered'. Furthermore, the historical narrative found in Joshua–2 Kings also exhibits the same Deuteronomic style, and so there developed the view that a scribal school arose in exilic and post-exilic times that was responsible for the Deuteronomic history (Joshua–2 Kings) and also for the passages in Jeremiah which exhibit similar stylistic tendencies. Leaving to one side the matter of chapter 52, it was also noted that there were parallels in the contents of certain passages (39:1-10 compared to 2 Kgs. 25:1-12; 40:7-9 and 41:1-3 compared to 2 Kgs. 25:22-26). This further reinforced the notion of an authorial connection between Jeremiah and Kings that was widely identified as the product of the anonymous and otherwise unidentified Deuteronomistic school. This school moulded and applied the prophet's teaching in such a way as to give it relevance to the later conditions of their own times (Nicholson 1970). However, the relationship between the two sets of literature is not straightforward. Jeremiah employs many characteristic turns of expression that are not to be found in Deuteronomy or Kings. The simple notion that both in their own way are influenced by Deuteronomy in style and outlook is more robust and cogent than elaborate patterns of interconnection and redactional activity.

There is, however, one remarkable feature of 2 Kings that deserves consideration: it does not mention Jeremiah even though he had been a figure of major importance in the years before Jerusalem fell. This is a significant omission in that the previous history in no way avoids references to prophets. Indeed, its central section is devoted to stories about Elijah and Elisha (1 Kgs. 17–2 Kgs. 8:15), and it also gives extensive detail about Isaiah (2 Kgs. 19–20). Why then does it keep silent about Jeremiah? Two factors may be of relevance. One is that Kings was written later than Jeremiah, and, aware of what was already available about the prophet, the author of Kings felt that there was no need to mention him. That certainly fits in with the relative dates of the composition of the books, but it fails to account for the inclusion of references to Isaiah, whose work was also already well known. Another suggestion is that the author of Kings did not mention Jeremiah because there was a substantive divergence between the ultimately optimistic view of the prophet regarding the future of the people and their restoration, and the view advanced in Kings. McConville explores the extent to which Jeremiah develops the message of Deuteronomy 30:1-10 that there is hope beyond judgment because of the sovereign intervention of the LORD, whereas the approach of Kings is to suggest that the history of the people is at an end (1993:19-20).

2.5 Poetry and Prose. English versions of Jeremiah generally set out the book as a mixture of poetry and prose, and there is remarkably little variation between the standard translations in their delimitation in this respect. However, what significance is to be attached to this feature of the text? Critical analyses generally approached the matter in terms of differences in authorship and sought to use the distinction as a basis for determining the prehistory of the work.

Modern analysis of the phenomenon began in 1901 with Bernard Duhm who, assuming that there was an affinity between prophetic inspiration and poetic inspiration, claimed that the original utterances of Jeremiah were confined to 280 verses of poetry. As regards the prose in Jeremiah he distinguished, mainly on the basis of content, between what was contributed by Baruch (220 verses) and what came from a long line of exilic supplementers (about 850 verses). Secondary material in poetry or prose was recognised as being stylistically akin to Deuteronomistic literature, and a similar exilic or post-exilic provenance was assumed for such prose in Jeremiah.

The Scandinavian scholar Sigmund Mowinckel studied the same material and refined Duhm's approach. He identified four basic literary sources which were incorporated into the present text of Jeremiah. Source A was the poetry in the book, which (along with certain first person narratives in chapters 1–25) was accepted as mainly the authentic oracles of the prophet. This material stops substantially at chapter 25, with chapters 30–31 and 46–51 constituting special cases of their own. The biographical prose narratives, B (generally considered by others as contributed by Baruch, and frequently identified as chapters 19:1–20:6; 26–29; 36–45), were distinguished from autobiographical prose, C, which he considered to be a late Deuteronomistic production reflecting an origin in early Babylonian Judaism. This was the least reliable of the sources. There were also other later contributions of minor interest, D, especially found in chapters 30–31. C type material is anticipated in 1:1-13 and 3:6-18, but is identified as beginning at chapter 7 and including 7:1–8:3; 11:1-4; 18:1-12; 21:1-10; 24:1–25:29; 31:23–32:44; 35. This basic division has been widely accepted by subsequent scholars, though there are inevitable variations in detail. This is particularly seen in the extent to which the later editors are adjudged to have composed the C material from scratch or to have developed it from genuine reminiscences of what Jeremiah said. Of course, if the poetry and prose are from different sources, then there is also opened up the possibility that the portraits they present of the prophet and his ministry differ as well.

Now at a formal level the differences between these types of writing are fairly readily identified and unexceptionable. However, the theories that are advanced to account for them are highly speculative. There is much to be said for the view that the prose of Jeremiah is not some distinctive Deuteronomistic brand but represents the ordinary, formal written Hebrew of the period. There are, for instance, similarities with the (admittedly fragmentary) prose of the Lachish Ostraca which come from this period. The obvious stylistic connections with Deuteronomy and the Book of Kings are readily accounted for by supposing that the Book of the Law was a major text in the scribal schools of Judah and that adoption of Mosaic diction was the mark of a good education. Indeed this probably had been the accepted style for formal written communication from a much earlier period, and it continued to be influential in later writings.

Furthermore, if we start from the premise that, with the assistance of Baruch and others, Jeremiah was his own editor, what requires elucidation is why he used such different styles of writing. The B material principally found in the biographical narratives of chapters 26–45 is most easily accounted for as contributed by Baruch (and possibly others; see on chaps. 27–29). But what motivated the switches between poetry and prose in earlier sections of the prophecy? Why, for instance, is 16:1-18 in prose, but 16:19–17:18 in poetry before 17:19-27 reverts to prose?

Hebrew poetry is distinguished from prose by the higher frequency with which terseness, parallelism and imagery occur (Longman 1996:169).

By its evocative use of language, poetry speaks more ambiguously and calls for greater input on the part of the listener to work out what it means. Indeed even when the overall message is clear, there will often be unresolved features of its detail. Prose on the other hand is a more suitable medium for greater clarity of expression. Wilson (1999) argues that the switch to the prose of C material is motivated by a desire to set out the message in simple, clear-cut terms. For instance, he notes that the language of 3:13–6:30 is evocative and ambiguous with the identity of the addressees and the allegations made against them not being clearly spelled out. The didactic prose of 7:1–8:3 suddenly removes the ambiguities and amplifies the preceding poetic oracles. Wilson treats this as primarily a function of the present literary context of the C prose.

In terms of our discussion, however, the analysis needs to be set on a broader base. The initial communication of the prophet was an oral one. It is possible to understand poetic passages as originally delivered in a setting where there was an overriding need to gain a hearing from a potentially dismissive audience. Reconstructions of prophetic activity generally suppose their main platform to have been in the Temple precincts where they addressed those who passed by. Brief poetic utterances suited the occasion: their compactness and rhythm made them memorable; their tantalising and evocative language required that they be mulled over before their full significance could be appreciated. It is therefore possible to see Jeremiah's poetic utterances as originating in such a setting.

However, there were times when the people in the Temple were not just passing through but gathered for some specific ceremony. It is perhaps significant that on such occasions (7:2; 11:2; 17:19; 26:2) Jeremiah speaks in prose. On feast days longer addresses could be given to those who had assembled, and at such a time the cadences of Mosaic/Deuteronomic prose would be a more suitable medium for delivery. But prose is also used in divine speech to Jeremiah (13:1-14; 14:11-16; 16:1-17). Certainly when Jeremiah came to incorporate his oracles into larger units, he also on occasions incorporated prose passages, which may serve to clarify the poetic sections, but we no longer know their original setting which may have given rise to the use of prose.

2.6 The Septuagintal Text of Jeremiah. There is a third strand of evidence adduced to counter conservative proposals regarding the composition of Jeremiah and that is the existence of a variant text of the book. This at least has the merit of being objective evidence, not critical reconstruction, though it is generally interpreted against the background of critical presuppositions.

The existence of two text types, a longer represented in Hebrew by the Massoretic Text (MT) and a shorter represented in Greek by the Septuagint (LXX), has long been known about. There are two major differences between the LXX and the MT. Firstly, the LXX is substantially shorter, with perhaps one-seventh of the MT not being represented in the LXX. Thus in the MT but not in the LXX we find 8:10[b]-12 (= 6:13-15); 10:6-8, 10; 11:7-8; 17:1-4 (17:3-4 = 15:13-14); 27:7, 13-14[a], 17; 29:16-20; 30:10-11 (= 46:27-28); 30:15; 33:14-26; 39:4-13; 48:40[b], 42[b] (= 49:22); 51:44[b]-49[a]. There are also headings in the MT which are additional to those found in the LXX: 2:1-2[a]; 7:12; 16:1; 27:1; 46:1; 47:1. Secondly, the LXX has a different arrangement of the material. This is mainly concerned with the Oracles against the Nations, which in the MT are located at the end of the book (chaps. 46–51) but in the LXX come in the middle of the book after the oracles against Judah (25:14–31:44, LXX). Furthermore, the order of the oracles is different (for details see commentary on chap. 46).

However, the LXX is a translation and not an original text. It is probable that variations between it and the MT arose at least in part because of the translator. In his discussion of the poetic text of the Confessions, for instance, Diamond argued that the differences between the text types are not matters of expansions or dislocations, but are primarily a matter of different vocalisation or division of a common consonantal text (1990:35). He considers that the MT exhibits more sensitivity to the context in determining the reading to follow.

To variations arising from a different understanding of the same original text there may also be added variations arising from the translator's attempts to make his text more intelligible to his original readership or conformable to their normal modes of speech. Archer (1991) argued that most of the words omitted singly from the LXX result from a translator's policy of abridgement. The Hebrew introductory formula, 'This is what the LORD Almighty, the God of Israel, says', is often shortened to, 'This is what the LORD says'. Similarly when patronymics are added to individual's names in the MT, the LXX generally omits them. Also, Nebuchadnezzar frequently loses his title, 'King of Babylon', in the Greek version. 'Since this same policy is found in the LXX translation of Isaiah and other OT books dealing with historical events, it is quite unsafe to assume that the Hebrew *Vorlage* likewise omitted these additional patronymics and titles. The Alexandrian translators tended to prune the impressive but somewhat ponderous style of the Hebrew document in order to make it flow a little more easily and smoothly in the ears of the Greek-speaking audience' (Archer 1991:143).

There are other features of the Greek translation that go some way towards accounting for the differences between the text types. Frequently the LXX will omit passages that are doublets of what is found elsewhere, and when there are four lines in the parallelism of a Hebrew verse, the last line or colon was dropped as not adding substantially to the information already given. 'This policy was much more noticeable in the LXX rendition of Isaiah, but it does occur in Jeremiah as well, and it therefore raises a real question as to whether we may validly infer that the omitted colon was actually missing in the *Vorlage* itself. All this serves as a caution against overemphasising the discrepancies between the MT and the LXX' (Archer 1991:143-44).

However, such factors do not account for all the divergences between the MT and LXX as regards the text of Jeremiah. Nowhere else in the LXX are substantial blocks of material omitted in a way which suggests that this was done to conform to what a Greek-speaking readership would expect, and it is improbable to surmise that this was done in the case of Jeremiah alone.

Furthermore the discovery at Qumran of six fragmentary manuscripts of Jeremiah supports the view that the LXX translators were genuinely attempting to translate a markedly different Hebrew text. The manuscripts 2QJer, 4QJer[a], and 4QJer[c] reflect substantially the same text as MT, but 4QJer[b] (containing parts of a number of verses from chaps. 9 and 10) and 4QJer[d] (which contains parts of 43:2-10) preserve features of word and verse order that agree with what is found in the LXX. Of itself this does not establish that all major omissions and variations in order in the LXX reflect what the translators found in the Hebrew text before them, but it does show that the text of Jeremiah was current in two principal Hebrew forms in the third century BC.

The majority explanation for this phenomenon is that the LXX text type preserves an earlier form of Jeremiah and that the MT represents the outcome of a process of development in which the tradition evolved over a period of time and other matter was added to the proto-Septuagintal text. This has fitted in with the prevailing critical consensus of the prophetic books as the product of an extended period of textual transmission and literary formation. However, against the background of the substantial similarity of the two texts and the possibility of explaining some of the differences as resulting from the translation process, other approaches to the matter may be developed.

Lundbom (1986:108) advanced the view that Baruch was responsible for the earliest arrangement of Jeremiah and that this corresponded to the order now preserved in the LXX in which the oracles against the nations come after 25:13. In this arrangement the book ended with chapter 45 (51:31-35 in the LXX order of the material), and Lundbom identifies this chapter as being a development of an ancient scribal practice whereby whoever copied a text added a note of who he was and when he had written the text. Such a note is technically called a colophon, and Lundbom considered that chapter 45 was Baruch's expanded colophon which he added when he completed copying out the collected works of Jeremiah. At that time Baruch was located in Egypt, and the Egyptian provenance of the LXX may account for its use of a locally preserved text type.

More speculatively, Lundbom identifies 51:59-64 as performing a similar function as an expanded colophon which points to the involvement of Seraiah, Baruch's brother, in the reordering of Jeremiah's material into the sequence now found in the Massoretic Text. We are told that Seraiah was in Babylon in 594/3 BC, and leaving Babylon to the last of the nations mentioned in the oracles favours some connection between Babylon and the reordered text. Whether or not Seraiah was responsible for the reworked text is incapable of proof. It seems to me equally plausible that it was done by Baruch for the use of the exiles in Babylon. There is a Jewish tradition that Baruch himself went there, and it is certainly the case that he would have wished them to be aware of the finished work of Jeremiah. If Kings originates in Babylon, then the addition of chapter 52 fits in with the preservation of the text there. It must be supposed that the proto-Septuagintal text was subsequently modified by a similar addition of this concluding chapter.

It is therefore possible to account for the evidence regarding Jeremiah and still maintain that the book originates from around 580 BC and is an accurate reflection of the ministry of Jeremiah. It is not simply a stenographic record of Jeremiah's preaching, but a work that developed throughout his later ministry and was shaped to address the needs of the community in Judah both before and after the fall of Jerusalem.

§3. THE WORLD OF JEREMIAH

3.1 Introduction. The geography of the Middle East has always exerted a substantial influence on the politics of the region, and this was undoubtedly so in the time of Jeremiah. The Fertile Crescent stretches up from the Persian Gulf through the valleys of the Tigris and the Euphrates (Mesopotamia), down along the eastern seaboard of the Mediterranean (Syria–Palestine), and on into the Nile valley in Egypt (see Map 2). Control of the central strategic zone of Syria–Palestine, where there were a number of small states including Judah, was always high on the agenda of the superpowers to the north or south as they vied for total domination of the area. It called for considerable diplomatic and military skills on the part of the rulers of the buffer states to know how to adapt their policies to changing circumstances around them. This was particularly true in Jeremiah's day when there was a succession of major political upheavals in the region: the decline and demise of the Assyrian empire, a temporary spell of independence for Judah, a brief period of Egyptian domination, and then the iron grasp of the neo-Babylonian empire under Nebuchadnezzar. To know whom to back and when to do so required the exercise of considerable shrewdness and sagacity, something that the rulers of Judah proved incapable of, and as a result their state was eventually wiped from the map in 586 BC.

It was also the case that Judah in Jeremiah's day experienced internal upheaval when King Josiah introduced sweeping religious reforms which only partially won the support of his subjects, so that during the subsequent reigns the reforms were allowed to lapse and various foreign influences reasserted themselves. While Josiah himself ruled wisely and equitably, the same cannot be said for his successors. Increasing external pressure and ongoing internal disquiet and confusion meant that in its final years Judah lurched from one crisis to another.

It was against such a background that Jeremiah exercised his prophetic calling. The prophets did not engage in abstract theological speculation, but were divinely instructed to apply the revealed law of the LORD to the specifics of the situation of their own day. Their theology was an intensely practical, applied theology, and many lessons can still be drawn from it for current application. To do this sensitively requires an appreciation of the background circumstances of the times, many features of which are not expressly stated in the prophetic literature because their contemporaries were already familiar with them. As we become aware of such information shared by the prophet and his audience, not only are we in a position to understand better the prophet's original message, but also, by detecting the similarities and dissimilarities between his times and ours, we can apply that message more surely to our own situation. In this way we can develop a hermeneutical bridge between earlier and later times, enabling us to grasp the relevance of Jeremiah's message for the present.

The modern reader is fortunate in the considerable amount of detail that is available concerning the world of Jeremiah's day. At many points the book makes contact with historical events regarding which we have other information and are able to assign precise dates to them (for a more detailed discussion of the chronological information see the Appendix to Volume 2). What is contained in the book itself is supplemented by the narratives in 2 Kgs. 21–25 and 2 Chron. 33–36, and there is further background material available from the writings of the contemporary prophets Zephaniah, Nahum, Habakkuk and Ezekiel. To the scriptural data there has been added over the past century information provided by archaeology. In 1923 data from the Babylonian Chronicles for 616–609 BC was published, and in 1956 this was augmented by the publication of further material from the same source for the years 626–623 BC, 608–595 BC and 556 BC (Wiseman 1956). The Babylonian Chronicles are not a single document, but a set of texts recorded in tightly packed cuneiform writing on clay prisms. They were composed in the style of a detached observer presenting straightforward summaries of royal reigns, based apparently upon year-by-year records of events kept in Babylon. We thus have an outline for the major events for parts of the reigns of the Babylonian kings Nabopolassar (626–605 BC) and Nebuchadnezzar (605–562 BC). Archaeological discoveries of one kind and another, including some small but important written items, add to our knowledge. While there are still many gaps, we are able to present a remarkably full picture of what occurred. In this section we will look at the general history of the times, and in the next section we will attempt to set Jeremiah's life into this framework.

3.2 The Fall of Samaria. When Tiglath-Pileser III came to the Assyrian throne in 745 BC, there began a period of highly successful imperialistic expansion which led to this Mesopotamian power dominating for over a century the ancient Near East (confusingly this is much the same area as is now termed the Middle East). By 740 BC Tiglath-Pileser had conquered all of northern Syria, and in 738 BC he subjugated the Aramean city-state of Hamath, forcing other small kingdoms nearby to pay tribute. Included among them was Israel under Menahem (2 Kgs. 15:19-20). This represented the first stage of Assyrian control in which a vassal relationship was established with the minor state, obligating it to pay tribute and also to provide military manpower as required. The satellite state continued to be ruled by its own king, but should he engage in any subversive activity, there was immediate Assyrian military intervention to depose him and install a more compliant ruler (still often from the native royal house). At this point the territory of the state would be reduced, tribute requirements would be increased, the foreign policy of the ruler more closely monitored, and numbers of the nobility would be transported to distant parts of the empire to act as hostages against the future behaviour of the country and its regime. The third stage of Assyrian domination followed quickly upon any suggestion of further unrest from the vassal territory. Then its ruler would be removed and its independence totally eliminated. An Assyrian governor with support staff would be assigned to what was now a totally integrated province of the empire, and there would be additional substantial deportations, particularly of the upper classes of the nation, and also the introduction of foreign peoples into the region to dilute further the possibility of effective rebellion against Assyria.

Before advancing Assyrian might Damascus was captured in 732 BC, and the territory of the northern kingdom of Israel was eroded in stages by Assyrian annexation, under which it was divided into three provinces. Hoshea, the last king of Israel, was left in charge of a small kingdom centred on Samaria, but then in an act of grave folly, probably incited by the Egyptians (2 Kgs. 17:3-4), Hoshea decided to withhold tribute from Shalmaneser V (727–722 BC). This provoked the inevitable Assyrian response. Hoshea himself was quickly captured, but his capital withstood siege for three years before being taken in 722 BC and incorporated into the Assyrian province of Samerina.

There were immediate deportations from Samaria to various parts of Babylonia and Media (2 Kgs. 17:6), followed by forced settlement of foreigners in the land (2 Kgs. 17:24). At later times in the reigns of Esarhaddon (681–669 BC; Ezra 4:2) and Ashurbanipal (669–627 BC; Ezra 4:10), there were further settlements of foreign peoples. These all brought their own gods with them and set up shrines to them in the former territory of Israel (2 Kgs. 17:29-33). Although the Assyrians sponsored a priest of the LORD who settled in Bethel (2 Kgs. 17:25-28), the situation in the north was one of religious confusion.

3.3 Assyria and Judah. Judah was not swept away at the same time as Samaria because in 733 BC it had already become a vassal state of Assyria. Ahaz of Judah (743–715 BC) had refused to join a coalition of nations organising themselves to resist Assyria, and when the coalition had instead turned against Judah, Ahaz rejected the advice of the prophet Isaiah and sought help from Tiglath-Pileser (2 Kgs. 16:7-9). As a result of this policy Judah was compelled to undertake the obligations of a normal vassal. Tribute was paid to the Assyrian ruler by taking the gold and silver found in the Temple and the royal treasury (2 Kgs. 16:7-9). There was also recognition of Assyrian gods in the Temple in Jerusalem. Ahaz was obliged to appear before Tiglath-Pileser in Damascus and to pay homage to the Assyrian gods at a bronze altar that stood there. A copy of this altar was then made and set up in the Jerusalem Temple (2 Kgs. 16:10-15). When Ahaz died in 715 BC, he left to his son, Hezekiah, a kingdom virtually surrounded by Assyrian territory and a kingdom itself at the first stage of vassalage to the empire.

In 729 BC, when Hezekiah was eleven years old, he had come to the throne as co-regent with his father. On assuming sole kingship he immediately initiated several religious reforms, reopening the Temple and reinstituting the Passover. He made moves to integrate any remaining Israelites in the north into the worship at Jerusalem (2 Chron. 30:1), and also had a measure of success in reclaiming Philistine territory which had been considerably weakened by Assyrian invasion (2 Kgs. 18:8). After making extensive diplomatic and military preparations, Hezekiah, encouraged by unrest all over the empire on the accession of Sennacherib (705–681 BC), revolted against Assyria. A response was delayed while Sennacherib dealt with trouble elsewhere, but when it did come, it was devastating.

In a strong campaign Sennacherib overwhelmed various states in Syria–Palestine that were allied with Judah. He crushed Sidon, and caused Ashdod, Ammon, Moab and Edom to pay tribute. Assyrian records report that he took forty-six walled and strong cities in Judah. Lachish was besieged (shown in a relief in the royal palace at Nineveh), Hezekiah was 'shut up like a bird in a cage' (*ANET*, 288) and forced to pay tribute to Sennacherib (2 Kgs. 18:13-16). More of his land was annexed and given to the Philistine kings, and Padi, king of Ekron, who had been imprisoned by Hezekiah, was released. But biblical and Assyrian records agree that Jerusalem was not taken in 701 BC. The miraculous preservation of the city was to become an important feature in the thought of the nation during the following century. It was interpreted as an indication of an absolute commitment of the LORD to the preservation of Jerusalem, no matter how ominous the circumstances and no matter how flagrant the misconduct of her citizens. This encouraged them to think of themselves as different from the northern kingdom in that they had the Temple and the Davidic dynasty to ensure divine blessing on Judah.

It would be wrong to think of the Assyrian withdrawal from Jerusalem as in some sense a victory for Judah. Hezekiah's efforts to break free from Assyria had failed, and he was left on the Judean throne only after agreeing that he had 'done wrong' and that he would pay whatever the Assyrian king imposed on him (2 Kgs. 18:14). Surprisingly in the light of the central role he had played in the revolt, Hezekiah's kingdom was not reduced in status to an Assyrian province. This may have been because of an Assyrian desire to have buffer states between their own territory and Egypt.

3.4 The Reign of Manasseh. After Hezekiah's death, his son Manasseh (687–642 BC; he had already been coregent since the age of 12 in 697 BC) inherited a land which still had not recovered economically from the devastation of invasion and which remained a vassal to Assyria, paying tribute and providing military manpower. During Manasseh's reign the Assyrian empire reached its zenith. Sennacherib's successors Esarhaddon (681–669 BC) and Ashurbanipal (669–627 BC) were able to invade Egypt and even to sack its ancient capital of Thebes in 663 BC. With such massive forces moving south near, or through, his territory Manasseh had no option but to remain a loyal vassal of Assyria.

But Manasseh did more than that. He returned to the pro-Assyrian policy of his grandfather Ahaz. This involved not merely political subservience but also recognition of the gods of Assyria. Indeed he went much further and opened the door to all kinds of irregular religious practice. He cancelled the reform measures of Hezekiah, allowed the restoration of local shrines, gave full rein to old Canaanite practices including Baal worship and the erection of an Asherah, and tolerated the fertility cult with its sacred prostitution even in the very Temple precincts (2 Kgs. 21:4-7; Zeph. 1:4-5). By offering his own son, the king went further still by participating in the cult of Molech with its practice of human sacrifice (2 Kgs. 21:6). All these actions were heinous offences against the LORD, and throughout Manasseh's long reign there was an increasing openness to, and adoption of, pagan practices throughout Judah. This wholesale disregard of covenant law was tantamount to a rejection of the sole sovereignty of Yahweh, Israel's covenant God. Once the law of the covenant was rejected, violence and injustice abounded (2 Kgs. 21:16) The enormity of Manasseh's religious and social misconduct constituted adequate grounds for the judgment that subsequently befell the nation (2 Kgs. 21:9-15; 24:3-4).

Although Manasseh's life ended with a personal return to the LORD (2 Chron. 33:12-13) and a correction of religious abuses in the land (2 Chron. 33:15-17), this situation prevailed for only a short time because his son Amon (642–640 BC) evidently followed his father's pro-Assyrian policy and promoted his former religious policy. Amon reigned only briefly before being assassinated, probably by high officials who may have been trying to organise an anti-Assyrian revolt. The 'people of the land' intervened and the assassins were executed and the eight-year-old Josiah, grandson of Manasseh, was placed on the throne (2 Kgs. 21:23-24). Around this time Jeremiah was born.

3.5 The Decline of Assyrian Power. It is always difficult to point to a particular event that marks the end of an empire. What is obvious in hindsight may well not have been so to contemporary observers. But when the Assyrians changed their policy of maintaining buffer states between themselves and Egypt, and decided instead to attack Egypt, they overreached the capability even of their efficient military and administrative machine.

Before the start of the reign of Esarhaddon in the early seventh century BC, Assyria had broken the power of the kingdom of Urartu to the north of its territory (see on 51:27), but that left it directly exposed to incursions from the Cimmerians (Gomer) and then the Scythians (Ashkenaz) whose territory lay further north. By military and diplomatic means Esarhaddon was able to divert these peoples westwards into Asia Minor, and then having had some success against the Medes to the north-east and having made a treaty with Elam to the south-east of Mesopotamia, what else was left for an active and aggressive emperor to do but to turn to the other end of the Fertile Crescent and campaign against Egypt? The battles he fought were even by his own account very bloody, but he did win. When the Egyptian pharaoh Tirhakah fled to his native Ethiopia, many native Egyptians were pleased to see the ousting of the southern dynasty, and several of them were recognised as local princes, loyal to Assyria. But the Assyrians could not hold Egypt. Whenever their army withdrew, Tirhakah returned, and two years later Esarhaddon had to come back to fight in Egypt—but he fell ill and died on route. He left his kingdom divided between his two sons, Ashurbanipal as king in Nineveh, and Shamash-shum-ukin as an independent but subordinate king in Babylon.

Ashurbanipal (668–627 BC) continued his father's campaign, drove Tirhakah south again, and took Thebes in Upper Egypt, some 435 miles (700 km) from the Mediterranean. But it was impossible for Assyria to hold Egypt, however many battles might be won. The supply lines were very extended, there were insufficient Assyrian troops to garrison the land effectively, and revolt followed on revolt. Psammetichus I (Psamtek, 664–610 BC), one of the local princes through whom the Assyrians had hoped to control Egypt, spread his influence from the city of Sais in the Delta throughout Egypt, drove out the last Assyrian soldiers in 655 BC, and took control of Egypt, founding the 26th Dynasty.

By then Ashurbanipal was fully occupied in a fresh war with Elam, where a hostile king had ascended the throne. No sooner had the Elamites been crushed than in 651 BC there was a revolt in Babylon led by Ashurbanipal's brother who, though a foreigner, held the loyalty of the local people. Shamash-shum-ukin had also taken steps to create a wide-ranging conspiracy, and there are those who suggest that Manasseh's imprisonment in Babylon (2 Chron. 33:11) indicates that even Judah was implicated. It took three years of hard fighting before Ashurbanipal secured victory. Shamash-shum-ukin died in the flames of his own palace in Babylon (648 BC). The Arab tribes who had joined in the confederacy were dealt with next, but not easily. Elam was finally crushed (639 BC) and its capital Susa sacked. But though Ashurbanipal had restored a semblance of control to his scattered domains, all this had taken its toll on Assyria militarily, economically and politically.

Scarcely anything is known of the last decade of Ashurbanipal's reign, but the Assyrian army was exhausted with constant hard fighting, and the emperor had no real friends in any quarter. Babylon in particular was very antagonistic, and beyond the eastern mountains the Medes made little secret of their hostility. Civil strife broke out in Assyria itself probably even before Ashurbanipal's death in 627 BC.

Assyria's last governor in Babylon, a Chaldean named Nabopolassar, revolted as soon as he heard of Ashurbanipal's death, and after defeating Assyrian forces in October 626 BC, he declared himself king of Babylon. Subsequent kings of Assyria, Ashur-etil-ilani (627–623 BC) and then Sin-shar-ishkun (623–612 BC), fought Nabopolassar as aggressively as they could, but gradually he proved the stronger. The old capital Asshur was briefly besieged in 616 BC, and Assyria in desperation sought the help of Egypt, but assistance did not arrive soon enough to turn the tide. Babylon's armies were suddenly reinforced by the Medes, whose king Cyaxeres invaded Assyria without warning in 615 BC. Cyaxeres captured Asshur in 614 BC, and then the two allied armies joined forces for the final assault on Nineveh which they captured in 612 BC. On the death of Sin-shar-ishkun, an army officer made himself king under the name Ashur-uballit, and set up court at Haran in Syria, with Egyptian support. Two years later that last stronghold fell to the Babylonians and their allies, who subsequently repulsed a counter-attack in 609 BC, and with that defeat the last embers of the Assyrian empire were extinguished. Peoples throughout the region shed no tears over the demise of a cruel and hated conqueror, but they waited in bewilderment to see what would happen next.

3.6 The Reforms of Josiah. It was during the period of the rapid collapse of Assyrian power that Josiah became king in 640 BC when he was only eight years old. During his minority, government of the land would have been in the hands of leading courtiers. As far as we can ascertain these men were not only anti-Assyrian in their sentiments (and so well disposed towards anything that asserted Judah's national identity over against their hated overlords) but also genuinely in sympathy with the worship of the LORD.

There are two extensive narratives about Josiah in 2 Kgs. 22–23 and 2 Chron. 34–35, which mainly focus on his religious reforms. While both accounts mention his removal of pagan cults, the finding of the Book of the Law and the renewal of the covenant, and the celebration of the Passover, this last item receives more attention in Chronicles, while Kings emphasises the first. 'The writer of Kings does not attempt anything in the nature of a consecutive, exhaustive account of Josiah's reign. He reigned for thirty-one years, but the writer's theme is sufficiently and strikingly illustrated by a spot-light on one significant incident which occurred about the middle of his reign' (Robinson 1951:5). From the Chronicles account, however, it is evident that Josiah's reforms took place in stages.

In the eighth year of Josiah's reign (633/32 BC), when he was sixteen years old, he began to seek the LORD, and four years later, in his twelfth year (629/28 BC), when he was twenty, he began to purge Judah and Jerusalem (2 Chron. 34:3). After another six years, it was in the eighteenth year of his reign (623/22 BC) that repair of the Temple was begun (2 Kgs. 22:3; 2 Chron. 34:8) and there was found 'the Book of the Law' (2 Kgs. 22:8) or 'the Book of the Law of the LORD that had been given through Moses' (2 Chron. 34:14). 'The Chronicler makes explicit what is probably implied by the Kings account, that the book was actually found *before* the repair of the Temple began, and presumably in or near the place where the money had been kept' (Robinson 1951:7). The book was a single scroll, which probably contained the text of Deuteronomy. Though the descriptions given of it are identical to those often employed for the whole five books of Moses, the fact that it is a single scroll that the accounts refer to makes it more likely to be one book. From the reaction of those involved it is obvious that the book possessed unquestioned authority and that its contents had not been read in any assembly of Israel during the lifetime of those present (Robinson 1951:31-2). 'The main emphasis in the account in Kings of the discovery of the book is not on a demand for a revolution in religious practice, but the *revelation of doom* which is imminent because of Manasseh's sin, *even in spite of* Josiah's humility. Josiah does not send to ask what he should do, so much as to find out if the threat is really true. Huldah gives no order to Josiah to begin a great reform, but simply avers that the threat is exactly as the book states' (Robinson 1951:11).

When Josiah became interested in religious matters, we may presume that he was informed of the essential demands of the Law through the instruction of a faithful few remaining among the priests or prophets, but these men were relying only on oral teaching and tradition. When the discovery of the scroll was made, it seems particularly to have been the curses of the broken covenant found in Deut. 27–28 which brought home to the king the dire peril the nation was in because of the apostasy of the preceding seventy years. He therefore continued and extended his previous efforts at reform. The use of the high places for the worship of the LORD was suppressed. On the analogy of what Moses had done at the plains of Moab, Josiah solemnly renewed the covenant of the people with the LORD and required everyone in Judah and Jerusalem to pledge themselves to it (2 Kgs. 23:1-3; 2 Chron. 34:29-32). He convened a Passover in Jerusalem, which would have reminded the people of the way in which they had been divinely liberated from Egypt. No doubt the theme of freedom also fitted in with the prevailing nationalistic sentiment of the nation as they regained control of their own affairs while the Assyrians withdrew. Josiah also sought to extend his purge into the territory of the former northern kingdom, destroying the idols found there (2 Kgs. 23:15-20; 2 Chron. 34:6-7, 33). This was, of course, only possible because of the collapse of Assyrian control in that area. Even so, it is by no means established that Josiah was able to annex these areas; only that he exercised influence over them. Archaeological evidence also suggests that Josiah was able to make his presence felt in the area of Philistia. This did not, of course, happen overnight. As Assyrian influence receded, so Josiah's moves became more confident and extensive.

It is probable that this expanded influence is a factor to be taken into account in seeking an explanation for the final puzzling incident in Josiah's life where he met his end at the hand of Pharaoh Neco II (610–595 BC). Egypt under Psammetichus I had for many years been building up its resources with a view to re-establishing its influence in Syria–Palestine. It was this aim, rather than any sympathy towards the Assyrians, that drew Egypt into the conflict with Babylon, and Egyptian forces began to assist the Assyrians as early as 616 BC. Josiah probably grasped the long-term significance of this for the independence of Judah. Though Neco assured him that he had no hostile intentions against Judah (2 Chron. 35:21), Josiah persisted in attacking him as he moved north in 609 BC. This may have been a pro-Babylonian gesture in the hope that when they were victorious (they had already dealt a severe blow to Egypt and her allies in the previous year), the Babylonians would respect Judah's independence and also Josiah's sovereignty over Israelite and Philistine territory. His move tragically failed, Josiah was killed, and Judah fell under Egyptian hegemony.

3.7 The Reign of Jehoahaz/Shallum (609 BC). With Josiah's death the 'people of the land' placed his son Shallum on the throne (2 Kgs. 23:30-31), bypassing his elder brother (2 Kgs. 23:36). Shallum took the throne name Jehoahaz, but his reign lasted only three months. Though Neco was unsuccessful in his aim of retaking Haran from the Babylonians, the latter were too occupied with other matters to follow up their victory and Egyptian control of Syria–Palestine persisted for several years. When Neco returned from northern Syria, Jehoahaz presented himself to him at

Riblah, voluntarily recognising Judah's subservience to Egypt. In spite of this, he was placed in bonds and deprived of his rule. A modest fine of a hundred talents of silver and a talent of gold was imposed on Judah, and Jehoahaz was taken into exile in Egypt, where he eventually died (2 Kgs. 23:33-34). Though Jehoahaz had not favoured religious reform (2 Kgs. 23:32), Jeremiah expressed sympathy for his fate (22:10-11).

3.8 The Reign of Jehoiakim/Eliakim (609-598 BC). Jehoahaz's elder brother, Eliakim, was then placed on the throne as an Egyptian appointee and given the throne name Jehoiakim. He was a determined, irreligious man whose focus was on his own power and prestige. The nation was already aware of his character and policies, and had deliberately passed him over three months earlier. His pro-Egyptian stance and tyrannical rule were deeply unpopular, an attitude that was intensified by the levy he raised to pay the tribute demanded from Judah by Neco. Jehoiakim did not raid the royal or Temple treasury but instead extracted the silver and gold from the people of the land in special taxation (2 Kgs. 23:35).

Acutely aware of how he had come to power and of his own citizens' dislike of him, Jehoiakim sought to boost his prestige by surrounding himself with the trappings of monarchy. At some point in his reign, probably during the early years when he was an Egyptian vassal, he began the construction of a new royal palace, but not at his own expense (22:13). A seal, probably from this time, has been found with the inscription: 'Belonging to Palayahu who is over the compulsory labour'. Possibly Jehoiakim in seeking to emulate Solomon's building achievements had also resumed his practice of using conscripted labour. Whatever it was, Jeremiah was scathing in his denunciation (22:13-19).

The religious state of the nation rapidly deteriorated under Jehoiakim. Even during Josiah's reign the reform movement may already have run out of steam, but now it was brought to a halt, if not reversed. It was not that Jehoiakim tried to introduce any particular pagan practices. In 2 Kgs. 23:37 he is condemned in the general phrase that he did evil in the sight of the LORD as his fathers had done, and no specific charge of spiritual malpractice is laid against him. There is, for instance, no accusation that he restored the high places and encouraged worship there. The central sanctuary continued to be the focus of organised and recognised religious life in the nation. But Jehoiakim was not a religious man; he took little interest in promoting or opposing any religious view in and of itself. It was his political position that was the focus of his interest. When he had the prophet Uriah extradited from Egypt and assassinated (26:20-23), it was because he regarded his utterances as seditious (not heretical), liable to undermine the regime.

The impetus behind the reform programme of Josiah had always been the king's personal involvement. Without it, the people soon showed how superficial their attachment to the LORD was and how little impact had been made on them despite all Josiah's endeavours. Pagan practices, which had probably never been totally suppressed, were again openly espoused. While Judah claimed to adhere to the covenant, the superficiality and nominalism of their religious practice revealed the extent to which the national psyche had been warped during the years of Manasseh's apostasy. The resurgence of other cults was not, however, a matter that caused Jehoiakim any concern.

For the first four years of Jehoiakim's reign the battlefront between Egypt and Babylon lay to the north of Palestine along the river Euphrates. During this period Jehoiakim remained a loyal ally of Egypt, but that all abruptly changed with the Egyptian defeat at Carchemish in the summer of 605 BC. The overwhelming victory of the Babylonian crown prince Nebuchadnezzar completely reversed the balance of power in Syria–Palestine, and he ruthlessly drove home his advantage, defeating the Egyptians again at Hamath and driving the survivors back to their own border. 'The king of Egypt did not march out from his own country again, because the king of Babylon had taken all his territory, from the Wadi of Egypt to the Euphrates River' (2 Kgs. 24:7). The way in which the ferocious Babylonian invasion would undermine local morale was anticipated in the description of Hab. 1:6-11. Before such a force, Jehoiakim had no option but to submit. Following the earlier Assyrian practice, this submission seems to have taken place in two stages. In Nebuchadnezzar's first pursuit of the Egyptians southwards, he took hostages and tribute from the states that has previously been under their rule, and Judah was not exempt from this, the hostages including the young Daniel (Dan. 1:1-3; see also Appendix §7 in Volume 2). After his enthronement, Nebuchadnezzar seems for a time to have returned each year to Syria–Palestine, most notably in late 604 BC when he seized the Philistine city of Ashkelon, which had refused to surrender, and took its king into captivity. During one of these campaigns arrangements with Judah and Jehoiakim were put on a more formal basis, because 2 Kgs. 24:1 records that Jehoiakim became Nebuchadnezzar's vassal for three years. As this ended in 601 or 600 BC, it probably relates to circumstances in 604 or 603 BC.

The Babylonian record of the campaign that Nebuchadnezzar waged in his fourth year (spring 601–spring 600 BC) is significant in that it records an attack on Egypt, where the two armies inflicted great damage on each other in the winter of 601/600 BC. Neither side could claim a victory, as the Babylonian Chronicle implicitly acknowledges by recording that in the following year Nebuchadnezzar did not campaign but spent his time at home building up his forces and re-equipping his chariotry. The Egyptians meantime felt confident enough to mount some show of strength in southern Palestine. These events induced Jehoiakim to transfer his allegiance from Babylon to Egypt. Nebuchadnezzar was unable to respond directly to the Judean rebellion for the next two years, using instead punitive raids by his allies (2 Kgs. 24:2). His main reaction came in the winter of 598/597 BC when the Babylonian army laid siege to Jerusalem. It would appear, however, that before the siege began Jehoiakim had died in December 598 BC. The events surrounding his death are unclear, and there is the possibility of treachery. His tyrannical rule had caused him to be generally hated, and his death, from whatever cause, was little mourned (22:18; 36:30).

3.9 The Reign of Jehoiachin (597 BC). The reign of Jehoiakim's son, Jehoiachin (also known as Jeconiah or Coniah), lasted for a brief three months and ten days. One of the most remarkable features of the Babylonian Chronicle is the account that it gives of the end of his reign.

> In the seventh year, the month of Kislev, the king of Akkad mustered his troops, marched to the Hatti-land, and encamped against the city of Judah and on the second day of the month of Adar he seized the city and captured the king. He appointed there a king of his own choice (literally, 'heart'), received its heavy tribute and sent [them] to Babylon. (Wiseman 1956:73)

'The king of Akkad' is the term employed in the Chronicles for the Babylonian king, in this case Nebuchadnezzar, and by Babylonian dating his seventh year began in the spring of 598 BC, so that the month Kislev in his seventh year fell between 18th December 598 and 15th January 597 BC. 'Hatti-land' is a Babylonian geographical term for Syria–Palestine (obviously here including Judah). The distance Nebuchadnezzar's army had to march to get to Judah makes it unlikely that it spent more than a week surrounding Jerusalem (certainly under a month) before the city capitulated. The fact that the Chronicle exceptionally records the exact date for this emphasises either the significance to the Babylonians of the capture of this rebel city or the speed with which it was done. Nebuchadnezzar appeared at the city once his army was in place (2 Kgs. 24:11) and captured 'the city of Judah' (i.e. Jerusalem; cf. 2 Chron. 25:28 for the expression) on 16th March 597 BC. Because Jehoiachin had preferred to surrender rather than continue resisting the Babylonians, he was deposed but his life was spared. His surrender also meant that Jerusalem was not ransacked and destroyed. Jehoiachin, along with the royal family and many of the nobility and leaders of Judah, including the prophet Ezekiel, were taken into exile. Though the king was kept in confinement in Babylon, he seems to have received special treatment and the royal family was not split up (*ANET*, 308). Indeed the Babylonians may have continued to regard him as the king of Judah. In the thirty-seventh year of his exile he was freed from prison (52:31-34) though not permitted to return to Jerusalem.

3.10 Zedekiah/Mattaniah (597-586 BC). Nebuchadnezzar did not leave Judah without a king, appointing Mattaniah, another son of Josiah and an uncle of the exiled Jehoiachin, to the throne and renaming him

Zedekiah. He appears as an irresolute and ineffective ruler, and he had been placed in a virtually impossible situation. Many of the people in Judah as well as those in exile in Babylon continued to regard Jehoiachin as their king, and there arose an expectation of his reinstatement (28:4). The land had lost its elite administrative class and also many of its skilled workmen so that the economy was in a weak condition. Furthermore there was a deep internal rift between those who favoured acceptance of Babylonian domination and a group including army officers and many prophets who were pro-Egyptian and urged rebellion. During the early part of his reign Zedekiah managed to check the pro-Egyptian party (no doubt the need to build up men and materials helped him in this by dampening their belligerence), but eventually they succeeded in dragging the king into rebellion against Babylon. In the fourth year of his reign (594/93 BC) there was a conspiracy with a number of neighbouring states (27:3) with the connivance of the newly enthroned Pharaoh Psammetichus II (595–589 BC). But for unknown reasons the plans fell through, and Zedekiah renewed his pledges of loyalty to Nebuchadnezzar, going to Babylon personally (51:59).

In 592 BC, shortly after Psammetichus II had returned from a victorious campaign over Nubia (Ethiopia), he went on some kind of tour through Palestine, where Nebuchadnezzar had not campaigned since 594 BC. Perhaps it was a victory celebration rather than a military incursion, but it must have been viewed as a reassertion of Egyptian interest in the area. Ezekiel refers to Zedekiah around this time as having reneged on his solemn commitment to Nebuchadnezzar and sending to Egypt for military help (Ezek. 17:11). He does not seem to have got the men or weaponry he asked for, but he certainly received assurances, and encouraged by this, in 590 or 589 BC Zedekiah failed to remit the usual annual tribute to Babylon (2 Kgs. 24:20) and in this way declared open rebellion. Lachish Ostracon III shows the extent of Egyptian involvement, in that it records that the visit of a Judean general to Egypt to negotiate for assistance (*ANET* 322). Josephus mentions that Tyre joined in this revolt (*Ag. Ap.* 1.21), and Ammon too rebelled (Ezek. 21:18-23).

Nebuchadnezzar did not take long to react to Zedekiah's rebellion. The siege of Jerusalem began on the tenth day of the tenth month of Zedekiah's ninth year (2 Kgs. 25:1), which is equivalent to 15th January 588 BC. Around this time the Babylonian forces spread throughout Judah, capturing and destroying its fortified cities and pillaging the land. Insight into the tension experienced during this period is revealed by the Lachish Ostraca. The commanding officer of one of the fortresses wrote to his superior in Lachish saying, 'And let [my lord] know that we are watching for the signals of Lachish, according to all the indications which my lord has given, for we cannot see Azekah' (Ostracon IV; *ANET* 322; cf. 34:7). It would seem that Azekah had already been taken by the Babylonians. The situation was exacerbated by divided counsels within the city of which Ostracon VI provides evidence (*ANET* 322; cf. 38:4). During the course of the siege Egypt under Pharaoh Hophra (Apries, 589–570 BC) did make a gesture of support, sending forces into Palestine, and also, it would seem, deploying their fleet (Herodotus *Hist.* 2.161). To meet this threat the Babylonians temporarily lifted of the siege of Jerusalem (37:6-10), but after some months the Egyptians withdrew without any major engagement of the Babylonians and the siege was resumed in earnest, dragging on until July 587 BC or July 586 BC when the supply of food totally ran out. When the fall of Jerusalem is dated as 587/86 BC, this is not an instance of an ancient year overlapping two of our years. There is genuine doubt as to the year in which Jerusalem fell, and whether the siege lasted eighteen or thirty months. For further details see Volume 2, Appendix §§11-12.

When the city wall had been breached, Zedekiah led a group of soldiers at night through a breach in the wall (39:4; 52:7), probably trying to make for Ammon on the other side of the Jordan because it had also revolted at this time. The king had not gone far before he was captured and taken to Riblah in Syria where Nebuchadnezzar had his headquarters. There Zedekiah's sons were killed in front of him, and then his own eyes were put out before he was transported to Babylon (39:5-7).

Jerusalem was systematically looted and destroyed before the Temple and other major buildings were burned down on 17th August 586 BC (52:12), a month after the fall of the city. The Babylonians continued the Assyrian practice of mass deportation of rebellious peoples, and so many of those captured in Jerusalem and also of those who had previously deserted to the Babylonians were taken into exile (39:9). However, in a departure from Assyrian policy, no settlers were brought in from other regions and a native governor was appointed for the land. Many of the poorer people who lacked skills that were in demand in Babylon were left in the land of Judah to maintain a subsistence economy there.

3.11 The Governorship of Gedaliah (586 BC). The governor the Babylonians appointed over the land was Gedaliah, a member of a prominent Jerusalem family which was pro-Babylonian in its outlook. Gedaliah previously had held a high position in Zedekiah's administration, and he seems to have approached the task allotted to him with considerable skill. He encouraged the survivors who had not been exiled and also those who had fled as refugees to neighbouring states to form a viable community in the land (40:7-11). He himself was stationed at Mizpah in the territory of Benjamin because it was one site which had not been destroyed in the recent fighting. However, Gedaliah's governorship was brief because he was assassinated by Ishmael, a member of the Davidic royal family, who was probably acting in concert with Baalis, the Ammonite king. Ishmael was unable to gain support from those left in the land, and he again fled to Ammon (41:1-14). Because the remnants of Gedaliah's supporters feared

Babylonian reprisals, they made their way south to Egypt and settled there (43:4-7). The situation they left behind them in Judah is unclear. Presumably there was some population eking out a minimal living in the ruins of the land whose defences and economy were wrecked. They lived passively under Babylonian control, concerned with survival, not rebellion. 'All her people groan as they search for bread; they barter their treasures for food to keep themselves alive' (Lam. 1:11).

3.12 The Exilic Community. Even before Nebuchadnezzar's time there had been a substantial community from Israel and Judah in Mesopotamia. Tiglath-Pileser II had begun the process by deporting Israelites from Gilead and Galilee in 732 BC (2 Kgs. 15:29), and Assyrian records listed 27,290 as exiled in connection with the fall of Samaria. Not long afterwards Sennacherib moved 200,150 persons from Judah (*ANET* 288). These groups were settled in various parts of Mesopotamia (2 Kgs. 17:6). Next to nothing is known about their subsequent history, but it may be presumed that while most merged into their new environment, some at any rate joined the groups of those later deported by the Babylonians. After the first fairly small scale deportation in 605 BC (Dan. 1:1-3), more substantial transportations occurred in 597 BC and 586 BC, and there were other smaller groups deported including one in 582 BC (52:28-30).

Babylonia itself was the main reception centre for the later deportees (Ps. 137:1; Ezek. 1:3). Nebuchadnezzar was engaged in major public works in the area and the skills of craftsmen could be readily used. There thus arose a viable community centred round the deposed king Jehoiachin and retaining its own social organisation including elders (29:1) and a certain measure of autonomy. The community seems to have enjoyed a fair measure of prosperity. Those artisans employed on state projects would have been paid from the royal treasury. At first the exiles received grants of land which they cultivated as tenants (29:5), and it is known from other records that there were many who soon engaged in commerce. The size of the offerings sent to Jerusalem after the Exile show a community that was by no means impoverished (Ezra 1:6; 2:68-69). Indeed, the fact that so many did not return but were content to remain in Babylonia shows how comfortably off they considered themselves to be. The community adopted the Aramaic language as their ordinary means of communication and gave up the older Hebrew script as their mode of writing. Other cultural assimilation included the adoption of the Babylonian names for the months of the year, and also the use of many Babylonian-style personal names. However, they did retain their ethnic and national identity largely because they kept their religious practices such as circumcision and the Sabbath. Many locate the origin of the synagogue in the way worship was organised among the exiles.

3.13 The Fall of Babylon. Details about Nebuchadnezzar's closing years are sketchy because the Babylonian Chronicles for the period have not been discovered. Josephus (*Ant.* 10.9.7) mentions that in the twenty-third year of his reign (582/81 BC), after defeating Moab and Ammon, Nebuchadnezzar attacked Egypt, killed its king and installed another ruler there as well as transporting the Jewish refugees to Babylon. This account is not without problems; for instance, there is no record of any transition of power at this time in Egypt. However, continuing Babylonian activity is not improbable. From over a decade later a fragmentary cuneiform text (Wiseman 1985:39-41) indicates that Nebuchadnezzar took advantage of the confused transition of power from Hophra to Ahmose II (Amasis) to invade Egypt around 568 BC, not to occupy the country but to deter it from becoming further involved in overseas adventures in Cyprus and Phoenicia (cf. 43:13). Thus, as far as we can tell, Nebuchadnezzar maintained till the end a strong presence throughout the area.

However, after Nebuchadnezzar's death in 562 BC, the neo-Babylonian empire rapidly disintegrated. He was succeeded by his son, Amel-Marduk (Evil-Merodach, 52:31), who ruled for under two years in 562–560 BC, during which time he treated Jehoiachin kindly (52:31-34). He was assassinated by his brother-in-law, Nergal-šar-uṣur (Neriglissar, 560–556 BC), who is probably to be identified with the Nergal-sharezer of 39:3. During his reign he campaigned in Asia Minor, but on the way home succumbed to a mysterious disease. His young son, Labashi-marduk, reigned only for nine months before being ousted by a military coup.

Nabonidus (556–539 BC), a military commander from Haran in northern Syria, was very unpopular in Babylon because of his religious policies which focused on supplanting the traditional Babylonian worship of the sun god Marduk with the moon god Sin, which was the principal deity of his home town and many other places in the empire. Indeed, Nabonidus did not care much for Babylon, or else he found conditions there too hostile for comfort. For most of his reign he lived at Tema (25:23), an oasis on the western edge of the north Arabian desert, and left the conduct of affairs in Babylon to his son Belshazzar.

Militarily Nabonidus and Belshazzar were no match for one of the greatest kings and conquerors in history, Cyrus II, who had inherited the throne of Persia and Anshan, two small states on the Persian Gulf, in 559 BC. In 550 BC he defeated the much larger state of Media to the north to create the Medo-Persian empire, and then step by step consolidated his position to the north of the Babylonian zone of influence (see on 51:27) reaching across to the Greek cities of Asia Minor, capturing Sardis, the capital of Lydia in 547 BC and then extending his realm eastwards into India. After that Cyrus was in a position to move south against the Babylonian empire. Though Nabonidus had belatedly returned to Babylon, neither he nor Belshazzar had real support from their subjects. The main battle against the Medo-Persian forces was fought and lost at Opir on the Tigris late in September 539 BC, and on 12th October the troops of Cyrus entered Babylon without having to meet real opposition (see on 50:24). Belshazzar was killed, and Nabonidus was captured and exiled. On 29th October (dates as in *ISBE* 3:469) Cyrus himself entered the city in triumphal procession, being greeted by its inhabitants as their liberator.

The religious policies of Cyrus were remarkably tolerant for the times. He instituted a programme of repatriating deported peoples and restoring the images of their gods to their temples. As part of this enlightened policy the Jews were permitted to return to Jerusalem and to begin work on reinstating the Temple (Ezra 6:13). Cyrus also returned to them the articles of silver and gold which the Babylonians had looted from it (Ezra 1:9-11; 6:14). In this way there came about the prophesied release of the Jews and a new era in their history began.

§4. THE LIFE OF JEREMIAH

Though we know more about the circumstances of the life of Jeremiah than we do for Isaiah or Ezekiel, and a great deal more than we know for any of the minor prophets, it is still not sufficient to allow us to compose anything like a biography in the modern sense of the term. On the other hand it is not possible to dismiss the details of Jeremiah's life as largely irrelevant on the grounds that what matters is the message he delivered and not his *curriculum vitae*. The record we have gives us significant access to the inner life of the prophet and shows Jeremiah as a living embodiment of his proclamation. In this he resembles most closely the earlier prophet Hosea, the circumstances connected with whose marriage are very much part of the message he had to convey. In the case of Jeremiah also, the man plays a substantial role in the prophetic presentation of the LORD's message to his rebellious people.

4.1 Jeremiah's Early Years

	BC
Jeremiah born	*c.* 639
Josiah's reformation started	628
Jeremiah called	627
Book of the Law found	late 622
The Great Passover	April 621
Fall of Nineveh	612
Battle of Megiddo; death of Josiah	609

Jeremiah records very little about his early life. We know that he was the son of Hilkiah, a priest who lived in Anathoth, and that when his father was told about his birth, it was an occasion of rejoicing for him (20:15). As it had been to Anathoth that the high priest Abiathar had been sent into internal exile by Solomon (1 Kgs. 2:26-27), there is a possibility that Hilkiah and Jeremiah were descended from him, but other Levitical families would have resided in such a priestly city so close to Jerusalem. At any rate the family possessed property in the area (32:9), and there is no reason to suppose them to have been in economically straitened circumstances.

But when was Jeremiah born? This is a crucial factor for reconstructing his life and determining the background to the prophecies of chapters 1–20. The traditional view has been that 1:2, 4 tell us that Jeremiah was called to be a prophet in the thirteenth year of Josiah, that is, 627 BC, and that this date is also vouched for by the evidence of 25:3. There are two other verses (3:6 and 36:2) that mention the days of Josiah in connection with Jeremiah's ministry, and corroborate this general impression.

To establish Jeremiah's age when he was called, attention is directed to the fact that Jeremiah describes himself as 'a youth' at the time of his call (1:6). However, the Hebrew word employed for a 'young male' is of fairly wide application. An upper limit of around twenty years for the term as applied by Jeremiah is suggested by two considerations. (1) Though Jeremiah was of a priestly family, there is no indication that he ever functioned as a priest. Twenty years old was the age at which the Levites began their service (cf. Num. 4:3; 8:24; 1 Chron. 23:3, 24), and so we might well conclude that Jeremiah fell under this threshold. (2) Also given that Jeremiah was not married (16:2) and that marriage would have been expected in a priestly family by the time a man was twenty years old, it was generally concluded that Jeremiah was around 18 years at the time of his call, having been born in 645 BC in the closing years of Manasseh's reign.

Since the 1920s such a reconstruction of Jeremiah's birth and call has been frequently challenged on the grounds that it is difficult to find passages in the prophecy which fit in with what we know about conditions in Josiah's reign. The bleak picture presented in the early chapters of the prophecy does not correspond in any easy way with conditions under Josiah whose purge of idolatry had begun the year before Jeremiah's call. In particular it is argued that it is surprising that Jeremiah passes over in silence the momentous events centring on the finding of the Book of the Law in the Temple in 622 BC and the great Passover held a few months later. Further it is pointed out that when Josiah looked for prophetic help in elucidating the significance of the scroll found in the Temple the royal delegation turned not to Jeremiah but to Huldah (2 Kgs. 22:14; 2 Chron. 34:22). Indeed it is only by inference and guesswork that anything can be said about the prophet's attitude towards Josiah's reform movement. Also it is argued that now that the Scythian hypothesis has been dismissed (see introduction to 4:5), there is no likely identification for Jeremiah's foe from the north during those early years. Further the major international event of Josiah's reign, the fall of Nineveh, is passed by without a mention in the prophecy.

These silences and seeming inconsistencies led a number of scholars to suspect, with differing emphases, that Jeremiah's call was dated too early and that his ministry did not really begin until the reign of Jehoiakim. The few passages that indicated otherwise were either dismissed as late additions to the text or were emended. One favourite change was from 'thirteen' in 1:2 to 'twenty-three', and so Jeremiah's ministry was dated as beginning a decade later. But when arbitrary textual change went out of scholarly fashion, proposals for the late dating of Jeremiah's ministry came to be based on accepting 'thirteen' in 1:2 and taking 627 BC not as the beginning of Jeremiah's public ministry but as the year of his birth, inasmuch as he was divinely set apart as a prophet from the womb. His prophetic ministry then began in his late teens around the time of Josiah's death. This view is argued for, with various elaborate supporting hypotheses, by Holladay (1986, 1:1-10). He supposes that Jeremiah began to preach in 615 BC at the age of twelve. Based on his understanding that there was a septennial covenant renewal ceremony initiated in 622 BC at which Deuteronomy was formally recited, Holladay argues that the sermons of Jeremiah were preached on the same occasion in 615, 608, 601, 594 and 587 BC. This is the kind of precision which the data do not enable us to substantiate.

A more significant reassessment of Jeremiah's early career is that presented by Lundbom (1993; 1999:107-109). It is based on a literary analysis of chapter 1 which separates 1:4-12 from 1:13-19 and claims that Jeremiah's call took place in 627 BC when he was around the age of thirteen, but that he did not accept this call until after the scroll was found in the Temple, when he was eighteen. It was at this stage that the LORD spoke to him for a second time to commission him (1:13-19), and so Jeremiah's ministry begins in 622/21 BC. On this basis Lundbom points out that Jeremiah would have been divinely called at the same age as Samuel (1 Sam. 3:1, where 'boy' is the same word as Jeremiah uses in 1:6; Josephus *Ant.* 5.10.4).

It cannot be said that late dating of the start of Jeremiah's ministry has been accepted even by the majority of critical scholars. There does, however, appear to be some weight in the arguments for Jeremiah's age in 627 BC being taken as about twelve. This need not be accompanied by acceptance of the particular analysis of chapter 1 advocated by Lundbom. There is no good reason for denying that right from the start of his ministry Jeremiah was told of the general tenor of the message he had to deliver. Even young Samuel had had revealed to him a solemn message regarding the future of Eli and his line (1 Sam. 3:11-14). Jeremiah began to present that message over subsequent years so that a ministry that gradually developed after 627 BC seems not improbable.

The arguments for a start to his ministry in the closing years of Josiah's reign are inadequate to counter the evidence of the text. The lack of an immediate referent for the foe from the north derives from modern critical perceptions which see the prophet more as a political commentator on current events than as a recipient of divine disclosure. Once the critical predisposition to narrow the gap between prophetic announcement and historical event is discounted, there is no difficulty in 1:13-19 being dated in 627 BC. Further, Jeremiah's relative youthfulness in 622 BC explains why the royal delegation went elsewhere. At that time he was probably still a student at the scribal school in Jerusalem. The perceived difficulty regarding Jeremiah's attitude to Josiah and his reforms probably reflects the nature of the First Scroll. It was not written as a contemporaneous historical document but as a tract for the times, and those times were the deteriorating situation in Jehoiakim's reign. The tenor of Jeremiah's ministry over the previous twenty-three years had remained remarkably constant, and he summed up his message in a way that applied it clearly to Jehoiakim rather than gave a chronicle of his preaching throughout Josiah's reign.

Jeremiah's Upbringing. Jeremiah seems to recall his youth as a time of joy (8:18). With Hilkiah being a priest, Jeremiah would have received from his earliest days instruction in the sacred traditions of Israel. As Anathoth lay within the territory of Benjamin and not far off from Shiloh, it is probable that Jeremiah would have learned of the history of north and south, as well as becoming familiar with the solemn reminder that Shiloh gave regarding the consequences of apostasy. He would also have been aware in his formative years of the more recent history of his people, including what had occurred during the reigns of Manasseh and Amon.

What would the priests at Anathoth do? It is unlikely that they ministered at a local high place. Their proximity to Jerusalem suggests that they would have participated in the service of the Temple there.

It is likely that during the years after 627 BC Jeremiah as a trainee priest would have attended the scribal school in Jerusalem over which Shaphan presided. It was at this time that there was probably forged the bond between Jeremiah and the family of Shaphan that was to stand him in good stead in later years (26:24; 29:3; 36:11-12, 25; 39:14; 40:5-6). We do not know if during this period Jeremiah went to stay permanently in Jerusalem, but the more he engaged in prophetic ministry, the more probable it is that he lived in the city itself where the Temple provided the main platform for his declarations.

In his training Jeremiah would have become familiar with the traditions of the covenant community. In particular he reveals an extensive knowledge of the Psalms that were sung in the Temple, and an appreciation of them. During this time Jeremiah would also have become aware of the prophetic ministry of Zephaniah who was then active in Jerusalem.

4.2 During Josiah's Reign. Was Jeremiah a supporter of Josiah's reforms? Rowley argued that after first advocating support for the reforms, the prophet then criticised and opposed them. 'There is nothing inherently improbable in his first hope that Josiah's reform would lead to purity in religion and in life being followed by disillusionment, and turning to opposition when he found men putting their trust in the written law and in obedience to the letter, rather than the acceptance of its spirit' (1950:173). Ellison notes, however, that there is no clear evidence either for the prophet's support or for his opposition to the reforms. He argues that from the first Jeremiah realised that official reformations could never meet God's requirements. Although a view of the development of the prophet's thought does have an appeal, 'this view is really based on a forgetting of that strange and indefinable factor that made a prophet. He was more than a godly and God-fearing man of deep spiritual insights. He had stood in God's council (23:18, 22), and had gained an entirely different viewpoint from which to see man's strivings and efforts' (1962:161). 'I do not doubt that the first impulse of Jeremiah's heart was to leap with joy, when the news of a clean sweep of all heathenism was first received. But as a prophet, viewing it from God's standpoint, he could see that it never had any chance of success' (1962:162).

Jeremiah's teaching was consonant with previous revelation, and since Josiah's reform movement was based on a renewed appreciation of the instruction of Deuteronomy, there is a basic similarity in the structure of the teaching to be found in both. This is seen in the emphasis on covenant loyalty. Both Jeremiah and Deuteronomy insist that the way forward for the people is in terms of obedience to the stipulations of the covenant (6:16-21; 7:1-15; 11:1-15; 34:14-22; Deut. 5:1-33; 7:12-16; 18:9-14). This obedience is undermined by any attempt at syncretism, accompanying the worship of the LORD with service of other gods (1:16; 2:9-13, 27-28; 3:9, 24; 7:6-10; 16:10-20; 22:9; 25:6; Deut. 12:1-7, 29-32; 13:1-18; 17:2-7; 18:9-14). In exposing the sin of the nation Jeremiah aims at the same response as Deuteronomy, namely repentance, in which the people turn to the LORD and are permitted to continue enjoying the blessings of the covenant, especially occupation of the land of promise (7:3, 7; 25:5; 35:15: Deut. 11:8-12; 12:1; 16:20; 19:8-9; 23:21; 25:15; 26:1-11; 30:4-5). It is true that Deuteronomy is written more in terms of instituting the basic structures of Israelite society, particularly its cultic practice, whereas Jeremiah is frequently critical of the religious establishment (6:16-21; 7:21-23; 11:15; 14:11-12). However, this is largely a matter of differing historical situations and not a fundamental divergence about what the role of king, priest and sacrifice ought to be. It is necessary to insist on this essential harmony between Jeremiah and Deuteronomy because of the variety of hypotheses that have been propounded concerning the relationship between them. The prophet builds on and seeks to apply the Mosaic vision of how the covenant people should live before the LORD.

During Josiah's reign, therefore, it seems as if Jeremiah's ministry was broadly supportive of official policy regarding religious reformation. It was not that public policy was going in the wrong direction; it was rather that it was not, indeed could not, go far enough. The prophet was always aware that changing outward religious structures was no substitute for inner heart change. The record of his early ministry shows that it was this spiritually fundamental feature that was the essence of Jeremiah's message as he called for repentance and inner reorientation towards God. Only in this way would Josiah's covenant renewal ceremony come to true fruition at the level of individual and national reconsecration to the LORD. Jeremiah had grasped the two-part structure of the covenant. Blessing would flow from obedience. But if there was only superficial, nominal change, then disobedience to the basic demand of the covenant for complete loyalty to the LORD would result in divine judgment. Jeremiah had been divinely made aware of the dire prospects that awaited the people if they did not display true loyalty. The imminence of the foe from the north gave urgency to the prophet's proclamation. However, the nation was content with the trappings of religion and unable to see the need for repentance. After all, had the land not already been purged of the offensive practices of earlier times and the Temple restored? Rededication of a building had taken the place of personal devotion to the LORD.

A Northern Ministry? As has been remarked in §3.6, when Assyrian power began to wane, Josiah extended his influence into the territory of the former northern kingdom of Israel. It is an unresolved question whether in connection with this Jeremiah engaged in a ministry specifically to the population that remained in the north. Arguments for such a ministry have focused on passages such as 3:12-18; 4:1-2; 30:10; 31:1-21. The focus in these verses on Israel or Ephraim as distinct from Judah has suggested that Jeremiah may be recalling earlier occasions when he had spoken directly to survivors from the north. However, the language need involve no more than a vivid attempt to bring home to Judah the lessons of what had happened to Israel a century previously. At a time when renewed interest in Deuteronomy brought back memories of the united kingdom, there was an obvious point of contact in the experience of the north to impress upon the south what her history had to teach them.

Jeremiah's Personal Circumstances. During this period Jeremiah was not alone in sharing with others the hope that Judah would seize the opportunity afforded by Josiah's reformation and truly return to the faith of their fathers. There was an inner group of courtiers around Josiah who shared the king's vision. There were prophets like Zephaniah and Habakkuk. However, Jeremiah is already a figure who is in measure distanced from his contemporaries. No doubt the politicians thought that their policies would make a difference; Jeremiah was aware of the need for heart change. The prophet was already forbidden to marry, and did not attend ordinary social gatherings whether in Anathoth or Jerusalem. Even at this stage Jeremiah would have known opposition sparked by the spiritual demands of his life and preaching. Those who were challenged, whether high or low, would not have felt comfortable under his indictment (2:8; 3:12-14; 5:30-31; 6:13), and his warnings of impending doom were rejected by a people who wanted to be congratulated on their conduct and reassured that all would be well with them (5:12-13, 31; 6:14-15). There is no mention of the fall of Nineveh because Jeremiah's focus is on the impending fall of his own nation. It would seem that Jeremiah felt frustration at the lack of success which attended his calls for repentance (6:10-11, 16-17). No real repentance has taken place (5:20-31; 8:4-7).

Increasingly the prophet brought out that the LORD's judgment would come upon the nation if it proved obdurate in its rejection of the message he brought, though he was personally grieved by what he had to say. He cannot anticipate the downfall of his people with equanimity, and tells them of his distress to intensify the pathos of the warnings he conveys to them (4:19-21). Jeremiah did not automatically and unthinkingly relay the messages that were given to him. The impact of what he was foretelling came home to him and caused him grief. Invasion would lead to a shriek of lament throughout the land and not only would the prophet himself participate in that grief, he already knew the pain of what is looming over his people. At this time also there are increasing rifts between Jeremiah and his contemporaries who are proclaiming peace for the land on the basis of a superficial analysis of her spiritual condition (4:9-10; 5:12-13, 30-31; 6:13-15). There is an element of dissatisfaction and disillusionment in Jeremiah's teaching (6:16-21).

The prophecy says nothing of the death of Josiah. It was an event which caused consternation at the time, and puzzlement ever since. It is through the pagan king Neco that the LORD's word of warning came to Josiah (2 Chron. 35:20-22)—were there no prophets in Judah? Jeremiah provided a lament for the dead king (2 Chron. 35:25), but had he given him any advice, either to support Egypt or Babylon? Probably at this period Jeremiah's posture was one of non-involvement in the international crises of the times. During Josiah's reign Jeremiah's ministry was, if not part of the official reform movement, at any rate broadly supportive of its aims. In part this may explain the absence of records of direct contact with Josiah. With Josiah's death, however, that was to change because Jeremiah's loyalty to the spiritual aims of the reform brought him into increasing conflict with the religious and political establishment.

4.3 During the Reign of Jehoahaz. The short reign of this king chosen by the people on hearing of Josiah's death gave little scope for prophetic intervention. Insofar as he represented an anti-Egyptian policy and so continued the action adopted by Josiah, Jeremiah probably was as much in sympathy with him as with his father. It is in a tone of respectful sorrow that the prophet speaks of his exile (22:10), which contrasts markedly with the tone in which he addresses his successor (22:13-19).

4.4 During the Reign of Jehoiakim

	BC
Jehoiakim enthroned by Neco	October 609
Jeremiah's Temple Sermon (chaps. 7, 26)	606
Battle of Carchemish	May 605
First Deportation (Daniel)	July/August 605
Nebuchadnezzar enthroned	September 605
First Scroll written (36:1)	early 604
Fall of Ashkelon	November/December 604
First Scroll read (36:9)	November/December 604
Jeremiah and Baruch in hiding; Second Scroll written (36:32)	December 604 on
Nebuchadnezzar defeated in Egypt	winter 601/600
Jehoiakim revolts	spring 600
Judah raided	December 599–February 598
The Rechabites (chap. 35)	598
Death of Jehoiakim	December 598

Jehoiakim's reign witnessed a marked deterioration in Jeremiah's circumstances. Although his message had previously met with hostility, it had been muted because of the ethos of Josiah's regime. That now changed, and the prophet had to face open opposition.

From the early part of Jehoiakim's reign when he was still an Egyptian vassal, Jeremiah's Temple Address (chaps. 7 and 26) contains a scathing indictment of the shallowness of popular religion and the formalism that attended it. The people were expecting divine deliverance in return for ritual observance without heart engagement. They were placing their trust in the Temple, not in the LORD himself. Therefore when they heard Jeremiah announce that the Temple would become a ruin like Shiloh, this was a shocking and blasphemous attack on their core beliefs.

Jeremiah was summoned before the authorities to answer for his utterance. The religious establishment consisting of the priests and prophets were particularly enraged by what he had to say, and they demanded the death penalty. The royal officials seemed to be more sympathetic towards him. Jeremiah escaped the death penalty because he claimed to be speaking on behalf of the LORD, and his message was similar to that which had been earlier uttered by an acknowledged prophet, Micah. Though Jeremiah survived the trial, he needed the special protection of Ahikam, son of Shaphan (26:24).

Many of the Confessions fit in with Jeremiah's situation in the early years of Jehoiakim's reign, when the prophet was at odds with the authorities of Judah. The very basis of Jeremiah's faith was being tested in those times of opposition and hostility, when even his close friends no longer wanted to know him. What the prophet was wanting to find out was where the LORD was in all that he had to undergo. Though Jeremiah did receive assurances which enabled him to continue, his personal situation was to deteriorate further. However, Jeremiah did not abandon his calling and persisted in acting as the LORD's witness to the people.

It is possible that the incidents of chapters 19–20 occur after the Temple Sermon and express the hostility of the priests that the verdict had not gone as they desired. It could well be that Jeremiah's banishment from the Temple Precincts is part of the same response (36:5). In that case the indictment of Judah in chapter 25, which Jeremiah was able to address to the people of Judah and inhabitants of Jerusalem (25:2) in Jehoiakim's fourth year, must precede chapters 19–20.

The year 605 BC marked a turning point in the affairs of the region, the land and the prophet. Egypt was defeated, and Babylon was the new super-power. Jeremiah addressed its situation in a series of oracles (46:3-12). It was at this time that the prophet also prepared a written scroll of his oracles with the help of a scribe Baruch. After the scroll was publicly read in November/December 604 BC, Jeremiah and Baruch had to go into hiding. It is probable that during the ensuing years of Jehoiakim's reign the material in the scroll was extended in various stages (36:32) while Jeremiah was unable to engage in public ministry. Like the earlier prophet Isaiah, Jeremiah concluded this phase of his ministry by preparing a scroll containing his prophecies which would function as an enduring public record of the word of the LORD (cf. Isa. 8:16-17).

The Confessions of the prophet give us a glimpse into his inner struggles during those years. They do not tell us about his public face. Though at times he seems to have kept silent, in general he spoke out against the increasing degeneracy of the land. Jeremiah was perplexed as to why preaching the divine word brought him so much anguish. Possibly the anguish would have been more bearable had there been any results to show for his efforts. Jeremiah ended this era in his ministry rejecting his birth, his call and the assurances that the LORD had given of his presence to deliver him from all his foes. It was a dark and depressing period.

4.5 During the Reign of Jehoiachin. Jehoiachin's short reign did not allow any major ministry by Jeremiah. The prophet had probably come out of hiding during the final months of the previous reign (35:1, 10), and now he warned the young king of what lay ahead of him (13:18-19; 22:24-30). He would not return home from exile and none of his offspring would sit on David's throne. Jeremiah did not record any direct denunciation of this king. It is in the deportation that took place at the end of Jehoiachin's reign that the twenty-five year old Ezekiel of priestly descent was taken captive to Babylon. Possibly Jeremiah's known pro-Babylonian stance led to the Babylonian authorities leaving him in Jerusalem.

4.6 During the Reign of Zedekiah

	BC
Zedekiah enthroned by Nebuchadnezzar	597
Vision of Baskets of Figs (chap. 24)	between 597 and 594
Letter to Captives (chap. 29)	between 597 and 594
Jerusalem Conference (chap. 27)	594
Confrontation with Hananiah (chap. 28)	594
Zedekiah goes to Babylon (51:59)	594
Scroll sunk in Euphrates (51:59-64)	594
Siege of Jerusalem begins (39:1)	589
Capture of Jerusalem (39:2)	18th July 586
Destruction of the City (39:8)	14th August 586

A third period of ministry followed in the reign of Zedekiah and is described in chapters 21–24, 27–29, 32, 34, 37–39, which cover the years before the fall of Jerusalem. Jeremiah was active in Jerusalem in the years between 597 BC and 593 BC. Certainly the prophet gave Seraiah, Baruch's brother, a scroll to take with him to Babylon in 594 BC. However, there is nothing that can be definitely dated between 593 BC and 588 BC, though perhaps some of the Oracles against the Nations may have originated then.

Zedekiah's reign was a time of serious conflict between Jeremiah and the false prophets (chaps. 27–29) and of persecution by the authorities in Jerusalem that culminated in imprisonment (chaps. 37–39). We are told a lot about Jeremiah's relationship with Zedekiah, who was reasonably well disposed towards the prophet and who frequently sought his advice—quite a different situation from that which had prevailed under Jehoiakim. But receiving advice and acting on it are not the same, and Zedekiah exhibited a chronic inability to grapple with the problems that affected a city in turmoil. He lacked the courage to resist the fanatical pro-Egyptian party in his own court and was eventually swept by them into rebellion against Babylon. Jeremiah repeatedly warned him that the only way to mitigate the disaster that would surely follow this unwise move was to surrender to the Babylonians, but Zedekiah could never steel himself to cope with the backlash that result from his own officials. His respect for the prophet was such that he ameliorated the conditions of his imprisonment, but would not order his release.

During these bleak years Jeremiah had revealed to him the encouraging visions of chapters 30–31, and also the token of better times for the future that was embodied in the purchase of the field at Anathoth (chap. 32). Even so his situation was dire as famine gripped the besieged city more tightly and he remained in confinement.

4.7 After the Capture of Jerusalem. The final stage of Jeremiah's ministry starts with the fall of the city, when the Babylonians treated him

The Sequence of Events During the Siege of Jerusalem

Event	Reference
Siege begun	39:1
Message to Zedekiah	34:1-7
First Consultation of Jeremiah	21:1-7
Freeing of the Slaves	34:8-10
Lifting of the Siege	37:5
Second Consultation of Jeremiah	37:3
Recapture of the Slaves	34:11-22
Jeremiah Arrested	37:11-16
Zedekiah's First Interview with Jeremiah	37:17-20
Imprisoned in Courtyard of the Guard	37:21; 32:1-2
Jeremiah's Continuing Witness	32:3-5; 38:1-3
Purchase of the Field in Anathoth	32:6-44
Imprisonment in Cistern	38:4-6
Rescue by Ebed-Melech	38:7-13
Zedekiah's Second Interview with Jeremiah	38:14-27
Return to the Courtyard of the Guard	38:28
Message for Ebed-Melech	39:15-18
Capture of Jerusalem	39:2-14

well. He refused their offer of being looked after in Babylon, and instead he was permitted to stay with the remnant of the people left in the land under Gedaliah who had been appointed governor of Judah (39:11-14; 40:1-6). However, Gedaliah was soon assassinated, and the group of Jews who had gathered round him were afraid of Babylonian reprisals (41:16-18). They asked Jeremiah to obtain divine guidance for them as to what they should do next, but despite being told to remain in the land, they rejected the prophet's message and decided to move to Egypt (43:1-7). Surprisingly they took Jeremiah and Baruch along with them. The last scriptural record regarding them is Jeremiah faithfully preaching to the Jewish community in Egypt, but meeting with opposition and a lack of response similar to that which he had faced before the fall of the city (chap. 44).

If Jeremiah was twelve years of age in 627 BC, then he would have been in his early fifties when he arrived in Egypt. Although he had suffered considerably during the siege, it is possible that he lived for some time after that. There are traditions recorded in Jerome and Tertullian that he was stoned to death by a Jewish mob in Tahpanhes in Egypt, but these are late and of uncertain worth. We simply do not know where or when he died.

4.8 The Character of the Prophet. Jeremiah has been traditionally identified as the weeping prophet and portrayed as having a naturally sensitive and timid character. 'He was not a second Elijah; he had a soft disposition, a lively sensibility; his eyes were easily filled with tears' (Hengstenberg 1856, 2:369). But that is to take a one-sided view of both Elijah and Jeremiah. True, Elijah was the valiant and indomitable adversary of false religion at Carmel (1 Kgs. 18:16-40) and the stern opponent of king Ahab in his land grabbing and connivance in murder (1 Kgs. 21:20-24). But equally there is Elijah under the broom tree saying, 'I have had enough, LORD. Take my life; I am no better than my ancestors' (1 Kgs. 19:4). Jeremiah is just as complex a character. He too speaks out boldly against false religion (for instance in chaps. 7 and 26) and risks the wrath of kings and officials in his unwavering dedication to the proclamation of God's word, which condemned their conduct. Still there is also the other side to his character. He did not fulfil his commission in a cold and heartless fashion. Far more than any of those he addressed, he appreciated the extent of the suffering that lay ahead of his people, and was perturbed and aghast at the prospect. In assessing his character we must not underestimate the difficulties he had to face and the severe strain he came under as his pleas for repentance were repeatedly rejected. Even strong men weep when entreaties motivated by love are trampled on, and dire catastrophe engulfs the people whose welfare they have at heart.

Assessments of Jeremiah's character have, therefore, to do justice to the blend of steadfastness and reluctance that he exhibited, both of which have to be understood in terms of his deeply committed faith—for, above all else, Jeremiah was a man of God. His piety is seen in the account of his call. The LORD does not approach one who is a stranger to him. Whatever hesitation Jeremiah displays in accepting the divine call, the narrative reveals an underlying sense of his familiarity with God, his acceptance of divine sovereignty and recognition of the LORD's particular shaping of his life. So when we first meet Jeremiah, he already is an individual who is loyal to the LORD. No doubt his upbringing in a pious and conservative priestly family in Anathoth meant that from his earliest days Jeremiah possessed considerable knowledge of the LORD and his dealings with his people. The teaching of his home would be reinforced by the training he would have received in the scribal school of Jerusalem as one destined for the priesthood. Jeremiah exhibits a profound acquaintance with previous revelation in the Pentateuch, the Psalms and prophets such as Hosea and Isaiah. He could truly say, 'When your words came, I ate them; they were my joy and my heart's delight, for I bear your name, O LORD God Almighty' (15:16).

It is against this background of informed piety that we may also assess Jeremiah's reliance upon prayer, particularly in situations of distress. This can be seen at times of intellectual difficulty such as when he did not grasp the divine reason for purchasing the field at Anathoth (32:16), but especially in his emotional dejection and distress as recorded in the

Confessions. Here Jeremiah speaks out of the intensity of his grief and suffering in terms that verge on the blasphemous. He likens the LORD to a 'deceptive brook' (15:18) and questions his whole prophetic vocation by cursing the day he was born (20:14-15). But it is vital to note that Jeremiah persists in bringing all his inner turmoil and doubts before the LORD. He cannot deny him nor can he understand his own experience without relating it to the divine purpose in his life. Insistently Jeremiah is a man of faith who recognises that he can only quell his inner anguish by struggling through to assessing his life from the divine perspective. For much of his ministry he shows us that he did not know inner peace; yet he maintained a resolute witness to a degenerate community.

In all this Jeremiah reveals himself as having an introspective nature which was sensitive to the message he was proclaiming and which was frequently in turmoil and under pressure. It may be that this did not set him apart from other prophets of the LORD. We cannot tell, for it is Jeremiah who alone bares his soul for us in the way he does. Since this has been recorded in Scripture, it is to be viewed not just as an almost accidental aspect of his character but as a vital constituent of his ministry and message. Jeremiah does not merely announce the word of the LORD; he ponders its significance and proclaims it as one who has grasped its implications, not only for the people but also for God himself.

Even at the time of his call Jeremiah, though just on the verge of adulthood, appreciated that it was no easy matter to be a prophet of the LORD. He protested his inadequacy for the task allotted him on the grounds of his age. While that objection was far from specious, there can be no doubt also that he was aware of the personal cost that would be involved. His upbringing had probably already led him to look askance at the religious confusion and degeneracy prevailing in the land and to wonder how it might be righted. When he was told that the LORD intended him to play a key role in forwarding his purposes, he immediately grasped that this would be difficult and demanding. It was therefore not unnatural that he shrank back from it and required to be persuaded. 'O LORD, you induced me, and I was persuaded; you are stronger than I, and have prevailed' (20:7, NKJV). Youthfulness and inexperience were no doubt factors in his reluctance, but the personal cost would be high even with the divine guarantee, not of exemption from trouble and distress, but of deliverance out of them.

Throughout his life Jeremiah's struggles with his prophetic vocation continued. There are two main levels at which this occurred: inner anguish and physical danger. His warnings regarding the calamities to come upon the people caused him personal sorrow. 'Since my people are crushed, I am crushed; I mourn, and horror grips me' (8:21; cf. also 4:19; 9:1). Even more distressing was the rejection of his calls for repentance. As the royal assayer assessing the condition of the people, Jeremiah could only report on their corruption (6:28-30). Their unfaithful behaviour and their spiritual folly distressed him (9:2). He felt isolated, and his sense of loneliness was increased by the restrictions on marriage and social contact that the LORD imposed on him in the light of the judgment that was to come upon the land (16:1-9). His natural temperament was not that of the ascetic, and the example he had to give to reinforce his proclamation intensified the suffering he endured on account of his vocation.

When Jeremiah's message was rejected, he personally became the target of attacks by his countrymen. The people of Anathoth, including his own relatives, conspired to kill him (11:18-19; 12:6). There were plots to slander him (18:18) and to assassinate him (18:23). He was put in peril of his life on a charge of being a false prophet (26:11). He was beaten and held up to public ridicule in the stocks (20:2). Later king Jehoiakim sought to arrest him and he had to go into hiding (36:26), and under Zedekiah he was imprisoned for a considerable period in various places (37:16; 38:6, 28). Jeremiah's personality was not such as to derive satisfaction from having to face opposition and to welcome being rejected. It hurt him that he had become a laughing stock (20:7), especially since he was acting for the good of those who were spurning him. Being the repeated object of harassment, derision, and plots on his life almost broke the prophet. He became depressed. He called down God's judgment on those who opposed him. More than once he wished that he would be relieved of his task (20:9). He knew inner despair at being unable to get through the barrier of obduracy that affected his fellows. He tried all the rhetorical skills that he had at his disposal to alert them to the danger of their circumstances, and all to no avail. He bitterly felt his lack of success.

It was not merely natural wisdom that Jeremiah displayed in his analysis of the spiritual condition of Judah, and it was not political insight that led him to predict the coming of the Babylonians and the iron hold they would have over the nations for seventy years. Jeremiah's natural intelligence and perceptivity were heightened by the divine revelation given to him and by the sensitising guidance of the Spirit. In the same way the steadfastness which he exhibited in carrying out his commission was not the product of ordinary determination. He shrank inwardly from confrontation and hostility (1:7-8, 17) but was divinely empowered to maintain his witness in the face of intense opposition (1:18-19). Those who fought against him encountered an individual who would not yield in any way, because he had been entrusted with the LORD's message (37:17; 38:17-18; 43:1). His honesty would not let him be bribed, threatened, cajoled or beaten into compromising the message that had been given to him. But the Spirit's empowerment was not a totally new characteristic added to one who was naturally timid, but rather a heightening and reinforcing of what was naturally there. In this way he was given the strength to lay aside the dictates of his immediate comfort and self-interest and to maintain his witness without publicly flinching from his task for over forty years.

In many respects Jeremiah answered the description of the Servant in Isaiah's prophecy. 'He was despised and rejected by men, a man of sorrows, and familiar with suffering. Like one from whom men hide their faces he was despised, and we esteemed him not' (Isa. 53:3). In this he was a precursor of the one who completely fulfilled Isaiah's prophecy. The one was rejected by his home town of Anathoth, the other in Nazareth (Luke 4:16-30); and both faced attempts to kill them. The one enduring the opposition of the priests and prophets of his day, the other also contradicted and rejected by the religious establishment of later times as represented by the chief priests, the teachers of the Law and the elders (Luke 20:1). Both were subject to the unjust condemnation of the civil authorities.

What was more both Jeremiah and Christ spoke out of a compassionate concern. If Jeremiah is indeed the weeping prophet, he is doing no more than the Messiah would in weeping over Jerusalem as he approached it, and is not much of what Christ said on that occasion equally at home on the lips of Jeremiah. 'If you, even you, had only known on this day what would bring you peace—but now it is hidden from your eyes. The days will come upon you when your enemies will build an embankment against you and encircle you and hem you in on every side. They will dash you to the ground, you and the children within your walls. They will not leave one stone on another, because you did not recognise the time of God's coming to you' (Luke 19:41-44). Furthermore while neither concealed the ominous time that lay ahead for the generation they addressed, they did not keep silent either about the vista that divine grace provided for renewal and restoration.

§5. PROPHETS AND PROPHECY

5.1 The Prophetic Office. When the LORD informed young Jeremiah that he was to be his prophet, there was no need to explain what that entailed because prophets had played a significant role in the life of God's covenant people for centuries. Indeed, pagan nations also claimed to have prophetic figures who acted as spokesmen for the gods. However, in Deuteronomy Moses had set the divinatory practices of Canaan (Deut. 18:9-12) in direct contrast to what the LORD instituted in the prophetic office for Israel (Deut. 18:13-22). The function of the prophet was twofold: to be the recipient of divine revelation and to be the communicator of that revelation to the covenant people. The need for such a figure is traced back to the scene at Sinai where Israel were overwhelmed by the immediacy of the theophanic presence of the LORD and felt themselves unable to endure the reality of direct divine revelation. They therefore asked that Moses be permitted to act as their intermediary (Exod. 20:18-19; Deut. 5:23-31;

18:16). Subsequently the LORD raised up a series of men who were granted prophetic privileges which in measure reflected those accorded Moses (Num. 12:6-8).

In the earliest stage of Israel's history as the covenant people the prophetic office often provided leadership for the nation at times when it was struggling to cope with unforeseen difficulties. This is most notably evident in the figure of Moses himself, but also later in characters such as Deborah (Judg. 4–5) and Samuel (1 Sam. 3–16). But with the establishment of the monarchy the scope of prophetic activity changed. It now focused on bringing the LORD's advice to the king as the one he had set over his people and whose conduct would influence the nation for good or ill. The court prophets such as Nathan (2 Sam. 7:2; 12:1-14) or Gad (2 Sam. 24:11-14) acted as policy advisers to the king, and in this their role came closest to prophetic figures in surrounding nations. However, when later kings became more and more resistant to the divine word, the prophets turned to speak directly to the people at large. They were still emissaries of the covenant king, but conditions had become so dire that all the nation needed to hear the LORD's word concerning their misconduct and his condemnation of it. The classical or writing prophets were thus given a ministry that addressed the whole land in a way that was unique in the ancient world both in its scope and in its message. The LORD as the sovereign ruler of creation had a purpose which he was working out through human history. Israel's privileged position as the nation to whom he had revealed himself did not guarantee them exemption from judgment, but was rather a summons to further the divine programme. When Israel persistently misinterpreted her election, the LORD sent the prophets to rebuke the people for their deviation from the covenant and to warn them of impending disaster and exile.

The men whom the LORD used as his spokesmen to proclaim his message came from various backgrounds within the covenant people. Being called as a prophet was not a matter of heredity or education. The divine heralds were individually chosen by God and directly commissioned by him when he called them. A prophet's call was therefore the defining event in his life, and it placed upon him new and solemn responsibilities as well as initiating him into the privilege of special access to the mind and purposes of God.

The prophetic call also ushered an individual into a vocation which encompassed his whole life. Being a prophet was not an occupation that could be left behind once working hours were over. It demanded total dedication of a prophet's thought and life. The LORD's ambassadorial messenger had to be in sympathy with the demands of the covenant and the proclamation to be uttered. The substance of the message might at times grieve him personally, but he could not deny its appropriateness or the justice of the warnings he gave. Equally, his vocation required that the prophet had to yield his whole life to the LORD's service. Hosea, for instance, was directed into a marriage that was doomed to failure through his wife's infidelity (Hos. 1–3). In this way his marriage mirrored the relationship between the LORD and Israel so as to bring home to the nation their fickle ingratitude and disloyal attraction to pagan gods, while also portraying the LORD's gracious constancy and determination to allure them back to himself. With Jeremiah the divine call to prophetic office interposed in his personal life an opposite requirement, that he abstain from marriage (16:2), so that his life as well as his words would announce impending divine judgment.

Furthermore, although a prophet might gather round him a group who supported him and who were in sympathy with his message (1 Sam. 19:20; 2 Kgs. 4:38; Isa. 8:16), the prophet himself was always a lonely figure, for it was to him personally that the word of the LORD had come. But the succession of the prophets that the LORD raised up over the centuries did constitute a genuine prophetic movement, and that not simply because they were each divinely called and experienced this inescapable compulsion to declare the LORD's word. Rather the progression in the LORD's dealings with his people meant there was a corresponding continuity in the message the prophets were given to deliver. Their proclamation built on what the LORD had previously said to the people, and often it would seem that they were consciously aware that it did so. They shared a common commitment to the maintenance of the covenant and to exhorting their contemporaries to live in accordance with its terms, condemning departures from its standards both in the area of social ethics and also as regards cultic deviation in worshipping strange gods. They realised how empty the prescribed rituals of the sanctuary were if they were not accompanied by heart allegiance to the LORD. But the themes of their ministry were not all negative, for they were also permitted to glimpse the future provision that the LORD had decided to make for his people in terms of the Messianic age of blessing that would come.

5.2 Prophetic Revelation. A prophet was one who received direct revelation from God. 'No prophecy of Scripture came about by the prophet's own interpretation' (Greek *epilusis*, 'release', 'unloosing'), that is, true prophetic utterance was not the product of the prophet's personal discernment of the significance of current events and what their outcome was likely to be. 'For prophecy never had its origin in the will of man, but men spoke from God as they were carried along by the Holy Spirit' (2 Pet. 1:20b-21). It was not a matter of superior human insight that generated the substance of what the prophets had to say; their message was directly derived from God. They possessed insider information because they had been granted access to the council of the LORD to see or to hear his word (23:18).

Many analogies for the prophetic experience in the reception of revelation have been sought in the abnormal or the psychotic. Frequent reference is made to 'prophetic ecstasy', but one must be careful to observe that the sense in which different writers use this term varies enormously. Certainly the classical prophets did not enter into some trance-like state during which they mouthed words without themselves being aware of what they were doing. On the other hand they did undergo some profound supernormal experience, the nature of which we can only dimly conceive. One analogy that seems to have some explanatory power is that of prayer. Here there is a heightening of our ordinary, but low-level, spiritual perception to permit genuine communication, genuine conversation, between God and the individual. It is possible to think of this process being amplified in the case of a prophet when he was made inwardly aware of the reality of God's presence and of the message that was being conveyed to him. The experience may well have been so focused and intense for the prophet that he was not as conscious of his physical surroundings as he would ordinarily have been, being absorbed in what was being conveyed to him inwardly. But his personality and consciousness were not suppressed, rather they were sensitised to an extraordinary degree. His mental processes were not suspended, as some definitions of ecstasy imply, and he was able to interact with what was being disclosed to him. Since the prophet did not control the content or timing of the matter revealed to him, this intensified his conviction and certainty as to its divine origin.

So there was no suppression of the personality and being of the prophet. He was passive in that he was receiving the message, but he was not inert. Rather his potential was being used to the full because the process of receiving revelation was not a mechanical one, but organic, involving the whole psychical being of the prophet. Since he was not originating the substance of the message, its content was revelation to him which he also had to absorb and understand. It could leave him struggling to grasp the significance of what he had perceived. Indeed, there were times when a prophet found himself astounded by what God had revealed to him (Isa. 21:3-4; Dan. 10:16-17); indeed, it was possible that the prophet could not fully understand what he saw (Dan. 8:15, 27).

5.3 Prophetic Inspiration. But the prophetic task was not exhausted with the reception of divine revelation. After all it was a message, and one that was not addressed primarily to the prophet himself but to others. The prophet was supremely a divine spokesman who was commissioned to relate whatever the LORD had commanded him (1:7). This commission was initially fulfilled through proclamation to his own generation, and also through a written ministry designed to reach later generations.

Prophetic inspiration concerns the process by which the prophet communicated with others, whether verbally or in writing. In many prophetic writings this does not differ markedly from the process of inspiration that underlies other parts of Scripture. For instance, in chapters

37–44 there is an historical narrative concerned with events that took place in the days immediately before and after the fall of Jerusalem. Most of the facts that are recorded there could have been provided by ordinary observation, and it would have been possible for an historian to write up those facts in the way in which they are now found. But the narrative of Scripture is more than ordinary history. It comes to us as part of the word of God, and the self-testimony of Scripture as to its 'God-breathed' origin (2 Tim. 3:16) informs us that the writer of the narrative was specially guided by the Holy Spirit to write in the way he did. Not only is the accuracy of the narrative guaranteed, but what is recorded also conforms to what the Holy Spirit wished to be set down. All historical presentation involves selection and emphasis. That process occurred under the control of the Spirit in such a way that even in the historical portions of the Old Testament, including narratives in the prophetic writings, there is a genuine revelation bearing testimony to what God wanted to relate regarding these events.

However, there is obviously another type of prophetic writing where the subject matter has not been obtained by historical research. When the prophets repeatedly use phrases such as 'The word of the LORD came to me, saying', 'This is what the LORD says', or 'declares the LORD', it is evident that they are claiming access to more than would be available to a contemporary spectator or historical investigator. Their proclamation has been specially revealed to them by the LORD, and the prophets are explicitly disclaiming that they are the ultimate originators of their message. But are they then claiming that they are just mouthpieces, uttering verbatim what they have heard? Are they posing as scribes who are reading out a message they have taken down from divine dictation? Such a mechanistic view of the process of inspiration does not do justice to these prophetic passages. For instance, in reading the various prophetic records that we possess it is evident that the style of each prophet is different. It is clear, for example, that the three major prophets, Isaiah, Jeremiah and Ezekiel, have left on their prophecies the impress of their individual characters and personal style. But how was this achieved?

We do not really know. The concept of concursive inspiration covers those forms of revelation in which no human activity—not even the control of the will—is superseded. When we analyse a Pauline epistle or a Davidic psalm, we can readily appreciate that we are following the thought of Paul or David. We are happy to say, 'Paul argues this way because ...' or 'David then moves on to say, or adds this word, because ...'. The level of human involvement is evident, and it is possible to envisage the active participation of the human author combined with the Spirit's activity not only in guiding the author's thought processes but in ensuring that he had just that character and experience which in the outworking of God's providence would lead him to think and say precisely what he did.

It is, however, difficult to extend concursive inspiration to what is uniquely prophetic. Certainly it may be done if what is involved is the prophet giving a verbal description of a scene revealed to him in vision, and equally it may apply to prophetic ordering of already existing oracles so that their written form may have overall rhetorical shape and impact. But the nub of the problem is the distinctively prophetic, the declaration of the divine purpose. It is difficult to conceive of that as existing even in the mind of the prophet without it being embodied in some verbal form. One explanation is to argue that what was revealed to the prophet was couched by an act of divine condescension and supreme communicative skill in precisely the speech forms that the prophet himself would have used. Divine revelation came not just in the Hebrew language that Jeremiah spoke, but in the vocabulary and idiom that were naturally his. This was a testimony to God's intimate knowledge of the prophet, and also to the way in which the prophet had been prepared as one who would be in a position to convey the message just as God desired. An alternative emphasis is to argue that the prophet was actively involved in reporting what had been communicated to him in general terms. Since he had been divinely chosen from birth and was concursively borne along by the Spirit, this again means that the record he has given us is precisely that which God wished us to have. When an ambassador conveys the policy of his government to another nation, he is not restricted to the precise wording of what he has been told, but he is not permitted to add to the substance of the message he is conveying.

Neither of these explanations is totally satisfactory. The first approaches closely to dictation theories of inspiration which fail to do justice to the individuality of the prophet and his intelligent involvement in the commission given to him. The second explanation seems to involve the prophet being made generally aware of the divine purposes whereas statements such as, 'I will put my words in his mouth' (Deut. 18:18; cf. Jer. 1:9; 5:14), arguably require more specific divine involvement in a way that goes beyond the later apostolic style of interpretation.

However, no matter how we may grapple with analysing the mode of divine inspiration, the reality is undeniably present. The word of God which is revealed through the prophet comes as the pure and unmixed word of God from God to the prophet, and is also by the operation of the Spirit recorded for us in such a way that we too have the word of God. Throughout this process of reception and delivery of revelation the intelligence of the prophet is alert. The process is not merely mechanical, and so the prophet's declaration also becomes his personal message which he delivers by the authority of God.

5.4 False Prophecy. Because the prophetic call was experienced in the inner life of the prophet, it was not directly accessible to others. This opened up the possibility of individuals fraudulently claiming to have received such a call, or sincerely misunderstanding their own spiritual experience and interpreting it as constituting a divine call. The problem of false prophecy was one that Jeremiah had to face in severe and protracted form.

It is not just the modern reader who has to reflect on the genuineness of the prophets. Perhaps today we have questions that would not have perplexed the ancient Israelite for whom there was no doubt that the LORD did exist and that he did speak through prophets. Their perplexity arose from the conflicting claims of those who said they were the LORD's spokesmen, but who did not bring the same message. Certain tests could be applied to ascertain the authenticity of a prophet and his message. The Israelites had long been warned that if a prophet spoke in the name of any other god than the LORD, even though he substantiated his claims with the prediction of a sign that should come to pass or by performing some miracle, he was not to be believed (Deut. 13:1-5; 18:20). A true prophet's word would not contradict previous revelation, and he would by his conduct show himself to be loyal to the standards of the covenant. Equally if a prophet's predictions did not come true, then he could not be a true prophet (Deut. 18:21-22).

But these tests did not cover every situation. Waiting for the fulfilment of a prophecy concerning the distant future was not a practicable method of determining the genuineness of a prophet today. Furthermore there was the phenomenon of conditional prophecy where an absolute announcement of judgment might well have an implied condition of repentance (18:7-10). A clear instance of that is Jonah's proclamation, 'Forty more days and Nineveh will be overturned' (Jonah 3:4). A false prophet might easily use this to allege that changed circumstances had led to his message not coming true. At the end of the day detecting the false prophet was often a matter of spiritual perceptivity, and when those being addressed were accused by one prophet of lack of spiritual insight and judgment it was all too easy a matter for them to look instead to another messenger who flattered them with attractive and appealing words.

§6. THE THEOLOGY OF JEREMIAH

Having thought about how Jeremiah received his message, we must now consider the content of that message. This involves identifying the main themes of what he proclaimed, and assessing how they fit into the flow of prophetic revelation. In doing so it needs to be remembered that the prophets were not systematic theologians. They were speaking to very particular situations and their theology was always applied. There is therefore an element of artificiality in abstracting and ordering the principles they espoused. It is also the case that though the prophetic ministry was in many respects an individual one, the prophets were also part of a God-directed movement that had that links backwards and forwards, especially towards the coming of the Messiah. These interconnections are essential components of the message of Jeremiah.

6.1 God. The prophets were not so much concerned with imparting new truth as with the implementation of existing truth. In practice this meant that they exhorted the people to return to, and to maintain, the standards of the covenant delivered through Moses. Jeremiah's theology was therefore applied *covenant* theology, and this suggests that it is appropriate to set out his thought in terms of the parties to the covenant relationship which had been divinely instituted between the LORD and Israel.

The God of Creation. Jeremiah's shared outlook with the Pentateuch means that foundational to his thinking is the realisation of the LORD's role as the Creator of the universe. 'But God made the earth by his power; he founded the world by his wisdom and stretched out the heavens by his understanding. When he thunders, the waters in the heavens roar; he makes clouds rise from the ends of the earth. He sends lightning with the rain and brings out the wind from his storehouses' (10:12-13; 51:15-16). The Creator has not abandoned his creation, but acts as its sustainer, particularly in respect of the gift of rain which is so much appreciated in the dry conditions of the east.

The repeated use of the term LORD Almighty/LORD of hosts (2:19) reinforces the fact that he is in control of all the forces and beings that are in the created realm. For instance, at one stage Jeremiah is instructed to inform ambassadors who had come from surrounding nations, 'This is what the LORD Almighty, the God of Israel, says: "Tell this to your masters: With my great power and outstretched arm I made the earth and its people and the animals that are on it, and I give it to anyone I please" ' (27:4-5). The LORD who created the world is sovereign over nations whether weak or strong. It is he alone who determines their destiny.

So fundamental was the perception of God as Creator in Israelite thought that Jeremiah used this truth as a basis for pleading with his fellow countrymen regarding their inconstancy. It is the LORD who could truly say, 'I made the sand a boundary for the sea, an everlasting barrier it cannot cross. The waves may roll, but they cannot prevail; they may roar, but they cannot cross it' (5:22). In doing so there is a contrast drawn between the stormy sea, which nevertheless keeps to its ordained boundary, and the conduct of Jeremiah's contemporaries who acknowledged no God-given restraint. The permanent order of nature also provided a guarantee for the permanence of all that the LORD undertakes (31:35; 33:20). Supremely the reality of the LORD's work in creation provided a striking contrast with the ineffectiveness and impotence of pagan gods and their idols. In his polemic against idolatry Jeremiah ridiculed the worship of idols because they are incapable of action either for good or ill. Indeed they do not even have the power to move but have to be carried about; they are just like scarecrows unable to speak; they hang together only because they are fastened with nails. 'These gods, who did not make the heavens and the earth, will perish from the earth and from under the heavens' (10:11). 'But the LORD is the true God; he is the living God, the eternal King. When he is angry, the earth trembles; the nations cannot endure his wrath' (10:10).

Furthermore, Jeremiah sets out how God is both transcendent—the one who stands apart from mankind and who fills heaven and earth—and immanent, the God who is always nearby (23:23-24). He is the God who is omnipresent, and from whom no human secrets can be hidden because he tests heart and mind (11:20), and so can say of their misdeeds, 'I know it and am witness to it' (29:23). He is also the God who is omnipotent—for him nothing is too hard (32:17, 27).

The God of the Electing Love. But the covenant which the LORD made with Israel introduces new dimensions of the divine character which are not obvious through an examination of creation. Jeremiah draws on the message of Hosea to set out the love the LORD displayed in electing Israel, 'the one I love' (12:7) and 'my beloved' (11:15), to be in a special relationship with him. 'I have loved you with an everlasting love; I have drawn you with loving-kindness' (31:3). Time and again Jeremiah reminds his hearers of how God had expressed that love in what he had done for the nation at the time of the Exodus. 'You brought your people Israel out of Egypt with signs and wonders, by a mighty hand and an outstretched arm and with great terror. You gave them this land you had sworn to give to their forefathers, a land flowing with milk and honey' (32:21-22; cf. also 11:5). Indeed, the LORD's activity continued down to the present (32:20). Jeremiah recognised the privileges thus bestowed on Israel as the nation brought near to God, 'the spring of living water' (2:13), and had the nation drunk deeply at that spring they would have realised their potential to become 'like a tree planted by the water that sends out its roots by the stream. It does not fear when heat comes; its leaves are always green. It has no worries in a year of drought and never fails to bear fruit' (17:8).

Yet, while recognising the special role accorded to Israel in the divine purpose, Jeremiah is true to the universal note of the Mosaic covenant ('the whole earth is mine', Exod. 19:5; cf. Gen. 12:3; 22:18). The LORD is no mere national deity, but 'King of the nations' (10:7) and 'the God of all mankind' (32:27). Indeed, the prophet's calling was one that extended 'to the nations' (1:5, 10). Undoubtedly the LORD has the authority and knowledge to bring charges against the nations for their misconduct (25:31), and Jeremiah had repeatedly to announce that judgment in the Oracles against the Nations (chaps. 46–51). But both there (46:26; 48:47; 49:6, 39) and elsewhere (3:17; 12:16; 16:19) he holds out the prospect of the LORD's gracious intervention on behalf of those who are not the covenant people. This is a significant, though minor, aspect of Jeremiah's proclamation.

The God of Covenant Standards. Israel's election was not a piece of divine favouritism designed to secure her peace and prosperity no matter what her conduct was. It was the essence of pagan thought that a national deity was bound on all occasions to promote the interests of those who occupied his land. Provided they continued to bring offerings to his temple and to engage in all the ceremonies of the cult, the deity was taken to be committed to fostering their happiness and security. This pagan delusion had gripped the heart of Judah in Jeremiah's day, and he strove earnestly to correct their superstitious concept of God. By repeating 'This is the temple of the LORD, the temple of the LORD, the temple of the LORD!' (7:4) and venerating the ark of the covenant (3:16), they had substituted mere objects as the focus of their security rather than a living relationship with the LORD. Zion was inviolable only if Zion was obedient. Neglect of covenant standards evoked divine wrath. Even the rites instituted by the LORD were ineffective if there was not obedience. 'When I brought your forefathers out of Egypt and spoke to them, I did not just give them commands about burnt offerings and sacrifices, but I gave them this command: Obey me, and I will be your God and you will be my people. Walk in all the ways I command you, that it may go well with you' (7:22-23).

Jeremiah had repeatedly to remind the people that the covenant obligated them to holy living because it gave God's required structure to the bond-relationship the LORD had instituted between himself and his people. Over the years the LORD had time and again sent prophets to exhort the people, 'Do not do this detestable thing that I hate!' (44:4). But the people succumbed to the allure of Baal worship (2:20), adoration of the Queen of Heaven (7:18; 44:17-19) and worse (7:31). Their conduct deteriorated as they forgot the moral imperatives of the covenant, which were not arbitrary but based on the character of the LORD himself as the one 'who exercises kindness, justice and righteousness on earth, for in these I delight' (9:24). When this was forgotten, the LORD would act against those who had made light of his requirements.

Jeremiah had no doubt that the LORD would punish those had violated his standards. 'The LORD is a God of retribution; he will repay in full' (51:56). He asserts his majesty and power over all that opposes him. This is particularly seen in the imposition of divine vengeance on Babylon for the desecration of the Temple (50:28) and for the attitude it had displayed towards the nations, and especially towards Judah and Jerusalem. 'It is time for the LORD's vengeance; he will pay her what she deserves' (51:6). However, it was not just foreign powers who came under the judicial scrutiny of God. He will punish his own people for their misconduct as it too was an affront to his dignity (5:29).

The God of Salvation. It would seem that the holy wrath of the LORD against the sin of his people would be the end of the message that Jeremiah could bring to them. When the LORD says, 'I have withdrawn my blessing, my love and my pity from this people' (16:5), there seems to be no way of avoiding the catastrophe of enemy invasion that was the LORD's means of punishing the people. After the land is devastated, the Temple burned and the people deported, what future could there be?

But it is at this very point that Jeremiah is brought to see the astounding impact of the LORD's graciousness. Truly he is the God of salvation, who may be addressed as, 'O Hope of Israel, its Saviour in times of distress' (14:8). Once his fierce anger has accomplished his purposes (30:24), he acts to build up again (31:4), a truth that had been implied even in Jeremiah's commission (1:10) but which was brought out more clearly in the dark days before Jerusalem fell and recorded in the Book of Consolation (chaps. 30–33). 'I will hide my face from this city because of all its wickedness. Nevertheless, I will bring health and healing to it; I will heal my people and will let them enjoy abundant peace and security' (33:5-6). The covenant bond was not a temporary phenomenon (31:35-36) and would not be divinely ignored. The LORD still yearned after Ephraim and was grieved by his folly (31:20). Though the covenant brought the curse of heaven on those who infringed it ('I will not let you go entirely unpunished', 30:11), yet it held out also the possibility of restoration through divine grace ('I will not completely destroy you', 30:11). 'Search will be made for Israel's guilt, but there will be none, and for the sins of Judah, but none will be found, for I will forgive the remnant I spare' (50:20). The vista of future restoration arose not from human achievement but was the consequence of divine love and grace.

6.2 The Covenant People. Turning to the other party in the covenant relationship, we find that the covenant instituted at Sinai had placed special obligations on the people to whom the LORD said, 'I will be your God and you will be my people' (7:23; 11:4; 24:7; 31:33; 32:28). At the time of Josiah's reforms the nation had pledged itself anew to the terms of the covenant. 'The king stood by the pillar and renewed the covenant in the presence of the LORD—to follow the LORD and keep his commands, regulations and decrees with all his heart and all his soul, thus confirming the words of the covenant written in this book. Then all the people pledged themselves to the covenant' (2 Kgs. 23:3). But the sad fact about Judah and Jerusalem was that they were not living up to the terms of these obligations. The covenant was two-sided not just from the fact that it structured the relationship between two parties, but also because it determined the course of that relationship towards one or other of two outcomes: divine blessing on the people if they adhered to what the LORD required of them, and divine curse and abandonment if they breached the terms of the relationship (5:15). Jeremiah repeatedly called their attention to their covenant violations both by formal addresses (7:1-15; 11:1-17) and by object lessons, including the incident of the linen belt (13:1-11) and that involving the Rechabites (chap. 35).

The Covenant Ideal. Jeremiah shows his awareness of how Israel should have responded to the overtures of God. There had been a time when they could truly call God, 'My Father, my friend from my youth' (3:4; cf. also 3:19). Ephraim (the northern tribes) had been God's dear son, the child in whom he delighted (31:20). If their behaviour had conformed to what he desired to find in them, then this would have led to the enjoyment of covenant blessing. 'Obey me and do everything I command you, and you will be my people, and I will be your God. Then I will fulfil the oath I swore to your forefathers, to give them a land flowing with milk and honey—the land you possess today' (11:4-5). But rather than living as obedient children, the people of Israel and Judah, like the prodigal son of Jesus' parable (Luke 15:11-31), strayed from their Father's ways.

Frequently it is to the relationship between a husband and wife that Jeremiah likens that between the LORD and Israel (3:1). He sets out the devotion they displayed at the time of their departure from Egypt as his bride (2:2), for not only had the LORD sovereignly elected them to be his people, they had willingly aligned themselves with him. They had abandoned all other gods and committed themselves wholly to him. He had provided for his people a suitable home in the land of promise. Jeremiah recognised that there had once been a time when the land and all its towns had been filled with 'the sounds of joy and gladness, the voices of bride and bridegroom, and the voices of those who bring thank-offerings to the house of the LORD, saying, "Give thanks to the LORD Almighty, for the LORD is good; his love endures for ever" ' (33:11).

The Blighted Ideal. But though the LORD had provided that Israel would be 'a thriving olive tree with fruit beautiful in form' (11:16), though they had been planted 'like a choice vine of sound and reliable stock' (2:21), the people had turned against the LORD and become a corrupt, wild vine. They were not true to their covenant commitments, not only abandoning the true source of spiritual health and vitality, but substituting in place of their affection for the LORD allegiance to worthless idols (2:11). They no longer saw the uniqueness of the LORD and failed to appreciate all that he had done for them.

The major aspect of Judah's breach of covenant was her rejection of the uniqueness of the LORD and her violation of the requirement that she worship him alone. The worship of idols was a course of sheer folly because they were quite unable to meet the needs of their devotees. A number of pagan deities and practices proved particularly attractive to the people. They turned to the gods of the Canaanites and indulged in the licentious practices associated with the worship of Baal (2:8). They even offered their children in fire sacrifices to this god (19:5) and also to the Molech (32:35). Mesopotamian influences seem to have given rise to the worship of the Queen of Heaven, which involved baking cakes with her image on them, burning incense on the housetops and pouring out drink offerings (7:18; 44:17-19, 25). So great a hold had this practice taken of the people that they continued to indulge in it in Egypt after the fall of Jerusalem, claiming that it was the abandonment of this ritual that had caused the calamity (44:15-19).

Jeremiah employed the imagery of prostitution and adultery (3:1-10) that had been previously used by Hosea (Hos. 1:2; 2:2) to emphasise how heinousness the people's behaviour was. Their worship of Baal under the spreading greenery of the sacred trees at the high places was like an adulteress giving herself to her lovers (2:19). Because of the nature of the rites at such sites the comparison was telling. What was more the northern kingdom of Israel had already engaged in such wayward behaviour and had suffered the inevitable consequences, but Judah had proved incapable of learning the lesson that had been so tragically set before it.

Rampant Paganism. The demands of the covenant ran counter to the philosophy of paganism which was both amoral and immoral. Pagan rituals were humanly devised to satisfy the cravings of depraved human nature and, as a consequence, worship of a pagan deity gave rise to no moral demands on the conduct of the worshipper. With the ingress of pagan thought into the ethos of Judah, social injustice and religious nominalism had become rampant in the land. Some other prophets (notably Amos and Micah) say more about social injustice than Jeremiah, but he was not unaware that the nation which had effectively abandoned the LORD had also set aside the social standards of his covenant. He notes that the rich violently oppressed the poor and failed to maintain standards of social justice (2:34; 5:26-28; 7:5-6). In particular he scathingly attacked Jehoiakim for the way in which he conducted himself as king, compelling craftsmen to build a fine palace for him but not paying them for their work (22:13-14). In the final siege of Jerusalem, the action of Zedekiah and the upper classes in first solemnly granting liberty to their slaves and then going back on their agreement when it no longer suited them was a clear example of the shameless opportunism that characterised the community (34:8-20).

Equally Judah's religious conduct had been corrupted by pagan attitudes. Though they continued to worship the LORD in the recently refurbished Temple, they considered the essence of religion to lie in the performance of outward rituals and had no appreciation of the fact that they were intended to be expressions of inner heart allegiance. They thought that the Temple in their midst (7:4) with its sacred objects (3:16), the number and costliness of their sacrifices (6:20), and their possession of God's law (8:8) were sufficient to ensure their good standing before the LORD. More perniciously this outlook was promoted by the priests and prophets who set the tone of the nation's religious life. Against these pagan corruptions in the ostensible worship of the LORD Jeremiah reminded the people that obedience had always been more important than sacrifice (7:21-22) and that mere possession of the law was insufficient without observance of it (8:7-9). What caused greatest offence to the ecclesiastics of his day was Jeremiah's observation that the presence of the Temple was no guarantee of divine preservation of the people. 'Remember Shiloh' was a message that seemed to them to be utter blasphemy (7:12-14; 26:6, 9).

Heart Corruption. A marked feature of Jeremiah's prophecy is the extent to which he emphasises the moral and spiritual deviousness of mankind, and traces its prevalence to inner human corruption. 'The heart is deceitful above all things and beyond cure. Who can understand it?' (17:9). This inner deceitfulness is also alluded to in the phrase 'the stubborn inclinations of their evil hearts' (7:24; cf. 13:10; 23:17).

As the inner life of the individual is not merely tainted but polluted, it required radical inner change (not merely Josiah's spring cleaning of the Temple and its ritual) before the people could conform to the requirements of the covenant relationship. Only by such personal spiritual transformation could reform become revival. Jeremiah presented the requisite change in terms of the metaphor of heart circumcision (again a figure drawn from Deuteronomy, Deut. 10:16; 30:6) to emphasise the need for true inner dedication to the LORD. 'Circumcise yourselves to the LORD, circumcise your hearts, you men of Judah and people of Jerusalem, or my wrath will break out and burn like fire because of the evil you have done—burn with no one to quench it' (4:4).

It was the lack of inner allegiance to the LORD, that is, a lack of faith, that blighted all Israel's acts of religious devotion and possession of the symbols of religion. They had the shell of religion but not the kernel, and without hearts deeply committed to the LORD the externals of religion were of no avail. The lack of heart awareness of the LORD left them quite comfortable with their own watered-down ideas of what true religion was all about. By confining the presence of the LORD to the Temple and by viewing him as irrevocably committed to their welfare, they considered themselves free to live as they pleased, but their security was a sham (3:10; 13:25).

Repentance. But though the people had become fundamentally corrupted by their inner condition, there was still the possibility of restoration if only there was a right response to the prophet's message. Jeremiah has much to say about the theme of repentance which he characteristically expresses in terms of the spatial metaphor of 'Return', that is, a return from the ways the people had chosen for themselves to the ways the LORD had mandated for them.

Jeremiah showed that the LORD's verdict on a nation reflects what it does. The way in which a potter could remould clay until it conformed to what he wanted to produce (18:1-11) provided an illustration of how the LORD would react. If a sinful nation repented of its wickedness, then the LORD would graciously accept them. On this basis the LORD through his prophet urged his wayward people to abandon their wicked ways and to return to him. The most basic aspect of this was worship of the LORD alone. If the people returned to this, then he would show them mercy (3:12), heal their backsliding (3:22), and avert the disaster that was looming over them (26:3). Their outward conduct in matters such as Sabbath observance would provide a litmus test for their inner convictions (17:19-27). Jeremiah informed the people of how they should repent by providing them on three occasions with examples of the sort of confession they should make of their sin (3:22-25; 14:7-10; 14:19-22).

But the call for such a change went unheeded, and over the years Jeremiah's message changed from one of warning about the doom that their conduct would bring upon them to the inevitability of the LORD's judgment from which he would not turn back (4:28). This was dramatically indicated by the LORD's prohibition on Jeremiah's intercession for the people (14:11). Their conduct had degenerated so far that neither fasting nor sacrifice would be sufficient to avert the coming catastrophe (14:12). In the final days of Jerusalem Jeremiah could only counsel King Zedekiah to submit to the Babylonians. In no way could the destruction of the city be avoided (21:1-7), though submission would mitigate the disaster by avoiding much slaughter and destruction (21:8-10; 27:11, 13).

6.3 The Future. But the covenant commitment of the LORD to the people he had called was irrevocable (31:36-37). While he would punish his people for their iniquity, he did not abandon his commitment to them and he graciously held out through the prophet the prospect of restoration. Over the years of his ministry Jeremiah came increasingly to recognise that there would be no immediate response to his proclamation, and his hope focused on the future after the imposition of judgment.

Restoration. The banishment of the people from the land was the most obvious sign of their estrangement from the LORD. It was a sign of his grace that the period of Babylonian domination was limited to seventy years (25:11), and then there would come a time when the LORD would show compassion to his people and bring them back to Palestine. The weeping of the people in their wretchedness at the deportation from the land would be at an end (31:15). A great throng would come, even of those normally considered unfit to travel (31:7-8). What was more, it would be a time when ancient hostilities and tension would be removed, and both Israel and Judah would participate in the return from exile (30:3-4). This act of deliverance would be placed along side the Exodus; indeed it would replace it in the thinking of the people as the epitome of the LORD's redeeming action on their behalf (16:14-15; 23:7-8).

In this connection too Jeremiah was called on to reinforce his message by prophetic action. To show how certain it was that the land would be repossessed by the people, the prophet was instructed to buy a field even while the siege was under way and the land involved probably already under Babylonian control. Even Jeremiah seemed puzzled by the significance of the action he had to perform, but again the LORD pointed to the blessings he would provide in the everlasting covenant he would make with the people (32:40). The people would enjoy fruitful harvests and abundant flocks and herds (31:4-5; 33:10-13). They would be united in worshipping at Jerusalem (31:6), which would be rebuilt and purified (30:17; 31:38-40). The city would be repopulated and filled with sounds of joy (30:17, 19-20). Jeremiah describes not a few features of the return. The towns of Judah would be reoccupied by their lawful inhabitants. Above all, the Holy City would be built again on its own hills (31:38-40). The Temple, with its sacrifices and services, would be restored; so would the royal house (33:17-26). There would also be a renewed and purified priesthood.

The New Covenant. All this would be part of the provision of the new covenant (31:31-34). It was not that the basic demands of the covenant were going to change: the same law would prevail as before. Nor was the basic relationship going to be altered: they would be God's people and he would be their God. The focus is on the people's capacity for obedience which the LORD will ensure by placing within them the desire to remain loyal to him and by strengthening them to do so.

This would remedy what had proved to be the weakness of the old covenant. God had been faithful to the relationship he had instituted, but Israel had ceased to love and obey. Israel's unfaithfulness had breached the terms of the covenant. But would the reinstitution of the covenant prove to be any more lasting than the old covenant? No change was required on God's side, but a more potent influence towards commitment would be required as regards the people's response. This is provided for in the declaration, 'I will put my law in their minds and write it on their hearts' (31:33). Israel's heart failure would be directly dealt with by divinely bestowed effective inner change. 'They will be my people, and I will be their God. I will give them singleness of heart and action, so that they will always fear me for their own good and the good of their children after them' (32:38-39). There will be an internalisation of the covenant, and obedience will spring out of affection. The law of the old covenant had been written externally on tablets of stone, but in the new covenant God will work inwardly a right disposition towards himself which will ensure compliance with his law.

This is reinforced by the additional description of the new covenant: 'No longer will a man teach his neighbour, or a man his brother, saying, "Know the LORD," because they will all know me, from the least of them to the greatest' (31:34). This does not predict that there will come a time when religious instruction will prove unnecessary, but when the covenant community will be characterised by a deep and genuine inward intimacy with the LORD. Knowledge of God had been emphasised by Hosea to distinguish true covenant allegiance of the LORD from the 'knowledge'

Israel acquired through involvement in the cultic prostitution of Baal worship (Hos. 2:20; 4:1, 6; 5:4; 6:6). Jeremiah repeats the same allegation that the people do not know the LORD (2:8; 4:22; 9:3, 6, 24; 22:16). But conditions will be totally changed in the era of the new covenant.

There can be no doubt that the new covenant was not fully instituted in the immediate aftermath of the Exile. True, many of the survivors of Israel and Judah returned to the land, and there were tokens of divine blessing, but it was still perceived as 'the day of small things' (Zech. 4:10). It was only with the coming of Jesus Christ that the new covenant was properly inaugurated because only then did it become evident how its final component would be effected: 'I will forgive their wickedness and will remember their sins no more' (31:34). On the night on which the Son of Man was betrayed into the hands of sinners, he took the cup and, giving it, said, 'This cup is the new covenant in my blood, which is poured out for you' (Luke 22:20). In this he showed that Jeremiah's prediction was fulfilled in his cross where his blood was 'poured out for many for the forgiveness of sins' (Matt. 26:27). The new age was introduced, drawing into the church of Christ all who are true children of Abraham whatever their national background. However, the consummation of the new covenant is still not complete as it awaits the return of Christ.

The Righteous Branch. Closely connected with Jeremiah's proclamation of a new covenant is his Messianic hope. Though in fact Jeremiah does not mention the Messiah in his new covenant prophecy (31:31-34), he does show that in the time of restoration the LORD would provide a king to rule his restored people. 'They will serve the LORD their God and David their king, whom I will raise up for them' (30:9). It is not that David would rise from the dead, but rather the king would realise the ideal of David, ruling in the spirit of his illustrious ancestor. He would be 'a righteous Branch, a King who will reign wisely and do what is right and just in the land' (23:5; 30:9; 33:15). His conduct would be in sharp contrast to the unjust rulers who were to be found in Jeremiah's later ministry, and would inaugurate a time of prosperity and security for Israel and Judah.

Jeremiah provides further detail about the coming king in 30:21 where he is described as a distinguished 'leader' and as the 'ruler' of the people. His origin from among the people themselves is emphasised in line with earlier requirements (Deut. 17:15; 2 Sam. 7:12), so that he will be quite different from the foreigners who had oppressed them. Most surprisingly, Jeremiah goes on to describe the privileges divinely accorded this kingly figure in terms that are usually associated with the priesthood: 'I will bring him near and he will come close to me, for who is he who will devote himself to be close to me?' (30:21). This anticipates the sacerdotal work of the Messiah.

As Jeremiah was taught regarding the LORD's future provision, these matters were presented to him in terms of already existing realities, and it is in the same language that he has perforce to describe them to his contemporaries. But the form which God's rule upon earth then took was going to be moved forward in a way in which preserved its essential continuity with the promises of the past and yet broke through the restricted perspective that had previously existed. The coming of the Messiah and the inauguration of the new covenant grandly fulfilled what the LORD had promised his people, and yet surpassed even their most profound anticipation.

§7. TRANSLATIONS AND TRANSLATING

7.1 In this commentary the English text quoted is the New International Version (Anglicised Edition), which is a lively and accessible translation. To save space, line divisions in poetic sections are not reproduced. Also, there are times when an alternative, generally more literal, translation has been offered after an oblique. Other standard English translations were also consulted and are on occasions quoted.

However, the commentary is primarily concerned with the significance of the Hebrew text of Jeremiah. It is appreciated that many readers will not be able to access this, but for those who can footnotes contain details of how it may be understood, including discussions of significant textual variations or obscurities, and also of passages where the *kethibh* (the traditional Hebrew consonantal text) is accompanied by a *qere* (a marginal annotation giving the reading preferred by the Massoretes).

When it is the sound of Hebrew words that is significant or where reference is facilitated by citing the basic Hebrew word employed, this has been done in the text using a standard form of transliteration. Attention is also drawn to the use of the symbol √ to indicate the base or root form of a Hebrew word, especially in the combination <√ to indicate that a word is derived from a particular root. Underbrackets are employed to indicate words that have been added as supplements in English to bring out the significance of the text.

It is also convenient to mention here two common features of the text that require further comment.

7.2 The prophetic perfect. Unlike English where the form of a verb is varied by the use of tenses to indicate differences in the time at which an action occurs, the verb in Hebrew is inflected to distinguish the aspect or modality of the action that is being described.[1] Though the details of what is involved are a matter of ongoing controversy, the main distinction that is present is between an action that is viewed as complete and an action that

1. For further details of modern discussions regarding Hebrew verb forms, see *IBHS* chapter 29. For the prophetic perfect see *IBHS* §30.5.1e.

is viewed as incomplete. The perfect form of the Hebrew verb represents an action that is considered as complete, the imperfect one that is thought of as non-complete. In many instances this may be conveyed in English by the use of a past tense to render a perfect verb form and a future tense to render an imperfect form because the majority of complete actions are those that have occurred (that is, been completed) in the past and the majority of non-complete actions lie in the future (or are currently underway and await completion).

However, there are many exceptions to such a simple translation rule, and one of these that is of significance in translating prophetic passages is known as the 'perfect of certainty' or the 'prophetic perfect'. This does not refer to a change in the grammatical form of the verb that is used, but to a rhetorical device in which a future event is conceived of as being so certain and complete in itself that it is expressed using a perfect verb form. This was intended to impress the hearer with the certainty of what is predicted, and use of the prophetic perfect was not an idiom confined to prophetic speech.

The main problem with the perfect of certainty is identifying it with certainty! There are passages where the context makes the meaning of the verb form indisputable, but often there is considerable ambiguity. Standard translations frequently differ in their renderings. For instance, in 2:35 the verb *šāb* is perfect in form. It may indicate a completed action in the past, 'Surely his anger has turned from me' (NRSV). Many English translations use a present to convey the sense of a definitive past action ('he became not angry') with ongoing consequences, 'He is not angry with me' (NIV). But it is possible to identify the verb as a prophetic perfect in which the unrepentant people brazenly declare their innocence and state, 'Surely his anger shall turn from me' (as in NKJV). It is part of the translator's exegetical skill and feel for the sense of a passage to choose between options that are grammatically plausible.

7.3 The Hebrew particle *kî*. The NIV frequently does not translate the common and versatile Hebrew particle *kî*. It is not always clear whether this translation policy is motivated by an understanding of how *kî* functions in Hebrew or by the requirements of modern English style—perhaps indeed by both. However, from an exegetical point of view it is frequently worthwhile to wrestle with the precise way this particle functions in leading forward from one statement to another, and to facilitate this I have noted in the commentary where *kî* is found in the Hebrew.

For a brief statement of the options regarding its function see *IBHS* §39.3.4e or *NIDOTTE* 4:1030. An excellent extended discussion is to be found in Aejmelaeus (1986), who distinguishes between (a) connective functions of *kî* and (b) nonconnective, emphatic functions. Group (a) is further divided into (i) those where the *kî* clause precedes the main clause and sets out circumstances (conditional, temporal or causal) relating to the following clause (e.g. in 2:26; 5:19), and (ii) those where the *kî* clause follows the main clause. Group (ii) may be further subdivided into three main categories.

(1) Where the *kî* clause functions as a noun clause, after for instance a verb of speech or perception, its significance is generally unambiguous, and it may be translated by the subordinating conjunction 'that' (as in 2:19).

(2) *kî* may also be found introducing a positive alternative after a negative statement, in which case a translation such as 'but' may be appropriate (as in 1:7; 2:25; 18:15; 22:17).

(3) In causal clauses *kî* has traditionally been rendered 'for'. It may indicate a link that is strictly causal (as in 1:6), motivational (as in 1:8), or loose and indirect. In this use *kî* may not introduce the reason for what is stated in the preceding clause, but may rather function indirectly to express the reason why the statement in the previous clause has been made.

There is disagreement as to the extent to which (b), the emphatic function of *kî*, possibly to be rendered as 'indeed' (cf. 2:20; 14:13), occurs. Many modern scholars consider the proportion of emphatic occurrences to be higher than traditionally identified. However, Aejmeleaus in general finds limited scope for the emphatic use of the particle, and with this conclusion I tend to agree. But whatever viewpoint is adopted, considerable insight into the nuances of the text may be gained by trying to identify the function performed by *kî*.

COMMENTARY

I. INTRODUCTION AND CALL

(1:1-19)

OUTLINE

A. Superscription (1:1-3)
B. Jeremiah's Call (1:4-19)
   1. A Prophet to the Nations (1:4-10)
   2. The First Vision: An Almond Branch (1:11-12)
   3. The Second Vision: A Boiling Pot (1:13-16)
   4. Get Ready! (1:17-19)

Introductions are important because first impressions frequently linger, even when they are in fact mistaken. The Book of Jeremiah begins with what are in effect two introductions: the first (vv. 1-3) is the literary introduction to the book in the form in which we now have it; the second (vv. 4-19) is the record of the way in which Jeremiah entered on his prophetic ministry. One did not become a prophet of the LORD by family descent or by popular choice. It was the LORD alone who selected and appointed his prophetic messengers. Therefore the call by which God made known to them his purpose for their lives was the constitutive moment for their entire ministry. They could no longer live as they had previously; they had an inescapable divine directive to comply with. Moreover, the fact that a prophet had been divinely called was of vital significance to the people to whom he ministered. He was no longer a man uttering a message that reflected his own perception of their current situation, but one who came with a divinely originated message which was ignored at one's peril. In presenting the account of his call to the people, Jeremiah was accrediting himself as a spokesman of the LORD, publicly committing himself to act in accordance with that commission, and claiming the right to demand their attention to what he said to them.

A. SUPERSCRIPTION (1:1-3)

Unlike many works from the ancient Near East where matters such as the title of the work and the scribe who recorded it are dealt with in a colophon, a concluding paragraph containing such annotations, all the prophetic books of the Old Testament have introductory material naming the prophet and showing that his message was given by God. This may be done explicitly by using the formula 'the word of the LORD' (as in v. 2), or indirectly through phrases such as 'he saw' (Amos 1:1) or 'the vision' (Isa. 1:1; Obad. 1). Often there is also an indication of the period when the prophet was active, for example 'in the days of Jotham, Ahaz and Hezekiah, kings of Judah' (Mic. 1:1), and there may be a summary of the theme of the prophecy, such as 'concerning Judah and Jerusalem' (Isa. 1:1). Jeremiah has a fairly full introduction. It tells us who Jeremiah was (v. 1), where his message came from (v. 2), and how long his ministry lasted in a very turbulent period of Judah's history (vv. 2-3). Of the introductory elements found elsewhere only that of the prophetic theme is not found, though it is strongly hinted at in the closing words 'when the people of Jerusalem went into exile' (v. 3). As subsequent generations approached the book of Jeremiah, they did so in the knowledge that he was the prophet whose word had come true: the LORD did enforce his sentence of deportation from the land.

But this inevitably raises the question of how these words came to placed here at the beginning of the prophecy. The view taken in this commentary of the process by which the book of Jeremiah was composed has been set out in the Introduction §2.2. The way in which v. 2 begins strongly suggests that the superscription originated in two stages. The title of v. 1 may be taken as the heading which Jeremiah dictated to Baruch when the First Scroll was written in the fourth year of Jehoiakim (36:2). Obviously v. 3 originated after the fall of Jerusalem in 586 BC, and may well have been added by Jeremiah when he re-edited his prophetic works in Egypt some years later, not long before his death. The grammatical structure of v. 2 suggests that it was added at the same time as v. 3. Jeremiah wished to set before the disoriented and despairing survivors of the catastrophe that had engulfed Jerusalem the record of his ministry so that they would understand why these events had taken place and so that they would also find hope for their immediate future and for the long-term.

1. There are two different ways of understanding the phrase, **the words of Jeremiah.** 'Word' (*dābār*) may also signify 'event', 'act' or 'chronicle', as it frequently does in the books of Kings and Chronicles. For instance, in 2 Chron. 33:18 'the words of Manasseh' refers to his actions as king, 'the words of the seers' are their utterances, and 'the words of the kings of Israel' are the written annals of their reigns. Since much of Jeremiah (and especially chapters 27–44) is taken up with an account of what happened to him, it has been suggested that this phrase is equivalent to 'the history of Jeremiah' ('legacy of Jeremiah', Lundbom 1999:222). This, however, is unlikely. A similar introductory phrase, 'the words of Amos', occurs in Amos 1:1, and the idea of a history of Amos is improbable there. Furthermore this phrase 'the words of Jeremiah' is used in 36:10 to describe Jeremiah's message as found on the first scroll. Since the prophet's primary task was to relay the word of God, it undoubtedly refers here to the message that the prophet brought.

The name Jeremiah itself is used of ten different men in Scripture. Two of them are listed among David's warriors (1 Chron. 12:4, 13), and another two are in the book of Jeremiah itself (35:3; 52:1). Archaeology also attests the frequency of the name, in that three Hebrew bullae, seal impressions preserved on hardened clay, from around this period have been found with it. Its meaning is uncertain: probably 'May the LORD exalt' (with the verbal component of the name from the hiphil of *rûm*, 'to make high'); or possibly 'May the LORD hurl down ⌞his enemies⌟' (<√*rāmâ*, 'to cast down');[1] or even 'May the LORD loosen ⌞the womb⌟' (again from the root *rāmâ*, but now meaning 'to loosen the womb' on the basis of a cognate root in Aramaic). The fact that it is a common name makes it unlikely that it has significance for the nature of Jeremiah's ministry.

The prophet is identified as **son of Hilkiah**, another fairly common name, meaning 'The LORD ⌞is⌟ my portion'. While there have been commentators who considered this to be a reference to the famous Hilkiah who was high priest at the time of Josiah's reformation (2 Kgs. 22:4), that seems improbable because a reference to him would most probably have been explicitly indicated, and the high priest presumably lived in Jerusalem at this time. The additional information given that he was **one of the priests at Anathoth in the territory of Benjamin** seems clearly designed to rule out the possibility of confusion with the high priest. But to whom does this phrase refer: Hilkiah or Jeremiah? Jeremiah clearly came from a priestly family, but the expression does not require that he himself had ever been consecrated as a priest. Indeed Jeremiah's claim to be 'a youth' (1:6) indicates he was not yet old enough for office. Rowley's verdict still seems sound: 'It would certainly be strange for Jeremiah to be described in this way if he actually served as a priest, but the phrase is unexceptionable as the description of one who came of a priestly family' (1963:139).

Anathoth was located near the modern Anata, three miles (5 km) north-east of Jerusalem (see Map 1). The town is also mentioned in 11:21, 23; 29:27, and 32:7-9. It was a very ancient settlement, its name being derived from that of the Canaanite goddess Anat. At the conquest of the land by the Israelites, it became a levitical city in Benjamite territory (Josh. 21:18; 1 Chron. 6:60). Solomon sent the high priest Abiathar, the last representative of the house of Eli, into internal exile in his home town of Anathoth (1 Kgs. 2:26-27). There is the possibility that the priests at Anathoth had kept alive memories of the sanctuary which had previously existed some miles further north at Shiloh—only Jeremiah among the prophets mentions it (7:12, 14; 26:6, 9). Living as he did at the northern border of Judah, Jeremiah would have grown up with an awareness of conditions in the territory of the former northern kingdom of Israel. Though there was no direct route to it, the sanctuary at Bethel was only eight miles (13 km) away.

But the dominant influences on life in priestly circles in Anathoth

1. For the significance of the underbrackets and other symbols, see the Introduction §7.1.

would have come from Jerusalem, as the capital city was only an hour's walk away. Some have supposed that there was a high place at Anathoth where Jeremiah's family served as country priests. The reforms of Josiah severely curtailed the activities of such country priests (2 Kgs. 23:8-9), and it may be that this provides the background for the tensions Jeremiah had to contend with in his local community (11:18–12:6). However, it seems improbable that Anathoth was associated with some local centre of worship. It was close to Jerusalem, and the priests of Anathoth would have gone regularly to the city to take part in the worship at the Temple. In the religiously bleak days of Manasseh's reign, or during that of Amon, all the priests of Judah would have been compromised by their acquiescence in the practices promoted by the state cult. Jeremiah would therefore have grown up in a home where the traditional beliefs of the people were known, but which probably was affected by the religious confusion of the times.

2. Although English translations generally smooth out the construction of this verse, it is introduced in Hebrew by the relative *ʾăšer*, 'which', followed later by a resumptive *ʾēlâw*, 'to him', referring back to the antecedent Jeremiah. It is the resulting remoteness of 'Jeremiah' from the relative which suggests that the clause may have been used to add matter to an existing title.

What is to follow is declared to be not merely the message of a man. It is made clear right from the start that this is the message of God. **The word of the LORD came to him** reflects a standard expression for the reception of divine revelation by a prophet (Isa. 38:4; Ezek. 1:3; 3:16; Hos. 1:1; Joel 1:1; Zeph. 1:1; Hag. 1:1). The phrase indicates the completeness of the experience by which Jeremiah was informed of the divine message. Although the verb *hāyâ* is traditionally glossed as 'to be', its usage only partially overlaps that of the English word. In this expression with the preposition *ʾel*, 'to', it does not describe an on-going state of divine-word consciousness, but an experience which could be, and was, repeated (1:4, 11, 13; 2:1; 14:1; 46:1; 47:1; 49:34). It makes the claim that these words which are the words of a man are also the words of God. Consequently the prophet is not to be viewed as an astute individual whose insight into the spiritual and political conditions of his day equipped him to become a perceptive social commentator. Even if additionally we suppose that the prophet had a profound personal commitment to the LORD and that he urged the people of his day to maintain their loyalty to the LORD, our assessment would still fall short of the claim of Scripture. The prophet was one to whom the word of the LORD came, making the prophet directly aware of the divine assessment of the current situation and giving him information about it and the future propects for the nation that went beyond anything he could say on the basis of merely human insight. We do not know the details of how this was done; we cannot explain the mechanics of it (see Introduction §5.2). But we accept their testimony that God spoke to them and commissioned them to take his message to others. That is the fundamental claim. It was controversial even during the course of Jeremiah's career as he confronted others who claimed to be prophets but who presented a message that was contrary to what had been revealed to him (23:9-40; 28–29). The claim that in Scripture we have the record of such direct revelation from God remains controversial, but that is what the self-witness of Scripture asserts, and it is only by acknowledging the truth of that claim that we can do justice to the message that is before us.

The introduction also provides us with information about the duration of Jeremiah's ministry. **In the thirteenth year of the reign of Josiah son of Amon king of Judah** may be identified as a reference to 627/6 BC. It is also found in 25:3, and marks the start of Jeremiah's ministry. Because so few of his sayings are explicitly dated to Josiah's reign, there have been those who argue his call ought to be dated later (see Introduction §4.1). But there is no textual evidence to support a later date here, and the supposition that the reference is not to the start of his public ministry but to his birth ('called from the womb', 1:4), is strained, and also contradicts a passage such as 3:6 which is clearly dated in Josiah's time. Equally fanciful is the notion that the reference was back-calculated from 586 BC to give a forty-year ministry, symbolic of completeness and perhaps reflecting Moses' public ministry in Israel.

3. Only the three major kings are mentioned in this summary of the period of Jeremiah's ministry. Jehoahaz (609 BC) and Jehoiachin (598–597 BC), who each reigned for about three months, are omitted. **And through the reign of Jehoiakim son of Josiah king of Judah** refers to the period from 609 to 598 BC during which Judah passed from Egyptian to Babylonian control after the decisive victory of Nebuchadnezzar at Carchemish in 605 BC. At the end of his reign Jehoiakim rebelled against Babylon. On his death his son Jehoiachin quickly submitted to Nebuchadnezzar, probably to spare the land more suffering. He was taken to Babylon and his uncle Zedekiah (Mattaniah) was put on the throne as a puppet ruler. His reign (597–586 BC) also culminated in rebellion against Nebuchadnezzar, and again Jerusalem was besieged. **Down to the fifth month of the**

eleventh year of Zedekiah son of Josiah king of Judah involves a certain re-arrangement of the text, where 'down to the completion of the eleventh year' is separated from the 'fifth month', which is specifically mentioned as the time of the deportation (52:15), **when the people of Jerusalem went into exile.** The city fell on 18th July 586 BC, and a month later its walls were razed and the Temple, the palace and much else were burned to the ground, and many of the inhabitants of the city were deported to Babylon.

There is, however, the question: Did not Jeremiah's ministry continue after this? We see him in chapters 41–44 ministering among those who fled to Egypt and took him with them. It is not that this later period is being disparaged, but rather that it is viewed as an appendix to his main ministry. Through forty years of frequently difficult circumstances Jeremiah had not deserted his post, but had warned Judah of the impending execution of the LORD's judgment. When this came to pass with the fall of the city, it was a devastating climax to, and vindication of, Jeremiah's ministry. The people had not accepted his warnings, and had rather given credence to those who proclaimed that somehow or other Jerusalem would escape the worst. But the people's continuing rebellion against the LORD ensured that there could be no mitigation or avoidance of the sentence against them. Their dreams of security were shattered by the fall of the city, when Jeremiah was shown to have been right after all. Subsequent generations had to accept and live with that reality. It was for them that the prophet recorded the warnings God had given over the years so that they might acknowledge that their nation had brought disaster on itself. But there was still hope, because along with the many solemn warnings there had been given indications of a new age and a new covenant (31:23-40; 33:6-26). If Jeremiah's ministry had not been able to turn Judah from its disastrous course in the years leading up to 586 BC, then it could still be blessed to those who grappled with the aftermath of their national folly.

However, Jeremiah's prophetic mission was in the first instance to a religiously blind and decadent age, trying to arrest its decline before it became totally plunged into disaster. This is the most remarkable fact about the book: that even when God's message had been spurned, he continued to speak; even when his people stubbornly refused to respond to his entreaties, he was still concerned for them and addressed them. There was the possibility that some might be snatched from the fire (Jude 23). There was also the reality of God's ongoing commitment. After the imposition of the covenant curse on their continued disloyalty, there would through divine grace be a restored relationship in which the people would hopefully have learned the grim lessons of the past.

B. JEREMIAH'S CALL (1:4-19)

When Jeremiah set out his prophetic credentials at the beginning of the scroll written in 605 BC, it is clear that he brought together four different literary units. The heading 'The word of the LORD came to me', which begins the account of his call in vv. 4-10, is repeated in vv. 11 and 13 where it clearly marks the beginning of two vision reports, that of the almond branch (vv. 11-12) and that of the boiling pot (vv. 13-16). The change in subject between vv. 16 and 17 from the fate of the nation to personal directions to the prophet serves to delimit the final section of the chapter. The divisions of the passage are fairly widely agreed.

Jeremiah is not primarily concerned with giving autobiographical information. This record is a presentation of his prophetic credentials, and is intended to validate his claim to the office of prophet. His inner experience was not of course subject to direct verification by others, but he set out his personal testimony to provide a suitable background for others to assess his ministry. These are the directions he was given by the LORD, and they explain why he persevered with his task despite all the difficulties to be faced.

1. A Prophet to the Nations (1:4-10)

Form critical studies have analysed the various elements in the narrative of 1:4-10 and have shown the existence of parallels with other accounts of divine calls in the Old Testament, such as those of Moses (Exod. 3:1-12), Gideon (Judg. 6:11-23), Solomon (1 Kgs. 3:7), Isaiah (Isa. 6:1-13) and Ezekiel (1:1–3:15). The major divisions of the literary structure of the call accounts have been set out as: 1. divine confrontation, 2. introductory word, 3. commission, 4. objection, 5. reassurance, 6. sign (Habel 1965:298), though the relevance of the first two to this passage has been questioned (Holladay 1986, 1:27). There can be no doubt that many parallels do exist; the question is rather one of their significance. Those who see the book of Jeremiah as the product of an involved process of redactional activity tend to claim that the formal parallels are an editorial technique to show that Jeremiah stood in an on-going line of prophets who had been genuinely called by God. The parallels are then largely a literary device, and the stylised and stereotypical literary form so dominates the record that 'it is virtually impossible to analyse the psychological dimensions of the prophetic calls' (Habel 1965:317). However, accepting that this narrative goes back to Jeremiah, the existence of the literary parallels can be otherwise explained. Most significantly, the literary similarity arises from the actual existence of a similar response to the overwhelming reality of a divine call. That, for instance, the recipients of such a call felt unworthy of it and inadequate to fulfil it cannot be appropriately analysed merely as a literary phenomenon; it reflects the nature of the divine-human encounter that is involved. Further, it is no doubt an aspect of divine condescension to use procedures and language familiar from accounts of former calls to assist later individuals in grappling with their own experience. Equally, when Jeremiah tried to record what was really inexpressible, it is not surprising that he resorted to words and categories that he and his audience were already familiar with from Scripture, and which would convey some meaning to them. The existence of literary parallels points primarily to the existence of real parallels in experience.

Why then were prophets given this unique initiatory experience by God? Their office was not hereditary like that of the priests, and so inevitably there came a time when they were first made aware of what the LORD wished them to do. Given that they were to function as the LORD's messengers testifying against a spiritually careless nation, bringing to it a message that often was one of condemnation, and that they inevitably had to stand out against the consensus outlook of their day, their experience was made unforgettably vivid to them so that they would be in no personal doubt that their task was not one that they had projected themselves into. Furthermore, by communicating the experience of their call to their contemporaries, the prophets were presenting their credentials as divine ambassadors so that they would be recognised by others and the legitimacy of the message they brought might not be questioned.

In his discussion of Jeremiah's call Skinner makes two points, one of which can readily be accepted as true. Indeed it is of considerable significance in understanding the prophet. 'We cannot but feel that though this may have been Jeremiah's first vision of Yahwe [*sic*] it was not the beginning of his fellowship with him. It is the consummation of a genuine religious experience, rooted probably in the pieties of home and early life, of growing self-knowledge and knowledge of God' (Skinner 1922:27). On the other hand when he goes on to argue that the prophet's awareness of his call 'is not of course a truth suddenly injected into the mind from without—no such process is conceivable—but a conviction formed within, an intuitive perception of the divine ideal and meaning of his existence, of his true place in the divine order of the world, of the work for which he is "cut out" in the service of God and his kingdom' (Skinner 1922:27), this has to be totally rejected. The prophetic call was that precisely because it came unexpectedly and cut across preconceived ideas and expectations. It shared elements of self-discovery and self-surrender to God that continue to be elements in the experience of all God's servants, but it was uniquely distinguished by the personal revelation of God and his direct commissioning, which, though taking account of the previous experience of the individual called, constituted an entirely new element in it.

4. The word of the LORD came to me, saying essentially corresponds to the phrase in v. 2, and makes the claim that the message and activity about to be described did not originate with Jeremiah, but was the result of specific divine communication, 'divine confrontation' (Habel 1965:307). Jeremiah did not set himself up as a prophet, as if it were a career option he might or might not follow. It was a matter of divine selection that was suddenly, intrusively, made known to him. We are limited in what we can say about the mode of divine communication, but it is clear that certain interpretations can be ruled out, such as that Jeremiah personally convinced himself that this was to be his vocation in life. No amount of psychologising can do justice to what Jeremiah here claims. We may reject his claim—although that would be misguided—but to reject his claim is more honest than to reinterpret it into something other than what he intended. Furthermore, 'to me' indicates that Jeremiah himself is the source of this account. So significant was this in his life that he would have made a written record of it before it was later incorporated into the scroll he dictated to Baruch.

5. In the first part of the verse God reveals to the prophet that his call was no sudden divine decision, but a matter that had long been planned. Indeed God was already active in his life, though he had not been aware of it. This was Jeremiah's destiny, and there could be no escaping it. **Before I formed you[2] in the womb, I knew you**. The divine speech presents the reality of the divine origin of Jeremiah's call

---

2. The kethibh seems to be *ʾăṣûrəkā* from the root *ṣûr*, a by-form of *yāṣar*, found in Exod. 32:4 and 1 Kgs. 7:15. The qere reads *ʾeṣṣorkā* (with a short *o* because the stress is on the pronominal suffix) from the root *yāṣar*, with the same meaning, 'I formed you'. *NIDOTTE* 3:792 suggests that *ṣûr* may possibly have a homonym 'to summon', though that does not fit so well here.

in three statements which substantially overlap in meaning.[3] The LORD's speech focuses on three divine actions, the first two of which relate to action which took place before Jeremiah's birth. 'Formed' (<√*yāṣar*, 18:2, 6) describes the work of a craftsman, particularly a potter. It was used for the LORD's creative work in Gen. 2:7. Not only do we have here the assertion that the LORD is the sovereign controller and originator of all life, even life before birth, but that he has also determined what destiny should be for each (Ps. 139:13-16). That is true in measure of everyone, but it was especially true of Jeremiah (44:2, 24; 49:5; cf. Gal. 1:15). Such knowledge was given beforehand of Samson (Judg. 13:3) and also of John the Baptist (Luke 1:13-17), though there is nothing to suggest that was so as regards Jeremiah. Though other prophets such as Moses and Samuel were divinely designated from birth, their call is not traced so far back. However, in Isaiah the Servant is 'formed in the womb' (Isa. 44:2, 24; 49:5) and 'called from the womb' (Isa. 49:1). In Jeremiah's case there had been the same divine superintendence of his life, preparing him for the task that would be assigned him, but Jeremiah (and others) were unaware of God's special purpose in his life until his call in 627 BC.

'Know' (<√*yādaʿ*) here is used in its fuller Hebrew sense, which covers not merely factual information about someone, but approval, choice and personal commitment. Hence the translation 'choose' in the NIV margin (see also the REB and Amos 3:2). From the very start of Jeremiah's life God had sovereignly recognised him as his subject and his servant who would play an important part in the outworking of the divine purpose. Being made aware of his status in God's sight provided Jeremiah with an encouraging and secure basis for compliance with what God would require him to do.

Before you were born/'came out of the womb'[4] **I set you apart**

3. Translations vary significantly from the NIV which identifies verse only in v. 5. The REB has prose throughout vv. 4-10, whereas the NRSV uses poetry also for the divine speeches in vv. 7-8 and vv. 9-10. The NASB and NKJV even print Jeremiah's reply in v. 6 as verse. There is much to be said for all three divine speeches being presented similarly. If that is as verse and Jeremiah's speech is set out as prose, this would effect a contrast between the speech of the divine king and the response of his courtier, though whether the equivalent of that in our diction is a poetic layout is another matter.

4. *reḥem*, which is found in the second clause, is a more specific word for 'womb', whereas *beṭen* in the previous line is a more general term for 'inner parts of the body', which in specific contexts may indicate 'womb' (*NIDOTTE* 1:650).

indicates that God had selected him for his own. 'Set apart' (<√*qādaš*, 6:4; 17:22) is also used for the setting apart of the priests and everything connected with the worship of Israel, hence 'consecrated you' (NASB, NRSV). While the term indicated that people and items were for use in the worship of the sanctuary, the emphasis was not on personal holiness as such, but on being designated to perform a specific function in divine service. It was therefore sacrilege and rebellion for one set apart to turn to other pursuits. The combination of set apart/holy and divine choice is also found in Deut. 7:6 as regards Israel and in 1 Sam. 16:5, 8-13 in respect of kingship. Note also the use of 'holy one' in Luke 1:35. Ahead of Jeremiah were times of depression, of doubt and of despair. Right from the start, God was teaching him how he should look at his life. Rather than being overwhelmed by the pressures of the moment, his self-perception was to be that he was one shaped and appointed for his master's use.

Jeremiah's commission is then expressed in words which refer to it as already an accomplished fact, or more probably as then sovereignly bestowed. **I appointed you** gives more specific details as to how God had set him apart in his own service. *nātan*, 'to give', followed by two accusatives has the meaning 'to set' or 'to appoint' (Gen. 17:5; Exod. 17:1). The perfect here may be used in a performative sense, 'I hereby appoint you', in which an action carried out by one with appropriate authority coincides with, and is effected by, the word that is spoken (*IBHS*, §30.5.1c; cf. 1:10). It may not be inappropriate to see a parallel between the three steps in this divine statement regarding Jeremiah and Paul's use of 'foreknew', 'predestined' and 'called' in Rom. 8:29-30.

But Jeremiah's calling was not just as a member of the people of God. It was specifically **as a prophet.** The original significance of *nābî'*, 'prophet', is still a matter of scholarly dispute (*TWOT* 2:544-5; *TDOT* 9:129-135), but the scriptural use of the term is decisively set by Exod. 7:1, 'Then the LORD said to Moses, "See, I have made you like God to Pharaoh, and your brother Aaron will be your prophet (*nābî'*)",' especially in the light of Exod. 4:15-16. The prophet was God's spokesman, his messenger, divinely selected for the task of conveying to the LORD's people the message which had been communicated to him by God (see further Introduction §5).

It is here, however, that there is a surprising aspect to Jeremiah's call: he is denominated not just a prophet to Judah, but **to the nations**. 'Nations' (*gōyīm*) ordinarily refers to the heathen nations as distinct from Israel or Judah, though in the singular the word is occasionally employed of the chosen people also (e.g. in Gen. 12:2; Exod. 19:6). But the main theme of Jeremiah's ministry was the fate of his fellow countrymen in Judah. However, v. 10 sheds further light on the sense in which this expression is to be taken. It refers to more than the fact that in Jeremiah's day the affairs of Judah were inextricably linked with those of surrounding nations, so that saying something about Judah's future also meant saying something about the nations around her. Judah was not just flotsam swept along by the current of prevailing international affairs. As the prophecies against the nations show (chaps. 46–51), what the LORD was permitting to happen in the world scene arose out of, and was determined by, what he was doing for his own people. His control over events ensured that his messenger had something to say of relevance to their destiny also. That this international dimension to his ministry was not unique to Jeremiah is clearly shown in 28:8 where Jeremiah talks about earlier prophets who 'prophesied war, disaster and plague against many countries and great kingdoms'.

The approach advocated by Skinner that Jeremiah's call was the outcome of a process of personal spiritual maturation has to face the problem of how such a conception of his mission could have come naturally to such a diffident personality as that of Jeremiah. Resorting to expedients such as emending the text or suggesting that this is written from the perspective of his later life merely evades the claims of the text that this was a mission divinely assigned to Jeremiah.

6. Jeremiah was overwhelmed and dismayed by the task that he was called to. It is to underestimate the significance of the situation to suggest that this is a conventional refusal. 'Ah!' (*'ăhāh*) is a cry of bewilderment at being in God's presence (Josh. 1:7; 6:22; cf. also Isa. 6:5) and also consternation at the duty assigned to him (Josh. 7:7; Judg. 6:22; 11:35), because Jeremiah is aware of the tension between his own will and the implications of the divine pronouncement. A similar cry also appears in 4:10; 14:13; 32:17.

However, it would be wrong to suggest that Jeremiah is refusing to comply with his mandate. He uses the term **Sovereign LORD** (*'ădōnāy Yhwh*, 'Lord LORD') which acknowledges God's rights as the sovereign ruler of all, and also as Yahweh, the covenant God of Israel. He does not seek to evade the task, but feeling his incompetence, he looks for a delay on the grounds of his age. **I said, 'I do not know how to speak;** 'for' (*kî*, omitted by the NIV) **I am only a child.'** The reasons recorded for the reluctance shown by those called by God varied (see Judg. 6:15; Isa. 6:5; Ezek. 2:1). Although Jeremiah's reason seems to be patterned on that of Moses, 'I am slow of speech and tongue' (Exod. 4:10; see also 3:11; 4:1), it is in fact different.

Jeremiah's inability to speak is not a matter of physical impediment, as seems to have been the case with Moses, but rather a genuine lack of skill in public speaking because of his youthfulness. 'Child' (*na'ar*) does not really capture the Hebrew word in this context because it sounds too young. Though the word can be used to refer to an unborn child (Judg. 13:5, 7, 8) as well as a three-month-old infant ('baby', Exod. 2:6 NKJV), its range of reference can extend well into middle age. Solomon uses it of himself in his speech of protestation, when he was at least thirty (1 Kgs. 3:7). It is used of Joshua in Exod. 33:11 in the sense of 'attendant' when he was aged 45! Though earlier scholars took Jeremiah's age to be around twenty, it is probable that he was as young as twelve (see Introduction §4.1).

Public meetings in Anathoth would be no different from other assemblies and councils at that time. They looked to the aged to speak (cf. Job 12:12; 32:4-7), and Jeremiah had as yet had no opportunity to acquire skills in public speaking and debate. And it was not just a matter of experience. He would not have easily received a hearing because no one would have taken a youth seriously if he did try to speak. So Jeremiah's problems are not feigned: he foresees genuine difficulties in carrying out the task allotted to him. He felt the situation was one that was beyond him, and was perplexed because he did not know how to cope with it. No doubt there was also a genuine element of apprehension. The prophet as God's spokesman had to be one able to present God's case before the nation, and Jeremiah would have well known the reception accorded previous prophets of the LORD, such as Amos at Bethel (Amos 7:10-13) or even the great Elijah at the hands of Jezebel (1 Kgs. 19:2), and seemingly others whose innocent blood according to Jewish tradition had been shed in more recent times in the atrocities perpetrated in Manasseh's reign (2 Kgs. 21:16). Jeremiah's response is also evidence that he did not seek the role assigned to him; so it was misunderstanding the situation to accuse him of enjoying bringing words of woe (17:16). He was acting under divine constraint (1 Cor. 9:16).

7. The LORD then spoke to reassure Jeremiah. No great significance can be attached to the fact that the words, **But the LORD said to me**, are also to be found in Deut. 18:17, in the passage about the prophet like Moses which is alluded to later. The expression is an ordinary one, and its use unremarkable (*contra* Lundbom 1999:233).

God does not dispute the accuracy of Jeremiah's claims about his age and inexperience. He disputes their relevance: **Do not say, 'I am only a child.'** Since the LORD had selected Jeremiah from before his birth, he would be the one to provide him with what he needed. Also, there was no lack of clarity about the instructions he was being given. The next clause begins with the Hebrew particle *kî*, usually glossed as 'for' and generally introducing a reason (for a fuller discussion regarding this particle see Introduction §7.3). When it is found, as here, after a negative, it can bear the sense 'but rather', and so introduce the alternative scenario that the LORD envisages. 'Instead' **you must go to**[5] **everyone**[6] **I send you to and say whatever I command you.** There is a balance between *ʿal-kol-ʾăšer*, 'to everyone that', and *wəʾēt kol-ʾăšer*, 'and everything that', which is not brought out in the NIV or NRSV, but is found in the REB: 'You are to go to whatever people I send you, and say whatever I tell you to say.' The emphasis is not on the limitation of Jeremiah's commission, as if he were not to go to those he had not been commanded to, though no doubt that was true. Rather it is on the completeness of the obedience that is expected—everyone and everything, without exception. Because that is his divine commission, he has no option or discretion in the matter: the choice of recipients was not his, nor was the message to be delivered to them. So Jeremiah need not worry about having to work out what he was to say. He was a commissioned messenger whom the LORD had sent. 'Send' plays an important part in the prophet's perception of his task (23:21, 32; 28:15; cf. 43:2), as does 'go' in terms of his fulfilment of that commission (Exod. 3:10-11; Judg. 6:14; Amos 7:15; Isa. 6:8-9; Ezek. 2:3-4). A prophet who is not sent by the one he claims to represent is necessarily a fraud and an impostor (23:21).

There is a further element to the situation. The LORD uses words already employed in Deut. 18:18, 'He will speak to them all that I shall command him', where they describe the prophet like Moses whom God promises he will raise up. By using words with which Jeremiah was familiar from Scripture, God calls on him to see his life's work as following in the footsteps of those who had gone before (cf. also Exod. 7:2; notice the similar terms in the Apostolic Commission of Matt. 28:20). This is not evidence of a later Deuteronomic redaction, in which an editor rewrites the life of Jeremiah to conform the history of the prophet to what is found in Deuteronomy. Rather it is part of the LORD's using of Jeremiah's training in prior revelation to give him a

5. *ʿal*, 'against', here as often in Jeremiah is used with the same meaning as *ʾel*, 'to', that is, there are no hostile implications. Elsewhere also *ʿal* after *hālak*, 'to go', differs little from *ʾel* (2:11; 1 Sam. 15:20; Neh. 6:17).

6. 'Everywhere' (NASB) is a possible rendering of the Hebrew, but it tends to make the introduction of 'them' in v. 8 unnecessarily abrupt.

frame of reference within which he can begin to understand his own experience and encounter with God. This would have been reinforced for Jeremiah if the scroll found five years later was in fact a copy of Deuteronomy (see Introduction §3.6). What was then read out (2 Kgs. 23:2) would have seemed like a second call, encouraging him in his mission.

8. Jeremiah need not have been overly prone to timidity, but his call at such a young age and in the circumstances of his day obviously led to a fearfulness that was boosted by a sense of personal weakness and inadequacy. The LORD next acts to counter this (Ezek. 2:6; Luke 5:10; Acts 18:9), but not by rewording his orders or reshaping the response Jeremiah would encounter. **Do not be afraid of them**[7]**.** 'Them' refers to those to whom Jeremiah is sent in the previous verse. He is not to let their opposition get through to him and undermine his nerve. God helps him in this by giving him a twofold promise.

The first reason Jeremiah is given for overcoming his fear is, **For** (*kî*) **I am with you.** The promise of the special divine protecting presence was often given to God's servants in these words (cf. also v. 19 and 15:20). In this phrase the 'am' is a translator's supplement which in many respects is contrary to English usage which would require 'I will be with you' in conformity to the tense of the following verb. But the Hebrew expression is tenseless, and the promise is without temporal limitation. Such assured presence and support is found in other call narratives also (Judg. 6:16; Exod. 3:12; Ezek. 3:2), and in combination with deliverance in Deut. 20:1; 31:8; Isa. 41:10. This is in fact the second reason why Jeremiah could banish his fears: God promises that he **will rescue you.** 'Rescue' is the hiphil stem of *nāṣal*, 'to snatch away, remove from danger', suggesting not avoidance of situations of danger, but release from the grasp of distress. It is the word that is rendered 'save' in Amos' graphic description, 'As a shepherd saves from the lion's mouth only two leg bones or a piece of an ear, so will the Israelites be saved' (Amos 3:12). Jeremiah was not being promised immunity from difficulties, but there was a measure of reassurance for the trying days ahead. The promise of presence and rescue recalled what God had done for his people in former days at the time of the Exodus (Exod. 3:8; 18:10), and what was related by David as his own experience in later days (Pss. 18:17, 19; 22:21; 143:9). So whatever the future held in store for him, Jeremiah is being assured

7. 'Of their faces' (NKJV) is an overly literal rendering of *mippənēhem*, and is probably unwarranted in this context. The idiom is frequent elsewhere meaning simply 'because of' (see, for instance, the NKJV rendering of 4:4).

that his life will be preserved from his enemies, as in fact it was.

Declares the LORD (*nə'um-Yhwh*) occurs 168 times in the book (Holladay 1986, 1:35), at the middle or end of divine sayings, and functioning somewhat like a signature to authenticate the message that has just been given by naming its originator. As this message comes from the LORD, the phrase embodies the claim that it is accurate and authoritative. The same note of authority is found in the introductory phrase, 'This is what the LORD says' (*kōh 'āmar Yhwh*), which points away from the messenger who is merely the mouthpiece of the one who has commissioned him to deliver it. For further discussion of the root *ne'um*, see on 23:31.

9. The divine word revealed to Jeremiah's inner consciousness was accompanied by a confirmatory sign which presumably occurred in a vision, that is, Jeremiah was not only inwardly aware of auditory data, but also of visual information. However, a third party at the prophet's side when this vision was given would not have been aware of any phenomenon; it was granted to the prophet's psyche alone. But the visionary nature of the sign would not have lessened the vividness with which it would have impressed itself on Jeremiah. **Then the LORD reached out his hand and touched my mouth.** The 'hand' is the member of action and power. It also occurs in a number of passages which speak of the way in which the LORD communicated his message to the prophets (15:17; Isa. 8:11; 2 Kgs. 3:15; and frequently in Ezek. 1:3; 3:13, 22; 8:1; 37:1). Notice specifically its role in the call of Ezekiel as a concluding experience (Ezek. 2:9). It is a sovereign action which accompanies divine bestowal of blessing. There is a hint that Jeremiah was aware of much more in the vision, but that revelation is not accessible to us.

'Touched' renders the hiphil of *nāga'* (as in Isa. 6:7) and perhaps is used instead of the qal to convey the deliberateness of the action, 'He caused it to touch'. The root conveys the idea of contact being made between persons or objects, and in certain contexts is used of a severe blow. Some have therefore suggests that 'touch' is too weak a translation, and that Jeremiah received a blow corresponding to the contact with burning coal experienced by Isaiah (Lundbom 1999:235), but this seems unnecessarily violent and traumatic after the encouragement of the previous verse.

The significance of the action is explained by the divine word. He **said to me, 'Now, I have put my words in your mouth.'** Lundbom argues that the verb here is a prophetic perfect, the reckoning of a future event as if it were already past (Lundbom 1999:235; see

Introduction §7.2). Because the LORD has determined that it shall be, it is treated as already certain. This is to fit in with his theory that Jeremiah's ministry does not actually begin until 622 BC when he eats the words written on the Temple scroll (15:16). But this seems to be special pleading. The words more naturally serve to explain the action being experienced, albeit in vision, and may be taken as a performative perfect (cf. vv. 5, 10). The prophet now has a message to relay, not one of his own devising, but one divinely provided (2 Pet. 1:21). Again, Jeremiah is reminded of Deut. 18:18 where the words 'I shall put my words in his mouth' are also to be found with the same verb but in a future construction.

10. In **See, today I appoint you** the combination of the perfect verb and 'today' shows that here again we have an instance of a performative perfect, 'I hereby appoint you'. The verb used for 'appoint' (*pāqad*) is different from that used in 1:5 (*nātan*). *Pāqad* is a verb which requires quite a variety of translations in English. Basically it refers to the action of a superior with respect to an inferior, and here (in a hiphil form) it conveys the idea that Jeremiah has been divinely appointed to an office and invested with all the authority associated with it ('I give you authority', REB). As far as God is concerned, Jeremiah is a man under orders to whom authority has been delegated (Josh. 10:18; 2 Chron. 34:12; Isa. 62:6). This helps explain the power of the prophetic word. It is misconceived to think of the word as possessing inherent power as is argued by Lindblom: 'Here it is said that Jeremiah's message, whether of judgement or salvation, would be not only a statement about doom or salvation, but also a power which really created ruin or prosperity for the nations' (1962:117-8). The power of the prophetic word is not in the word per se; it arises from the fact that it is the word of the vice-gerent who has been divinely appointed; and indeed it is only as that word faithfully reflects the determination of the heavenly council that it is effective. The power of the word inheres in its divine originator.

However, the sphere of the prophet's authority is wider than might have been expected. It is **over nations and kingdoms**. The LORD's dominion knows no bounds (10:6-7, 10, 12-16; 32:17), and so he is in a position to delegate to others international responsibilities. Jeremiah has a message to deliver that impacts on the destiny not only of Judah but also of neighbouring nations. The prophet speaks for God, and as he utters his words, so the divine purpose is put into execution. The prophet's task is presented in terms that go beyond a messenger merely announcing a decree, to a governor given effective authority by God to implement his decrees throughout the territories under his sway.

The international aspect of Jeremiah's ministry was no new thing. Previous prophets had proclaimed messages regarding the conduct of surrounding nations. For instance, though Amos' vision particularly concerned Israel (Amos 1:1), he proceeded to announce the LORD's verdict on Israel's neighbours (Amos 1:3–2:5) before focusing in on conditions in Israel itself. Furthermore, when Jeremiah addresses Hananiah, he acknowledges this international aspect of previous prophetic ministries. 'From early times the prophets who preceded you and me have prophesied war, disaster and plague against many countries and great kingdoms' (28:8).

The divine rule, and Jeremiah's administration of it, are described in six terms: four of which are negative (1-4), and two positive (5-6); three of which are from an agricultural background (1, 3, 6), and three from a building one (2, 4, 5), though 'to destroy' is used in a variety of contexts. (1) **To uproot and** (2) **tear down,**[8] **and** (3) **to destroy and** (4) **overthrow,** (5) **to build and** (6) **to plant.** NLT suggests that this ministry is distributed over various nations, 'to uproot some … to build others up', but a sequential arrangement seems more plausible. The negative terms precede the positive because of the order in which Jeremiah's ministry as regards Judah would be carried out: the overgrown field of the nation will first have to be cleared of thorns and weeds before true crops can be planted; the unsteady structures of the land would have to be demolished to make room for future construction. That there are four negative terms and two positive may well reflect the balance of Jeremiah's ministry—more demolition work was needed than reconstruction. There is probably also here the tension between expressions of condemnation and expressions of praise that is needed in any ministry that would reflect the balance of God's word. The words are repeated in a number of forms throughout the book and evidently formed a theme round which Jeremiah perceived his ministry to centre (12:14-17; 18:7-9; 24:6; 31:28, 40; 42:10; 45:4).

The impact of this section is not confined just to those who are called to the public ministry of God's word. At Pentecost the day dawned when all the LORD's people are prophets, as Moses desired (Num. 11:29). Still we are not at the same level as Jeremiah, with the same immediacy of divine revelation. Nonetheless the completed canon of Scripture provides us with a message of utmost significance, of divine origin and of international relevance.

---

8. The first two verbs are brought together because of the assonance involved between *nātaś*, 'to pluck up', and *nātaṣ*, 'to pull down'.

2. The First Vision: An Almond Branch (1:11-12)

The next two sections of the chapter (vv. 11-12 and vv. 13-16) present visions which follow on from the prophet's call and set out basic aspects of the task to which he was called. In neither vision is there any elaboration of the details of what was seen, but one key aspect is emphasised and explained.

A vision is divinely given revelation experienced in the form of visual perception where there is no external, publicly accessible phenomenon, but where God directly stimulates the inner capacities of the recipient so that they experience the same inner sensation as they would have done had there been appropriate external stimuli. A vision is thus private to the recipient, but not merely the product of the recipient's own imagination or mental faculties. It is not a hallucination, but objective divine communication.

A vision is also to be distinguished from a dream in that the recipient is not asleep, but conscious, in possession of his mental faculties, and able to interact with what is perceived.

Lindblom differentiates between *pictorial visions* in which the attention is simply directed towards objects or figures which are seen by the recipient, and *dramatic visions* in which the stress is upon what the people who appear in the vision undertake and do (1962:124). In terms of that distinction these two visions are pictorial. Lindblom, however, prefers to class these visions as instances of symbolic perception, where there is a real, objective phenomenon, accessible (at least potentially) to a third party, which then is interpreted as a symbol of a higher level of reality (1962:139).

Care must be taken not to minimise the level of divine involvement in symbolic perception. Lindblom writes as if what happened were merely due to Jeremiah's innate powers of perception.

> One day when Jeremiah was walking in the field he noticed a twig of an almond tree which captured his attention. We may imagine that he walked in prophetic reverie. He pondered over the problem if his preaching of doom really would be fulfilled. … This association of ideas came to him as an answer to the question he was just pondering. Had not Yahweh let him see this almond tree in order to show him that He at all events would watch over the accomplishment of His words spoken by His prophets? … The whole had for the prophet the character of a revelation. The trivial impression was by inspiration from God lifted up to a higher level. The everyday observation was sublimated, carried over into the divine and supernatural sphere. (1962:139)

Quite apart from the question of what constitutes 'prophetic reverie', the phrase 'the character of a revelation' is significant in this description for not conceding a true divine disclosure but stopping short with something that is human insight.

The information presented in the text is not sufficiently detailed for us to be certain whether they are instances of pictorial visions or symbolic perception. On balance, visions supernaturally introduced into his mind seem more likely. But if this is symbolic perception of an external phenomenon, then it must be maintained that there was also audition, the inner perception of divine speech, so that the prophet knew the significance of what he saw was not the precipitate of his own consciousness, but was directly and divinely communicated to him.

11. Both visions are introduced by the formula, **The word of the LORD came to me** (1:11, 13). This does not of itself settle the question in favour of symbolic perception as distinct from pictorial vision, because the phrase emphasises the revelatory nature of the experience, rather than reflecting on its mode.

The revelation proceeds by way of a conversation. **What do you see, Jeremiah?** (cf. Amos 7:8; 8:2; Zech. 4:2; 5:2). This is to evoke a response from the prophet, and involve him as more than a passive recipient of the vision. **'I see the branch of an almond tree,' I replied.** The words used may refer to physical sight or inner vision. As regards interpretation of the event, the question to be answered is if there is any significance to be attached to the fact that it is only a branch, and not the whole tree, that is seen. There are a number of Hebrew words that signify a 'branch', and this one (*māqqēl*) may also be used of wood taken from a tree and made into a stick or staff (1 Sam. 17:40, 43). Naegelsbach (1871:22-3) accepted the view of certain earlier interpreters that the staff was a 'threatening rod of castigation' and not a branch with twigs and leaves, arguing that stick or staff is the meaning of the word rather than branch and that it would be possible to recognise it as being from an almond tree even though stripped of leaves since almond trees were common in the neighbourhood of Anathoth, and Jeremiah would be familiar with their wood. This view is not as far-fetched as many subsequent commentators have assumed (indeed the REB rendering of the next verse, 'I am on the watch to carry out my threat', also introduces a negative note into this vision), but it must be conceded that the explanation of the vision does not develop the significance of the portion of the tree that is seen, but rather of the type of tree involved.

12. The focus of the disclosure is a play on words through which the message is given (cf. Amos 8:1-3). **The LORD said to me, 'You have seen correctly[9], for I am watching to see that my word is fulfilled.'** Jeremiah's response is correct, and the significance of the vision is explained in terms of a word association that is easily made in Hebrew. The almond tree was called *šāqēd*, 'the watchful one'/'the alert one', because early in the season, before other trees, its blossom and the buds of leaves appeared. Sometimes its characteristic white blossom could be seen as early as January, even before its leaves developed (King 1993:152-3). The LORD used the almond branch as a symbol of what he himself was doing: 'I am watching', 'I am wakeful' (*šōqēd*). This verb describes divine activity in 31:28 and 44:27, but in 5:6 it is employed of a leopard lying in wait to tear the unwary to pieces. However, the word itself does not have negative overtones. It is the intensity and vigilance of the divine scrutiny that is being emphasised.

Various explanations have been advanced as to the significance of this vision for Jeremiah. Most presuppose that it was given at a later stage in his ministry when he was concerned that his prophecies of doom had not been fulfilled, and he was being reassured that the LORD was maintaining watch over circumstances and would act to realise his announced purpose. Further it is argued that it is artificial to date this vision at the start of Jeremiah's ministry because it would then be dealing with a hypothetical future situation and not meeting an immediate need.

But does that do justice to the situation in which Jeremiah found himself? The long years of Manasseh's suppression of the true worship of the LORD had not long ended. There had been no obvious response from God to the atrocities the people committed during those years. Did his word, that is, the covenant stipulations of Israel's divine king, still hold? The fact that Manasseh's rebellion had not met with divine retribution, that previous prophetic warnings of judgment on the rebellious seemed to have been as misguided as their opponents maintained, would have been puzzling the pious in the land for many years. When called on to be the bearer of the king's word, Jeremiah would undoubtedly have had unresolved questions about how that word worked itself out in practice. Right from the start the LORD acted to convince the young prophet that his word for the people had not been discarded and that its warnings would be implemented if there was no suitable response forthcoming.

---

9. In *hêṭabtā lirʾôt*, 'you have done well with respect to seeing', the principle idea is contained in the infinitive and the governing verb is best rendered adverbially in English (GKC §114n[2]; Joüon §102g).

The divine explanation does not attach any significance to the word 'branch', but at least the word itself is in the text. Since there is no mention at all of leaves or blossom, it is incorrect to make the focus of the vision an almond tree covered in blossom as a sign of spring ahead. That imports a sense of joy and anticipation which is lacking in the text itself. If anything, a mere branch without any sign of life is an emblem of a situation in which there was nothing to suggest that God was active to ensure the fulfilment of his word. But by the verbal connection between the almond branch and the thought of watchfulness Jeremiah is alerted to the LORD's scrutiny of what is taking place and the inexorability of the process by which the divine purpose will be worked out. Immediate inaction should not be confused with lack of interest. The Lord of history who has announced his will to his people is taking steps to ensure that what he has purposed will surely come to pass.

3. The Second Vision: A Boiling Pot (1:13-16)

13. In the second vision, the focus shifts from the actualisation of the divine message entrusted to the prophets to the content of the message. **The word of the LORD came to me again**. Since the introductory formula, 'The word of the LORD came to me', has already occurred twice (1:4, 11), the reference in 'again' (*šēnît*, 'a second time') is not immediately clear. Lundbom (1975:98; 1999:227) argues that the sequence in the chapter is rhetorical rather than historical in origin, that is, while not denying that these incidents occurred, their presentation here is structured according to the impact they should have on their original hearers and not to preserve chronological data. The reference in 'again', he argues, is to 1:4 since 1:4-12 form a unit relating to Jeremiah's call in 627 BC, whereas 1:13-19 relate Jeremiah's subsequent commission when he began his public ministry in 622 BC after the Book of the Law had been found. More commonly, however, the reference in 'a second time' is taken to be to 1:11, and understood to link the two vision accounts, which together form a subsidiary, explicative role to the call of 1:4-10. The two visions are similar in form and content (see previous section), but now the focus is clearly on the content of Jeremiah's message.

Either while the content of the vision is divinely presented to the prophet's inner faculties, or while the prophet was looking at an externally perceptible pot, the LORD gives to it a symbolic significance which is brought out through question and answer. The LORD encourages Jeremiah to look more closely at what is before him and to verbalise his experience by asking, **What do you see?** (cf. 1:11, though here without the vocative). The question calls for a description by the prophet. The similarity of language with v. 11 indicates a similarity in the experience.

'I see a boiling pot, tilting away from the north,' I answered. A pot was a large vessel for cooking for a number of people. It was usually spherical, and made of pottery, though here more probably of metal. There might have been handles for carrying it, and the opening would have been at the top (King 1993:171). The pot is described as 'boiling', literally, 'blown upon', referring in the first instance to the fire under the pot being fanned into life, perhaps by the wind, if the scene is outdoors. But all is not going well. Though the contents of the pot have begun to boil, the pot itself has settled unevenly on the fire so that it is tilting. The pot is said to have 'a face', either a reference to the rim of the pot, or to the surface of the liquid within it, and its face is 'away from the north'.[10] Because of this, the pot was liable to spill its contents out onto the fire or hearth. The more it boiled, the greater the overflow, if indeed the pot itself did not tip right over.

14. The scene might be one of a minor domestic accident in which someone is liable to be scalded, but the divine explanation associates the boiling pot with what the LORD is about to do.[11] **The LORD said to me, 'From the north disaster will be poured out on all who live in the land.'**[12] 'Poured out' comes from the root *pātaḥ*, which generally signifies 'to open', but 'to let loose' seems to fit in Isa. 14:17, and the niphal here would then mean 'be let loose', 'break out' (NRSV). The focus is on 'from the north' (fronted in the Hebrew for emphasis). This

10. *ṣāpônâ*, originally 'northwards', hence 'toward the north' (AV), but there was a general weakening of the original directive force of the final *he*, GKC §90e.

11. The paragraphing of the NRSV seems suspect in that vv. 11-19 are divided into two paragraphs between vv. 13 and 14. This unnecessarily separates the second vision from the divine explanation of it, and obscures the fact that vv. 17-19 are directly addressed to Jeremiah.

12. The subjective nature of many decisions about where the text is prose and where it is poetry can be seen in the treatment of the closing part of this chapter. The NRSV and NASB treat vv. 11-19 as prose throughout; the REB and NKJV change after v. 14a from prose to poetry. The NIV delays the change to poetry until the middle of v. 15, but then takes vv. 17-19 as prose. Such changes frequently reflect judgments not only about the quality of the Hebrew verse but also about the continuity of the thought between the sections.

was the direction from which invaders from Mesopotamia would advance into Palestine since to avoid marching across desert they would move up the Tigris/Euphrates before turning south down the Mediterranean coast. There may also be an ominous resonance in the use of 'north' in that it was the traditional home of the gods in Canaanite myth, and on occasions there may be reflections of such a use in the Old Testament (Ps. 48:2; Isa. 14:13; Joel 2:20), but that is unlikely to be the case here. What had come upon Syria–Palestine from Mesopotamia over the previous century or so was itself sufficiently sinister and threatening without finding overtones of anti-pagan polemic.

Holladay objects to the understanding that the pot is about to boil over on the grounds that it focuses on the contents of the pot, which are not mentioned in the prophet's reply: indeed, there is no explicit mention anywhere of there being anything in the pot. Instead he supposes that the pot is empty, and that it is being heated to burn off charred material adhering to its inner surface, and that this process of cleansing is similar to what the people will have to undergo (Ezek. 24:11). 'The vision communicates either a judgment on the northern tribes or a summoning of those tribes to stand judgment along with the south' (Holladay 1986, 1:40). Holladay has to assume that the passage has been subject to secondary reinterpretation, probably by Jeremiah himself after the battle of Carchemish in 605 BC when the 'foe from the north' took a more definite form. The complexity of the hypothesis makes it difficult to sustain in the face of the traditional interpretation.

However, there remains the question of just what historical event gave rise to this vision of disaster coming from the north. Commentators often used to associate this with the threat of Scythian incursions, though this is now largely dismissed (see introduction to 4:5). But the significance of the Scythians is often misinterpreted. It was not that, in the light of Scythian invasions, Jeremiah spoke of a foe from the north, whom he wrongly identified as the Scythians. This is a word from the LORD, and the foe is not identified at all in the early chapters of Jeremiah. However, if the Scythians were active in Palestine in the decade before Nineveh fell, then it may well have been the case that the people wrongly assumed that they were the ones of whom Jeremiah was speaking, and on that basis dismissed his message when the threat soon passed.

The picture is one of an ominous threat. Just as the spilled contents of the pot would scald anyone they touched, so those involved in what is let loose by the LORD from the north will be engulfed in catastrophe. The message Jeremiah is given to proclaim is that a time of general calamity is impending for Judah and Jerusalem.

15. How the calamity will occur is further specified by the divine message: **'I am about to summon**[13] **all the peoples of the northern kingdoms,' declares the LORD.** The current international situation was soon to be divinely changed, and there would be disastrous consequences for Judah. The identity of those to be involved is not clearly stated. In 627 BC the scene in Mesopotamia was confused; Assyria was declining, and it was not yet clear which nation, if any, would come to dominate the region. The plural 'peoples' is rather 'clans' or 'families' (*mišpəḥôt*), often referring to tribes or parts of the tribes of Israel, but here to the variety of foreign groups (10:25) that will make up the force invading Judah. Typically the armies of the empires of the east were composed of contingents drawn from subject peoples. **Their kings** (literally, 'they', but kings is a reasonable inference from the subsequent mention of thrones) **will come and set up their thrones** (the Hebrew emphasises that they will each do so) **in the entrance of the gates of Jerusalem**. This picture may be interpreted in two ways: of a siege in progress, or of the capture of the city. 'The entrance of the gates' is used on a number of occasions when the enemy got no further than the city walls (Judg. 9:40; 2 Sam. 10:8; 11:23; similarly '⌊at⌋ the entrance of the gate' means outside Jerusalem in 19:2), but 'the gates of the city' referred not just to the opening in the wall, but also to the area typically within the gate which served as a market place and forum for the conduct of business, including the administration of justice. 'Come' (<√*boʾ*) may also be rendered 'enter', and setting up their thrones in the entrance of the gates implies not that the enemy forces are outside the city, besieging it, but inside the captured city, administering its affairs. The concluding phrases of the verse are also ambiguous. The preposition *ʿal* may be rendered 'against'—and so fit in with a siege—or 'upon', suggesting capture and domination. **They will come against all her surrounding walls and against all the towns of Judah.** This contrasts with the view that was prevalent in Jerusalem that all would be well with Judah, and that the land was guaranteed immunity from capture—an expectation that would have been reinforced by the evident decline in Assyrian power. Jeremiah is instructed to disabuse the people of these false hopes. Prosperity from God will not come without obedience on their part as required by the covenant.

---

13. This construction with *hinnēh*, 'look' (traditionally 'behold'), with a first person singular suffix, followed by a participle occurs 58 times in Jeremiah. It is used to denote imminent action which the LORD will take.

16. But though the enemy kings impose their rule on the chosen city, there is another hand at work behind and above their action. What is going on is ultimately determined by the LORD. **And I will pronounce my judgments on my people**/'on them'[14] uses a phrase that is found a number of times in Jeremiah to indicate the whole judicial process terminating in sentence being given (4:12; 12:1; 39:5; 52:9), rather than as the REB renders, 'I shall state my case against my people'. Its clearest use is in 39:5 where Nebuchadnezzar judicially reviews the relationship between himself and Zedekiah, and passes sentence against him. 'On them' would have been ambiguous—was it Judah or her enemies being judged?—were it not for the following indictment of covenant disloyalty. **Because of their wickedness** involves a play between 'their wickedness' (*rāʿātām*) and 'disaster' (*rāʿâ*) in v. 14. The use of this word in two different senses is a common Old Testament technique to emphasise that judgment flows from the offence committed and is commensurate with it (see on 6:19).

'Namely that', (*ʾăšer*; not translated in the NIV), introduces the threefold specification of their wickedness. Firstly it is **in forsaking me** (2:13). This refers to general breaches of the requirements of the covenant. The people of God were no longer loyal subjects of their covenant king, but have rebelliously dissociated themselves from him. This was evidenced by the way they had chosen to follow their own preferences as to conduct and lifestyle. More particularly it was obvious from their religious disloyalty and apostasy. **In burning incense to other gods.** Translators are divided in their rendering of this verb, *qiṭṭēr*, a piel form which does not occur in the Pentateuch, though the hiphil stem is frequently used there to describe the way in which legitimate sacrifice is 'made to go up in smoke' (e.g. 'burn' in Exod. 29:13, 18, 25). Some translations take this to be the significance of the piel stem also ('made offerings', NRSV; 'burning sacrifices', REB). However, the emphasis on smoke (a common related noun refers to incense) has led to the piel being translated as 'burn incense', though it seems on occasions to go beyond that to burning parts of a sacrifice (1 Sam. 2:16; Amos 4:5). The piel is, however, reserved for worship knowingly offered to false gods or for worship considered to be in some respect cultically improper, particularly in Kings of illegitimate worship of the LORD (*TWOT* #2011). Here it is offered to

---

14. *ʾōtām*, 'them', is rendered 'my people' in the NIV to make clear the reference is to Judah, and not to her attackers. The idiom seems to use the object (4:12; 12:1) or the preposition *ʾittām*, 'with them' as in 39:5 and 52:19, and as many manuscripts in fact have here (*IBHS* §10.3.1c).

'other gods', a reference to the first injunction of the Ten Commandments (Exod. 20:3) where the LORD demanded the exclusive fealty of his people. The charge against them of breaching covenant loyalty is not then related to some secondary detail of their practice, but to an offence that was a basic violation of the relationship and furthermore one that was blatantly committed. The people wanted freedom to live as they pleased and were prepared to accept any ideology that provided a cover story for their actions. **And in worshipping what their hands have made.**[15] 'Worship' (<√*ḥāwâ* hishtaphel, 7:2) refers to the physical action of prostrating oneself before a superior, whether human or divine. The reference here is to a breach of the Second Commandment (Exod. 20:5), emphasising the foolishness of idolatry when people bow down to physical objects which they themselves have crafted (Deut. 4:28; Ps. 115:4; Isa. 2:8; Hos. 14:3). A similar accusation is to be found in the words of Huldah in 2 Kgs. 22:17, 'Because they have forsaken me and burned incense to other gods and provoked me to anger by all the idols their hands have made, my anger will burn against this place and will not be quenched.' There is no need to assume dependence in either direction as the indictment concerns basic breaches of covenant norms which had been described in similar terms for centuries (Deut. 32:15-22).

4. Get Ready! (1:17-19)

After the two visions, this section looks back to the narrative of the call in vv. 4-10. There is a renewed recognition of Jeremiah's fearfulness ('Do not be terrified', v. 18 and 'do not be afraid', v. 8) and of the divine promise to counter it ('I am with you and will rescue you', vv. 8, 19). While 'today' (v. 18) does not require that 1:4-19 be understood as having occurred on a single day, the text certainly implies that these incidents all occurred very early in Jeremiah's ministry. Although he had not yet faced opposition, Jeremiah was well aware of what had occurred in the recent past during the reigns of Manasseh and Amon, and of the fact that the underlying spiritual conditions in Judah continued to be unfavourable for the reception of the divine message and messenger. And if he was not aware of it already, he was left in no doubt about it by the charge given to him. Difficult times lay ahead for the prophet of the LORD.

---

15. The REB translation 'the work of their own hands' is based on reading *maʿăśeh*, 'work', as is in fact found in many manuscripts, but the plural is also used in this phrase (44:8), and there is no need to change it here. The meaning remains the same.

17. There is a balance between v. 17 which begins *wəʾattâ*, 'and ⸤as for⸥ you' and v. 18 which begins *waʾănî*, 'and ⸤as for⸥ me'. On the one hand there is Jeremiah's responsibility as regards the commission given to him, and on the other there is the LORD's commitment to assist his messenger in the execution of his duty. The task before him is one that requires immediate preparation for strenuous activity: **Get yourself ready!** The phrase used, 'gird up your loins' (NRSV), refers to the custom whereby the long robes worn in the east would be tucked up under a belt so as to allow for easy movement when working (Prov. 31:17), running (1 Kgs. 18:46; 2 Kgs. 4:29), going on a journey (Exod. 12:11; 2 Kgs. 9:1), or engaging in physical activity in general. The belt was a significant piece of military dress (1 Sam. 25:13; Isa. 8:9; Ezek. 23:15), and so in the light of v. 18 one might wish to view Jeremiah here as the warrior in the divine cause. If so, it is significant that his role is defensive rather than offensive. However, it is more likely that the idea in this verse is that of the prophet getting ready to act as a messenger (2 Kgs. 4:29; 9:1).

Two specific aspects of his task are identified. (1) **Stand up and say to them whatever I command you.** The prophet is above all else the LORD's spokesman, and so his task is to deliver the message entrusted to him (cf. v. 7). Faithful transmission of the divine word was the mark of a prophet who corresponded to Moses (Deut. 18:18). (2) But the message must also be delivered in a specific way. When the LORD's spokesman encounters opposition and hostility, he is not to apologise for his message or present it half-heartedly. He is not to cringe but to be forthright and bold in his presentation. The injunction, **Do not be terrified by them**, recalls similar pronouncements given to earlier leaders of the people (Deut. 31:6-8; Josh. 1:6-9), but Jeremiah is presented with an unusually grim alternative **or I will terrify you before them.** There is a wordplay in the verb forms used in the two parts of this charge: 'Do not break down (<√*ḥātat*[16]) because of them, lest I break (hiphil of *ḥātat*) you before them.' The REB renders, 'Do not let your spirit break, or I shall break you before their eyes.' *ḥātat* is used in its literal sense of 'to break' or 'to be in a state of brokenness' in 14:4 to describe how the ground is cracked due to prolonged drought. Here it is used to describe the psychological condition that arises when circumstances so press in on a person that he is inwardly

16. BDB (369) analyse the verb form as the qal of *ḥātat*, pointing to a state of brokenness rather than the action of breaking, but its form could also be that of a niphal (*HALOT* 365), presumably a *niphal tolerativum*, 'do not let yourself be broken'.

broken and unable to function. 'Be afraid' (NLT, GNB) is perhaps too weak a rendering: one can be afraid and still act. 'Be dismayed' (RSV, NKJV), not to have the strength or courage (the 'may') to act through fear, is more accurate, though archaic. Jeremiah is not to let human opposition undermine his nerve and alter the demeanour that is appropriate to the deliverer of the LORD's word of warning. If he does, then the LORD will let him experience real abandonment in which he will indeed tremble within and without. 'Before them' carries the idea of public humiliation in his loss of nerve. This stern word is a call to faith and continuing trust in the LORD rather than giving way to feelings of panic. A wordplay on the same verb occurs in 10:2, and Jeremiah later offers a prayer using these words (17:18).

18. The LORD then turns to set out what he will do for Jeremiah so that he will be able to withstand the pressures that he will be under as a result of his commission. **Today I have made you** may be another instance of a performative perfect (cf. v. 5). It is at the moment of the LORD's announcement and in virtue of his declaration that Jeremiah becomes **a fortified city, an iron pillar and a bronze wall** (literally, 'walls', perhaps an intensive use). Jeremiah's fate will be quite different from that of Judah and Jerusalem (v. 15) because the LORD will make him impregnable. Just as a besieged city had to withstand external pressure, so Jeremiah will be able to endure sustained opposition. Enemy forces are not able to breach a well-fortified town. The image may be one of wooden gates covered with bronze ornamentation off which weapons bounce ineffectually. The 'iron pillar' may indicate a building support (Judg. 16:29), or it may reflect later usage and be the bar used to close the city gates (Craigie et al. 1991:14). The LORD is going to protect his prophet so that he is able **to stand against the whole land**. The promise is not that opposition will be cleared out of his path, but rather that Jeremiah will be given the inner resources to stand up to and endure the antagonism that he will have to face, even though it comes from every quarter.

The extent of the anticipated opposition is clearly spelled out. **Against**[17] **the kings of Judah, its officials, its priests and the people of the land.** 'Kings' in the plural are mentioned probably because of the long time span of Jeremiah's ministry. The 'officials' (*śārîm*, 26:10) are those who constituted the inner circle of the court, advising

17. This is probably an instance of *lə* used in apposition (*IBHS* §11.2.10h; Joüon §§125l, 133d). Alternatively, the meaning of *lə* may have become so weak that it takes on the meaning of the preposition it serves to continue (Joüon §133d).

the king on policy and overseeing its execution. The priests were of course in charge of the religious institutions of the land. It is uncertain whether 'the people of the land' refers to everyone else in Judah, or is a technical term for the upper, landed classes, not the common folk (34:19; 37:2; 44:21; *ABD* 1:168). The opposition was certainly going to involve the most influential classes in the land, and Jeremiah was going to be an isolated figure, opposing the establishment of his day and its ideology. On his own he would not have the resources to cope with his situation. Indeed, the book makes clear that even with divine assistance he was hard pressed to deal with it. But what a difference there is between Jeremiah's experience and that of Jerusalem: the one equipped to stand in obedience to the word of the LORD, and the other doomed to fall because of her disobedience.

19. They will fight against you (a clear instance of *ʾel*, 'to', being used in the sense of *ʿal*, 'against') makes clear that the aggression would not be initiated by Jeremiah, but by his opponents. However, even though they take the initiative in attacking him, the outcome is: **'but will not overcome you, for** (*kî*) **I am with you and will rescue you**/'with you to rescue you',**' declares the LORD.** The LORD's presence with him would be particularly evident in his situation of difficulty when the promise of rescue already made in v. 8 would be fulfilled. Carroll's comment, 'It is not possible to extract from the book of Jeremiah a confirmation of v. 19 in relation to the life of Jeremiah' (1986:110), is perverse in the light of 20:13, 39:11-14, and 40:1-6. This is the abiding feature of the lives of all the people of God. It is not their wisdom or strength that ensures their survival, but God's protecting presence with them to ensure their deliverance.

Now, where does that leave us? It is one thing to see the *then* of the text: what it meant for Jeremiah. But a message for Jeremiah is in itself merely a message for yesterday. We need a message for today. How does the text apply to our circumstances? Well, we are not prophets in the way Jeremiah was. We will not have divine visions and direct revelation as he did. But there is one obvious way in which this text may apply at the level of the church as a whole. There is the universal prophethood of believers, which is unitedly focused on carrying out the Great Commission, 'All authority in heaven and on earth has been given to me. Therefore go and make disciples of all nations, baptising them in the name of the Father, and of the Son, and of the Holy Spirit, and teaching them to obey everything I have commanded you. And surely I am with you always, to the very end of the age' (Matt. 28:18-20). It is in essence the same role as that of Jeremiah: the same *everyone* and *everything*; the same divine message to be announced, the same promise of divine presence; and the same possibility of failure, underachievement and lack of success. It is not just Jeremiah who had to face a hostile age, intent on doing things their own way and making light of divine claims upon them. There are many adversaries, and the danger is the same. The challenge given here is not confined in its relevance to Old Testament times; it lies behind Paul's words 'without being frightened in any way by those who oppose you' (Phil. 1:28), where 'frightened' renders a term equivalent to 'not letting oneself be intimidated', a word used of the terror of a startled horse.

It is through God's presence and the resources that he makes available by his Spirit that the people of God are able to withstand the pressure exerted by the adversary and to persevere until success is achieved. 'I will build my church, and the gates of Hades will not overcome it' (Matt. 16:18).

Stalker in reflecting on the call of Jeremiah likened his recoil from the task set before him to the experience of John Knox.

> When John Knox was called to be a Preacher by the acclamation of his fellow-prisoners in the church of St. Andrews, he was so overwhelmed that, after an ineffectual attempt to address the congregation, he burst into tears, rushed out, and shut himself up in his chamber, persuaded that he could never appear in the pulpit again. ... Not infrequently those who are most timorous at the first, when they are called, are the bravest at the last. When it is made perfectly clear to them that it is their duty to go, they are all the more fearless because they are sure that they are going, not in obedience to their own fancy or vanity, but because they cannot disobey a divine command. The best antidote to the fear of man is the fear of God. Knox shed tears and trembled and fled, when first called to preach, but over his open grave this witness was borne, 'There lies one who never feared the face of man.' So Jeremiah's was naturally a sensitive and shrinking nature, but God made him to his age 'a defenced city and an iron pillar and brazen walls,' that is, a heart which no task could tire and no opposition terrify. (1895:69, 70-71)

Though we too may initially feel overwhelmed, we should pray for enabling to speak with great boldness in the face of threats and of indifference (Acts 4:29).

II. JEREMIAH'S EARLY MINISTRY

(2:1–6:30)

OUTLINE

A. The LORD's Indictment of Judah (2:1-37)
  1. Israel's First Love (2:1-3)
  2. Israel's Forgetfulness (2:4-8)
  3. The Divine Complaint (2:9-13)
  4. The Bitterness of Apostasy (2:14-19)
  5. Ingrained Sin (2:20-25)
  6. Judah's Disgrace (2:26-28)
  7. Why? (2:29-37)

B. Plea for Repentance (3:1–4:4)
  1. What Follows Divorce? (3:1-5)
  2. The Greater Sin (3:6-10)
  3. Repent and Return (3:11-13)
  4. The Blessings of Repentance (3:14-18)
  5. Disappointed Hope (3:19-20)
  6. The Way Back (3:21-25)
  7. Heart Circumcision (4:1-4)

C. Impending Judgment (4:5–6:30)
  1. Threat from the North (4:5-31)
  2. The Corrupt City (5:1-31)
  3. Impending Devastation (6:1-30)

In this section we have the record of Jeremiah's earliest ministry as it was preserved in the First Scroll (see Introduction §2.2). It is therefore possible to identify four audiences Jeremiah addressed using this material.

(1) These prophetic sayings originally formed the substance of the prophet's ministry to the people in the time of Josiah. It is noticeable that the background of chapters 2 and 3 is one where external threat is absent and the land is enjoying a time of tranquillity and peace—which fits the reign of Josiah, but not later. At that time there was a royal sponsored reform movement which met with considerable popular support not because of heart allegiance to the LORD, but because it was an expression of resurgent nationalism after years of having to submit to Assyrian hegemony. People went along with Josiah's changes in religious matters because they fitted in with the national mood of the moment. Jeremiah was not opposed to what Josiah was doing (Introduction §4.2), but he was divinely made aware that reformation in religious structures and rites did not go deep enough. The people as a whole were content with the outward performance of religious duty; they did not have a true covenant allegiance to the LORD arising out of heart dedication to him. Jeremiah's ministry during this period was therefore directed at deepening the response of the people through true repentance to bring them into heart fidelity to the LORD.

(2) The second audience for this material is to be located 604 BC when the First Scroll was read. Many of the pagan practices which had been suppressed by Josiah resurfaced during the laxer conditions of Jehoiakim's reign; increasingly the land was outwardly displaying its inner heart alienation from the LORD. The circumstances of the time were ominous with the Babylonians already dominating the land after their victory at Carchemish in 605 BC. Jeremiah's previous preaching which had been generally dismissed, if not derided, was now repeated, and in collected, concentrated form challenged the situation to be found in the land. Where did their true loyalty lie? Would they accept that disaster awaited them if they did not heed the prophet's warnings? This was the same problem that Jeremiah had wrestled with over the previous twenty years. The impact of the First Scroll did not come from the fact that his message was new, but that it was the same and its relevance had now become even more obvious. The objective of the First Scroll was that 'each of them will turn from his wicked way' so that God would forgive their wickedness and their sin (36:3).

(3) When Jehoiakim decisively rejected the warnings of the First Scroll, he represented majority opinion in Jerusalem. The Second Scroll which recorded the same material plus additions addressed a

nation now set on a course that would inevitably lead to disaster, but it was still possible that individuals would respond to the prophetic warning.

(4) After the predicted fall of Jerusalem, Jeremiah continued to minister to the spiritual needs of his own and future generations as they adjusted to their changed circumstances. It remained appropriate to incorporate these early messages into the final edition of his work. There were some who were not convinced by the trauma that had come on the city; the conduct of the Jews in Egypt gives evidence of that (44:17-18). So the call for repentance and genuine reform was one that was still needed. Equally to move forward there had to be a correct understanding of the past. The record of Jeremiah's ministry acted as a testimony to the righteousness of God. The people had brought the disaster upon themselves, and they had been repeatedly warned about the folly of the course of action they were pursuing. By providing a rationale for past events which still shaped the lives of the people, Jeremiah helped them adjust to the tragedy brought on by their national folly. More than that: because Jeremiah's mission had never been exclusively one of proclaiming judgment and impending catastrophe, his message also provided a beacon of hope. The LORD's commitment to his covenant meant that he would not permit even the rebellion of the covenant people to frustrate his salvific purposes. The due punishment that had fallen on them would be exhausted and reversed by divine grace.

In these chapters therefore we have words that were originally intended to reprove the covenant people for withdrawing from displaying loyalty to the LORD (2:1-37), to urge them to repent of their conduct and show a genuine commitment to the LORD (3:1–4:4), and to warn them of the certainty of the disaster that the LORD would bring on them if they continued intransigent (4:5–6:30). When they were first uttered, the fate of Judah as a nation was not yet sealed, but disaster would only be averted if they recognised the gravity of their situation, if they appreciated that it was heart loyalty to the LORD, not merely nominal allegiance, that was required of them, and if they radically changed their conduct to conform to what God desired. These addresses continue to set the parameters for individuals and nations to live in a right relationship with God.

A. THE LORD'S INDICTMENT OF JUDAH (2:1-37)

Although the word 'covenant' is not found in this section, it is in fact applied covenant theology. Indeed, that is true of most of the Old Testament because the covenant was the basis of Israel's relationship with the LORD. It was to preserve the integrity of that bond that the LORD sent his prophets to warn the people when their actions and attitudes were jeopardising fellowship with him. So here, Jeremiah before moving on to call the people to repentance in the following chapter, first of all establishes that their conduct has fallen far short of what was required of them. In vv. 1-3 the standard that was expected of them is described; in the following six sections of the chapter instances are given of various ways in which their behaviour was deficient. In vv. 4-8 the focus is on their forgetfulness of what the LORD had done for them and given to them; in vv. 9-13 the LORD sets out his complaint that in abandoning him Israel had sinned more heinously than the heathen nations; the warning given to Judah through what happened to the northern kingdom of Israel is presented in vv. 14-19; the extent to which rebellious behaviour had become part of the national character is vividly exemplified in vv. 20-25; the disgrace they have brought upon themselves is described in vv. 26-28; and finally there is a rebuttal of the people's protestations regarding their conduct (vv. 29-37).

One feature of this chapter that is not evident in translation is the frequency with which changes occur in the way the people are addressed, sometimes using masculine second person pronouns but at other times feminine ones, sometimes in the singular but also in the plural. In vv. 2-3 the pronouns are second feminine singular, as they are also in vv. 14-28 and vv. 33-37 (though it is a masculine singular that is found in v. 14) suggesting that what was originally one oracle might have been interrupted by other material. In vv. 4-13 and vv. 29-32 the references are second masculine plural. Though a singular form of address was obviously viewing the people as a national entity, whereas a plural tended to bring out their individual roles in what was happening, the original motivation for the repeated switches is not clear. It does, however, suggest that here we have a collection of individual sayings which were initially given in a variety of settings and which Jeremiah has now skilfully incorporated into a unified structure that sets out the divine indictment in terms of a legal challenge to the people.

There are two metaphors which illumine the language used to present this challenge. One derives from the basic covenant metaphor of the relationship between a king and his people, and the other draws on the bond between husband and wife. As regards the first metaphor, this chapter, along with a number of other Old Testament passages such as Ps. 50, Isa. 1 and Mic. 6:1-8, have been analysed in terms of 'covenant lawsuit' (*rîb*), in which several shared features have been identified: (1) an introduction, summoning heaven and earth as witnesses to the original covenant undertakings (cf. v. 12); (2) a statement of the case against the people, often including interrogation of them (vv. 5-6, 8-11, 13-19, 20-25); (3) an accusation of ingratitude in the light of past benefits received (vv. 2-3, 7-8, 11); (4) rejection of recourse to merely formal worship, or to other gods, as being of assistance to the people (vv. 26-28). It is also argued that while such covenant lawsuits may mention the possibility of judgment (vv. 31-37), that is not their major emphasis. Rather the background for the covenant lawsuit is to be found in the procedures commonly followed in the contemporary enforcement of international treaty arrangements. When a vassal people rebelled against their overlord, or otherwise offended him, he did not necessarily immediately send his army on a punitive expedition against their country, but might first send a royal envoy with a statement presenting his grievances against the errant people and urging them to mend their ways. If they did, then at the political level there was the benefit for the overlord that he had not to spend time and resources in a military campaign.

The LORD followed a similar procedure with Israel. His ambassadors were the prophets, and in the covenant lawsuit they were trying to win the people's loyalty back to the LORD without them having to undergo the curse of the covenant. 'Lawsuit' is therefore an unfortunate term for this procedure because it does not involve hearing the case before a third party whose decision on the matter would be final. This is a dispute resolution procedure that exists before formal legal action. It is alerting the other party to the existence of a grievance, and urging them to recognise the legitimacy of the complaints held against them. 'The harmed party seeks restitution for his grievance by his own means, according to his own concept of justice. He does not ask a third party to mediate, nor does a judge issue a binding decision. The picture portrayed in these *rîb*-oracles is not that of a judicial process before the courts—be it civil, cultic, international, or any other—but of two contending parties arguing their cases amongst themselves' (DeRoche 1983:370-1). The *rîb*, the accusation of covenant disloyalty, did not preclude the possibility of amendment on the part of the accused. It thus fits in with the intention announced: 'Perhaps when the people of Judah hear about every disaster I plan to inflict on them, each of them will turn from his wicked way; then I will forgive their wickedness and their sin' (36:3). The divine king demands an account from his people for their rebellion and waywardness over many years.

The other analogy that Jeremiah develops from the prophet Hosea likens the relationship between the LORD and his people to that between a husband and wife. Through the difficulties he encountered in his own marriage Hosea was made aware that Israel's misconduct had disrupted their relationship with the LORD. 'She is not my wife, and I am not her husband' (Hos. 2:2). The LORD, however, did not abandon Israel because of her faithlessness but intended to allure her back to himself (Hos. 2:14; note also Hos. 11:8-11). The prophet in his own life and in his ministry was to proclaim that not divorce but reconciliation was the way forward for the broken marriage. 'Go, show your love to your wife again, though she is loved by another and is an adulteress' (Hos. 3:1).

1. Israel's First Love (2:1-3)

At the Exodus the LORD had given clear evidence of his commitment to the welfare of Israel by delivering them from the oppression of Egypt and providing for them as they travelled through the wilderness. Israel was designated as different from all the nations (Exod. 19:5-6). At that time the people acknowledged their utter dependence upon the LORD for all they were and had. They were content to move out of Egypt and into the wilderness when he commanded them, and they willingly and wholeheartedly committed themselves to the care of the one who had decisively intervened on their behalf. The deliverance from Egypt constituted the Old Testament paradigm for salvation and the response that should accompany it. The LORD had acted as the king of his people and at Sinai he formally instituted the terms of the relationship between them in the covenant given through Moses. The events of the Exodus therefore provide the norm to which the LORD refers in presenting his disapproval of the current conduct of the people.

1. The phrase, **The word of the LORD came to me**, occurred also in 1:4, 11, 13. As it does not occur again until 13:3, it may well function in parallel with 1:4 to indicate the second main beginning in the book. After the account of Jeremiah's divine call and the visions subsequently given to him, the focus now turns from the prophet himself to the message which he was commissioned to deliver to the people at the start of his ministry. Although introductory formulae in the third person are not to be taken as indicating a lack of personal involvement on the part of the prophet in the composition of the book, 'to me' emphasises that he did play a significant role, and it is insubstantial hypothesising to dismiss it as editorialising verisimilitude.

2. The command **Go**[1] is addressed to Jeremiah himself. Although 'go' is often used in Hebrew as an imperative conveying general encouragement, without necessarily implying motion, the impression is that its use here indicates that Jeremiah has to travel. This is reinforced by the subsequent mention of Jerusalem on its own. Although Jerusalem is addressed directly in 4:14; 6:8; 13:27 and 15:5, in an introductory formula such as this a link with Judah is normally found (4:3; 11:2, 6; 18:11; 25:2). This may therefore be a feature that has been retained from the time when the young prophet was commanded to travel from his home town to Jerusalem to act as the LORD's spokesman there. There is no hint here of any reluctance on Jeremiah's part to carry out these instructions, but given what he already knew of the opposition awaiting him (1:18-19) and given the suffering he had already endured by the time the First Scroll was written, there is almost an element of self-exculpation in this record. Jeremiah did not leave Anathoth of his own volition. He went only because of the compelling divine mandate that had been addressed to him.

And proclaim[2] **in the hearing of Jerusalem**. 'Proclaim' (<√*qārā'*, 'to call out') is used in a technical sense for the public announcement of the LORD's message (1 Kgs. 13:32; Isa. 40:2; Jon. 1:2; Zech. 1:4. *NIDOTTE* 3:972). The phrase 'in the hearing of'/'in the ears of' also indicates public proclamation. It may well be significant that the only other context in Jeremiah with the expression is chapter 36.

The second part of v. 2 begins the message Jeremiah is to deliver. 'Thus says the LORD' (inexplicably omitted in the NIV) is a standard introductory phrase used in prophetic speeches, occurring over 80 times in Jeremiah. Its use reflects the prophets' role as messengers of the LORD (cf. 1:8). A similar formula is found in secular contexts where messengers are being employed (Gen. 32:3-4 [4-5]; 45:9;

---

1. *hālōk*, 'go', is an infinitive absolute used to convey an emphatic imperative (GKC §113bb; *IBHS* §35.5.1).

2. The construction where the infinitive absolute is followed by the *waw*-consecutive perfect (expressing an action to be performed after the first, *IBHS* §32.2.2a) is characteristic of Jeremiah where it occurs 10 times (2:2; 3:12; 13:1; 17:19; 19:1; 28:13; 34:2; 35:2, 13; 39:16) and only twice elsewhere in the Old Testament (2 Sam. 24:12; Isa. 38:5).

2 Kgs. 18:19, 28-29).[3] Here Jeremiah is told to begin his address with this phrase to establish his right to speak as a prophet of the LORD (Lindblom 1962:103-4). The covenant king is addressing his people through the messenger he has commissioned to present what he wants said to them.

The message itself contains three main thoughts. Firstly, to recall the people to a right disposition towards himself, the LORD favourably reviews their early relationship with him. It speaks of a specific action of the LORD in calling to remembrance the early attitude shown by Israel. Though Keil (1873, 1:50) argues that **I remember** (*zākartî*, a perfect form) is an action completed in the past and so no longer reflects the LORD's attitude ('I remembered your devotion'), the perfect of this verb is used to indicate a past act of recall which has ongoing consequences. The root *zākar* frequently involves more than mental recollection: there is also action appropriate to that recall. When God remembered Noah, he took action so that the waters receded (Gen. 8:1). The LORD pledged that whenever he would see the rainbow, he would remember his covenant with Noah and take action to ensure that there will never again be such a flood (Gen. 9:15). So here, the LORD as the covenant king of the people, and also as the one who is married to them, recalls their behaviour with a view to fulfilling his obligations in the relationship. Of course, this intention to bless may be frustrated if the attitude of the people has subsequently changed. The remembering that could have been a source of blessing then becomes a threat.

About you, or 'in your favour' (REB), indicates the positive way the relationship had begun. The addressee is viewed as feminine, probably because of a reference to Jerusalem.[4] It also fits the depiction here of the covenant between the LORD and his people in terms of marriage, the metaphor previously developed in Hos. 1–3.

The devotion of your youth: it is well known that it is difficult to find a suitable rendering for *ḥesed,* 'devotion', which is employed here of the people's conduct. Although frequently used to describe God's loyal, committed love for his people (9:24), *ḥesed* also encapsulates the

3. This explains the translation of the perfect *ʾāmar*, 'he said', as 'he says'. This is an epistolary use of the perfect (*IBHS* §30.5.1d). Hebrew views the speech of the LORD to his messenger as past from the point of view of the recipients of the message, whereas English views the action as still taking place when the messenger relays it to its recipients.

4. Cities in general are treated as feminine in Hebrew, probably because of a suppressed reference to *ʿîr*, 'city', which is a feminine noun (*IBHS* §6.4.1c,d).

attitude that should characterise the response of the covenant people towards their God. It denotes a loyalty which goes beyond mere adherence to the legal terms of the covenant and undertakes wholeheartedly every obligation arising out of the bond that has been created, acting in the spirit of the covenant, and not merely the letter of its stated requirements. *Ḥesed* is grounded in an inner disposition of love, but it is not confined to inner affection. In the Old Testament the typical phrase is 'to do *ḥesed*' (9:24). It is an inner devotion that manifests itself in acts of loyalty.

The covenant relationship between God and his people is here viewed in terms of the marriage bond. This requires a disposition to stick with the pledge entered into through good times and bad, a commitment characterised by undivided allegiance to the covenant partner. Jeremiah's allegations against the people are not initially expressed in terms of injustice within the community, and only in passing is there condemnation of unwarranted international alliances. His focus is on religious apostasy, on the vertical dimension of life which Israel was forgetting or distorting. The covenant required Israel to adhere to an exclusive attachment to the LORD, with an accompanying lifestyle of obedient trust, but these were no longer attributes that the nation displayed. Although Jeremiah does not mention *ḥesed* again in chapters 2 or 3, it provides the backdrop against which Israel's disloyalty may be more starkly seen.

But at what stage in the past had Israel displayed such loyalty? 'Youth' (*nəʿûrîm*) is a plural form (<√*naʿar*, 'child', see on 1:6) used to form an abstract noun (*IBHS* §7.4.2b; Joüon §136h). It is an indefinite expression, which as regards a woman might refer to any point in her life up to her marriage. Here it looks back to the period of the Exodus when the nation first came into existence ('as in the days of her youth, as in the day she came up out of Egypt', Hos. 2:15). It reinforces the picture of an unaffected eagerness and simple devotedness. Perhaps there is also a hint of the vulnerability of the people at the time when they were afforded divine protection.

The second phrase, **how as a bride you loved me**, is literally 'the love of your betrothal' (NKJV), another plural formation used in an abstract sense. 'Betrothal' is based on the word for a bride or for a woman about to be married, and may refer, in modern terms, to either the engagement or the honeymoon. The distinction would not have been so significant in ancient Israel where betrothal implied a commitment virtually as binding as marriage. The problem again arises as to the time that is referred to. It is difficult to understand this passage if the reference is to the whole forty years of the wilderness period when there were many incidents of rebellion and apostasy, including engaging in Canaanite Baal worship (Num. 25:1-5). However, 'history knows of no apostasy of Israel from its God and no idolatry of the people during the time from the exodus out of Egypt till the arrival at Sinai, and of this time alone Jeremiah speaks' (Keil 1873, 1:51).

Covenant relationships between an overlord and his vassals were frequently expressed in personal terms. Hiram's attitude towards David is said to be that of being on friendly terms with him (literally, 'loving him', 1 Kgs. 5:1). Such language lies behind the covenant demand placed on Israel to 'love the LORD' (Deut. 6:5), though it was to be more than a political euphemism for acknowledging a superior's authority. Here the marriage analogy brings the covenant terminology back to its original reference to a personal emotional response.

The third item in the declaration of this verse shows how Israel expressed the love of her covenant commitment. **And followed me through the desert** is the evidence that proves her loyalty. 'Follow' (literally 'go/walk after') is a key term in this chapter (2:2, 5, 8, 23, 25). Elijah's challenge on Mount Carmel, 'If the LORD is God, follow him; but if Baal is God, follow him' (1 Kgs. 18:21), is the classic example of the use of this expression, where it is opposed to going after other gods (Judg. 2:19). The basic picture seems to be that of moving along a path which God has set before his people (Deut. 11:28) in an obedient lifestyle, responsive to his covenant demands (Deut. 13:4; 2 Kgs. 23:3). Loyalty requires that choices be made and consistently adhered to.

Because 'desert' suggests a vast area of sand dunes, it is not the best translation of *midbār*, 'wilderness', a place where, though the terrain was rough and rocky, there were areas of grass and shrubs suitable for pasturing flocks. However, there was insufficient rain to permit cultivation of crops. It was literally **through a land not sown**, and so it was a testimony to the strength of their commitment that they had been prepared to leave the agriculturally well-endowed land of Egypt and embark on such a nomadic lifestyle because the LORD directed them.

3. The second theme of this initial message relates to the special status of Israel as 'firstfruits', a people set apart for the LORD himself. This too looks back to Israel's early history. Here Israel is simply a reference to the covenant people of God as a whole, and does not indicate that these words were intended for a northern audience. **Israel was holy**/'holiness' (*qōdeš*) **to the LORD** comes out of the context of the worship of the sanctuary (Num. 18:8-19, 26-29), and especially as summed up by the inscription on the gold plate that hung across the high priest's forehead (Exod. 28:36). The principal idea is that of being set apart for divine service (1:5). It does not particularly emphasise personal qualities, but rather the standing of the people, that they were those who were separated for the special ownership and possession of the LORD (Exod. 19:5-6), and who should have conducted themselves accordingly. The emphasis in this verse is on the protection the LORD provides for those he has chosen for himself.

There follows another motif derived from the ritual law. This may reflect Jeremiah's own priestly upbringing as the LORD speaks to and through him in terms that came naturally to him. Certainly this imagery shows how false it is to suggest that the prophetic message opposed all that was involved in the ceremonial worship of the temple. What was rejected was the abuse of the stated observances of priestly worship. All Israelites would have been familiar with analogies from the practices laid down by the LORD and would have understood such language.

The firstfruits of his harvest[5] is based on the regulations of the Mosaic law whereby the firstfruits were held sacred to the LORD. At each harvest the first produce of plants was set aside from common use and offered to the LORD in acknowledgment of his ownership of the land, and to express gratitude for his provision (Num. 15:20; 18:12-13; Deut. 26:1-11). Only after this had been done could the remainder of the harvest be used by the people. What was offered became sacred and as such could be consumed only by the priests.

It is not the usual word for firstfruits that is found here, but one that does occur in Prov. 3:9 (cf. Num. 18:12-14[6]). Israel is the beginning of God's harvest. There are two implied consequences: this gave her a special status which ought to be recognised; and there would in the future be a further harvest from other nations. The figure of firstfruits is later employed of Christians of Jewish extraction (Jas. 1:18), but supremely it is used of him who is the embodiment of the people of God, the Lord Jesus (1 Cor. 15:20, 23). In this passage it indicates the

5. The kethibh can be read as *təbûʾātâ*, 'her harvest', with the feminine suffix perhaps referring to Canaan (not the land mentioned in v. 2, because that was wilderness). The qere *təbûʾāô*, 'his harvest', makes it quite clear that the reference is to the LORD; but this could also be understood from the kethibh because final *he* can occur for the third singular masculine suffix (GKC §§7c, 91e).

6. *bikkûrîm* is more often found for 'firstfruits' than *rēʾšît*, 'beginning' or 'chief', which is used here.

significance of Israel in the outworking of God's redemptive purpose. Through Israel the first-born son (Exod. 4:22) blessing would flow to others (Gen. 12:3). How jealously ought Israel to have guarded all that pertained to her special status!

The third theme that is taken up in this first message is the divine protection Israel enjoyed and the consequent fate of those who attacked her. There is a double change of expression in v. 3: the LORD is referred to in the third person rather than the first as previously; and now Israel is treated as masculine, though the NIV use of 'her' in **all who devoured her** to refer to the personified nation might suggest otherwise. Such changes of person are frequent in Hebrew, and particularly Hebrew poetry, and need not be treated as indicators of different sources, but rather reflect the change in the grammatical gender of the subject. 'Devoured' (<√*ʾākal*, 'to eat') is a participial form and may be used in a conative sense, 'tried to devour'. 'Eat' was used for more than consumption of food by man and animals. It was also employed for unjust treatment by oppressors (Ps. 14:4; Prov. 30:14), for death by the sword (Deut. 32:42; Isa. 1:20), and for the hostile action of one nation against another (Num. 24:8; Deut. 7:16). Its use here for the hostile attitudes Israel faced in the wilderness is especially appropriate after the use of the analogy of the firstfruit.

They **were held guilty**. As the verse is reviewing Israel's experience in the wilderness, the use of imperfects here and in the next clause refers to what happened repeatedly in the past (GKC §107e; *IBHS* §31.2b). The verb used (<√*ʾāšam*) can refer to the action by which the offence is committed, the state of guilt the offender brings on himself, or the punishment his guilt entails (*TWOT* #180). The last meaning is a possible rendering if this expression is treated as synonymous with the next clause, but it seems more likely that there is a progression in the thought here: first their offence, 'they devoured'; then the divine verdict on their conduct, 'they were held guilty'; and finally the judgment the LORD imposed on those who had opposed his people. **Disaster** (*rāʿâ*) **overtook them** uses language similar to that found in 1:16 to show that the LORD did not act arbitrarily in vindicating his people. As a result of the evil actions of their opponents, evil/disaster results for the perpetrators. This was borne out by the annihilation of the Amalekites (Deut. 25:17-19; 1 Sam. 15:8), the overthrow of the Amorites (Num. 21:21-31), and the condemnation of the Ammonites and Moabites (Deut. 23:3-6).

Declares the LORD (*nəʾum-Yhwh*, cf. 1:8) is the recurring phrase which indicates the sovereign and authoritative pronouncement of the LORD. Characteristically the phrase occurs, as here, at the end of a unit of discourse and functions as a verbal seal or signature. It reminded those who listened to the prophet as he spoke that though it was the voice of a man that they heard, the message was that of their divine king whose word was ignored at their peril.

The main question that arises from this section is that of assessing if this is an adequate description of Israel's attitude towards God at the time of the Exodus. According to Carroll (1986:120) the tendency to idealise the past in order to criticise contemporary society and possibly raise hopes of return to former idyllic situations is particularly characteristic of a period of disintegration and ruin. To avoid the charge that Scripture suppresses or overlooks awkward facts such as the incident with the golden calf (Exod. 32), it is possible to restrict the description to period from Egypt to Sinai. The relationship between Israel and the LORD was not then without difficulty, but it was not so much a matter of fundamental disloyalty to the LORD as of a weak and immature faith in him being tried and strengthened through testing.

However, it must be admitted that there are two sides to the scriptural evaluation of Israel's standing during the wilderness period as a whole. Israel is viewed positively in Balaam's speeches (Num. 23:21), enjoying close fellowship with the LORD and responding to him (Deut. 32:10-14; Hos. 2:14-15; 9:10). Yet elsewhere the presentation is that of a time of almost constant rebellion (Num. 14–17; Ps. 95:8-11; Amos 5:25; Hos. 11:1-2; Ezek. 20:5-26; 23). For all of Ezekiel's stress that Israel's corruption went back to Egypt and continued in the wilderness, yet in Ezek. 16:8-14 he too can portray the early days as a time of close fellowship. It may be that the whole of the forty years can, from a certain angle, be presented positively, as when a marriage has just started, the relationship is fresh and special. Though there were real problems in adjusting to the responsibilities of their new status, Israel was still willing to try to make things work, especially when challenged to do so. They were still in the period of their 'first love' (Rev. 2:4), meeting the problems of the situation with real, though faltering, faith, in a way that was increasingly not found as time went by. 'The sins of the wilderness are due far more to a failure of nerve than of loyalty. We are apt so to magnify the wonders of God at the Exodus and in the wilderness that we forget the very real greatness of the people's response' (Ellison 1960:6).

2. Israel's Forgetfulness (2:4-8)

The second item in the LORD's remonstrance with his covenant partner, Israel, is the forgetfulness that has characterised their attitude towards him, particularly in past generations, 'your fathers' (2:4). The land that should have been the place of fellowship and blessing had in fact been polluted by their behaviour.

4. The renewed call for attention suggests that this passage was originally separate from what precedes. **Hear the word of the LORD** presents the prophet as the LORD's messenger, demanding the attention of the people to what he has to say, because he is delivering God's message to his people.

There are two descriptions given of the people, **house of Jacob** and **all the clans of the house of Israel**. Since 'Jacob' can function as a description of the northern kingdom (Amos 7:2, 5; Hos. 12:13), it has been suggested that this is part of Jeremiah's early ministry to the remnants of Israel. In the present context, however, these synonymous terms refer to the people of God as a whole in terms of their covenant privileges. 'House' indicates that Jeremiah's hearers are part of a larger, intergenerational body with which they can identify and in whose covenantal privileges they share. 'Clan' denotes a community of individuals who share a common relationship. They all belong to God's chosen people, and it is because of that relationship this message is conveyed to them. Judah's heritage is to be traced back to the endowment conferred on the people of God as a whole.

5. The LORD's remonstrance begins with a rhetorical question, uttered in hurt and puzzled tones: **What fault did your fathers find in me?** It is not indicated which generation of Israelites are in view; the description of the following verses includes the history of the nation from the time of their settlement in the land. The question does not, of course, presuppose that there is any doubt about its answer. It is posed to encourage thought about their forefathers' behaviour because it is always easier to see the faults of the past and to assess what their standing was before God, than to assess our own behaviour in the same critical light. So the history of the nation is being used to challenge Jeremiah's generation to think about their own attitude towards the LORD.

Although 'wrong' (*'āwel*) occurs only here in Jeremiah, use of this word and its cognates is common, particularly in Job and Ezekiel, to refer to actions that deviate from what is right. It describes unjust and dishonest behaviour that is the opposite of 'righteousness', and which is consequently detested by the LORD as contrary to his character (Deut. 25:16). He is 'a faithful God who does no wrong (*'āwel*), upright and just is he' (Deut. 32:4; see also Job 34:10; 2 Chron. 19:7). The response that should be given to the question has to be that their forefathers found no ground for complaint, and it then follows that the LORD is justified in his complaint that their behaviour was unwarranted and unreasonable.

That they strayed so far from me. *kî*, 'that', may be used to introduce a result clause, especially after a question implying surprise (GKC §166b; *IBHS* §38.3). The consequence of their critical attitude towards the LORD was that they strayed/went from him: they became spiritually distant and aloof from him. Distance is used as a spiritual metaphor in many of the psalms (Pss. 22:12, 20; 35:22; 38:22; 71:12), but there it describes the spiritual separation of God from his people. Here it is the reverse process that is in operation: the people disparage what the LORD has done for them and withdraw themselves from fellowship with him.

How previous generations had distanced themselves spiritually from God is then spelled out in greater detail. **They followed worthless idols and became worthless themselves.** To 'follow'/'walk after' is a term of covenant commitment and obedience, already used in 2:2. Here what is in view is not just a matter of a lessening of their zeal for the LORD, but a spiritual attachment to idolatry.

'Worthless idols' renders *hahebel*, 'the breath', though it rarely is used in this literal sense (Isa. 57:13). *Hebel* is Ecclesiastes' word in his favourite refrain 'vanity of vanities' (AV), 'utterly meaningless!' (NIV), but it had also long been used to describe the insubstantial nature of pagan idols and worship, occurring as early as Deut. 32:21, where it is found in parallel with 'what is no god.' Jeremiah frequently used the term as a collective reference to idols and idolatry, conveying the illusory nature of pagan idols, which despite their physicality had no spiritual reality behind them to give substance to heathen worship. Why idols may be considered *hebel* is explained in detail in 10:2-10.

But though there was no substantive reality behind the idols, the effect of worshipping them was not neutral. It tended to make the worshippers like the objects of their worship, rendering them spiritually ineffective and of no value to God. Canaanite religion viewed the gods behind the idols as beings to be manipulated, and it did not inculcate any sense of moral obligation to its adherents. Because of this, human conceptions of deity were degraded, and human aspirations and standards were left to determine behaviour patterns and conduct. By associating with such a religious system, the people had been contaminated. This is brought out by the play between *hebel*, 'worthless', and the cognate verb form *wayyehbālû*, 'became worthless' (2 Kgs. 17:15 records a similar verdict on the northern kingdom). It is difficult to bring across such wordplay from another language, but the NKJV rendering, '[they] have followed idols, and have become idolaters', seems particularly banal.

Throughout the Old Testament prophets the theme of poetic justice is frequently expressed through a declared correspondence between the sin or crime and the judgment or punishment for that act. There are a number of ways in which this correlation occurs. For instance, there may be consequences inherent in the act itself, or the correspondence may be divinely imposed. In any event judgment is seen to be retributive and appropriate; there is nothing capricious in the way in which penalty follows on the heels of transgression. The prophet seeks to heighten one's perception of this link by the rhetoric of correspondence whereby the root *hbl* is used first in a noun and then in a verb (Miller 1982:126). Going after *hebel* leads to becoming *hebel.* This is technically not a formulation of punishment, but a further manifestation and consequence of their sin.

hebel is also the Hebrew form of the name Abel, and the use of the noun with the definite article along with the unusual use of the verb here and in 14:1-18 is identified by Lee (1999) as an important rhetorical device in Jeremiah's presentation. The noun plus article combination has become the equivalent of a proper name, suggesting in addition to the insubstantiality of what is characterised as *hebel* that it is a description of one who will shortly disappear after a fleeting, possibly futile, life.

6. So infatuated had their fathers become with the emptiness and moral laxity of idol worship that they forgot not only the LORD's past blessings to the people but also the ongoing requirement of seeking the LORD's presence in every part of their lives. The catalogue of past misdemeanours continues with, **They did not ask, 'Where is the LORD?'** Though a similar question is often found on the lips of the heathen as they ridicule the people of God for the seeming inactivity of the LORD (Pss. 42:3; 79:10; Mic. 7:10), what is represented here is the neglect of what was essential to the practice of faith. The link in 2:8 between this expression and the priests may well suggest that the question was part of the traditional vocabulary of worship, though we have no specific example of it in that sense. However, quite apart from possible liturgical usage, remembering the LORD and what he had provided for his people was a basic element in Israel's piety (Deut. 8:2, 18; Pss. 105:5; 106:7), not just as a tribute for former benefits received, but as an invocation of the LORD's intervention and help in ongoing difficulties (2 Kgs. 2:14; Job 35:10). He was the one **who brought us up out of Egypt** (literally 'land [*'ereṣ*] of Egypt'; contrasting with the threefold use of 'land' later in the verse), which had involved a display of his power over Egyptian military might (Exod. 14:26-28) and over Egyptian deities (Exod. 12:12). Should he not then have been trusted to provide deliverance from all similar adverse circumstances? He was also the one who **led us through the barren wilderness** (this double term being used to translate *midbār*, see on 2:2). This was an experience which revealed more than the ability of the LORD to control the elements of nature; there he had shown himself not to be dependent on nature at all, and the people were educated into complete trusting reliance upon him (Exod. 16; Num. 20:2-11). Both these descriptions are participial expressions in Hebrew, pointing to historical actions, but also suggesting an enduring potential in the LORD's being and character: he is the one who typically acts in this way and can still be relied upon to do so. 'Led' (<√*hālak* hiphil, literally 'caused to go/walk') may involve an implicit contrast with the going the people had chosen for themselves ('follow' also <√*hālak*, 2:5). The use of 'us' in these confessional statements is part of the intergenerational solidarity of the people of God, but it also begins to raise the question of what the attitude of the current generation was and to point to the extension of the allegations of misconduct to include them as well.

There then follows a graphic description, whose grammatically rough expression matches the rugged terrain being described. (Three successive lines begin without any conjunction; there are construct chains with unusual double absolutes; the last line is extremely terse with a relative term twice omitted.) More significant theologically is the threefold repetition of *bəʾereṣ*, 'in a land of'. The wilderness experience was the LORD's training route for the people from the land of Egypt to the 'fertile land' (2:7), designed to make them ready to inhabit the land in dependence on the LORD. The harsh conditions they endured should have intensified their appreciation of the goodness and graciousness of God's provision and motivated their subsequent loyalty. **Through a land of deserts** (*ʿărābâ*, 5:6) **and rifts** seems to refer more particularly to the rift valley which stretched from the Dead Sea to the Gulf of Aqaba. 'Rift' indicates what is 'sunk down', and so may indicate the physical difficulties involved in getting into and out of the valley itself. The same word is, however, used of a 'pit' which was dug and camouflaged to catch larger animals (Ps. 35:8), so that the idea of troublesome obstacles which constituted a danger to unwary travellers may also be present (Ps. 57:6, cognate noun). **A land of drought and darkness** refers to the dryness and inhospitality of the region and also to its awe-inspiring nature. Much scholarly ink has been expended on the meaning *ṣalmāwet*, 'darkness'. Traditionally it had been taken as a compound noun from *ṣal*, 'shadow', and *māwet*, 'death'; hence 'shadow of death' (NKJV). This was often viewed with suspicion because of the lack of compound nouns of this sort in Hebrew, leading to an alternative derivation from an Akkadian root signifying 'darkness'. Increased evidence about the occurrence of compound nouns in Ugaritic has rendered the traditional analysis more plausible, and the rendering 'shadow of death' brings out the emphasis on the dangerous and oppressive nature of the experience of being in the wilderness (*NIDOTTE*, 3:809). **A land where no one travels and no one lives.** The two verbs found here are perfect in form, which might be a gnomic use, expressing an ongoing truth (*IBHS* §30.5.1c), though participles might have conveyed that more clearly. It is just as plausible that they are descriptions of the past situation: 'where no one ever travelled, where no one made his home' (REB).

7. But the wilderness experience was never intended to be the end of the story, and by divine guidance it was not. **I brought you into a fertile land** (*karmel*, 'fruitful land', 4:26). Indeed it was '*the* fruitful land' (the construct chain is definite), the only land of divine blessing, in contrast to '*the* wilderness' (2:6). Palestine was indeed a garden land (Deut. 8:7-9), and after the rigours of the desert the LORD intended that they should enjoy all that it provided them with: **to eat its fruit and rich produce.** 'Rich produce' translates *ṭûbâ*, 'good things' or 'goodness', which may just be a general expression of bounty, but more probably picks up on the use of 'good' in covenant contexts as descriptive of the Overlord's provision for his people ('a good land', Deut. 8:7).

'I brought' (<√*bôʾ*, hiphil 'to cause to enter') is followed by **you came** (<√*bôʾ*, qal 'to enter'). English translations generally add the contrast, **But**, which in Hebrew is not linguistically marked. The stark contrast with the outcome which might have been expected is left to speak for itself: you **defiled my land and made my inheritance detestable.** 'Defiled' (<√*ṭāmēʾ*, 3:2; 16:18; cf. Ps. 106:38) and 'detestable' (<√*tāʿab*) reflect the language of the cult as found in Leviticus and Numbers. For instance, both roots occur in Lev. 18:19-30, where 'defile' is used in reference to rendering someone or something ceremonially polluted so that they could not be permitted in the sanctuary, and 'detestable' refers to behaviour that is loathsome in the LORD's sight and so prohibited in his worship. What is being referred to here are moral rather than ritual abominations. Just as one set of conditions debarred from access to the sanctuary where the LORD was pleased to presence himself, so moral pollution was inconsistent with living in the land of the LORD's presence. Their rebellious behaviour, which is recorded as early as Judg. 2:10-17, transformed the land from what it should have been, and their offence was all the more culpable because they were not the absolute owners but only the appointed guardians of what remained 'my land'. The suzerain's land should have been used in accordance with his requirements, and their conduct on his property was doubly offensive to him.

Traditionally the noun *naḥălâ* has been translated as 'heritage' or 'inheritance', but it is more probable that the idea is rather that of landed property granted as a reward for past loyalty and in expectation of future service (Block 2000:79). However, the LORD is not a vassal who has received land from another, and the term conveys instead the thought that he has gained the land by right of conquest from the Canaanites and now holds it inalienably as his own special possession (Exod. 15:17). 'My inheritance' is not one that God has made over absolutely to Israel, but one in which he has given them rights of settlement as his tenants.

8. The leaders of the community are held responsible for the collapse of life in the land. Far from functioning to reverse the apostasy that was prevalent, their poor example contributed to it. Four times the Hebrew clause structure begins with *waw*-disjunctive (that is, *waw* followed by a non-verb), indicating that what follows is not a sequential account but a catalogue of concurrent practices. Four groups are identified:

(1) the priests who were set apart to the service of the LORD. **The priests did not ask, 'Where is the LORD?'** This re-echoes v. 6, and perhaps indicates the cultic origin of the phrase. They had seriously failed in understanding the nature of the task assigned to them, which included the duty of teaching the people regarding the requirements of the law. 'For the lips of a priest ought to preserve knowledge, and from his mouth men should seek instruction—because he is the messenger of the LORD Almighty' (Mal. 2:7; see also Lev. 10:10-11). But the priests had become happy with the routine of the sanctuary and the temporalities they enjoyed, and had no concern for the spiritual realities of religion or for encouraging the people to deepen their faith.

(2) **Those who deal with** (<√*tāpaś*, 'to handle', perhaps 'to be skilled in') **the law did not know me**. 'Law' refers to the covenant instructions of the LORD (whether moral, ceremonial or judicial). While this description may apply to the priests (certainly 18:18 speaks of the teaching of the law by the priests as did Deut. 33:10), the structure of this verse fits in with the view that in the years before the fall of

Jerusalem there emerged a scribal group whose duties were particularly closely involved with 'handling', that is, 'reading' the law so as to inform the current generation, and recording and transmitting the teaching of the LORD for subsequent generations. These men may have been priests and may also have overlapped to some extent with 'the wise', but they are brought to task for their lack of true understanding. 'Know' (*yādaʿ*) is a word of personal intimacy and relationship, as well as of political recognition. It indicates not a lack of cerebral knowledge of the LORD, but of personal commitment to him. However skilled and erudite their discussions of the law, however great their desire to promote the cause of religion, their lack of heart loyalty to the LORD undermined their effectiveness in promoting the standards of the covenant in the community so that the nation as a whole did not have a true heart commitment to the LORD. Jeremiah was later to prophesy that this deficiency would be remedied under the arrangements of the new covenant (31:33-34).

(3) **The leaders rebelled against me.** 'Leaders'/'shepherds' refers to political rulers (23:1-4), here either successive rulers in Judah or the ruling classes as a whole. 'Rebellion' (<√*pāšaʿ*) is basically a political term, but was applied to religious offences against Israel's covenant king. They were no longer seeking to live after and rule in accordance with the LORD's covenant mandates for them, but were acting in defiance of the LORD.

(4) **And the prophets prophesied by Baal**, the Canaanite god of fertility. *baʿal* was originally a common Hebrew noun for 'lord', 'master' or 'owner', but it became a recognised title of, effectively a name for, Hadad, the storm god who was the most active and significant male deity in the Canaanite pantheon, though technically of inferior status to El, the supreme god. Baal was also worshipped as a god of agricultural fertility, and the Baal cult provided the greatest religious challenge Israel had to face in the period from their entrance into Palestine until the Exile.

The reference to the prophets is primarily to what we now term 'false prophets' (see on 23:9), who had not received a genuine call from the LORD. 'Prophesying by Baal' could mean either that these prophets got their oracles by activities such as those practised in the Baal cult, or that they openly spoke in the name of Baal as well as that of the LORD. They promoted a composite religion, continuing lip-service to the LORD and yet at the same time accepting Canaanite ideas that the ground and natural phenomena like wind and rain were caused by the power of Baal. To most Israelites these practices would have seemed natural and attractive, being part of the accepted norms of the culture that surrounded them. That was, of course, precisely why the LORD was lodging his complaint against them. Their world-view was no longer exclusively focused on him, and they were not according him the unique place in their lives and in their thinking which he demanded.

Following worthless idols[7] picks up the theme of v. 2 and especially v. 5. The NIV translation takes the clause as referring specifically to the prophets, but it may also be understood as summing up the behaviour of all four groups. 'Worthless' is not the word that was used in v. 5, but a synonymous expression, *lōʾ-yôʿālû*, 'they do not profit', perhaps chosen for its similarity in sound to 'by Baal', *babbaʿal*. Idol worship provided no real benefit for its devotees, only the trouble involved in its rituals. Again there is a correspondence between the form of their deviant behaviour and their resulting condition.

But were such accusations fair? Should this language be understood to be as sweeping as it might first sight seem? Were there no loyal priests, or scribes, or kings, or prophets? Probably the intention is to indicate the overall impact of each of these four groups, and not to pass judgment on every single individual. The history of the people of Israel down to Jeremiah's contemporaries in Judah was a story of deviation and unfaithfulness rather than of loyal devotion to the LORD.

3. The Divine Complaint (2:9-13)

Having completed his historical retrospect of Israel's relationship with him—their early love (vv. 2-3) and his abundant provision for their defence and well-being (vv. 3b, 7a), despite which the people were thankless and became involved in idol worship, both individually (v. 5) and corporately through the leading members of the community (v. 8)—the LORD now sets out his complaint against the current generation of his people. It is indeed difficult to be certain whether v. 9 is to be associated with the preceding rather than the succeeding verses. Both 'therefore' and 'declares the LORD' favour the view that v. 9 concludes the historical review, but the actual statement of the complaint is not found until v. 11b, and the logic of the situation supports the NIV paragraphing which associates v. 9 with what follows.

9. In prophetic speeches **therefore** (*lākēn*) frequently functions to introduce the divine sentence of judgment (see on 5:14), but here it

7. Unusually the relative clause follows the preposition without an expressed relative pronoun (GKC §155n; *IBHS* §9.6d; Joüon §129q).

rather provides the link between the behaviour of the past and the fact that a formal complaint is being lodged against the present generation. They have perpetuated and not remedied the grievous situation they inherited from their fathers, and so on the basis of their own conduct the LORD has no option but to initiate proceedings against them by formally stating his grievance.

I bring charges against you again indicates that the LORD is starting proceedings: but what sort of proceedings are in view? The verb used is *rîb*, and it and the corresponding noun have often been related to a covenant lawsuit. Undoubtedly most of the occurrences of this root in the Old Testament are in the legal-judicial sphere, and it may be used of a tripartite process in which two parties bring their dispute before a court for adjudication (Exod. 23:5; 'dispute', Deut. 19:17; 'complaint', 2 Sam. 15:2). However, the word may be used more generally of 'strife' (Prov. 17:1) and what is in view here is a bilateral process in which the LORD formally informs the people of his grievance with them. It is an invitation to them to consider their situation and argue it out with him. There is an openness about the outcome: if they acknowledge the error of their ways, then reconciliation will be possible; if they persist in their misconduct, then the matter will require formal adjudication and sentence. No doubt there is an analogy with the way in which the emperors of old sent plenipotentiaries to remonstrate with recalcitrant subject peoples. If they were open to verbal persuasion to see things their emperor's way, then this would spare him the expense and trouble of sending an army to coerce them back into line, but there was no escaping the threat that punitive measures would be taken if persuasion was unavailing. So too the prophet as the LORD's covenant spokesman begins his mission by arguing for a response from the people before matters proceed to the next stage of the process.

'I bring charges' is an imperfect representing an ongoing situation (*IBHS* §31.3b) rather than one still to start, 'I will bring charges' (NKJV). The matter is of such gravity that it is being pursued now and in the future until it is resolved one way or another. 'Again' (*'ōd*) does not relate to any previous message conveyed by Jeremiah, but rather to the ongoing ministry of the prophets. Isaiah (Isa. 1:10-20) and Micah (Mic. 6:1-8) had previously pled with the people, and the outcome had been a favourable response—at least in measure—so that the imposition of the ultimate sanction was avoided.

The formula, **declares the LORD**, here occurs in the middle of a verse. 'It is also a mark of lively rhetorical style that the Yahweh utterance formula can even stand parenthetically within a clause, as in

Jer. 2:9' (*TDOT* 9:111). There are twelve instances of this use in Jeremiah (e.g. 7:30).

There is now no doubt that the divine grievance is against the people of Jeremiah's day. 'You' refers to the prophet's audience, and the complaint is viewed as encompassing their descendants also. **And I will bring charges against your children's children.** Jones (1992:84) views this as a gloss written at a later time when it was clear that the complaint against the people had not been satisfactorily resolved. The NIV variation in translating *ʾārîb* from 'I bring charges' to 'I will bring charges' unnecessarily introduces the thought of another, future complaint. It is the one action that is in view: all those who constituted the house of Jacob (2:4) are jointly been cited to answer for their collective behaviour.

10. The next verse begins with *kî*, 'for', indicating the basis on which the complaints procedure is based. Plural commands are issued, **Cross over to the coasts of Kittim and look**, but it is not immediately clear who are being addressed. It might be the people themselves who are being urged to do so, so that the unreasonable nature of their actions would be brought home to them. It is improbable that the subject of the imperative is the heavens, which are not formally introduced until v. 12. However, it may be that in an apostrophe the subject is deliberately unspecified as a rhetorical device to call upon any and all to make the journey in their thoughts (18:13). Consideration of the behaviour of other nations provides the evidence needed to impress upon one the unreasonableness of the conduct of the LORD's people, and so justification is provided for presenting this complaint.

'Coasts'/'coastlands' (25:22; 31:10; 47:4; Ps. 72:10; Isa. 41:1, 5) refers to the islands and shores of the Mediterranean, viewed it would seem originally from a seafarer's point of view as a place where one could find rest. 'Kittim' at first referred to the Phoenician settlement at modern Lanarka in Cyprus, but the term became one for Cyprus itself, and indeed for those who dwelt anywhere in the Mediterranean littoral. It is not geographical precision that is required here. The figure is an example of merism, involving the idea of going as far west as you can, and then going as far to the east, and at the same time taking in everything that is found lying between those extremes. **Send to Kedar** involves dispatching a messenger into the deserts of northern Arabia and reporting how the prominent nomadic tribe of Kedar behaved there (49:28). **Observe closely** how the people of these very different life-styles, the maritime and the nomadic, behave. This is an injunction not to come to a snap judgment, but to weigh up matters. It is not that it is hard to reach a conclusion, but time should be taken because of the consequences of the observations made. **See if**[8] **there has ever been anything like this**, which is then specified in the next verse.

11. The rhetorical question, **Has a nation ever changed its gods?**, strongly asserts that no instance will be found of a nation switching gods. Such loyalty was not just a matter of historical observation. It was also fostered by the accommodationist thinking of polytheism. Because worship of more than one deity was commonplace, there was no need to offend the gods by abandoning any of them. It was accepted that others could be worshipped as well. But for all the difference it made, these peoples could have left their national gods and patron deities because the gods they chose to worship were non-entities. **Yet they are not gods at all.** The phrase 'not gods' links back to Deut. 32:17, 21. The fact that they were incapable of conferring good might well have been an excuse for changing them, but that did not happen.

In contrast 'my people', the only ones who had a God who was able to make a real difference, had deserted him. Those who had experienced the LORD's goodness and who should have been strongly attached to him exhibited utter folly in deserting the one true God. The ethically undemanding requirements of pagan religions meant that their devotees felt no need to change. But the religion of the LORD was not a human construct; it came from without and created a bond of love that was restrictive and demanding. Israel frequently sought to evade the requirement of self-surrender integral to a living relationship with the LORD, and so in ironic tones it is recorded, **but my people have exchanged their Glory**[9] **for worthless idols.** 'Their glory' is what

8. The translation of *hēn*, 'if', here has been a matter of some dispute. It can introduce a conditional clause, but what is here is an interrogative clause. BHS consequently proposes repointing the consonants of *hēn hāyətâ* into one word *hănihyətâ*, the interrogative particle, followed by the niphal of *hāyâ*, meaning 'to occur, to happen'. The feminines are functioning as English neuters, and the translations is much the same.

9. There is some problem as to what should be the reading here. The kethibh reads *kəbôdô*, 'his glory', where the masculine singular agrees with the collective noun *ʿam*, 'people'. But the Massoretes marked this as a *tiqqun sopherim*, what they thought was an early scribal correction that had been made to avoid a disrespectful reference to God. The margin suggests the original reading was *kəbôdî*, 'my glory'. It is not clear in what direction the change has occurred, but in Ps. 3:3 [MT 4] the Psalmist appears to address God as 'my glory' (but compare the NIV translation). This would support the kethibh as meaning that 'their glory' is the God that they adore.

they should reverence, respect and adore, that is, the LORD himself (cf. Ps. 3:3). 'Exchange' suggests a process of bartering, striking a bargain, but their sense of value was such that though they thought they were getting a good deal, they were in fact self-deceived. They traded in the glorious self-revelation of God in their midst (Exod. 40:34; 1 Kgs. 8:11; Isa. 6:3; Ezek. 10:4), and what they got in return were 'worthless idols'/'something that has no worth', a singular phrase corresponding to the plural used at the end of v. 8, and again involving a play on the name Baal. Indeed, Thompson (1980:166) suggests that this is in effect a proper name, 'The Useless One'.

12. 'Be appalled at this, O heavens, and shudder with great horror,' declares the LORD. The heavens are personified and treated as a witness to what has been going on, who can be cited to vouch for the accuracy of what has been said. In the covenants of the Ancient Near East divine witnesses were called on to supervise the conduct of the partners to the treaty. Such a polytheistic option was not open to Israel, but there is often personified address to various features of the created realm, heaven, earth, mountains to witness what has happened (Deut. 32:1; Isa. 1:2; Mic. 6:1-2). Here the conduct of Israel is presented as so atrocious that even the inanimate creation will react with horror to this affront to the majesty of the Creator, and what it will entail for those who have turned their backs on him.

Three verbs are used. 'Be appalled' (<√*šāmēm*, 'be desolate, laid waste'[10]) describes one who is paralysed by a physical or psychological blow. The heavens are depicted as aghast as they consider the outrageous behaviour that Israel has perpetrated. The verb 'shudder' is a denominative from *śaʿar*, 'hair' (*NIDOTTE*, 3:1261-2) and graphically portrays the reaction by which one's hair stands on end with shock. 'With horror' renders a third verb, 'to be in ruins', from a root indicating dryness, and then the desolation of arid areas or the devastation caused by war. It is used here in a transferred sense for the reaction of the heavens being like those whose land has been devastated by calamity. The enormity of what will occur would induce an intense traumatic reaction from any unbiased spectator who is able to appreciate what has been done—but God's people did not view things in that way. **Declares the LORD** stands outside the metrical structure of the poetry at this point. As such it is not clear whether it is part of the divine message, or the prophet's reinforcement of it.

10. The assonance between *šōmmû* ('be appalled') and *šāmayim* ('heavens') reinforces the impact of the message.

13. The complaint is then formally enunciated. An introductory 'for' (*kî*) presents it as a further explanation as to why the preceding horrified reaction is appropriate. The charge is twofold: **My people have committed two sins**/'crimes' (*rāʿôt*, 'evils'), used here of moral misconduct. When heathen nations worship idols, that in itself is an offence before God; but when the LORD's people, 'my people', do so, they are sinning against light. Their offence is therefore compounded in that they have first to turn away from the LORD in rebellion against their covenant Overlord. It is the extent of their covenant privilege that reveals the depths to which human folly can go in rebellion against God. (1) In **they have forsaken me** 'me' (*ʾōtî*) is fronted in the clause for emphasis, 'I am the one whom they have forsaken.' 'Forsaken' (<√*ʿāzab*) is a covenantal term that involves legal infringement of the stipulations of the covenant (Deut. 29:25), but even more than that, it is an act of personal disloyalty to the LORD, their covenant king. There is then a metaphorical description of the LORD as **the spring of living water.** 'Spring', *māqôr* (<√*qûr* I, 'bore, dig', *TWOT* #2004), indicates a source of flowing water that is available through human effort. In this, it differs from *ʿayin* II ('spring', *TWOT* #1613), which denotes a flow of water from a natural opening. But the focus of the image is not on the engineering of the situation, but on the provision of 'living water', flowing freshly from some underground source and available all year round. This is water that is perpetual and pure.

(2) **And have dug out their own cisterns.** An adequate water supply was a matter of considerable concern in Palestine, and frequently this was secured by excavating in the rock a cavity with a narrow neck opening out into a considerable lower reservoir, which would be lined with a lime-based plaster. In the rainy season, water would be stored up in the cistern (*bōʾr*; cf. *bôr*, 37:16). Months later, it would have become flat, and be contaminated with algae. As such it served a purpose, but was much inferior to running spring water. W. M. Thomson was a missionary for 45 years in Syria and Palestine during the nineteenth century and he provided a first hand description of the water from such sources, little changed since the prophet's time.

> The best cisterns, even those in solid rock, are strangely liable to crack, and are a most unreliable source of supply of that absolutely indispensable article, water; and if, by constant care, they are made to hold, yet the water, collected from clay roofs or from marly soil, has the colour of weak soap-suds, the taste of earth or the stable, is full of worms, and in the hour of greatest need it utterly fails. Who but a fool positive, or one gone mad in love of filth, would exchange the sweet, wholesome stream of a living fountain for such

> an uncertain compound of nastiness and vermin! I have never been able to tolerate this cistern-water except in Jerusalem, where they are kept with scrupulous care, and filled from roofs both clean and hard. (Thomson 1872:287)

There was a further potential problem; the lining of the cistern could be faulty or a crack could occur in the rock itself. **Broken**[11] **cisterns that cannot hold water**[12] must have often disappointed the farmer coming for water in the dry season. So too the man-made expedients of religion will prove ineffectual and seriously flawed when in time of testing they are called upon to provide the help their devotees seek. At best what they give is flat and contaminated water; but there is the very real danger that they will have no water at all to give. This vivid metaphor drawn from conditions in Palestine points out the futility of their course of conduct.

Coming to a true knowledge of God is frequently likened to having thirst quenched by a drink of cool water (17:13; Ps. 36:9), and the need to be refreshed in this way becomes all the more intense under adverse conditions. The people of Jeremiah's day had previously been invited to come to the source of true spiritual water (Isa. 55:1), but they felt that they had made ample provision for their needs in other ways. The imagery of life-giving water is one to which we can still relate, and the New Testament continues to issue the same invitation to find this spiritual water in Jesus Christ (John 4:13-15; 6:35; 7:37; Rev. 22:17). Unfortunately there remain many who prefer to hew out broken cisterns and adopt lifestyles that neglect God's requirements and provision, being satisfied with alternatives that reflect their own priorities and preferences. As then in Jerusalem, so now, such conduct is the basis for divine complaint and will become subject to the reality of divine judgment.

4. The Bitterness of Apostasy (2:14-19)

This section begins without any formal device to mark the transition, though there is a standard concluding formula in v. 19. The theme of the section is what happens to the LORD's people when they forsake

11. Whereas the qal passive participle denotes a completed action or state, the niphal participle (as here) denotes an action in process, 'cisterns which tend to develop cracks', not '(already) broken cisterns' (Joüon §121q).

12. The hiphil imperfect of *kûl*, 'to contain', is here used modally to indicate capability (*IBHS* §31.4c). The article with *hammāyim*, 'the water', is used to make the noun definite in the imagination, that is, 'the water you would expect to be in such a cistern' (*IBHS* §13.5.1e).

him (vv. 17, 19) and lose the protection he bestows on his children. The fate of the former northern kingdom of Israel is presented as a warning to Jerusalem (vv. 14-15), which is urged to avoid entangling political alliances with nations to the north or south. The need to stand firm in their faith, trusting in the LORD's provision for them at a time of external confusion and threat, was just as great as it had been in Isaiah's day (Isa. 7:9). Though foreign alliances might appeal to their political instincts, they were inconsistent with true reliance upon divine resources (Ps. 20:7), and would bring dire consequences.

14. In the first of a series of questions that occur down to the end of the chapter (the NIV has twelve question marks in this section), the LORD probes the position of a nation that was insensitive to the reality of its situation, to see if they can be made to view things in a proper light. First, in vv. 14 and 15 they are called to reflect on the example of the northern kingdom of Israel. The question **Is Israel a servant, a slave by birth?**, though rhetorical and expecting the answer 'No', is not asked in an accusing way, but rather in a bemused, quiet manner. The Hebrew question does not specify any temporal perspective: 'is' is a translator's supplement. Was that really Israel's status: to be a slave? The Hebrew word *ʿebed* denotes a subordinate and is used for a variety of relationships. It may be translated 'servant' or 'slave', but what is envisaged here is the even lower status of 'a slave by birth' (*yəlûd bayit*), one whose mother was already a slave in a household and so her child was doomed to lifelong servitude. It was possible for individuals to sell themselves into slavery because of poverty or debt, but they had the hope of releasing themselves from the period of their indenture (34:8). A home-born slave, however, was his master's property. But surely that did not apply to Israel who had been the LORD's covenant partner, his bride?

In the third member of a typically Jeremianic construction (see on 8:22), the puzzled question is posed, **Why then has he become plunder?** The answer is clear: it was by their defection from the ways of the LORD that the fortunes of Israel deteriorated in such a sorry way. They had been seized by their enemies, deported from their land, and their goods and resources spoiled. The NASB renders *baz* as 'prey', looking forward to the metaphor of the next verse, but this seems to be a clear statement of the fate Israel suffered (*terep* would have been the expected word to use for an animal's prey). Judah had only to look a few miles north to see what had happened there: could they not learn the lesson?

15. Lions (the plural of *kəpîr*) is rendered 'young lions' in the NKJV, and no doubt this is strictly speaking correct, so long as it does not suggest lion cubs but strong and aggressive animals in late adolescence, lacking only the experience of an adult. The reference is to the might of Assyria which brought about the capture of the northern kingdom. Lions were common decorative features in the temples and palaces of Mesopotamia, and were associated with their gods of war. The lions of Assyria **have roared**. There is a grammatical problem in that the verb 'roared' (*yišʾăgû*) is imperfect, but rather than pointing to a future action, this indicates repeated action in the past (*IBHS* §31.2b) whereby the Assyrians from the rise of Tiglath-Pileser in 745 BC made successive inroads in the north until they captured Samaria in 722 BC (see Introduction §3.2).

The roar of a lion can be heard as far as five miles (8 km) away, and close up it is extremely intimidating. But when does a lion roar? Lions do not typically roar when hunting or stalking prey. The lion's roar is usually heard in the evening and again before sunrise, and it is uttered to mark out the territory of a pride and to help the animals locate one another. Lions also roar as an aggressive gesture during violent interaction with other lions. The idea here seems to combine territorial assertiveness and aggression against another state.

As regards **they have growled at him**, commentators, generally not having much experience of lions, are at odds over whether this is a paralysing threat before the lion pounces on his prey (and so parallels the first statement), or an act of triumph over the dying prey, though the latter is much more probable. But there could be no doubt about the facts of history. **They have laid waste his land**/'made his land into a desolation' (*šammâ*). *Šammâ* and *šəmāmâ* (4:27), 'desolation', are both found frequently in Jeremiah, and are derived from *šāmēm*, 'to be desolate' (see 2:12, 'be appalled'). They differ in that *šəmāmâ* focuses on the physical devastation caused whereas *šammâ* also involves the reaction of horror caused by witnessing such devastation. **His towns are burned**[13] **and deserted**[14]. 'Town' translates *ʿîr*, 'city', a settlement

13. The kethibh is *niṣṣətâ*, 'she (i.e. the land) was burned', a feminine singular niphal from *nāṣat*, 'to burn', whereas the subject is plural. The qere suggests *niṣṣətû*, 'they (i.e. the cities) were burned', agreeing with the subject (GKC §44m). It may, however, be a collective usage of the feminine singular (GKC §145k; Joüon §150h). *NIDOTTE* (3:137) takes the root as *nāṣâ*, 'to fall in ruins', niphal 'to be destroyed, devastated'.

14. In the phrase *mibbəlî yōšēb*, 'from not one inhabiting', *min*, 'from', is used in a privative sense to denote what is missing (*IBHS* §11.2.11e), and so the compound with *bəlî*, 'not', an adverb of negation, is pleonastic.

of any size which was physically distinguished by having defensive structures of some sort. That they had been set on fire indicates that there was no possibility of further resistance to the enemy. All had fallen before him, and what had once been regarded as places of refuge were now defenceless and uninhabited.

16. Also, combined with a switch in Hebrew to second feminine singular pronouns for those addressed (last found in 2:3 and continued until 2:25), indicates a move to discussing more recent affairs in the south. **The men of Memphis and Tahpanhes**[15] **have shaved the crown of your head** is a clear reference to Egypt. Memphis is the better known Greek name for Noph (*nōp*), which was situated about thirteen miles (21 km) south of modern Cairo. At one stage it had been the capital of Egypt, and still remained a significant city. Tahpanhes (Greek, Daphne) is a reference to a major town situated in eastern delta near the mouth of the Pelusiac branch of the Nile, and so the first significant settlement encountered on entering Egypt from Palestine. 'The men of' (literally, 'sons of') refers to the inhabitants of Noph, and is possibly to be understood with Tahpanhes also. Together they are used to refer to the might of Egypt.

It is not, however, clear what precisely the Egyptians are said to do, or when, because there is difficulty with the pointing of the Hebrew text which reads *yirʿûk*, 'they were shepherding you' (<√*rāʿâ*, 'to shepherd, pasture'). Although the verb may be used to refer to rulers, 'they were ruling you as to the crown of your head' does not yield any tolerable sense. However, retaining the consonants of the text and pointing them as *yərōʿûk* gives the sense 'they were breaking you' (<√*rāʿaʿ* II, piel, 'to break'), which may correspond to the English idiom, 'to crack one's skull'. Transposing two consonants and repointing to *yəʿārûk* (<√*ʿārâ*, piel, 'to lay bare') yields the sense 'they were shaving you bald' as in the NIV, which was a mark of enslavement throughout the ancient world, or might refer to mourning customs. It must also be noted that whatever the root of the verb, the form is that of an imperfect and divergences of translation reflect different views as to the original setting of this passage. The imperfects might be of customary action extending over a period in the past (*IBHS* §31.2b), or of a present ongoing situation (*IBHS* §31.3b), and so continue the past references in v. 15 (so NIV, NRSV). But equally, the imperfects may be futures (so REB, NJPS), prophesying what was yet to occur.

---

15. The qere yields the form *wətaḥpanhēs*, 'and Tahpanhes', whereas the kethibh would be read *wətahpənēs*, 'and Tahpenes'. The difference is only that of a minor variation in spelling the name of this town.

'Crown of your head' is just a way of referring to the top of the head and has no explicit royal overtones. Even so, many find here an oblique reference to the death of Josiah at Egyptian hands in 609 BC, either by 'breaking you with respect to the top of your head' being a rough way of saying 'killed your king' or by understanding shaving your head as a reference to putting you into deep mourning. If this has already happened, then what we have is a report of Jeremiah's preaching originating during the early years of Jehoiakim. But there is no compelling reason to take the saying as late. The thought may easily be that just as Assyria brought disaster to the north, so relying on Egypt will bring disaster (or understanding the idiom in other ways, slavery or mourning) from the south. Egypt would be unreliable as an ally: despite a friendly welcome she would just as easily turn and attack them if she thought such a change of policy suited her interests. Egypt was committed to Egypt, not to the interests of Judah. Such a lesson in the realities of power politics was no new theme in the prophetic repertoire of warnings. Already back in Hezekiah's days Isaiah had forecast 'Woe to those who go down to Egypt for help' (Isa. 31:1; see also Isa. 30:1-7), and Jeremiah too was shown how futile Egyptian alliances would be (2:18, 36). In the period of his early ministry, the perceptible decline in Assyrian power would have strengthened the hand of the pro-Egyptian party, which was always present in Jerusalem. Jeremiah's early warning that Egypt did not provide the answer to the problems of Judah would have been reinforced by the time the First Scroll was written through the impact of Josiah's death and also the levy imposed by Pharaoh Neco (2 Kgs. 23:33-35).

17. A series of questions is used to bring home to the people that what was happening to them was their own fault. **Have you not brought this on yourselves?** They are asked if this scenario is not one they are making for themselves, with the imperfect verb indicating ongoing action extending into the present. The root cause of their problem is not, however, inadequate political insight, but lack of covenant commitment to the LORD. Echoing the words of 2:13, **by forsaking the LORD your God when he led you in the way**/'path' refers back to the Exodus (for 'led' see 2:6) when the right way spiritually and politically was divinely set before them, yet they had deserted the LORD. The reforms of Josiah meant that there was a renewed awareness among the people of the LORD's past dealings with them, and they are being urged not to repeat the errors of their history. The LORD was still providing for them and pointing the way forward, but were they truly committed to him? The question may well point to an attempt to deepen the spiritual basis of the reform movement by bringing home the fact that total loyalty to the LORD was required and not just cultic reform. The lack of such allegiance had brought (and would bring) disasters on them. Although Jeremiah could doubtless have said much more about the political folly of those years, the focus of his preaching remains stubbornly where it ought to be—on the root cause of all their troubles, their sinful defection from the LORD.

18. Now (*'attâ*) functions to indicate both temporal and logical sequence, but in combination with *wə*, 'and', as here, it is usually logical in force, moving the argument on to its next stage (*IBHS* §39.3.4f) in which the nation is challenged as to its current behaviour. **Why go to Egypt?** is literally, 'What to you with respect to way of Egypt?', instituting a comparison with 'the way' of the LORD in the previous verse. **To drink water from the Shihor** is to rely for the restoration of their national fortunes on the support and resources that might come from Egypt, particularly military aid with a view to protecting them if there should be a resurgence of Assyrian might. (Around 620–616 BC it was clear that Assyria was down, but not that she was out.) However, the question posed also echoes 2:13 with reference to the LORD as the true support and only reliable sustainer of his people. Shihor used to be explained as 'blackness', a name for the Nile coming from the mud in its waters during the annual inundation, but there is now evidence that it is a Hebrew form corresponding to a name for the easternmost distributary of the Nile in the Delta region (notice its use in 1 Chron. 13:5 with reference to entering into Egypt), and that it is here used by synecdoche to refer to the river as a whole.

It is not immediately evident whether the second part of the verse reinforces the first part, or whether it presents an alternative policy. Up to 616 BC there was a real choice to be made in Judah between continuing subservience to the northern power of Assyria or an alliance with the southern power of Egypt, and there were two parties in the land, favouring the different options. After 616 BC, Egypt became an ally of Assyria and that particular policy option was no longer present. **And why go to Assyria to drink water from the River?** The River is a reference to the Euphrates (Isa. 8:7), and drinking its water is again adopting a policy of relying on its resources and help. Though 'Assyria' may be used to refer to whatever nation was in control of the Mesopotamian region even after the Assyrian empire was defunct (Ezra 6:22), that is not the case here. This is posed as a real policy option being debated in Jerusalem (and so comes from before 616 BC). But the prophet's challenge is not one that relates to political expediency, as if to say, 'Assyria is on the decline and might not recover, why then make an alliance with her?' It was not a matter of 'side with the south' or 'side with the north'; it was rather a radical call for covenantal realignment of their thinking so as to give the LORD his due place.

19. Rejection of covenant loyalty inevitably brings consequences in its train. **Your wickedness will punish you** implies that their behaviour will issue in unintended results. It is only here that *yāsar*, 'punish', is found with an abstract subject. Elsewhere in Jeremiah, *yāsar* has the LORD as a personal subject (e.g. 30:11; 31:18), and here too it obliquely points to the way in which the LORD disciplines and instructs Judah. **Your backsliding will rebuke you.** For 'backsliding' (in fact here a plural, 'repeated acts of apostasy'), see the discussion at 3:6. 'Rebuke' is often used with an educational motive in view, and occurs in the context of covenant remonstrance (Ps. 50:8, 21; Hos. 4:43; Mic. 6:2). Again the thought is that there are inner connections between Judah's actions and their consequences which will make themselves evident over time and serve to chastise and correct her. But this does not mean that the LORD is uninvolved in the process. 'Yahweh is seen as the one who sets the connection between act and consequence in force' (Miller 1982:127).

The covenant Overlord then calls his people to awareness of the consequences of their abandonment of him (2:13, 17) **'Consider then**[16] **and realise how evil and bitter it is for you when you forsake the LORD your God and have no awe of me,' declares the Lord, the LORD Almighty.** The two commands 'consider and realise' (literally 'know and see', followed by *kî*, 'that, how' introducing a subordinate noun clause after the verbs of cognition) intensify each other: it is complete realisation that is commanded, not some half-perception. 'Evil' (*raʿ*) accompanied by 'bitter' points forwards to the repercussions of their actions rather than to the inherent wickedness of their apostasy. Although stated negatively, there is a clear indication given of how they should be acting. 'Dread' (<*pāḥad*) is a strong word that may point to an external source of terror or, as here, to the consequent inner emotional response. It is often found in parallelism with the root *yārēʾ*, 'to fear', which describes the essence of Old Testament piety.

There is also found here a number of key titles for God which emphasise the heinousness of the offence of spurning him. 'LORD' is

---

16. The force of the *waw* in *ûdəʿî*, 'and know', is illative, pointing to the conclusion that should be drawn.

Yahweh, the personal, covenant name of God (Exod. 3:14-15; 6:2-3), with 'your God' serving as a reminder of the bond that the covenant had brought into existence between Yahweh and his people (7:23; Exod. 6:7). 'Lord' (*'ădōnāy*) is derived from *'ădōn*, a term used of human and divine superiors, to acknowledge their status and authority. 'LORD Almighty' (*yhwh ṣəbā'ôt*, traditionally 'LORD of hosts') is a term which seems to have originated in the conception of Yahweh as the commander of his people's army and to have been extended in the light of Gen. 2:1 to include the thought of Yahweh as the one who controls every being and force that exists in the whole created realm (*NIDOTTE* 4:1297-8). Before him and his purposes Judah should bow in reverential awe. Since all affairs in heaven and on earth are under his control, it is futile to adopt policies that run counter to what he requires.

5. Ingrained Sin (2:20-25)

This section brings out the extent to which rebellion against the LORD had become an automatic, deep-seated response on the part of the people. It is characterised by the use of a series of images—an ox ploughing (v. 20); a prostitute (v. 20); a vine (v. 21); a washerwoman (v. 22); a camel (v. 23); and a wild donkey (v. 24). There are also three quotations placed on the lips of the people: 'I will not serve you' (v. 20); 'I am not defiled' (v. 23); and 'It's no use! I love foreign gods, and I must go after them' (v. 25). It would be pressing matters too far to require that these words were actually uttered by the people. It is difficult to imagine a situation in which they would jointly agree to prepare such statements and have them issued on their behalf. These are words that are put on their lips as a way of setting out vividly what their conduct declared the tendency of their life to be and how distorted their view of reality had become. They are not sheer invention, because their impact depended on the authenticity of the attitudes they portrayed. The objective is still to bring the people to realise the futility of their actions in abandoning the LORD and in seeking to find spiritual satisfaction elsewhere. The exposure of their sin now moves on from their lack of fidelity to the gross sensuality of their conduct.

20. The verse begins with *kî*, and at the beginning of a section it is often not easy to discriminate between the logical use of the particle ('for', NRSV) and the emphatic use ('indeed'). The NIV treats it as an emphatic, which need not be represented in English. But it is just as easy to see it as connecting back to 'You have no awe of me' in v. 19.

It is not that what follows explains why they lacked reverence for God; rather this brings forward the evidence to substantiate that assertion.

Long ago (*mēʿôlām*, 'from of old') is a composite expression based on *ʿôlām* which is generally glossed as 'ever', but may be used of an extended period, whether past or future. Here it looks back to the early stage of the people's existence as a nation. The force of *min*, 'from', seems to be not just to locate the action of the following verb in their past but to suggest that such attitudes continued thereafter. This corresponds to its use in 5:15 (see also Gen. 6:4; Josh. 24:2). The complaint is against the present generation as well as their forefathers.

The first of two main translation problems in the verse concerns the statement, **you broke off your yoke and tore off your bonds.** This understands the verbs to retain the older perfect second feminine singular ending *-tî*, a form that was preserved in Aramaic and which seems from there to have been used on a number of occasions by Jeremiah and Ezekiel (GKC §44h[1]). The feminine subject retains the mode of address that has been in use since v. 16. However, the verb forms may also be taken as first person singular ('I have broken your yoke *and* burst your bonds', NKJV). In that case v. 20 would look back to the deliverance from Egypt, when the LORD effectively dealt with the Egyptian yoke of political subjugation of Israel and the leather thongs that held it in place (for the imagery see on 27:2). Jeremiah uses similar language in 30:8 to describe the release of those in exile from Babylonian domination. On the other hand, this metaphor of an animal unwilling to yield to the requirements of its owner is used in 5:5 to describe Israel's flouting of the Sinai covenant, which would favour the NIV rendering.

Related to this is the second translation problem. Should it be, **you said, 'I will not serve you!'** or 'You said, "I will not transgress" ' (NKJV). The NIV reflects the kethibh of the Massoretic Text, *lōʾ ʾeʿĕbōd* (<√*ʿābad*, 'to serve'), whereas the marginal qere (*lōʾ ʾeʿĕbōr* <√*ʿābar*, 'to transgress'; cf. 5:22) is followed by the NKJV. The interchange of a *daleth* and a *resh* was a common scribal mistake, probably arising here when the previous verbs were mistakenly understood as first person. The NIV rendering seems more probable.

The people are portrayed as viewing their covenant undertaking, 'We will do everything the LORD has said; we will obey' (Exod. 24:7; 2 Chron. 34:32), as burdensome and intrusive. Therefore they are presented in language similar to that of the rebels in Ps. 2:1-3 who renounce their allegiance to the LORD and abandon any practice of *ḥesed* (see on 2:2). But their claim, 'I will not serve you!' is an illusion if they think that they can achieve absolute freedom to do whatever they want. Those who rebel against the good and generous provision and requirements of the LORD are in effect submitting themselves to another master who will not hesitate to oppress them. Spiritual neutrality is not an option for humanity. The house swept bare invites occupation by the enemy (Matt. 12:43-45).

So it was with the people of Judah. **Indeed** treats the particle *kî* as an emphatic. It is unlikely to be a subordinating use, 'when' (NKJV), following the main verb, but it is possible to take it as introducing a justification for representing the people as saying, 'I will not serve!' Their conduct provides the evidence for asserting what their inner attitude was. **On every high hill and under every spreading tree you lay down as a prostitute.** The idolatrous worship of Canaan was conducted at shrines known as high places, which had originally been sited on hill tops, but later on artificially elevated sites elsewhere were used, so that a high place could be in a valley. 'Spreading' (*raʿănān*, 17:8) refers to a leafy, profusely growing tree whose greenery testifies to its vitality. As such it was often planted at the sites of Canaanite idol worship which had long been described by this phrase or a variant of it (Deut. 12:2). The ritual at such sites frequently involved sexual activity, which was assumed by a sort of sympathetic magic to induce the gods to behave in a similar way and so assure fertility for crops and livestock. Israel had been commanded to eradicate such worship from the land of promise (Deut. 12:2-4), and it was repeatedly condemned by the prophets (Isa. 1:29; 57:5; Ezek. 6:13; Hos. 4:12-13). 'Lay down' is a euphemistic expression for what the REB renders more graphically as 'sprawled in promiscuous vice'. Though the participle *zōnâ* is often used as a noun, 'a prostitute' (see on 3:1), here it follows another participle and this probably reinforces its original function of indicating ongoing activity. These deviations from the standards of the covenant happened early and they happened often.

21. The image changes to that of the LORD as a vineyard owner and the people as a vine. The verse begins *wəʾānōkî*, 'yet I' (NRSV), strongly contrasting his behaviour with that of the people. **I had planted you like a choice vine of sound and reliable stock**, literally, 'all of it (i.e. the vine), seed/offspring of faithfulness', that is, a plant with no deviant growths so that no aberrant behaviour should have occurred. The image of the vine for the people of God occurs a number of times (Ps. 80; Isa. 5:1-7; Ezek. 17:6-8; Hos. 10:1), but this particular word, *śōrēq*, 'choice vine', is used in this way only here and in Isa. 5:2, where it is also applied metaphorically to Judah. The soreq vine was a plant with choice dark red grapes which was cultivated in Wadi al-Sarar, located between Jerusalem and the Mediterranean Sea (cf. Gen. 49:11). This description resembles the ideal portrayal of Israel in earlier verses, though 'planted' looks to the time of the settlement under Joshua rather than the Exodus. **How then did you turn against me**[17] **into a corrupt, wild vine?**, literally, 'ones of turning aside of the vine, a foreign one', a somewhat tortuous expression grammatically, but one whose meaning is nonetheless clear. 'Turn' (<√*hāpak*) often has a negative sense as here (23:36). The question is one of puzzlement, reproaching the people that such degeneration should have occurred in what had been a promising plant. There were now foreign branches of alien stock in the vine, just as the people were indulging in practices which the LORD had sought to prune out of their national life. It was no longer a vine he could recognise as his own. Why then should it have a place in his vineyard? It is in contrast to such a portrayal of a degenerate vine that Jesus presents himself as 'the true vine', the genuine one who does his Father's will (John 15:1).

22. The metaphorical kaleidoscope is twisted once more, and the people are compared to a washerwoman trying to eradicate a stain from a garment. **'Although you wash yourself with soda and use** 'for yourself' **an abundance of soap, the stain of your guilt is still before me,' declares the Sovereign LORD.** 'For yourself' indicates that they were acting to further their own interests. 'Wash' (<√*kābas*) is the normal word for 'fulling', that is, laundering clothes rather than washing the body (*TDOT* #946), but it is found in Ps. 51:2, 7 as a spiritual metaphor (a different word is found in Isa. 1:15-20, though the idea is comparable). The people have realised that their clothes are contaminated with dirt (the early Jewish interpretation found in the Targum is that it is a bloodstain they are dealing with) and are trying to wash them clean. But relying on human resources does not provide a suitable strategy for rectifying the situation. 'Soda' (*neter*) was an alkali obtained from mineral deposits and probably imported from Egypt for use as a detergent (see *ISBE* 3:191). 'Soap' is an anachronistic rendering of *bōrît*, 'lye, potash', which was a local product obtained from the ashes of various plants. But no matter what cleansing agent they used or how much of it they employed, it would be unable to remove the stain that had been ingrained into the fabric of the material. 'Their guilt' renders the noun *ʿāwōn*, from a root indicating 'twisted/bent' and so used of crooked behaviour (*TWOT* #1577; cf. 9:5). The noun may refer to a misdeed, or to the guilt arising from it, or

---

17. A *dativus incommodi*, indicating the one to whose detriment their change occurred (*IBHS* §11.2.10d).

to the punishment that was duly imposed. 'Before me' indicates that though they might be able to cover things up as regards human tribunals, the Sovereign LORD, the ruler of all (1:6), is not deceived, and until matters are properly dealt with, they will be debarred from acceptance with him. For cleansing to be spiritually effective inner renewal was required (Ps. 51:2, 10).

23. Verses 23-25 deal with a supposed rebuttal from the people when these accusations are made against them. They protest that it is inaccurate to say they are in need of spiritual cleansing, or have acted with disloyalty, but Jeremiah in the name of the LORD robustly undermines their attempt to evade responsibility. **How can you** (feminine singular) **say, 'I am not defiled; I have not run after the Baals'?** The covenant complaint has failed to induce in Judah and Jerusalem any spirit of real self-examination, and their response is a brazen denial of the facts. In that case Jeremiah represents the people as being inconsistent when in v. 25 they acknowledge their infatuation. This is a plausible interpretation, in that those who are set on defying God are prepared to use every argument that seems to stave off the day of reckoning. As they turn and twist, it is not logical consistency they are striving for. On the other hand, it may be that, while not denying the facts of their behaviour, what the people are arguing is that it has not polluted them. Are we to hear them protesting in a voice of injured innocence, 'I am not defiled' (<√*ṭāmēʾ*, v. 7), because they had not become devotees of Baal ('run after'/'go after', v. 2)? 'The Baals' is a plural reference to different manifestations of Baal found in various localities (9:14). 'Presumably, they defend and deceive themselves with appeals to their orthodoxy, the Solomonic temple, the functioning Levitical ministries. They perceive themselves as respectable Yahwists, and they resent the prophetic challenges to their integrity' (Ortlund 1996:86).

Their response is further challenged by the injunction, **See how you behaved in the valley!** Literally, it is 'Look at your way in the valley' (NRSV), where the 'way'/'path' resumes the theme of vv. 17 and 18. Indeed it may go further than their behaviour in general and point to the well-worn route they had taken to the sites of idol worship. Cannot they see their footprints in the dust? Is that not evidence enough against them? 'The valley' would then be the valley of Hinnom to the south-west of Jerusalem (see on 7:31), where the abominable rites associated with the worship of Moloch were practised (7:31; 2 Kgs. 23:10). **Consider what you have done.** It was not that they were unaware of the facts of their conduct. Rather they lacked the discriminating knowledge to be found by assessing their behaviour in the light of the demands of the covenant LORD on them.

There is then yet another change of metaphor to the unsteady movement of a young camel. **You are a swift she-camel running here and there**. The mention of a female camel simply reflects the feminine references to the nation in this passage. 'Running here and there' comes from the root *śārak*, which also yields the word for a sandal thong (Gen. 14:23; Isa. 5:27) as it too goes this way and that, though doubtless with greater regularity than the lurching of a young camel. 'The point of the camel image here is that the camel is young, and young camels cannot walk straight; when a young camel gets loose in the marketplace, everyone scrambles out of the way, because no one knows where the camel will step next' (Holladay 1974:41). In a similar fashion the nation's behaviour has been quite inconsistent, tottering from one extreme to another so that no one could predict where they would go next. This may well reflect the political as well as the spiritual situation in the land (vv. 17, 36). Since there was no real ideological base for their actions, they were always ready to follow the latest trend, and so they lunged from one seemingly attractive expedient to another.

24. Judah's irresponsible and unrestrained conduct is then pictured using another animal metaphor as she is said to be **a wild donkey accustomed to the desert.** The wild ass[18] roamed wilderness areas (*midbār*, 'desert', 2:2), and was renowned for its independence and intractability (Gen. 16:12; Job 39:5-8). It is used as a figure for a lifestyle that abandons the conventional and focuses on self-satisfaction (*NIDOTTE* 3:672). Here Judah is portrayed as gripped by an infatuation from which she cannot be dissuaded. **Sniffing** (literally, 'she sniffs', a gnomic perfect <√*šā'ap*, 'to pant, gasp') **the wind in her craving**[19], she picks up the scent of a male and is off down the road after him. **In her heat who can restrain her?** So overwhelmed is she

18. Although the animal is a she-donkey, the noun and following adjective are masculine. *pereh* (usually spelled *pere'*) is probably being treated as epicene, used indifferently of the male and female of the species (GKC §122d).

19. Literally, 'longing of her throat', *bə'awwat napšô*. *nepeš*, traditionally glossed as 'soul', probably originally signified 'throat' as an organ of breathing. The qere reads *napšâ*, 'her soul', for the kethibh *napšô*, 'his soul'. The kethibh is the more difficult reading, which, if the epicene use of *pereh* was not recognised, might naturally be changed to a feminine. The translation is unaffected.

by her longing, it is impossible to make her turn back. **Any males that pursue her need not tire themselves; at mating time they will find her.** No need for the male donkey to weary himself searching for the female; she is making tracks straight for him. So too Judah in her obsession for finding foreign allies does not have to be approached by them; she is always ready and looking out for potential partners in some league or other, no matter how inappropriate or misguided. For an instance of this propensity, see 27:3.

25. Developing, it would seem, from the picture of the donkey in the wilderness, there is added, **Do not run until your feet are bare** (that is, you have worn holes in your sandals) **and your throat**[20] **is dry**. This seeks to dissuade the people from such reckless and exhausting conduct. If they discern any reflection of their behaviour in the descriptions given, then they will stop wearying themselves in the pursuit of what is alien to the covenant, whether foreign alliances or pagan gods. But words of advice, no matter how compellingly or arrestingly put, are not heeded by an addict.

No longer do the people (contrast v. 23) seek to deny the facts of the situation. Such self-awareness might be construed as a hopeful sign, because recognising that there is a problem can be the first step towards dealing with it. But the speech here is probably to be understood as a prophetic representation of their attitude rather than as a direct quotation of what they actually said. They reject the good counsel that has been given them by admitting in effect that they are in the grip of an overwhelming impulse which cannot be gainsaid. **But you said, 'It's no use!'** (<√*yā'aš*, niphal 'to despair'; *IBHS* §40.2.5b). 'Useless!' is a cry of hopelessness and misery, rather than of defiance. The impulse to go after what they desire is so strong that no warnings of the dangers involved are of any avail. 'No, but' (*kî* after a negative) introduces the alternative course of conduct that they find so alluring: **I love foreign gods, and I must go after them.** Their addiction is such that there is no way they will be restrained. 'Love' contrasts with the commitment they once showed to the LORD (2:2) and which they ought still to have. 'Foreign gods' is a particular interpretation of 'strangers' (NRSV), outsiders (<√*zûr*, 'to be a stranger') who do not belong to the group with which the speaker is associated. As such, the reference may be either peoples ('foreigners', 30:8) or their gods (3:13). It is difficult to be certain whether religious or political overtones are dominant

20. The kethibh *wgwrnk* seems to be an obvious error. The only possible pointing seems to refer to *gôrēk*, 'threshing floor', which does not fit the context. The qere is *ûgərônēk*, 'and your throat', transposing the *resh* and *waw*.

here; possibly the ambiguity of the phrase is deliberately chosen to cover both. In either case Judah is seen to be wilfully intent on pursuing its own perception of what is for its good, having rejected the service of the LORD. But it was not freedom they had achieved; rather they were trapped in an even greater slavery.

6. Judah's Disgrace (2:26-28)

The consequences of the addiction of the people of God to what was prohibited by the covenant is set out in greater detail. (1) The people will experience disgrace because the evidence of their turning to the nature religion of Canaan is so evident (vv. 26-27a). (2) The irrationality and inconsistency of their behaviour is further shown by their attempt to invoke the help of the LORD in time of real crisis (vv. 27b-28).

26. As a thief is disgraced when (*kî* in a clause preceding the main verb to set out the circumstances in which it occurs) **he is caught**/ 'found'. The Hebrew concept of 'disgrace/shame' (<√*bôš*, 'to be ashamed') focuses more on the outward loss of status and reputation than on inward feelings (see on 7:19). If a thief who has taken another's property without their knowledge or consent is caught red-handed, or if it is a matter of his being traced at a later stage, he still may not in fact experience the embarrassment and shame he ought to feel about his conduct. However, his personal response does not prevent his situation from being one in which the clear evidence of his improper act leads to a loss of reputation and standing within society. This would be very obvious in the close-knit community structure of ancient society. So here shame here relates to disgrace and loss of reputation consequent upon Judah's open involvement in Baal worship and rejection of the LORD. **So the house of Israel is disgraced.**[21] The reference is not to the northern kingdom, as the mention of Judah in v. 28 clearly shows, but to the people of the south as the remaining representatives of the covenant community. They may not be embarrassed by their behaviour, but there is no doubt about their disgrace since their behaviour has been exposed for what it is. **They, their**

21. The hiphil of *bôš*, 'be ashamed, fall into disgrace', has two grammatical forms: (1) *hēbîš* has the expected causative sense 'be put to shame'; (2) *hôbîš*, as here, carries the sense not so much of finding oneself engulfed by a situation of disgrace as of bringing it upon oneself by one's own action (*TDOT*, 2:59). The NRSV translation 'shall be shamed' treats *hōbîšû* as a prophetic perfect, but that seems unnecessary. The perfect is used in a stative sense to indicate the condition that has already definitively come upon them.

kings and their officials, their priests and their prophets returns to the theme of v. 8, that there was an especial culpability on the part of those in leadership positions in the land. Their influence and conduct had set the negative note which the rest of society had readily adopted. Notice here the mention of 'kings'; if first uttered in Josiah's days, this would look back to Manasseh and Amon. Later in Jeremiah's ministry, the list of such kings would be expanded.

27. There then follows a scathing caricature of Baal worship. **They say** translates a participle *ʾōmərîm*, 'saying', which indicates habitual action, 'who keep on saying.' It is not one lapse that is in view but repeated involvement in illegitimate cults, where they were found saying **to wood, 'You are my father,' and to stone, 'You gave me birth.'** Though the description may be of pagan worship in general terms, where idols made of wood and stone are worshipped as the gods who are responsible for life, in this context the focus is clearly on Canaanite worship practices. The wood found at Canaanite shrines refers to a wooden pole or Asherah used to represent the female deity, and the stone to a standing stone associated with the male deity. The god of Canaanite religion was originally thought of as the one who had begotten the race, but later use of the term 'father' relates to protection and support of the worshipper (*TDOT*, I, 7). However, the main feature of the description is the ironic inversion of the references, 'You are my father' being addressed to the female deity symbolised by the wood, and 'You gave me birth'[22] to the male deity represented by the stone. Jeremiah deliberately puts them the wrong way round to mock these perverse beliefs and to show that there is no substance to them. Nonetheless the people engage in them, 'for' (*kî* introducing the reason for their perverse behaviour) those who turn from the living and true God readily become involved in what contradicts reason and is an affront to their humanness. **They have turned their backs to me, and not their faces.** Both *ʿōrep*, 'neck, the back of the body from the neck to the legs', and *pānîm*, 'face', are probably accusatives of limitation rather than objects after the verb (Joüon §126g), describing their rebellious gesture of complete dissociation from the LORD.

But as with so many who deny the existence or the supremacy of God, times of pressure reveal their inner inconsistency. **Yet when they are in trouble, they say** (an imperfect of past habitual activity, 'they would say' on repeated occasions, *IBHS* §31.3e), **'Come and save us!'** These singular imperatives are addressed to the LORD, urging him to

---

22. The kethibh represents *yəlīdtinî*, 'you gave me birth', whereas the qere suggests *yəlidtānû*, 'you gave us birth', but the change seems unnecessary.

'rise up', that is, to respond immediately, and save them (4:14; Ps. 3:8). Having neglected God in time of prosperity, their behaviour shows their remaining consciousness of the emptiness of Canaanite religion. Its great attraction lay in the fact that it imposed no moral restraints on their conduct, but when the going got rough the gods of Canaan were unable to provide real assistance and so the people were forced back to the LORD and the provisions of the covenant in an implicit recognition that there was a substantive reality behind the worship of the LORD that was lacking in their alternative faiths. However, their desperate turning to the LORD for help also showed that they considered him to be as indifferent to their misconduct as they were themselves.

28. But the lesson of such inconsistent behaviour must not be side-stepped. **Where then are the gods you** (masc. sing. in this verse) **made for yourselves?** It is not as if the evidence of their idolatrous worship suddenly vanished. To ask, 'Where are the gods?' is to ask for evidence of their power; it is to focus the discussion on their reality and effectiveness. They are challenged: **Let them come if they can save you when you are in trouble.** Furthermore it is not just a matter of their power. Consider their number; surely that will be the basis for adequate intervention on behalf of their devotees. **For** (*kî*) **you have as many gods as you have towns, O Judah.** In accordance with typical Canaanite practice each place had its own deity. 'One of the most difficult features of ancient mythologies for those who study them is the wide variety of often contradictory stories told of the same gods. This is only in part due to syncretism. Nature tends to be protean. As long as men worshipped its powers, they might well vary in their interpretation of them. It is only through revelation that we can obtain a unitary and coherent picture of God' (Ellison 1960:13).

Although it was basically the same nature forces that were being worshipped throughout the land, the various idols used in their worship led them to be conceived of in different ways in each place, and so Jeremiah mocks them as so many different deities. But surely because there are so many of them, their numbers will make up for any lack of power on the part of one.[23] However, no matter how long the string of zeros you add or multiply together, the result never changes from zero.

---

23. The LXX text, presumably on the basis of 11:13, adds at the end of the verse 'and according to the number of the streets of Jerusalem they sacrificed to Baal.' Although many interpreters favour it as being original here (e.g. Ellison 1960:13; Holladay 1986, 1:54), there is no Hebrew manuscript evidence to support such an insertion.

7. Why? (2:29-37)

The final address in the covenant complaint consists of the LORD's rebuttal of what the people have said in protesting their innocence. It would appear that they sought to justify themselves by bringing counter-accusations against the LORD (v. 29). While one cannot describe the passage as dialogue, the citations of the people's attitudes (vv. 30, 35) enable us to ascertain their confident and spiritually insensitive approach to matters. 'Why?' (2:29, 31, 36) re-echoes through the passage as God tries to induce the people to self-examination and bring them to realise the futility of their attitude and conduct.

29. Although they were deluding themselves in thinking they were innocent (v. 35), the people of Judah no doubt felt genuinely aggrieved at the charges Jeremiah was levelling against them. This prompted them to respond to the LORD's complaint by alleging that any breakdown in the covenant relationship was his fault. In the light of v. 30, it may be that they were remonstrating with the LORD by interpreting the chastisements he had brought on them, not as a heavenly rebuke intended to turn them back to the right way, but as divine incompetence: should not the covenant king protect his people? The LORD's question constitutes an indignant repudiation of such outrageous thinking. **Why do you bring charges against me?** 'Bring charges' (<√*rîb*) corresponds to the LORD's complaint in v. 9. The verb is an incipient imperfect, relating to a action already begun and continuing at the time of speaking (*IBHS* §31.3d). In this and the next verse 'you' is masculine plural. There was no substance to their complaint, as the evidence all pointed in the opposite direction. So the LORD does not permit any obfuscation of the fundamental issue. **'You have all rebelled against me,' declares the LORD.** 'Rebelled' (<√*pāšaʿ*), rather than 'transgressed' (NKJV), catches the right note. The word refers to a subject people's repudiation of their overlord's authority (v. 8). As rebels, they have no basis for accusing God of having acted counter to the terms of the covenant which they have repudiated.

30. The LORD then recounts what he had done to try to recall his errant people. Although the Greek translations represent substantially the same text as the Hebrew, two features of this verse ('your *sons*', rendered 'your people' by the NIV, and '*your* prophets') have caused sufficient uneasiness among commentators to lead some to emend it. But the text as it stands is quite intelligible. **In vain I punished your people.** 'Punish'/'strike' (<√*nākâ* hiphil, 5:3) is used of various disasters the LORD brought on his people when they broke the covenant

(Lev. 26:14-15; Deut. 28:15-68). They should have recognised his displeasure and turned back from their sin. The use of 'sons' rather than, say, 'fathers' indicates the intergenerational solidarity with which the people are being viewed (as in v. 2, 'your youth'). But incredibly they were not prepared to respond to the LORD's action. It was 'in vain' (*šāwʾ*), a word which designates what is ineffective, and often also what is consequently false and worthless because unable to live up to the hopes placed in it. It occurs five times in Jeremiah (also 4:30; 6:29; 18:15; 46:11). Here it denotes measures which proved ineffectual because the people were not prepared to react appropriately to their Overlord's action.

They did not respond to correction. 'Correction' (<√*yāsar*) may include both physical chastisement and verbal rebuke, and so provides a link to the next element of their rebellion because admonition on its own is insufficient to rectify the deteriorating relationship. The people had to accept and act on the criticism of their conduct, but they were not prepared to do this. So far were they from accepting the message of those who brought them the word of the LORD, that **your sword has devoured your prophets**. 'Your prophets' is an unusual expression, which might at first seem to indicate false prophets. But that does not fit the train of thought here. 'Your prophets' are the ones sent to them, the ones whose word they were obligated to respond to. Instead there was bitter persecution. This is usually assigned to Manasseh's reign (2 Kgs. 21:16), but the same attitude would be evinced later in Jehoiakim's treatment of Uriah (26:20-23). Although 1 Kgs. 18:4 suggests it was Jezebel who cut off the prophets of the LORD, Elijah's complaint in 1 Kgs. 19:10, 14 is that the people of Israel had slain the prophets. Here is the beginning of the belief that Israel as a whole is corporately responsible for the death of her prophets and must bear the guilt corporately (cf. 2 Chron. 36:15-16 with respect to ridicule). Their spiritual hardness and lack of discernment (Prov. 17:10) led the people throughout the centuries to react to those bearing the word of correction with savage intensity (Neh. 9:26; Matt. 23:37; Acts 7:52). **Like a ravening** (<√*šāḥat* hiphil, 4:7) **lion** likens them to a ferocious animal seeking to kill and destroy, from whom no mercy can be expected. This is an aspect of their behaviour that Jeremiah had not previously mentioned. Those who present themselves as tolerant of the beliefs of others frequently respond quite differently when exposed to the searching critique of divine truth. Then it is seen that their inclusiveness extends only to all varieties of error, not to the truth.

31. The word of exhortation with which v. 31 begins, **You of this**

generation, consider the word of the LORD, is treated by the NIV as part of the divine word Jeremiah is given to relay, but it may well be Jeremiah's own comment. Its authenticity has been challenged because the LXX has the more standard formula: 'Hear the word of the Lord: Thus says the Lord', but there is no good reason for adopting this. 'Consider'/'see' is unusual, but not impossible, with 'the word of the LORD' (cf. 23:18). The people of Jeremiah's own day might well have thought persecution of the prophets was a thing of the past, part of the excesses of Manasseh's reign. There had been a reformation under Josiah since then. But Jeremiah here emphatically brings the matter back to challenge them. The people are called on to consider the LORD's past goodness toward his own. There is a need for every generation to 'see', to consider afresh what God has already done, so that faith may be strengthened. 'Could Jeremiah have introduced this note deliberately, as he dictated his prophecies of an earlier generation to Baruch, in order that they might be seen by the later generation as on the point of fulfilment?' (Jones 1992:93).

The challenge is presented in the threefold question formula frequently used by Jeremiah (cf. v. 14; 8:22). **Have I been a desert to Israel or a land of great darkness?** The language recalls the time of the Exodus when the LORD had led them 'through the vast and dreadful desert' (Deut. 8:15). The wilderness was not of course literally a place of darkness. The word *ma'pēlyâ* occurs only here, and rabbinic analysis decomposed it into *ma'ăpēl*, 'darkness' and *yah*, 'the LORD', so as to mean 'darkness sent by the LORD' (*TDOT* #145f; *NIDOTTE* 1:480). The thought resembles that of v. 6, with the wilderness being a place that yielded no produce or comfort, and darkness signifying a time of disorientation and danger. That was not the destiny the LORD planned for his people. Rather he had led them through it to give them the bounty of Canaan, where they did not have to live in danger or deprivation. He had lavishly provided them with everything they needed, but with incredible blindness they did not acknowledge this (Hos. 2:8). The question has to be asked, **Why do my people say, 'We are free to roam;[24] we will come to you no more'?** The thought is similar to v. 20. In their ingratitude the people displayed a desire to go off and do as they pleased. They wanted the excitement and thrill of doing their own thing, and had no intention of ever coming back.

---

24. *rûd*, 'to wander, roam', occurs in the same sense in Judg. 11:37 and Hos. 11:12 [12:1]. 'We are lords' (NKJV) reflects a derivation from *rādâ*, 'to rule'. In either case the people are showing ingratitude and going their own way.

32. The theme of forgetfulness is taken further in v. 32. Two instances are cited where in human terms forgetfulness is unlikely. Looking back to Israel as the bride in v. 2, the question is posed, **Does a maiden forget** (a gnomic imperfect, referring to situations that occur over and over again, *IBHS* §31.3e) **her jewellery, a bride her wedding ornaments?** 'Maiden' (*bətûlâ*; 18:13) refers to someone of marriageable age. The jewellery would be silver or gold ornaments, and a source of considerable pride to their possessor. 'Wedding attire'/ornaments occurs only here and in Isa. 3:20, and seems to refer to special items of adornment (the idea conveyed is something bound on a woman, but precisely what is not clear) associated with a wedding (cf. Isa. 49:18). No woman forgets all that is involved in her wedding day, **yet my people have forgotten me, days without number.** They did not value the solemn covenant relationship they had entered into with the LORD. 'Days without number' probably indicates a long history of this forgetfulness rather than repeated occasions. The people had fallen into the very trap that they had been solemnly warned about (Deut. 8:11).

33. Lundbom (1997:98) argues that the poem of vv. 33-37 'can be shown to be one of the most fully and intricately balanced in the book', consisting of two longer stanzas (vv. 33-34; vv. 36-37) enclosing a half-length stanza (v. 35). In the first stanza two aspects of covenant forgetfulness are examined. Reverting to a feminine singular form of address, the prophet initially seems to be conveying congratulations to Judah with the words, **How skilled you are**[25] **at pursuing love!**, but in reality they are heavily ironic. 'Skilled' (*ṭôb*, 'good') carries no moral overtones, but indicates that the people have served their apprenticeship in these matters and are now master craftsmen in going astray. 'Love' refers back to v. 2, but here it is illicit love that is being spoken about, and that went beyond their affection for, and allegiance to, other gods. The Canaanite worship of nature and fertility gods, like many ancient pagan religions, relied on symbolic action and gesture to induce the gods to provide good health, fruitful harvests, offspring, or whatever other benefit was desired. It involved those who participated in such cults in sexual debauchery, but so knowledgeable were the LORD's people when it came to debasing themselves in the worship of such cults that **even**[26] **the worst of women can learn**

25. The imperfect in *mah-têṭbî darkēk*, 'What/how you do well with respect to your way', denotes an ongoing situation. NKJV translates it as 'Why do you beautify your way?'

26. 'Even' takes *lākēn* in an emphatic sense (*HALOT* 530; see on 5:2), but there is no difficulty in understanding 'therefore' as ironic (cf. NKJV, NASB).

from[27] **your ways.** As a consequence of the effort they had expended on the matter, they could pass on quite a few tips about this way of life to those who made it their trade, the cult prostitutes. Pagan worship had made such inroads into the life of Judah that she was leading the way in it.

34. But it is not just desertion of the religious norms of the covenant that was involved. Moral and social evils arose from the corrupting influence of acceptance of pagan lifestyles, which debased human life. **On your clothes**[28] **men find** (an indefinite use of the third person plural, *IBHS* §4.4.2) **the lifeblood of the innocent poor**. In 'lifeblood'/'blood of the life' *nepeš*, 'life', indicates the whole sentient being of an individual. The word originally seems to have denoted the throat (cf. v. 24 footnote), and developed a metaphorical application to the desires of a person before also being used to refer to the whole being of an individual possessed of life and particularly with overtones of weakness and vulnerability. In many contexts the word developed a pronominal sense and is equivalent to 'self'. The traditional gloss of 'soul' derives from Greek thought and introduces ideas which are foreign to the holistic Hebrew conception of the individual. 'Lifeblood' indicates that through bloodshed the poor are no longer alive.

The picture is one of flowing eastern robes with bloodstains on their hems because those who wear them have passed by scenes of violence or have been involved in the foul play. Perhaps the stains were not obvious to those wearing the robes, but their presence alerted others to where they had been. Whether the stains are real or metaphorical, the picture is one of misuse of power within society. While 'poor' may be used of those undergoing ill-treatment for their faith (Ps. 86:1), the reference here is probably to the poorer sections of society whose deaths are being caused through miscarriage of justice or through oppression (7:6; 22:3, 17; cf. Ps. 94:21). Other possible backgrounds to the thought are the practice of child sacrifice (19:4; Ps. 106:38), or perhaps Manasseh's persecution (2 Kgs. 21:16; 24:4). 'Innocent' (<√*nāqâ*) is not used absolutely, but refers to those who had

27. The kethibh *limmadtî*, 'you have taught', has the older spelling of the second feminine singular perfect, which is identical with the first person form. The qere gives the ordinary second singular feminine form *limmadt*. The translation is the same. (See on 2:20.)

28. The LXX (similarly Syriac) has *en tais chersi sou*, 'on your hands', reflecting a reading *bəkappak*, 'on your palms', rather than *biknāpayik*, 'on the edges of your robes'. The meaning is much the same. *kānāp* originally meant 'wing', and then became used of the flowing hem or edge of a robe.

not committed any offence for which they could be brought before the courts. The fact that they are innocent is brought out in the next clause **though you did not catch them breaking in** (<√*ḥātar*, 'to dig'),[29] which refers to forced entry through a wall. The word only occurs elsewhere in Exod. 22:2, 'If a thief is caught breaking in and is struck so that he dies, the defender is not guilty of bloodshed', and it is this regulation that is the basis for what is said here. If they had interrupted a thief at night digging through the brick wall of their house, and he had been killed in the ensuing fracas, there would have been extenuating circumstances for their conduct. But no such excuse was possible.

It is not immediately clear how the last words of v. 34, **Yet in spite of all this**, *kî ʿal-kol-ʾēlleh*, are to be related to the context. Their obscurity has given ample scope for the display of ingenuity by commentators and translators. The NIV rendering 'Yet in spite of all this' (similarly NASB and NRSV) makes reasonable sense of them by taking them with the following verse, 'Yet in spite of all this, you say, "I am innocent".'[30] Other translations adopt a different rendering of the previous line, and link the phrase to that: 'I have not found it by secret search, but plainly on all these things' (NKJV). Strangely it does not put 'plainly' in italics, though it is difficult to see where it is expressed in the text.

35. The central, shorter stanza starkly states the people's refusal to recognise what is wrong, and the LORD's inevitable response to such recalcitrance. **You say, 'I am innocent'** (<√*nāqâ,* niphal; cf. v. 34) emphasises their contention that they were exempt from judicial condemnation or penalty. They protest that their conscience is clear, and in doing so show up their lack of perception of what the LORD required of his covenant people. They further add with emphasis, 'indeed' (*ʾak*, 3:13), a particle used to introduce an additional statement which qualifies what has preceded. Here it denotes what made them certain of their innocence: they were in a right relationship with God. **He is not angry with me**/'his anger has turned from me' (NRSV) or, treating the verb as a prophetic perfect (see Introduction §7.2), 'his anger shall turn from me' (NKJV). 'Anger' is *ʾap*, the same word

29. The NKJV rendering 'I have not found it by secret search' treats *məṣāʾtîm* as a first person form and places a different interpretation on 'digging'.

30. This understands *kî* as introducing a contrast, and *ʿal* as indicating attendant circumstances so that it may be rendered 'in spite of' (BDB 754 (f)). This rendering does, however, suffer from the awkwardness of not really accounting for the *waw*-consecutive at the beginning of v. 35.

which Hebrew uses for ‘nose’ and so suggesting the heavy breathing of intense emotion. They seem to have quite misunderstood God’s providential dealings with them and considered there was nothing offensive in continuing to worship the LORD along with the Baals. It may be that they interpreted the evident decline of Assyria as a token of the LORD’s favour towards them, but if so, they were quite mistaken and instead they are warned of the imminence of divine action against them. **But I will pass judgment on you because you say, ‘I have not sinned.’** ‘Pass judgment’ (<√*šāpaṭ*, ‘to judge’) is a niphal participle which does not here indicate ‘plead my case’ (NKJV), but ‘execute justice’ (25:31). It would seem to indicate that the next, more formal, stage of proceedings is about to begin because the suzerain has not obtained a suitable response from his people through the complaint about which the prophet has notified them. Instead they maintained their innocence, saying they had not sinned (<√*ḥāṭāʾ*), that is, missed the mark or a path. In Judg. 20:16 the root is used in its most basic sense of those who could sling a stone ‘and not miss’. The same verb occurs in Prov. 19:2 in the expression ‘miss the way’. It refers to a failure to comply totally with any regulation or requirement, civil or spiritual. Here despite all that has been said to them the people continue to claim that their conduct meets the standards God has set for them.

36. The final stanza of the poem in vv. 33-37 reverts to the earlier theme of the inconstancy and inconsistency of Israel’s behaviour. **Why do you go about[31] so much, changing your ways?** It is difficult to determine the historical circumstances suggested by the words, **You will be disappointed** (<√*bôš*, v. 26) **by Egypt as you were by Assyria.** Certainly Ahaz had volunteered entering into a relationship with Assyria to counter the threat of the Syro-Ephraimite coalition (2 Kgs. 16:7-9), and that had only resulted in disillusionment and woe (2 Chron. 28:20-21). Perhaps now with the demise of the Assyrian empire, there were those who were promoting a policy of seeking help from Egypt. But that too is a policy doomed to disaster. The precise time of the original saying is subject to similar considerations to those applicable to v. 18, though here Egypt and Assyria are not viewed as contemporaneous options.

37. The beginning of the verse, **You will also leave that place**, is

31. The early versions read *tazēllî*, ‘belittle’, <√*zālal*, ‘be frivolous, despised’ for the MT *tēzlî* (<√*ʾāzal*, ‘disappear, go away’), and hence ‘Why do you treat it as of no significance to change your ways?’ The root *ʾāzal* is infrequent in the Old Testament, but common in Aramaic.

obscure, but presumably 'that place' is Egypt, and perhaps the idea is that the envoys who had gone on their behalf to seek assistance would depart frustrated. The next clause is introduced by *waw* plus a non-verb, indicating a set of accompanying circumstances (Joüon §159d): **with your hands on your head**. Craigie et al. (1991:44) point out that ancient Egyptian monuments depict this as the posture of prisoners of war (with their hands tied above their heads) and of those about to be slain. Egyptian help therefore would be presented as leading not just to shame in general but to captivity and death. The pronouns are feminine singular, and the people are being depicted as a young woman led off by her captors to an unknown fate. However, this gesture is here presented as accompanying departure from Egypt, not arrival there. It seems better therefore to interpret it as a general gesture of shame and deep sorrow (2 Sam. 13:19). Their envoys will be unable to conclude an agreement with Egypt and so they as the people's representatives will leave frustrated at having failed to achieve their aim. The ultimate reason for this was that a higher hand was at work in the situation. **For** (*kî*) **the LORD has rejected** (<√*mā'as*, 6:30) **those you trust**, the plural taking in many particular situations in which they have put their trust in others (Joüon §136g). **You will not be helped by them.** What the precise punishment was going to be did not matter so much. They had to grasp that it was divinely determined and therefore inescapable. This acted as a solemn warning to which Jeremiah's original audience should have responded. It also helped to explain to the remnants of the nation after the catastrophe had occurred how and why it was that the LORD had dealt in such a way with his covenant people.

In assessing the relevance of this chapter to current conditions we have to recognise that with the personalisation of religion that is prevalent nowadays, the focus of our thinking is generally on where an individual stands in relation to God. Here, however, we have what is primarily a national indictment addressed to the people as a whole and taking in individuals only as they are part of that nation. Undoubtedly there are aspects of Judah's position as the people of God that involved what is now thought of as two separate spheres, church and state, but that should not obscure the reality of national sin and of the corporate sin of the visible church of Christ on earth. Every generation is responsible for its collective lifestyle and the standards that are promoted by public policy. There is a recurrent need to assess national behaviour in the light of divine truth.

But it is not only the wider social and political arena that has to be scrutinised. It is imperative that the professing church also examines itself in the mirror of God's law. It is all too easy for the church to cloak itself in Christian garb while at the same time assimilating to the prevailing patterns and lifestyle of its age, and to be ready to utter pious phrases while losing hold of the fundamentals of the faith that gives them meaning. Unperceived discrepancies in actions and words can still lead to an assertion, 'I have not sinned', while the reality is quite otherwise. So the call for reassessment must still be heard and the response of repentance must still be urged.

B. PLEA FOR REPENTANCE (3:1-4:4)

The second division of Jeremiah's early ministry begins at 3:1 and extends to a bridge passage in 4:3-4 where it shades into the next division of his presentation. The main topic of this division is the need for repentance, which is largely explored through the metaphor of a broken marriage (resuming a theme already found in chap. 2). In its present form this material is shaped according to Jeremiah's concerns when he was composing the First Scroll, and he has so thoroughly integrated his former sayings that it is not possible to be certain about the form they originally had. The most obvious difference is between the prose of vv. 6-12a and vv. 14-18 and the poetry of the remainder of the passage. (The REB also treats v. 1 as a prose introduction, a view favoured by Craigie et al. [1991:47], but not common otherwise.) Scholars such as Bright (1965:25) took 3:1-5; 3:19-25; 4:1-4 as originally comprising a single unit, while others argued that the initial proclamation had been more substantially reshaped, e.g. it might have been 3:1-5; 3:19-20; 3:12b-13; 3:21–4:2 (Jobling 1978). There is often associated with this the view that the prose is less directly attributable to Jeremiah than the poetry. However, such hypothetical analyses fail to account for all the features of the passage, which is tightly integrated in its present form and can confidently be attributed to the work of Jeremiah in 605 BC when the prophet skilfully and movingly reworked material spoken on earlier occasions into a final plea that the people would return.

The early part of Jeremiah's ministry was a time of real spiritual choice for Judah. Outwardly the reform movement superintended by King Josiah provided a suitable religious climate for a true relationship with the LORD to flourish once more. But on their own, improvements to the Temple buildings and desecration of the sites of pagan worship did not ensure spiritual revival. For there to be reconciliation between Judah and the LORD heart change was required, and that would only come through deeper personal and spiritual reassessment. During the period of Josiah's reforms Jeremiah was led to see beyond the outward changes that were taking place and to proclaim the need for repentance. He was able to do this with complete sincerity. If the people responded as they should, then even though reconciliation seemed impossible (vv. 1-5), the way ahead was still hopeful because of the character of the LORD (v. 12), and in that case the outlook was extremely encouraging (vv. 14-18). The prophet had, however, to warn them that continued rebellion would issue in judgment (4:4). But such an outcome was as yet by no means inevitable. There was an openness not dissimilar to that described in Isa. 1:19-20, 'If you are willing and obedient, you will eat the best from the land; but if you resist and rebel, you will be devoured by the sword.'

One of the significant integrating features of the passage is the recurrence of key terms, which occur through poetry and prose alike, e.g. 'live as a prostitute' (*zānâ*, 3:1, 6, 9) and 'defiled' (*ḥānap*, 3:1, 2, 9). However, the main repetition involves variations on the remarkably versatile root *šûb* (3:1, twice; 3:7, twice; 3:8, 10, 11; 3:12, twice; 3:14, twice; 3:19; 3:22, three times; 4:1). Its basic meaning is 'to turn', that is, to move back to a point previously departed from (*HALOT* 1427-34). When used in a theological sense, it denotes turning back to God in repentance. However, it also came to be used for 'to apostatise', that is, to turn away from God and reject him. A significant additional use is when *šûb* functions in conjunction with another verb to convey the adverbial sense of 'doing again', that is, repeating the action of the second verb. By extensively playing on these meanings Jeremiah reinforces his message of the need for repentance.

1. What Follows Divorce? (3:1-5)

This section builds on the metaphor of the union involved in marriage as an analogy for the relationship between the LORD and his people. Hosea 1–3 had already developed this metaphor extensively, and Ezekiel would later continue such a treatment (Ezek. 16). In terms of Jeremiah's First Scroll the matter had already been set out in 2:2. But if there is marriage, then there is also the possibility of a breakdown in marital relationships, and beyond that there looms the possibility of divorce. In this scenario the LORD is the innocent party who has been betrayed by his unfaithful wife. Indeed, it is his unfaithful *wives* because the split of the northern and southern kingdoms had led to two nations/'denominations' both of which had a recognised claim to be considered the LORD's bride. This is used to point out that the southern kingdom of Judah should learn from the mistakes which had already brought ruin to Israel in the north.

However, the section begins by exploring the implications of divorce for a subsequent resumption of the marriage relationship, and so poses the question of how the people and the LORD may be reunited in the bond of the covenant. Initially the argument is not encouraging because, judged by human possibilities and even by the standards of the LORD himself in the Mosaic law, it does not seem possible.

1. The Hebrew text of this verse begins with the word 'saying', which cannot grammatically occur in isolation. Therefore either 'saying' has been wrongly inserted here, or other words have been omitted from the text. Some interpreters have sought to relate it back into the previous context, perhaps as a follow-on from 2:35, but this is improbable. Nor is it likely that the word has crept into the Hebrew by mistake. Its omission in the rendering of many early versions is understandable, because its function could not be readily determined. It seems to indicate that a fuller introductory clause, such as 'The word of the LORD came to me' has fallen out of the text at some early stage. It is of course impossible to say what the clause in fact was, though Naegelsbach (1871:46) adopts the proposal that the introductory phrase, 'During the reign of King Josiah, the LORD said to me', has been inadvertently transposed from this verse to v. 6. Whether or not this is accepted, it does seem reasonable to conclude from the presence of 'saying' that a new section starts here, despite the NIV quotation marks indicating that the divine speech is continuous.

The verse looks back to the ancient covenant provision of Deut. 24:1-4, whereby a man was permitted to give his wife a certificate of divorce and send her away (<√*šālaḥ*, piel 'send away'). If, however, she subsequently married another man, and he either divorced her in turn, or died, then her first husband was debarred from marrying her again (<√*šûb*, in the sense of repeat an action). This was to prevent abuse of the marriage bond. Otherwise a man could divorce and remarry with the connivance of the second man. In Israel there ought to have been no doubt that divorce was a serious and irreversible procedure.

The Deuteronomic proscription underlies the three rhetorical questions posed here. **If a man divorces** (<√*šālaḥ* piel, 'send away') **his wife and she leaves him and marries another man, should he return** (<√*šûb*)[32] to her again? The initiative both in marriage and

32. The LXX reverses the roles with the woman returning to the man, probably because the root *šûb* has overtones of repentance as well as return. But the MT is more consistent with the language of Deut. 24:4.

divorce rested with the man, though 'she leaves him' seems to imply that the woman is acquiescing in the arrangement. Jeremiah's hearers would have agreed in answering 'No', that was not what the Mosaic law required. This answer would have come to them all the more readily because of the recent emphasis on Deuteronomy in Josiah's reform. **Would not the land be completely defiled?**[33] The second question too would readily elicit a negative response, because it also looks back to Deuteronomy, where behaviour infringing the regulation was viewed as that which would 'bring sin upon the land the LORD your God is giving you as an inheritance' (Deut. 24:4). Here 'be completely defiled' (<√*ḥānap*, intensified by an infinitive absolute, GKC §113q) uses a different expression for the consequences on their offence from Deuteronomy, which effectively presents the same outcome using three terms 'defiled' (<√*ṭāmēʾ* hiphil, a weaker word; cf. 2:7), 'detestable' and 'bring sin'. 'Land' is not here being used simply as equivalent to 'society', as if to say that a society which is lax as regards the sanctity of the marriage bond is living in a way that is unacceptable to God (true though that is). The land of promise was the LORD's gift to his people, and it was part of their covenant duty towards him to treat his land with respect, by conducting themselves in a way of which he approved. Their attitude towards marriage and the pledge of trust and loyalty given in it was not merely a matter of individual, personal conduct. It reflected on their relationship with God through the view they took of their pledge to him and had repercussions for the nation as a whole.

The situation that has been posed as a legal problem in the abstract is now brought round to focus on Judah with 'you' (fem. sing.) being expressed twice in Hebrew for emphasis. **But you have lived as a prostitute** (<√*zānâ*), a broad term for sexual misconduct in general. The people had abandoned their pledges of troth to the LORD. Their misbehaviour was political, religious and sexual all at the same time. Seeking foreign alliances revealed mistrust in the LORD, and their religious affections had been attracted by the lure of the Baals, which involved not only the worship of false gods, but also illicit sexual practices. The religious prostitution of Baal worship meant that Judah's offence was compounded because she had consorted **with many lovers.** 'Lovers' (< *rēaʿ*, 'neighbour, friend, companion') is possibly a

33. The LXX has, 'Will not that woman be completely defiled?', perhaps misreading the Greek *gē*, 'land', as *gunē*, 'woman'. Possibly the translators in Egypt were no longer aware of the link between land and people in the changed circumstances of their own setting.

euphemistic usage, but the point is that, unlike the case referred to in Deuteronomy, she had not been remarried just once. Her conduct had been promiscuous because she considered any other form of alliance better than being faithful to the LORD and relying upon him.

The resolution of the argument of this verse may be grammatically construed as a command, 'Yet return to me' (NKJV), which would signify that despite the increased heinousness of Israel's behaviour, the LORD is still pleading with her. However, it is fairly certain that the construction is a formally unmarked question, **Would you now return to me?** 'Return' (*šôb*) is an infinitive absolute. Joüon (§123w) suggests it is the equivalent of an imperfect, 'Will you return?', but it probably indicates an indignant question (GKC §113ee). The people were failing to realise how untenable their situation had become. Just as there was no way in which a marriage broken off by divorce could subsequently be resumed, so too there was no provision within the covenant for Judah's behaviour to be condoned. The people were making light of the situation they had got themselves into, and the LORD is trying to bring home to them the gravity of their predicament.

In terms of Jeremiah's early ministry this at first sight seems incongruous. How can he be inviting the people to repent if he is also telling them that there is in effect no way to return? If the analogy cited is taken as a binding precedent, then Judah has been divorced, and the LORD cannot be expected to receive back one whose shame has become a matter of public notoriety. If the analogy from Deuteronomy is decisive, then there is no way forwards. But Deuteronomy has not been cited to provide a precise parallel. In terms of v. 8 the LORD had not yet given Judah a certificate of divorce by sending her into exile. Nonetheless, the comparison stresses the gravity of the people's plight. It also provides a dark background against which the graciousness of the LORD may shine more brightly. The impossible may after all be possible once the compassion of the LORD is operative (v. 12).

If Israel sought to come back to the LORD without reforming her conduct, it would show that her attitude towards the LORD and his covenant demands remained frivolous and irresponsible. Marriage and the family are essential elements in the structure of a stable society and neither can survive without ongoing mutual loyalty and trust. If one partner ignores and disparages the pledges of loyalty that have been exchanged, that places an intolerable strain on the relationship. It is on the verge of collapse. So too was Judah's relationship with the LORD.

2. There were two flaws in Judah's perception of her relationship with the LORD: she did not consider that she had done anything so very seriously wrong at all; and, even if there was a problem, it could easily be rectified. It is the first facet that is taken up in vv. 2 and 3 where Judah is confronted with her own behaviour so as to bring her to appreciate that the LORD's assessment of it is well justified. **Look up to the barren heights and see.** The word translated 'barren heights' (<√*šāpâ*, 'to sweep bare') caused considerable problems for early translators, and it cannot be said that the difficulties have been entirely resolved. However, it is now generally recognised as a description of a bare spot, probably without trees or vegetation (*HALOT* 1628). Although there are those who would argue that it describes a bare *plain*, it was more probably an elevated site (12:12; 14:6). In this context the reference is obviously to the high places where the sacred sites of Canaanite religion were located (2:20). Looking at any of them would soon establish what the people's conduct had been. **Is there any place where you have not been ravished?**[34] The prophet's language is forceful and explicit: it was designed to shock. Israel had been subject to inconsiderate ill-treatment from those to whom she had pledged allegiance, and she had not found her desertion of the LORD brought the benefits she had been expecting. **By the roadside you sat waiting for lovers.** Literally it is just an ambiguous *lāhem*, 'for them', but is resolved by many translations into 'lovers', though it may well be that 'anyone at all' is the thought. Israel had demeaned herself by aping the behaviour of prostitutes (Gen. 38:14-16; Prov. 7:12-15; Ezek. 16:25). So desperate was she to get away from the LORD, she would become involved with any who came by. **Sat like a nomad in the desert.** The word *ʿărābî* suggests the translation 'Arab' (RSV, REB, NIV margin), but modern use of that term means this translation is no longer considered appropriate, hence 'nomad' or 'Bedouin'. This phrase has traditionally been understood as a picture of marauding tribesmen waiting in ambush for any who would pass by their way, but that imparts a measure of aggression and initiative to Judah that is lacking in context. More plausible is the suggestion that the Bedouin tribes of the desert would wait near the trade routes for passing caravans to whom they could sell their wares. This would fit in with Israel waiting for any who would pass by, to whom she could sell her favours.

The conclusion to be drawn is found at the end of v. 2: **You have defiled the land with your prostitution and wickedness.** 'Vile

34. The kethibh *šuggalt*, 'you have been ravished', was considered too strong and vulgar by the Massoretes, who substituted for it the qere *šākabt*, 'you lay down' (cf. NKJV).

harlotry' (RSV) takes this as an instance of hendiadys, but a distinction is probably to be made between 'prostitution' as their specific offences in Canaanite religion and 'wickedness' being their attitudes and conduct in general. 'Defiled' (<√*ḥānap* hiphil, 'cause to be defiled') looks back to v. 1. Again it points out that the consequences of their actions were not confined to the individuals involved. The prevalence and toleration of such behaviour impacted on their relationship with the LORD and so affected the land as a whole.

3. One consequence of their moral delinquency in its national impact is then specified: the LORD had afflicted the land with drought. We do not know when this took place, but Jeremiah does refer to other droughts later on (12:4; 14:1-6). It was one of the many curses that had been forecast as a consequence of covenant disobedience (Deut. 28:22). **Therefore** ('and') **the showers have been withheld, and no spring rains have fallen.** 'Showers' refers to rain in general as providing water for crops, while the 'spring rains', or late rain, refers to the final rain of the rainy season. This fell in March and April, and was vital to a successful harvest in Palestine because without it the yield of crops would be severely diminished in quality and quantity. That was the very thing the rites of Baal worship were supposed to prevent, and the drought was therefore not an arbitrary divine affliction but one that showed how ineffective the Baal rites were and challenged the fundamental perceptions of Judah's religious delusion.

But such providential signs of divine displeasure failed to bring about the desired result. **Yet you have the brazen look of a prostitute** (*'iššâ zōnâ* clearly refers to one whose 'profession' is prostitution). 'Brazen look'/'forehead' describes the appearance of an individual who has no embarrassment and is contemptuously obstinate in defying public standards of conduct. We do not know how this was associated with the forehead; it may have been by being uncovered. **You refuse to blush with shame** (<√*kālam* niphal). The root *kālam*, 'to be disgraced, humiliated', generally occurs in conjunction with the root *bôš*, 'to be ashamed', which describes the experience or condition of loss of honour and position as a result of sinful conduct, defeat or distress. It would involve more than 'blushing'. What was looked for from Judah was inner acknowledgment of how their conduct had brought shame on them. But the people had lost her capacity to reflect and learn, even to care. Without this sense of shame there would be no turning to the LORD in true repentance that leads to a restored relationship.

4. Their shameless attitude is illustrated in this verse which also picks up on the second part of the application of the illustration begun in

v. 1—the prevalence in Judah of the view that it was an easy matter to return to the LORD. They had come to him (probably in the Temple) and used the words and phrases of religion with ease. **Have you not just called**[35] **to me, 'My Father, my friend from my youth'?** 'Just' renders *mēʿattâ*, 'from now on', but combined with a perfect verb some other understanding seems to be needed, such as 'from now' or 'just now'. There is nothing in the text to make clear whether this reflects pledges of loyalty given in Josiah's reformation or if it is a more general reference to the speech used in worship. Though the use of 'father' as a description of God goes back to the time of Moses (Exod. 4:22) and occurs elsewhere (Isa. 63:16; 64:8), it was generally avoided because it was liable to be perverted in the light of the Baal cults into the notion of physical derivation (as can be seen in 2:27). It is therefore possible to see this use here as tainted with the thinking of Baalism. But given that the LORD acknowledges they have called to him, it may well be that what is described was intended as a proper act of Temple worship. Though there is no recorded instance of the use of the phrase in the cult, it is the basis of the entreaty in Isa. 63:7–64:12. The problem here is that though the words are formally correct, they are uttered without true heart loyalty. 'Father' was primarily an acknowledgment that they owed their existence as a nation to him (Deut. 32:6, 18). On that basis their respect for him should have taken concrete expression in acts of obedience. Since the father/son relationship preceded the Exodus, it contained within itself an element of permanence, which gave grounds for hope even within a ruined covenantal situation. But God's fatherly relationship with them was being misused and presumed on by their rebellion and faithlessness. 'Friend (*ʾallûp* indicates one who is known and familiar) from youth' is a phrase to describe a husband ('partner of her youth' Prov. 2:17; it is parallel with *rēaʿ*, 'neighbour', in Mic. 7:5). It may convey the idea of guide and adviser. Here there is hidden apostasy: they protest their loyalty, but their outward actions will not suffice to cover up the heart defection that has already taken place.

5. Their speech to God was one that traded on his benevolence, and did not rightly appreciate the extent of the breach in relationship. The people ask two questions which expect negative answers. **Will you always be angry?** changes the Hebrew 'Will he always be angry?' in the interests of English idiom where such a transition from second to third person is unnatural. Alternatively, there may in fact be a change

35. The kethibh *qārāʾtî* is the old second person feminine singular form (and not a first person form) of the perfect. The qere gives the normal form *qārāʾt*.

from address to God to speech about him. In either event the people are treating God as a capricious monarch who has to be humoured. 'Be angry' (<√*nāṭar*, 'to keep, watch over') is often used of maintaining an attitude (Lev. 19:18). **Will your wrath continue for ever?** Literally, 'Will he guard/maintain ⌞it⌟ for ever?' If we interpret these questions as arising in the time of drought (v. 3), then the people are almost challenging the LORD with caprice and unpredictability. This is not the language of those who acknowledge their own wrongdoing.

This is how you talk[36]**, but you do all the evil you can** treats what precedes as hypocritical speech. Approaching God correctly requires more than having the right words. There must also be appropriate conduct, which involves a realignment of total life activity in covenant loyalty and sincerity. Despite what they have said, the actions of the people speak louder than their words. They are as far off from God as ever.

The concluding words of the verse are more literally, 'Look! you have spoken and have done evils and you were able' (<√*yākōl*, 'to be able, prevail or endure')[37], and so there are alternative translations such as 'have done evil things, and you have had your way' (NASB), or 'you have done evil and gone unchallenged' (REB). Taking 'you have spoken' as a characteristic perfect (as in the NIV), the translation might well be, 'This is how you talk and do evil, and are able ⌞to go on doing so⌟.' Because of their persistent refusal to accept that they were in the wrong, the situation is going to get worse, not better!

The people had radically failed to recognise the unique character of God and the implications that had for their covenant relationship with him. They saw nothing incongruous in placing him alongside other deities as one worthy of worship; in effect their thinking had become conformed to that of their polytheistic environment. What is more, mere talk of devotion, even of repentance, will not suffice to establish a proper relationship with the LORD. What he demands in relation to himself and what he requires from his people proceed from what he is unchangeably within himself. Consequently his requirements are non-negotiable. The only appropriate response was humble and complete acceptance.

---

36. The qere *dibbart* again corrects an old style second feminine singular perfect form, *dibbartî* as given in the kethibh.

37. *wattûkal*, 'and you were able', looks like a masculine rather than a feminine form, *wattûklî*. But there are occasions when the distinctive feminine form is avoided (GKC §§47k, 69r, 145t).

2. The Greater Sin (3:6-10)

This section is written in prose rather than poetry, a feature which is commonly taken to indicate the activity of someone other than Jeremiah. Although acknowledging that this passage is subtly woven into the theme of the chapter as a whole, Jones argues that, 'We may suppose that when the exact wording of a poetic oracle was not remembered, it was natural to give its substance in prose. More probably prose was the means of expression normal to Baruch and his successors as they gave the content of their master's work in their own words. There is no reason to suppose that this chapter ever existed in any other written form' (1992:99). Others identify Baruch's successors more precisely as the Deuteronomistic school whose reapplication of Jeremianic material gave rise to the sermonic prose material in Jeremiah (Nicholson 1970:10-16). But there is every reason to suppose that Jeremiah was as skilled in writing prose as Baruch was, and capable of using either prose or poetry as the occasion warranted. It is probable that the difference between prose and poetry was not as significant then as it is in modern western culture. Certainly there is no evidence to establish what the significance of the distinction was to Jeremiah and his contemporaries. Furthermore, eastern styles of argumentation do not always conform to what the western mind considers logical. The text is therefore best interpreted as coming from Jeremiah himself, as being in prose for reasons we are no longer able to determine, and as incorporated by him into this section when he wrote the First Scroll in 605/4 BC.

The comparison in this section between Israel and Judah is the basis of an object lesson for Judah from the experience of her sister, the northern kingdom, whose faithlessness resulted in her ruin. Nothing could have made clearer to Judah what awaited her if she persisted in her current course than the view to the north. What more compelling motive could there be for Judah to reassess her position and change her conduct! Whatever she did, Judah should avoid the path that Israel had gone down.

6. The introductory note, **During the reign of King Josiah, the LORD said to me,** is not to be dismissed as late editorial addition. It does not seem to mark the start of a major section of the prophecy, because the text through to 4:4 follows the themes of *šûb*, 'return/repent' and of divorce. The note itself is a mark of the way Jeremiah assembled his material, presumably from written records that he had made at various stages of his ministry. It is not, however, clear when in the reign of Josiah this revelation was first given, but it might well be prior to

622 BC during Josiah's earlier attempts at reform, at a time when the people were not responding fully. The attention paid to the territory of the former northern kingdom of Israel by Josiah between his twelfth and eighteenth years (629/28–623/22 BC; 2 Chron. 34:5) may have given comparisons with the north greater immediacy. One other feature of this introduction that is somewhat unusual is the fact that it is not followed by an injunction to make this message known to the people. It may be that was just taken for granted, but it is at least possible that this section incorporates what was originally information for the prophet himself, and only later made public. As he brought together the material for the First Scroll, Jeremiah noted when this message in particular originated to indicate that the wrong attitudes of the people were no new problem, but had existed even at a time when they thought they were progressing under Josiah.

In the section from v. 6 to v. 10 we find the LORD addressing the prophet. **Have you** (masc. sing.) **seen what faithless Israel has done?** *Hă*, the interrogative particle, may be used with an exclamatory force before *rā'îtā*, 'have you (masc. sing.) seen!' (Joüon §161b). The designation 'Israel' can occasion difficulty as to whether it represents the northern kingdom of the ten tribes, or whether it draws attention to the privileged status of the southern kingdom as the remaining representatives of the true people of God, or indeed whether it encompasses all the covenant people of God whatever their origin. Here, however, there need be no difficulty because the contrast with Judah shows it to be the northern kingdom that is in view. Jeremiah is invited to consider the behaviour that Israel displayed.

'Faithless Israel' does not quite catch the significance of *məšubâ yiśrā'ēl*, where we do not have the usual noun plus adjective combination, but adjective plus noun, with the adjective lacking the article which as an attributive adjective it would ordinarily have in connection with the proper name Israel. It is effectively a title that is being given to the north, 'Apostasy' (GKC §132b). Israel is the virtual embodiment of apostasy and defection. *məšubâ* is a noun derived from the root *šûb*, and denotes 'falling away, backsliding, apostasy', that is, rebellion against the covenant requirements of the LORD by deserting his path and going back to a life of disobedience.

The aspect of Israel's behaviour that is singled out to substantiate this allegation is that **she has gone up on every high hill and under every spreading tree and has committed adultery there.** 'Has gone up' is the participle *holəkâ*, 'going', and this implies such action was her habitual practice, not just something done on one occasion. The phrases referring to Baal worship are similar to those in 2:20, except that 'mountain' (NKJV) is substituted for 'hill' (though no change is shown in NIV or NRSV). The concluding clause is literally 'and you (fem. sing.) committed prostitution' (cf. GKC §75ii). It is unfortunate that the NIV uses 'committed adultery' here to render *zanâ* (v. 1). There is a different root, *na'ap* (cf. v. 8), for breach of the marriage bond, but the NIV does not maintain the distinction between them.

7. The divine reaction to Israel's conduct may be interpreted in two ways. It might be taken as a summary of the prophetic message sent to the north, pleading that she truly repent. 'I said, after she had done all these *things*, "Return to me" ' (NKJV). Alternatively, the emphasis may be on divine long-suffering in the expectation that after Israel had worked her rebelliousness out of her system and had become disillusioned with its emptiness and futility, she would come to her senses and return to the LORD: **I thought that after she had done all this she would return to me.** 'She would return' (*tāšûb*<*šûb*) is not an imperative in form, but an imperfect, and may be translated in either fashion. However, in the approach adopted by the NKJV the verb is somewhat removed from the words of the divine invitation. Although the verb 'thought' (<√*'āmar*, to say) does ordinarily denote speech, it can also indicate internal speech, that is, thought (see also v. 19), and this seems preferable since on the NIV approach the content of the thought begins immediately after the verb without the intrusion of an additional clause. The LORD in his role as the offended husband is musing with Jeremiah over his past hopes for reconciliation with Israel his unfaithful wife. It is clear that it was not her treacherous behaviour that was the ultimate obstacle in the way of rapprochement but her continuing intransigence.

But she did not (*wəlō'-šābâ* <√*šûb*), that is, 'she did not return'. Again we have the use of the 'return/repent', but because of Israel's obstinate insensitivity that was not to be. However, what happened in the north should have conveyed a clear warning to the south. **And her unfaithful sister Judah saw**[38] **it.** 'Unfaithful', *bāgôdâ* <√*bāgad*, 'to act deceitfully/treacherously/unfaithfully' (for the form of the word, cf. GKC §84ᵃk), refers to betrayal not only in the marriage relationship, but also in covenantal relations generally (3:20). It is a somewhat stronger word than 'apostate', as is perhaps brought out by the rendering 'treacherous' (NKJV). There is no play in the Hebrew between '*faithless* Israel' and '*unfaithful* Judah', though 'unfaithful', like 'faithless' in v. 6, is also used as virtually a title, 'the unfaithful one,

38. The kethibh is *wattir'eh*, the fuller later form for the *waw*-consecutive imperfect. The qere has the regular contracted form *wattēre'*.

Judah' (*TDOT* 1:470-73). The destinies of the two sisters were later to form the basis for the extended portrayal in Ezek. 23.

'Sister' is a reminder of the common origin of the two kingdoms. But despite their links Judah learned no lessons from what had occurred in the north. Up to the time of the capture of the northern kingdom, Judah in the south had remained relatively loyal in her espousal of Yahwism, but not long after the fall of the north the horrendous years of Manasseh's long reign saw Judah fall far away from the LORD (see Introduction §3.4). The reform movement under Josiah seems to have been accompanied by a popular feeling of superiority over the north, which is here combated because Judah had drawn the wrong conclusion that she was exempt from her sister's fate.

8. I gave faithless Israel her certificate of divorce[39] and sent her away because of all her adulteries. Yet I saw that her unfaithful sister Judah had no fear; she also went out and committed adultery. The structure of the verse is not immediately clear, and some understand it of what Judah saw, rather than the LORD. However, the manuscript evidence for reading *wāttēre*ʾ, 'and she saw', (so NRSV, REB) is slight. The NIV delays *wāʾēre*ʾ, 'and I saw', which begins the Hebrew verse, until after the description of background circumstances, understanding what the LORD saw was not what he himself had done, but Judah's reaction to it—or rather, lack of a suitable reaction. This is probably correct, though it does obscure the contrast between what Judah saw at the end of v. 7, and what the LORD saw. The action that the LORD had taken against Israel was to give her a certificate of divorce (Deut. 24:1) and to send her away from the land of promise ('sends her from his house', Deut. 24:1) where he was near to his people (Deut. 4:7). The ground for the divorce was her repeated spiritual adulteries, from the root (*nāʾap*) used in the Ten Commandments (Exod. 20:14) to refer to a breach of the marriage bond, specifically having sexual intercourse with the spouse or betrothed of another. But the capture and deportation of Samaria had not the impact they should on the south. Judah 'had no fear' does not deny that events in the north had traumatised the south. There is no doubt that Judah was badly shaken with fears for her own safety and survival. However, Judah, the one who is treacherous in her relationship with the LORD, had not learned from the fate of the north that she should display

39. *kərituteyhā* seems to combine the singular noun *kərîtût*, 'divorce', with a plural style pronominal suffix; GKC §91 l lists this as an anomaly. An alternative understanding found in *HALOT* 497 is that there is another noun form *kərîtâ* here used in the plural.

exclusive fealty towards him. Instead she also followed a similar course of conduct, committing spiritual prostitution (<√*zānâ*)—and doing so despite the warning evident from the history of the north.

9. Because[40] **Israel's**/'her' **immorality** (<√*zānâ*) **mattered so little to her, she defiled**[41] **the land and committed adultery with stone and wood.** Who is being spoken of? The flow of thought from v. 8 would suggest that 'she' and 'her' refer to Judah, but the connection into v. 9 favours a reference to Israel, which the translators of the NIV adopt, inserting 'Israel' at the start of the verse. The thought of the beginning part of the verse is also problematic. The word *qōl*, rendered 'little' in the NIV, may be taken as a defective spelling of *qôl* ('sound, noise'); hence 'fame' (AV margin), that is 'report' (Naegelsbach 1871:49), or perhaps used pejoratively, 'the racket' (Keil 1873, 1:89). Hence, 'it came to pass through the report of her immorality she defiled the land'. However, the prevalent interpretation of the expression is to derive it from the root *qālal*, meaning 'something light', and indicating 'her casual prostitution' (REB, cf. NKJV), or else the offhand way in which she dismissed her conduct as something trivial. But it was not, and the land was defiled in God's sight because Israel had 'committed adultery' (<√*nāʾap*, v. 8) by her involvement in Baal worship. For 'stone and wood', see on 2:27.

10. In spite of all this refers to Israel's behaviour at the pagan shrines and the resultant spiritual pollution of the land as well as to the judgment that God sent on them for their disloyalty. **'Her unfaithful sister Judah did not return** (<√*šûb*) **to me with all her heart, but only in pretence,' declares the LORD.** Ellison (1960:113) maintains that it is questionable if 'return' is an appropriate rendering and favours 'turn' instead because the Hebrew 'thinks less of distance and more of disloyalty and disobedience.' He also considers that there is no reason in v. 12 for not bringing out the full force and inner meaning of the word by rendering it 'repent'. There was a turning to the LORD in the land but not 'with all her heart' (24:7; 29:13; 32:41), a phrase often used in Deuteronomy to indicate an unfeigned and total spiritual

---

40. Unusually the verse begins *wəhāyâ* (*waw* plus perfect) and not *wayhî* (*waw*-consecutive imperfect). The use of the perfect may indicate a continuing past state (GKC §112ss), or an event going on at roughly the same time so that this is a further description of Israel's behaviour before 722 BC.

41. The MT reads *watteḥĕnap*, the qal of *ḥānap* (v. 1), 'she was defiled', presumably taking the next phrase as 'with/along with the land'. But there is versional evidence (generally accepted by English translations) that the consonants should be pointed as a hiphil, *wattaḥnēp*, 'she defiled'.

commitment (e.g. Deut. 4:29; 6:5). 'But only (*kî 'im*) in pretence' introduces the word *šeqer*, 'deception, a lie' (5:2), which Jeremiah uses repeatedly in his critique of Judah's religion and conduct. Here it indicates that repentance, which is normally viewed with approval, was not on this occasion all that it should have been. What Judah professed was a mere sham because there was no underlying heart commitment, the reference presumably being to the superficiality of Josiah's reformation. 'Declares the LORD' marks the close of this section.

Jeremiah has been told of the significance of the events that took place in the north and the fact that Judah has not learned all that she should have from them. There is the clear implication that Judah faces the same fate if she does not learn the lesson, but even so there is no direct statement of approaching judgment. When Jeremiah passes on to the people the substance of what has been revealed to him, it is still the case that his aim is to bring the people to a right understanding of their spiritual situation rather than to present a message of inevitable and impending doom.

3. Repent and Return (3:11-13)

Though this section is composed of prose (v. 11-12a) and poetry (v. 12b-13), it is a unit in its theme, which surprisingly seems to contain a call to repentance addressed to Israel, the northern kingdom that had been swept from the map over a century before. Scholars have struggled to find an adequate background against which to hear these words. Some, such as Bright (1965:26) and Holladay (1986, 1:118), envisage Jeremiah engaging in a preaching mission to the north, possibly associated with Josiah's interest in that area (2 Kgs. 23:15-20; 2 Chron. 34: 6-7; 35: 17-18). Others, such as Carroll (1986:145), consider it more appropriate to relegate this passage to the post-exilic era and take as reflecting the tensions and conflicts that existed then. While a northern ministry for Jeremiah is not impossible, it seems best to view Jeremiah's ministry as concerned with the south and using Israel as a means of inducing spiritual reassessment in Judah (McConville 1993:33-41). What he is commanded to do is not to go to the north, but to engage in prophetic symbolism (see on 13:1) by preaching towards the north (v. 12).

The message of this section is a further attempt to make clear to all what the pathway to blessing entails—and that is repentance. These verses present the essence of Jeremiah's teaching on the subject, showing that reconciliation between the repentant and the LORD is a possibility only because of the character of God, and that it is not a formal or automatic fact but requires acknowledgment of guilt.

11. The LORD said to me marks the beginning of a new section, particularly after the 'declares the LORD' with which v. 10 ends. What was related to the prophet, however, was a summary of the verdict of the previous section: **Faithless Israel is more righteous than unfaithful Judah.** 'Is more righteous' translates, *ṣiddəqâ napšāh* (< *nepeš*, 2:34), 'she has justified herself'. The piel verb may have a delocutive sense here, indicating Israel's action in presenting her situation, 'she has declared/shown herself righteous' (*IBHS* §24.2g). The judgment is not based on any absolute standard of righteousness. Israel's guilt could not, and was not being, denied. But Israel has been shown to be held in higher esteem in the divine court than Judah. Judah had possessed greater spiritual privileges than Israel because of the Jerusalem Temple and the relative purity of worship there. Judah had been more favourably circumstanced than Israel in that she had the example of the northern kingdom to learn from. Her conduct was therefore more despicable because she had sinned against greater light. What was more, not only had she engaged in syncretistic religion as Israel had done, Judah had pretended to turn to the LORD, but her repentance was feigned and insincere. It is this last factor in the conduct of treacherous and deceptive Judah that decisively brought her lower than Israel in the LORD's esteem.

The verdict of v. 11 seems designed to undermine the superior attitude that Judah seems to have adopted towards the north. After all, it was the kingdom of Israel that had been exiled in 722 BC, and Judah had been miraculously preserved from such devastation at the hands of Assyria in 701 BC. The south also had the Temple and the Davidic dynasty: did that not give them security? Was not the territory to the north now inhabited by a mixture of peoples with no true concept of religion at all? Was there really anything that they should be expected to learn from the history of the north? However, as their situation is adjudged to be in fact worse, the LORD's dealings with the north really presented them with much food for thought.

12. On this basis the prophet is commanded to address Israel. **Go, proclaim this message towards the north**. 'The north' represented the direction from which disaster was going to come (1:14; 4:6; 6:1, 22), and it was also the place to which the Israelites had been taken in exile (3:18; 16:15; 23:8; 31:8). But in this action of prophetic symbolism Jeremiah seems to be directed to turn away from his audience (at the Temple?) and go to a north-facing gate of the courtyard or perhaps of the city and speak from there. 'Northwards' rather than 'in/to the north' does not so much suggest a northern ministry of Jeremiah as point to the posture of the prophet as he speaks in Jerusalem. In effect the people hear him speak to the north, and are left to work out the implications of what is said for themselves.

The message is a summons to repentance. **'Return, faithless Israel,' declares the LORD.** This is a play on *šûb*, 'to turn/return' (see comment on v. 10), used in the sense of 'faithless'/'backsliding' in relation to Israel and also to give the command to 'return'. Bright tries to bring out the wordplay in *šûbâ məšubâ yiśrā'ēl* with 'Come back, backsliding Israel' (1965:22). But in what sense are they to 'come back'? If it is viewed as geographical relocation from exile, then we would have to suppose that Jeremiah conducted a mission in Mesopotamia. The emphasis is, however, on the spiritual response of a return in repentance, as can be seen from the fact that Israel is designated 'faithless', not 'exiled'. 'Return' is a masculine second person imperative so that the analogy of divorce has receded somewhat. The invitation to the north, both those remaining in the land and those exiled from it, constituted a graphic presentation to Judah of the LORD's willingness to be reconciled with his people no matter what the circumstances, but it has to be on his terms not theirs. This invitation would, of course, take on a deeper significance for Jeremiah's audience when he issued the final edition of his prophecy after the fall of Jerusalem.

I will frown on you no longer, literally, 'I will not let fall my face against you (masc. pl.)' (Gen. 4:5-6; Job 29:24), shows that the LORD will lift the sentence that had been imposed on them. It is not an attempt to say that the sentence was misguided in the first place, but is rather an indication that the punishment for their waywardness has been exhausted. **For** (*kî*) shows that the change in the LORD's attitude towards them is not capricious, but flows from what he is in himself: **I am merciful.** *Ḥāsîd* ('merciful') is only rarely employed with respect to God (Ps. 145:17), as the one whose actions are characterised by *ḥesed*, 'steadfast love' (2:2). This raises the question of how we are to conceive of the divine *ḥesed*. Does it arise out of the covenant and reflect God's commitment to his people even when they have abandoned him? Or, is his *ḥesed* an aspect of his love, which exists prior to the covenant, indeed which gives rise to, and expresses itself in, the covenant? (For a useful summary of various views, see *TWOT* #698.) The way forwards will not be found in any human achievement; it is only possible because of the character of God. Israel's inexplicable and chronic unfaithfulness is outweighed by the LORD's incomprehensible and steadfast love which acts in terms of perceived need, not perceived demerit. **I will not be angry** (<√*nāṭar*, v. 5) **for ever.** The LORD's anger is proportioned to the offence. The same dependence on the LORD's willingness not to retain his anger for ever which gave the people of Judah a false sense of confidence is offered as the basis of Israel's hope of being reunited, redeemed and restored if they truly repent.

This call to return raises the fundamental question of how it can be reconciled with the analogy of the first part of the chapter where the divorce is represented as irrevocable. If the LORD has divorced his people by sending them away into exile, then the argument seems to be that the marriage relationship has come to an end. But here backsliding Israel is still addressed as Israel and invited to return. The link had not been severed, merely put into abeyance. Many have assumed that this betrays the interests and perspectives of a later editor, and does not reflect what Jeremiah said at all. But the difference in viewpoint is not great, and it does reflect the problem posed by ruptured covenant relationships. Is there any future for the party who has violated the covenant relationship? Have they not forsaken everything? Their future is resolved not by anything that they on their own initiative can do to ingratiate themselves into the favour of the Overlord, but solely by his good pleasure. But does not this undermine the basic analogy of the metaphor in vv. 1-5, because the point is that in Israelite law the husband was not permitted to take his wife back if she had been divorced and become another man's? However, the LORD is not bound by legal protocol. Yet the restoration even of those who have truly recognised that their rebellious conduct led to their downfall can never be treated as a foregone conclusion. It awaits the good pleasure of the covenant king; the basis for hope is that he is the one who is merciful.

13. Restoration to divine favour does, however, require that those who have sinned against the LORD recognise their error. **Only** translates the emphatic particle *ʾak* (2:35), which may serve to reinforce a previous statement or be used, as here, in a restrictive sense to introduce a qualification to what has gone before. The experience of divine mercy awaits their contrite acceptance that they have done wrong. The address in **acknowledge your guilt** is feminine singular. 'Acknowledge' (<√*ydʿ* 'to know'; 'consider', 2:23) points to Israel's need for serious reflection and spiritual honesty regarding herself before God. For 'guilt' see on 2:22. 'For', *kî*, introduces the three grounds of their culpability. (1) **You have rebelled against the LORD your God** with 'against the LORD your God' preposed for emphasis. Israel had been taught to think of her relationship with the LORD in terms of the covenant, which used the language and institutions of the political arrangements of ancient emperors with their subject peoples as a structure for understanding what the LORD required of them. The basic charge against them is that they have rebelled (2:8, 29), that is, they have repudiated the terms of the covenant they entered into and in doing so they have dishonoured him. (2) **You have scattered your favours to foreign gods under every spreading tree.** 'Scattered your favours', literally 'ways', is a euphemistic expression with sexual undertones, referring to their behaviour in Baal worship (Thompson 1980:197, 201; Holladay 1986, 1:59, 119-20; see also Ezek. 16:15, 33). For 'foreign' in reference to gods, see on 2:25, and for 'spreading tree' as a site of orgiastic worship, see on 2:20. (3) You **have not obeyed me.**[42] 'No less than 13 times the prophet declares that the people have not heeded the voice of God, a commonplace expression deeply woven into the fabric of his prophecy' (*NIDOTTE* 3:900). The covenant with the LORD required compliance with his commands no less than an international treaty with a human emperor set the parameters for the behaviour of subject peoples. Israel's lack of allegiance to the LORD revealed itself in disobedience. **Declares the LORD** again marks the end of a prophetic message.

4. The Blessings of Repentance (3:14-18)

This passage, which is generally but not universally treated as prose, presents the future positively. Questions inevitably arise as to its time of origin and of incorporation into this chapter. The difficulties seem to increase in v. 18 which mentions Judah returning from exile. Before treating this as a later insertion, either by Jeremiah himself or by his post-exilic editors, it is better to try to interpret it as a part of the First Scroll of 605/4 BC. It continues the theme of indirectly urging the people of Judah to repentance by presenting to them what the LORD is prepared to do for Israel. The envisaged restoration of Israel might well have made them envious (Rom. 11:11, 14), and stirred them up from their spiritual lethargy. It is possible to use carrots as well as sticks to provoke a spiritual response. It is also made clear that the transformation in the people will only come about because of the LORD's intervention.

42. There is now a switch from feminine singular forms to a masculine plural form in *šəmaʿtem*, 'you heard/obeyed'. While the masculine plural form is often used instead of the rarer feminine plural, this does not explain why it is a plural form that is found. The form does, however, ease the flow into the mention of 'sons' in the next verse.

14. There is no distinct indication as to whether the subject of this verse is Israel or Judah. **Return, faithless people** (*šûbû bānîm šôbābîm*, 'Return, backsliding sons', also found in v. 22), looks back to v. 12b where there is a similar play on the root *šûb*, but a different word is used here for 'faithless/backsliding' and so it does not necessarily identify them. The lack of specificity and the use of second person masculine plural through to the end of v. 18 permits this message to be addressed to the whole of the covenant people, from north and south. It is unnecessary to find in 'return' principally a return from exile. This is still a call to repentance, to a spiritual return to the LORD.

The summons to the people is based on God's relationship to them: **for** (*kî*) **I am your husband.** The NIV rendering of *bāʿaltî* as 'I am your husband' (cf. 31:32) has in its favour the preceding references to divorce, but is unlikely in view of the use of 'sons' and the masculine pronouns in this verse. 'Master' is found in the NRSV and NASB,[43] and is an obvious play on the word Baal. The LORD is saying, 'I (expressed in two ways for emphasis) am your true lord and ruler.' He claims them as his own. Furthermore, the LORD is not saying he will initiate a new relationship or revive an old one; it is rather that he has not on his side considered the covenant relationship to have gone out of existence at all. Events have not annulled his sovereignty over them and so he will sovereignly act to restore them to his favour.

I will choose you—one from a town and two from a clan. 'Choose' (<√*lāqaḥ*, 'to take') points to the LORD's initiative in the matter: it is his action that will bring about this return. 'One from a city, and two from a family' as in NKJV is unnecessarily paradoxical, in that it seems to indicate a greater number from a smaller unit, which is not the intention. The 'clan' refers to a major subdivision of one of the tribes. 'The implicit recognition that Israel has become scattered in distinct cities and in small family groups points us to the recognition that these words were formulated after the deportations of 598 and 587 had taken place' (Clements 1988:35). This, however, is to forget what had already happened in the north after the fall of Samaria a century before. It is also uncertain what the stereotyped numerical saying actually implies. Although generally understood as pointing to how few would be involved in the return, the 'one … two' sequence might instead indicate a growing number of unspecified magnitude (for a discussion of the numerical idiom involved, see GKC §134s), which would fit in with 'a great throng will return' (31:8). Certainly the

43. The basis for the REB rendering 'I am patient with you' is unclear.

expression brings out that no part of the people would be forgotten about; every town and clan would be represented. There is possibly also the thought that the national return would be based on particular divine favour extended to individuals, who together constitute the restored people.

The LORD also adds, **and bring you to Zion.** For the people of the north and south their destination is not to be the polluted shrines of syncretistic worship or of blatant Baalism. Rather there will be a refocusing of the people in unity at the one true shrine in Zion, the place the LORD had appointed and had graced with his presence. Zion originally referred to the citadel in Jerusalem that David captured (2 Sam. 5:6-10), but it was later used of the city of David and the Temple area. Geographically Zion might also point to the whole city of Jerusalem, particularly considered in its religious significance. Although Jeremiah's contemporaries had a distorted notion of that significance, Zion would be the centre of the restored covenant nation (31:6, 12; 50:5), where they would be able to live in true harmony and fellowship with the LORD and with one another. This would be the true consummation of reforms such as those which Josiah had initiated.

15. The restored people are pictured as living in true harmony and fellowship, where the defects of the past will be remedied by divine action. **Then I will give you shepherds after my own heart.** 'Shepherd' was a metaphor used throughout the ancient Near East for a political ruler (2:8), but it could apply to officials in any sphere. Indeed Jeremiah calls himself a shepherd in 17:9. 'After my own heart' points to the character and conduct of the future kings as fully in accordance with God's will (contrast 7:31). The phrase recalls the way the LORD approved of David ('a man after his own heart', 1 Sam. 13:14) and indicates that these rulers will correspond to the Davidic ideal in a way in which previous kings of Israel and Judah had rarely succeeded in doing. Unlike the kings of the past, who had let the people down by their inadequate and compromising policies, these will be rulers **who will lead you with knowledge and understanding.** The NKJV translation 'who will feed you with knowledge and understanding' leaves open the possibility that the rulers are viewed as giving the people knowledge and understanding. But 'lead'/'feed' (<√*rā'â*, 'to shepherd') is not used in Hebrew with an accusative signifying the food that is provided (GKC §113h). Rather, as in the NIV, the phrases are adverbial, qualifying the manner in which the rulers carry out their tasks. Knowledge and understanding/aptitude were precisely the two qualities desired in a true statesman, and will characterise the coming Messiah (23:5). No longer will kings seek to rule through the wisdom of their political counsellors, but they will know the source of true insight and perceptivity in obedience to the commands of God (Deut. 4:6; 1 Kgs. 2:3).

16. Verses 16-18 are linked by a series of temporal phrases 'in those days', 'at that time', 'in those days' which set out three distinct aspects of the future situation that is envisaged. In v. 16 we have a picture of population increase, an important index of national strength and prosperity. **In those days** is a characteristically Jeremianic expression occurring eight times (3:16, 18; 5:18; 31:29; 33:15, 16; 50:4, 20) and four times elsewhere in the Old Testament. The plural 'days' tends to bring out that it is a future period that is being described rather than an event, as conveyed by the more common prophetic formula, 'in that day'.

It will be a time **'when** (*kî*) **your numbers have increased greatly in the land,' declares the LORD.** It is unclear whether there are one or two aspects of blessing envisaged here. Generally the Hebrew phrase is 'be fruitful and multiply'; here it is reversed to 'multiply and be fruitful'. It is possible to understand the second phrase as indicating general blessing quite apart from population increase, a feature found in many descriptions of future blessing (23:3; Hos. 2:1; Ezek. 36:11). The formula 'declares the LORD' occurs 26 times in Jeremiah (19 times elsewhere in the Old Testament) in conjunction with the mention of a future day or days. 'The point is to indicate that Yahweh knows the future, that he governs the course of world history and controls future destiny' (*TDOT* 9:112). This is the authoritative and definitive disclosure of the will of the one who alone knows what the future holds. 'This context is one of restoration and future bliss. Not only will there be a re-instatement of theocratic rulers, or shepherds, but there will be felicity and fertility of paradisaical proportions' (Woudstra 1965:37-8).

But there is also a major spiritual change indicated: **Men will no longer say, 'The ark of the covenant of the LORD'.** 'They will no longer say' is used by Jeremiah in other contexts (23:7; 31:29; cf. 31:23) to indicate that an earlier phase of revelation has made place for a later one, but without invalidating the earlier (Woudstra 1965:38). The implication is that such a phrase as this was used in Jerusalem to express wonder and gratitude at the LORD's provision. The ark had been constructed in the time of Moses according to precise divine requirements and was placed in the Most Holy Place in the tabernacle (Exod. 25:10-22). It was called the ark of the covenant or of the testimony because it contained the two stone tablets which had the covenant Overlord's requirements inscribed on them (Exod. 25:16; Deut. 10:1-5; 1 Kgs. 8:9). The ark continued to play a very significant role in the worship of the Temple, being the throne of the LORD, the place of the presence in power of the king of the covenant people, and also the centre of Israel's sacrificial system, being sprinkled with blood on the Day of Atonement. The later history of the ark is obscure. Despite the desecration of the Temple in Manasseh's reign, it existed in Josiah's day, as the reference in 2 Chron. 35:3 indicates, but there is no record of it after that. It seems to have vanished during the Babylonian sack of the city in 586 BC. However, it is not listed among the booty that was taken from the city (52:17-23), and so may have been hidden and never recovered.

But why will there be no ark in the future restoration? Does Jeremiah wish to convey the thought that mankind, in order to obtain communion with the living God, is no longer going to be dependent on a material symbol? Woudstra argues that the true thought is not that the use of symbols in the worship of God is incompatible with the spiritual character of that worship; they have a place as long as these symbols are God-ordained. But what is envisaged here is such a radical change of circumstances that use of a material object as a focus for religious sentiment is rendered unnecessary. 'A separate cult-object will be superfluous when the cultus will have permeated all of culture' (Woudstra 1965:38). Jeremiah's attitude towards both ark and Temple is similar (7:4), and it corresponds to what is found elsewhere. Isaiah, for instance, presents heaven as God's throne and earth his footstool (Isa. 66:1; cf. Pss. 11:4; 103:19).

To Jeremiah's hearers used to emphasising the privileged status of Jerusalem in that it had Temple and ark it would have been shocking to say that the ark would not exist in future. It would have been tantamount to saying that there would be no religion, no presence of God with his people. But the ark had been popularly redefined into a religious talisman which reinforced an optimism among the people that was unwarranted on the basis of their spiritual conduct. Since a true perception of the ark had been perverted by an automatic, mechanical view of religion, Jeremiah is prophesying that in the restored times he envisages ahead the element of formalism will have vanished and there will be no need for sacramental symbols as a focus for the worship of the people. **It will never enter their minds** (<*lēb*, 'heart', 4:4) **or be remembered.** It is possible that the use here of the phrasal verb *zākar bə*, 'to remember on', indicates not a complete forgetfulness of the ark, but rather an absence of a nostalgic clinging to it. The blessings of their new condition will be such that they will feel no loss in not having the presence of the ark in the Temple. **It will not be missed,**[44] **nor will another one be made.** The non-existence of the ark will not be a drawback in the future because of the spiritual nature of the worship that will prevail and because of the sense of the divine presence that the worshippers will have.

17. Next there is presented a positive description of the spiritual glory that will prevail in Jerusalem: no ark because all ark. **At that time they** (an indefinite subject, equivalent to a passive construction, 'Jerusalem will be called') **will call Jerusalem The Throne of the LORD.** As the ark was the place where the LORD's presence had been specifically manifested between the two cherubim over the covering on top of the ark, in the future there will be no spiritual restriction of the LORD's presence among his people. The whole of Jerusalem will function as the place where the LORD will manifest himself (Ezek. 48:35).

What is more, it is envisaged that this will not just involve Israel, but will embrace the heathen nations also. **And all the nations will gather in Jerusalem to honour the name of the LORD.** It is frequently forgotten just how international the Old Testament vision of the future is (Isa. 2:1-4; 56:6-8; 60:11-14; Mic. 4:1-3; Zech. 14:16-19). While 'gather' does convey the idea of being gathered together (<√*qāwâ*), it is frequently used in connection with water (Gen. 1:9, 10; Exod. 7:19), and it may well be that underlying imagery is similar to that of the peoples flowing together to Jerusalem (Mic. 4:1). 'To honour' attempts to bring out the significance of 'with respect to the name of the LORD', a term that stands for all that he has revealed himself to be. This is an attitude of submission, and fits in with the picture found in the prophets of the nations being taught by Israel and coming in true acknowledgment of the LORD to worship him in sincerity. **No longer will they follow the stubbornness of their evil hearts.** Eight of the ten Old Testament occurrences of *šərîrût*, 'stubbornness' (from a root attested in Aramaic with the meaning 'to be firmly set') are in Jeremiah. The term describes those who are certain they have the capacity to make decisions for themselves, and once they have made them, there is no deflecting them from their resolution even though it can be shown to be contrary to the way of God. In Deut. 29:18 the person who persists in going his own way ('walking in the stubbornness of his heart') is described as a root that

44. This is another instance of the versatile root *pāqad* (1:10). This is a secondary sense based on the idea that the careful inspection of a superior has not detected anything amiss or deficient in his subordinate.

produces bitter poison in the community. Generally the term is used of the obstinacy of God's people that led them into idolatry, but here the nations are said to have been characterised by the same attitude because of their inner, heart corruption. In Jeremiah human sin is clearly traced to the perverted inner disposition of the individual (17:9). Thoughts and desires are not morally neutral.

18. There is a third aspect to the scene of future blessing. It will be a time of harmony and union for the people of God because the division that had marred their fellowship will be overcome. **In those days** (cf. v. 16) **the house of Judah will join**/'come in addition to' **the house of Israel.** There will no longer be separation and tension, but a time of united blessing (cf. Isa. 11:12; Ezek. 37:16-28; Hos. 2:2). **And together they will come from a northern land to the land I gave your forefathers as an inheritance.** If we accept that mention of return from exile for Judah requires that she has already experienced exile, then we might well conclude with Ellison that this oracle cannot be dated earlier than the time of Jehoiachin's deportation in 597 BC (1960:212). Presumably that should be moved back to 605 BC in the light of Dan. 1:1-3 which records a first deportation in that year of hostages from the upper classes in Jerusalem as a means of ensuring the good behaviour of the others. On that basis it is not impossible to see this verse as a last minute addition to Jeremiah's First Scroll. However, all that is required by these words is that Jeremiah had previously mentioned that exile awaited Judah as a punishment for her rebellion, and in presenting this picture of future blessing he views it as a time of joint restoration. The people will again enjoy the blessings of the Sinai covenant under which they had been granted occupancy of the land. 'Give as an inheritance' (<√*nāḥal*) sums up the benefits of the covenant to Israel (Deut. 4:21; 12:9-10; 21:23).

5. Disappointed Hope (3:19-20)

Having set out what the LORD had shown him of the future prospects of the people, Jeremiah brings in material which continues the earlier discussion of the blessings that the LORD as their husband/master had intended would flow to people as a result of the covenant, but which were forfeited by their infidelity. There is a switch back to poetry and the people are again addressed in the second person feminine singular.

19. The section begins strongly, 'But' **I myself said.** Many have felt that this connects back to the thought of v. 5, 'Will you always be angry? Will your wrath continue for ever?' (e.g. Bright [1965:25] who takes v. 19 as following on from v. 5), and the answer now being given is a decided 'No.' Another possibility that has been put forward is that the connection is with the poetry of v. 13 (Jobling 1978). However, the link between vv. 18 and 19 based on inheritance (√*nāḥal*) is not merely verbal, but thematic, leading into the closely and carefully worked sequence of 3:19–4:4 which elaborates on the need for repentance before they will be permitted to participate in the good that may be bestowed on them through the covenant. The contrast involved seems to be that the pathway towards enjoying the LORD's blessing had not been intended to be by way of exile and restoration. When the LORD had presented the people with the blessings of the covenant at Sinai, it was with a genuine desire that they immediately enter into enjoyment of them. 'Said' (<*ʾāmar*) may also denote inner speech ('thought' NLT, NRSV).

How gladly would I treat you like sons, (literally, 'How I would set you among the sons'). 'You' is feminine singular (= house of Israel, v. 20), and has led to the thought that what is being presented here is an unusual donation of land to daughters as true heirs: they would be treated 'among the sons' (Num. 27:1-10). More probably this reflects the special status the LORD bestowed on the Israelites as his 'firstborn son' (Exod. 4:22; reflected also in Hos. 11:1; Jer. 31:9). This has the implication that the LORD as Creator of all mankind has other sons, but this is not followed up in the Old Testament (unless possibly in Deut. 32:8-9, cf. NIV footnote) because of the naturalistic interpretation liable to be put on it through the ideas made prevalent by paganism. The focus is not on the existence of other sons or the privileges accorded them, but on the special standing extended to the Israelites as his 'treasured possession' specially selected from among all the other nations (Exod. 19:5). There had been no reluctance on the LORD's part to treat the people in accordance with the status he had conferred on them, and he would **give you a desirable land** (*ʾereṣ ḥemdâ*, 'land of longing'; 'pleasant land', Ps. 106:24; Zech. 7:14). *ḥemdâ* emphasises the outward attractiveness of an object, **the most beautiful**[45] **inheritance of any nation.** 'Most beautiful' (*ṣəbî ṣibʾôt*, 'ornament of ornaments', 'beauty of beauties') is a Hebrew idiom for expressing a superlative (*IBHS* §14.5.b; GKC §133i; Joüon §141l).

The LORD sets out the response he had expected to his unmerited

45. *ṣibʾôt* is the construct plural of *ṣəbîʾ*, 'host, army', and this is reflected in the NKJV rendering 'a beautiful heritage of the hosts of nations'. But most translations understand the same form as the construct plural of *ṣəbî*, 'ornament, glory', with an *aleph* substituted for a *yodh* in the expected plural form, *ṣəbāyîm*.

and overwhelming generosity: **I thought you would call**[46] **me 'Father'** (*'ābî*, 'my Father', cf. 3:4) **and not turn away**[47] **from following me.** 'Thought' renders *'āmar* (normally 'to say'), but it can also be used of inner speech to oneself (see 'said' at the start of the verse). Here too it might be rendered 'I said, "You shall call me"' (NKJV), which would be a divine command addressed to the people, but the note of wistfulness in the NIV rendering seems just right. Some responses ought to be so spontaneous that there is no need to give instructions regarding them. True fellowship with the LORD, recognising his status and the benefits he had conferred, should have been accompanied by devoted obedience to his commands. Acknowledgment of his fatherhood implies a readiness to be loyal and obey him. Such a response is in contrast to turning away, where the term reflects the use of the root *šûb* in the sense of 'apostatise'/'turn from' what is true rather than turn to the LORD from rebellion.

20. But (*'ākēn*) introduces an emphatic statement which may either, as here, reverse or restrict what has preceded (='nevertheless'), or may provide emphasis (='undoubtedly'; *IBHS* §39.3.5d). **Like**[48] **a woman unfaithful to her husband, so you have been unfaithful to me.** 'Husband' renders *rēaʿ*, 'companion', 'friend'. **O house of Israel** is formal language addressed to the covenant community, which both reflects the promises set before them in the covenant, and, through allusion to the conduct of the northern kingdom, it hints at the degree of estrangement that their behaviour has now entailed. **Declares the LORD** marks the end of the section.

Jeremiah has again urged the people to acknowledge that they owed everything to God who had provided so bountifully for them. Gratitude for gifts already received as their inheritance should have characterised their whole lifestyle. Equally they were to anticipate still greater and grander provision in the future. He calls on them to act in accordance with the demands of the covenant and enjoy the blessings their covenant Overlord provides.

46. The kethibh is *tiqrə'û*, 'you will call' (masculine plural), while the qere is feminine singular *tiqrə'î*, 'you will call'. The Massoretes proposed the qere to conform with the feminine suffix on *'ăšîtēk*. They evidently considered that the masculine forms were a scribal error under the influence of 'sons' earlier in the verse.

47. The kethibh is masculine plural *tāšûbû*, while the qere is feminine singular *tāšûbî*.

48. Unusually in this comparison the protasis has no introductory particle (GKC §161b; *IBHS* §38.5a)

6. The Way Back (3:21-25)

Jeremiah then switches from presenting the LORD's declaration of the future he had intended for his people to what are probably instructions to them as those who had strayed from the ways of the covenant as to how they should act if they wished to re-enter a loyal relationship with the LORD.

21. It is not clear how this description should be read. At first it seems to depict the sort of conduct that substantiates the divine allegation of their unfaithfulness. **A cry is heard on the barren heights.** 'Barren heights' (3:2) refers to the sites of Baal worship, and from there comes the noise of **the weeping** (<√*bākâ*) **and pleading of the people of Israel** (*bənê yiśrā'ēl*, 'the sons of Israel/the Israelites', and hence following instances of 'they' and 'their' are masculine plural). The language probably is intended to cover the covenant community from both north and south. But what is it that the prophet sees them as doing? Are they seeking to induce the Baals to respond to their need? Is this what they have been reduced to **because** (*kî*) **they have perverted**[49] **their ways** ('taken to crooked ways', REB, <√*ʿāwâ*, 'to bend, twist, distort', cf. *ʿāwōn*, 2:22) **and have forgotten the LORD their God.** For 'forget' see on 2:32.

It is, however, possible to interpret the scene more positively, and this perception is reinforced by the following verses. Then the scene is not one of pagan worship but an anticipation of what will happen when the people come to their senses. 'Barren heights' indeed points to former sites of Baal worship, which are now simply bare and waste. The cries are no longer the ecstatic and frenzied shouts of the devotees of the Canaanite god, but rather the bewildered lamentation of the sorrowful remnant at the devastation that has engulfed them. They speak in their misery, conscious of the fact that the ruin and havoc that surround them is the result of their abandonment of the LORD and his covenant. This is not an historical description, but a pedagogic picture which sets the scene for what is presented in vv. 22b-25. 'The closing verses of chapter iii must be read as a confession put into the mouth of Israel in its ideal unity, as the unfaithful spouse of Yahweh, convinced at last of her guilt and folly. On any view the description is an ideal one; for we may be sure that no such spontaneous cry of penitence as is described in the following lines ascended from the high places of Judah in the lifetime of Jeremiah' (Skinner 1922:84).

---

49. Most manuscripts have only one dagesh, reading *heʿĕwû* rather than *heʿĕwwû*.

22. Into this scene the voice of the LORD is heard bringing a message of hope: **Return, faithless people** (cf. v. 14); **I will cure**[50] **you of backsliding.** There is a threefold play on the root *šûb* in 'return' (*šûbû*), 'faithless' (*šôbābîm*), and 'backslidings' (*məšûbōtêkem*). The two statements are presented asyndetically, but as in v. 14 the possibility of return in repentance is only present because of the action of the LORD, who is here presented as the divine physician, 'the LORD who heals you' (Exod. 15:26). The people are unable to provide the remedy for their own incorrigible departures from the LORD, but he is able to do so (30:17; 33:6; Deut. 32:39; Isa. 53:5; Hos. 14:4), and because of that there is a way forwards. He comes as a father to reclaim his wayward children.

The prophet then presents the response the people should give. Assurance is being given to penitent Israel that if they return in repentance, they will find the LORD ready and willing to meet them and provide for them. The words put into the lips of the community are, of course, teaching for Judah so that they may progress beyond their superficial spiritual response to Josiah's reforms, and genuinely seek the LORD. They are then portrayed as reacting positively to the divine summons: **Yes, we will come**[51] **to you, for** (*kî*) **you are the LORD our God.** This is acknowledgment of the sovereignty of the LORD over them. Their rebellion is now a thing of the past, and they pledge their loyalty to their God and king.

23. This is no empty or shallow confession because it is accompanied by a realisation of what had been wrong in their previous involvement in the fertility cults. *ʾākēn* ('surely' cf. 3:20) is here used twice with strong assertive force, firstly reversing their previous perception and then restricting salvation to its one true source. **Surely the ⌊idolatrous⌋ commotion on the hills and mountains is a deception.** The Hebrew is very terse: 'surely, for the deception (*šeqer*, 5:2), from hills, commotion, mountains.' But it is clear that the people are revising their judgment on what was involved in idol worship. 'Deception' may just be a phrase indicating 'in vain' (so many English translations), but the use of *šeqer* brings with it decided overtones of the delusiveness of idolatry. Lundbom suggests reading the last two words in combination as 'Noise of the Mountains', possibly another disparaging name for

---

50. *ʾerpâ*, 'I shall cure' is a mixed verb form, being final *he* and not final *aleph* as would be expected (GKC §75pp; Joüon §78g).

51. *hinənû ʾātānû* might also be rendered, 'Here we are. We are coming to you' (*IBHS* §40.2.1b). For the long *a* in the second syllable of *ʾātānû*, an imperfect <√*ʾātâ*, 'to come', see GKC §75rr; Joüon §79l.

Baal (1999:322). They acknowledge what they have been involved in as the sham that it in fact was. Baal worship on the hilltops was mere commotion, the uproarious orgies of idolatry (cf. vv. 2, 4, 9; cf. also 1 Kgs. 14:23-24; 15:11-13; 2 Kgs. 23:4-15; Ps. 106:35-40; Isa. 28:7-8; Hos. 4:9-14; Amos 2:7-8). In contrast to that, the only hope of real spiritual blessing is to be found in the LORD. **Surely** (*'ākēn*) **in the LORD our God is the salvation of Israel.** He alone is therefore worthy of trust and worship.

24. The people are then viewed as reflecting on their past experience, and confessing the deleterious effect of the idol worship. **From our youth shameful gods have consumed the fruits of our fathers' labour**. 'Youth' refers back to Israel's emergence as a nation at the time of the Exodus and settlement (2:2). 'Shameful gods'/'the Shame' (*bōšet*, 2:26) is an oblique reference to Baal (11:13; Hos. 9:10), for whom the title 'Shame' was used by pious Israelites. 'Labour' (*yəgîaʿ*) is not just the product of one's work, but the result for which one had strenuously toiled, thus making its loss all the more bitter. There are two views as to what is meant: (1) our worship of Baal involved our fathers in sacrificing to him **their flocks and herds, their sons and daughters.** What they had worked for was used up in pointless and ineffective offerings to the Shameful One. There would seem to be a reference to the murderous rites of the valley of Hinnom (7:31; 19:5; 2 Kgs. 16:3; 21:6). (2) More probably, their words reflect on the judgments that had come on the land because of their idolatrous behaviour. They are recognising that from the time of the judges enemy invasions, coming as divine punishment, had devastated their land that should have yielded them fruit (Deut. 28:30, 33). By departing from the LORD they had not gained but lost. Involvement with Baal, the fertility god whose worship was supposed to secure the productivity of the land, had only succeeded in bringing repeated and intense damage on the country.

25. So overwhelmed are the people as they realise their folly that they acknowledge that their misconduct constituted a terrible indictment against them. **Let us lie down**[52] **in our shame, and let our disgrace cover us**, as a cloak or a blanket on a bed (Pss. 35:26; 109:29; Mic. 7:10; Obad. 10). They are in no doubt why this reaction is appropriate. 'For' (*kî*) **we have sinned** (cf. 2:35) **against the LORD our God, both we and our fathers; from our youth till this day we**

52. *niškəbâ*, 'let us lie down', is a cohortative and may express a resolution formed under compulsion (GKC §108g).

have not obeyed the LORD our God.[53] The people are acutely aware of the hold that sin had taken of them and the fact that their conduct was a personal affront to the LORD. The phrase 'We have not obeyed the voice of the LORD our God' occurs 65 times in the Old Testament of which eighteen are in Jeremiah. Such a repentant acknowledgment of the wrongfulness of what they had done throughout their national history (cf. 2:5; 11:10) had not in fact been made up to that point. This is ideal language dramatically put on Israel's lips by the prophet to show what she should have said and done. The principal target of this exercise was Judah, the southern kingdom. If she could see how recovery was possible, perhaps she might act appropriately before it became too late.

Only if those who have wandered far from the LORD come to their senses and recognise the folly of what they have done can there be the possibility of a true return to the LORD (cf. the 'Father, I have sinned' of the lost son returned from the distant country in Luke 15:21). The confession put on the lips of those who have recognised the folly of the lifestyle of their fathers and of themselves is an acknowledgment that what they had hoped to give meaning and purpose to their lives proved elusive even in their very efforts to gain it (Mark 8:36). Once there is an open and unreserved admission of where things have gone wrong, there is the possibility of experiencing the restoration to spiritual health that is available because of divine mercy. Repentance is not urged as a goal in itself, but as a necessary prerequisite for a restored relationship and enjoyment of divine blessing.

7. Heart Circumcision (4:1-4)

This section ends the division of the prophecy which began at 3:1 and which focuses on the rupture of relationship between the LORD and his people, mainly using the metaphor of marriage and divorce. The concluding section continues to emphasise that genuine repentance is needed if the broken relationship is to be mended. Thematic unity with what has preceded is maintained by the use of *šûb*, 'to turn, return', to point to the need for a heartfelt response (v. 1) after which the people

53. The NIV takes a different division of the verse from the Massoretic Text and most English translations, e.g. NRSV 'for we have sinned against the LORD our God, we and our ancestors, from our youth even to this day; and we have not obeyed the voice of the LORD our God.' The athnach is found under *hazzeh*, indicating that the Massoretes took the main break within the verse to occur after 'to this day'.

will be in a position to enjoy the blessings of the covenant (v. 2). Then Jeremiah begins to move on towards the next division of his material by citing a message to the people of the south in which they were urged to reconsecrate themselves to the LORD, with a solemn warning that if they do not, they will experience divine wrath (vv. 3-4).

1. In vv. 1 and 2 there are seven verbs in Hebrew, only the first ('you will return') and third ('you remove') of which are preceded by *'im*, 'if'. Translators understand the structure of the passage in various ways. The NRSV and REB have five successive conditional clauses with the last two verbs expressing the consequences. This is grammatically possible, but the repetition of 'if' before the third verb gives grounds for thinking that the element of conditionality is being re-expressed there, and that the first two verbs are a separate conditional sequence. The NKJV treats only those clauses introduced by 'if' as conditional. Thus its treatment of the first two verbs is as in the NIV, but verbs four to seven are treated as an extended apodosis to the third clause. However, as reasonable an approach as any is that of the NIV where verbs three, four and five are taken as part of a complex protasis, and verbs six and seven as its apodosis.

'If you[54] will return, O Israel, return to me,' declares the LORD. Interpretation of this saying depends on the sense given to 'return' and to 'Israel'. In both occurrences 'return' is *tāšûb* (<√*šûb*), but in the first instance the direction of the movement is unstated. For a moment the situation is ambiguous: are we to understand it as 'lapse into backsliding', 'return from exile' or 'turn in repentance'? The apodosis clarifies the matter by adding 'to me', which is brought forward for emphasis, as if to say, 'If you are going to move in any direction at all, it is to me alone that you must turn.' There is therefore no direct reference to backsliding. Israel, however, may point to the remnants of the former northern kingdom so that they are being told that the route back to their land geographically is by way of spiritual return to the LORD. However, the openness of Israel as a sacral form of address for the covenant community by no means excludes reference to Judah. The words are probably best understood as the anticipated response of the LORD to the confession of 3:22b-25 which Jeremiah envisages as appropriate for those from either north or south who are convicted of their sin. The primary demand of the covenant was exclusive commitment to the LORD and those who wish a restored relationship with him had to make sure that he alone was the focus of their faith.

54. The personal references in this section to the people are masculine, singular in vv. 1 and 2, and plural in vv. 3 and 4.

Since genuine repentance has to be distinguished from the self-indulgence of mere regret, which wishes for the removal of the consequences of the past but does not exhibit deep abhorrence of past conduct by adopting a radically distinct pattern of behaviour, three characteristics of an acceptable response are set out in vv. 1b-2a.

Firstly, abandonment of idolatry, that is pagan practices and thinking. **If you put your detestable idols out of my sight.** 'Detestable' (*šiqqûṣ*) is used to refer pejoratively to idolatrous worship, frequently to the idol itself (1 Kgs. 11:5; 2 Kgs. 23:13, 24; 2 Chron. 15:8; Isa. 66:3; Ezek. 20:7-8), but also to associated practices (Nah. 3:6; Zech. 9:7). 'It is unlikely that it is merely a strong synonym for idolatry, though it may be so used by Ezekiel. It probably referred in the first place to images of beasts and lewd sex, and the bestiality, ritual prostitution and perverted sexual practices that sprang from them' (Ellison 1962:99). Revulsion at the fertility cults was in the first place the divine attitude, but if the people adopted the standards of judgment of the covenant, then they would associate themselves with God in his disgust at such perversions and act accordingly. 'Out of my sight' is not an invitation to worship them covertly (where is there that the LORD does not see?), but to cleanse the land of them completely.

Secondly, living close to God. **And no longer go astray** (<√*nûd*, 'to move backwards and forwards, wander'; 'restless wanderer' Gen. 4:12, 14; 'sway' Isa. 24:20) may refer to straying into idol worship, but probably is more general in its reference, urging them to live in the divine presence in obedience to God's commands and not to lurch from one expedient to another as the whim took them (cf. the camel of 2:23 or 'we are free to roam' 2:31).

2. Thirdly, **And if in a truthful, just and righteous way you swear, 'As surely as the LORD lives,'**[55] presents the condition of a consistent covenant lifestyle to control the way in which they conduct themselves in everyday life. This is looking particularly at the fabric of mutual trust that sustains the covenant community in the light of their shared acceptance of the LORD as their God and his moral standards as the rule of their lives. Although the combination does not seem to occur elsewhere, the three nouns that are rendered 'truthful, just and righteous' here express the essence of covenant living. 'Truth' (*'ĕmet*) looks for reliability and dependability. It is quite the opposite of 'in pretence' (3:10) or 'delusion' (3:23). 'Justice' (*mišpāṭ*) is action in accordance with what is permitted and usual (5:1; 7:5), and

55. Another way of rendering *ḥay-yhwh* is, 'The LORD's life!' (cf. *IBHS* §40.2.2b).

'righteousness' (*ṣədāqâ*) is conduct in accordance with the norms stipulated by the LORD. Together they emphasise in a solemn and impressive way the need for upright living, which would maintain covenant relationships and harmony, particularly as focused on one's word being one's bond. What is especially enjoined here is avoidance of a light and unthinking use of the divine name to pledge the veracity and sanctity of a commitment. There had always been an injunction against misusing the name of the LORD (Exod. 20:7). It was no sign of true piety to have his name on one's lips if it was a mere trickery that was in one's heart. Those who solemnly used his name were required to be aware of the nature of the one by whom they pledged their word.

The series of conditional clauses is then resolved in a joint protasis which sets out the role of the covenant people as channels of blessing towards other nations. This is the development of the gentilic promise in the Abrahamic covenant, 'all peoples on earth will be blessed through you' (Gen. 12:3). **Then the nations will be blessed**[56] **by him** is a deliberate reflection on that promise, and also looks back to the international scenario of 3:17. The one referred to in 'by him' is the LORD rather than Abraham, because it was always the LORD who was going to use Abraham as the channel of divine blessing, so that this is really a development of that pledge (cf. Gen. 22:18). Thus the repentant people are promised that they will be reinstated in their role of providing covenant blessing (Isa. 42:6; 49:6). **And in him they will glory** (<√*hālal* II hithpael). The verb is used in the piel for expressing admiration and praise of another being either human or divine, whereas the hithpael stem involves a reference to oneself, either in the sense of boasting (9:22; 49:4) or in a statement recognising the personal benefits that accrue from the excellent qualities of another. It is the last sense that is present here. This is a description of the nations joining in a united expression of joy and thanksgiving at the excellence and supremacy of the LORD who has made this provision for their salvation (Ps. 105:3; Isa. 41:16). Their exultation is not focused on God in general or abstract terms but on what he has wonderfully done *for them.*

Stressing the absoluteness of the divine rejection of Judah in 2:5-37, Carroll argues that no amount of theologising can adequately account for the incompatibility between the material urging repentance and return, and the message of rejection which has preceded it

56. The verb *wəhitbārəkû* is a hithpael and may be translated reflexively, 'bless themselves' (NRSV margin; cf. REB), or, perhaps less plausibly, as a passive 'be blessed'. The NIV follows the pattern of New Testament citations of the Abrahamic blessing which treat it as a passive usage (e.g. Acts 3:25).

(1986:147-8). But that style of argument rules out any form of salvation; it denies that there can be a gospel. There is the stark reality of divine condemnation of those who rebel against his rule, but the whole outworking of salvation history is based on the revealed fact that what seems juridically impossible to human wisdom—the righteous judge of all the earth justifying the ungodly—can, and is, achieved by divine wisdom and power through the mediatorial intervention of the God-man. It is the mark of the prophet's access into the council of the LORD that he holds to both aspects of the truth of God's plan of salvation.

An attempt is often made to argue that here Jeremiah links a southern tradition of the absolute promises of the Abrahamic covenant to a northern conception of the covenant where blessing was contingent upon obedience. This is to make a distinction where none really exists. Undoubtedly there are differing presentations in Scripture of the way in which the covenant will unfold, but as it is the vehicle for the LORD's furthering of his purposes, there can be no doubt about its eventual success. The covenant king guarantees his promises and has the power to secure all that he proposes. However, there is the ongoing challenge of individual participation in the blessings of the covenant. Even in the Davidic covenant his descendants' enjoyment of their privileges was contingent upon obedience (2 Sam. 7:14). So Jeremiah here is not combining two different traditions, but bringing out the implications and demands inherent in the covenant relationship.

3. The verse begins with *kî*, 'for'. This is not to be dismissed as merely 'an editor's effort to join this section to what precedes' (Jones 1992:105), but shows Jeremiah drawing to a conclusion and setting out the reason he had for presenting this material. Though it has been ostensibly about Israel, he says in effect, 'I have proclaimed these messages to you, Judah and Jerusalem, because in them the LORD is speaking to you as part of the covenant community.' **This is what the LORD says to the men of Judah and to Jerusalem**. 'Men' is literally 'man' (*'îš*), and on this basis Harrison argues that 'the MT indicates that each man of Judah and Jerusalem is challenged to repent. It must thus be on an individual basis, not a corporate one as in the religious rituals of the day of atonement. This emphasis on personal religious experience is especially important for the theology of the new covenant' (1973:68). However true Harrison's comment may be at a spiritual level, it does not seem justified grammatically. The plural of *'îš* is rarely used, and so the singular is often found as a collective, as in the next verse where it is joined with a plural, 'people of/inhabitants of Jerusalem'. Moreover, the verbs here are plural. The covenant community collectively and individually is being challenged to assess how they stand before the LORD. The need for a deep-seated change in their attitudes is then pressed home in two further metaphors.

The first metaphor in v. 3 is drawn from contemporary farming practices. **Break up your unploughed ground** (*nîrû lākem nîr*) is also found in Hos. 10:12; indeed Holladay argues that Jeremiah is probably quoting the earlier prophet (1986, 1:129). *Nîr* may refer to 'fallow' ground, that is, ground previously ploughed, but left uncultivated for a while and so having weeds growing in it, or to 'virgin' ground that has never been cultivated. There is insufficient evidence to limit *nîr* to unbroken soil (Craigie 1991:67; Thompson 1980:214), but the point is that the ground has been covered by some of the seventy different types of thorny plant found in Palestine. So the command is given, **Do not sow among thorns.** Generally in Palestine after the crop was harvested, the weeds were gathered at the edge of the field and burned. The next season the seed was scattered on the surface of the ground before it was ploughed and the seed covered by soil. In the process many of the weed seeds were also ploughed in and grew up along with the crop. Sowing among thorns is then indicative of sowing on ground which by the practices of the day had not been properly prepared. It would seem that an additional ploughing prior to sowing is being urged to remove noxious weeds that would inhibit a fruitful harvest.

Spiritually, Judah is being told that her condition is like that of a field that has been left untended. Her religious activity has been contaminated by practices that are flawed and detrimental to her spiritual health. There is no point in trying to establish a new relationship with God unless radical action is taken first of all to clear away what will stifle the genuine crop. 'Still others, like seed sown among thorns, hear the word; but the worries of this life, the deceitfulness of wealth and the desires for other things come in and choke the word, making it unfruitful' (Mark 4:18-19). It was all very well for Judah under Josiah to turn towards God professing new obedience to him, but first they had 'out of a true sense of their sin' (Westminster *Shorter Catechism*, 87) to turn from it. It was folly to expect devoted allegiance to the LORD without first eradicating the alien growths from their life. Judah proved unable to do this, and it took the Babylonian Exile to clear the weeds from their national life. However, in its fullest sense the command looks forward to the promise of the new covenant (cf. Ellison 1960:217, but he takes *nîr* as new ground).

4. The people of Jeremiah's day derived considerable spiritual comfort from all that had been done under Josiah to reform the Temple and the worship of the LORD throughout the land. The second illustration used to reinforce the need for more than superficial change in their religion draws from the symbolism of the cult itself. First they are enjoined, **Circumcise yourselves to the LORD**. Circumcision had been instituted as the mark of the covenant in Abraham's time (Gen. 17:9-14) and it continued to be practised under the Mosaic covenant as an act of dedication to the LORD (Josh. 5:2-8). The language here sounds like a ritual formula for covenantal dedication, something that the men of Jerusalem would have been happy to acknowledge: 'We are circumcised'. 'To the LORD' points out that it was not merely the ceremony that mattered but the attitude of self-dedication to the LORD that it symbolised. The call was not for a national ceremony as such but for individual reconsecration that would be found throughout Judah.

This is further emphasised by the reminder that the external rite on its own was insufficient. **Circumcise your hearts, you men of Judah and people** ('inhabitants') **of Jerusalem.** Moses had clearly taught the need for more than a male surgical operation. The metaphor of heart circumcision directed the whole community to exercise spiritual commitment. Passages such as 'Circumcise your hearts' (Deut. 10:16) and 'The LORD your God will circumcise your hearts and the hearts of your descendants, so that you may love him with all your heart and with all your soul, and live' (Deut. 30:6) would have spoken all the more clearly to them if it was in fact the book of Deuteronomy that had been rediscovered in the Temple. At a time of intense nationalistic feeling, ritual circumcision might well be seen as a national badge, without the people grasping the ethical demands that the LORD made of his people (9:25-26; Ezek. 44:9; Rom. 2:28-29). The sacramental ritual fell short of achieving its true significance if it was separated from inward spiritual commitment to the LORD of the covenant. They were being commanded to consecrate their hearts to the service of the LORD. 'Heart' (*lēb*, 58 times in Jeremiah, or *lēbāb*, 7 times) is used throughout the Old Testament in a transferred sense not just for an individual's emotional life but for the entire inner psychical and spiritual life including feelings, thoughts and will (cf. 17:1). It was a foundational imperative that the LORD's rule be established there, and the call is one for complete and unconditional dedication to the LORD.

Integral to the structure of the covenant is the possibility of the highest blessing on obedience but also the polar possibility of the most dire curses upon disobedience. Nothing is hidden from the people; there is now set before them the alternative outcome awaiting those who fail in their duty towards the covenant King. **Or my wrath will break out and burn like fire because of the evil you have done—**

burn with no one to quench it. 'Wrath' (*ḥēmâ*, from a root conveying the idea of heat) conveys a stronger emotion than 'anger' (*'ap*, 2:35) when used without modifiers, and there can be no doubt about the intensity of the LORD's displeasure at their misconduct. His wrath is compared to a raging fire storm that cannot be put out and consumes all before it (7:20; 17:27; 21:12; Isa. 1:31; Amos 5:6). The reality of divine anger awaiting the impenitent may not be dismissed as just an outmoded part of the Old Testament. All too often, like the people of Judah, we act as if it will never really take place, but the New Testament solemnly repeats these warnings (Matt. 18:8; 25:41; Mark 9:43; 1 Cor. 3:13; Jude 7, 23). And the reason for the judgment remains the same: 'the evil you have done' (26:3; 44:22). It is not an arbitrary imposition of the Sovereign, but derives from the high honour he has bestowed upon mankind in that he treats us as responsible creatures. However, that honour is transformed into a nightmare if we do not exercise our God-given responsibility within the parameters that have been set out by our Creator.

The note of impending judgment which concludes the application of the object lesson of the two 'sisters', Israel and Judah, leads directly into the presentation of that judgment in the following division, where details about how it will come upon Judah and Jerusalem are set out. In the form in which the prophecy was finally issued by Jeremiah this presentation addressed the exilic community at two levels: it enabled them to interpret their plight through realising that the people had not responded to these impassioned pleas for repentance; and it gave them a measure of hope for the future by indicating that the way forwards was not through continuing rejection of the LORD, but rather by genuine contrition for their sin and by showing fidelity to their covenant lord/husband.

C. IMPENDING JUDGMENT (4:5-6:30)

The third major division of the material from Jeremiah's early ministry focuses on the judgment that was looming over impenitent Judah. It would be a mistake to view this primarily as foretelling what would inevitably occur when the Babylonians invaded the land and Jerusalem was captured. These words were not originally uttered as mere prediction, and they were not incorporated by Jeremiah into the First Scroll of 605/4 BC as such. Their primary function was that of warning. The aim of Jeremiah's ministry was still to stir up the people to a true discernment of their spiritual plight and to admonish them to return to the LORD before it was too late. It was still a ministry of mercy that the

LORD desired towards his errant people (cf. 4:14), seeking to stir up those who were 'complacent in Zion' (Amos 6:1).

The first use of the material in this division cannot be precisely dated during Jeremiah's early ministry. Indeed, it can be difficult to decide on the shape of the original poetic material that the prophet has incorporated here. But that is no great loss. What we have is a skilfully constructed message that invites us not to concentrate on its literary prehistory but to assess its effectiveness in alerting Judah to the divine judgment that was going to fall on impenitent and stubborn people.

The Foe from the North

One feature that is recurrent throughout this division is 'the foe from the north' (4:5-9, 13-17, 19-21, 29-31; 5:15-17; 6:1-8, 22-26). The threat from the north had originally been revealed to Jeremiah at the start of his ministry in connection with the vision of the boiling pot (1:13-16). In his description of the enemy Jeremiah identifies them as coming from the north (4:6; 6:1, 22) and from a distant land (4:16; 5:15; 6:22), being an ancient nation (5:15), speaking a foreign language (5:15), being merciless (6:23), taking captives, having armies consisting of great warriors and armed with bows and spears (4:29; 6:23), riding on swift horses and chariots (4:13), attacking unexpectedly (4:20; 6:26), using battle formations (6:23), and being bold enough to attack a fortified city at noon (6:4-5). From this picture it might be expected that their identity could be definitively established. Certainly the northern enemy is stated to be Babylon in chapter 25, but that relates specifically to the situation around 605 BC following the Babylonian victory at Carchemish (25:32). There has been much scholarly discussion regarding the identity of the foe in Jeremiah's original presentation before that period. Was the foe another historical enemy prior to Babylon? Or was the description 'the foe from the north' not historical at all, but rather one that described a mythical or eschatological enemy? After all, the same style of description is used in chapters 50 and 51 to speak of the enemy who would conquer Babylon. Or was it the case that the foe was originally an unspecified enemy whom Jeremiah was only later able to identify as Babylon?

There is no doubt that Jeremiah's presentation of the foe from the north depicts a looming menace that threatens the life of the nation. The term 'north' may be used not for geographic reasons but because, being associated in surrounding cultures with the dwelling of the gods, it had mysterious, terrifying overtones. The most plausible argument for detecting an apocalyptic element in what Jeremiah says is the picture of cosmic dissolution in 4:23-26. But every judgment of the LORD in the flow of human history is a precursor of the final Day of the LORD, and for Jeremiah that ultimate background does not dominate, though it may colour (cf. 4:9), the immediate catastrophe facing the nation. There seems little doubt that Jeremiah anticipated the attacks of an historical enemy to come from the north.

Attempts to identify an early historical context for the foe from the north draw on Mesopotamian texts which indicate that as Assyrian power waned, bands of marauding Asiatic tribesmen known as the Umman-Manda (generally equated with the Scythians of classical authors, though Miller and Hayes argue that it is instead an archaic expression revived by Babylonian scribes primarily in reference to the Medes [1986:387]) moved from the area north and west of the Black Sea into Asia Minor and Syria–Palestine and that they played a part in the downfall of Nineveh in 612 BC. The Greek historian Herodotus (*Hist.* 1:103-106) relates that these invaders dominated the area for twenty-eight years and marched through Palestine intending to attack Egypt, before they were bought off by Egyptian gold. On their way back north they looted a temple at Ashkelon. One independent piece of evidence regarding their presence is the fact that during Hellenistic times the town of Bethshan was known as Scythopolis, an indicator that they settled for some time in the area (Rowley 1963:144; but see Cazelles 1984:144).

During the eighteenth century the view arose that Jeremiah's foe from the north should be identified with these Scythian invaders. However, there are various improbable features in Herodotus' narrative. It is difficult to establish a precise chronology for the twenty-eight years of Scythian domination and there are various aspects of his story which do not quite tally. There is no record of any ravages of Judah during Josiah's reign. Furthermore Jeremiah's description contains details that do not match what we know of the Scythians. The foe from the north was an ancient nation, used chariots, fought in battle formation, besieged cities and took captives. It is unlikely that Jeremiah was thinking of the Scythians.

This does not mean that the general outline of Herodotus' account is to be dismissed. It seems probable that the Scythians were present in the area during Jeremiah's early ministry and possibly before 616 BC. But it is one thing to establish the presence of the Scythians and another to show that Jeremiah had them in mind when he talked about the foe from the north. As Welch pointed out, however, the basic problem with much of the earlier discussion 'lies in the mistaken idea that the prophets were roused to activity by outward events in the national history. The theory of their having needed some crisis in the world or in the fate of their own people to stir them to intervention does not correspond with the facts of the case' (1928:107-8). The prophet was divinely given his message, and there is no need to suppose that Jeremiah himself initially identified the foe from the north with any particular world power. Indeed early naming of the foe might have diverted the people into thinking about the specifics of how they would counter this identified threat. Ultimately it did not matter precisely who the human agent was; the real threat came from the fact that the LORD was their opponent. The matter they had to address was not appropriate strategies against invasion but turning back to the LORD.

It was, however, not difficult for the nation to dismiss Jeremiah's message of doom from the north as alarmism. If the enemy had been popularly identified with the Scythians, then their departure from Palestine might well have undermined his standing in popular esteem. Certainly in the years before Josiah's death there was no menace from the north. Such threats as existed against Judah came from Egypt to the south. Assyria was in collapse, Mesopotamia was in turmoil, and there was no menace on the northern horizon. For long enough Jeremiah seems to have had to face the problem that there was no obvious foe from the north, which doubtless led to consequent scepticism on the part of his countrymen regarding his message. But that had changed by the time the First Scroll was written and read. By then there could be no doubt about who this mysterious foe in fact was. Little wonder then that the re-presentation of these old oracles which had been largely dismissed over the years had such a profound impact on Jehoiakim and his advisers. In the light of the crisis in which they were engulfed, they saw with intense clarity what the prophecies had to say about the future of Judah.

1. Threat from the North (4:5-31)

OUTLINE

a. The Lookout's Alert (4:5-9)
b. Divine Deception? (4:10)
c. Swift Advance (4:11-18)
d. The Prophet's Anguish (4:19-22)
e. Uncreation (4:23-28)
f. The Mortal Anguish of Jerusalem (4:29-31)

'Although these poems must have been composed at intervals, and under many fluctuations of feeling, they seem to have been carefully selected and artistically arranged so as to form a complete cycle, beginning with the first warning blast of the trumpet and reaching an overpowering climax in the death-shriek of the doomed capital, with which the chapter closes' (Skinner 1922:38). That is a sounder evaluation than 'a miscellaneous collection without a clear ordering or structure' (Brueggemann 1998:53). The description given is a generalised one made in anticipation of a future reality. It lacks explicit historical references, but great artistry is evident in the way in which various scenes and speakers are woven together into a vivid tapestry of war with the approach of a menacing but unidentified army and the scattering of a panic-stricken populace. The whole section was primarily designed to get the people of Judah to alter their perception of existing reality of Jerusalem as possessing divinely guaranteed security. Instead they were to realise how precarious and threatened the existing state of affairs was. To later readers the message was one of how the LORD was forced into punishing the nation for its intransigence.

a. The Lookout's Alert (4:5-9)

5. After the bridge-passage of vv. 3-4 which links the section about repentance with this section about disaster, there is no formal indicator of a new start and instead we abruptly find the words, **Announce in Judah and proclaim in Jerusalem and say.** These are all plural commands, not addressed to Jeremiah but constituting part of 'what the LORD says to the men of Judah and to Jerusalem' (4:3). The unrepentant citizens of the doomed land are being shown their destiny in advance. So real and certain is the judgment that is going to come on them in the form of a devastating enemy invasion that they are called on now to mobilise their forces and take up defensive positions.

The first message concerns the newly detected invader. The alarm has to be raised. **Sound**[57] **the trumpet throughout the land!** The trumpet was an instrument made of horn, which was not intended for musical performance (it emitted a raucous blare) but to give a signal. It was used in time of invasion or emergency to alert the populace throughout the land to imminent problem (Amos 3:6; Joel 2:1). There follows a series of imperatives, reflecting the breathless urgency of the

57. The kethibh *wetiqʿû*, 'and blow', seems to have a redundant initial *waw* by dittography of the final letter of the preceding word, and the qere reading *tiqʿû*, 'blow', is preferable, making it the start of the message.

situation. **Cry aloud** represents one interpretation of two asyndetic imperatives, 'Call out! Make full!', taking the second verb as an auxiliary to the first, referring to the complete nature of the cry, i.e. its loudness (GKC §120h; Joüon §177g). 'Make full' might also refer to filling the hand with a weapon ('take your weapons', NRSV footnote), or since 'call out' may be used in a military context for army service (Judg. 8:1), the two verbs might be an injunction for a full mobilisation of the defence forces. **And say: Gather together! Let us flee to the fortified cities!** This would have been the normal procedure in times of invasion. The people scattered throughout the villages and fields were called to assembly points. If they remained in the unwalled villages of the land, they would be easy prey to invading forces. So for their own safety they are urged to go to the fortified towns, whose walls would provide a measure of security against the enemy. There were several fortified cities in Judah apart from Jerusalem. When Sennacherib had invaded the land in 701 BC, he boasted he had captured forty-six fortified cities in Judah (*ANET*, 288), and there is some archaeological evidence that Josiah had strengthened sites such as Lachish (King 1993:79).

6. As well as the trumpet and the loudly shouted news, a visual signal would be used to alert people to the danger (Joel 2:1; Hos. 5:8). **Raise the signal** (*nēs*) **to go to Zion! Flee for safety without delay!** The signal would have been a pole with a flag which was erected on a prominent site such as a hilltop and would complement the sound of the trumpet (4:21; Isa. 5:26; 18:3; for a different technique see on 6:1). 'To go' is a translator's supplement; the text reads simply *ṣîwōnâ*, which would originally have meant 'to Zion'. So the hoisting of the signal-flag was a directive to move there, or possibly to pass the news on to Zion. Alternatively, the force of the ending as indicating movement may have become weakened (cf. 1:13) and the word may have simply locative force, 'in Zion', which would have been at the centre of any national system of warning signals. At any rate it is a picture of intense activity in the face of invasion with people being urged to make for safety as speedily as they could.

Verse 6, however, concludes on an ominous note. A people warned about invasion or impending disaster so that they could take appropriate action might have expected to be told that there was some likelihood of success for their defensive measures. But instead the need for their action is spelled out, **for** (*kî*) **I am bringing disaster from the north, even terrible destruction.** This reference to disaster from the north goes back to the message of 1:13-14, but its truly ominous note is that the disaster is divinely instigated. The enemy they see is not their true antagonist; it is the LORD himself who stands opposed to them.

Over one-third of the Old Testament occurrences of *šeber* ('destruction'/'breaking') are in Jeremiah. The phrase found here, *šeber gādôl*, 'great breaking', is also used by Zephaniah (Zeph. 1:10), a prophet whose ministry overlapped that of Jeremiah, but the direction of adoption of the term, if any, is unclear. Holladay (1986, 1:153) identifies three ways in which the prophet uses the root *šābar*, 'to break, shatter': for the fracture of a bone (and hence metaphorically for the spiritual condition of the people, 6:14; 8:21; 10:19); for the shattering of pottery (18:10); and for the breaking down of walls in a town or village (19:11). The breaking of the land describes the demolition of the physical infrastructure of the country, and evokes a picture of crashing buildings and tumbling walls, of farms shattered and widespread ruin. How then would its inhabitants fare?

7. The NIV takes vv. 7 and 8 as the speech of the prophet as he describes a vision he has seen. The change from masculine plurals of v. 6 to feminine singular in 'your land' and 'your towns' suggests that v. 7 was not originally linked with v. 6. In the present context it is difficult to explain why the feminines of v. 7 occur, because in v. 8 the commands revert to being masculine plural.

Jeremiah describes the aggressor as **a lion**, *ʾaryēh*, a different word from that found in 2:15, but in no way diminishing the overtones of cruelty and rapacity. It **has come out of his lair**, the 'thicket' of trees and shrubs in which it lies to sleep. A prowling lion would ordinarily constitute a threat to an individual or small group, but it is more than an animal that is involved here. **A destroyer of nations has set out** (<√*nāsaʿ*, 'to pull up one's tent pegs' and so 'to start a journey') moves from rhetorical to plain speech and makes clear the political and military nature of the menace that is advancing upon Judah, indeed upon the nations generally. 'Destroyer' (<√*šāḥat*, hiphil; 51:1) derives from a term that denotes not casual looting but thorough devastation. The identity of this individual/nation has been variously assessed, but it does not appear that Jeremiah need be supposed to have had any particular enemy identified for him when he first passed on this message. That we are talking about a movement from Mesopotamia is clear from the use of 'north', but the vision conveys a general sense of menace rather than identifying a specific attacker (cf. 2:30).

He has left his place to lay waste your land. For 'lay waste', see on 2:15. It is not a random unpremeditated attack that is envisaged but a deliberate movement of enemy forces with a definite strategy. The result of this is stated in: **Your towns will lie in ruins** (<√*nāṣâ*, II 'to fall in ruins')**, without inhabitant.** The conventional policy of seeking refuge in the cities will prove ineffective in this case, because rather than providing protection, the cities themselves will fall before the enemy and no one will be left alive in them.

8. So certain is the impending disaster that the people may as well get ready for the inevitable. What they are urged to do is not to repent, but to mourn. **So** (*ʿal-zōʾt*, 'on account of this') **put on sackcloth.** The verb 'put on' (<√*ḥāgar* 'to gird oneself') suggests that they wear it round the waist. Being clothed in this coarse material made of goat or camel hair might be associated with repentance (Jon. 3:5), but it was also commonly worn as a sign of mourning or disaster (6:26; 49:3; 48:37; Joel 1:13). Even though the disaster has not yet occurred, Jeremiah warns the people that they may as well begin mourning right away. Still, within that prognosis there is a chink of light, in that any who accept the accuracy of the prophet's warning and begin to mourn will be turning in repentance, and as the threatened catastrophe has not yet engulfed them, it might not yet be too late to avert it. However, Jeremiah's principal theme is the inevitability of the looming judgment. **Lament** (<√*sāpad* 16:4) **and wail** (<√*yālal* hiphil, used of shrill cries of sorrow, but not mourning for the dead)**, for** (*kî*) **the fierce anger of the LORD has not turned away from us.**[58] 'The fierceness of his anger' (*ḥărôn ʾap*, a frequent combination, with *ḥārôn* possibly coming from the human reaction of becoming hot and red-faced when angry) is a burning anger that arises from Israel's continuing apostasy. The 'us' betrays the prophet's identification with the people. He cannot see their fate in prospect without reacting as one of them, recognising his solidarity with the people of his day. As the LORD's prophet he has not received any exemption from the distress that is going to come on them, and so he feels for and with them. Earlier in 2:25 they had glibly assumed that the LORD's anger had passed from them, but without true repentance this could not be. 'Turn away' (<√*šûb*, 'turn/return') reminds of the previous warnings. If they do not turn back to the LORD, then his fierce wrath will not turn back from them. Where is now the immunity that the Jerusalem ideology assured them of?

9. The formula, **'In that day,' declares the LORD**, raises the question of whether or not 'that day' is here used as a technical term or just as a

58. The NRSV takes *kî* not as a causal connector but as introducing speech, so that 'The fierce anger of the LORD has not turned away from us' is the content of what they will wail. So also Holladay (1974:48).

link-phrase relating the LORD's message to the preceding description of invasion and sweeping devastation. Isaiah had already extensively used 'that day' as a way of referring to the coming time of divine intervention when his enemies would be subdued and his people delivered (for instance, Isa. 2:11, 20, and compare Isa. 26:1 and 27:1). But there was another side to 'that day' or 'the day of the LORD', as Amos had shown. He had presented it as a time when the LORD would also punish his own people for their waywardness. 'Why do you long for the day of the LORD? That day will be darkness, not light' (Amos 5:18; cf. also Amos 2:13-16; 3:13-15; 5:20). Zephaniah developed the same theme extensively (Zeph. 1:7-18; 2:1-3; 3:8, 11-20; see Mackay 1998:258-9). Jeremiah too employs 'that day' to refer to God's action in judgment and deliverance (30:7, 8; cf. similar phrases 'day of slaughter' 12:3; 'day of despair' 17:16; 'day of disaster' 17:17-18; 'day of their disaster' 18:17). Although these references refer primarily to the time of divine judgment against Judah, they are to be set against the background of the final intervention of the LORD (see on vv. 23-26 below).

The day of divine intervention will reverse all merely human expectations and lead to the psychological disintegration of a society whose value system and aspirations are based on them. The leading groups in the land (for their identity see on 2:8, 26; they are again grouped together in 8:1; 13:13; 17:25; 25:18; 32:36; 44:17, 21) will be unable to cope with a crisis that turns upside down their whole way of thinking: and if that is so, what of those under them whose lives they have ruled and shaped? Jeremiah was conscious that his message ran counter to the consensus expectations of his times because he is predicting how the LORD's action will undermine the prevailing power structures of the land. Even when re-presented in the First Scroll, it still awaited its final fulfilment. It is little wonder that Jeremiah's preaching was treated as seditious and demoralising.

The Jerusalem establishment held to the belief that they were divinely guaranteed peace and security. When their presumed immunity from disaster is shattered by the advance of so overwhelming an enemy, **the king and his officials will lose heart.** The very groups who should organise the defences and boost the people's resolve to resist will be so taken aback by the turn of events that they are unable to function properly. 'Heart' here refers to their nerve, courage and firmness of resolve (Deut. 20:2-3; 2 Sam. 17:10; Pss. 22:14; 73:26). The religious leadership of the country will also crumble: **The priests will be horrified, and the prophets will be appalled.** The root *šāmēm*, 'be horrified' (2:12), sums up their emotional response to a scene of devastation, and implies that the shock received is such as to leave them discouraged and at a loss to know what to do or say. Their whole theological outlook would be nullified by the catastrophe. The root *tāmâ*, 'be appalled', which is often found along with *šāmēm*, relates to a stunned surprise at unanticipated events (Job 26:11; Ps. 48:5[6]). The prophets who had made such confident predictions about the future based on their religious and social presuppositions will be unable to gather their wits and organise a response to the decisive falsification of their presuppositions and forecasts.

The unqualified picture of doom presented in the preceding section might suggest that Jeremiah is proclaiming that judgment is unavoidable. That, however, fails to do justice to the conditional nature of much prophecy (18:7-11). The description that is given is of what will inevitably happen if repentance is not forthcoming, and the objective in setting out such a scenario is to avoid it by alerting the hearers to the peril of their situation and inducing them to change their attitudes by repentance.

b. Divine Deception? (4:10)

Jeremiah was the LORD's messenger whose primary task was to relay what was revealed to him. As we have seen (e.g. in vv. 7-8), he also pressed upon the people the need to respond to the message he was conveying to them. The prophet approached neither of these tasks in a cold or distant fashion. He saw himself as part of his people, with his hopes and destiny very much part of theirs. It is therefore not surprising that he reacted to what had been divinely revealed to him. No doubt other prophets did so also. But what is surprising in Jeremiah's case is the extent to which he has recorded his personal reaction. It is difficult to tell if these personal notes formed part of Jeremiah's preaching before 605 BC. That he included them in the First Scroll is perhaps a response to allegations made by his opponents that he was callous and indifferent to the welfare of the people, perhaps even that he secretly revelled in the horrors he predicted for them. By intruding so much of his own attidtude into the record of his ministry and of the divine revelation given to him, Jeremiah was attempting to sway the people to reassess their attitude towards him, but more importantly he was trying to lead them to respond more positively to the message he brought.

10. This verse records Jeremiah's private feelings at what he was given to announce to the people.[59] **Then I said**[60] introduces a note of personal bewilderment: **Ah, Sovereign LORD** (cf. 1:6). Jeremiah completely accepts the status of the LORD and the fact that it is his prerogative to proceed as he sees fit. But at the same time he was aware of the inner tension he felt between the message revealed to him and his own instinctive reaction to it.

How completely you have deceived this people and Jerusalem. *ʾākēn*, 'how' (3:20), is used here in an emphatic sense. 'Deceive' (<√*nāšāʾ* II hiphil, cf. Gen. 3:13) raises questions about the nature of Jeremiah's speech. Calvin supposed that the speech was ironic, bitterly taunting and deriding those who had falsely prophesied in the LORD's name (1850, 1:213-4). Others have suggested that at an early stage in his ministry Jeremiah supposed that the other prophets were sent by God. After all, they were associated with the Temple and were widely regarded as true spokesmen of the LORD. It is noted that even as late as the events of chapter 28 Jeremiah had difficulty when confronted with the message of a false prophet promising peace. He wished their message was indeed true even though it conflicted with his own, and so it is argued that this early prophecy reflects his thinking before he came to appreciate fully the character of the false prophets. Most probably, however, Jeremiah's speech reflects the Hebrew mode of thought in which all is ultimately ascribed to God. He had permitted the false prophets to arise. 'God not only permits these lying spirits to appear and work, but has ordained them and brought them forth for the hardening of the people's heart; as he once caused the spirit of prophecy to inspire as a lying spirit the prophets of Ahab, so that by promises of victory they prevailed upon him to march to that war in which, as a punishment for his godlessness, he was to perish; 1 Kgs. 22:2-23' (Keil 1873, 1:109). 'This people' may involve a note of dissociation. Though Jeremiah is prepared to identify with the people, he can also stand over against them and perceive their failings. Here he is functioning as an intercessor between them and God, effectively pleading that the people's doom consequent on their rebellion had arisen because of

---

59. The verse is generally taken to be prose, though BHS and the NKJV treat it as poetry. Indeed v. 9 is also presented as prose in the NRSV. This illustrates how poetry shades off into elevated prose and poetry, and raises doubts as to whether any major interpretative significance should be attached to the distinction, particularly in marginal cases.

60. There is some weak textual evidence in the Codex Alexandrinus and the late Arabic version for reading 'and they will say', referring to the priests and prophets. As textual evidence goes, this is flimsy to say the least, but there are those who would adopt the reading as a conjectural emendation.

what God had allowed to happen.

By saying, 'You will have peace.' This was the message that the false prophets brought (6:14; 14:13; 23:17). It played a significant part in the popular theology of the day that the LORD would provide peace (*šālôm*) for Jerusalem (*yərûšālēm*). 'Peace' undoubtedly implied absence of warfare, which is always a major blessing (see on 23:17), but the term stretched beyond exemption from the turmoil caused by foreign aggression. It denoted personal well-being and economic prosperity along with the concomitant feelings of satisfaction and contentment. Peace was indeed what the LORD aimed to provide for his people as part of the prosperity associated with the blessings of the covenant (see on 2:7), because he 'delights in the well-being (*šālôm*) of his servant' (Ps. 35:27). 'Covenant of peace' would be used to describe the total restoration the LORD would provide for his people (Ezek. 34:25; 37:26).

The message the false prophets propagated with the approval of the religious and state authorities was a distortion of this because it defined peace as the continuation of the political status quo without any acknowledgment of the covenantal dimensions of peace. So there had occurred the contradiction of the preaching of an assured peace at a time **when the sword is**/'touches, reaches as far as' **at our throats.** 'Our' is an NIV supplement, and 'their' would fit better in with the note of distance in 'this people'. For 'throat' as a rendering of *nepeš*, see 2:24 footnote and *TWOT* #1395a. Less probable is the rendering 'heart' (NKJV), which is deduced from the more common meaning of the word, 'self, inner being, person'. They had been lulled into a false sense of security and this was going to be rudely shattered when the risk to their lives was made starkly obvious.

c. Swift Advance (4:11-18)

In this unit Jeremiah again reverts to describing the enemy invasion, before recording his personal reaction to the vision of judgment (vv. 19-22). Traditionally the speaker in vv. 11-12 has been identified as the LORD, and the NIV identifies vv. 16-18 also as divine speech, though v. 18 is less certain. Verses 13-15 may then be Jeremiah's own speech, combining a report of visions he has received and advice as to the appropriate response to it.

11-12. After the prophet's own reaction, **at that time** resumes from 'in that day' of v. 9, but particularly introduces an extension of the invasion scene of vv. 5-7. Although the NIV treats these verses as prose, others (BHS, NKJV, REB) present them as poetry. **This people**

and Jerusalem (as in v. 10) **will be told** is a somewhat oblique expression and Jones suggests that it may be 'a saying which had been spoken before, perhaps not originally by Jeremiah, but will be spoken in circumstances which make it cruelly relevant' (1992:113). Henderson argues that the identity of the speaker is left deliberately obscure (2002:200).

The impending judgment will come like **a scorching wind from the barren heights in the desert**. For 'barren heights', see on 3:2. The wind is the sirocco (13:24; 18:17; Hos. 13:15) which blows in from the desert to the east of Palestine. But it is not the direction of the wind that is significant (the enemy will come from the north), but its effect: carrying dust and sand with it, it is low in humidity, and searingly suffocating and oppressive. It **blows towards** (there is no word for 'blows', but rather *derek*, 'way', which taken as an accusative of respect implies 'towards') **my people, but not to winnow or cleanse; a wind too strong for that** (literally, 'full from these', probably referring to the two functions of winnowing and cleansing) **comes from me.** After grain had been harvested, it was threshed to separate the kernels, which were left on the threshing floor mixed with particles of straw and chaff. At an exposed site with a good current of air, this mixture was then tossed up using a winnowing fork, and the lighter straw and chaff would be blown away while the kernels fell to the ground. This might happen a number of times before the ears of grain were finally shaken in a sieve. The strength of the sirocco made it unsuitable for this purpose—both grain and chaff would be blown away. The sirocco is thus a suitable metaphor for the indiscriminate destruction brought on the land by the inrush of the enemy forces. It will not be a beneficent breeze, but a gale bringing havoc. There will be no attempt to distinguish between the good and the bad—all will be blown away before it. But the most devastating feature of the invasion is not the ferocity of the enemy, but the fact that it is 'from me'. God is acting against his people, but he is not going to chastise them so as to purify them. His determination is to sweep them away.

There are, however, two features of the NIV translation that require further consideration. The translation 'my people' obscures the fact that there is another word (*'ammî*) that is similarly translated (e.g. in v. 22; 2:11, 13, 31-32; 5:31). That expression conceptualises the people as a group of individuals, who are then frequently referred to by a masculine plural pronoun. The phrase here is literally 'daughter of my people' (also found at 6:[14], 26; 8:11, 19, 21, 22; 9:1, 7; 14:17) where the imagery is that of an individual woman, who is generally in Jeremiah in a situation of distress, and who is subsequently referred to by a feminine singular pronoun. The phrase may well not be a construct chain as traditionally understood, 'the daughter of my people' (NKJV), but two nouns in apposition, 'daughter, my people'. The use of 'daughter' to refer to the people is found elsewhere in Jeremiah (4:31; 6:2, 23; 31:22), and this particular mode of address is an endearing personification of the nation—'my very own people', 'my dear people'. The NRSV translates the phrase as 'my poor people', which brings out the note of sympathy in its use, but loses the relational overtones of 'daughter'. But despite the acknowledgment of the close bond between them, the LORD adheres to his purpose, **Now I** (emphatic; 'it is I who', NRSV) **pronounce my judgments against them.** For the phrase, see on 1:16. Behind the destructive wind which symbolises the enemy stands the LORD himself and he is the real force to be reckoned with as he passes sentence against his people.

Henderson presents another plausible interpretation of the passage based round the fact that 'from me' (*lî*) in the description of the wind would be more naturally rendered 'for me' (2002:200).[61] He argues that in this case the speaker is the prophet who both speaks against the people and shares in their fate. The reader is forced to the shocking realisation that the prophet who had formerly interceded for the people now says, 'Now even I will pronounce judgment against them.' However, reading 'for me' is more likely to refer to the LORD and indicate that the wind comes at divine direction (cf. NASB).

13. Jeremiah next dramatically describes what he has seen of how the destroying army will come and put the LORD's sentence into effect. **Look!** is a gasp. The prophet's own breath has been taken away by the vision, and he is trying to communicate his consternation to the people. The subject of the vision is not explicitly identified, but it is obviously the invading army. Three terse images are used to reinforce the theme of ominous speed. **He advances**[62] **like the clouds.** It is a picture of a mass of dark storm-clouds sweeping across the sky (Joel 2:2; Ezek. 38:16) and enveloping the land in dark foreboding. **His chariots come like a whirlwind.** The 'whirlwind' (*sûpâ*) is a strong wind that causes destruction. It is the picture of the dust of their wheels (the 'stour', if one may be permitted a Scotticism) stirred up by the speed at which they advance (Isa. 5:28; 66:15). **His horses are swifter than eagles.**

---

61. The NIV margin and the NASB render *lî* as 'at my command'.

62. A problem arises as regards the tense to use in translating the verb. The imperfect may be a true future, 'he shall come up' (NKJV), but it is more likely to convey a present continuous action, 'he is coming up', describing what was immediately before the prophet's eye in vision.

Horses were a major component of ancient armies. 'Eagles' (or 'vultures', *nešer* covers both) swoop down to snatch their prey (Hab. 1:8). As well as being a picture of swiftness, the imagery contains an element of revulsion as both birds are unclean (Lev. 11:13), probably because of their contact with carcasses and blood. Here is the implementation of the covenant curse of Deut. 28:49, 'The LORD will bring a nation against you from far away, from the ends of the earth, like an eagle swooping down.'

Jeremiah does not rely just on visual imagery to set out the future scene. He reports the sounds that will be heard, for he has already witnessed the cry of alarm and dismay that will be uttered by the people on that day, and joins them in it. The wail of the people, **Woe to us!** is linked to, **We are ruined!** by *kî*, 'for', setting out the reason for their panic stricken cry (but compare Holladay 1986, 1:157). They see no hope for themselves as the enemy war forces come speedily upon them. 'Ruined' (<√*šādad*, 'to destroy', generally of the damage caused by a marauding army as it loots and plunders; 51:1) occurs 26 times in Jeremiah out of a total of 50 in the Old Testament.

14. Jeremiah then interrupts the description of the enemy advance to address Jerusalem directly. This is not part of the vision but an attempt by the prophet to bring the people to their senses. Will they not learn before it is too late? **O Jerusalem, wash the evil from your heart.** It is a call for deep and effective repentance with the removal of all the moral defilement that affected them. 'Wash' (<√*kābas* piel) is used for ritual washing of garments, and such external action had already been pronounced ineffective (2:22). The 'heart' refers to the whole interior being where Hebrew psychology located the feelings, thinking and willing (v. 4). The thought is reminiscent of the words of Ps. 51:2, 7, though there the washing is done by God. Here the people are called on to act (cf. v. 4) so that the LORD would accept them. The NIV **and be saved** does not really do justice to *ləmaʿan*, a particle indicating purpose or result; 'so that you may be saved' (NRSV) is to be preferred. What they are urged to do is to wash not in pretence or superficially, but with the solemn intention of being divinely saved (<√*yāšaʿ* niphal). The root *yāšaʿ* is used for deliverance from danger of all sorts. Here the thought is principally rescue from the impending disaster. This can only be achieved by turning away from all that offends the only one who is able to effect that salvation.

Jeremiah follows his plea with a rhetorical question, which can only be answered with some admission of guilt: **How long will you harbour**[63] **wicked thoughts?** The picture is that of lodgers staying as guests within the city. 'Thoughts' (<*maḥăšābâ*, 11:19) refers to plans that may be for good or ill. 'Wicked' (*'āwen*), however, refers to conduct that corruptly misuses power in any situation. It is not a spontaneous action, but deliberate, and is morally heinous and damaging to one's relationship with God and others. The phrase 'wicked thoughts' may focus on thoughts harmful to their neighbours (Prov. 6:18; Isa. 55:7; 59:7), but it is more probable that it is their conduct generally that is in view. 'Within you' (not directly translated in the NIV) refers in the first instance to within the city, but it is also used of the interior of the person, not anatomically but psychologically (31:33). The situation already exists, but will the citizens of Jerusalem continue to tolerate it any longer in view of the impending judgment of God?

15. Again the description switches back to the advancing enemy. It begins with 'for' (*kî*) which may convey the thought: 'How long will you persist in such behaviour? for be assured disaster is already on its way.' Participles are used to indicate that this is taking place before the prophet's very eyes. **A voice is announcing from Dan.** Dan was a major city, lying near the source of the Jordan. It was traditionally taken as the northernmost limit of the land of Palestine (Judg. 20:1), and so it was most vulnerable to invasion from Mesopotamia. But word of the advancing foe does not stop there. News comes in from further south**, proclaiming disaster from the hills of Ephraim.** The reference may not be to a specific peak, but to the hill country of Ephraim which was situated rounded Shechem, and so lay just north of Jerusalem. The news that is brought is of 'disaster'/'harm' (*'āwen*), the same word as in v. 13. It is used to emphasise the proportionality of the retribution that the LORD is bringing on his errant people (cf. the similar use of *rāʿâ* in 1:14, 16; 23:10, 12).

16. 'Against me' and 'declares the LORD' in v. 17 clearly identify that verse as divine speech. Since v. 16 closely links in with v. 17, it too may be taken as divine speech. In that case, **Tell it to the nations**, which is a plural command, probably indicates the LORD's instructions

---

63. The verb is *tālîn* (<√*lûn*, 'to lodge, pass the night'). The form may be third feminine singular or second masculine singular imperfect, and may come from either the qal or the hiphil. The hiphil ('to cause to rest/stay') is less unusual for this verb, and to suit the passage where Jerusalem is taken as feminine would have to be second feminine singular: 'How long will you cause wicked thoughts to lodge in your midst (*bəqirbēk*)?' The qal verb might be taken as 'How long will wicked thoughts lodge in your midst?' Though this has the problem of a plural noun with a singular verb, this is not unknown in Hebrew (GKC §145k; Joüon §150g).

to those bringing the message. What is happening in Palestine is not merely of local significance: it has international implications (cf. 1:5) because the LORD is bringing judgment upon his chosen people. All should watch and consider their own fate if this is what happens here (1 Pet. 4:17-18). **Proclaim it to Jerusalem,** where it would of course be headline news. *ʿal* is treated by the NIV as a variant of *ʾel*, 'to', but a note of hostility 'against' may be present (so NKJV, NRSV). **A besieging army is coming from a distant land**. 'A besieging army' is literally 'watchers' (<√*nāṣar*, 'to watch over, guard'). The idea seems that they come and tightly monitor the situation around the city so as to prevent movement in or out (cf. 'a city under siege' Isa. 1:8). The reference to a 'distant land' fits in with the idea of a foe from the north, rather than an Egyptian invasion. **Raising**[64] **a war cry against the cities of Judah**/'giving their voice against' conveys the menace and intimidation of the shouts of the advancing army.

17. They surround[65] **her like men guarding a field.** The occupation forces are depicted as going about their task with careful thoroughness as they deploy 'against her all around' (NKJV), enclosing her as effectively as farmers trying to keep their crops or animals safe from the depredations of marauding animals or thieves. Here, however, it is the marauders who have done the surrounding, and they are intent on taking the city. The reason for this is inescapable. The city the LORD chose and blessed is to experience this, **'Because** (*kî*) **she has rebelled against me,' declares the LORD.** 'Against me' is brought forward for emphasis; this is more than a matter of international politics. Notice how the NIV punctuation makes it clear that this is part of the message that is to be conveyed to the nations. It is not just a matter of warning them also of a possible military threat; they are to be informed of the theological reasons for what has happened.

18. This is an additional word addressed by the LORD to Jerusalem (here referred to in the feminine singular) to make abundantly clear how this situation has been arrived at. **Your own conduct** (*derek* 'way') **and actions have brought**[66] **this upon you.** The LORD's action is just and merited. **This is your punishment** (<*raʿ*, 'evil, disaster').

64. The *waw*-consecutive imperfect *wayyitənû* continues the sense of the preceding participle.

65. The perfect *hāyû* ('they are') is used here as a prophetic perfect in connection with a future event seen as so certain that it is described as completed.

66. The Massoretic Text reads the infinitive absolute *ʿāśô*, but Hebrew manuscripts do vary, some having the form *ʿāśōh* (a variant spelling) and many others the perfect *ʿāśû*, 'they have done/made'.

The wickedness they had thought and done had brought this disaster on them as their punishment. **How bitter it is! How it pierces to the heart!** In both exclamations 'how' renders *kî* in an emphatic sense. A causative sense is possible if the preceding clause is understood as, 'This is the ⌊outcome of⌋ your evil'. 'For it is bitter, for it reaches through to your heart' then presents a tolerable line of thought connecting the extent of their wrongdoing with the nature of their punishment. However, 'bitter' (2:19) relates more to the consequences of their acts than the acts themselves. 'Bitter' is associated with the sour taste of wormwood (Prov. 5:4; Lam. 3:15). It is not just a disagreeable taste that is left in their mouths by what they have done. The punishment associated with breach of the terms of the covenant strikes deep into their inner being. It is difficult to see why the NIV prefers 'the heart' to 'your heart' as in the Hebrew, because that emphasises the personal impact of what is to happen.

d. The Prophet's Anguish (4:19-22)

There have been various changes of speaker in the preceding passage and this raises the question as to who is speaking in these verses. The options explored have been: (1) the LORD, (2) Jeremiah and (3) the people. In favour of (1) is the fact that v. 22 is undoubtedly divine speech. 'They do not know me' can hardly be interpreted otherwise. Equally vv. 16-18 have, as has been argued above, to be taken as divine speech, and on this approach the one speaker would be found throughout this section. The LORD would be expressing his intense distress at the lack of response on the part of the people and at the fact that they are as a consequence having to suffer. One does, however, wonder if the language, taken as anthropomorphic, has really any proper reference when applied to God, e.g. 'My heart is throbbing within me; I cannot keep silent.' There is also the problem of interpreting 'my tents', 'my shelter' in v. 20, although this could be taken as divine identification with the people.

It is of course one of the strongest arguments in favour of option (3) that the terms 'my tents' and 'my shelter' can then be readily understood as those of the personified nation viewed as one individual. Further the people were already introduced abruptly as speakers in v. 13b. Carroll argues that 'the land (Judah) or the city (Jerusalem) would be the most fitting subject of the lament in vv. 19-21 (cf. 30.12-15), and the poem should be understood as an expression of the community's disturbance and disintegration under the onslaught of the enemy from the north' (1986:167). Perhaps the words could be understood as those of a loyal few within the land, but that would make the transition to the LORD speaking of his people as fools in v. 22 rather harsh.

Most interpreters favour option (2). We have already seen in vv. 10 and 14 that the prophet was no unthinking mouthpiece of the message he delivered. He felt intensely the distress and disaster which he knew was about to come on his people, and on later occasions also we find him pouring out the anguish of his heart to God. These words would then express his dismay as he contemplated what the LORD had revealed to him of his judgment coming on the people. It is easier to take 'my tents' and 'my shelter' in v. 20 as prophetic identification with the people than as divine identification. Even so, the conclusion of Keil is worth remembering: 'The prophet certainly is expressing his personal feelings regarding the nearing catastrophe, but in doing so he lends words to the grief which all the godly will feel. The lament of v. 20 ... is unquestionably the lament not of the prophet as an individual, but of the congregation, i.e. of the godly among the people' (1873, 1:115).

19. In uttering **Oh, my anguish, my anguish!** Jeremiah expresses his distress at what he has been permitted to preview as certain to happen when the LORD's judgment is executed upon the land. His description of his personal anguish is not an interruption to the proclamation of the invasion and its associated suffering. It is an intensification of the scene because the prophet is no idle spectator but one who identifies with his people and suffers along with them. Visions from God can turn into nightmares of extraordinary impact and intensity when they describe the outpouring of divine judgment (see on vv. 23-26). Because of his experience of the intransigence of the people Jeremiah has deep foreboding that they would not repent and that the threatened judgment would take place. The repeated 'my anguish' is literally 'my bowels' (*mēʿay*, 'bowels, intestines', 31:20; Lam. 1:20; 2:11). The repetition serves to intensify the emotion behind the cry. The inner organs of the abdomen were considered by Hebrew speakers to be the seat of various emotions; here bewilderment, astonishment and anguish (see McKane 1986, 1:102-3). The problem for translators is to know how to render this in English, where references to 'bowels' verge on the indelicate, and are certainly obscure. Using the corresponding emotion fails to do justice to the linked emotional and physical reaction conveyed by the Hebrew. Jeremiah so identified with his people that anticipating what they were about to experience affected him physiologically too.

I writhe in pain.[67] 'Writhe' (<√*ḥûl*) refers to uncontrollable trembling and physical distress on witnessing God's judgment. This very disturbed condition is due to the emotional shock he has sustained as a result of what he has been shown. No doubt telling the people about his personal reaction was intended to impress on them the severity of what was to come. It was not a cry for sympathy for himself so much as an anguished plea for their repentance.

Jeremiah continues to give vent to his inner turmoil. **Oh, the agony of my heart!** is literally 'walls of my heart' (*lēb*, 17:1). Though 'wall' (*qîr*) is only attested of physical walls, the metaphorical use is easily understood as conveying that Jeremiah is experiencing such inner turbulence and pressure that he feels it is about to rip him apart. **My heart** (*lēb*) **pounds within me** attempts to make sense of another obscure expression. The participle used is from the root *hāmâ*, which combines the notions of loud noise and movement (e.g. the roaring of the waves in 5:22). It is probable that in neither expression are we to understand a reference to the heart as a bodily organ, as if Jeremiah were saying the stress is so much I am about to have a heart attack. Heart refers to his thought and emotions, which are in turmoil, shrieking a thousand and one things within him so that he has to let it out: **I cannot keep silent.** But still it is not just physical relief for his inward agony. He must tell the people what it is that he has been told (20:9; 6:11; Ps. 39:3-4; Amos 3:8).

He then makes clear the reason for his intense distress as he talks to himself, 'You have heard, O my soul' (NKJV). **For** (*kî*) **I have heard**[68] **the sound of the trumpet; I have heard the battle cry** (cf. 20:16)**.** The prophet emphasises that through the divine vision granted to him he has already in his inner being experienced what is to come on the people as a whole. For trumpet, see on 4:5; the trumpet sound here is probably that of the enemy troops as they advance (see also v. 21). The din of battle horns and the shouting of combatants are also referred to in 49:2.

20. The verb *qāra'* found in the first clause of this verse is homonymous with the two meanings 'to call' or 'to meet'. It is

---

67. The kethibh is *'ḥwlh* and the qere is *'ōḥîlâ*, 'I will wait', but this yields no good sense. Taking the verb as a byform of *ḥûl*, 'to writhe', and understanding the cohortative form as conveying necessity, the meaning 'I must writhe' is suggested (GKC §108g; Joüon §114cN).

68. The qere is *šāma'at*, the second feminine singular perfect, 'you have heard'. The kethibh *šāma'tî* is probably an old second feminine singular form (cf. 4:30; 2:20), with the same translation, in both cases the feminine reference is to the noun *nepeš*, 'self' (2:34).

therefore possible to take the verb *niqrāʾ* in the first line as 'is called': 'Destruction upon destruction is cried' (NKJV), continuing the description of the battle sounds of v. 19. The next clause introduced by *kî*, 'for', then states the reason for these cries being made, namely that the whole land is plundered, and the second part of the verse could be understood as continuing the distressed cries of the people.

Adopting the other meaning of *qāraʾ* leads to a translation such as **disaster follows disaster** (*šeber*, 'breaking', see v. 6), which describes waves of catastrophe following close behind one another as towns and villages fall and are destroyed in succession until **the whole land lies in ruins.** In this case the *kî* introducing the second clause may be understood as an emphatic (not translated in the NIV) or it may state the grounds on which the statement regarding disaster has been made. The enemy forces have wrought havoc as they passed through the land.

It is emphasised that the invasion has been swift. **In an instant** (*pitʾōm*, 'suddenly', is frequently used in contexts of calamity or invasion, 6:26; 15:8; 18:22; 51:8) **my tents are destroyed** (<√*šādad*, v. 13), **my shelter in a moment.** 'Shelter'/'curtains' refers to the sheets, often made from goat hair, that were stretched over a wooden frame to form the sides of the tent, and so they are used by synecdoche for the whole tent (10:20; Isa. 54:2). Ellison points out that tents here will not refer either to military tents, since there would be no attempt to meet the invading forces in the field, or to ordinary dwellings, for even the Rechabites took refuge in Jerusalem (35:11). 'The tents must stand for defencelessness, and it is probably the prophet's own isolation that is implied; he sees himself swallowed up in the storm which he has in God's name called upon the land' (1960:219). Thompson takes it of the prophet's physical defencelessness in view of the calamity: 'his flimsy shelter was thrown down and its curtains torn to shreds' (1980:228). But it is more probable that the prophet is identifying with the people and using traditional language to talk about the devastation brought on the land.

21. Jeremiah then sighs in emotional weariness and perplexity at the tragedy the LORD has revealed to him. **How long must I see**[69] **the battle standard and hear the sound of the trumpet?** 'The battle standard' (*nēs,* v. 6) may well refer to the signal flags of the defenders as they warn of the approaching army, and in that case the trumpet sound might well be theirs too (in contrast to v. 19). We may picture

69. The following *ʾešməʿâ*, 'let me hear', is a cohortative, and so parallelism indicates that *ʾerʾeh* is to be read similarly; for the translation 'must' cf. footnote 67 above.

Jeremiah, hands to his ears, with the din of battle on both sides, crying out in distress as to how long this will continue. 'How long?' is often heard in the Psalms as a cry of perplexity, pleading for the end of an ongoing situation of trouble and turmoil (Pss. 6:3; 74:10; 79:5; 80:4; 82:2; 94:3). These words are uttered by faith which grasps that the negativity of judgment and affliction will not be the LORD's last word on the destiny of his people.

22. After the emotional intensity and confused upheaval of the previous verses, Jeremiah inserts an oracle in which the LORD speaks in measured and cool tones reminiscent of the language of the wisdom teachers as found in Proverbs or Ecclesiastes. The switch may well have been designed to shock the people into an appropriate response. The verse begins with *kî*, but it is difficult to know what to make of the translation 'for' (NKJV, NRSV) without there being a considerable supplement, 'This has come about and will continue, for …' The NIV may well be correct in taking the term as emphatic here.

My people are fools. The 'fool' (*ʾĕwîl*) is mentioned 19 times in Proverbs and twice in Job, not as one who lacks intellectual prowess, but one who is spiritually insensitive. In the language of Scripture there are many very intelligent fools. The essence of their folly is **they do not know me** (cf. 9:2). The object 'me' (*ʾōtî*) begins the clause to emphasise that knowledge in other ways is not being denied to them, but they are deficient in this one respect in particular. 'Know' is used in its fullest sense (2:8; 9:24; Hos. 4:6; Isa. 28:9) as that recognition of the LORD as their covenant Overlord which has bound up with it submission to him and his requirements (22:15-16). **They are senseless children.** 'Senseless' (*sābāl*) occurs six times in Ecclesiastes where it is synonymous with 'fool' (*kəsîl*), one with a tendency to make wrong choices. Here 'senseless' points to their inability or unwillingness to discriminate between what is right and what is wrong so that they advise and act inappropriately. **They have no understanding.** There is a wordplay between *bānîm*, 'sons' and *nəbônîm*, 'understanding' (the niphal participle of *bîn*, 'to understand', which occurs nine times in Proverbs). They lack discernment to appreciate what information is relevant and to understand its implications so as to form appropriate decisions as the basis for their action. **They are skilled in doing evil; they know not how to do good.** 'Skilled'/'wise' (<*ḥākām*) indicates their practical ability when it comes to activities that are divinely frowned upon. 'The *ḥākām* ['wise one'] was the man who could devise a policy which was intellectually coherent and was an effective means of reaching a desiderated goal, and it was by this and not any ethical criterion that the "wisdom" of such a policy was judged' (McKane 1965:89). They had abandoned the way of the LORD where true wisdom (that is practical ability combined with ethical competence) is to be found, and had become spiritually blinded. Not only did this bring divine condemnation on them, it also caused their senseless indifference to the warnings which Jeremiah was so urgently communicating to them.

e. Uncreation (4:23-28)

There are two parts to this unit: vv. 23-26, a poem of exquisite formal beauty, followed by an explanatory and reinforcing word from the LORD in vv. 27-28.

The poem of vv. 23-26 is rendered all the more poignant by its stark coldness. This vision must have been received by Jeremiah at some other time than those related in vv. 5-7, 11-18, because here the prophet is not as in the earlier part of the chapter the involved and reactive observer. Perhaps one might liken his condition to the shell-shocked whose capacity to respond has been so drained by the trauma they have experienced that they speak in detached tones. The poem is all the more impressive for the distant perspective from which it is composed.

Each verse begins 'I looked' and also contains a 'behold', at the beginning of the second clause in vv. 23-24, but following immediately the verb in vv. 25-26. Understanding the vision requires determining what the key word *ʾereṣ* signifies in v. 23: is it 'the world' or 'the land', that is Judah? Lindblom is probably on the right lines when he argues, 'It was in a real vision that the prophet saw the chaotic disorder in the world, and that he then interpreted this vision as alluding to the devastation of Judaea' [rather, Judah] (1962:127). So this vision is not eschatological or apocalyptic in the strict sense, in that Jeremiah was not instructed to prophesy about the remote future or the end of the age. What has been revealed to him is a picture of the dissolution of the cosmos as a sign of how dire the impending desolation of Judah was to be and also as a sign of how structurally significant the divine action was. There was no incongruity or exaggeration involved: dissolving, however temporarily, the covenant bond between the LORD and Israel was a step of the same magnitude as undoing the divine creative purpose for the earth and reverting to pre-creation chaos.

23. Jeremiah reports on a vision he had received. **I looked at the earth, and it was formless and empty.** The language used is drawn from the creation account of Genesis 1. The 'earth ... and heavens' inverts the order of Gen. 1:1; 'I looked' (<√*rāʾâ*, 'to see') reminds of the repeated divine scrutiny when 'God saw' (<√*rāʾâ*, Gen. 1:4, 10, 12, 18, 21, 24, 31) but no longer reaching a climactic 'it was very good'; 'formless and empty' repeat the description of Gen. 1:2. It all indicates that the impact of God's judgment is to reverse the process of creation. He undoes it, by bringing it back not to nothingness but to the disordered state that prevailed after the initial creative act. **And at the heavens** might suggest that this is completely parallel with the first clause, but 'at' now is *ʾel*, 'to', and not the object marker as before. Jeremiah speaks as one who is located on earth. **And their light was gone.** This is a picture of the darkness on the face of the deep that prevailed before the first creative word (Gen. 1:2).

24. I looked at the mountains, and they were quaking. The mountains were frequently regarded as the 'everlasting foundations of the earth' (Mic. 6:2) whose roots stretched out under the ocean (Jon. 2:6). They were firm and unmovable, something that could be relied upon to be there. Only the power of the LORD could cause the ancient mountains to crumble and the age-old hills to collapse (Hab. 3:5). So when here they are said to 'quake' (<√*rāʿaš*, often associated with the onset of disintegration and chaos, Isa. 13:13; 24:18; Joel 2:1; Nah. 1:5; Hag. 2:6, 7, 21), there is no doubt as to how this has been brought about. **All the hills were swaying!** (<√*qālal* hithpalpel, probably meaning 'move backwards and forwards', but Lundbom [1999:360] suggests 'tossed about as if they had little or no weight') in the upheaval of the LORD's presence in judgment.

25. I looked, and there were no people. The second phrase (*ʾên hāʾādām*) is similar to that in 'there was no man to work the ground' (Gen. 2:5). The earth that was made to be inhabited is now forlorn and empty. It has also become a scene of terrifying quietness. **Every bird in the sky had flown away** (<√*nādad* 9:10). One might have expected a reference to the animals as in Hos. 4:3, but Jeremiah, who frequently mentions birds (9:10; 12:4; 17:11), uses them in a representative manner to bring out the lifelessness of the scene.

26. I looked, and the fruitful land (*karmel*, 2:7) **was a desert.** This may suggest a typical piece of fruitful land had become characteristically wilderness, but more probably the focus is on Canaan, the fruitful land of God's giving (2:6-7), which had reverted to wilderness. This is all the more likely as Jeremiah's focus moves from a scene of cosmic dissolution to one that focuses on Judah. **All its towns lay in ruins** introduces a feature that had not been present at creation. Here is what mankind achieved in their rule over creation, but now it lies in ruins

(<√*nātaṣ*, 'to pull down, tear down', cf. 1:10). Their cities with their fortifications are dismantled because the final judgment on human endeavour is that passed by the LORD. Two stark phrases sum up how creation is reversed: **before the LORD, before his fierce anger.** For 'fierce anger', see on 4:8. Jeremiah's vision incorporates various elements that are found in other prophetic descriptions of the day of the LORD's judgment (Joel 2:1-11; Amos 8:9-10; Nah. 1:2-8; Zeph. 1:2-3). It would be wrong to view his language simply as prophetic hyperbole used to describe a national situation of great distress. The vision of the ultimate judgment of God was the prism through which Jeremiah was led to see the catastrophic and expectation-shattering infliction that was to come on Judah.

27. 'The terrifying vision of vv. 23-26 with its message might have sounded obscure and undecipherable to the people, and so the message is repeated in clear and plain terms: God's anger, aroused by their contrasting ways, will not relent; neither will he change his mind, but will bring desolation and mourning to the land' (Castellino 1980:400). 'For' (*kî*) introduces the divine word that substantiates what has preceded. **This is what the LORD says: 'The whole land will be ruined.'** Although it is *ʾereṣ* ('land' or 'earth', cf. v. 23) that is used, it seems certain that the focus is back on Judah, explaining that it as part of the 'fruitful land' (v. 26) 'will become a desolation', *šəmāmâ*, a scene of utter ruin (2:15).

There then follows the clause **though I will not destroy it completely**/'but I will not make a full end', that is, bring it utterly into the state of uncreation described in vv. 23-26. 'Make a full end' (<√*kālâ*, cf. 5:2) connotes finality and completeness. But that the LORD commits himself to holding back from this has been felt to be at odds with the surrounding picture of total, indeed of cosmic, dissolution, and many attempts have been made at emendation or deletion. There is no textual evidence to support deletion of 'not' (*lōʾ*) but some would emend it to 'in it' (*lāh*): 'and I will make its destruction complete' (McKane 1986, 1:109; BHS; and seemingly Thompson 1980:230-31). Others, encouraged by Ugaritic usage, explore the possibility of an emphatic use of *lamedh* (*NIDOTTE* 4:1040): 'and a complete destruction I will surely make'. However, it seems best to retain the negative. Although in no way mitigating the severity of the LORD's chastisement of his people, nor suggesting that grace might be presumed on as if it permitted sinning with impunity, it had been revealed from earliest times that his punishment of them was within bounds: 'I will not reject them or abhor them so as to destroy them completely (<√*kālâ* piel), breaking my covenant with them' (Lev. 26:44). It is to this principle of divine covenant retribution that reference is again made in 5:10, 18. These passages must be interpreted in the light of the unambiguous statement in 30:11, 'Though I completely destroy all the nations among which I scatter you, I will not completely destroy you'. Here the parenthetic comment (brought out by the NIV use of 'though') serves notice that this principle is not infringed even though there has been a portrayal of the sweeping nature of divine judgment.

28. Therefore/'on account of this' refers back to the devastation and ruin of v. 27a. **The earth will mourn and the heavens above grow dark**. 'Mourn' (<√*ʾābal*) is often understood in the sense 'be dried up' when it is applied to inanimate objects. There is scholarly dispute as to whether there are two homonymous roots (*HALOT* 6-7 notes the existence of an Akkadian root *abālu*, 'to dry out'), or whether applications to objects such as 'the earth' are metaphorical (*NIDOTTE*, 1:244). Here we seem to have earth and heaven personified in celebrating funeral rites over the destruction that has taken place. Darkness or blackness is also associated with mourning in 8:21 and 14:2. In this passage it is particularly appropriate in view of the absence of light mentioned in v. 23. Darkness does not seem to have been connected with wearing of dark clothing as a sign of mourning, though it may refer to an unkempt appearance indicative of deep grief (2 Sam. 19:25).

There is no doubt that the cosmos will mourn over the impact of the LORD's decree, **because** it is irrevocable. The combination *ʿal kî*, 'because', has often felt to be difficult, and the *ʿal* has been taken as a dittography with the final syllable of the preceding word *mimmāʿal*. But the words are also found together in Deut. 31:17; Judg. 3:12; Ps. 139:14 and Mal. 2:14, and from this the sense of 'inasmuch as' is established. **I have spoken and will not relent, I have decided and will not turn back.** The NIV (following the LXX) changes the order of the verbs from 'I have spoken, I have purposed; I have not relented nor will I turn back' (NRSV) in order to make a neater set of contrasts. The repetition of the thought drives home the point that the matter is certain. 'Relent' (<√*nāḥam* niphal) was translated 'repent' (AV), but in relation to God who does nothing wrong this raises unnecessary questions as to whether he had previously made a wrong move or decision (cf. 8:6). In working out his purposes God does not change what he had decreed. 'He who is the Glory of Israel does not lie or change his mind; for he is not a man, that he should change his mind'

(1 Sam. 15:29). However, from a human perspective which lacks full knowledge of the divine purpose and of events on earth, it often appears that God relents. Here, however, the LORD makes clear that he will not deviate from the course of action he has decided on (<√*zāmam*, often used of the divine determination to act in judgment); he will punish his rebellious people. The final ironic twist is contained in 'will not turn back' (<√*šub*). The people have not repented and turned back to him, so there can be no divine turning back from imposing the penalty for their misconduct on them.

f. The Mortal Anguish of Jerusalem (4:29-31)

The closing verses of the chapter describe what will happen when the enemy army arrives. The inhabitants of the towns of Judah will flee in panic, and Jerusalem will not be exempt either. None of the political wiles that had worked before will be able to deflect the enemy from wreaking the havoc he has planned, and the city is depicted in her death throes.

29. The NKJV continues the divine speech of vv. 27-28 to the end of the chapter, though v. 31 is improbable, but it is more likely that this is Jeremiah continuing his presentation of the visions he has received. **At the sound of horsemen and archers** (in the Hebrew text these are singular nouns being used generically) points to the cavalry and bowmen, the main body of the invading army. The civilian population no longer flee to the cities for safety (v. 5) because they realise that their defences are insufficient to withstand the might of the enemy. So **every town takes to flight** (<√*bāraḥ*, used of secret escape). While we would undoubtedly expect *kol-hāʿîr* to be 'the whole city' (NKJV), it recurs later in the verse along with *bāhēn*, 'in them', which requires the rendering 'every city', or 'all the cities' (Joüon §139g). **Some go into the thickets; some climb up among the rocks.** 'Thickets' refers to dense, intertwined shrubs, which impede movement and therefore also provide good cover. In Palestine the crevices and caves of the hilltops frequently provided sanctuary for those escaping hostile forces (Isa. 2:19, 21). 'Let those who are in Judea flee to the mountains' (Mark 13:14). There is no attempt to maintain their dignity. Like startled animals their aim is mere survival wherever that may be possible. As a result of this panic-stricken evacuation **all the towns are deserted; no one lives in them.**

30. In the closing two verses the prophet turns and addresses Jerusalem directly.[70] **What are you doing, O devastated one?**[71] It is a mocking portrayal of how the city will behave when disaster has struck. It will revert to the techniques employed before, but the old trickery will not be successfully in obtaining mercy from these invaders. The attitude may be that of people who have massively misjudged the situation and cannot see that the devastation (<√*šādad*, v. 13) which has overtaken them represents the end of the story, or, perhaps more plausibly, what is depicted may be the hardened bravado of those who, having played the game this way so far, will play it out to the end. Are there overtones of Jezebel here (2 Kgs. 9:30-33)? The people will do anything rather than turn to the LORD.

Jerusalem is likened to a prostitute seeking to attract clients. There are three clauses describing her behaviour, each introduced by *kî*, which serves to specify the content of 'what', and so is equivalent to 'in that' (NRSV). The NKJV prefers to take the series of *kî* as introducing a series of concessive clauses preceding the following verb, 'although you do these things, you act in vain.' The repeated interrogatives of the NIV bring out the tone of outrage at her insensitivity. **Why dress yourself in scarlet and put on jewels of gold? Why shade**[72] **your eyes with paint?** lists the ways in which she would usually try to make herself attractive to prospective clients, but now they will not meet with success. Scarlet dye obtained from insects was used to produce costly and beautiful clothing (2 Sam. 1:24; Prov. 31:21). **You adorn yourself in vain.** 'In vain' (*šāwʾ*, 2:30) shows that her actions are futile; they will have no positive consequences. **Your lovers despise** (<√*māʾas*, 'to reject' 6:30) **you; they seek your life** (*nepeš*, 2:34). Her 'lovers' (<√*ʿāgab*) are not idols, but the foreign nations with whom she had tried to make alliances. Far from acting in her interests, they are now attempting to murder her.

31. The verse is introduced by *kî*, not translated in the NIV because it was understood either as an emphatic or as indicating a change of speaker. It may be functioning causally to indicate the evidence that is cited to substantiate the claim that the very life of Jerusalem is at risk. The prophet knows this because of what he has perceived in his vision. At first he thought what he heard were cries like those of a woman

---

70. The kethibh *weʾattî*, 'but you', is an archaic form of the second feminine singular pronoun (GKC §32h), for which the qere has substituted the usual spelling *wəʾat*. Its position at the start of the sentence makes it emphatic.

71. The masculine passive participle *šādûd* is used instead of a feminine form as sometimes happens (GKC §145t).

72. *tiqrəʿî*, 'you enlarge', is literally 'you tear'. The idiom seems to be of attempts to make the eyes seem larger by applying cosmetics of some sort.

giving birth: **I hear a cry as of a woman in labour, a groan** (literally, 'distress', perhaps 'cry of distress') **as of one bearing her first child.** This is a picture of vulnerability and helplessness coupled with intense agony at sudden pain never experienced before. But then the prophet revises his assessment of what he is hearing: it is really the cries of a murder victim that are reaching his ears. **The cry of the Daughter of Zion gasping for breath, stretching out her hands and saying, 'Alas!** 'for' (*kî*, introducing the reason for her cry of woe) **I**/'my being' (*nepeš*, 2:34) **am fainting; my life is given over to murderers.'**[73] 'Daughter of Zion' is a personification of Jerusalem and its inhabitants (cf. v. 11). It is unlikely that this language implies that Zion is described as God's daughter (contra *NIDOTTE* 2:780) because expressions such as 'daughter of Tyre' (Ps. 45:12), 'daughter of Babylon' (50:42; 51:33; Ps. 137:8) and 'daughter of Edom' (Isa. 4:21) are also found. The idiom arises from the fact that the Hebrew words for 'city' (*ʿîr*) and 'land' (*ʾereṣ*) are both feminine and lead naturally to such a personification. Jerusalem is entreating any who will listen to take pity on her (Lam. 1:17). 'Fainting' (<√*ʿîp*, 'to be weary') refers here to the ebbing away of Jerusalem's life as she is overcome by hunger and fatigue. 'Murderers' (<√*hārag*, 'to kill, slay', extending also to include 'to murder') may not refer to an immediate act of homicide, but to the effects of an extended siege.

2. The Corrupt City (5:1-31)

OUTLINE

a. Searching for the Upright (5:1-9)
b. Judgment, but not a Complete End (5:10-19)
c. Heart Failure (5:20-31)

Chapter 5 stands somewhat apart from chapters 4 and 6 where the focus is on the devastation that will be caused by the enemy forces whom the LORD will use as his instruments of judgment. While the impact of this judgment is not absent from chapter 5 (note especially

73. Translators are undecided whether Zion makes one or two statements. It could equally well be 'My being is fainting with respect to murderers' (cf. NKJV, NRSV).

vv. 10-11 and vv. 15-17), the main theme reverts to that of the guilt of the people. The horrors of the impending invasion are not disproportionate to the behaviour exhibited by the rebellious community. The chapter is therefore by way of theodicy, justifying God's sweeping action against his own people. Although the case against the corrupt city is open and closed, there are still suggestions that the situation might be reversed if only they would come to their senses and abandon their intransigence. This can be seen in the possibility, albeit remote, of forgiveness in v. 1 and the repeated question of vv. 9 and 29 where there is a note of wistfulness—if only there was some evidence of change that would give grounds for calling a halt to their punishment. But alas! such evidence is lacking.

When then did Jeremiah compose this material? Carroll, of course, opts for a setting after the fall of the city (1986:174), but this does not do justice to the prophet's words which clearly presuppose a situation where the judgment is still prospective (e.g. v. 6). Holladay distributes the material in the chapter, 5:1-9 and 5:20-29 coming from the period between the writing of the First Scroll and its being burned, and 5:10-17 coming after the destruction of the First Scroll and being incorporated into the second (1986, 1:135-36). On the other hand, writers such as Skinner (1922:139-142) adopted the viewpoint that this chapter comes from Jeremiah's early ministry, perhaps around 620 BC, when he first made close study of the moral situation in Jerusalem and was shocked by it. Underlying this is Skinner's view that it is the prophet's experience, and not divine revelation, that gave rise to the prophecy.

It is difficult to be certain as to when this material originated. The charges brought against the people mention idol worship (vv. 7, 19) but do not focus on it in the way chapter 2 does. Possibly this suggests that the background is to be sought in the later reign of Josiah or the early years of Jehoiakim. Jones argues that Jeremiah's positive appreciation of Josiah makes it questionable whether the prophet would have uttered this judgment until after his death (1992:119). But there is no critique here of the king; it is the populace in general who are in view. The social and religious conditions that underlie the material fit in well with a time of outward religious reform when idol worship was largely suppressed, but when the people as a whole had no true commitment to covenant standards in their ordinary life. Jeremiah could well have presented this message between 615 BC and Josiah's death as a means to widen and deepen the response to Josiah's reforms. It is not difficult to see it incorporated into the First Scroll.

The passage has three main sections. First, there is a dialogue that exposes the corruption in the city (vv. 1-9). Then the nature of the judgment that is to come upon Judah is set out (vv. 10-19). The concluding section brings out the contrast between the way in which the natural realm keeps the LORD's creational ordinances and the way in which Judah breaches his covenant requirements (vv. 20-31).

a. Searching for the Upright (5:1-9)

When does a nation become so corrupt that there is no hope for its recovery? This was a matter that Scripture reflected on from earliest times. When the LORD entered into covenant with Abraham, he told him that it would not be until the fourth generation of his descendants that they would inherit the land of promise, 'for the sin of the Amorites has not yet reached its full measure' (Gen. 15:16), implying that there was a level of wickedness beyond which divine judgment could not be restrained. Also, in the context of Abraham pleading for the cities of the plain, it was revealed that if even ten righteous men were to be found in Sodom, it would not be destroyed (Gen. 18:32). Later Isaiah perceived that it was the LORD's preserving of such a remnant in Judah that had withheld the outpouring of his wrath. 'Unless the LORD Almighty had left us some survivors, we would have become like Sodom, we would have been like Gomorrah' (Isa. 1:9). Here the LORD makes graphically clear that Jerusalem can no longer pass such a test—even with a lowered requirement!

The dialogue of this section has two speakers: the LORD in vv. 1-2 and again in vv. 7-9, and Jeremiah in vv. 3-6. There are many verbal links binding the speeches together: 'forgive' (vv. 1, 7), 'strike' (v. 3) and the same word rendered 'attack' (v. 6), 'truth' (vv. 1, 3), 'swearing' (vv. 2, 7). Lundbom (1997:102-03) recognised a more elaborate chiastic structure in this section by noting that v. 3 and vv. 5b-6 are Jeremiah's speech to the LORD, whereas in v. 5a Jeremiah is addressing himself.

1. The speaker in vv. 1-2 is the LORD, as the concluding words of v. 1, 'that I may pardon her,' show. There is less certainty regarding who is addressed because the commands, **Go up and down the streets of Jerusalem, look around and consider, search through her squares**, are plural, and so are not in the first instance addressed to Jeremiah. As the chapter divisions were only introduced into the text much later, those who were originally present when Jeremiah's scroll was read might have thought that these were commands issued to the invading troops, but it becomes evident as the picture emerges that the scene is set before the city is captured. The invitation seems to be a general one. 'God here permits the whole world to inquire diligently and carefully what was the state of the holy city' (Calvin 1850, 1:252). Included in the invitation, of course, are the people of Jerusalem themselves. They more than any others are urged to look at themselves and take stock of their real condition.

'Go up and down' (<√*šûṭ*, 'to twist, weave', and so 'range through') here renders a polel form of the verb, which occurs elsewhere four times, twice of God's eyes ranging through the whole earth (Zech. 4:10; 2 Chron. 16:9. See also Amos 8:12, Dan. 12:4.). The idea of 'run' (NKJV) originates in the LXX translation, 'run about'. 'Stroll' (Craigie et al. 1991:85) seems to introduce too casual a note. The picture is not one of haphazard or aimless motion, but rather of thorough scrutiny of Jerusalem's streets, the narrow alleys that lay outside the houses of ordinary folk, and of her squares, found at the intersection of the streets or else the open spaces within the city walls, generally near the gates, where people conducted civic and commercial business. The focus is particularly on the public conduct of Jerusalem.

The command to search the city obviously recalls the LORD's scrutiny of Sodom (Gen. 18:23-32). Zephaniah had described how the LORD would 'search Jerusalem with lamps and punish those who are complacent' (Zeph. 1:12). Later Ezekiel also saw a search party which would mark those in Jerusalem who were weary of iniquity, followed by another group with orders to kill those without the mark (Ezek. 9). All these searches occurred over two centuries before the unsavoury cynic philosopher Diogenes (*c.* 400–323 BC) lit a lamp in broad daylight and walked through Athens 'looking for a man'(Diog.Laer.vi 41).

Sodom would have been spared if there had been ten righteous men found in it (Gen. 18:32), but now the test is made easier: **if you can find but one person**. This is obvious hyperbole for rhetorical effect. Was it true that not one could be found? What about Jeremiah himself, or those like Baruch or the prophet Zephaniah who were in the city at this time? One sort of explanation that has been advanced is that this 'gives but the simple truth, as is seen when we consider that it is not Jeremiah who speaks according to the best of his judgment, but God, the searcher of hearts. Before the all-seeing eye of God no man is pure and good. They are all gone astray, and there is none that doeth good, Ps. 14:2-3' (Keil 1873, 1:121). While that is so, it seems to be a strained explanation of this passage. The focus is on the extent to which behaviour in the city has deviated from the conduct required by the covenant.

Specifically what is sought is an instance of one **who deals honestly and seeks the truth.** The first characteristic is 'doing judgment' (*mišpāṭ*; see on 7:5), and was one of the three divine requirements that Micah had set out (Mic. 6:8). It is the action of one who directs his affairs in accordance with the demands of God's covenant, living the manner of life required by the LORD (4:2; 8:7). 'Seeks the truth' (*'ĕmûnâ*, 'what is steadfast/reliable') is a parallel expression, which refers not to a philosopher's quest for some abstract definition of truth, but to the trustworthiness and reliability that are evident in a life that gives practical expression to the LORD's covenant requirements. Both qualities should be evident in the relationship between individuals and God, and in their dealings with their fellow countrymen. It was not sufficient that the cultic practices of Jerusalem had been reformed. The LORD himself was just and faithful (Deut. 32:4), and it was the same characteristics that he wished to see reflected in his people. But such practical examples of covenant living were lacking, and so the promise **I will forgive this city**[74] cannot be claimed. The tone is ironic. It is not expected that the search, however diligently carried out, will achieve success.

2. A specific instance of their lack of fidelity is then cited. **Although they say, 'As surely as the LORD lives'** portrays the people as acting as pious believers in the LORD and solemnly using his name in taking an oath to seal a transaction (Deut. 6:13; 10:20). The LORD's name was being invoked (4:2; 12:16) so that he became a witness to the deal struck, and would be the one who would punish any who defaulted on their agreement. Outwardly the life of the city seemed to be conducted in a God-fearing fashion by those who, true to their covenant commitment, held the sanction of the divine name as utterly binding. **Still**[75] **they are swearing falsely.** *laššeqer*, 'by the lie'/'in falsehood', is unlikely to be a concealed reference to Baal as 'the Lie'. The idiom with *lə* is found as early as Lev. 19:12. The term *šeqer*, 'falsehood, lie', is frequently employed by Jeremiah to denote words or actions that are without basis in reality. It is used of deliberately uttering falsehood to the injury of one's neighbour (Exod. 23:7) and about words designed to mislead (Exod. 5:9). It is therefore the opposite of 'in honesty' (9:2). Those who do *šeqer* are those who practise wrong (6:13; Hos. 7:1). So

74. The verb is *wə'eslaḥ* with ordinary *waw*, and so indicates a consequence, 'so that I may pardon' (NRSV; cf. REB).

75. 'Still' is used to render *lākēn*, usually 'therefore', but that hardly fits here. Some commentators argue that the word might also have the sense, 'notwithstanding, yet' (NRSV), introducing a contrast (cf. the rendering 'however' in 16:14; see also 2:33). Here many translations read on the basis of many Hebrew manuscripts, *'ākēn*, 'surely' (NKJV, NASB).

it indicates that despite appearances the people had no respect for the LORD and were using his name in vain, to commit perjury, or give undertakings they had no intention of fulfilling. Although later it is used regarding the teaching of the false prophets, here it reflects the basic covenant requirement not to bear false witness (Exod. 20:16; Deut. 19:18). Their conduct was a sham.

3. Jeremiah now responds to the LORD's challenge. It is not clear whether the prophet mentally surveyed the contemporary situation before reporting on the people's behaviour or whether (as might be suggested by v. 5) he conducted a symbolic search through the streets of Jerusalem. In any event he finds he can only present a negative verdict on what he perceives going on around him.

O LORD, do not your eyes look for truth (*ʾĕmûnâ*)**?** There is no verb in the Hebrew where the idiom implies relationship or belonging: 'Do not your eyes belong to the truth?'/'Are not your eyes for the truth?' Bringing this clause forward before v. 2 (Holladay 1986, 1:177) is an unnecessary attempt to make the flow of thought conform to western idiom. 'Eyes' is an anthropomorphism for divine scrutiny (32:9; 2 Chron. 16:9; Ps. 11:4). The outcome of a search for 'truth', that is, practical trustworthiness and covenant integrity in living, is a foregone conclusion. There is no doubt as to the standards that the LORD looks on with approval—and there is no doubt as to what would be found by searching the bazaars and law courts of Jerusalem.

What is more, this situation of covenant unfaithfulness has persisted despite divine warnings. **You struck them** (<√*nākâ* hiphil, 2:30) refers to a physical blow, but not necessarily one that is so severe as to cause death. The precise form this took is not stated, **but they felt no pain.**[76] They did not interpret God's action as a divine danger signal, but continued as if nothing had happened. **You crushed them** (<√*kālâ* piel, 'to bring to an end, finish') often conveys a note of finality. 'Crushed' and 'pierced them to the heart' (REB) are attempts to express the dire impact of the divine chastisement. **But they refused correction** (<√*yāsar*, 2:30). The people stubbornly refused to live in terms of their covenant obligations, no matter what divine action was taken to alert them to the need for change. Jones (1992:120) takes this verse as a brutally relevant reminder of what had happened after Josiah's death at Megiddo. Quite apart from the implications that has for the original date of the passage (it was obviously of relevance as an application when incorporated in the First Scroll), it is too particular an

---

76. *ḥālû* is from *ḥālâ*, the accent being drawn back in pause. The verb form could be either *ḥûl*, 'to writhe', or *ḥālâ*, 'to be ill', cf. Prov. 23:35.

interpretation for a summary of the whole history of the people. Equally interpretations which apply these words to the personal conduct of individuals within the nation are too narrow. 'Men give themselves to their selfish and lawless pursuits with a feeling of security' (Skinner 1922:143). What is in view is the series of national judgments (defeats by enemies, disasters such as plague and famine) that had occurred throughout their history.

The people had wilfully declined to respond (2:30; 7:28; 32:33; 35:13). **They made their faces harder than stone and refused to repent.** 'Made … harder' (<√*ḥāzaq* piel) refers to spiritual stubbornness. The rebellious people were pharaonic in their obduracy (Exod. 7:13, 22). The picture is one of those who had been left in no doubt as to the gravity of their situation, but who were adamant in their refusal to take the course of action urged on them and repent (<√*šûb*).

4. The 'but as for me' (*wa'ănî*) with which the verse begins marks a transition between Jeremiah's report to the LORD and the prophet's own inward musing, **I thought** (<√*'āmar*, 'to say', but here used of inward speech with oneself; 3:19). He records that he sought some extenuating factor to explain the people's lack of response. **These are only the poor.** 'Only' renders *'ak*, a restrictive adverb, that clarifies what precedes (3:13). 'But I was wrong to look there; they are the poor who are foolish' (*IBHS* §39.3.5e). The poor (*dallîm*) generally refers to those who are 'the have-nots' in society. It is not that they always lack basic necessities, but comparatively speaking they lack wealth (Finley 1985:414). Ellison, however, suggests that the poor here are not the broken population of slaves and landless in Jerusalem, but the skilled artisans and shop-keepers, the ordinary folk of the city (1961:29). This would reflect a two-level classification of society, and 'poor' (*dal*) would be those who were not part of those who considered themselves socially superior. Note the contrast between poor and rich in Ruth 3:10, and with the 'leaders'/'great ones' here in v. 5 (cf. also Lev. 19:15). Presumably the lower class would consist of those who had not received any training in the elite scribal school at Jerusalem, and therefore might not be expected to have a good grasp of what behaviour was expected from them. **They are foolish** (<√*yā'al*) does not refer so much to their character (for which we might have expected an adjective to be used) as to their conduct. They are those whose actions display their lack of true understanding of what the LORD requires. The reason for this state of affairs is: **for** (*kî*) **they do not know the way of the LORD, the requirements of their God.** The 'way of the LORD' refers to the direction he gives in the covenant (Gen. 18:19; Deut. 5:33;

2 Kgs. 21:22). 'Requirements' renders the word *mišpāṭ*, 'judgment' (NKJV; cf. 4:2). It may function here as a juridical term pointing to the 'justice' of God which will surely have the final say in their lives, even though they do not recognise it. However, the root *šāpaṭ* takes in all aspects of government, and may refer to the divinely given norms which should guide the conduct of the people. It is equivalent to their manner of life, their characteristic behaviour. Jeremiah considers the possibility that the wrong behaviour of the ordinary people arises from the fact that they had had neither time nor opportunity to be educated in God's ways and so were acting in ignorance.

5. So Jeremiah resolves to see if the assessment of Jerusalem's moral character would be bettered by considering those at the other end of the social scale. **So I will go** renders a cohortative, 'let me go' (NRSV), indicating the course of action he wishes to take for himself. Holladay (1986, 1:178) suggested that the great ones might live in a different part of Jerusalem and would not be mingling with the common folk going about their daily business, so that Jeremiah has to visit another quarter of the city. Still mindful of the directions the LORD has given him, the prophet will take the trouble and go **to the leaders**/'great ones', possibly 'the rich' (NRSV), but more probably the powerful and influential. He does not merely observe their conduct, but resolves also to **speak to them**[77]**; surely** (*kî*, 'for', stating the reason why he speaks to them) **they** (emphatic: 'they are the very ones who') **know the way of the LORD, the requirements of their God.** Presumably Jeremiah is arguing that given their privileged background and greater responsibilities they would have taken great care to live in accordance with the stipulations of the covenant. No direct mention is made of the king (whether Josiah or Jehoiakim) or his officials so as not to alienate them unnecessarily, but there is no doubt that courtiers, priests, temple officials and scribes are in view.

The second part of the verse is not part of Jeremiah's inner thinking but relates his report on the search that had been carried out. **But** (*ʾak*, contrary to what I expected, cf. v. 4) **with one accord they too** (bringing out the emphasis of the expressed pronoun) **had broken off the yoke and torn off the bonds.** 'With one accord' (*yaḥdāw*) may refer to the leaders as a group being united in their rebellion, or it may refer to them 'alike' (NRSV), as a group sharing the attitudes of the poor, so that the whole of Jerusalem society is seen as condemned. For a similar

77. It is the object marker *ʾōtām* that is found where we might have expected the preposition *ʾittām*, cf. 9:7. The verb seems to take an accusative of person in Gen. 37:4 as well.

metaphorical use of yoke and bonds, see on 2:20; for a description of these items, see on 27:2. They were behaving like refractory animals unwilling to submit to the yoke and so be in a position to be useful in their master's service. Later 'yoke' was used to refer to the binding nature of the Torah, the law of God, and probably does so here also. Indeed their behaviour is worse than that of untrained animals. They had entered into covenant with the LORD and now have gone back on their word, opting for a spurious freedom from the demands of the divine Overlord. They had concurred with the form but not the spirit of Josiah's renewal of the covenant, and their conduct remained unreformed. Consequently the prophet is frustrated in his attempts to find a basis on which to plead for the city in the way that Abraham pled for Sodom.

6. Although it is possible to understand vv. 5b-6 as a divine judgment speech, there is no marker in the text, such as 'Thus says the LORD', and so it is easier to read them as a continuation of the prophet's words. The divine messenger can only report to the LORD that based on scrutiny of the behaviour of Jerusalem there is no basis for withholding divine judgment. **Therefore** (*'al-kēn*, 'on account of this') introduces a statement of established facts as distinct from *lākēn* ('therefore') which introduces a declaration of intention or command based on preceding information (BDB 486-7). The judgment has already begun. It is presented using animal imagery. **A lion from the forest will attack them** or 'has struck them' (√*nākâ* hiphil, v. 3). The perfect verb form is generally taken by English translations in a future sense as a 'prophetic perfect' (see Introduction §7.2). Keil, however, argued that 'the verbs are used aoristically of chastisements which have partly already taken place, which may be partly yet to come' (1873, 1:123). But there may well be a deliberate use of the verb forms to distinguish what the lion has already done from the future reality, **a wolf from the desert**[78] **will ravage them,** expressed using an imperfect, and from the ongoing threat posed by the leopard: **a leopard will lie in wait near their towns to tear in pieces any who venture out.** 'Lie in wait' is a participial form of the verb *šāqad*, which was actually used of the LORD watching over his word in 1:12. Here the idea is that of an animal prowling about the city ready to seize as prey any going out.

78. *'ărābôt* is not the plural of *'ereb*, 'evening', an understanding reflected in the AV rendering and going back to the early Jewish Targum, but of *'ărābâ*, 'wasteland, steppe', not true desert (wolves would not be found there), but a waterless and inhospitable region such as that on the east of Jordan, or to the south of Judah (cf. 2:6).

The participial form might well denote action ongoing at present and in the future, as well as simple futurity. Early commentators such as Jerome and Rashi tried to equate the animals mentioned with particular foes such as the Babylonians, the Persians and the Greeks. Since there is nothing obviously metaphorical in the description, it is also possible to take the references as being to literal animals in fulfilment of the covenant curse of Lev. 26:21-22, 'If you remain hostile towards me and refuse to listen to me, I will multiply your afflictions seven times over, as your sins deserve. I will send wild animals against you, and they will rob you of your children, destroy your cattle and make you so few in number that your roads will be deserted.'[79] However, foreign aggressors are often pictured as animals (2:15; 4:7; Hos. 13:7-8; Amos 5:19; Zeph. 3:3; Hab. 1:8). The threefold depiction of the fierceness of the lion, the ravenous nature of the wolf, and the prowling ambush of the leopard probably does not refer principally to different enemies, but to the full extent of the LORD's judgment upon them—the judgment that is expected to come through the foe from the north.

The reason for these divinely imposed calamities is the covenant disloyalty of the people. **For (*kî*) their rebellion is great and their backslidings many.** The noun 'rebellion' (*pešaʿ*, in fact a plural form, 'acts of rebellion') occurs only here in Jeremiah, but for the root see 2:8. For 'backslidings'/apostasies, see on 3:6. Their offences are countless (for similar expressions, cf. 30:14-15) and therefore judgment is inevitable. They have rejected the covenant and refused to return (Deut. 28:15-46).

7. And yet despite the clear acceptance that punishment was due, the prophet (and the LORD who sent him) continue to explore the matter of forgiveness. So overwhelming is the penalty that will be imposed on those who have despised the LORD and his covenant, that every effort must be made, every avenue of approach no matter how unlikely must be explored, in an attempt to bring them to their senses before the

79. 'Commentators have often taken these lines as figurative for the enemies of Judah, but there is no real need to do so. Consider these curses from the long list attached to the first Sefire treaty (eighth century BC): "May the gods send every sort of devourer against Arpad and against its people! [May the mo]uth of a snake [eat], the mouth of a scorpion, the mouth of a bear, the mouth of a panther. And may a moth and a louse and a [...] become to it a serpent's throat!" The second Sefire treaty is badly broken at this point, but the legible portions contain a similar list, adding the lion: "[And may] the mouth of a lion [eat] and the mouth of [a ...] and the mouth of a panther ... " ' (Hillers 1969:132-3).

catastrophe overtakes them. Having then recorded the conclusion he had reached about the city's condition, Jeremiah now presents the matter from a different angle as in vv. 7-9 the LORD challenges the people to overturn the verdict that has been reached concerning them.

Why? (*'ê lāzō't*) is a phrase which occurs only here, conveying the thought: 'Where with respect to this? on what basis? how?' (*IBHS* §18.4b). Why **should I forgive**[80] **you?** uses the feminine singular to address Jerusalem (perhaps Judah) as a mother figure. 'Pardon' (NKJV, NRSV) is a more formal expression than 'forgive', which deals more with interpersonal relationships. 'Pardon' probably fits the official level of the situation envisaged as the divine judge inquires of the convicted if there are any grounds for modifying the penalty that is justly due. Jerusalem is being challenged to answer on behalf of her children before sentence is put into effect. But there does not seem much she can say because the allegations against them cannot be refuted. **Your children have forsaken me** (<√*'āzab*, cf. 2:13; Exod. 32; Num. 13–14; Deut. 32:15-18). The citizens of Jerusalem had deserted the covenant as a basis for their living, and they had spurned the LORD of the covenant. Their religious defection had gone further than that in that they conformed their practices to those of the heathen. They had **sworn by gods that are not gods.** The extent of their departure from covenant standards is seen in their using the name of other gods in taking oaths; the folly of their conduct derives from the fact that the deities they name are mere figments of the polytheistic cultural consensus of the day. In no way could they judge the conduct of those who broke their solemn undertakings (cf. 4:2). Since the people so openly and deliberately flouted the requirements of the covenant, how could they expect to be pardoned?

I supplied all their needs[81]/'fed them to the full' (NKJV, NRSV) proves how bountifully the LORD had provided for them (<√*śāba'*, 31:14). But while they enjoyed the gifts, they did not acknowledge the giver (Hos. 2:8). The danger of ingratitude had been set before the

80. The kethibh *'eslôaḥ*, 'I shall forgive' is an older form, written plene, for which the qere gives the usual form *'eslaḥ,* 'I shall forgive', cf. GKC §65b.

81. Some manuscripts read *wā'ašbia'*, 'I caused them to swear', which would refer to the oath of covenant fidelity, despite which they committed adultery and so breached the covenant in another way. Most manuscripts, however, and the early versions read *sin* rather than *shin*. The hiphil of *śāba'*, 'to be satisfied', may indicate solicitude: 'I took care to satisfy them' (*IBHS* §27.5b). The play between *šāba'*, 'to swear', and *śāba'*, 'to be satisfied', emphasises how contrary their conduct was.

people by Moses when he described the bounty of the LORD's provision (Deut. 8:7-10) and warned them lest their heart became lifted up in pride and they forgot the LORD, attributing their prosperity to their own power and strength (Deut. 8:11-20; cf. also Deut. 32:15).

But it was not just a spirit of thanklessness that affected them. **Yet they committed adultery and thronged**[82] **to the houses of prostitutes.** 'Commit adultery' (<√*nāʾap*, 3:8) may refer either to their involvement in Baal worship or to breaches of their marriage vows, but the reference to adultery in the following verse favours the interpretation found in most English translations that it is sexual misconduct that is in view. The second clause begins with a non-verb and either gives an explanation of the first clause or indicates action taking place at the same time (*IBHS* §39.2.3). The verb 'thronged' is understood in various ways. It might be translated 'gashed themselves', which would refer to the orgiastic excesses of Canaanite worship (cf. 16:6; 41:5). In that case 'a prostitute's house' would indicate a Canaanite shrine where sexual licentiousness was commonplace. The previous mention of 'no gods' and the fact that it is a singular 'house of the prostitute' would then suggest the focus is on the spiritual rebellion of the people. However, the verb can also be understood as 'thronged'/'frequented', and such openly and shameless conduct might well refer to other sorts of breaches of the marriage bond in defiance of the covenant.

8. They were well-fed, lusty[83] **stallions, each neighing** (13:27) **for another man's wife** (cf. Ezek. 23:20) has always provided difficulties

---

82. *yitgōdādû*, 'they gash themselves', is a hithpolel form from *gādad*, 'to cut'. Perhaps there is another root *gādad* II, which means 'to band together' as in Ps. 94:21 and Mic. 5:1 (cf. the noun *gədûd*, 'a troop'), and hence 'they trooped' (NASB, NRSV). Since *daleth* and *resh* were similar and easily confused, a third possibility is to read *yitgōrārû*, from *gûr* I, 'to dwell as a stranger', which seems to be reflected in the LXX *kateluon*, 'they were resting, or taking up quarters' (Holladay 1986, 1:180). Of course, that explanation could work in the other direction, namely that the LXX was trying to make sense of a difficult word. On balance it is best to retain the Massoretic reading.

83. *məyuzzānîm*, 'well-fed', and *maškîm*, 'lusty', occur only here, and have given rise to much speculation. For the first word many modern versions accept the reading of the Occidental text, *mûzānîm*, a hophal participle of *zûn*, 'to feed'. BDB suggests a meaning 'furnished with weights (i.e. testicles)' for the root *yāzan*, based on Arabic evidence. *maškîm* seems to be a hiphil participle from *šākam*, 'to rise early'. The LXX translates both words by *thēlumaneis*, 'mad for women', abandoning the metaphor but conveying the correct sense.

for translators. The pagan religions of Canaan were deeply involved in sacred prostitution, but the marriage bond was part of the LORD's special requirements for his people. Breach of it was viewed as rebellion against him. The picture is that of men driven by sexual impulses and disregarding any obstacle in their way, whose conduct was blatantly contrary to the covenant.

9. This verse seems to lie outside the main structure of the poem, but it has been added to bring the section to a conclusion with two rhetorical questions, which are repeated in 5:29 and in slightly different form in 9:9. The people's behaviour is at variance with the standards of the covenant, and so, **'Shall I not punish them for this?' declares the LORD.** This question is the obverse of 'Why should I forgive you? (v. 7). 'Punish' (<√*pāqad*, 'to visit'; 1:10) describes a superior's scrutiny of the situation or conduct of a subordinate, and the consequent action he takes. The situation here was one that obviously called for punitive measures in the face of continuing intransigence.

Again the LORD asks, **Should I not avenge myself on such a nation as this?** Literally, 'will not my being/soul avenge herself?' where *nepeš*, 'being', is used as an emphatic way of referring to 'self' (6:8). The use of *gôy*, 'nation', rather than the more personal *ʿam*, 'people', suggests a degree of alienation between the LORD and Judah. It has become just another nation which has repudiated his authority, and divine vengeance asserts God's rights over them. 'Avenge myself' (<√*nāqam* hithpael), however, has now such a negative connotation, and 'revenge' even more so, both being used of unwarranted blood feuds among mankind over imagined affronts and injuries. It is preferable to translate, 'Shall I not bring retribution on a nation such as this?' (NRSV, NJPS), though that loses the note of personal affront denoted by the verb. The action involved is the prerogative of one in authority who acts to ensure that his position is not infringed. It is a legitimate use of power to vindicate his rights and punish those who have violated them. 'I will take vengeance on my adversaries and repay those who hate me' (Deut. 32:41). Such action is a necessary correlate of divine holiness, since the God of purity cannot remain true to himself if he permits sin and iniquity to go unpunished, especially when the offences are directly against known commands. The offer of grace and forgiveness is not held open indefinitely: if repeatedly spurned it will be withdrawn, because the Sovereign God must act to promote his dominion over his people and over the nations. So he cannot overlook the violations of his covenant that are to be found in Jerusalem.

b. Judgment, but not a Complete End (5:10-19)
Although it is clear that this section was composed from a number of smaller blocks of material, it is not without thematic continuity provided by the subject of judgment. The first and last units (vv. 10-11 and vv. 18-19) restate the fact that although judgment is certain and will be severe, yet it will not result in total annihilation of the covenant people. Note the recurrence of *kālâ*, 'complete end', in vv. 10 and 18. The second unit (vv. 12-14) forms a judgment speech relating to the false expectations held by the people, while the third unit (vv. 15-17) gives further details about the devouring foe whom the LORD will use as his instrument of judgment.

10. The LORD continues to speak, but now he addresses the enemy armies and commands them to get on with their task. **Go through her vineyards and ravage them.** *šārôtẹ̄hā*, 'vineyards', has caused translators problems. Formerly the word was rendered 'walls' (Vulgate, AV, NKJV still), but these are now understood not as citywalls but those round a vineyard, or else forming part of the hillside terraces which were used to permit cultivation (hence the imperative *'ălû*, 'go up'). Since vines were often grown on these terraces, the translation 'vineyards' or 'rows of vines' (REB) by metonymy seems warranted in the light of the mention of branches later in the verse. 'Her' could refer to either Judah or Jerusalem. 'Ravage' (<√*šāḥat* piel, 'to spoil, ruin, destroy; 4:7) is a good word for a verb that need not imply utter destruction, but does involve something being so spoiled that it can no longer function properly ('ruined' 13:7; 'marred' 18:4).

The vineyard represents the nation (2:21; Ps. 80:8; Isa. 5:1-7; Matt. 21:33-41), which had been intended to provide spiritual fruit pleasing to the LORD. Since that has not been forthcoming, it is going to undergo severe judgment which will leave it unable to function as a nation. However, there is a limit to what will happen: **but do not destroy them completely.** There is much discussion as to whether *'al*, 'not', can have an asseverative function here: 'Surely you will make a complete end' (Lundbom 1999:388). Others such as the REB and McKane (1986, 1:120) have simply deleted the *'al*, arguing that the negative, or the negative understanding of *'al*, is a later reinterpretation of what was originally a prediction of complete disaster. But such approaches fail to do justice to the nature of the covenant commitment which brings the curse of punishment on the disobedience but does not permit the vassal's disobedience to thwart the suzerain's commitment (see on 4:27).

The figure is further developed in **Strip off her branches, for** (*kî*)

these people do not belong to the LORD. 'Branches' may refer to the trailing tendrils of the vine, or to its extended branches, but the command is not to destroy or uproot the vine. Stump and roots are left and there is the possibility of new growth. 'If "strip away her branches" likens the judgment to a thorough pruning, a "full end" has not been made' (Bright 1965:40). The NIV takes the explanatory clause as interpreting the metaphor, but 'these people' is literally 'they' and could simply refer to the branches (NKJV, NRSV). In this case it is left to the hearer/reader to infer that the vine is the nation and the branches growing on it are the people who constitute the nation. It is no light pruning that is in view: the severity of the cure reflects the severity of the disease.

11. The reason for the LORD ordering this drastic action against his people is again stated: 'for' (*kî*) **'The house of Israel and the house of Judah have been utterly unfaithful to me,' declares the LORD.** The LORD's explanation of his action may be addressed to the destroyer, or to the prophet, and so to the people. Mention of both the northern and the southern kingdom is probably made to tie in with the link that has already been made between what had befallen the north and what was then impending for the south. 'Unfaithful' (<√*bāgad*, 3:7) applies the description formerly given to Judah to both kingdoms, reinforcing the idea that their offence and therefore their judgment would be the same.

12. Following the declaration of the people's unfaithfulness, Jeremiah records another instance of their spiritual incapacity and rebellion. This takes the form of a judgment speech with the evidence cited in vv. 12-13 and the verdict pronounced in v. 14. In **they have lied about the LORD** the unspecified 'they' is most naturally taken as referring back to the house of Israel and the house of Judah in v. 11, and particularly to the latter. Jones (1992:123) represents the viewpoint that the 'they' are in fact the false prophets, who otherwise would appear abruptly in v. 13, and that their sudden introduction here arises from the editorial incorporation of a different segment of material. Also the words cited in the charge are characteristic of the message of the false prophets (12:4; 14:13-15; Mic. 3:11), about whom Jeremiah will have a great deal to say later. However, those prophets were just reflecting and reinforcing the consensus of the day; so there is no difficulty in understanding this verse as referring to the false views held by the people in general. It should also be noted that resolution of who speaks in v. 12 is linked to the identity of the prophets in v. 13. Further the mention of the people in v. 14 may favour the idea that they are the ones who speak here.

They said, 'He will do nothing!' renders a very terse expression, 'Not he' (*lo'-hû'*). This enigmatic statement was not an attempt to deny the existence of God, rather it was an expression of practical atheism: 'He does not matter' (REB). God does not really intervene in the affairs of earth (Zeph. 1:12), and so we can leave him and his prophets out of consideration in deciding what it is that we want to do. **No harm** (*rāʿâ*, 'evil, disaster') **will come to us; we will never see sword or famine.** The people who were insensitive to the warnings of divine providence (v. 3) are now shown to be equally complacent in the face of the warnings of the prophetic word (2 Chron. 36:16). 'Sword or famine' represents two of the three items in the Jeremianic triplet, 'sword, famine and plague' (14:12). The threefold repetition of 'not' presents the people as dismissing out of hand the judgments that the LORD has threatened will come on them. This false sense of security was to be their downfall because famine and sword would come upon them from the LORD (v. 17).

13. Who then are **the prophets** to whom this verse refers? If it has been the people speaking at the end of v. 12, then, as they continue to speak, the reference is probably to the true prophets of the LORD, whose message they reject (so Jerome; Calvin). In saying they **are but wind and the word**[84] **is not in them**, the people are dismissing figures such as Jeremiah himself, Zephaniah and Uriah (26:20-23) as impostors. They repudiated their message because of their confidence in the security afforded to them by Jerusalem. There is a play here in that 'wind' (*rûaḥ*) is also the Hebrew word for 'spirit' or 'Spirit'. Though Jeremiah himself does not present matters in this way, it was widely acknowledged throughout the Old Testament that the Spirit of the LORD inspired the prophets and their message (Num. 11:17, 25; 1 Kgs. 22:24; Neh. 9:30; Ezek. 11:5; Joel 2:28-29; Zech. 7:12), but in their spiritual blindness the people dismiss the true prophets as mere wind. The relationship between the prophets and the word is discussed at 23:18, 21, 30. They then seek to divert the threatened warnings of the prophets from themselves and onto the LORD's messengers: **So let what they say be done to them.** 'What they say' is literally 'thus',

84. *wəhaddibbēr*, 'and has he spoken?', seems an impossible pointing. One manuscript has *wəhaddābār*, 'and the word', which is also supported by the Septuagint. The same translation is also argued for by understanding *dibbēr* as a noun on the analogy of post-biblical Hebrew (Lundbom 1999:390; GKC §52o). Alternatively, the article before the verb may be functioning as a relative, 'he who speaks is not in them' (Keil 1873, 1:128). Other renderings include 'that which he speaks is not in them' (GKC §138i).

that is, in accordance with the threats they had uttered in the name of the LORD. This is then in effect a curse formula, calling down on them what they had threatened would befall others (Lehmann 1969:82).

Alternatively, it must be recognised that these words may be Jeremiah's and reflect his assessment of the false prophets. This is also a view that is found early, being in the Targum, and the medieval rabbinic commentators, Rashi and Kimchi. It is supported by the fact that 'the prophets' is regularly Jeremiah's designation of the contemporary prophets (e.g. 4:9; 5:31), not a designation of the people for prophets like Jeremiah (but note 28:8 and the phrase 'my servants, the prophets', 7:25). Adopting this interpretation is much easier if the speakers in v. 12 are understood to be the false prophets. But 'thus' ('what they say' NIV) is unlikely to refer to the message of the false prophets which Jeremiah on this view would be dismissing, and has to find a remoter reference, possibly in the judgment of v. 10. If v. 13 ends with Jeremiah calling down judgment on these prophets, then the LORD in v. 14 accepts that verdict.

14. Therefore (*lākēn*) introduces the sentence that the LORD imposes on the people: **This is what the LORD God Almighty says.** The extended title in which 'Almighty'/'of hosts' (2:19) is linked not to LORD but to God (as in 15:16; 35:17; 38:17; 44:7; 46:10; 50:25, 31) renders the verdict more solemn. Furthermore by indicating the LORD's power over all forces that exist it answers the thought that he is doing nothing because he can do nothing.

The LORD rebuts the allegation that he does not care, and he acts to reinforce the effectiveness of the word he has given to this prophet. **Because the people have spoken these words** is literally, 'because of your (plural) speaking this word'. The NIV rendering is an attempt to avoid successive 'you' having different referents which is not a natural English idiom. 'Your speaking' could easily be misunderstood as pointing to Jeremiah's speaking and not, as the plural requires, to what the people have said (or on the alternative interpretation to what the false prophets have said). The LORD addresses the people and the prophet in turn. The link between action and consequence indicated by 'therefore' and 'because' is not merely one of judicial interposition; the consequences flow from and arise out of the particular offence committed. **I will make my words in your** (*singular*) **mouth a fire and these people the wood it consumes** (<√*'ākal*, 'to eat, devour'; v. 17). Their repudiation of the prophetic word from the LORD leads to that very word being the judgment imposed on them.

The technique of formulating a judgment corresponding to the sin does not produce a notion of judgment that is extraordinary or

> trivial. On the contrary, the prophetic word of Yahweh did consume the people, and their judgment came at the hands of a distant nation (Yahweh's *rā'āh* upon the people) who brought famine and sword. And while the judgment that ensues arises in part out of the sinful actions of the people, the correspondence described by the prophets is not one of a fate-effecting deed but one wrought out by the action of Yahweh, which the prophet perceives to be directed toward a particular sin and therefore appropriate punishment. (Miller 1982:66-67)

The people had thought they were dealing merely with the wind, but the LORD will show that his word is in reality fire, not here an instrument of refining, but of destruction (23:29; Isa. 1:29-31). Jeremiah as the LORD's spokesman is reassured that his message is genuine and will be backed up by a display of divine power. As this judgment comes upon them rather than false prophets, it seems to reinforce the view that the previous verses were talking about the general reaction of the populace to the message being brought by the true prophets. This was no doubt one of the passages that made such an impact on Jehoiakim's cabinet, because they had the spiritual perceptivity to recognise the truth of the allegations being made.

15. The unit consisting of vv. 15-17 is an amplification of the consuming judgment that the LORD will bring upon the people. **'O house of Israel,' declares the LORD.** This is a reference to Judah who were now the remaining representatives of the covenant people, and who are now directly addressed and warned. **I am bringing a distant nation against you**, a masculine plural though other references in vv. 15-17 are masculine singular. Behind the movements of history and the analyses of political developments lies the reality of the sovereign hand of God. He is already at work, so it is no idle threat that is being discussed.

The graphic description of the invaders emphasises how dire the punishment awaiting Judah will be. Perhaps the message will get home and the people turn back to the LORD before it is too late. Four times the word 'nation' is repeated, each time with a different attribute. They are 'distant'/'from far away' (4:16). The language deliberately echoes Deut. 28:49-52 where Moses set out the covenant curse that would come on the people if they disobeyed the covenant: 'The LORD will raise against you a nation from far off, from the end of the earth, just as the eagle swoops down, a nation whose language you will not understand: a nation fierce of face, that does not respect the old and does not pity the young. He will eat up the fruit of your livestock and the fruit of your ground until you are destroyed, inasmuch as he will not leave to you grain, new wine or oil, the increase of your herds or the young of your flock until he has made you perish. He will lay siege to you in all your gates until your high and fortified walls in which you are trusting come down in all your land.' Isaiah had also described the Assyrians as 'from afar' (Isa. 10:3), but there is still no positive identification of this foe—and the description is all the more menacing for that.

An ancient and enduring nation ('it is an enduring nation; it is a nation from of old') is one which has maintained its existence over many years. 'Enduring' (*ʾêtān*) is an epithet typically applied in Scripture to mountains (Mic. 6:2) or rivers (Ps. 74:15). Furthermore they are 'ancient' (*mēʿôlām*, 'from long ago'; 2:20). The existence of this nation can be traced back as far you care to go into the mists of history. It is no upstart power, but can be treated as a permanent feature of the international landscape—which fits in with the early references to Babylon/Babel in Scripture (Gen. 10:10; 11:9). Though in the event the nation proved to be Babylon (and certainly not the Scythians), here matters of identity are not clarified, and it need not follow that this oracle originates as late as the beginning of Jehoiakim's reign (contra Thompson 1980:242). This is prophecy and not the insight of an astute political commentator. Jeremiah may not at first have known for sure who it was, though by the time of the writing of the First Scroll no doubt remained.

For a fourth time the nation is described as **a people** (lit. 'nation') **whose language you do not know, whose speech you do not understand.** The inability to communicate with them would render the occupation forces even more terrifying as misunderstandings would abound. Is there a hint here of the confusion of language at Babel (Gen. 11:9)? More significant is the fact that this description reflects Deut. 28:49-53. It is the curse of the broken covenant that is going to come upon the disobedient people.

16. The strength as distinct from the alienness of the invaders is then emphasised. **Their quivers are like an open grave** is a very terse expression which some have sought to alter[85]. But its meaning seems clear. 'As the open grave gapes for its victim (Prov. 30:16), so the quiver of the bowmen gapes relentlessly for ever more victims (cf. Hab. 2:5). The arrows fired by the enemy deal out death, and so their container is described as an open grave' (Laetsch 1952:77). Alternatively, the thought may be that the open grave will be filled with

85. 'Their jaws are a grave, wide open' (REB) is conjectural, following the rendering of the Vulgate. It involves reading *ʾăšer pîhû*, 'whose mouth', instead of *ʾašpātô*, 'his quiver', in the light of Ps. 5:10.

corpses and the quivers of the enemy are filled with arrows just waiting to create more corpses. Archers were a major part of an ancient army: not only did the arrows kill in combat, but they could also shoot firebrands over city walls to start a conflagration. The troops who come will not be raw recruits, but **all of them are mighty warriors.** Ancient armies often comprised a motley collection of conscripts from various backgrounds who were only with great difficulty melded into a coherent fighting force. This invading army, however, will consist of experienced and formidable soldiers.

17. The havoc they wreak is described in v. 17 using a fourfold repetition of 'devour'/'eat up' (<√ʾ*ākal*; 3:24; 10:25) which expands on 'consume'/'eat up' in v. 14. The first and last references are to the enemies' impact on the cultivation of the land, and the centre two items refer to their impact on its populace and their animals. **They will devour your harvests and food.** The army going through the land will not only eat up its resources; coming early in the year, they will destroy the grain harvest of April–June. Ancient armies lived off the territory they invaded, so this is not just a matter of their manoeuvres destroying fields. It is foraging and plundering as well as sheer wanton destruction, making it difficult for any left alive to survive until the following harvest. They[86] will **devour your sons and daughters.** This points to the slaughter of the population that will take place; it does not imply cannibalism. **They will devour your flocks and herds.** Again, the devastation of the rural economy is pointed out. They will **devour your vines and fig-trees.** The ingathering of fruit took place in July–September and it too would be affected disastrously. The invasion was not going to be over in a few weeks, but was going to ruin the land. Their wealth and resources in which they had placing their trust as a substitute for relying on the LORD would be wiped out. **With the sword they will destroy**[87] **the fortified cities** (4:5) **in which you trust** (Deut. 28:52). 'With the sword' is strangely delayed until the very end of the Hebrew sentence, which to some suggests it may be an interpolation. More probably 'sword', standing for military might, is

86. Apart from this verb, the enemy is referred to in the Hebrew of vv. 16-17 by the singular 'he'. At this point the plural 'they' is used, a switch which is much more elegant in Hebrew than English. The NIV uses plurals throughout as being more suited to references to a collective noun 'nation' in modern English.

87. The verb *rāšaš*, 'to break in pieces', occurs only here in polel (pual, Mal. 1:4). The LXX rendering *aloēsousin*, 'they will thresh', suggests that there may be an agricultural background to the word.

deliberately delayed for emphasis. Earlier prophets had scorned Israel's readiness to trust in her military preparations (Isa. 31:1; Hos. 10:13). In 4:5 they had been exhorted to take refuge in these very fortified cities. Now that expedient is no longer open to them; the crisis has intensified and their plight is extreme.

18. Verses 18 and 19 revert to discussing the nature of the LORD's judgment, and raise again (v. 10) the question of its extent. The verses are generally identified as prose, and many consider them to be an exilic or post-exilic comment to explain why the judgment of Jerusalem took the form it did. 'Just because the previous passage presents a picture of unmitigated destruction, this verse must be understood as part of the build-up of the tradition, modifying the judgment and so making sense of the fact that Judah did survive, though in exile' (Jones 1992:126). However, if due allowance is made regarding the nature of covenant chastisement (Lev. 26:44; see v. 10 and 4:27) and also of the use of language, there does not appear to be any significant obstacle in taking these words as they stand here as coming from Jeremiah's teaching in the First Scroll. Lundbom reminds us that prophecies of a complete end need not necessarily be absolute 'any more than "holocaust" has to be absolute when referring to the mass killings of Jews during World War II' (1999:388).

The previous unit had presented judgment coming in the form of an enemy invasion of unmitigated severity. But though what was in prospect was awesome, the nature of the covenant bond meant that even such devastation would not spell the utter end. **'Yet even in those days,' declares the LORD, 'I will not destroy you completely.'** 'In those days' (3:16) refers here not to the time of renewed blessing but the time of judgment, though even then there would still be grounds for optimism. The basis for this expectation is not stated, but it will eventually be seen to lie in God himself. Calvin indeed took the words in the sense 'I will not destroy you completely' but explained them as a threat that after the invasion there would be yet further kinds of punishment that God would inflict upon them (1850, 1:289-90). That is, the present judgment will not be the last; there will be more to come after it. However, the context favours the idea of a divinely spared remnant which would ensure that the divine purpose in choosing a people and entering into covenant with them was not totally frustrated by their disobedience (Deut. 30:1-5).

19. There is then envisaged what will happen in the situation after judgment has been imposed. There are survivors, among them the prophet. **And when** (*kî*) **the people** (lit. 'you' plural, as in v. 14) **ask,**

'Why has the LORD our God done all this to us?' you (*singular*) **will tell them, 'As you** (*plural*) **have forsaken me and served foreign gods in your own land, so now you** (*plural*) **will serve foreigners in a land not your own.'** There is again a contrast between second person singular (the prophet) and plural (the survivors) as was found in v. 14. That their question is phrased as it will be subsequently after the event does not lead to this being an exilic or post-exilic saying (contra Jones 1992:126). The survivors are pictured speaking in tones of puzzlement and injured innocence. 'Why?' (an unusual expression: *taḥat meh*, 'in return for what?') suggests they still did not recognise that God had acted justly in what he had done in bringing 'all this', the disasters set out in v. 17, on them. But they are to be left in no doubt about the righteousness of God or about the fitting nature of the penalty. Again it is made clear that the punishment will fit the crime. In 'forsaking' the LORD (1:16; 2:13) they had abandoned their covenant king and transferred their allegiance to foreign gods (*nēkār*, that which is not recognised as belonging to a community or nation), worshipping them and paying them tribute so that they would provide security and fertility. Since they had compounded the guilt of this defection by perpetrating it in the land the LORD had given them as their covenant inheritance, they will be consigned to a land not theirs, one in which the gods they have chosen are reputed to hold sway. There they will learn what is really involved in serving 'foreigners' (*zārîm*, 'strangers', those who are not known and to whom one is not related), either 'strange gods' (2:25; 16:13) or foreign masters (30:8). The NIV play on 'foreign' is not present in the Hebrew, but the clear and forceful equivalence between the misdeed and its punishment certainly is. Because of that, it is noteworthy that in the divine sentence there is no 'I will forsake you' corresponding to 'you have forsaken me'. There might well have been, but its absence fits in with the prevailing concept of overwhelming judgment but not total eradication.

The repeated references to the Exile do not mean that it had already happened. The example of Samaria in 722 BC reinforced the warnings given in the covenant curses that had been promulgated through Moses. But because what is spoken about is covenant disobedience, there is still an element of hope built into the presentation. Let there be no doubt that if there is no repentance, the land will surely be devastated and the people carried off to foreign lands. However, that will not be the end of the story. Unlike many other people groups, which in similar circumstances lost their identity, the people of Judah will maintain theirs. Their God has not given up on his purposes, and there is held open the possibility that he will do more to and through them in the future. But right in front of them is the horror of the devouring enemy and the anguish of their land being conquered and ravaged. For Jeremiah's audience, first in the time of Josiah, and again when the First Scroll was read, their personal concern was what the immediate future held. The challenge to them was to turn their allegiance back to God.

c. Heart Failure (5:20-31)

Again the prophet's message reverts to exposing and denouncing the folly of the people. The LORD is identified as the speaker in vv. 22 and 29, and the NIV is undoubtedly correct in identifying the whole section as divine speech. After the introduction of v. 20, there are three subunits, vv. 21-25, vv. 26-29, and vv. 30-31.

20. The formal introduction, **Announce this to the house of Jacob and proclaim it in Judah**, separates off this section from the preceding. 'Proclaim' is literally 'cause to be heard', which is a plural command (as were those in 4:5; 5:1). It presumably is spoken to a group of people, but we do not know the identity of those who were to act as the LORD's heralds in this matter. Might this phenomenon reflect an early stage in Jeremiah's ministry when he was instructing those who were promoting Josiah's reforms as to what they should say? 'House of Jacob' only occurs elsewhere in Jeremiah in 2:4, which may also indicate a similar background near the beginning of his ministry. As in 2:4 the term is synonymous with Judah, rather than a reference to some early ministry to the north.

21. Hear this (*šimʿû-nāʾ*) links back to 'announce' in v. 20. It is a plural form, though the accompanying collective noun 'people' is grammatically singular, perhaps implying that a personal response was sought from each individual in the group being addressed. The precative particle *nāʾ* usually indicates deferential speech, but that is quite lacking here as the audience are addressed as **you foolish and senseless people.** Such blunt talk is used to shock them and pierce through the defences they have erected against the truth. For 'foolish' (*sābāl*), see 'senseless' (4:22). 'Senseless' here renders 'and there is not heart ⌞to them⌟', where 'heart' is used of human capacity to think, reflect, feel and decide (4:14); they have no understanding. 'Heart' functions as a keyword in this section, linking with vv. 23-24. It is their 'heart failure', their inability to discern the spiritual significance of what is going on around them, that is the root of the problem. This is further spelled out in: **who have eyes but do not see, who have ears but do not hear.** Similar language is used of the people in Isa. 6:9-10 referring to their spiritual insensitivity (cf. also Ps. 94:7-9). However, these words are descriptive of idols in Pss. 115:5-7; 135:15-18, and it may well be that the description of the people in the same terms endorses the thought of those psalms that the people have become like the idols of the alien gods whom they have been serving (Calvin 1850, 1:249).

22. Two rhetorical questions are employed to focus the argument. **'Should you not fear me?'[88] declares the LORD** is a reference to the attitude of reverence and awe that should characterise the LORD's people. It is the essence of Old Testament piety (Exod. 20:20), and is presented as the beginning of true wisdom (Prov. 1:7). 'Me' is fronted in the Hebrew sentence to render it emphatic. **Should you not tremble in my presence?** also has emphasis on 'in my presence', referring particularly to times of worship. 'Tremble' (<√*ḥûl*, 'writhe', 4:19) refers to a violent physical reaction accompanying mental apprehension, presumably with overtones of guilt and not just the due reverence of worshippers.

It was not enough to denounce the folly of idol worship; there had also to be a true appreciation of the character and power of the LORD. This is done using participles in a Hebrew style reminiscent of the language of praise (e.g. Ps. 104:2-4). **I[89] made the sand a boundary for the sea, an everlasting barrier it cannot cross.** 'Sand' (*ḥôl*) forms a nice play with the preceding 'tremble'. 'Barrier' (*ḥoq*) is basically a 'statute/decree' and so came on occasions to indicate a set limit or border. The Creator gave structure and form to his creation, and that continues to be observed by the physical universe. His decrees are everlasting in duration and are respected by the sea. **The waves may roll, but they[90] cannot prevail; they may roar, but they cannot cross it.** The repetition of 'cross' (<√*ʿābar*) makes clear the significance of what is being said. This word which initially points to movement across or through a physical zone is also used in the sense of 'transgress' an overlord's commands ('violate' 34:18), and it invites reflection on the different behaviour of Judah. Unlike the unruly sea Judah repeatedly oversteps the boundaries he has set for her behaviour.

---

88. Possibly there is a wordplay between *yirʾû*, 'they see', in v. 21, and *tîrāʾû*, 'you fear' in this verse.

89. *ʾăšer* may have a causal significance here, 'in that', or it may simply be a relative, 'who', somewhat separated from its antecedent in 'in my presence'.

90. The Hebrew verbs are plural, and have as their subject 'waves' which is not expressed until the next line. The LXX has singular verbs and takes 'sea' as the subject.

The particular illustration chosen from the natural realm may also challenge prevailing conceptions of the sea as an untamable power in its own right. Not only is it under the control of the LORD; he does not exist on the same level as it. He is the one who is above his creation, and therefore worthy of its fear and trembling respect.

23. In vv. 23-24 the LORD addresses Jeremiah, and not the people directly. We often find this phenomenon in Jeremiah, whereby we hear the prophetic word as it comes to the prophet, rather than in the form in which he delivers it as the spokesman of the LORD. **But these people have stubborn and rebellious** (<√*mārâ*, 4:17) **hearts**. This picks up the mention of 'heart' from v. 21, and develops further a theme that is often found in Jeremiah, that the basic human problem is not political, sociological or economic, but spiritual, deriving from the inner being (4:4, 14, 18, 19). The combination of 'stubborn and rebellious' is found in Deut. 21:18, 20, which deals with the case of a rebellious son whose offence had to be dealt with by stoning. Judah was acting in the same stubborn fashion (<√*sārar* which describes a persistent refusal to alter behaviour that is contrary to a norm established by due authority). They were obstinate and self-willed children who would not move from the position they had adopted for themselves, and who were thus defying God and rebelling against him (see also Ps. 78:8). **They have turned aside**[91] **and gone away** from following after the LORD and walking in his ways. They refuse to respect the bounds that the LORD has set for their behaviour.

24. Their defiant attitude is further indicated by the fact that **they do not say to themselves, 'Let us fear the LORD our God'.** The inward root of their behaviour is identified in 'say to themselves', literally, 'say in their heart' (cf. vv. 21, 23). Their hearts were not right with God, and so they did not conduct themselves with due fear and reverence towards him (v. 22). This inner alienation results in a spiritual blindness which again prevents them from discerning the lessons that the natural world might teach them. They do not recognise the bounty of God **who gives autumn and spring rains**[92] **in season,**

91. Notice the play between *sôrēr*, 'stubborn', and *sārû* (<√*sûr*), 'turn aside'.

92. The qere deletes the 'and' before autumn rain and, interchanging the initial consonants, reads an unchangeably long *ô*, *yôreh*, as if the text were wrongly listing three items: rain, autumn rain, and spring rain. The kethibh *wîreh* may, however, be retained, treating the repeated use of *wə* as indicating 'both … and' so that the generic word *gešem*, 'rain', is then explained more particularly by the two types.

who assures us of the regular[93] **weeks of harvest.** The Canaanite gods were primarily fertility gods, and in worshipping them Israel was led to attribute to them the bounty of the land. The people's inability to perceive the LORD as providing for them is a frequent ground of complaint in the prophets (cf. v. 7) The autumn rains fell between mid-October and mid-December and softened the ground after the heat of summer to permit sowing to take place; the spring rains in March and April (3:3) permitted the growth that ensured a good harvest. The weeks of harvest refer to the seven-week period between the Feast of Passover and Feast of Weeks during April and May. The presentation of the first sheaf of barley (Lev. 23:10) and the first sheaf of wheat (Lev. 23:17) was an acknowledgment of their indebtedness to God for the harvest.

25. The LORD breaks away from speaking to the prophet and again directly addresses the people: **Your wrongdoings** (< *ʿāwōn*, 2:26) **have kept these away**. 'Keep away' refers to the deflection of rain from their fields. There were droughts about this time (3:3; 12:4; 14:1-6), and this passage may reflect on that. **Your sins have deprived you of good.** Their wrong-doing had resulted in a reversal of the proper order of things in which they should have enjoyed divine favour as those with whom the LORD had entered into covenant. (Similar arguments are found in Isa. 59:1-2 and Hos. 2:8-9.) 'The good' is specifically rainfall (Deut. 28:12; Ps. 85:12), and so also the bounty of harvest which came from it. But the blessings of the covenant were conditioned on obedience. The curse of the covenant fell on the disobedient.

It is significant that the arguments presented here are not from the word and promises of God, or his past deeds of salvation, but from his natural power (over the sea) and goodness (harvest). This is testimony that is available even to those without special revelation (Rom. 1:20). Its use here indicates that because of their spiritual immaturity the covenant people have to be approached by the prophet at a very elementary level.

26. In vv. 26-28 the LORD again speaks to Jeremiah about the people and directs an indictment against a certain section of society. The people as a whole are now viewed more favourably as 'my people' rather than 'this people' (v. 23). The verse begins with 'for' (*kî*), which

93. *ḥuqqot* normally means 'ordinances, statutes', but note Jeremiah's use in 31:35 and 33:25 to imply 'dependable pattern', as also his use of the related term *ḥôq* in v. 22 for the limit set for the sea.

here seems to specify a particular area in which the sinful behaviour of the nation may be clearly seen: **among my people are wicked men** (<√*rāšaʿ*). This refers particularly to social oppression, and takes up the theme of social injustice which was common in the earlier prophets (Isa. 1:23). It is difficult to date the original setting of this oracle, but it may be from the early reign of Jehoiakim when matters were again allowed to get out of hand in the community. (Compare the description of Josiah in 22:16 with that of Jehoiakim in 22:13, 17.) Such behaviour showed that covenant standards were not being upheld by those who were the most influential in the land, because the king and his officials were failing in their duty of promoting the standards of justice throughout society. 'Are' is literally 'are found', often used in legal contexts for a misdemeanour being found out (2:26, 34). Perhaps there is an echo here of the fruitless search for an honest person in v. 1. However, it did not take long to identify those who were acting dishonestly and unscrupulously.

The well-known figure of the fowler is used to identify those witihin the community who are oppressing others. They are those **who lie in wait like men who snare birds.**[94] Here they are pictured 'lying in wait'/'observing intently' the nets they have spread so that when the birds have entered them they may pull them together and trap them. **And like those who set traps to catch men.** 'Trap' is literally 'a destroyer' (*mašḥît*, 4:7), one who has more in mind than capturing birds. A similar analogy is found in a number of places (Ps. 124:7; Prov. 1:11; Isa. 8:14-15; Amos 3:5).

27. Like cages full of birds refers to willow baskets with lids (Amos 8:1) which may have been used to catch the birds though the comparison with houses suggests that here they are for storage and fattening before consumption (so Rashi). **Their houses are full of**

94. The English translation covers over a number of features in the Hebrew. Whereas *rəšāʿîm*, 'wicked', and *yəqûšîm*, 'fowlers' (which the MT accents read in the same clause as *yašûr*) are plural, *yašûr*, 'he waits', is singular. The singular may be used indefinitely of a large number (Hos. 13:7), or it may reflect the fact that only one individual would be left to watch. *kəšak* may be composed of the inseparable preposition *kə* and an infinitive construct *šak* (for its form, see Joüon §82l) <√*šākak*, 'to recede, subside', and so with a meaning such as 'bend down as fowlers beside a net to pull it tight'. The NRSV offers, 'They take over the goods of others'. Emerton (1981) read *śōk* with a meaning 'booth'. As Jones remarks, 'It is of course possible that the word *šak* is an unknown Heb. word rather than a corruption of the text, perhaps meaning "net", or better "as in a hide" (J. A. Emerton)' (1992: 129).

deceit. 'Deceit' refers presumably to their ill-gotten gains that have been acquired by ensnaring the unfortunate. Similar metonymy is found in Zeph. 1:9 and Amos 3:10. Because their houses are filled with such spoil, 'on account of this' (*ʿal-kēn,* v. 6) **they have become rich and powerful.** As they have managed to carry off their schemes with impunity, their wealth has inflated their arrogant self-esteem.

28. The description of the wicked continues in terms similar to those found in Ps. 73:4-9 and Ezek. 34:8. **And have grown fat and sleek.** Fatness in the ancient world was viewed as a sign of prosperity (Deut. 32:15; Ps. 92:14; Prov. 28:25), but it had negative overtones when the wealth was viewed as excessive or improperly acquired or used. 'Sleek' conveys the thought of those who are smooth, well filled out, and in no way suffering from malnutrition. **Their evil deeds**[95] **have no limit** is literally either 'they pass by deeds of evil/an evil one' (hence, 'They turn a blind eye to wickedness', REB; cf. NASB margin), or 'they go beyond bounds ⌞with respect to⌟ deeds of evil'. Whichever way it is taken, it paints a picture of the lawlessness in the land. 'Pass by/cross' forms a verbal link back to its occurrences in v. 22.

The description of their sin does not remain generalised, but specific examples are cited from the area of extortion and oppression, defrauding others of their rights. **They do not plead the case** (the root *dîn* is repeated in the verb and a cognate noun; cf. 22:16) **of the fatherless.** This was expected in the covenant community, where concern for one's fellow and neighbour, particularly the disadvantaged who were unable to help themselves, should have figured prominently in their actions (Exod. 22:21-22; 23:6; Deut. 24:14, 17-18). In Josiah's covenant renewal ceremony there might well have been recitation of the curse, 'Cursed is the man who withholds justice from the alien, the fatherless or the widow', to which the people would have added their 'Amen!' (Deut. 27:19). But such obligations were treated with disdain. **To win it** (literally, 'and they succeed/thrive') is better than 'yet they prosper' (NKJV) in that the construction is not *waw*-consecutive, but ordinary *waw* followed by the imperfect, presumably indicating purpose. The rich were becoming richer and intended to keep things that way; and so **they do not defend the rights of the poor.** There was prevalent neglect of the rights (*mišpāṭ*, 'justice'), the judgment that should be given in their favour. The 'poor' (*ʾebyôn*, 2:34) are those who lack the physical necessities of life and whose economic deprivation leaves them without resources to stand up for themselves. The

95. As there is no mention of the speech of the wicked in this context, it is apparent that *dābār* is here used in the sense of 'action' rather than 'word'.

courts and administration of justice in the land were not providing them with the legal redress that was theirs by right.

29. There are then repeated the questions of v. 9, **'Should I not punish them for this?' declares the LORD. 'Should I not avenge myself on such a nation as this?'** This sums up not just the particular cases cited in the previous verses. There would be a measure of incongruity in the whole nation being punished for the evils of the few. Rather it looks back to the whole section from v. 20, and reflects on the conduct that had been described there.

30-31. The concluding unit of this section turns from the economically powerful in the land to those who were influential in its religious life: the priests and the prophets. **A horrible and shocking thing has happened in the land** expresses in words of considerable intensity the repulsive nature of what has occurred. For 'horrible ... thing' (*šammâ*), see on 2:15. It normally refers to the horror-stricken reaction arising from the destruction involved in the LORD's judgment of his people. 'If this is the case, then the lie being proclaimed by the prophets is seen as being itself a destructive force' (Overholt 1970:73). 'Shocking thing' (*šaʿărûrâ*) is derived from a stem denoting filthiness. Here and in 23:14 it is used of the behaviour of false prophets, though in 18:13 a closely related form describes how the people have conducted themselves. The same root is used in 29:17 of figs which are too rotten to be edible. The two words combine to describe what is loathsome and abhorrent: those who should have been guiding the people in their attitudes to the LORD have instead been perverting his way. The precise nature of the false prophesying is unclear, as is the relationship of the priests and prophets.

As the threefold indictment is read out, there is an emphatic foregrounding of the three groups: prophets, priests and people. **The prophets prophesy lies** (20:6; 29:9). It is also possible to understand this as 'the prophets prophesy by the Lie' (*baššeqer*), a reference to Baal (cf. v. 2). Whatever deity the invoke, it is certain they are not proclaiming the message of the LORD, and so the people are not hearing the truth as it applied to their particular situation. **The priests rule by their own authority** could be either 'on their own authority', or more probably at the prophets' direction (33:13; 1 Chron. 25:2, 3, 6)[96].

96. Holladay suggests the translation 'the priests deconsecrate themselves' (1986, 1:201). The technical term for the ordination of the priests was 'filling their hand' ('ordain', Exod. 29:9), and by taking the verb as *rādâ* II, 'to scrape out, scoop out', Holladay envisages their action as being one by which they removed from their hands whatever had been placed there.

There may well have been a measure of collusion between the two groups. The incidents described in 27:16 and 29:25-29 illustrate the interplay between prophet and priest at this time. Rather than applying the norms of God's word, they were relying upon man-made rules as they sought to guide the people. Although Temple prophets were nominally under the control of the priests (20:1-2; 29:26), it may well have been that a situation had arisen in which, through their influence with the people, the prophets were able to exercise a more influential role in shaping public perceptions (20:3-6; 27:16; 29:24-32). **And my people love it this way.** This perhaps goes a long way toward explaining why the prophets and priests were acting as they did: it brought them popularity. They no longer had the hard task of presenting the people with the LORD's censure on their immoral and rebellious behaviour. They were speaking pleasing words to them, and the people were only too ready to hear that all was well with them—even if that involved them being the victims of a measure of exploitation, and others in society being oppressed. The immoral actions of the ruling elite were only able to be perpetuated because the people as a whole were disinclined to take any corrective action. Although they were living in a fool's paradise, that was just what they wanted.

However, it made no allowance for what was still to come. **But what will you do in the end?** Literally, 'her end' with a feminine suffix which may have a neuter force, referring to the end of that sort of conduct, or which may refer to Jerusalem (Calvin 1850, 1:311). Matters would not always continue as they had done. The people are being called on to reflect on the culmination of their present course of conduct. 'If only they were wise and would understand this and discern what their end will be!' (Deut. 32:29). 'What will you do in the day of reckoning, when disaster comes from afar?' (Isa. 10:3).

3. Impending Devastation (6:1-30)

OUTLINE

a. Jerusalem under Siege (6:1-8)
b. No Peace (6:9-15)
c. The Good Way (6:16-21)
d. The Ruthless Foe (6:22-26)
e. The Royal Assayer (6:27-30)

In drawing this first main block of material (2:1–6:30) to a conclusion Jeremiah again brings to the forefront of his presentation the devastation that will be caused in the land by the incursion of the unidentified foe from the north. The invasion itself is graphically described in vv. 1-8 and vv. 22-26. But though the LORD has announced that the people's conduct merits sweeping judgment, the presentation is still conditional in that the possibility of repentance has not been foreclosed. Jerusalem is pled with to respond to the warnings that have been issued and alter her conduct (vv. 8, 16), even though the overall presentation holds out little hope of a positive reaction. The people refuse to listen (v. 10, 17); they spurn the LORD's way (v. 16) and reject his law (v. 19). Because they fail the test that the LORD has imposed on them, the outcome will be that they are discarded as useless in the same way as a refiner of ore discards dross and slag (vv. 27-30). Even so there are hints that the people are not to be totally rejected in the use of the metaphor of gleaning (v. 9b).

a. Jerusalem under Siege (6:1-8)

1. Picking up from 4:5-6, the LORD's message is that the alarm should again be raised because of the enemy invasion. **Flee for safety, people of Benjamin! Flee from Jerusalem!** But the advice is now different in that it is no longer a call to find safety in the fortified cities—they had already been viewed as deserted (4:29). The enemy campaign has been so successful that Jerusalem itself is about to be besieged and will not be able to withstand it. The only course to avoid capture or death is to leave what had seemed a secure citadel. 'Flee for safety' (<√*ʿûz* hiphil) implies that immediate action is required: 'Run for your lives' (NLT). But why is this entreaty addressed to the 'people of Benjamin' (*bənê binyāmin*[97])? One factor might well have been the assonance involved in the description, a technique used repeatedly in the passage. In that case the vocative would simply point to the inhabitants of the city, because although Jerusalem was later associated with the tribe of Judah, it had originally been in Benjamite territory. However, another factor cannot be overlooked. Jerusalem was dominated by a mind-set that thought the city inviolable, and therefore there would be an unwillingness to act on such advice. Possibly those who had just escaped to the city from Benjamite territory to the immediate north would be more open to the prophet's message that it was going to fall.

---

97. BHS faithfully reproduces the Leningrad Codex here in that it has no *šəwā* under the *nun*, as would be expected grammatically, and indeed is found in most manuscripts.

The picture of imminent invasion is continued with the command, **Sound the trumpet in Tekoa!** For the use of the trumpet, see 4:5. The assonance involved in the phrase *ûbitqôaʿ tiqʿû*, 'and in Tekoa sound', probably accounts for it being selected for special mention. Tekoa lay eleven miles (18 km) south of Jerusalem and six miles (10 km) south of Bethlehem. It was the birthplace of the prophet Amos (Amos 1:1) and, more significantly in this context, it had long been a fortified site (2 Chron. 11:6). This indicates that the whole area round Jerusalem was to be in a state of military readiness, rather than that the invasion was expected from the south (for the contrary view see McKane 1986, 1:139-40). **Raise the signal over Beth Hakkerem!** The word used for 'signal' differs from that found in 4:6, permitting a play on the sound of *śəʾû maśʾēt*, 'raise signal'. These signals were most probably fire beacons whose flames and smoke would attract attention at a distance (Judg. 20:28, 40). The Lachish Ostraca (IV:10) from this period show that use of fire beacons was a contemporary military practice (King 1993:83; *ANET* 322). Beth Hakkerem (named also in Neh. 3:14) is literally 'house of the vineyard'. As vineyards were commonly situated on hillsides, its raised elevation would make it a suitable place for signalling. Its location is still a matter of conjecture with a site just west of Jerusalem on the road to Bethlehem and another near Tekoa both being proposed. The picture, however, is quite clear. The unrelenting advance of the enemy has necessitated a national alert. **For** (*kî*) **disaster looms out of the north, even terrible destruction.** 'Disaster', 'out of/from the north' and 'terrible destruction' recall 4:6b, but there is an interesting change. Disaster is virtually personified, and 'looms' (<√*šāqap* niphal, 'to look down') would be used of a person who looks down over someone or something from a height, perhaps even leaning out from a window to do so. 'Looms' brings out well the ominous note in this scrutiny.

2. This verse has long been acknowledged as one of the most difficult to translate in Jeremiah. The two main approaches are well illustrated by the NIV, **I will destroy the Daughter of Zion, so beautiful and delicate**, and the NRSV, 'I have likened daughter Zion to the loveliest pasture' (the NRSV footnotes the alternative translation). The NKJV opts for a mixture of the two approaches: 'I have likened the daughter of Zion to a lovely and delicate woman.' The different translations arise especially from the ambiguity of two Hebrew words. The first approach takes *nāwâ*, 'beautiful', as a by-form of the root *nāʾâ*, 'to be pleasing, delightful'. However, it may equally well be understood as a feminine form corresponding to *nāweh*, 'grazing place, settlement'.

The second ambiguity arises from the root *dāmâ* where lexicographers identify two (BDB 197-198) or three (*HALOT* 225) homonyms (cf. also 8:14). 'I will destroy' renders the verb *dāmîtî* as a prophetic perfect from √*dāmâ* (III), in which case Zion is personified as a beautiful and pampered woman, but even so (or is there a note of condemnation, echoing Amos 4:1?) the LORD is going to destroy her. Certainly likening the city to a woman intensifies the sense of her weakness and vulnerability before the onslaught. However, the presence of the homonym *dāmâ* (I), 'to be like', cannot be entirely ruled out, though it usually requires the use of *ʾel* or *lə*, 'to', rather than the accusative as here. If the form is taken as an archaic second person feminine, this would yield the sense 'You, daughter of Zion, are like a beautiful and delicate ⌞woman⌟' or 'fine pasture'. Repointing the form to a first person piel from the same root, *dimmîtî*, yields the NRSV rendering quoted above. On the understanding that vv. 2-3 are a picture of what the LORD intended Zion to be, v. 4 breaks the idyllic scene with a harsh intrusion of what her sins have brought her. For 'Daughter of Zion', see on 4:31.

3. Depending on one's interpretation of v. 2, this verse may continue a nostalgic picture of the peace and prosperity Zion might have enjoyed (so NKJV, AV, following Vulgate). Most translations, however, render v. 3 as the start of an invasion. **Shepherds with their flocks will come against her; they will pitch their tents round her.** 'Against' (<*ʾel*, 'to') need not be translated as indicating hostile intent, but it is brought forward for emphasis and that in itself may indicate a contrast is involved. 'Shepherds' may be used metaphorically for 'rulers' (2:8), so that what at first seems to be a picture of shepherds and their flocks coming and pasturing around the city is transformed into a hostile army laying siege. 'Pitch' (<√*tāqaʿ*, echoing its use in a different sense, 'sound', in v. 1) implies pounding tent pegs into the ground. They are there to stay till they have achieved their aim—and it is not a matter of sheep-rearing. **Each tending** (<√*rāʾâ*, 'to tend, shepherd') **his own portion,** 'his hand', what lies next to him or has been placed under his care (cf. 4:17). Again this may be equally well taken as describing true pastoral care or as an ominous picture of how closely the besieged city will be beleaguered as each contingent of the enemy army watches over the sector of the perimeter assigned to it.

4. Jeremiah then abruptly switches to a description of the siege. Although the NIV presents the report as that of one voice, it is easier to understand the words as the excited comments of three speakers in the confusion of the engagement. The first voice sets out the proposed action of the enemy. **Prepare** (plural) **for battle against her! Arise, let us attack at noon!** 'Prepare' (<√*qādaš*, piel 'to sanctify/consecrate') is used to denote the cultic preparations for going to war (22:7; 51:27, 28; Joel 3:9; Mic. 3:5). Neither in Israel nor in the surrounding nations was war considered to be a secular pursuit. The invading armies are called on to seek propitious omens from their astrologers for the time to attack, and to make appropriate sacrifices to the gods to ensure success. Ordinarily armies of the day engaged in combat when daylight became sufficiently clear, and the battle would continue until nightfall. But here battle is to commence at noon. Perhaps that was the time the omens indicated as propitious, or perhaps it conveys a note of impatience, not being prepared to wait until the following day. This is a self-confident army, ready to engage in combat.

Who then utters the second speech: the attackers or the defenders? Calvin argued that this is the speech of the besieging army, reflecting the rough language of soldiers who were ready to make a forceful assault and take the city in the remaining moments of the day (1850, 1:318). The REB, 'Too late! The day declines and the shadows lengthen', supposes that the soldiers express their frustration at the coming of dusk preventing them from pressing home their advantage against the city. That, however, does not fit in with the portrayal of the invader as confident and successful. It would seem preferable to take this as the viewpoint of the defenders. **But** (a translator's supplement)**, alas** is a cry of personal despair, 'woe to us!' (NKJV, NRSV), indicating disappointment and foreboding (4:13). From the defenders' point of view things are not going well, and that is for two reasons both introduced by 'for' (*kî*), **the daylight is fading** (<√*pānâ*, 'to turn, turn away)**, and** (*kî*, reinforcing the previous instance) **the shadows of evening grow long.** Darkness would ordinarily have afforded a measure of respite to the besieged, but faced with opponents of such overwhelming strength they are uncertain what surprise measures might be launched against them during the night.

5. And that is just what they will have to face. Another voice—that of the enemy—is then heard: **So arise, let us attack at night and destroy her fortresses!** So well has their campaign gone that they see no obstacle as capable of impeding their progress. Why not have a night attack? Their mood is one of self-assurance and they are eager to bring matters to a conclusion. 'Fortresses'/'citadels' were small elevated defensive structures either as part of a city wall or incorporated into the royal palace (1 Kgs. 16:18).

6. The enemy forces are not acting merely on their own initiative. The veil is again drawn aside to permit the underlying cause of the invasion and siege to be revealed. 'For' (*kî*) **this is what the LORD Almighty says: 'Cut down the trees**[98] **and build** (lit. 'pour' of the stones and soil used) **siege ramps against Jerusalem.'** The LORD of hosts (2:19), the one who has all power in his control, is in command of the enemy army/hosts also, and he is heard issuing orders to them as to how to proceed with the siege. This is a complete reversal of what was expected of the LORD when it came to warfare involving his people. The trees are those that surrounded Jerusalem and they would be used in various ways such as making scaling ladders to mount the city walls, or as battering-rams. These were protected by wooden structures, which also formed suitable platforms for archers to shoot fire brands into the city. Wood was also used to support the sloping siege-mounds of earth and large stones, heaped up against the wall of the city to form a ramp to allow attacking forces access over the top. Of course, such attacks would be stoutly resisted by those inside the city.

The reason for this action is given. **This city must be punished** or 'This is the city that must be punished' (NRSV) is a grammatically difficult construction,[99] but what is involved seems fairly clear. The LORD as the city's suzerain has inspected his subordinate and reached the only verdict that was possible: the city has violated the instructions given it and must be punished. **It is filled with oppression.** 'Oppression' (<√*ʿāšaq*) was a breach of the covenant in which the LORD's people were to respect each other's rights because all were equally answerable to their common Overlord. So it was an abuse of power to deprive others of their property or rights, perhaps with a semblance of legality but in fact without thought for the morality of the situation, and oppression had been prohibited from earliest times

98. *ʿēṣâ*, 'trees', is an otherwise unknown feminine collective form of *ʿēṣ*, 'tree'. A few manuscripts and the versions support reading a *mappiq* in the final *he*, *ʿēṣāh*, 'her trees' (cf. Deut. 20:20).

99. The feminine noun 'city' is followed by a masculine verb, and further the verb is not a niphal which would more naturally convey the thought 'must be punished', whereas the hophal which is found here would mean 'he has been visited (with punishment)', or '⌞which⌟ has been inspected' (<√*pāqad*, 1:10), possibly an impersonal usage. The NRSV marginal reading, 'This is the city of license', emends *hopqad* to *happeqer* for which the meaning of 'licentiousness, dissoluteness' is derived from post-biblical Hebrew. The LXX 'O false city' seems to be a guess at what the obscure expression might mean based on what follows.

(Lev. 19:13) and was vehemently criticised by the prophets (Isa. 30:12; 59:13; Ezek. 22:7, 12, 29).

7. At v. 7 there is a marginal note in the Hebrew Bible indicating that this is the middle verse of the Old Testament. **As a well**[100] **pours out its water, so she pours out her wickedness.** This presents a picture of the copious supply of wickedness in the city ('pour' <√*qûr* hiphil, 'to overflow', cf. Hess 1991). Alternatively, deriving the verb from a different root, the thought may be of an ever-fresh supply: 'As a well keeps its water fresh, so she keeps fresh her wickedness' (NRSV; 'keep fresh' <√*qārar* hiphil, 'to keep cool'). Just as the supply of water from a deep well is cool and refreshing to drink, so Jerusalem keeps a cool and well-preserved stock—of wickedness! So much in use was this well that there was no opportunity for its waters to stagnate. **Violence and destruction resound in her.** The fact that the accompanying verb is singular suggests that 'violence and destruction' may be an example of hendiadys, with both nouns referring to the same phenomenon, and so equivalent to 'violent destruction' (*IBHS* §4.4.1b). It has also been suggested that violence (*ḥamas*) is more focused on the person, while destruction (*šōd*) has to do with the destruction of property (Holladay 1986, 1:208). The sounds of social unrest and disruption re-echo in her streets. **Her sickness and wounds are ever before me.** Isaiah had used similar language to describe the desolation of the land as a result of foreign invasion (Isa. 1:6-9), but here the description is of the internal condition of the city (cf. v. 14). 'Ever' ('continually' NKJV) brings out the same fact as the illustration of the well: this is an ongoing, deep-seated problem. It is not merely 'before me'; it is 'against me' (*ʿal-pānay*), causing offence to God.

8. Even so, the situation is not yet totally beyond recall. **Take warning, O Jerusalem**. 'Take warning' (<√*yāsar* niphal, 2:30; 5:3) is perhaps a reflexive usage, a *niphal tolerativum*, 'let yourself be warned' (cf. Ps. 2:10; GKC §51c). There is still the possibility of an appropriate response by Jerusalem if she will only learn the lesson that she is being taught and correct her attitudes. However, the alternative is clear: **or I will turn away from you**/'lest (*pen*) I (<*nepeš*) turn' (<√*yāqaʿ*, 'to wrench, twist, turn away in disgust', partly echoing vv. 1, 3). When *nepeš* is used of human beings, there are overtones of weakness and vulnerability which are no longer present when the word is

100. The kethibh is *bôr*, 'cistern' (m.); the qere is *bayir*, an otherwise unattested variant spelling of *bəʾēr*, 'well' (f.). The pronominal suffix on 'its water' is also feminine, favouring the qere, as does the sense of the passage. Cisterns do not pour out water, and certainly do not provide fresh water.

extended to describe God. It may function in a referential sense, 'self', or it may, as here, have overtones of desire. 'My being will no longer desire you and will turn from you' implies a violent rupture (Gen. 32:26) and also conveys a strong sense of revulsion and loathing (Ezek. 23:17). If God reacts in this way, then it will be more than absence of blessing they will experience. A second consequence of her unresponsiveness is again introduced by 'lest' (*pen*). The LORD warns them of the severe judgment he will bring on them: I will **make your land desolate so that no one can live in it,**[101] a variation of the condition described in 4:7 (cf. also 10:22). For all that this verse warns of the dire outcome of a ruptured relationship with the LORD, it also captures the essential quality of the early preaching of Jeremiah in that this is an outcome that God does not desire. There is an openness and prospect of potential reconciliation. The warnings are real, but an appropriate response may still be made so that disaster is averted.

b. No Peace (6:9-15)

9. A new section is indicated by the absence of any linkword at the start of v. 9 (compare v. 6), and by the introductory formula. **This what the LORD Almighty says: 'Let them glean**[102] **the remnant of Israel as thoroughly as a vine.'** The LORD is speaking to the prophet regarding the enemy who will devastate the land. The imagery continues earlier references to Israel as a vine (5:10); but who are the 'remnant of Israel'? It is not the usual use of remnant to refer to the small proportion of the people left after the judgment of the wrath has come upon the land as a whole (Isa. 6:13; 10:22). Rather Judah is taken as constituting the remnant left of the original people of God after disaster had overtaken the north. That kingdom had already been harvested, and all that was left was the smaller southern kingdom, which would now be subject to gleaning. Harvesting of grapes is the final stage of the summer's work when the late fruits and the vintage are gathered. Gleaning the vineyard happened last of all. The owner of the vineyard was not allowed to perform this task himself. It was the privilege of the poor and the resident alien in Israel to take what was left by the harvesters (Lev. 19:10). So too outsiders will function as the LORD's gleaners of Judah.

The verb in the second part of the verse is singular, **Pass your**

---

101. *nôšābâ*, 'habitable', is a gerundival use of the niphal participle (cf. *IBHS* §23.3d).

102. The NRSV emends the text to read *ʿôlēl ʿôlēl*, 'glean thoroughly', an infinitive absolute followed by a singular imperative addressed to Jeremiah.

hand over the branches[103] **again, like one gathering grapes.** Calvin (1850, 1:326) views the words as addressed by one gleaner to encourage another. Such use of direct speech without formal attribution would not be unusual in Jeremiah. However, if only to make sense of the transition to v. 10, this saying has apparently to be understood as referring to the prophet, so that we have two contrasting sayings from the LORD, each of which develops the imagery of the grape harvest in a different way. Jones argues that 'there seems here to be an unexpressed assumption that the LORD's instruction is to look for a faithful remnant' (1992:134). Jeremiah is to go through the branches of the vine, that is, move through the people with his message, doing so with a thoroughness that is like one looking for fruit on the vine. It was his task to confront all with the LORD's warning, and to do this before the enemy came. 'Israel will be stripped clean like a vineyard from which every grape has been picked. So you must rescue everyone you can while there is still time' (GNB). Though this approach does not totally account for the juxtaposition of the two sayings of v. 9, it does provide a connection into the prophet's response in v. 10.

10. The LORD's assignment to Jeremiah to search for those who may be rescued leaves the prophet in perplexity. **To whom can I speak and give warning?** The cohortative *ʾădabbərâ*, 'let me speak', may be used here either for its fuller sound (GKC §108g) or in an optative sense in which the speaker recognises he may not be able to carry out his wish, 'To whom may I speak?' (cf. *IBHS* §34.5.1a; Joüon §114cN). 'And give warning' (<√*ʿûd* hiphil, 'to testify, give solemn assurance, warn') is also a cohortative form expressing the intended result of his speaking (*IBHS* §34.5.2). It is a juridical term that indicates the formality and gravity of what was being said to the people regarding the consequences of their conduct.

But Jeremiah expects his actions to be fruitless. **Who will listen to me?** The imperfect expresses another consequence of Jeremiah's speech, 'that they may hear' (NKJV, NRSV). Going through the land again with another word of warning seemed to him to be quite futile. He points to the fact that **their ears are closed so that they cannot hear.** 'Closed' is literally 'uncircumcised' (Acts 7:51). The metaphor (4:4; 5:24) is being used to indicate a covering of a spiritual nature which blocks off reception of the message of God. They may have

103. *salsillâ*, 'branch', occurs only here in the Old Testament. On the basis of *sal*, 'basket', the LXX and the Vulgate render it as 'basket'. But the meaning 'branch' or 'tendril' may be argued for either as a by-form of *zalzallîm*, 'tendrils' (Isa. 18:5) or from the post-biblical Hebrew *silsêm*, 'to curl the hair'.

outwardly received the mark of membership of the covenant community, but they are strangers to the corresponding inward grace of spiritual sensitivity to the word of the LORD. 'There is a hard unwillingness to believe that a threat of judgment can be a word of Yahweh, and when Jeremiah speaks he gives deep offence. The image of uncircumcised ears does not indicate total deafness but selective deafness—receptivity to illusions and an incapacity to hear the truth' (McKane 1986, 1:145). Lacking the insight to comprehend the divine word (4:4), the people were unable to hear it in the sense of 'respond in obedience' to it (5:21). The community beyond the reach of the word is described in a way reminiscent of Isa. 6:9-10, though the language is different. Again the prophet points to the reality of the situation he is having to deal with: **The word of the LORD is offensive to them; they find no pleasure in it.** 'Offensive' (*ḥerpâ*, 'a reproach') refers to something that is viewed as contemptible and worthless, and which is treated accordingly. Frequently, this attitude of disparagement is translated into scornful speech (Ps. 79:4). They despised what was their greatest covenant privilege, one which they should have held in special esteem (Ps. 119:35). 'Has anything so great as this ever happened, or has anything like it ever been heard of? Has any other people heard the voice of God speaking out of fire, as you have, and lived?' (Deut. 4:32-33).

11. Jeremiah then considers his own situation as his message continues to meet with no response. **But I am full of the wrath of the LORD, and I cannot hold it in.** Though his ministry is to an unreceptive people, yet he is so gripped by the enormity of the tragedy coming upon them that, try though he might, he cannot be silent about it and must give warning no matter how his message is treated. 'Hold' is used of cisterns in 2:13. Jeremiah has been so filled with an inner awareness of the LORD's wrath (*ḥēmâ*, 4:4) that he compares himself to a container whose capacity for retaining liquid has been exhausted and consequently its contents are spilling out. It is possible to detect here for the first time a theme that will become prominent in Jeremiah's Confessions. The words are very similar to those of 20:9, where Jeremiah relates that he had tried to stop proclaiming the LORD's message. It is unlikely that something similar had occurred at this earlier stage in his ministry, but still there is a note of reluctance. Jeremiah wished he had something else to proclaim other than the message of impending ruin.

There is then a sudden change of speaker, as the LORD turns to Jeremiah and exhorts him to carry through his task to completion:

Pour[104] **it out on the children in the street and on the young men gathered together; both husband and wife will be caught in it, and the old, those weighed down with years**/'full of days'**.** There is to be no limit to those whom Jeremiah is to address. 'Children' (*ʿôlāl*) refers to toddlers, able to be out playing in the streets (9:21). It is a picture of a dire catastrophe that will affect all age groups; none will be exempt. We may shrink from the reality of the indiscriminate nature of warfare, but the centuries have not lessened the misery it brings. 'Pour' is the opposite of 'hold in' in a vessel. But what is it that Jeremiah is to pour? It is the message of impending judgment, which since it will be ignored will turn into the very judgment itself.

12. The judgment will be as comprehensive as the misconduct. **Their houses will be turned over to others, together with their fields and their wives.** It is not merely a scenario of enemy occupation of their land that is envisaged, but the horror of a community devastated by rampage and pillage. And yet it is not just brutal enemy action that they suffer. It is the curse of the broken covenant (Deut. 28:30) imposed by the covenant suzerain. **'When I stretch** (or better, 'For (*kî*) I will stretch out, NKJV, NRSV) **out my hand against those who live in the land,' declares the LORD.** The LORD's hand refers to his active intervention in power. The hand that had been stretched out before to save them (Exod. 3:20; Deut. 7:19) is now stretched out in judgment against them, to strike them (compare 15:6).

13. The words of vv. 13-15 will be repeated in 8:10b-12, following words in 8:10a similar to those found here in v. 12a. These verses demonstrate that the inhabitants of the land will experience the LORD's judgment because of their materialism. 'For' (*kî*) introduces the reason for the impending punishment. **From the least to the greatest** uses adjectives 'small' and 'great' as superlatives (GKC §133g; *IBHS* §14.5c) to express how widespread corruption was in the community (cf. 16:6; 31:34; 42:1, 8; 44:12). **All**[105] **are greedy for gain.** They were all on the make, trying to squeeze whatever they could for themselves out of any situation they encountered (22:17; cf. Hab. 2:9; Prov. 1:19; 15:27).

But the flaw in the life of the community is not simply that people in general are just out to make themselves as prosperous as they can.

104. The verb *šəpōk* is an infinitive construct. BHS proposes reading the infinitive absolute *šāpōk*, presumably in an imperatival sense. The LXX reads 'I will pour' (hence NKJV).

105. 'All' renders *kullô*, 'everyone of him', where the suffix may be used vaguely to convey the idea of totality (Joüon §146j).

The same attitude towards life has permeated the thinking of their religious leaders who should have known better and who should have expostulated with the people regarding their behaviour. **Prophets and priests alike, all practise deceit**, is expressed by a participle to denote their repeated, ongoing sin. They too are so eager for gain that they will use any method to obtain it, especially 'doing falsehood' (*pāʿal šeqer*, 8:10; 2 Sam. 18:13). Earlier prophets had described the conduct of the false prophets: 'If one feeds them, they proclaim "peace"; if he does not, they prepare to wage war against him' (Mic. 3:5; see also Hos. 4:4-9 regarding the priests). Telling people what they wanted to hear and condoning their conduct ensured that the donations kept coming in, and it was temple revenue (and the prosperity that flowed to them personally from it) that was their number one target, not faithfulness to God. Consequently they avoided their proper task of recalling the people to their covenant obligations (no money to be made by doing that), and this rendered the priests and prophets ultimately culpable for the socially destructive practices prevalent in the land arising from the community's deficient awareness of their responsibility before God.

14. How they carry out their duties is spelled out more fully in v. 14. **They dress**[106] **the wound of my people as though it were not serious.**[107] 'Deceit' (*šeqer*, v. 13) has led to 'wound'/'breakage' (*šeber*, 4:6). The word *šeber* is used for a broken arm or leg (Lev. 21:19) as well as for brokenness of spirit (Prov. 15:4; Isa. 65:14) and the collapse through shattering of a building or city (*HALOT* 1404-05). The community was physically and spiritually in a dire situation, and according to many manuscripts[108] the LORD views them with a measure of sympathy as 'the daughter of my people' (4:11). To a people who had a life-threatening condition their religious leaders were

106. The *waw*-consecutive imperfect, *wayərappəʾû*, 'and they have healed', after a predicate participle (*ʿōśeh*, 'doing' v. 13) may indicate a persistent perfective sense, 'have been healing' (*IBHS* §33.3.5c).

107. *nəqallâ* <√*qālal*, 'to be light' is a feminine niphal participle, and *ʿal* may be used of the standard to which something is done, so that the phrase is equivalent to 'by a standard of lightness' (Joüon §134n).

108. The textual evidence cited in BHS notes that many Hebrew manuscripts, some Greek translations, the Syriac, Targum and Vulgate all favour 'daughter of my people' as in 8:11. The AV acknowledged the textual uncertainty of 'of the daughter' by putting it in italics, and most modern English translations omit it, viewing it as having been introduced from the parallel passage.

applying totally inappropriate remedies. With bland optimism and an eye on the contributions that would flow into the Temple, **'Peace, peace,' they say**.

'Peace' (*šālôm*, 4:10) is a significant Old Testament concept which denotes completeness, well-being and tranquillity. Often this derives from an absence of external threats and extends to the mental equilibrium of the individual who is not experiencing vexation or distress. Durham further argues that the concept always involves the additional thought that this peace and contentment have arisen not merely or primarily by human effort but are the result of divine blessing. Often it refers to an individual's 'realisation, under the blessing of God, of the plan which God has for him and the potential with which God has endowed him' (Durham 1970: 280). He further shows that such peace was often associated with the divine presence with his people. For instance, in Ps. 29:11 where 'the LORD blesses his people with peace' (*baššālôm*) this points to the fulfilment the divine king provides for his people when he is present with them (cf. also Num. 6:24-26). This analysis need not be restricted to an exclusively cultic view of the origins of *šālôm* as Durham favours.

'Peace' then appealed to the theology of the political and religious establishment in Jerusalem. Their error was not in associating peace and blessing with the divine presence, but in assuming God's favour existed towards those who despised his covenant and in presuming that divinely provided peace was the same as endorsement of the existing regime. The repetition of 'peace' here suggests it is a quote of a slogan used to effect ideological inculcation and to stifle any glimmering perception of the reality of the situation in the city. The establishment theology preached in Jerusalem assured the people that all would be well, that is, that through the existing regime the blessing of God would rest upon their living and their actions. This was based on an inadequate appreciation of the covenant because they divorced the blessings of the Overlord from the obedience of his subjects and assumed there was an absolute divine commitment which automatically extended *šālôm* to Jerusalem and its inhabitants. But if the people of the covenant live in rebellion against God, they can expect not the blessings of the covenant but its curses. Those who should have been summoning the people to repentance were totally failing in their duty. As a result the community were unwilling to assess the totality of their lifestyle in the light of God's covenant demands, and did not appreciate the searching and inward dimensions of what he required from his people. The religious establishment were prepared to legitimate as the essence of the covenant an outward conformity to the (revenue generating) rituals of the Temple. Bright asserts that the verse 'clearly reflects the post-reformation complacency when priest and people alike imagined that the nation had by its action gained peace with its God and assurance of his continued protection' (1965:50). But though the formal restoration and perpetuation of worship seemed to deal with the fractures in the land, it was no substitute for true repentance (Ezek. 13:10-16). The wholeness, integrity and real prosperity of the land would not be established **when there is no peace**, that is, there is not a genuine, sound and harmonious relationship between the people and their covenant king.

15. The focus on the priests and prophets continues as the malaise which has ensured there will be no peace in the land is further analysed. **Are they ashamed of their loathsome conduct?** For 'ashamed' (*bôš* hiphil), see 2:26. They were unconscious of the fact that in God's sight their behaviour was loathsome (*tôʿēbâ*, 'detestable' 2:7). There is no formal mark of interrogation, and it may be that the REB is right in rendering, 'They ought to be ashamed because they practised abominations'. Either way their conduct is condemned in strong and unequivocal terms. The religious leaders of the land just could not see that their actions had disrupted their relationship with God. **No, they have no shame at all; they do not even know how to blush.** The debasing impact of the long years of Manasseh's reign had so seared the conscience of the nation, including (perhaps especially) that of its religious functionaries, that they had no compunction at all about their conduct or awareness that the changes brought about by Josiah fell far short of what was desired. As far as they were concerned there was nothing they should be uneasy about.

In such circumstances it is not surprising that the LORD pronounces their doom. **'So** (*lākēn*, 'therefore', introducing the sentence of condemnation) **they will fall among the fallen; they will be brought down when I punish them,'**[109] **says the LORD.** When judgment sweeps across the land, it will not just be soldiers who fall on the field of battle; there will be no exemption for the teachers and religious leaders who were ultimately responsible for the catastrophe. 'Brought down' (<√*kāšal* niphal 'cause to stumble', v. 21) refers to the ruin that will come on them. 'Punish' is undoubtedly the right rendering of the root *pāqad* here, but it should be kept in mind that the root implies that this is the consequence of divine inspection. It is not an arbitrary imposition that is being described, but one that arises from their king's scrutiny of their actions and his evaluation of their propriety.

109. Literally, 'at time of I punished them'; see Joüon §129p,2.

c. The Good Way (6:16-21)

The LORD speaks throughout this section to show how unresponsive the people are to his entreaties, and how futile are their efforts to ingratiate themselves with him. Because of their failure to grasp the serious nature of their misconduct, the LORD turns and calls for witnesses as he issues his threat of retribution. The people were determined to follow the trends of their day and what seemed currently popular. They were not prepared to learn from the experience of past generations, so sure were they of their own wisdom. Like the Athenians of old they wanted to hear what was new, what was trendy (Acts 17:21).

16. The nation is compared to a group of travellers who have come to a junction on their route, and they are counselled to consider well before they proceed. The decision they took would be crucial, for there would be no way of reversing it. **This is what the LORD says, 'Stand at the crossroads and look.'** Scripture frequently uses the metaphor of a path or road for the general conduct of one's life (18:15; 21:8-9; 23:12; Deut. 30:15-20; Ps. 1:6; Prov. 4:10-14). The crossroads refers to 'paths': a choice has to be made as to which route to follow. They therefore ought to stop and examine the options before them. But it is not just a call for reflection that is issued; they are also advised as to what they should be looking for. **Ask for the ancient paths.** 'Ancient' (*'ôlām*) refers to those that have existed from as far back as you care to trace (2:20), but it is not that there is any virtue in old practices as such. These words presuppose that the new ways which the nation is now going on are unsatisfactory. But there were many old ways and not all of them were approved by God. Therefore more particular inquiry must be made. **Ask where the good way is.** 'The good way' is 'the way of the good' (*derek haṭṭôb*), where the absence of the article with *derek* and the lack of agreement in gender (*derek* is feminine here—note the following *bāh*, 'in her'—and *ṭob* is masculine) show that this is a construct chain. 'Good' does not refer to the character or quality of the way so much as to its terminus. It is the path which leads to the enjoyment of covenant blessing from the LORD. Jeremiah was no innovator. As the messenger of the covenant king, he directs the people back to the requirements of the covenant that the LORD had instituted.

But it is not enough merely to know which way leads to the correct destination. They must also **walk in it.** Having examined the options and ascertained which path they ought to take, they must then actually move along it. The lip-service of the Temple with all its acclamation of the LORD and the deeds of wonder he had done had to be accompanied by lives reoriented in word and act to his revelation of himself. In that way **you will find rest for your souls.** 'Will find rest' renders an imperative which may be used after the preceding imperatives to express a consequence intended or desired by the speaker (GKC §110f; Joüon §116f). 'Rest' (*margôaʿ* <√*rāgaʿ* II hiphil 'to cease activity, be at rest') occurs only here but *margêaʿ* is found in Isa. 28:12 describing the promised land as the resting place the LORD gave his people. The reflection of this phrase in Matt. 11:29 is therefore not an improper application of what is in mind here, that true *šālôm* is found by following the path that leads to harmony with God. It is, however, doubtful if the New Testament application warrants the translation here of *lenapšəkem* as 'for your souls' (so also NKJV and NRSV; for *nepeš* see on 2:34) rather than 'for yourselves' (REB). The focus is not primarily on some inner spiritual repose. Having ceased to trust in their own wisdom and having committed themselves to the path of trust in God, they would enjoy all the blessings that flow from covenant obedience. Their desires would be met and in the totality of their beings they would be vulnerable no more.

The sound advice was, however, spurned, and here and in the next verse their own words are quoted as evidence against them. **But you said, 'We will not walk in it.'** They refused to be obedient and walk (2:2) in the LORD's way because there were other ways they found more attractive (2:33, 36; 3:2). Here and at the end of the following verse the Hebrew is literally, 'And they said' (so NKJV, NRSV). Either there is a break in the divine speech, and this is the prophet's record of the people's response, or else the LORD at this stage addresses the prophet. However, it is quite probable that such 'solutions' may represent a very logical Western approach and that the change of person may not really be a problem to solve. Certainly such shifts in the person of pronouns occur in a number of places and so may not have struck Jeremiah's hearers as odd. But it is not the grammar of the expression that is of ultimate concern; what matters is the spiritual intransigence. Their refusal does not focus on being unable to ascertain if a good way existed, or, if it did, where it was to be found. It is not a matter of knowledge, but of stubborn disinclination to acknowledge the LORD.

17. The LORD had taken other steps to alert the people to the perilous course they were following. **I appointed** is a *waw*-consecutive perfect (note the stress on the final syllable of *wahăqimōtî*; GKC §49h), which we might have expected would be translated, 'I shall set', but here it is more probably a past frequentative usage, 'I kept on setting/

appointing' (GKC §112dd; Joüon §118n). **Watchmen over you** refers to the prophets who acted as national lookouts on sentry duty to detect any deviation from the path of the covenant and to give due warning to the people regarding their conduct (Ezek. 3:17; 33:7; Hos. 9:8; Hab. 2:1). **And said** is an NIV supplement; the Hebrew does not make clear who said to the people, **Listen to the sound of the trumpet!** 'Listen' (<√*qāšab*) implies hearing with attention or with a view to action. Just as the trumpet gave warning of impending danger (4:5), so the prophetic word repeatedly alerted the people of what lay ahead of them if they did not heed the divine summons to an obedient response. **But you said, 'We will not listen** (<√*qāšab*).**'** The testimony of their own speech bore witness to the people's disobedience in refusing to take notice of the warnings they were given.

18. The LORD then turns and calls for witnesses to note that the judgment he is bringing on his people is as a consequence of their ways. **Therefore** (*lākēn*) introduces the first stage in the proceedings at the court of the covenant king. The witnesses to the LORD's righteous judgment are summoned: **Hear, O nations; observe, O witnesses, what will happen.** 'Witnesses' takes *ʿēdâ* as a feminine noun from the root *ʿûd*, 'to witness', applied collectively to the nations (so also REB). But the word is more frequently found in the sense 'congregation' (so NKJV, NRSV), in which case it is derived from *yāʿad*, 'to appoint'. This term is generally applied to Israel, and it is unusual for it to refer, as here, to Gentiles. But it can be used of other gatherings (Pss. 7:7; 22:16; Num. 18:5, 6, 11, 16), and even in Judg. 14:8 of a swarm of bees. Perhaps its use here hints at the thought that Judah may no longer be the LORD's congregation. 'What will happen' renders a very terse Hebrew expression, *ʾet ʾăšer bām*, 'that which on/among them'. It refers to their impending judgment.

19. How the LORD acts in respect of the transgression of his covenant people is of universal significance, and so the call is repeated: **Hear, O earth.** The fate awaiting God's people is the result of their rebellion. **I am bringing disaster** (*rāʿâ*, 1:16) **on this people, the fruit of their schemes, because** (*kî*) **they have not listened to my words and have rejected** (<√*māʾas*, 6:30) **my law.**[110] 'Fruit' is the common metaphor for the outcome or product of their plans (17:10). 'Schemes' (<*maḥăšābâ*, 4:14) probably indicates that what was wrong proceeded

110. *wayyimʾăsû*, 'and they rejected', has an unusual, almost independent use of the *waw*-consecutive imperfect (GKC §111h), because the 'and' has already been expressed before the fronted 'my law'. The *waw* may be with the verb because it is in pause (Joüon §176o), being joined by maqqeph to *bāh*.

from an inner alienation from the LORD and was evidence of the evil disposition of their hearts. The nation had devised plans without reckoning on the consequences, but the LORD will ensure that as they have done, so it will be rendered to them. 'My words' refers to the law and to the warnings relayed by the prophets. They 'have not listened' (<*qāšab*, v. 17) is repeated here for a third time as the basis for their condemnation. The rejection of the law (*tôrâ*) refers to more than divine instruction in general and looks back to the written ordinances of the Mosaic covenant, which should have been at the heart of their national life. But they have been set to one side (8:8-9), and so the people are unable to orient their living correctly.

> The fruit of *rāʿāh* is *rāʿāh*, i.e. the deed-consequence connection. But the passage is equally clear that the one who brings about that connection, who sees that *rāʿāh* brings forth a similar or corresponding fruit is Yahweh. He sets the relationship into effect and brings it to completion. One has to be careful about referring to inevitable or irrevocable consequences of human deeds of good or evil without recognising how thoroughly Israel understood the relationship being guided by the word of God. (Miller 1982:127)

20. No doubt the people thought that the refurbished Temple and the provision made for the sacrificial offerings there constituted a very adequate observance of what Moses had instituted. Now it is made clear that it has not been for the outward performance of their worship that the LORD found fault with them. **What do I care**[111] **about incense from Sheba or sweet calamus**[112] **from a distant land?** 'Incense' is here specifically frankincense, a white substance (as its Hebrew name implies) which was a gum resin from various trees (King 1993:112). It was an ingredient in the exclusive tabernacle formula for sacred incense (Exod. 30:34). Sheba was in the south-west of Arabia, roughly corresponding to modern Yemen, and from there and the African coast opposite incense was brought at great cost to be used at the sanctuary. Similarly sweet calamus or cane was imported, probably from India, to be incorporated in the oil used in anointing (Exod. 30:23). The people were taking great care over the details of the ritual prescriptions of the law, and in this way were seeking to please the LORD. But the rituals of the law had always been intended to act as a channel of expression for those who were loyal to the LORD. Heart obedience was the prior

111. *lāmmâ zeh lî*, 'why ever to me?'

112. The article in *wəqāneh haṭṭôb* shows that this is not a noun followed by an adjective, but a construct chain, 'cane of the goodness' (GKC §126x; but see also *IBHS* §14.3.1d).

requirement for acceptable worship. Mere observance of detailed rites could never render the people acceptable to the LORD. So although the LORD is not repudiating the law itself, he is not impressed with the spirit in which the people are acting. **Your burnt offerings are not acceptable; your sacrifices do not please me.** Burnt offerings involved the total offering of the sacrifice, whereas 'sacrifices' generally denotes those offerings where part of the sacrifice was returned to the worshipper. They are presented here together to cover the whole gamut of sacrificial worship. It was not acceptable. The term refers to what the priest would say in receiving an offering and adjudging it to be ritually acceptable (Lev. 1:3; 22:19; 23:11; Exod. 38:38; Isa. 56:7). There was no question about the quality of the animals being brought—something the religion of affluence no doubt emphasised. But the LORD rejects their sacrifice because without obedience it is a sham (1 Sam. 15:22). A religion that manipulates objects is easy; it is heart reorientation that is costly. Where sin is not forsaken, sacrifices are useless. Again we can detect that Josiah's reform programme had not managed to effect an appropriate inward response among the general population. Whatever measure of enthusiasm there was for outward reformation, on its own it was not enough (see also on 7:23).

21. Therefore (*lākēn*) introduces the statement of judgment. **This is what the LORD says: 'I will put obstacles before this people. Fathers and sons alike will stumble over them.'** 'Obstacles'/ 'stumbling blocks' are circumstances that the LORD puts before his people to test their loyalty. In themselves the obstacles do not induce the people to sin. Those who are living true to God's commands will detect the problem ahead of them and deal with it appropriately. Those who lack spiritual discrimination will be unable to see the true nature of the problem they have to face and will not be capable of responding adequately. They will therefore 'stumble' (<*kāšal*), that is, suffer serious injury because of their faulty action. The phrase 'this people' often denotes dissociation from them because of their rebellion. Here we have a divine word of judgment on those who are already obviously rebels, and the obstacles are enemy invasions into their land, the incursions of the foe from the north, which because of their obstinate refusal to give the LORD his rightful place in their lives the people will be unable to cope with and the whole community will come to grief. **Neighbours and friends will perish.**[113] Because they have wilfully

113. The kethibh is *yo'bēdû*, 'they will perish', whereas the qere reads a *waw*-consecutive perfect, *wǝ'ābādû*, which would have the same meaning. As the verb is final in the line, the kethibh seems preferable.

chosen the wrong path the whole nation will be enveloped in destruction.

d. The Ruthless Foe (6:22-26)

In this section Jeremiah returns to the theme of the invading army from the north, and in this way gives greater definition to the stumbling-blocks that are to be put before the people. Verses 22-23 are a divine description of the invader, who still remains anonymous. Indeed the depiction of vv. 22-24 is substantially reused to portray the downfall of Babylon before another invading army from the north (50:41-43). Verses 24-26 set out the impact of the invasion on the people.

22. Again the start of a new section is marked by a standard introductory formula without any formal connector. **This is what the LORD says: 'Look, an army is coming from the land of the north.'** 'Army' is *ʿam*, 'a people' (NKJV, NRSV) represented by their military personnel. 'From the land of the north' links back to earlier passages where the threat against Judah is depicted as coming from the north (1:13-15; 4:6; 6:1). The second part of the verse parallels the thought of the first: it would be wrong to think of a sequence of actions. **A great nation is being stirred up** (<√*ʿûr* niphal 'to be roused') describes them like one awakened from sleep with the obvious implication that the one doing the rousing is none other than the LORD himself. **From the ends of the earth** ('from the sides of the earth') is a somewhat unusual phrase that is not primarily a geographical term. It indicates very remote regions, and serves to evoke the ominous nature of the threat. The purpose of this description is, of course, that the people may be warned, and so turn in repentance. If they do not, no complaint can be raised against the justice of the LORD on the grounds that he acted without due cause or without due notice.

23. The foe that is coming on Judah is fearsome. **They are armed with** ('have gripped/seized') **bow and spear.** Archers were a major contingent in ancient armies, but the identity of the second weapon (*kîdôn*) is much discussed. It occurs nine times in the Old Testament, and was traditionally identified as a javelin (NRSV) or spear, a meaning which it has in later Hebrew. Both weapons have metal tips and wooden shafts, but the javelin was intended for throwing, often by charioteers, whereas the spear was an infantry weapon, used in hand-to-hand combat to kill one's opponent with a thrusting motion. However, for some years now the word has been identified in the Qumran Battle Scroll as referring to a short sword or sabre ('scimitar', REB). English translations are in general reluctant to adopt such an understanding, though commentators are less hesitant (e.g. Jones 1992:138). Holladay, however, argues that Assyrian and Babylonian reliefs do not provide evidence that such a weapon was in use in Jeremiah's day, and he retains the rendering 'spear' (1986, 1:224).

They are cruel (lit. 'he is') **and show no mercy** (<√*rāḥam* piel, 'to have compassion'). The people of Judah could expect no clemency from these invaders, for they are ruthless, determined to achieve their objective. **They sound like the roaring sea as they ride on their horses.** Again Jeremiah uses sound to convey the impact of the scene: powerful, deafening, awe-inspiring. The main military use of horses at this period was in chariot teams rather than as cavalry. Monumental evidence shows chariots carrying three or four men drawn by teams of three or four horses. The speed with which they could move and the weapons they carried made them a formidable element in any major army. To the relatively immobile countryman the speed and manoeuvrability of the enemy forces would have been ominous indeed.

They come like men in battle formation to attack you, O Daughter of Zion. The subject again switches to the singular, referring to the people/army as a whole. But the point of what is said is not immediately obvious. Would not an army be in battle formation? Why then the 'like' to institute a comparison? 'Equipped like a warrior for battle' (NRSV) does more justice to *ʿārûk*, 'set in battle array, made ready' than 'come', though the nature of the comparison is still not obvious. But the threat is clearly spelled out in 'to attack you' (lit. 'against you', feminine), the city which is the final target of their assault. For 'Daughter of Zion', see on 4:31.

24. The speaker changes to the people themselves as Jeremiah records what he has been shown of their reaction in the situation that is going to engulf them. Judah and Jerusalem will be quite unequal to the encounter. **We have heard reports about them** describes official information mixed with rumour that sweeps the land as word of the coming army spreads from place to place. The very lack of certainty arising from poor communications would have added to the confusion and no doubt magnified the ominous nature of the threat, but even so whatever they heard still would not match the reality. **Our hands hang limp** is a standard phrase to indicate that so great is the disaster envisaged the people feel helpless before it and unable to organise themselves to do anything effective about it. 'Limp' refers to the nervous and physical paralysis induced by the proximity of the enemy (Ezek. 21:12; Zeph. 3:16; the underlying physical action is clear from Neh. 6:9). Before they arrive, Jerusalem is already half-defeated and demoralised. **Anguish has gripped us, pain like that of a woman in labour**. The comparison here fits the context of the description of the people as Daughter Zion. It is a picture of sudden pain against which there is no effective remedy. It simply has to be endured; it is total in its impact. There is a wordplay here between the enemy of v. 23 who gripped his bow and spear, and the people gripped by anguish with the same verb, the hiphil of *ḥāzaq*, in both places. This enforces the contrast between the resolute and implacable enemy and the people helpless and panicking, unable to defend themselves.

25. In v. 25 the commands are given by an unnamed speaker; perhaps it is the prophet, perhaps it is the LORD. The commands are feminine and addressed to Daughter-Zion.[114] **Do not go out to the fields or walk on the roads.** The situation has advanced since that envisaged in v. 1, and the invading forces are now so close that leaving the city is too dangerous. Those who have stayed have now no option but to endure the dire calamity that is about to engulf them. There will be no safety in leaving **for** (*kî*) **the enemy has a sword**. This is in fact the first time that 'enemy' (*ʾōyēb*) is used with reference to the threat from the north. They are armed with swords, weapons used against individuals, and will not hesitate to employ them. Jeremiah then uses one of his favourite phrases: **there is terror on every side** (6:25; 20:10; 46:5; 49:29; also Lam. 2:22). The saying seems to be adopted from Psalm 31:13. Its use here does not date this passage after the incident with Pashhur in chapter 20, rather that is a specific application of the general expression. 'Terror' (<√*gûr* III, 'to dread') refers to a hopeless state of intense horror. Wherever the people of Jerusalem look they can only see the enemy waiting to destroy them.

26. 'Upon us' at the end of the verse indicates that it is spoken by Jeremiah, associating himself with his people in the coming tragedy. He addresses them with affection: **O my people**/'daughter of my people' (4:11). The prophet seeks to evoke a response from them by calling on them to mourn right now. The bitter calamity that is going to befall them is so certain that there is no point in delaying their reaction. **Put on sackcloth and roll in ashes.** These traditional activities were for mourners ('sackcloth', 4:8; for rolling in ashes as a mode of expressing great affliction, see Ezek. 27:30; Mic. 1:10). But this time there is to be greater intensity in the mourning. **Mourn** 'with respect to

114. The kethibh *tēṣəʾî*, 'go out', and *tēlēkî*, 'walk', are both feminine singular, whereas in the qere both verbs are changed to masculine plurals *tēṣəʾû* and *tēlēkû*. The change does not seem necessary, as the people are referred to in the feminine singular both in v. 23 and in v. 26.

yourself' **with bitter wailing** (cf. 31:15) **as for an only son.** The bereavement is not just the death of a loved one, but a family catastrophe that could hardly be exceeded in magnitude, possibly the end of a family line (Amos 8:10; Zech. 12:10). The only son was the one through whom a couple would expect their name to be perpetuated, and his death would lead to overwhelming grief. So devastating will the invasion be that it will evoke only the most intense grief response. **For** (*kî*) **suddenly the destroyer will come upon us.** Despite all the warnings they have been given, in the end they do not expect what happens, and the enemy is able to approach with devastating speed (cf. 4:20). For 'destroyer' (<√*šādad*), see on 4:13.

e. The Royal Assayer (6:27-30)

Jeremiah is given a royal commission to act as court assayer whose duty is to assess the purity of precious metals. Though the passage makes reference to various ancient metallurgical techniques, Jeremiah was not, however, in the business of assessing the quality of metal, but of people. That he holds his post by royal appointment means that when he scrutinises the world of his day and the conduct of his fellows, his evaluation is not to be based on personal preference or majority approval, but on the fixed and non-negotiable standards of the royal law. On the basis of the prophet's report the LORD discards the people as worthless dross (v. 30). Though there are a number of translation issues raised by the passage, the overall message is clear.

27. I have made you (<√*nātan*) recalls 1:5 where Jeremiah was appointed as a prophet to the nations. It is as an extension of that office that he is now divinely accorded the role of a metal tester. It is only here that the word **a tester of metals** or 'assayer' occurs, but the corresponding verb (*bāḥan*, 'to scrutinise, try, prove') is common (9:6; 11:20; 12:3; 17:10; 20:12), and there is little doubt about its meaning, though elsewhere it is the LORD who directly carries out the assaying. The same cannot be said about *mibṣār*, rendered 'fortress' in the NKJV and NRSV margin; 'tester' in the REB and NASB, 'refiner' in the NRSV; and 'ore' in the NIV. While 'fortress' is the ordinary meaning of the word (cf. 4:5), it seems out of place in this context. Repointing the consonants to a piel participle (*məbaṣṣēr*, <√*bāṣar* IV, not otherwise attested in the Old Testament) yields the translation 'tester of my people' (see also *HALOT* 148). The NIV would retain the MT pointing and connect the word with *beṣer*, 'gold ore/nuggets' (elsewhere only in Job 22:24-25), and so renders **my people the ore.** The picture is much the same on either understanding, as is the purpose of Jeremiah's appointment, **that**[115] **you may observe and test their ways.** As Jeremiah proclaims the LORD's word to the people, he will be able to 'observe' their reaction, literally 'know' in the sense of 'get to know', 'become acquainted with' (Job 21:19; Est. 2:11). 'Test' (<*bāḥan*) is the activity of the assayer as he scrutinises their 'ways', that is, conduct (2:33).

28. It is uncertain whether the divine speech stops at the end of v. 27 (so NASB) or whether it continues until the end of the chapter (NIV, NKJV, NLT. The REB and NRSV do not determine the point). It is no objection against the latter that there is the third person reference to the LORD in v. 30, because this does occur elsewhere in divine speech (e.g. 14:10). However, there is much to commend the break as in the NASB, so that vv. 28-30 are the assayer's report, as the prophet brings back to the LORD his verdict on the people after closely scrutinising them.

They are all hardened rebels renders the Hebrew superlative expression, *sārê sôrərîm*, 'rebels of rebelling ones' (an adjective followed by a participle from the same root), indicating those who are 'most stubborn' (GKC §133i) or 'hardened rebels' (*IBHS* §14.5b). The REB 'arch-rebels' is based on reading *sîn* for *samek* to yield *śārê*, 'officials of rebellions'. Holladay (1986, 1:228, 230) and McKane (1986, 1:154-55) adopt a similar emendation, which was known to, and rejected by, Calvin (1850, 1:356). The root *sārar* denotes defiant behaviour that resists all authority (5:23). This is true of Jerusalem as a whole and not just the upper classes. The people are also described as **going about to slander,** '⌊as⌋ a slanderer' (*rākîl* cf. 9:4). The phrase is used in Lev. 19:16 to condemn spreading false and malicious reports. Another understanding of this term is that *rākîl* means a 'peddler, huckster, hawker' who goes around from door to door, and hence the meaning is 'gossiping', which may be no less harmful (Prov. 11:13; 20:19) but lacks the idea of deliberate malevolence. This is a description of a society in which internal relationships have broken down.

Many have felt that the reference **they are bronze and iron** is out of place at this point (REB), but that is to try to force the metaphor along one stylistic line. Jeremiah the assayer is looking to see what sort of metal is before him. He has not found the more precious metals he sought, and has to conclude that the people are baser, more ordinary metals (Ezek. 22:18). Furthermore, these metals have particular metaphorical associations: bronze represents the people's defiance and

115. The second colon begins with *wə* + imperfect, which indicates a final clause.

indifference to criticism (15:12; Deut. 28:23); iron represents their hardness and the difficulty of making any impact on them. No wonder that despite all the prophet's ministry to them, his verdict has to be, **they all act corruptly** (<√*šāḥat* hiphil, 'to corrupt, destroy'). The inner life of the nation is presented as one where damage, devastation and destruction are promoted—and that is before the enemy army arrives. They cannot leave what is good alone but feel compelled to bring it down to their own level. What that level truly is will be seen in the judgment which will come on them, matching their sin.

29. The prophet's attempts to find something worth preserving are presented as a failure. The description is that of an ancient process for refining silver. The ore was heated up in a crucible along with lead, and then a jet of air was directed at the molten mass. The air oxidised the lead, which acted as a flux to take away the impurities. **The bellows blow fiercely.** *nāḥar*, 'to snort', usually describes horses, but here it is applied to sound of the bellows working full out. (An alternative explanation is to take the verb as the niphal of *ḥārar*, 'to burn', and so signifying that the bellows are burnt by the intense heat generated in attempting to purify the ore.) Considerable effort was involved in heating the ore up to the required temperature and also in directing the jet of air at the melted mass to stimulate the refining process **to burn away the lead with fire.**[116]

The assayer reports that he has carried out his task, but it has been unsuccessful. The problem was not lack of effort on his part, but the poor quality of the ore. **But the refining goes on**[117] **in vain; the wicked are not purged out.** 'Refine' (<√*ṣārap*) is found in parallel with 'assay' in 9:6; Zech. 13:9; Pss. 17:3; 26:2; 66:10. But instead of high quality metal, what is left is a mass of useless, impure slag. For 'wicked' the REB renders 'impurities': it could be either, as the transition from image to reality takes place. The goal had been pure silver, a people purified in obedience to the LORD. But the test proves the people a failure. There is no thought of reworking the refuse silver. Despite intensive efforts to refine the metal, it remains so contaminated with impurities as to be worthless.

116. The kethibh reads *mēʾeššātām*, 'from their fire', which the qere splits in two, *mēʾēš*, 'from fire' and *tam*, 'he is complete, he is finished'; perhaps 'he [the lead] is consumed by fire'. The verb is masculine, though nouns of the form *ʿōperet*, 'lead', are usually feminine.

117. The infinitive absolute *ṣārôp*, 'refining', following the verb indicates the continuance of the action (GKC §113r). *ṣārôp* may also be taken as a verbal noun for the agent: 'the refiner has refined'.

Jeremiah as the prophetic assayer is reporting that he has declared the LORD's word with vehemence and diligence, but it has failed to identify the righteous in the community. So deep a hold has wickedness taken on the life of the nation and of individuals that his ministry cannot separate the silver out, and so win a remnant for the cause of the covenant. This is a more probable interpretation of the metaphor than that there is no silver present in the ore at all. Elsewhere the prophets present the LORD himself as successfully refining the people (Isa. 1:25; Zech. 13:9).

30. The final report on the process is now recorded. **They are called rejected silver, because** (*kî*) **the LORD has rejected them.** 'They are called' is literally 'they call/name them', but it is an impersonal idiom which the NIV renders correctly as a passive rather than adding 'people' as in the NKJV. The wordplay on 'rejected' is a feature of the Hebrew which uses *mā'as*, 'to reject', twice here. This is all that can be said about the people of the covenant: Rejected by the LORD. The thought may well go beyond a statement that their condition is unsatisfactory to indicating feelings of aversion from them (note 'despise' for *mā'as* in 4:30).

We have now arrived at the end of the First Scroll. It concludes with the prophet recording the failure of his mission to bring the people back to the LORD. However, in terms of the commission that had been given to him, he has managed 'to uproot and tear down, to destroy and overthrow' (1:10). His exposure of the defection of the land and its corruption is thorough and mordant. There was no place left to hide from the light of his scathing critique of Judah and Jerusalem, of the people and particularly of the establishment figures in the land. When these prophecies were first issued, their message would have been far from welcome. But once Jeremiah has assembled the messages in the Scroll, it is far from surprising that the reading of the Scroll provoked such a hostile response from the king (36:23).

For Jeremiah himself there was the growing realisation that divine revelation was two-edged. 'For we are to God the aroma of Christ among those who are being saved and those who are perishing. To the one we are the smell of death; to the other, the fragrance of life. And who is equal to such a task?' (2 Cor. 2:15-16). The prophet Isaiah had already been made aware that his ministry would be one that would lead not to insight and conviction of the truth but growing spiritual insensitivity among his hearers (Isa. 6:9-13). It is often the way in the outworking of the kingdom that the expected outcome does not take place (Mark 4:11-12; John 9:39-41). Skinner aptly commented on this aspect of religious experience in the following terms:

> In the light of a fuller revelation of the character of God it is, indeed, impossible to think of His purpose except as a purpose of grace and mercy which, while respecting the independence of created personalities, and working patiently to evoke the free response of their will, genuinely seeks the salvation of all through the revelation of the truth. Yet on the other hand the moral universe is so constituted by its Maker that the sinful abuse of freedom brings its own punishment in hardening of the conscience, and a growing incapacity for fellowship with God. Thus it is true that God sent not His Son into the world to condemn the world, and yet by his coming the world is condemned. 'And this is the judgment, that light is come into the world, and men loved darkness rather than light, because their works were evil' (John iii.19). This is the permanent religious fact which underlies the stern predestinarian doctrine of the prophets, and is the basis of their assurance that the purpose of Yahwe will finally prevail in spite of the sin and unbelief of men. (Skinner 1922:161-62)

III. WARNINGS ABOUT WORSHIP

(7:1–8:3)

OUTLINE

A. The Temple Sermon (7:1-15)
   1. The Prophet's Commission (7:1-2)
   2. Reformation Required (7:3-7)
   3. Rampant Rebellion (7:8-11)
   4. Shiloh Revisited (7:12-15)

B. Do Not Intercede (7:16-20)

C. Meaningless Sacrifice (7:21-29)

D. The Valley of Slaughter (7:30-34)

E. Astral Worship (8:1-3)

There is a distinct difference in the mode of writing between chapters 6 and 7, for here we come upon the first extended portion of prose in the book. This is universally recognised, but its significance is a matter of ongoing debate and uncertainty. One fairly common perception is that this prose material is a later insertion into the original poetry of Jeremiah which continues at 8:4. It is argued that this material, possibly based on sayings that came from the prophet himself, was intended by the Deuteronomistic editors/preachers of the exilic period to make the people face up to the grim truth that the tragedies that had befallen the nation were the result of its grievous misconduct. Quite apart from the fact that others do not find a compelling case for Deuteronomic language in this section, there is of course from a conservative point of view the unproven assumption of the existence of such a body of men at all. This material purports to come from Jeremiah, and there is no reason to assign it anything but the closest relationship to the prophet himself. The Mosaic origins of Deuteronomy would have under any circumstances made it an important book in the shaping of religious perception and of literature in the land. The impact of Deuteronomy would have been significantly heightened if it, in whole or part, was contained in the Book of the Law which was so spectacularly found in the Temple during Josiah's clean-up operations (2 Kgs. 22:8-13). It requires no great leap of imagination to suppose that after that a Deuteronomic style of address became common in religious circles in Jerusalem—indeed it was probably reinforcing a style that had already been prevalent. It is also the case that though many eschew the simple notion that Jeremiah might have used both prose and poetry to communicate on different occasions, it remains virtually certain that he did so. The material of this division of the book may then without any sense of artificiality or contrivance be taken as coming from the prophet himself on occasions when he adopted a style of presentation that would have been common in the Temple, and with which he himself was undoubtedly familiar as a result of his priestly education.

When we seek to move on from that conclusion, however, matters become less certain. There are two interrelated questions: When did Jeremiah first utter these words? and, When did he incorporate them into the growing corpus of his prophetic memoirs? Answers to these questions depend upon our assessment of the Temple Sermon hypothesis. This is a relatively recent style of interpretation which was popularised by the German commentaries of Graf (1862) and Naegelsbach (1868; translated 1871), and widely adopted since. Basically it identifies the discourse of 7:1-15 with that mentioned in

26:1-6, and since the latter passage is dated, that enables this passage to be set 'early in the reign of Jehoiakim' (for the significance of the phrase, see on 26:1). The identification of the two passages is made on the basis of the location where Jeremiah was to speak (the gate/courtyard of the Temple, 7:2; 26:2), the shared use of Shiloh as a warning (7:12, 14; 26:6, 9), the recurrence of the phrase 'reform your ways and your actions' (7:3, 5; 26:13), and the general tenor of the passage (a call to repentance which, if not heeded, will lead to judgment). The precise relationship between the two passages may be understood in various ways, but the brief record of chapter 26 seems to originate with Baruch and focuses on the response to the sermon, whereas the vivid language and fuller account of chapter 7 show that it has come from the prophet himself. Whether we take 26:1 as referring to late 609 BC/early 608 BC, or more generally to the period between late 609 BC and 605 BC, the material of 7:1-15 was available for incorporation in the First Scroll. As the purpose of the Scroll was to elicit a change in the prevailing antipathy to Jeremiah's message, it would have been unnatural to exclude such a major feature of it—there could be no compromise on that. However it would have been prejudicial to the acceptance of the First Scroll to mention the response of the religious establishment to it. What mattered was presenting the LORD's warning. The background to material in 7:16–8:3 is assessed separately below.

But it is still necessary to keep the validity of the Temple Sermon hypothesis under review, and not merely endorse its widespread acceptance. Lundbom objects to the term 'Temple Sermon'—probably correctly; 'Notes of a Temple Sermon' would be more accurate—and emphasises the discontinuities that exist between the sections (1999:454-59). Earlier Keil (1873, 1:151) objected on the grounds that the similarities detected were not sufficiently compelling in a prophet who often repeated his leading thoughts and that the absence of any note of opposition to the prophet in the chapter and in the following chapters 8–10 was improbable if this is a record of a sermon that had aroused such vehement hostility. But 'it is hard to understand the blast of fury that greeted Jeremiah in chapter 26, if his message had already become familiar to the people' (Ellison 1961:222) during the reign of Josiah as proposed by Keil.

On balance then it seems that 7:1-15 record an outline of the address given by the prophet on the same occasion as chapter 26, early in the reign of Jehoiakim.

A. THE TEMPLE SERMON (7:1-15)

The early years of Jehoiakim were a time of great international uncertainty. The Assyrian empire had crumbled, and increasing Egyptian involvement in the affairs of Syria–Palestine severely impacted Judah. Josiah had been killed by Egyptian forces. Jehoahaz, who was the popular choice to succeed him, had been deposed by Pharaoh Neco who had installed Jehoiakim in his place. Babylonian power was becoming increasingly evident to the north, but not until the decisive events of 605 BC was it clear who would obtain hegemony over Syria–Palestine. Meanwhile in Judah the ruling elite were trying to discern the signs of the times and ensure that they backed the winning side.

But for Jeremiah—and for the LORD—the question was not primarily that of who would be the dominant superpower, but whether or not the people of Judah and Jerusalem would truly submit to God's rule. The religious establishment of the day pointed to the Temple, its worship and sacrifices, and the divine commitment to Jerusalem as guaranteeing the security of the city and the perpetuation of the Davidic dynasty. They argued that the LORD's favour had been bestowed absolutely and unconditionally, and they did not consider that there was any connection between it and the morality of the conduct of the people. Jeremiah was called upon to oppose this delusion that covenant blessing could be divorced from covenant obedience. True security can only be found in a right, living relationship with God.

1. The Prophet's Commission (7:1-2)

1-2. This is the word that came to Jeremiah from the LORD: 'Stand at the gate of the LORD's house and there proclaim this message: "Hear the word of the LORD, all you people of Judah who come through these gates to worship the LORD".' All that the Septuagint retains of these verses is 'Hear the word of the LORD, all Judah.' Since it is difficult to see why the other easily understood and non-contentious words would have been omitted, many conclude that the Massoretic Text here (which seems to be supported by a fragment of 4QJer[a]) represents a secondary expansion of the text, with the original being reflected in the LXX. It may simply be that additional information was added by Jeremiah in the later versions of his prophecy to clarify the terse annotation that had been employed in the First Scroll. When it was first issued, Jeremiah wanted to have his message heard again without it and not rejected out of hand because people associated it with the hostile response that is recorded in chapter 26. At a later date there was no need to omit these details about the divine origin of the prophet's message and the explicit instructions given to him regarding its proclamation in the Temple.

'The gate of the LORD's house' was the entrance way between the outer and inner courtyards of the Temple (36:10). By standing there Jeremiah would be able to address the people in the outer courtyard from the top of the steps. There is some evidence to suggest that this was a place where prophetic messages were ordinarily delivered (19:14; 28:1, 5). The practice of giving addresses in the courtyard of temple precincts is also exemplified by Amos at the Bethel temple (Amos 7:13) and by Christ (John 7:37). The place where the words were uttered gave extra significance to them. This in itself shows that Jeremiah was not mounting an attack on the Temple as such, but on the way it was being misused.

Jeremiah's address would not conform to the modern 'sermon' in that it would not be an extended discourse. The gateway was a public place, ensuring his message became widely known, but it was equally a place where people would keep moving. The prophet would present his message briefly and in a vivid and memorable form. It is probable that messages could be repeated several times as the crowds moved past the prophet.

The description of those to be addressed—'all you people of Judah who come through these gates to worship the LORD'—may just be a general form of address for a public proclamation (36:5, 9). But it is likely that this refers to a time when more were present than just the people of the city. Note the intervention of the elders of the land as recorded in 26:17. Jeremiah was to act at a festival or some other occasion when those from outlying areas would also attend the Temple, and in this way knowledge of his message would not be confined to the city.

It should also be noted that the people are addressed in their capacity as worshippers of the LORD. 'Worship' (<√*ḥāwâ* hishtaphel) denotes prostration before a superior. Such obeisance would occur as part of the etiquette of eastern courts when a vassal came before his overlord. The action was also considered appropriate in the worship of deities. In the Old Testament covenant context where the LORD was recognised as God and king of his people, it was an act that acknowledged his high status and the worshipper's lowly dependence upon him. This was what the people coming to the Temple were saying by their actions, but they were strangers to the reality of heart submission to the LORD.

The message itself is in three parts. There is first of all in vv. 3-7 a call to repentance so that the blessings of the covenant may be enjoyed. The next section (vv. 8-11) accuses the people of inappropriate, indeed incongruous, action and reminds them of the LORD's scrutiny. It is therefore no surprise that they are finally reminded (vv. 12-15) of the fate of Shiloh and of the northern kingdom, and what that implies for them if they remain intransigent.

2. Reformation Required (7:3-7)

3. The introductory formula makes it clear by whose authority Jeremiah speaks: **This is what the LORD Almighty, the God of Israel, says.** 'LORD Almighty'/'LORD of hosts' (2:19) points to the power and authority of the one who speaks. 'God of Israel' addressed the people as those who are in covenant bond with him and therefore obligated to hear his word. The covenant suzerain is issuing a summons to those who are his vassals, and who give at any rate formal acknowledgment of that bond by coming to worship him.

Their Overlord has a complaint against his people to which they must respond: **Reform your ways and your actions, and I will let you live in this place.**[1] 'Ways'/paths refers to their general lifestyle, their characteristic mode of conducting themselves, whereas 'actions', are the specific pieces of conduct that are carried out on the basis of this general pattern (18:11; 26:13). 'Reform/make good' (<√*yāṭab* hiphil) implies that their conduct currently does not correspond to what the LORD requires. But if an appropriate change is made in a spirit of repentance, then as a consequence[2] their Overlord will permit them to continue to occupy 'this place'. But where is referred to: the Temple, the city, or the land? 'Live'/inhabit, reside makes a reference to the Temple improbable here, though clearly that is what is intended in vv. 12 and 14. As the audience is said to have included those from Judah and not just Jerusalem, it makes the city a less likely referent. In v. 7 the phrase 'in this place' is explained as a reference to the land,

1. The NRSV text (as distinct from the margin which reflects the Massoretic reading) renders this as 'let me dwell with you' by repointing *wa'ăšakkənâ 'etəkem* (the piel of *šākam* followed by the object marker) to *wə'eškəhâ 'ittəkem* (the qal of *šākam* with the preposition *'et*) on the basis of the reading found in Aquila and the Vulgate. See also Calvin (1850, 1:362) and Holladay (1986, 1:236-37). On this understanding, 'this place' is clearly the Temple itself.

2. *wa'ăšakkənâ* seems to be ordinary *waw* + cohortative piel to express consequence.

which might well be the principal focus here. However, at one level it does not matter which it is, because all three are the gift the covenant God has given to his people, and in varying degrees they are all the place where he is present, dwelling with them. Their continued enjoyment of this privilege and their occupation of the city and the land depended on their remaining loyal to the LORD. It was precisely this point that had become obscured in the thinking of the day. The implicit threat is that persistent disloyalty will incur expulsion from the land of promise.

4. How they are to change their ways is then spelled out in some detail. Firstly, it involved a changed outlook on life and a reappraisal of what constitutes truth. In common with most English translations the NIV rendering, **Do not trust in deceptive words**, does not translate *lākem* ('with respect to you') indicating that the negative command requires that there be a determined dissociation from familiar attitudes and practices. (For further comment and explanation why it is left untranslated, see *IBHS* §11.2.10d.) 'Trust' (<√*bāṭaḥ* 'to put confidence in and so rely upon someone or something') is one of the recurrent themes of the Temple Sermon (vv. 8, 14). Upon what are the people to build as the foundation of their lives? The alternative to the LORD and his covenant is presented as 'deceptive words'/'words of the lie' (*dibrê haššeqer*). 'The Lie' was not open paganism, but the popular distortion of covenant religion that had lulled Jerusalem into a false sense of security. *Šeqer* (5:2) occurs fairly frequently throughout the Old Testament to point to something that is untrue, a lie (37:14; 40:16). Jeremiah, however, also uses the term to refer to this absolutised assurance that all would go well with Jerusalem and that consequently prophetic warnings could safely be ignored. This outlook was reinforced by, if indeed it did not originate with, the false prophets who promoted and perpetuated a one-sided presentation of divine truth in much the same way as the exclusive focus of 'God is love' theology turns truth into error.

The consensus approach to thinking about God encouraged them to say, **This is**[3] **the temple of the LORD, the temple of the LORD, the temple of the LORD!** The emphatic threefold repetition may be a religious formula such as Isa. 6:3, or it may be a vain repetition in the manner of a heathen incantation (cf. also 22:29). It was the latter that was an appropriate representation of their worship because in their thinking they had in effect converted the Temple into a lucky charm, a

3. The plural *hēmmâ* is found (cf. NKJV '*are* these'), perhaps indicating that the whole complex of buildings that constituted the Temple is in view.

talisman that would protect them come what may. This reflected one aspect of divine revelation. David had been told that the LORD had made with him 'an everlasting covenant, arranged and secured in every part' (2 Sam. 23:5) and had promised him, 'Your house and your kingdom shall endure for ever before me; your throne shall be established for ever' (2 Sam. 7:16). In this connection the LORD had designated David's capital as his 'resting place for ever and ever' (Ps. 132:13), and it was recorded of the city, 'God is within her, she will not fall; God will help her at break of day' (Ps. 46:5). Moreover it was possible to generalise from Isaiah's prophecy, 'I will defend this city and save it, for my sake and for the sake of David my servant' (Isa. 37:35), wrongly extending it from Sennacherib's invasion of 701 BC to later times. The miraculous deliverance of Jerusalem in 701 BC would have significantly reinforced the theological basis of Zion theology (2 Kgs. 19:35-36). The conclusion had been arrived at that, come what may, the name of the LORD was so bound up with Jerusalem that he had rendered it inviolable.

Furthermore, in the thinking of the ancient Near East a temple (*hêkāl*) was not primarily considered to be a place of public worship. It was rather the dwelling-place of the deity which protected the city, and it was considered an important aspect of a ruler's duties to maintain and extend the god's house so that he would be pleased with it, continue to dwell there, and consequently maintain his protection of the city. Israelite thinking had imbibed the outlook of those around them. Under Josiah they had refurbished the Temple, and so they concluded the city was secure. It is also apparent that the presumed inviolability of Jerusalem had impacted on popular perception of the public policy in Jerusalem. Zion theology imparted a sanctity to the political/religious consensus of the day. In challenging that viewpoint Jeremiah was seen as committing sacrilege so closely had the divine purpose become identified with policies promoted by king and priest.

But this obscured the demands of the covenant for ethical, God-honouring conduct. It had been clear from the start that the Davidic king was answerable to the LORD. 'I will be his father, and he shall be my son. When he does wrong, I will punish him with the rod of men, with floggings inflicted by men' (2 Sam. 7:14). Enjoyment of the blessings of the covenant was conditioned on covenant obedience. At the same time the covenant purpose of God could not be frustrated by the disobedience of one individual, one generation, or indeed the covenant people as a whole. The covenant provided responsible security but did not sanction presumption, and that was what had gone wrong in Jerusalem. The Temple guaranteed them nothing if they were living lives of rebellion. Rather than the Temple facilitating access to the LORD and fellowship with him, when its function was misunderstood and it was misused, it became a barrier to true access to God.

5. Therefore v. 5 continues with 'for' (*kî*[4]) to show why the prevailing outlook was deficient. Verses 5-7 are one sentence, in which vv. 5-6 set out the conditions for divine acceptance, and v. 7 the covenant blessing that will flow from covenant obedience. The first conditional clause sets out in general terms the change required: **if you really change your ways and your actions**. 'Change' (<√*yāṭab*, 'make good') repeats 'reform' (v. 3), and similarly 'your ways and your actions' resume the earlier theme. The requirement is of right behaviour, in accordance with the norms of the covenant. It is only when that is present that the worship of the Temple becomes meaningful and not a sham. Commitment to the LORD of the covenant has to go beyond maintaining a sanctuary for him and presenting the requisite offerings there. That commitment has to be reflected in the practices of their daily living. This is then further spelled out in four parenthetic conditional clauses which are jointly introduced by a single initial occurrence of *ʾim*, 'if' (not translated in the NIV). The verbs are imperfects, and the construction suggests that the conditions are viewed as capable of being fulfilled (GKC §158b1; *IBHS* §38.2d).

(1) The first stipulation is that they **deal with each other justly** (*ʿāśâ mišpāṭ*, 'do justice'). This refers to the whole process of legal and civil administration in the land. Indeed it goes beyond that to cover all transactions and relationships 'between a man and his neighbour' (literally; so NKJV). They have all to be conducted in terms of the norms set out in the covenant. It was particularly required of the king that he ensure that the public affairs of the land were carried out in this way (2 Sam. 8:15; 1 Kgs. 10:9), but the verbs in these clauses are all plurals and should not be seen as being directed principally at the king. It was equally expected that the people in general would know what the LORD demanded, and conduct themselves accordingly (5:1, 4, 28; 8:7). It was also the duty of the king to ensure that social justice prevailed in the community (21:12; 22:3, 13, 15; 23:5; 33:15).

6. (2) **If you do not oppress the alien, the fatherless or the widow.** 'Oppress' (<√*ʿāšaq*, 6:6; Deut. 24:14) has strong overtones of extortion, accumulating wealth that can only be done by robbing one's

4. Although *kî ʾim* frequently have to be read together as a logical unit 'but rather, except' (cf. v. 23), here they function separately, with independent force.

neighbour. This too reflects the requirements of the Mosaic covenant, where allegiance to the LORD required behaviour towards others that reflected how God himself behaved. The 'alien' was a temporary resident from another nation who was exposed to exploitation because he had become isolated from the support of family and relatives who would be expected to look after his interests if he could not do so himself. The orphan was generally one who had lost his/her father. There is no clear-cut case in the Old Testament of both parents having been lost. The widow too was liable to be maltreated by the unscrupulous. Having lost the breadwinner of the family and the one who would have defended its interests, she could easily be exploited. These three vulnerable groups all lacked natural spokesmen, and it was required of the covenant community that they took care of them (Exod. 22:21-24; 23:9; Lev. 19:33-34; Deut. 10:18; 16:11, 14; 24:17-18; 27:19; Ps. 146:9). However, those who were insensitive to the ethical demands of the covenant frequently failed to do so, and it became a standard theme of prophetic rebuke that consideration for those who had fallen on hard times was lacking (Isa. 1:17, 23; 10:2; Ezek. 22:7; Zech. 7:10; Mal. 3:5; Ps. 94:6).

(3) **Do not shed innocent blood in this place.** Again there is the problem of determining where 'this place' is, but probably it is the land (vv. 3, 7). Bloodguilt was incurred by slaying someone who did not deserve to die. The king was the one who was expected to ensure that did not happen (22:3, 17). If he was indifferent (or if he himself sponsored such action), then the nation as a whole became corrupt and polluted. Earlier Jeremiah had suggested that bloodshed was prevalent in the land (2:34). The reference here may again be to the evil of Manasseh (2 Kgs. 21:16) which led to the destruction of Jerusalem (26:15; 2 Kgs. 24:4), but it is more probable that the early part of Jehoiakim's reign saw a resurgence of such social malpractices (26:23).

These three requirements correspond closely to the demands made of the king in 22:3 and also to the ideal set out by/before Solomon in Ps. 72:1-4, 12-14. However, the same ethical standard was to be maintained by king and people, reflecting the fact that all were under the covenant and answerable to their common Overlord.

(4) **If you do not follow other gods to your own harm**. For 'follow/go after', see on 2:2. For 'other gods', see on 1:16. This is the first mention of idolatry in this sermon, which has focused principally on the need for covenant living. Right behaviour towards one's neighbour has to be joined with right behaviour towards the LORD. This shows that 'the Lie' (v. 4) was not just a distorted perception of

the social implications of the covenant, but also toleration of the worship of pagan deities. This is not surprising because a false perception of true religion and a weakened attachment to the LORD inevitably open the door for all manner of malpractice. Theological aberration is not just a matter of intellectual misunderstanding; it inevitably corrupts conduct and that ends up as being 'to your own harm'/'for evil/disaster for you'. Setting aside the LORD's demand for exclusive fealty and worship undermines the bond of the covenant and leads to catastrophe.

7. This verse brings the long conditional sentence to a conclusion by returning to the words of v. 3 and showing the blessings that will follow from correct observance of the stipulations of the covenant. **Then I will let you live in this place, in the land I gave to your forefathers for ever and ever**/'from ever to ever', that is, 'from long ages past to long ages to come', looking back to the days of Abraham, and viewing possession of the covenant inheritance as stretching forward into an indefinite future.

This grant of 'an everlasting inheritance to you and your descendants after you' (Gen. 17:8) must always be viewed within the bipolar covenant structure of blessing and curse, which are in turn conditioned on obedience/disobedience. From the beginning of Israel's existence as a nation this had been made clear to them (Deut. 27–30). Though there had been a resurgence of interest in Deuteronomy under Josiah, this aspect of the theology of the covenant had been filtered out of popular perception because of the dominance of Zion theology with its emphasis on unconditional blessing. That was why Jeremiah was divinely designated to bring this to the attention of the people. However, they did not want to know; they were more comfortable continuing to think that there was nothing seriously wrong in their relationship with the LORD.

3. Rampant Rebellion (7:8-11)

In this section the behaviour of the people is dramatically exposed as being inconsistent with the standards of the covenant and also as being self-deceived. They think they can live as they want and still claim the blessing and protection of the LORD. There is as yet no mention of judgment—although that is the obvious corollary, as the next section shows. The aim is to prod the people into realising just how incongruous their conduct has become.

8. But look turns the spotlight on to the people and urges them to engage in self-examination. **You are trusting** is a participial expression denoting their ongoing, characteristic attitude (v. 4), again with *lākem*, 'with respect to you'/'as regards your own interests'. But their reliance was **in deceptive words** (*dibrê haššeqer*, v. 4) **that are worthless.** What in v. 4 was presented as a warning is here repeated as a statement of fact. Possibly the deceptive words again refer to what follows in the declaration 'We are safe' (v. 10). 'That are worthless' is a similar expression to the one found in 2:8, and emphasises that no benefit or advantage can accrue from the false philosophy of 'the Lie'.

9. The dramatic language continues in v. 9 with a rhetorical question involving a staccato series of words. The first six verbs of the verse are infinitives absolute, emphasising the kind of action under consideration (without mention of time or agent), and probably conveying the indignation of the speaker at the lax attitude the people had developed towards the requirements of the covenant (GKC §113ee; *IBHS* §35.5.2a). **Will**[5] **you steal and murder, commit adultery and perjury, burn incense to Baal and follow other gods you have not known?** The prophets did not present a revolutionary new ethical code to the people, but recalled them to the standards of the covenant. Here there are listed breaches of the ten fundamental requirements of their covenant Overlord (Exod. 20), which carry all the more weight because of their ancient origin and the fact that they would have been recited at Josiah's ceremony of covenant renewal. In terms of the Exodus sequence they are cited in the order 8, 6, 7, 9, 2, 1. (Note that some variation in their order also exists in Hos. 4:2. This does not indicate that the order of the Decalogue had not yet been fixed, but rather the freedom with which the prophets quoted from such a well-known document.) 'Commit perjury/swear falsely' is 'swearing by the lie'. It may be a reference to the use of the name Baal in oaths, thus repudiating the LORD, or it may simply be to swear to what is false (v. 4; 5:2). For 'burn incense' or 'sacrifice', see on 1:16. Baal is representative of all the heathen gods in whose cult they participated. 'Follow after' is the language of life commitment and stated purpose (v. 6; Judg. 2:19; Ruth 3:10). They have not known them in the sense that they were intrusions into the national life of the people the LORD had chosen for himself. For further details on the significance of the commands, see Mackay 2001:338-355.

10. But it is the challenge of v. 10 that bears the thrust of the exclamation. **And then come**[6] **and stand before me in this house, which**

5. The interrogative particle *hă* may have exclamatory force (Joüon §161b). 'You steal! You murder!' etc.

6. The *waw*-consecutive perfect is used to express the sequel to the actions listed—a sequel that has frequently occurred (GKC §112o).

bears my Name, and say, 'We are safe'—safe to do all these detestable things? They thought it was possible to live as they pleased and then come and be accepted by God when they worshipped him in the Temple. They did not grasp how defiled they had become; they had forgotten that they had to do with the holy God. This is a clear example of dichotomous living in which the sacred and the secular are kept in insulated compartments and not seen as relating to each other. That outlook is alien to the covenant perspective of the LORD who claims total loyalty to himself in every area of life. His scrutiny goes beyond the details of cultic ritual to the heart attitudes of those who claim to be his followers.

This is true even when the rituals being performed are those which the LORD himself has appointed. There is no hint here of a repudiation of the stated worship of Israel. 'This house' (*bayit*) is acknowledged to be the one which legitimately bears the name of the LORD, that is, the one which he owns and has been pleased to recognise as his. On that basis it functions as a bridge between heaven and earth, and that is the factor which aggravates their offence. They were coming to the place of God's presence upon earth, and were thinking that the mere existence of the Temple in Jerusalem granted them immunity to commit all manner of evil ('detestable things' <√*tāʿab*, 2:7), here the covenant breaches of v. 9.

They boasted, 'We are safe'—a perfect of complete confidence (Ezek. 14:16, 18; Amos 3:12)—but it was a false confidence, based on a total misunderstanding of the covenant. 'Safe' (niphal <√*nāṣal*, 1:8) is a fairly common Old Testament term for deliverance, generally from physical peril. It is unlikely that this expression is put in the mouths of the people merely for rhetorical effect. This is language they might readily have used in worship, but what did they have in mind when they uttered these words? 'It seems only natural to assume that uppermost in their consciousness was the confidence that in time of political instability Yahweh would guarantee the safety of their national state. One gets the distinct impression that the message these men were conveying was simply this: Yahweh is our God and come what may he will never allow us, who come here and worship in his temple, to be completely overcome' (Overholt 1970:17-18). Such confidence allied to rank rebellion is detestable in the sight of God.

11. With outright indignation the LORD poses the question, **Has this house, which bears my Name, become a den of robbers to you?** 'Den of robbers' is fronted for emphasis. 'Robber' points to someone who confronts another and steals from them with violence, or the threat of it (Ps. 17:4; Ezek. 18:10; Dan. 11:4). Just as the robbers of Palestine would retreat to their caves and think themselves safe there until the next time they ventured forth to waylay and loot, so too the people of Judah came to the Temple, and without thought as to how they had been behaving, considered that in the Temple they had automatically been granted security. Would a notorious robber be any less so for coming into the Temple? Was it not the case that even the manslayer who fled to a city of refuge did not have sanctuary extended to him unless his action had been unintentional (Num. 35:25)? Why did they think that their behaviour was exempted from scrutiny? It could hardly go unnoticed when they were coming to the place that was claimed by the LORD as his own. The phrase **'But** (the expression is emphatic, 'But as for me, look!') **I have been watching!'**[7] **declares the LORD** shows that he is not fooled by their pretence of their piety and knows all that has been going on. His inspection cannot be evaded (16:17; 23:24), for he is the one who 'observes the sons of men; his eyes examine them' (Ps. 11:4). Even though they claim, 'The LORD does not see; the God of Jacob pays no heed', yet he who formed the eye does see and will repay them for their wickedness (Ps. 94:7, 9, 23).

Christ himself repeated the verdict of 'den of robbers' in connection with the Jerusalem Temple of his own day (Matt. 21:13; Mark 11:17; Luke 19:46), reminding us that improper attitudes towards the Temple were not confined to Jeremiah's generation. There should have been a holy carefulness regarding all that pertained to the place of the divine presence, and Christ in driving out the money changers and those who were selling doves was purging the Temple of what should not have been present. By doing so, he reinforced its divine institution. In the same way great care should be taken with respect to what corresponds to the Temple in the New Testament, the living building of the church of Christ (1 Cor. 3:16-17; 6:19-20).

4. Shiloh Revisited (7:12-15)

The LORD then uses two historical examples to disabuse the people of the idea that the mere presence of his sanctuary grants immunity from punishment.

12. The *kî* with which the verse begins is taken as contrastive, 'but', by NKJV. The link seems to be that what follows is the evidence to back the assertion that the LORD scrutinises what takes place in his

7. Or the verb may have present significance, 'I myself see it!' (Joüon §112a).

sanctuary. **Go now to the place** (lit. 'my place') **in Shiloh where I first made a dwelling for my Name**. The ironic command is not of course to move there physically, but to consider the circumstances of Shiloh, situated between Bethel and Shechem, about nineteen miles (31 km) north of Jerusalem. It too had been a place where the LORD had had a sanctuary, and at the end of the period of the judges when Eli and young Samuel had ministered before the LORD, the ark had been located there. Indeed the sanctuary was actually called a temple (1 Sam. 1:9; 3:3). But it too had been associated with great wickedness (1 Sam. 2:12-17, 22-25), and there had even been an anticipation of the mechanistic attitude towards religion in the way the people had thought the presence of the ark of the covenant would guarantee them victory in war (1 Sam. 4:3). But despite the status of Shiloh it had not been inviolable and had suffered destruction. **And see what I did to it because of the wickedness of my people Israel.** There is no historical record of the destruction of Shiloh in the Old Testament, though Ps. 78:56-64 reflects on it. The ark and apparently other sacred articles also were removed at that time, but the complex of buildings that surrounded the sanctuary were destroyed. Archaeological evidence has confirmed that Shiloh was consumed by a great conflagration about 1050 BC (probably by the Philistines) and that as late as 300 BC it had not really recovered, remaining at most a very small settlement (41:5). There had been no immunity for Shiloh because it was a site devoted to the worship of the LORD. It did not fall because of military ineptitude but because of covenant disobedience. The LORD demanded the loyalty of his people, and when that was lacking, their worship and their sacred sites became offensive to him.

13. While is a somewhat misleading rendering of *wəʿattâ yaʿan*. The first word 'and now'/'so now' (2:18) may indicate the next stage in an argument, but more probably here a switch from the circumstances of the past to those of the present, 'but now'. The second word *yaʿan* means 'because' (23:38; 35:17). So focusing on the current generation, not Israel of the past, 'because' **you were doing all these things, declares the LORD** refers back to the offences listed in v. 9, and shows that the LORD reacted to their behaviour, which had been against the norms of the covenant not by immediate punishment but by repeated warnings. **I spoke to you again and again, but you did not listen; I called you, but you did not answer.** 'Again and again' is used by the NIV to render the expression 'rising early and speaking', where the infinitives absolute signify repetition or continuance of the action (*IBHS* §35.3.2c; Joüon §123rN). 'Rising early' is used of God eleven times at various stages of Jeremiah's ministry (elsewhere of God only in 2 Chron. 36:15, but of human activity in a number of places, e.g. Gen. 20:8; Prov. 27:14). The word means first 'to incline', then 'to shoulder' a burden, and developed the sense of loading a beast to start a journey early in the day. The phrase is used three times in connection with divine speech (7:13; 25:3; 35:14), six times as regards sending the prophets (7:25; 25:4; 26:5; 29:19; 35:15; 44:4), and once each with regard to warning (11:7) and to teaching (32:33). The number of times the phrase is repeated raises the question of whether or not it is a dead metaphor conveying nothing more than the thought 'again and again'. But there does seem to be the additional thought of eagerness to do something about the situation. This refers to the ministry of the prophets though they are not explicitly mentioned in this context. Although the people were rushing away from God and making every effort to forget him, it is a mark of the LORD's covenant faithfulness in that dark era when the people abandoned the covenant that he put himself out to warn them of their danger and to recall them to himself (Isa. 65:2). The repeated warnings sent by God met, however, with no response. 'The light shines in the darkness, but the darkness has not understood it' (John. 1:5).

14. The consequence of their rebellion and their lack of response to the entreaties they had been presented with is then stated. **Therefore** (this is not *lākēn* which characteristically introduces a divine pronouncement of judgment; it is simply 'and')**, what I did to Shiloh I will now do to the house that bears my Name, the temple you trust in, the place I gave to you and your fathers.** Because the lesson of Shiloh has not been learned, the fate of Shiloh will be repeated in the case of Jerusalem and its Temple. 'The house that bears my Name' echoes v. 11. The question of trust in the Temple returns to the thought of v. 4 and the place given to their fathers reflects the description of v. 7. This seemingly unconditional announcement of destruction has often caused difficulties for those who felt it to be at variance with the message of vv. 5-7 where the possibility of repentance was set out, but there is no real tension between them once 18:7-8 is taken into account. Statements of judgment couched in seemingly absolute terms may in fact be made with an implicit condition and are designed to induce repentance. However, if the appropriate response is not forthcoming, then the situation becomes ominous.

15. Furthermore the people of Judah had not just the old example of the devastation of Shiloh to the north. They ought also to have appreciated the significance of what had happened more recently in

722 BC in the northern kingdom of Israel, here named after its most prominent tribe, Ephraim, when they too had rejected the requirements of the LORD. **I will thrust you from my presence, just as I did all your brothers, the people of Ephraim.** This solemn warning, being more recent, should have impressed them the more vividly. For the reaction to Jeremiah's proclamation, see chapter 26.

B. DO NOT INTERCEDE (7:16-20)

Though there is no mention of the Temple or its services in this section, it is related to the other material in this division by the theme of the worship of the people. It would seem that at the start of Jehoiakim's reign no immediate attempt was made to reverse Josiah's Temple reforms in which he had purged the sacred place of all traces of idol worship. But there was increasing laxity as regards what happened elsewhere. People could not see any harm in combining the Temple worship of the LORD with the worship of other gods at other sites. Jeremiah therefore exposed the inconsistency of popular practice and declares how heinous it was in God's sight. Temple ritual could never compensate for disobedience outwith its precincts.

The prohibition regarding intercession found in v. 16 raises two significant questions: What role did intercessory prayer play in prophetic ministry in general? and, Did this prohibition mark a turning-point in Jeremiah's ministry? Regarding the first question it is difficult to characterise intercession as a specifically prophetic function. Johnson (1962:58-60) argued that prophets were specialists in prayer who engaged in intercession in connection with the Jerusalem cult, particularly pleading for the peace of the city. However, it is not easy to relate this to the biblical record of prophecy. Possibly the clearest connection between prophets and intercession is to be found in the early divine word to Abimelech, where God says of Abraham, 'He is a prophet, and he will pray for you' (Gen. 20:7). But this does not seem to have been an integral part of prophetic ministry, no mention being made of it in the prophetic constitution (Deut. 18:14-22). Undoubtedly Moses (Exod. 8-10; Num. 21:7; Deut. 9:20) and Samuel (1 Sam. 7:5; 12:19, 23) engaged in intercessory activity (see on 15:1), but this does not seem to have originated specifically in their prophetic office. Of the prophets Jeremiah is the major intercessory figure, though a similar role is played on occasions by others (e.g. Amos 7:1-9; 2 Kgs. 19:4 = Isa. 37:4). On the other hand intercession is associated with royal figures (Hezekiah, 2 Chron. 30:18), national leaders (Nehemiah, Neh. 1:6), or even the people as a whole (29:7; Ps. 72:15).

If the prohibition of intercession is part of God's judgment on a faithless people who no longer deserve the privilege of divine-human dialogue, does this prohibition come at a stage in Jeremiah's ministry when the judgment threatened is so certain that it cannot be averted? If he knew that the LORD's judgment was irrevocably decreed, then Jeremiah would have been acting improperly if he requested what he knew was contrary to the divine will. But just as with the seemingly unconditional announcement of destruction in v. 14, making known to the people that he had been told not to pray for them may have been an attempt to convey how dire their circumstances were in God's sight. It does not seem possible to take the prohibition as absolutely delimiting a specific stage in Jeremiah's ministry, especially since it is repeated (11:14; 14:11), implying perhaps that it was in part a hortatory device and that Jeremiah had at first understood it that way. However, the seriousness of what is said should not be played down. Even the intimation of irrevocable doom became not a threat, but reality.

16. The introduction to this verse, **So**/'But as for you' (singular), does not mark a continuation in thought, but rather the start of a new section of speech, in which the LORD turns to Jeremiah and addresses him regarding his role. A threefold injunction is given to the prophet.

(1) **Do not pray** (<√*pālal* hithpael + *bəʿad*, 'intercede for') **for this people.** The verb *pālal*, 'to intervene on behalf of another, to intercede', occurs seven times in Jeremiah (7:16; 11:14; 14:11; 37:3; 42:2, 20; 29:7), and denotes not merely *prayer* but *prayer for* a person or persons. Here it is forbidden, but in itself the command is not a permanent one, being related to a specific situation. The negative used three times in this verse is *ʾal*, not the emphatic and frequently durative, *lōʾ* 'not' (GKC §107o). The prophet is being told that in the prevailing circumstances he is not to intercede for the people. The accumulation of terms by which the prohibition is enforced shows that the LORD was not treating their conduct as a light matter.

(2) The prophet is also told **nor offer any plea or petition** (<√*pālal*) **for them.** 'Offer' (<√*nāśāʾ*, 'to lift/raise') is only found three times elsewhere in connection with intercessory petition (11:14; 2 Kgs. 19:4 = Isa. 37:4). 'Plea'/'cry' (*rinnâ*) may be joyful and enthusiastic acclamation, but here it is an appeal to God for help in time of need (Pss. 17:1; 61:1; 142:6).

(3) **Do not plead with me.** 'Plead' (<√*pāgaʿ*) has a basic meaning of 'meet, encounter'. Apart from three occurrences in Jeremiah (7:16; 15:11 hiphil; 27:18) the only other time it is found in a prophetic book with the meaning 'intercede' is in Isa. 53:12 regarding the Suffering

Servant. Jeremiah is not to confront the LORD, coming across his path, with requests on behalf of the people. The reason for this is then stated: **for** (*kî*) **I will not listen to you**, or rather the durative statement 'I am not listening to you'. The LORD has made up his mind in respect of the punishment of the people, and therefore he has determined not to give audience to the prophet if he should seek to approach him on this matter.

This command not to pray for the people is repeated elsewhere (11:14; 14:11), and this raises the question of whether or not Jeremiah obeyed the command. One way of looking at the matter is to suppose that the three occasions are in effect variants of the one command and that they all relate to the aftermath of Jehoiakim's burning of the scroll. At that point the fate of the people was sealed, and so intercession would have been improper for Jeremiah because it would have been contrary to the LORD's known will. Later, however, near the final collapse of the city, he was able to pray not to avert the tragedy, but to mitigate its consequences for the people in their circumstances thereafter.

On the other hand, Jeremiah does pray for the people (18:20; 21:12; 37:3), and it may be that Jeremiah was given this instruction on a number of occasions. It is a specific prohibition, and related to specific circumstances as we shall see in the following verses. It may be that when these circumstances improved, or Jeremiah thought they had improved, it would have been proper for him to again engage in intercession. Presumably part of the reason why this information was conveyed by the prophet to the people was in an attempt to shock them into realisation of how critical their circumstances had become.

17. Do you not see what they are doing in the towns of Judah and in the streets of Jerusalem? It is not as though the prophet was unaware of what was happening around him. The question is to emphasise the reason for the LORD's unwillingness to listen to petitions on behalf of the people. There was paganism everywhere (2:28).

18. It is perhaps significant that it is the family religion of the day that is described, not the state sponsored and controlled worship of the Temple. That had been reformed by Josiah and though corruption spread again later (Ezek. 8:5-16), it is unlikely that it existed at the start of the reign of Jehoiakim. However, family religion too should have been focused round the LORD, but instead **the children gather wood, the fathers light** (<√*bāʿar*, cf. v. 20) **the fire, and the women knead**

dough and make cakes of bread for the Queen[8] of Heaven. When Jeremiah originally mentioned the 'children' it was doubtless part of the portrayal of how extensive the grasp of paganism was on society in Judah. After the Exile, however, it would have spoken powerfully to the consciences of the remnant as they remembered scenes from their childhood. It seems that rather than using an oven an open fire was employed with the dough being placed on the ashes. The women played a significant role in this cult (44:15-25) as they also did in the related Tammuz worship (Ezek. 8:14). The 'cakes' (<*kawwān*) is a Mesopotamian loanword which denotes a sweetened cake used in the cult of the mother goddess Ishtar, goddess of the planet Venus, the morning star, also known in Mesopotamia as Queen or Lady of Heaven (King 1993:103). The use of this word has been one factor favouring the view that the Queen of Heaven was not an indigenous goddess. Various proposals have been brought forward regarding the name used for the goddess in Judah; probably she was identified with the Canaanite goddess Asherah. But the content of her worship was strongly affected by Assyrian rites, possibly as early as the reign of Ahaz. Her cult became widespread in Manasseh's time (2 Kgs. 21; 23:4-14; cf. Amos 5:26) when it took a deep hold at a family level. 'The worship had been able the easier to go underground because of its nature, the pinch of incense, the libation, the cakes, either in the shape of a woman, or perhaps crescent moon or starshaped—these being Ishtar's symbols' (Ellison 1962:21). It enjoyed a resurgence after Josiah's death, and was not eradicated even by the Exile. It continued in Egypt (44:17), and there is evidence of it in the Elephantine Papyri. Mesopotamian beliefs related that Ishtar was courted by Tammuz, the deity of spring vegetation, whose cult was observed in the Temple during the reign of Zedekiah (Ezek. 8:14-15; King 1993:103).

They pour out[9] drink offerings to other gods to provoke me to anger. The mention of the Queen of Heaven is but one instance of far

8. The Massoretic Text is vocalised as *limleket* (so also four times in 44:17-25 as part of this phrase), as though to suggest *limleʾket* 'for the work' of heaven (this is in fact found in a number of manuscripts), referring to all the heavenly bodies. This may have been a device to avoid reference to the goddess, and should be pointed *ləmalkat*, 'to the queen'. Alternatively, the Massoretic pointing may indicate the existence of a by-form for 'queen' that was used in this phrase.

9. An infinitive absolute standing for a participle (*IBHS* §35.5.3a; Joüon §123x). The infinitive absolute is used rather than the infinitive construct because no preposition is present (GKC §113e).

more widespread corruption. 'Drink offerings' ('poured out offerings' from the same root as the verb 'to pour out') are not mentioned often in the Old Testament, but they would be more suited to a domestic situation, and pagan libations (offerings of wine) on the roofs of houses are mentioned elsewhere (19:13; 32:29). This would fit in with the worship of the Queen of Heaven; as an astral goddess she was typically worshipped in the open air. It may be that they were wittingly determined to insult the LORD by their espousal of such false worship, 'in order to (*ləmaʿan*) provoke me to anger'. Lexicographers are undecided as to whether *ləmaʿan* may denote the result of an action ('so that') as well as purpose. BDB suggest that in this passage the outcome of their action, though really unintended, is presented ironically as if it were by deliberate design. 'To provoke to anger' (<√*kāʿas*) shows that the sin of mankind can stir up an inner response within God, which leads on to judgment.

19. But am I the one they are provoking? declares the LORD. It is not that the LORD was not provoked. There can be no doubt but that their rejection of his sovereignty grieved and vexed him (25:6-7). The question, though expecting a negative answer, is not intended to deny such a reaction on the part of the LORD, but to indicate that the main impact of their behaviour was not on him but on themselves. **Are they not rather harming themselves**[10]**, to their own shame**/'shame of their face'**?** While this does refer to public shame that would be clearly evident to others, the phrase primarily points to personal awareness of shortcoming which is evident in their faces, as they can no longer look at others straight in the face but avert their gaze in embarrassment that they have been unable to achieve what they had hoped for. It is here predicted that the false worship the people have engaged in will rebound to their own confusion when the LORD intervenes to show up the ineffectiveness of what they have put their trust in.

20. Therefore (*lākēn*, introducing a word of judgment) **this is what the Sovereign LORD** (*ʾădōnāy YHWH*, 1:6) **says** brings the judgment of the king on his people. **My anger** (*ʾap*, 4:8) **and my wrath** (*ḥēmâ*, 4:8) **will be poured out on this place.** Again there is the ambiguity as to whether 'this place' is the Temple, the city, or the land, but given that the practices of the previous verses are spread throughout the land (v. 17) it seems it is the whole of Judah that is in view. The devastation will be all encompassing (4:25-26; 9:10), coming **on man and** ('on')

10. The accusative marker *ʾōtam*, 'them', is used instead of a reflexive pronoun to bring out the contrast with *ʾōtî*, 'me' (GKC §135k; Joüon §146k).

beast, on the trees of the field and on the fruit of the ground. Four times 'on' (*'al*) is repeated with ominous inclusiveness. The idea of heat that is involved in wrath is then further developed in the particular form of judgment that will come on them: **it will burn** (<√*bāʿar*) **and not be quenched.** While the people thought they were just kindling fires on roof tops (v. 18), they were in fact kindling a far more serious fire for themselves—God's wrath that will not be extinguished, but will consume them.

C. MEANINGLESS SACRIFICE (7:21-29)

The religious ceremonies of the Temple had been exposed as a sham because the conduct of the people of Judah was contrary to what the LORD demanded (vv. 1-15). The worship they really wanted to engage in was that of the Queen of Heaven (vv. 16-20). What they were doing in the Temple was therefore engaging in mere ritual, and that had never been what the LORD had instituted the sacrificial rites for. It is not impossible that these words could have been spoken early in the reign of Jehoiakim as part of the Temple Sermon, but all that seems to be required is that they reflect Jeremiah's ministry in the period before the writing of the Scroll as the emptiness of Temple worship became increasingly evident. The end of this section is indicated by the use of poetry in v. 29, and the start of a new section by the speech formula in v. 30.

21. Again the section begins with a full announcement formula to give impressive solemnity to what follows: **This is what the LORD Almighty, the God of Israel, says** (cf. v. 3). What follows is heavily ironic, as is indicated by the NIV supplement, **Go ahead!** There then follows the command, **Add your burnt offerings to your other sacrifices**, where the imperative is used to express an ironic challenge (GKC §110a). 'Burnt offerings', fronted for emphasis, refers to the sacrifices that were wholly consumed by fire on the altar, whereas the other ('other' is an NIV supplement) sacrifices referred to here were ones of which part was returned to the offerer to consume. The command is to treat them all alike. The sacred sacrifices no longer meant anything to God, and they could **eat the meat yourselves,** that is the flesh of the sacrifices, including what was usually dedicated to God. There is probably a hint here that all the offerers were interested in was in the feast at the end of the sacrifices, and not in the worship that was required, as if to say, 'Go on; have your feed. You don't understand what is happening anyhow.'

22. The divine repudiation of their sacrifices arose because the people had failed to grasp the most elementary principles of the covenant. To make this clear to them they are guided back to the initial constitution of Israel as the people of God. **For (*kî*) when I brought**[11] **your forefathers out of Egypt and spoke to them, I did not just give them commands about burnt offerings or sacrifices.** The NIV 'just' is a supplement to try to bring out the significance of what is otherwise a seemingly abrupt statement that at Sinai God did not give commands about sacrifice. There have been those who have used this passage (along with Amos 5:25) as evidence for the late origin of the Pentateuchal legislation regarding sacrifice, which would then be unknown to Jeremiah, or else as a denial that sacrifice had been practised at such an early date. There are more plausible explanations of what is being said. One is to focus on the particular time period that was involved. It was not immediately after the Exodus, nor yet at the first giving of the law at Sinai, that God spoke about sacrifice, but only later. 'Jeremiah is clearly indicating that the order of revelation is indicative of its relative value' (Ellison 1962:23). Another way of understanding what is said is to focus on the phrase translated 'about' (*ʿal-dibrê*, 'on account of words of'). There is evidence that it might be taken as 'for the sake of, in the interest of' (14:1; Deut. 4:21; 2 Sam. 18:5; 2 Kgs. 22:13; Ps. 7:1). In other words, though God did at that time speak about sacrifice, that was not his primary concern. A similar understanding can be achieved by focusing on the Hebrew use of a negative where we might more usually employ a comparative, so that the sense would be, 'I did not principally give them this command, rather I commanded'. The statement has to be read as a whole to be properly understood because the first relative is not to be taken absolutely, but only in relation to the second, emphasised part of the sentence. In Deut. 5:3, 'It was not with our fathers that the LORD made this covenant, but with us, with all of us who are alive here today', there is no denial that the covenant was made with their fathers, but rather than viewing it as an event of past relevance only, Moses is urging the people to accept its claims upon themselves. Such a relative understanding of the negative underlies the NIV rendering.

23. The alternative interpretation as to what occurred at Sinai is then stated. **But (*kî ʾim*) I gave them this command: Obey me, and I will be your God and you will be my people. Walk in all the way I**

11. The kethibh *hôṣîʾ* is a hiphil infinitive construct with no pronominal suffix; the qere adds the suffix, correctly, but not absolutely necessarily, to give *bəyôm hôṣîʾî*, 'in day of my bringing out'.

command you, that it may be well with you. 'Obey'/'listen to my voice' picks up on the use of 'listen' in vv. 13, 16. 'Obey me, and I will be your God' expresses a key theme in Jeremiah's theology of the covenant (11:4; 24:7; 30:22; 31:1; 32:38). True and single-minded devotion to the LORD would lead to the enjoyment of the blessings of the covenant from his hand. Jeremiah does not here cite any single passage of the Pentateuch, but instead brings together a number of significant phrases that are all associated with the giving of the law. 'Obey me' reflects Exod. 19:5. 'I will be your God and you will be my people' reflects Exod. 6:7; Lev. 26:12; Deut. 26:18. 'Walk in the ways I command you' is found after the ten words in Deut. 5:33, and 'that it may go well with you' (38:20; 40:9; 42:6) reflects on this verse also (see NKJV, NRSV) where 'good', that is the benefits bestowed by the covenant Overlord, is the consequence of covenant fidelity. 'All' (*kōl*) is used as practically equivalent to an adverb, 'totally, exactly'. 'Walk exactly in the way' (Joüon §139cN). It was this unconditional acceptance of his overlordship that the LORD had in view in Exod. 19 even before the terms of the covenant were detailed.

The point at issue is that the primary concern of the LORD was to have an obedient people. It is only on the path of obedience that they will enter into the full dimensions of the covenant relationship. It is only as they are totally committed that they will experience all the good that the covenant can bring to them.

In presenting this message Jeremiah is reiterating what had often been emphasised before him (6:20). 'Does the LORD delight in burnt offerings and sacrifices as much as in obeying the voice of the LORD? To obey is better than sacrifice, and to heed is better than the fat of rams' (1 Sam. 15:22). Sacrifice without obedience was totally misguided. Deuteronomy emphasised the need for heart obedience springing from a total inner commitment to the LORD which would then express itself in obedience to cultic requirements (Deut. 6:4; 10:12). For Hosea sacrifice without true knowledge of the LORD did not achieve anything (Hos. 4:1-3; 9:4), and Amos mocked sacrifices offered by a disobedient people (Amos 4:4-5). For Isaiah accumulation of sacrifices was just meaningless if there was not faith evidencing itself in covenant obedience (Isa. 1:11-17). Later Malachi shows how sacrifice offered without true respect for the LORD is unacceptable to him (Mal. 1:6-14).

24. However, the people had never been responsive to this message. **But they did not listen or pay attention; instead, they followed the stubborn inclinations of their evil hearts.** For 'listen', see on v. 13.

'Pay attention' is literally 'turn their ear', that is, to listen carefully to what is said and take appropriate action. To the phrase 'the stubbornness of their evil hearts' (3:17) there is added here 'inclinations'/ 'plans, schemes'. They decided to do what they wanted and refused to give obedience to the demands of their covenant Overlord. The next clause is variously understood. While the NRSV has 'looked backward rather than forward' and the REB 'they turned their backs and not their faces to me', a gesture of contempt, most English versions assume that the force of 'follow'/'walked' continues from the previous clause and translate with the NIV, **they went backward and not forward** (literally, 'they were with respect to back and not with respect to face'). This is either a description of their backsliding getting worse and worse, or else it has more particularly the LORD in view, and the thought is that they were walking away from him, on the path that departed from him, rather than moving towards him. This is a different perception of the early period of Israel's history from that presented in chapter 2; both loyalty and rebellion are presented in heightened terms for rhetorical effect. It is interesting that Jeremiah sees the current conduct of the people not as confined to one generation but as part of a process that stretched back to the earliest times of their history.

25. They were not left without warning. **From the time your forefathers left Egypt until now, day after day,**[12] **again and again I sent you my servants the prophets.** The covenant king had repeatedly sent his messengers to convey his warnings to 'you', his erring people of the generations from the Exodus. He had spared no effort to do this; for 'again and again' see on v. 13. 'My servants the prophets' were the officials he commissioned to carry out this task (26:5; 29:19; 35:15; 44:4; cf. 25:4). It was divine pity that impelled this action (2 Chron. 36:15), though repeated rejection of the warnings leads to condemnation.

26. However, all the effort that was made did not have the desired result. **But they did not listen to me or pay attention. They were stiff-necked and did more evil than their forefathers.** 'They' in the first part of the verse clearly refers to all previous generations. In the second part of the verse each past generation is thought of on its own and compared to the generation before it. Far from being a story of

12. The MT merely has 'day' (*yôm*). BHS recommends that the word be deleted as a dittography of the preceding plural ending. But there is sufficient early versional evidence (Greek, Latin, Syriac) to suggest that a second occurrence of *yôm* has been mistakenly omitted by haplography, or that the word was originally *yômām*, 'daily'.

human progress, the history of the people given so many privileges (and warnings!) by the LORD is one of ongoing downward slippage. It may perhaps be an indication of growing alienation of the LORD from the people of Jeremiah's day that he now talks about them rather than to them. 'Stiff-necked' (17:23; 19:15; also in various other places such as Deut. 9:6, 13) is a farming metaphor for an animal unwilling to bow its neck to have the yoke placed on it. Without that it could not be useful in its master's service (compare 27:11).

27. Jeremiah is directly addressed in vv. 27-28. He had already known that his message would not win acceptance (1:8, 17-19), and this is now restated with particular reference to what is found in vv. 21-26, possibly in the whole chapter. As the current servant of the LORD he has the task of bringing his warning to Israel (v. 25), but this generation will give no greater heed than those that went before. **When you tell them all this, they will not listen to you; when you call to them, they will not answer.** The expressions used echo those of v. 13.

28. Consequently it is no surprise that he is commanded to bring the message of the LORD's judgment to them. **Therefore** (this is not *lākēn*; it is simply 'and', cf. v. 14) **say to them, 'This is the nation that has not obeyed the LORD its God or responded to correction.'** The correction (<√*yāsar*, 2:30) is the word of warning that had been brought by the prophets. The use of 'nation' rather than 'people' probably indicates that they are now living on a par with all other nations and are no longer to be thought of as specially marked out as God's own. The epigrammatic statement, **Truth has perished; it has vanished from their lips**, sums up their condition. 'Truth' (*ʾĕmunâ*, 5:1) is reliable conduct in accordance with the standards of the covenant. It should characterise those who are the faithful people of the LORD, but it can no longer be found. Truth personified has died. 'Vanished'/'cut off' retains the figure, being the term used for expulsion from the covenant community (Gen. 17:14; Lev. 7:20). Here it is from the 'lips/mouth' of the community that it has been banished, and that raises the question of whether the people can truly be called the covenant people of the LORD.

29. This verse is generally recognised as poetry, though not by the NIV or NKJV. The imperatives used are feminine singular with reference to Jerusalem (hence the AV supplement, 'O Jerusalem', which could with advantage be retained). She is being commanded to engage in mourning rites in anticipation of her impending destruction. Even though it was probable that the message would be rejected, the inclusion of this speech to Zion shows that the message was still to be proclaimed. **Cut off your hair and throw it away.** 'Cut off' is literally 'shear, crop it close' (a different word from 'cut off' in v. 28, so that there is no linguistic link as might be suggested by the NKJV and NRSV), though what constitutes closeness is culturally determined. Cutting the hair was a gesture of mourning (41:5; 47:5; 48:37; Job 1:20; Mic. 1:16), but probably more than that is involved here. While 'hair' (<*nēzer*, 'crown') might refer to her hair as her crowning glory (a reflection of ancient hair styles?), the word was also used in connection with the Nazirites (Num. 6:7). As a sign of their consecration to the service of the LORD, they did not cut their hair. If, however, they became ceremonially unclean, they were required to cut their hair (Num. 6:9). If their hair were cut, it would signify a loss of consecration and power (Judg. 16:15-22). So Jerusalem is exhorted to mourn because she is no longer dedicated to the LORD. Her beauty is marred, and she cannot be called the holy city any more. All she can do is wait for divine judgment to fall on her.

Take up a lament on the barren heights. The lament (*qînâ*) is a poem of bereavement sung at a funeral. Jerusalem is urged to sing one in anticipation of the death and devastation that will occur because of the LORD's judgment. The mention of barren heights, previously associated with places of pagan worship (3:2, 21), probably has an ironic touch to it. The mourning is to take place on the very site of her deconsecration rather than McKane's suggestion that it is shearing of the hair and mourning for a dead god (1986, 1:177) with irony paralleling that of v. 21. The reason for this is given: **for** (*kî*) **the LORD has rejected** (<√*mā'as* 6:30) **and abandoned** (<√*nāṭaš* 12:7) **this generation that is under his wrath,** 'the generation of his wrath' (*'ebrâ*, 'intense, overflowing fury'). There is no hope for them, the LORD has given up on them. For 'reject', see 6:30.

D. THE VALLEY OF SLAUGHTER (7:30-34)

This collection of addresses relating to the worship practices of Judah ends with two sections (vv. 30-34 and 8:1-3) which set out the accursed nature of the degenerate practices which had become prevalent. While it is possible to argue that the addresses reflect the early years of Josiah before his reforms were fully instituted, it is more likely that the circumstances are those of the middle or late period of Jehoiakim's reign as Josiah's reforms were progressively eroded. Ellison indeed maintained that 'we may be certain from the silence of both Jeremiah and Ezekiel, as well as of Kings and Chronicles, that human sacrifice was not re-introduced in the last days of Jerusalem'

(1962:97-98), and that the verbs in this section should be translated as past tenses referring back to the time of Manasseh. This gives ground for pause, but is this passage not evidence from Jeremiah for a resurgence of such perversion?

30. The focus is on what has occurred in the Temple. The previous declaration of judgment is linked to a further description of what has given rise to it by *kî* ('for'). **'The people of Judah have done evil in my eyes,' declares the LORD. 'They have set up their detestable idols in the house that bears my Name and have defiled it.'** (This allegation is repeated in 32:34.) What has happened has taken place by popular instigation and not merely by royal decree. 'The house that bears my Name' (v. 10) is the Temple. Not content with idol worship at sites traditionally associated with it, the people have brought into the Temple cult objects ('detestable things', 4:1), and with them their associated evil practices, so that the place had been defiled (<√*ṭāmēʾ*, 2:7). The reference may have been to what happened in the past (Ahaz and Manasseh, 2 Kgs. 21:5-6; 23:10), but it is more probably to what happened in Jerusalem as Jehoiakim's reign progressed (cf. chap. 44; and further Ezek. 5:11; 8:6 regarding Zedekiah's reign). What Josiah had managed to remove from the official cult and to suppress in the outward conduct of the nation had not been totally eradicated from their hearts, or from their private practice. It was still the case that the religious degeneration of Manasseh's time exercised a baneful infuence on the thinking and attitudes of the people. Jehoiakim had no interest in enforcing his father's religious policies, and conditions quickly reverted to what they had been previously. The spiritual corruption of the people made itself evident in the religious perversions they engaged in. They were quite without loyalty to the LORD and heedless of the requirements of the covenant.

31. What happened inside the Temple was matched, indeed outdone, by what occurred outwith the sacred precincts. Further evidence of the religious corruption of the people was easily detected in an area outside the city, probably in the valley to the south-west of its walls (19:5-7). **They have built the high places of Topheth** contains a number of unusual features in Hebrew. 'High places' is plural, where we would expect a singular. Originally the word referred to a sacred site on a hilltop, often a wooded area, but by Jeremiah's day it had come to denote a pagan sacred site in any location, perhaps raised artificially from the surrounding area. We would not expect two high places at one site. The answer to this may perhaps be found in the verb which could denote repeated activity in the past,[13] and therefore the plural high places refers to their repeated re-erection, rather than existence of more than one simultaneously. Alternatively, the plural noun may be used to indicate the importance and significance of this one site, a type of honorific plural (*IBHS* §7.4.3)

Topheth as v. 32 makes clear is a place name, and not the name of a god, though the phrase 'high places of Baal' is also found (19:5; 32:25). The form Topheth is probably a deliberate deformation of a word meaning 'fire-place, cooking stove' (*təpāt*) so that it rhymes with *bošet*, 'shame' (King 1993:136), and also sounds the same as the word for spitting, a gesture of contempt (Job 17:6). In other words, the term is a deliberate rejection of all that went on **in the Valley of Ben Hinnom.** We do not know who Ben Hinnom was. Presumably the place had this name before it was used for these practices. The valley itself is probably to be identified with the southern section of the modern Wadi Rababi which runs to the west and south of the old city of Jerusalem. At its eastern end the Hinnom valley joined the other two major valleys of Jerusalem, the Central or Tyropoeon Valley, and the Kidron Valley, lying to the east of the old city. It has been suggested that the Tophet was located in the open area where these valleys met.

The horrific action **to burn their sons and their daughters in the fire** has caused controversy. Elsewhere the phrase 'to cause to pass through the fire' is used, and this has been interpreted as an act of dedication to the heathen god which did not actually involve the death of their children: a ritual ordeal or perhaps branding. Here and elsewhere (19:5; Ezek. 16:20-21; 23:37, 39), however, the use of 'burn … in the fire' (*śārap bāʾēš*) does not permit such an interpretation. Nothing less than child sacrifice is indicated. It was practised by surrounding nations (Deut. 12:31; 2 Kgs. 3:27; 17:31), a fact that has received archaeological attestation at Phoenician sites around the Mediterranean (King 1992:137-39). Once the people of God had deserted the standards of the covenant, this practice was no longer unknown among them (2 Kgs. 17:17; 21:6; 23:10).

Child sacrifice was particularly associated with the worship of

---

13. 'And they built' (*ûbānû*) is not, as might have been expected, a *waw*-consecutive imperfect, but ordinary *waw* with the perfect. This use of the perfect may indicate that it describes action contemporaneous with (and not subsequent to) the previous verb 'they set up', or it might be a frequentative perfect indicating what they did a number of times (so Holladay 1986, 1:264). The same verb form is found in the similar passage in 19:5; so it is unlikely to be a copyist's error.

Molech (Moloch). The traditional Jewish understanding of this is provided by Rabbi David Kimchi (*c.*1160–*c.*1235) in his comments on 2 Kgs. 23:10, where he says that the image of Molech was of hollow brass and located at a site outside Jerusalem in a shrine with seven chambers, separated by grated doors. If a worshipper offered fine flour, he was admitted into the first chamber; if he offered a turtle dove or young pigeon, he was admitted to the second; if a lamb, to the third; if a ram, to the fourth; if a calf, to the fifth; if an ox, to the sixth; and whoever offered his son was permitted entry into the seventh chamber where the idol stood. The face of the idol was like that of a calf, and it had hands stretched out like those of a man about to receive something from his neighbour. Fire was kindled, and the priests took the child and put it into the hands of Molech (presumably the metal was heated from within), where it burned to death. Meanwhile the priests kept beating on drums so that the father might not hear the cries of his child and take pity upon him. Our revulsion at the practice should not blind us to the fact that those who thus offered their children considered themselves to be engaging in an act of the highest piety and devotion. This was the measure of Judah's spiritual depravity. For a more recent assessment of what might have been involved in these rites, see *TWOT* #2539.

The concluding clause of the verse, **something I did not command, nor did it**[14] **enter my mind** (Lev. 18:21; Deut. 18:10), suggests by the emphatic and absolute nature of its rejection of this practice that there were those who were seeking to justify what they were doing as conforming to a divine commandment. A similar stance is also found in passages such as Mic. 6:7 where the example of Abraham and Isaac is adduced to justify their practice, and probably in Ezek. 20:26 where there is an appeal to the requirement that the firstborn of the womb were consecrated to the LORD—though certainly not in this way (Exod. 13:2; 22:29; 34:9). Whatever the reference, it is an indication that there was an attempted rationale for even the most evil practices. The people had become so spiritually imperceptive that they no longer grasped what the LORD truly required and had to be emphatically reminded of it. 'My mind'/'my heart' refers to the LORD's attitude towards what he approves of and sanctions, so that when used in a negative expression there is a rejection of any divine inclination towards the practice or authority for engaging in it (cf. 19:5; 32:35).

32. This state of affairs brings on a sentence of divine judgment. **So** (*lākēn*, 'therefore', introducing divine judgment) **beware** (*hinnēh*,

14. An impersonal use of the feminine (GKC §144b; Joüon §152c).

traditionally glossed as 'behold'; the note of warning comes from the context)**, the days are coming.** Jeremiah frequently (15 times; but also found earlier Amos 4:2; 8:11; 9:13) uses the phrase 'Behold! days ⌞are⌟ coming' to point emphatically to a time that will see a reversal of presently existing conditions. It carries with it the implication that matters are already in hand to ensure that this reversal will occur so that there should be no doubt about the reality of the events described. At the same time, there is a vagueness about the specific timescale. The prophet does not attempt to convey whether the matter will be resolved soon or late. But it is in hand. The reversal envisaged may, as here, be one from seeming prosperity to disaster, or from a time of distress to renewed blessing (as in 30:3).

When people will no longer call it Topheth or the Valley of Ben Hinnom, but (*kî ʾim*, 'but rather') **the Valley of Slaughter.** The impersonal construction 'it will be called' probably envisages the existence of a proverbial saying. The significance of the valley that was given over to such pagan and detestable practices will change, and this will be seen by the change of name. The slaughter (<√*hārag*, 'to slay', usually of people by violent means) envisaged is not that of the child sacrifices; it will be the result of enemy action. This change of name was not total, because the original Old Testament name survived in the form Gehenna, 'Valley of Hinnom', as a New Testament term for hell (Matt. 5:29). Furthermore, the valley will be dedicated to a different use in the day of the LORD's restoration (34:40). **For** (simply 'and') **they will bury the dead in Topheth until there is no more room** (or, with the RSV, 'because there is no room elsewhere'). The site outwith the city walls will be used for mass graves, but even they will prove insufficient because of numbers killed.

33. The scale of the slaughter is brought out in the fearful picture of v. 33 (for vv. 33-34 see 16:5-9). **Then the carcasses of this people will become food for the birds of the air and the beasts of the earth, and there will be no one to frighten them away**. Scavenging birds and animals would have their fill. For a corpse to be left unburied was viewed as a terrible curse (1 Sam. 17:43-46), but here there are so few survivors that they will have no time to chase animals away from the remains of the dead, let alone bury them. The curse of the broken covenant has come upon them: 'Your carcasses will be food for all the birds of the air and the beasts of the earth, and there will be no one to frighten them away' (Deut. 28:26). Furthermore, the site that they had dedicated to pagan gods would be desecrated by the bones that would inevitably be left lying there (2 Kgs. 23:16, 20).

34. The catastrophic consequences of enemy invasion are then presented in terms of what will no longer exist after the LORD's executioners have done their work. **I will bring an end to the sounds of joy and gladness and to the voices of bride and bridegroom in the towns of Judah and the streets of Jerusalem, for** (*kî*) **the land will become desolate.** Weddings were times of mirth and festivity, but the devastated community will have no inclination for rejoicing (16:9; 25:10). The NIV inverts the Hebrew 'bridegroom and bride' to conform to the usual English order. Weddings also opened up the prospect of the future growth and expansion of the community, but that has been stopped. Those who sacrificed their children will have no children. As the survivors looked around them, all they would be able to see is desolation, *ḥorbâ*, a term which in the first instance describes the dryness of the desert, and then was used for a scene of barren wasteland whether natural or brought about by enemy activity. The cities would be turned into rubble, their population dead or enslaved, and the land left uncultivated. This was their reward for covenant infidelity (Lev. 26:31-33). Such a prospect is also set out as the curse that will follow breach of secular treaties. 'Two treaties threaten rebels with the removal of all joyful sounds from their midst. Thus Sefire I: "Nor may the sound of the lyre be heard in Arpad and among its people." And in the treaty of Ashurnirari V of Assyria (754 BC): "May his peasant in the field sing no work-song" ' (Hillers 1969:134). But restoration of the LORD's covenant blessing would lead to the return of such sounds (33:11).

E. ASTRAL WORSHIP (8:1-3)

Following on from the denunciation of the Canaanite abomination of child sacrifice, Jeremiah brings to an end his collection of material concerned with the religious perversions of Judah by setting out the consequences that will ensue because of astral worship—worship of the sun, moon and heavenly bodies—which had also been explicitly forbidden by the LORD (Deut. 4:19; 17:3).

1. 'At that time,' declares the LORD resumes the description of future judgment which had already been envisaged in 7:32-34. The theme of the treatment of the dead continues, but whereas it had been mass burial in 7:32 and exposure of unburied corpses in 7:33, it now turns to grave desecration and the exhumation of remains. **The bones of the kings and officials of Judah, the bones of the priests and prophets, and the bones of the people of Jerusalem will be**

removed[15] **from their graves.** There is a fivefold repetition of the phrase 'the bones of' before each of the groups mentioned as being involved; this serves to cast a funereal gloom over the passage. The graves of the prominent were always an attraction to robbers on account of valuables that might have been buried with them. But this goes beyond the depredations of grave robbers. The Assyrians certainly, and the Babylonians probably, behaved in the way described here against vassals whom they considered had broken their covenant engagements with them. The exposure of the bones of the dead was considered to be extreme humiliation (2 Sam. 21:12-14; Ps. 53:5; Isa. 14:18-19; Ezek. 6:5; for violating the dead, cf. Amos 2:1.). It was the ultimate insult, an act of supreme contempt against a people who were so weak that they could not even protect the remains of their ancestors. In this passage there is probably the additional thought that even past generations of those who had rebelled against the LORD will be included in the outpouring of his wrath upon the people.

2. Here there is an ironic picture of the bones spread out in the open air where worship of astral deities generally took place. **They will be exposed to the sun and the moon and all the stars of heaven.** The combination of these three as objects of pagan devotion is found in Deut. 4:19; 17:3; 2 Kgs. 23:5. The 'stars'/'host' of heaven refers to the vast number of stars, each of which was considered to be governed by a deity and which in turn influenced the life of mankind on earth. Evidence of astral worship is found throughout this period (2 Kgs. 21:3, 5; 23:4; Zeph. 1:5; Ezek. 8:16). But these gods are impotent and unable to provide assistance when the bones of their former devotees are spread out before them in a macabre reconstruction of the worship they once engaged in.

There is another fivefold repetition in v. 2 (cf. v. 1) in which their acts of false worship are catalogued, each beginning with 'which' (*'ăšer*), adding a solemn cadence to the original, reproduced twice in the NIV. **Which they have loved and served and which they have followed and consulted and worshipped.** The verbs describing the corrupt worship are cumulated to emphasise the totality of their devotion to them. 'Love' is used of unfaithful, illicit behaviour (2:25; Hos. 9:1; 8:9; Ezek. 16:36-37). 'Serve' points to worship and also to obedience to what these gods required, for instance, as regards tribute/offerings (5:19). 'Followed' is 'to go/walk after' (2:2), indicating the lifestyle of their devotees. 'Consulted' (<√*dāraš*, 'to seek') is

15. The kethibh is *wəyōṣî'û*, 'and let them bring out', for which the qere, by transposing the first two consonants, substitutes *yôṣî'û*, 'they will bring out'.

used of inquiry through a prophet or other medium regarding the will of the deity. Rather than wanting to know what the LORD wished, the people had engaged in the forbidden practices of Canaanite cults (Deut. 18:9-13). 'Worshipped' (<√*ḥāwâ* hishtaphel, 7:2) shows the unlimited commitment they had pledged to these deities as they prostrated themselves before them. But the compendium of their past devotion is as complete as the powerlessness of these gods to act in defence of the interests of those who had formerly committed themselves so totally to their worship.

They will not be gathered up or buried, but will be like refuse lying on the ground. The tragedy will be so severe that in the aftermath of the invasion there will be no one able to rectify the situation, and the bones will be left exposed. For corpses becoming like refuse/manure, see on 9:22; 16:4; 25:33. 'The prophet alludes, perhaps, to the ancient practice of using bones (usually animal bones) as a form of fertiliser' (Craigie et al. 1991:127).

How was this prophecy fulfilled? 'The fulfilment of this prophecy is renewed time and again throughout the centuries. The greed of grave robbers, the excavations of the builders, the missiles of warfare, the plough and the hoe of peasant and gardener, the archaeologist's spade, all continue unwittingly in the fulfilment of this word of the eternal Lord' (Laetsch 1952:105-6). This seems to be an overly literalistic approach. What was being foretold was that the curse of the broken covenant would come on the disobedient people, and there is no doubt that it did.

3. But those who are the remnant will have a worse fate to endure than the dead (Rev. 9:6). They will be taken to many places.[16] **'Wherever I banish them, all the survivors of this evil nation will be prefer death to life,' declares the LORD Almighty.** The use of 'LORD Almighty'/'LORD of hosts' (2:19) contrasts with the stars/hosts of v. 2: he, not they, is really in control. It also provides a neat closure to this section which began with the same title (7:3). 'Nation' is *mišpāḥâ*, 'family, clan' (1:15), emphasising natural relationship rather than

16. The MT has *bəkol-hamməqōmôt hanniš'ārîm*, 'in all the places the remaining ones', a phrase which cannot easily be interpreted in the context of the passage. English versions omit *hanniš'ārîm* as erroneously repeated from 'the survivors'/'the remainder of the remaining ones' which occurs earlier in the verse in the Hebrew (the NIV has considerably rearranged the verse). It is, however, worth noticing that the plural of *māqôm* probably is intended to contrast to the previous references in chap. 7 to 'this place', now no longer the land, but the variety of places to which they have been deported.

political organisation. Here the link is through their shared wickedness, which is also found in the survivors, who are not the righteous remnant but simply those who were left alive. Every kind of hardship awaits them in exile (Lev. 26:36-39; Deut. 28:65-67). For death being preferred, see Lam. 4:9, and also 22:10. 'Banish' is from *nādâḥ*, 'to scatter, drive away', whose hiphil forms convey the idea of actions both forceful and expulsive, as decided as bringing an axe down on a block of wood (Deut. 19:5; 20:19; 2 Sam. 15:14).

In these addresses, probably delivered in the Temple on various occasions, Jeremiah castigated both the religious defection of the people and their delinquent social conduct. These were not two separate problems, but different symptoms of the one malaise, the estrangement of the nation from the LORD. Though various elements of Judahite society presented a different gloss on the situation and an altogether brighter scenario for their future, Jeremiah was utterly convinced by the divine revelation he had received that the course the nation was on led only to disaster. His message was blunt and controversial. It was designed to shock the people into realisation of how wrong prevailing sentiment was. But the reaction it provoked was principally directed against the prophet himself, as chapter 26 shows.

IV. DISOBEDIENCE AND PUNISHMENT

(8:4–10:25)

OUTLINE

A. Questions Requiring Answers (8:4-17)
   1. Unnatural Conduct (8:4-7)
   2. Unwise Conduct (8:8-12)
   3. The Unfruitful Vineyard (8:13-17)

B. Prophetic Grief (8:18–9:11) [8:18–9:10]
   1. The Physician of Gilead (8:18-22)
   2. A Fountain of Tears (9:1-2) [8:23–9:1]
   3. Social Breakdown (9:3-6) [9:2-5]
   4. Divine Refining (9:7-9) [9:6-8]
   5. Country and Town Ruined (9:10-11) [9:9-10]

C. Wisdom in the Face of Calamity (9:12-26) [9:11-25]
   1. Explaining the Ruin (9:12-16) [9:11-15]
   2. Death Coming through the Window (9:17-22) [9:16-21]
   3. Delusion and Reality (9:23-24) [9:22-23]
   4. Circumcision No Guarantee (9:25-26) [9:24-25]

D. The Four Contrasts (10:1-16)
   1. Weakness *v.* Power (10:1-7)
   2. Lifeless *v.* Living (10:8-10)
   3. Doomed Impostors *v.* The Creator (10:11-13)
   4. Man-made Frauds *v.* Israel's LORD (10:14-16)

E. The Coming Exile (10:17-25)
   1. Invasion and Destruction (10:17-18)
   2. Prophetic Intercession (10:19-25)

The evidence that we have does not permit us to identify categorically the contents of the Second Scroll, written after December 604 BC (36:32), but it is probable that 8:4–10:25 represents at least an initial block of material added by Jeremiah, using Baruch as an amanuensis, to the original scroll. There is no chronological information, and the largely poetic treatment of Judah's rebellion and inevitable doom is continued in terms that are similar to what was said in chapters 2–7. Unlike that earlier material, however, it is more difficult to discern any method in the way in which this section is structured, so that it is frequently referred to as a miscellaneous collection of sayings. This perhaps reflects the prophet's circumstances as he used his time of concealment from Jehoiakim to bring together various visions and revelations he had been given in the earlier years of that king's reign. In 8:4-17 the focus is again on the factors which led to judgment coming upon the land, whereas 8:18–9:11 moves on to explore the sorrow and mourning that Jeremiah already feels about this calamity and which the people will subsequently also share, a theme that is continued in 9:12-26 where wise counsel is also given to the people as to how they should behave. In an attempt to instruct them in basic theology, 10:1-16 sets out the vast differences between the LORD and idols, but in 10:17-25 exile is presented as the only realistic possibility facing Judah.

Again we may distinguish the various audiences who were addressed by these oracles. Originally the material was part of the prophetic proclamation designed to break through the spiritual obduracy of Jerusalem and make her face up to the reality and impending consequences of her sin. As time went on, however, such a general reappraisal became increasingly unlikely. The Second Scroll was written partly in the hope that some might see the error of the prevailing rejection of the LORD and his covenant and turn back before it became too late, and partly as a record of the warnings the LORD had given so that future generations would be able to understand what had been amiss in the rebellious nation. It is not known when copies of this Scroll became generally available, but it is likely that this happened during Zedekiah's reign.

There are many points of contact between this division of the prophecy and the preceding one. Indeed 8:10b-12 is an almost exact duplicate of 6:13-15, and the divine question of 9:9 repeats those of 5:9, 29. The connections also include general resemblances such as the descriptions of imminent invasion starting from Dan (4:13-17; 8:16), and the pictures of the tent of the people being destroyed (4:20; 10:20). Jeremiah also expresses his anguish at the prospect of what is to come upon the people (4:19-21; 8:18–9:2). Despite these similarities there is a change of tone. In the previous division the possibility of repentance is held out and urged (3:21–4:4; 4:14). Divine wrath and punishment may yet be avoided by a timeous response. This option has become less likely in the later division of the material. The conduct of the people is viewed as unnatural (8:7), deliberately deceitful (8:10) and brazen (8:12). The people are called on to prepare for exile (10:17).

A. QUESTIONS REQUIRING ANSWERS (8:4-17)

The message that is presented uses the technique of asking questions to probe the people's perception of their situation and to stir them up to a realisation of their danger. At first the focus is on the unnaturalness of their conduct (vv. 4-7), then on the unreasonableness of it (vv. 8-12), and finally in vv. 13-17, there is set out the penalty that will come upon them.

1. Unnatural Conduct (8:4-7)

This section makes use of three commonsense observations (about the actions of people, vv. 4-5; horses, v. 6; migratory birds, v. 7) to bring out how unnaturally Judah was responding to its circumstances. The note of amazement at how perverse their conduct was is reminiscent of 2:10-11.

4. The LORD's message begins with a series of questions to prod the people into thinking about their situation. **Say to them, 'This is what the LORD says: "When men fall down[1], do they not get up?" '** The language is general ('they'/'people') rather than specifically male. The natural response of someone who has slipped and fallen is to try to get up. **When a man turns away, does he not return?** An indefinite singular is now used, 'he', that is, 'someone', but the point of the observation is not so clear because of the ambiguity of the repeated verb, 'turn away'/'return', both <√*šûb*, which denotes either movement back to a point previously left or movement away from where one is. The picture may simply be that of someone going away from home, whether to work in the fields, or on a longer journey. If he goes away, you would expect him to come back. It may also depict an individual

1. The interrogative particle governs the first two clauses of the Hebrew; hence the NKJV rendering, 'Will they fall and not rise?' This is unnecessarily obscure. It is preferable to subordinate the first clause and take the interrogative only with the second as in the NIV (GKC §150m; Joüon §161k).

going off a path, and after getting lost, making every endeavour to retrace his steps back to the right route. This verb has already been used extensively in chapter 3 because it may be applied spiritually both to apostasy and to repentance. This use occurs here also: it is the same root that underlies 'turned away', 'turn away', 'return' (v. 5), and 'pursue' (v. 6). But though the spiritual application no doubt led to the employment of the word in v. 4, it is normal human behaviour that is in view here. Perhaps it is simply pointing out that someone who goes away from home is normally expected to return.

Interpreters have, however, found difficulty with the indefinite subjects of the verbs in this section and with the change from plural to singular. Medieval Jewish interpreters (Rashi and Kimchi) took the second part of the saying as referring particularly to the divine relationship with Israel: 'Does Israel turn back to God and God not turn back to them?' Holladay submits that it is more plausible to understand the plurals as referring to Israel and the singulars to the LORD in what is ironically cited as the preaching of the false prophets: 'If Israel falls, she will rise again, will she not? And if Yahweh turns away from us, he will turn back to us, will he not?' (1986, 1:278). Such approaches make the prophet's speech too terse. It seems better to take them as general statements, perhaps of the proverbial sort found in wisdom literature, which are not made specific in their application until the next verse.

5. It is a frequent feature of the style of Jeremiah that a sequence of two questions is followed by a third beginning 'Why?' using the situation posited by the previous questions to present a challenge (8:22). Here the further questions contrast the ordinary and expected reactions and behaviour of v. 4 with that displayed by Judah and Jerusalem. **Why then have these people turned away?**[2] that is, the people have performed the first action: left home or wandered from a path. But now it is applied spiritually: they have left their spiritual home, that is, a true reverence for the LORD, and are no longer walking in his ways. **Why does Jerusalem always** (<√*nāṣaḥ* niphal, 'to excel, endure') **turn away?** intensifies the matter. It is not a single instance of departure

2. 'These people' is a masculine singular collective, but *šōbəbâ*, 'turned away', is feminine singular. The final *he* may be an example of dittography with the following article, and then the reading would be *šôbāb*, which is what English translations usually follow. Alternatively, 'people' may be here treated as a feminine noun on account of the influence of 'Jerusalem' which immediately follows it in the Hebrew text and may be taken as in apposition to it (GKC §128c; cf. Exod. 5:16; Judg. 18:7).

that is in view, but of repeated slippage. It is not immediately clear if intermediate returns are implied in a cycle of apostasy and return, but it is more probably a description of a situation where every movement they make takes them further away from the LORD.

The NRSV (following one Hebrew manuscript and the LXX) omits Jerusalem and takes 'turn away' as a noun to yield, 'Why then has this people turned away in perpetual backsliding?' The evidence is not strong enough to permit deletion of Jerusalem, but treating v. 5 as one question rather than two, and the rendering 'perpetual backsliding' are commonly accepted. 'Backsliding' (*məšubâ*, 3:6) makes clear that the focus is now on their spiritual inconstancy.

After the questions comes the accusation. **They cling** (<√*ḥāzaq* hiphil, 6:23) **to deceit; they refuse to return.** Their grasp of deceit is as firm as that of a soldier's hold on the weapons he uses to keep himself alive in battle. 'Deceit' (*tarmît* <√*rāmâ* II, 'to betray') may just mean what is false in general (cf. Zeph. 3:13), but Jeremiah twice uses it (14:14; 23:26) in the context of false prophets, and it probably refers to the delusive beliefs that they promoted, namely, that there was nothing much wrong with Judah's relationship with the LORD and they could therefore confidently anticipate divinely guaranteed peace. This was what maintained the people in their rebellion. 'Refuse to return/repent' shows that they had been made aware of the situation, and had deliberately and unnaturally rejected moving back to the LORD. Should not those who turn away be expected to return?

6. While it is possible to treat v. 6 in isolation as the speech of the prophet, it is unnecessary to find here any break in the divine speech. The LORD states that, despite careful and extended examination of their behaviour, there are no hopeful signs. Their speech is flawed both in what they say and in what they do not say. **I have listened attentively** ('paid attention [<√*qāšab*, 6:17] and heard')**, but they do not say what is right**, or rather, 'they say what is not right' (*kēn*, 'correct, appropriate'). This is the same verdict as was to be found in 5:1-3. Regard for truth and proper conduct had gone by the board. And if that was true at the level of their dealings with one another, it was also the case at the spiritual level of their dealings with the LORD where they were equally oblivious to the error of their ways. **No one repents of his wickedness, saying, 'What have I done?'** 'Repents' (<√*nāḥam* niphal, 4:28) denotes reconsideration of previous conduct, recognition that it was wrong, and especially feelings of deep contrition and regret for it, such as the attitude of Job when he said, 'I despise myself and repent in dust and ashes' (Job 42:6).

Each pursues his own course[3] **like a horse charging into battle.** 'Pursue' is from the root *šûb* in the sense of turning towards something and immersing oneself in it (Hos. 12:7), 'having turned away and so become set in their ways' (cf. Holladay 1986, 1:279). 'Charging' (<√*šāṭap*) is elsewhere used of the rushing of water (47:2; Isa. 30:28; 66:12; Ezek. 13:11,13), but here it brings out the impossibility of restraining horses once they have started to charge into battle. Oblivious to the dangers around them, they sweep headlong in deliberate and vigorous action which is unstoppable. So too the people commit themselves not to a path through life, but a 'course'/'running'/ 'headlong career' (REB), something that is taken at a gallop so determined are they to get on with what they have started. There is no way they are going to be turned back.

7. There was a long-standing tradition in Israel that the natural world could be used to illustrate the divine message (Isa. 1:3; Prov. 30:24-31). Animal behaviour was not regarded as the product of instinct or an impersonal natural law, but of a divinely implanted norm. Because animals regularly follow this pattern, they provide an object lesson to humans whose behaviour is erratic. Here the focus is on the migratory instincts of birds: they know when to come and go. **Even the stork in the sky knows her appointed seasons, and the dove, the swift**[4] **and the thrush observe the time of their migration.** The variety of translations shows the difficulties that are encountered in precise identification of the birds involved. For instance, the REB has 'the wryneck' for 'the thrush', no doubt more accurately, but diverting attention from the main point of the illustration which is not ornithology. These birds observe[5] a regular pattern of migration. 'In the sky' refers to the height at which the stork (*ḥăsîdâ*) flies when migrating. The bird is probably mentioned ironically as its name derives from the same root as *ḥesed*, 'steadfast love' (2:2), because that was what the bird was considered to display in its relationships. But the behaviour of God's people reveals no such faithfulness. The birds observe the God-appointed pattern for their living, **but my people do not know the requirements of the LORD.** For the third person reference to the LORD in divine speech, compare 2:3. Now there could be no doubt that the people did know these requirements at an intellectual level, but 'know'

3. The qere transposes two consonants of the kethibh, *bmrṣwtm* (presumably a plural form), to yield *bimrûṣātām*, 'in their course', which is to be read.

4. For *sûs* the qere suggests *sîs*, perhaps to avoid *sûs* being taken as 'horse'. Both pronunciations may have been found.

5. The perfect is gnomic with a present/habitual significance (*IBHS* §30.4b).

here carries the sense of inward commitment. That was what was lacking. 'Requirements' translates *mišpāṭ*, 'judgment' (NKJV), but referring more widely to all acts of God's kingly administration, and so here that which he ordains as the standard of conduct for his people (5:4).

2. Unwise Conduct (8:8-12)

This passage reflects a period when Jeremiah was in conflict with the religious leaders of the community, probably during the early years of Jehoiakim.

8. The questioning begins again in an emphatic manner, but it is not immediately clear who is being interrogated. **How can you** (plural) **say, 'We are wise, for** ('and' of accompanying circumstances) **we have the law of the LORD'?** In v. 9 it seems to be a particular group who are being described as 'the wise', but here it is rather the people as a whole who are making the claim to be wise. Once again this need not be taken as a precise quote, but as a dramatic representation of the attitude they displayed (cf. 2:20). They felt in no doubt that their claim to be wise would stand scrutiny because they could say 'the law of the LORD is with us'. The words may point to more than a claim to possess copies of the law; there is also an implicit assumption that they have mastered the law: 'We know what it is all about, and so we have wisdom.'

The next part of the verse is notoriously difficult to exegete, not because of difficulty with any of the words used, but because its overall meaning is obscure: **when** (*ʾākēn*, 3:20, introducing a strong contrast to the behaviour expected of those possessing the law of the LORD) **actually** (*hinnēh*, 'look!', together these two words are highly emphatic) **the lying pen of the scribes has handled it[6] falsely.** Literally, 'to/for the deception (*šeqer*, 5:2) pen of deception of scribes has made ⌞it⌟.' The 'pen' was probably a reed sharpened to a point, used to write on papyrus or parchment (cf. 17:1). The mention of a pen reflects back on the law of the LORD to show that it is a written document that is in view, and not just oral tradition.

Scribes (literally, 'writers') were a class of people who became prominent in the period after the Exile, not for their writing abilities, but because they undertook to explain and teach what they copied,

---

6. The Massoretic Text reads *ʿāśâ*, 'he made', with the object to be inferred. It could be pointed with mappiq in the *he* as *ʿāśāh*, 'he made it (f.)', so that the feminine suffix referred back to the *tôrâ*, 'law' (cf. BHS).

principally the Law of Moses and the various regulations connected with it. Scribes are first mentioned in Scripture as military officers attending to the mustering of troops (Judg. 5:14; 2 Kgs. 25:19; Jer. 52:25). The need for documentation in royal administration led to scribes becoming prominent court officials (2 Sam. 8:17; 20:25; 1 Kgs. 4:3; 2 Kgs. 12:10; Isa. 19:11-12), and it is probably scribes who are referred to as Hezekiah's men in Prov. 25:1. Based on procedures in the ancient Near East generally, there would have been a school attached to the Jerusalem Temple/palace complex at which all scribes were educated, both those who went on to be royal officials and those who were involved in the preservation and transmission of religious documents. 1 Chron. 2:35 suggests that they were organised on the basis of families or guilds, and they are mentioned as a class of Levites in the reign of Josiah (2 Chron. 34:13). Possibly Shaphan the secretary/scribe, who plays a significant role in the finding of the Book of the Law (2 Kgs. 22:3-14), was the head of the Jerusalem scribal school at the time.

But what were the scribes doing? The answers given to this reflect one's views of the process by which the Old Testament came into existence. Earlier critical scholars suggested that they might have been writing up Deuteronomy for the first time, particularly Deut. 12:1-7, with a desire to centralise worship in the Jerusalem Temple, and that it was this of which Jeremiah did not approve. McKane (1965:102-112) argued that the scribes here were legal scholars, identifying them, as many have done, with 'those who deal with the law' (2:8). However, he goes on to develop this in terms of a particular view about the origin of wisdom literature. These scribes were conforming the old essentially amoral wisdom literature to the orthodoxy of the law. McKane argues that this passage shows that to the prophet what they were doing seemed a pen and paper exercise, ingenious no doubt, but largely irrelevant in the face of the imminent catastrophe facing Jerusalem. There is also the idea of the conformity that they sought to bring to wisdom in terms of the law being essentially spurious and misaligned. They used the vocabulary of wisdom, but they rejected the prophetic word, and so were unable to provide counsel of worth.

The traditional conservative view of the passage is that those who teach the Law have used its authority to present a message that is at variance with it. The problem with that understanding is that teaching at that time was conducted orally, and the deception attributed in the passage to the scribes is that which is wrought by their pen. It is essentially a written activity that is in view. Acknowledging this, Lundbom (1999:514) argues that we do not know what written law is being referred to, and rendering 'falsely' as 'for The Lie', he considers that 'the lying pen of the scribes has made some written Torah into a work honouring the Lie', that is, Baal. This is a highly speculative suggestion which lacks any substantive corroboration.

The variety of scholarly views may arise from a misunderstanding of what the passage is actually saying. Drawing on the insights of the medieval Jewish teacher Kimchi, the NJPS version renders the second part of the verse, 'Assuredly, for naught has the pen laboured, for naught the scribes.' This breaks up the three-part construct chain 'pen of deception of scribes' into three separate units, and understands *šeqer* not as 'falsehood' but as 'uselessly' (cf. 1 Sam. 25:21, and note AV translation 'in vain'). While this approach leads to an imbalance in the structure of the poetic line, it does yield a very appropriate sense. The scribes were not engaged in any deceptive behaviour, but in doing what they should, producing and making available copies of the Law. The incident of 2 Kgs. 22:8-13 indicates that copies of the Law had become scarce during the persecuting years of Manasseh, and so part of Josiah's reform would have been to make it available again. It would not, of course, have been widely available—the economics of the situation would have prevented that. But those whose duty it was to teach the people would no longer have themselves to rely on oral transmission of the Law, but would have been able to consult accurate written copies. However, all that activity was useless if the people treated the mere possession of a scroll of the Law as what was really important—as they did with the ark (3:16) or the Temple (7:4)—while refusing to practice what it commands. Salvation does not derive from the number of copies of Scripture one possesses; what matters is that one's life be responsive to its injunctions and shaped by its precepts.

9. The mention of the wise (*ḥăkāmîm*) in v. 9 is probably a reference to the group (9:23) who are the leaders and opinion formers of the community, acknowledged as competent and efficient scholars and administrators. They would all be scribes. Some might be teachers at the Temple school, but many would have been connected rather with the civil or political establishment. It was from their ranks that royal counsellors would be drawn (McKane 1965:38). At the time of Josiah's reform such men acknowledged the standards of the Law, but they did not practice them. **The wise will be put to shame; they will be dismayed and trapped.** 'Dismayed' (<*ḥātat*, 1:17) points to their psychological brokenness. 'Trapped' (<√*lākad*) may indicate capture by enemy forces, or being ensnared by adversaries more generally (5:26: 18:22; *HALOT*, 530). The verbs are generally taken as prophetic perfects describing a future situation perceived as certain. **Since they have rejected the word of the LORD, what wisdom do they have?**[7] Though it is possible to argue that the word of the LORD is a specific reference to Jeremiah's message, it seems better to take it to include all divine revelation. In rejecting what has been divinely disclosed the leaders of the community have acted unwisely; additionally they have cut themselves off from the fount of true wisdom.

10-12. The judgment to come upon the unwise leaders is then spelled out more fully, not directly in terms of foreign invasion, but through some of its consequences. **Therefore** (*lākēn*, of judgment) **I will give their wives to other men and their fields to new owners.** 'New owners' are 'those who dispossess', that is make themselves masters of a thing (49:2; Mic. 1:15), possibly but not necessarily 'conquerors' (NRSV). The reason for the covenant curse is then stated in words that correspond to what has already been said in 6:13-15[8]: 'for' (*kî*) **'from the least to the greatest, all are greedy for gain; prophets and priests alike, all practise deceit. They dress**[9] **the wound of my people**/'daughter of my people' **as though it were not serious. "Peace, peace," they say, when there is no peace. Are they ashamed of their loathsome conduct? No, they have no shame at all; they do not even know how to blush. So they will fall among the fallen; they will be brought down when they are punished,' says the LORD.** Most of vv. 10-12 are omitted in LXX, as it generally does with repeated passages, but the words fit well into this context. This is the conduct of the so-called wise, particularly those who act as religious teachers and officials. What they have their eye on is unjust 'gain'. They do not regard the word of the LORD, but act autonomously, making up the rules to suit themselves. This is the opposite of walking in the way of the righteous (Ps. 119:36; Isa. 33:15; 56:11; 57:17). So the LORD will act to bring them down/make them stumble. The groups who had duped the people will be caught up in the calamity which will overtake them all; there will certainly be no exemption for those who bear greater responsibility for what has happened.

---

7. *wəḥokmat-meh*: the interrogative is found in a construct chain, 'wisdom of what sort?' (*IBHS* §18.1e; GKC §137b).

8. The differences include 'daughter of my people' (v. 11) for 'my people' (6:14); 'even' (*gam*) omitted in v. 12, though present in 6:15; 'to blush' niphal of *kālam* (v. 12), hiphil (6:15); 'they are punished' (*pəqudātām*, 'their punishment' v. 12) in place of 'I punish them' (*pəqadtîm*, 6:15).

9. *wayrappû* for *wayrappəʾû* with the quiescent *aleph* omitted from the spelling (GKC §23f).

3. The Unfruitful Vineyard (8:13-17)

In this section the thought introduced at the end of v. 12 regarding the coming judgment of the LORD is developed further. Whereas 6:13-15 led into a continuing exploration of the causes of the situation described, when Jeremiah repeats the words here, he proceeds to show how delusive the false teaching was when it asserted that there will be peace, when in fact there is no peace. The catastrophe awaiting the deceived community is again portrayed in terms of the arrival of the foe from the north. The section is bracketed by two divine descriptions of the coming calamity (vv. 13, 17). However, vv. 14-16 describe the impending devastation of the land through a report placed on the lips of the people as the enemy forces his way into their country and the long-threatened disaster starts to engulf them.

13. Unfortunately the NIV note for the last sentence of this verse, that the meaning of the Hebrew is uncertain, applies in measure also to the introductory words. The Hebrew text as it stands may be rendered, 'Gathering I will make an end of them'.[10] Though an infinitive absolute before a verb from a different root cannot be ruled out (a very similar construction occurs in Zeph. 1:2), it would be an unusual expression. It has therefore been suggested that the consonants be repointed[11] to yield **'I will take away their harvest,' declares the LORD.** The agriculture of the land will be devastated, not by drought or pestilence, but by the enemy forces the LORD will bring on his people. **There will be no grapes on the vine** resumes the imagery of 5:10 and 6:9. **There will be no figs on the tree, and their leaves will wither.** The leaves of a well-watered tree do not wither; that this has happened perhaps suggests a drought. Similar figures are used in Isa. 34:4; 40:7-8 of the impact of divine judgment.

Another interpretation is possible by taking the LORD as the harvester coming on the people and finding them a fruitless vine and fig tree, and then saying by way of judgment that the land and blessings of the covenant which he had given them will be taken from them as a curse for their covenant unfruitfulness.

The last part of the verse is terse and obscure, and is omitted by the REB, following the LXX which did not understand it. It reads, 'and I

---

10. *ʾāsōp*, qal infinite absolute <√*ʾāsap*, 'to gather', followed by *ʾăsîpēm*, hiphil imperfect <√*sûp* hiphil, 'make an end of', with pronominal suffix.

11. Both BHS and *HALOT* (747) suggest reading the form *ʾōsēp*, a qal imperfect contracted from *ʾeʾĕsōp* (<√*ʾsp*), 'I will gather/bring in' followed by a noun form, *ʾăsîpām*, 'their harvest'.

gave to them they will pass by them.'[12] The NIV translation, **What I have given them will be taken from them**, is as good an attempt as any to render the words, taking the unexpressed object of 'give' as the land and its produce, which is also understood to be the subject of the second verb. It implies the reversal of the bounty that the LORD had given to his people in the land. They had broken his covenant, and so they can no longer enjoy the blessing he had provided for them in the land.

14. There is then a switch from the words of the LORD to the response the people will give in the envisaged time of judgment: **Why are we sitting here?** (cf. 2 Kgs. 7:3). They have heard the news of the enemy coming, and it has so confounded them that they were 'sitting' appalled and unable to do anything about the situation. They give counsel to each other to take such action as seems obvious. **Gather together! Let us flee to the fortified cities!** This advice had been given earlier (4:5). The cities were the obvious place to make for in the event of invasion. But this is no normal invasion, and when it comes on the people, they are going to recognise the hand of God in it and be overwhelmed by their situation. The action they take is not designed to organise their defence, far less a counter-attack; it is a pathetic gesture by those who have been totally unnerved. **And perish there**. 'Perish' is from the root *dāmâ* for which three roots are identified: (I) 'to be like, resemble' (cf. 6:2); (II) 'to stand still, be motionless/silent', which lies behind the NKJV rendering here; (III) 'to perish'. They will recognise that their fate is sealed, and state the reason for it to be: **for** (*kî*) **the LORD our God has doomed us to perish and given us poisoned water to drink.** 'Doomed ... to perish' (<√*dāmâ* III hiphil, 'to make to perish') acknowledges that their destiny is by divine decree. 'Poisoned water' is literally 'waters of *rōʾš*', a bitter and poisonous plant, from which an infusion could be made (9:15; 23:15; cf. Lam. 3:5-19). The expression always occurs figuratively, and the exact identity of the plant is unknown. Poisoned water may just be a reference to a deadly situation, particularly if, as here, they are gathered in a besieged city, but there may be a more specific reference to Num. 5:11-31, where a wife who was suspected of being unfaithful was given waters of bitterness to drink as a test of her fidelity. The people are belatedly recognising the hand of God in their circumstances, and they know they will fail any test of their fidelity. **Because** (*kî*) **we have sinned against him.** They acknowledge that the ultimate root of their problem

12. A clause as the object of a verb is sometimes added without relative or conjunction (Ps. 50:21; Judg. 9:48; Isa. 48:8; Hos. 7:2; cf. GKC §155n).

is that their conduct has been contrary to the requirements of their suzerain, and offensive to him (2:35).

15. The people are also portrayed as trying to get their befuddled thoughts straight as realisation dawns on them of what had undermined their relationship with God. They had entertained false expectations and desires. **We hoped for**[13] **peace** (6:14), that is, they had been completely taken in by the message of the false prophets (v. 11; 14:19). They had been sure things were all right with them, and that the message of Jeremiah could be safely ignored. The opinions of the experts had been listened to, and all the more readily because their advice reinforced the preferences of the people as regards the way they should live. But the outcome will prove the majority view and expert advice to be equally unfounded. **But no good has come.** It was not covenant blessing they were experiencing, but covenant curse. They say they had hoped **for a time of healing** (<√*rāpā'*, 'to heal'; used also in v. 11, 'dress'). Perhaps this recognises that something had been wrong, but they had thought that the LORD as the divine healer was so satisfied with them that he would sort matters out for them. **But there was only terror** (<√*bā'at*). This root predominantly expresses the terror of a lesser individual who is called before a superior. It does not always imply fear of judgment, but may be a response to something not fully understood (Isa. 21:4 NASB). Here it describes the horrible realities of judgment and unwelcome death as the enemy forces invade the land with speed and strength.

16. It is uncertain who speaks next. Perhaps Jeremiah himself adds this description of the situation he has been shown, or it may be that these are still words on the lips of the people as they explain their terror. **The snorting of the enemy's**[14] **horses is heard from Dan.** Dan was the northernmost point of the land (4:15). The invasion of the foe from the north has begun. **At the neighing** (<√*nāḥar*, used of bellows in 6:29) **of their stallions** (*'abbîr*, 'strong one', is here used for a mighty steed or charger; GKC §132[2]) **the whole land trembles.** The terrifying sound is that of approaching chariot forces relentlessly moving forward with irresistible might. **They have come to devour the land and everything in it, the city and all who live there.** 'Come' picks up 'flee' (v. 14; both √<*bô'*, 'to enter') at the start of the

13. The infinitive absolute *qawwēh* is used for the finite verb so that the Hebrew expression is more terse: 'hoping for peace, but no good.'

14. Literally, 'his horses'. The reference to the enemy has to be gathered from the context and knowledge of Jeremiah's previous statements, but 'His horses' (NKJV) is improbable despite Calvin (1850, 1:444).

central section. Probably the contrast here between land and city (both without the article) is intended to be taken as a comprehensive description like 'town and country'. Nothing escapes the attention of the invading forces as they sweep the land clean.

17. There is then added a saying of the LORD, which describes the impending invasion in metaphorical terms. The introductory *kî* indicates that disaster will happen because of the LORD's declaration against them. **'See, I will send venomous snakes among you, vipers that cannot be charmed, and they will bite[15] you,' declares the LORD.** *nəḥāšîm* is a generic word for snakes, which is then followed by *ṣipʿōnîm* in apposition to point out that a particularly poisonous variety is in view, 'vipers', but precise identification of the species is uncertain. Possibly more significant is the closeness of the word to *ṣāpôn*, 'north'. These northern-style snakes are a representation of the ominous foe from the north (4:6). 'Charmed' seems to indicate a process of conjuring by whispering, but these snakes will be impervious to such stratagems. The popular belief that vipers could be charmed is referred to in Ps. 58:5-6 and Eccl. 10:11 (cf. Isa. 47:11-12). Though real snakes may be part of the divine curse upon covenant breakers (Deut. 32:24), this is a metaphorical description of the invading army which will not be diverted from biting and spreading its poison. This may be a hint of a retrograde Exodus by mentioning a voluntary return through snake-infested territory (Isa. 30:6). Perhaps also there is a reflection of the incident in Num. 21:6-9, but on that occasion there was the possibility of a cure. This time there will be none.

B. PROPHETIC GRIEF (8:18–9:11) [8:18–9:10]

There is no dispute that this division expresses profound grief over the situation that has arisen in Judah and Jerusalem, and over what is still to come. The questions that arise are over the number and identity of the speakers, particularly who it is that gives voice to grief in 8:18, 21, 23 and 9:9: the LORD or the prophet? It is agreed that the voice of the people is heard in the 'we' of v. 20, but are they engaged in dialogue with the LORD alone, or is the prophet also a participant in these exchanges? The strongest argument for a dialogue with the LORD is that he is the only identified speaker in the division as is evidenced by 'declares the LORD' (9:3, 6, 9) and the full introductory formula in 9:7.

15. The use of the piel rather than the qal may suggest a plurality of incidents, or may reflect the metaphorical nature of the biting (*IBHS* §24.3.3c).

But that does not determine the passage as a divine monologue, particularly in 8:18-22 where there is no formal indication of any speaker. Though the motif of the weeping God has gained popularity in recent years and parallels have been adduced from neighbouring cultures (Roberts 1992), it remains difficult to integrate the strong expressions used here into the thought of the book as a whole. It is more cogent to see the expressions as primarily those of the prophet himself. However, this is not to deny that the LORD himself is grieved by his people's rebellion and the breakdown that has occurred in the relationship between them. The prophet's emotion here does not run contrary to what he has been made aware of in the divine council.

The cut-off between chapters 8 and 9 differs between English and Hebrew with 8:22 of English versions being equivalent to 9:1 of the Hebrew text, so that Hebrew verse numbers lag one behind the English throughout chapter 9.

1. The Physician of Gilead (8:18-22)

In this section the prophet tells of his grief at what he has seen. He cannot suppress his emotion because the dire ruin of his people pierces him through. There are those who argue that this section tells us nothing of Jeremiah's own feelings, and that what is presented here is a speech of a personified Jerusalem, or Zion, indicating how she felt over the destruction of the people. It is difficult to understand who this Zion is meant to be. The prophet, though part of the people, can stand over against them, but what group is indicated by Zion, as distinct from the whole people? This just seems to be an attempt to minimise the evidence regarding the person and personality of Jeremiah.

First Jeremiah speaks and we are brought into the thought-world of the prophet (v. 18). Then we overhear the prophet's portrayal of the people speaking as they will do in exile (v. 19a). A divine word of judgment intervenes in v. 19b, and this is followed first by further speech from the people (v. 20), and then by the prophet telling of his personal reaction (v. 21) before posing a puzzled challenge (v. 22), which flows into the words of 9:1-2. In this way Jeremiah communicates his own reaction to the message entrusted to him and seeks to evoke a similar response of perplexity from his audience. The possibility is still open that they will react appropriately to what they are being told, even though subsequent descriptions of the people (9:2-6) do not render that outcome very probable.

18. The beginning of the verse is difficult to construe. One way is to take the words as expressing the intensity of the prophet's grief: 'There is no cure for my grief' (REB, cf. RSV). This involves dividing one obscure word in the original into two with other adjustments.[16] Alternatively, the phrase points to God as the one who enables the prophet to bear up under the burden imposed on him. This is done by trying to find a meaning for the obscure word, as in the NIV, **O my Comforter in sorrow**,[17] or 'I would comfort myself in sorrow' (NKJV). Both approaches have in common the fact of Jeremiah's grief, not over his personal situation, but over what will come upon the people. The intensity of his reaction leads him to pray for relief (2 Cor. 1:3-4). **My heart is faint within me** (Lam. 1:22). A sickness which strikes at the heart is the most serious of ailments (Prov. 6:15; 29:1; 14:30; 15:13, 15); the prospect of what is about to happen has so inwardly overwhelmed Jeremiah that he has become weak and distraught.

19. Interpretation of the scene envisaged in this verse depends on the rendering of *mēʾereṣ marḥaqqîm*. The NRSV takes it as a description of Judah: 'from far and wide in the land' (cf. Isa. 33:17 NIV). What then follows is the confident speech of the people as they expect the LORD to intervene on their behalf, and v. 19b is divine remonstrance that such an expectation is inconsistent with their conduct. However, the people ignore such words of warning and blithely continue to expect the LORD to act in terms of the timetable they have set (v. 20). In the face of such obstinacy and spiritual blindness the prophet recognises that disaster will come upon them, and in anticipation of that already feels its impact himself (v. 21). He then wonders why there has been no cure for their fatal disease (v. 22).

The alternative translation is based round a scenario where the prophet has had revealed to him a future scene of the exiled people, who are perplexed by what has happened to them. He draws a vivid word picture of this for his hearers. **Listen to the cry of my people from a land far away: 'Is the LORD not in Zion? Is her King no**

16. The Massoretic Text has *mablîgîtî*. This, when divided in two and adjusted, would become *mibbəlî gəhôt*, 'beyond recovery'. Some treat this as part of v. 18; others following the LXX add it to v. 17 as descriptive of the snake bites, and begin v. 18, 'Grief has come upon me', adjusting *ʿălê* (a lengthened form of the preposition) to *ʿālay*, 'upon me'.

17. The root *bālag* occurs only in the hiphil. It is found in Amos 5:9 in the sense 'to cause to beam or shine upon', and intransitively in Ps. 39:14; Job 9:27; 10:20, 'to beam with joy'. Here the form is that of a noun derived from the hiphil of the verb, 'that which causes one to beam with joy' = 'comfort, consolation'.

longer there?' 'My people' is 'the daughter of my people' (as in v. 11; cf. 4:11), a tender and affectionate address which is used both by the LORD and by the prophet, and personifies the people as an individual woman. So these plaintive words have been revealed to the prophet as the reaction of those who have been taken into exile, perhaps in 605 BC or later in 597 BC. It is difficult to see them being used after the destruction of the city. In the distant land of their exile they are trying to rationalise what has happened. They had been sure that the Temple presence of the LORD in Zion guaranteed security for the city. It was his place; how then could he have permitted all these things to come upon his people? Could not the King (Isa. 33:22) defend his kingdom?

The exiles' two questions are then taken up by a question of the LORD which interrupts their chain of thought, but expresses clearly the fundamental factor in the situation: **Why have they provoked me to anger** (7:18) **with their images, with their worthless foreign idols?**[18] If they really believed that the LORD was present in Zion, then they would not have indulged in behaviour that was such a blatant contradiction of his presence there. The people are portrayed as being unable to see the discrepancy between their confession and their conduct. There was no way the LORD could be expected to stay in his abode in Zion if others were given residence there also.

20. The people then resume their lament. Their language is probably proverbial: **The harvest is past, the summer has ended** (<√*kālâ*, 5:3), **and we are not saved.** Our last chance has gone. The harvest is that of the wheat crop in May/June. If it proved to be a disaster, then the people could always look forward to the fruit crop that would be gathered in the late summer months of July/August. But once that has failed there can be no hope of deliverance from famine. But it is not agriculture that is at the forefront of their minds, but the conditions prevailing in Judah. The beliefs of Zion theology had led them to expect divine deliverance, even at the last minute. That has not happened, and the people in exile are not going to be able to account for what has befallen them.

21. Jeremiah then resumes from v. 18 his expression of how distraught he personally is by the disaster coming on his people. **Since my people**/'the daughter of my people' **are crushed, I am crushed**/'on account of the breaking of the daughter of my people (v. 19), I am

---

18. *bəhablê nēkār*, 'with nothingnesses (cf. 2:5) of foreign (cf. 5:19)' . Either idols is to be understood and *hebel* refers to the totality of foreign religion, or idols are referred to by the plural of *hebel*, 'with foreign idols' (NKJV).

broken' again uses the root *šābar*, 'to break', first in a nominal formation and then as a verb (2:13; 2:20; 5:5). The breaking of the people may be the physical disaster that will come upon them, but it goes beyond that to their spiritual condition (4:6). Jeremiah cannot keep himself aloof from the bewilderment that will come upon his fellow countrymen. What he sees engulfing them brings grief to him already. The horror of the tragedy is intensified for him because he knows it is all so unnecessary: they had been warned. **I mourn, and horror grips me.** 'I mourn' is literally, 'I am black' (<√*qādar*, 'to be dark, mourn', 4:28; cf. Pss. 38:6; 42:9). Dark thoughts oppress him. The burden of being the LORD's prophet to an unresponsive people lay not only in the difficulty of putting up with their rejection of his message, but also in his own vivid apprehension of what was coming upon them. 'Horror' (*šammâ*, 2:15) has him in its grasp. He did not exult over their fate; it grieved him because he was certain that the LORD's word was going to come true.

22. In terms of the metaphor of wounding that he has introduced, Jeremiah then wonders if nothing could be done for the people. **Is there no balm in Gilead?** Gilead lay to the east of the Jordan between the Sea of Galilee and the Dead Sea. It was a rugged and wooded area (Gen. 37:25; Ezek. 27:17) that had long been associated with an aromatic resin which was used as a soothing ointment and also gave a pleasant odour (46:11; 51:8). The plant from which it was extracted has not been identified. This rhetorical question expects the answer, 'Of course there is balm in Gilead'. **Is there no physician**/'healer' **there?** The area that produced the balm would of course have people who were experts at applying it effectively. Again the question expects the answer, 'Yes; there are those who can apply it.' There then follows the third question that makes up the characteristic Jeremianic triplet in which two ordinary questions set up a scenario, the consequences of which are then brought out with a third question beginning 'Why?' (2:14, 31; 8:4-5; 14:19; 22:28; 49:41; Holladay 1962a:48; 1962b:495-6). **Why then** (*kî* seems to be used emphatically here) **is there no healing for the wound of my people**/'the daughter of my people' (4:11)**?** 'Healing' (*'ărukâ*) refers to the 'lengthening' of the flesh over a wound as new skin grows in (30:17; 33:6). If the medicine exists, and the doctors exist, then surely a cure can be effected. But Jeremiah is not just talking about physical injuries, although they would abound during a military invasion. He is asserting the need for a spiritual cure, and is pointing to the LORD himself who was viewed as the Healer *par excellence* in Israel. So when he poses the question as to why there is no healing, there can be only one answer: 'There has been no repentance.'

2. A Fountain of Tears (9:1-2) [MT 8:23–9:1]

Arising from the idea that speech of the prophet and of God are frequently indistinguishable in poetry, several modern commentators have followed Heschel (1962:103-39) in taking these verses as expressing, if not the *pathos* (expressed suffering) of God, then a combination of the *pathos* of the LORD and Jeremiah. However, the Confessions, in which the prophet clearly speaks in his own name in a poetic section, militate against the idea of a fusing of divine and prophetic expression, and it seems more appropriate to read these verses as a dialogue in which both the prophet and God speak.

1. As the Hebrew enumeration recognises, this verse is clearly linked with what precedes, but it has even closer links with what follows. A chapter break does not fit naturally either before or after it. Though Jeremiah no doubt hoped that the intensity of his own emotion might have an impact on the spiritual insensitivity of his fellow countrymen, his expression of anguish was not an artificial exercise to stimulate a response, but reflects in hyperbolic language how deeply he was exercised by the situation he reported. **Oh, that**[19] **my head were a spring of water and my eyes a fountain of tears!** 'Spring of water' is just 'water'/'waters' (NKJV, RSV), possibly a 'pool' (41:12). 'Fountain' translates *māqôr* ('spring', 2:13), a constant and reliable source of water. If he had such an inexhaustible supply, then Jeremiah's feelings are such that he claims, **I would weep**[20] **day and night for the slain of my people**/'daughter of my people' (4:11). Although weeping (<√*bākâ*) is here connected with shedding tears, primarily 'weeping is associated with the voice; Semites do not weep quietly, but aloud' (*TWOT* #243). If he could, his grief would be unremitting so intense is the disaster awaiting the nation.

2. There are commentators who make the LORD the speaker in v. 2,

19. Verse 1 begins *mî-yittēn*, 'Who will give?' and v. 2 *mî-yittənēnî*, 'Who will give me?', both standard idioms for expressing a contrary-to-fact wish (GKC §151b).

20. The cohortative here (and in the same construction in the next verse, rendered 'so that I might leave' in the NIV) expresses the resolution of a wish, 'If I had …, then I would …' (GKC §108f). But though the cohortative indicates the inclination of Jeremiah's heart, there is an associated element of dubiety (*IBHS* §34.5.2b).

which they link closely with v. 3, which is undoubtedly divine speech (e.g. Craigie et al. 1991:143). But while there is a connection, the link is not so close as to require such a reading. The fact that the introductory words and the construction as a whole are so similar to v. 1 makes it clear that the speaker continues to be Jeremiah, expressing a second sincerely felt desire, but one which he recognises as impossible of fulfilment. There is no incongruity between this and the preceding verse. There Jeremiah had expressed his anguish over the fate that was going to overwhelm his people because of their intransigence in sin; now he expresses his revulsion at their sin. His sympathy for them was not a matter of condoning their conduct. The prophet had a commitment to the standards of the LORD's covenant, and he wished to see the people share it. But they do not, and he therefore wishes to get away from those who are so hostile to the LORD. **Oh, that I had in the desert a lodging place for travellers** (Ps. 55:6-8). The 'desert'/ 'wilderness' (2:2) does not indicate that he wished to live among sand dunes, but rather in an uninhabited part of the land. The lodging place would be a shelter of some sort where travellers would rest overnight before going on their way in the morning. Though it would generally be a very basic structure, the point of the observation is not that Jeremiah would be prepared to put up with discomfort. Instead it is the fact that there would be few, if any, permanent residents in such a spot. Jeremiah wants to get away from the people and their sin, but it is not the life of a hermit he is dreaming of, just a life without responsibility. At such a wilderness khan travellers would keep him as well informed as any about the events of the day, but he would feel no obligation towards those who, come morning, would be on their way.

So that I might leave my people and go away from them. There is still a basic identification with the people. They are 'my people', but his spirit is so grieved by their behaviour that he wants to abandon them, that is, his prophetic ministry to them. Of course, he did not. The expression of the difficulties under which he laboured in his prophetic work are a measure of the steadfastness Jeremiah displayed as a prophet of the LORD. He had been promised divine assistance in what had always been seen as a very heavy task, and though he here knows the urge to be quit of the responsibility, he did not in fact shirk the task, but kept at it for over forty years.

The reason for his revulsion is stated: **for** (*kî*) **they are all adulterers** (<√*nā'ap*, 3:8)**, a crowd of unfaithful people**. 'Adultery' has already been used as an expression for their spiritual entanglement with the Baal cults (2:20; 3:8-9), and it might be that is what is intended here. But the following verses bring out that as covenant loyalty to the LORD declined, there was a corresponding breakdown in the social cohesion of the land. Jeremiah may well have literal adultery in mind here as a sign of the breakdown in the marriage bond that cements society together. The second phrase 'an assembly (*ʿăṣārâ*) of unfaithful ones' employs a term that is ordinarily used for those gathered at sacred meetings, either consecrated to the LORD (Lev. 23:26) or to Baal (2 Kgs. 10:20). But the people are not a congregation of the faithful, but of the unfaithful (<√*bāgad*, 3:7). Their conduct with respect to each other lacked trustworthiness, and they had no true commitment to the LORD—that was their new religion.

3. Social Breakdown (9:3-6) [MT 9:2-5]

Jeremiah goes on to justify his description of the people as unfaithful by citing two divine sayings (v. 3, and vv. 4-6) which also portray the breakdown of social relationships in Judah. Both focus on sins of speech, which are particularly liable to occur in the context of intimate personal interaction. When truthfulness is no longer customary in ordinary speech, the fabric of everyday living is corrupted. But this is not just a matter of socio-political mores. It originates with lack of knowledge of the LORD (v. 3), and with deliberate rejection of such knowledge (v. 6). Ethical behaviour in the commonplace aspects of life can only be adequately sustained by acknowledging all of life to be before the LORD and subject to his standards.

3. The LORD describes the behaviour of the people, which he shows is despicable. It is difficult to decide how the Hebrew words should be split into clauses. The NIV text divides the lines in accordance with the Massoretic accents which take 'lies' with what precedes, 'like a bow, to shoot lies', where 'to shoot' is a supplement. Holladay (1986, 1:296), with greater plausibility, finds two clauses: 'They have drawn their tongue, their bow is falsehood.' In that case the tongue is metaphorically the arrow (cf. v. 8). If one ignores the Massoretic division, then 'They have grown strong in the land for falsehood, and not for truth' (NRSV) seems the most probable translation.[21]

They make ready their tongue like a bow, to shoot lies. The bow was prepared for use by stepping on it while the arrow was fitted, but in this case the arrows were the lies (*šeqer*) which their tongue shot

21. Other translations take 'falsehood and not truth' as the subject of 'are strong' (REB, NASB, RSV), but the verb *gābərû* is plural, not singular, and the preposition *lə* occurs before 'truth', though that may be treated as an emphatic *lamedh*.

out. A similar picture is found in Ps. 64:3-6. They are viewed as a force of mighty men who are misusing their power. **It is not by truth** (or 'in reference to/with regard to truth', GKC §119u) **that they triumph in the land.** The NIV margin translation 'they are not valiant for truth' preserves the traditional rendering of the verb (<√*gābar*, 'to be strong/mighty'), which is connected with the strength associated with a warrior. The truth that is being spoken of is trustworthiness one with another, so that the picture is of a society that has lost the capacity to function coherently, because speech no longer conveys truth and no one's word can be relied on. Instead they give expression to falsehood. But in Scripture the utterance of the mouth is indicative of what a person is within (Matt. 12:34-35). That is why these charges are of such grave significance. The lies they so easily tell reveal how far their inner lives are alienated from God.

Their power and influence in the land is set up on a false basis 'for' (*kî*) **they go from one sin to another.** 'Go from/out' may be used of an army going to battle, and that may be the thought here: these 'warriors' proceed from one act of evil (*rāʿâ*) to another. They are not satisfied with one display of wickedness, from evil speech they move on to the next outrage they can devise. The reason for such atrocious conduct is not hard to find. **'They do not acknowledge me,' declares the LORD.** The expression is the same as 4:22: 'They do not know me'. This lack of knowledge is not at a formal, intellectual level, but at the level of inner commitment to the LORD and consequent willingness to live by the expressed standards of his covenant.

4. The same theme is taken up again in vv. 4-6, but this time in the form of a general warning. Was the LORD giving Jeremiah a message which reflected his own experience (12:6; 18:18)? **Beware of your friends; do not trust your brothers**/'any brother'. 'Beware' and 'do not trust' are plural imperatives addressed to the community at large, to each man with respect to his 'friend'/'neighbour' (*rēaʿ*, v. 8). While 'neighbour' and 'brother' may be used synonymously here, it is probable that 'neighbour' refers to the 'covenant' community in general, and 'brother' to the more immediate family. But for both, the warning is the same: they are not to be relied upon. **For every brother is a deceiver,**[22] or as the NIV margin puts it, 'Every brother is a deceiving Jacob'. The name of Jacob is hidden in the Hebrew wordplay (Lee 1999:93) and so the comparison is more subtle than that found in

22. The verb *yaʿqōb*, 'he deceives/overreaches' is probably pointed this way (and not as *yaʿăqōb*) to distinguish it from the proper name *yaʿăqōb*, 'Jacob' (GKC §63c).

Hos. 12:2. The verb (<√ʿ*āqab*, 'to seize the heel, overreach, deceive') refers back to the behaviour of Jacob in Gen. 27:36, where Esau complains that Jacob supplanted him. The fact that it is particularly his brother he deceived probably points to 'brother' in this verse indicating more immediate family (Isa. 9:19; Mic. 7:6). The descendants of Jacob were living up to the reputation of their forefather; the social decay of Israel sprang from the outworking of a family trait whereby rather than seeking each other's good, brothers sought to hinder each other for their own advancement, a mark of societal disintegration in every age (Matt. 10:36). To complete the chiastic pattern (friend, brother: brother, friend) the verse concludes with **and every friend a slanderer**/'goes about ⌞as⌟ a slanderer' (*rākîl*, 6:28), which may well reflect on what is said in Lev. 19:16-18, but which also serves to pick up that the slanderer is not a static figure. He is one who has to carry his false tales from place to place to undermine the reputation of another.

5. The lack of personal integrity that prevails in the community is described further. **Friend deceives**[23] **friend, and no one speaks the truth.** 'Deceive' (<√*tālal*) 'seems to stress the lying or deception as a deliberate responsible act of the person involved' (*NIDOTTE*, 4:299). The basis for social trust and cooperation is undermined if speech no longer conveys truth (*ʾĕmet*); reliable communication is no longer possible when what is uttered becomes a device for concealing one's inner motivation. **They have taught their tongues to lie**, 'to speak falsehood (*šeqer*)'. The implication is that this was not something that came easily. Lying required effort and trouble, planning and fore-thought, to carry it out successfully. But they were willing—more than willing—to make this effort. **They weary themselves with sinning.**[24] The infinitive absolute 'sinning' (<√ʿ*āwâ*, hiphil 'to go astray, act wrongly/ twistedly'; cf. 2:22) precedes the verb to add emphasis. One might have thought such exertion would have been for a nobler cause.

6. The verse begins with a switch in reference from the people as a whole to Jeremiah. The LORD says to him, **You** (sing.) **live in the midst of deception.**[25] His place of residence is there. **'In their deceit they refuse to acknowledge me,' declares the LORD.** 'Deception'

23. For the hiphil with a non-elided *he*, see GKC §53q.

24. The NRSV rendering 'are too weary to repent' is based on the LXX.

25. In place of the awkward Massoretic reading, 'Your residing in midst of deception', the NRSV again follows the LXX and reads, 'Oppression upon oppression, deceit upon deceit!' (cf. REB), where oppression is more specifically imposing usurious interest charges.

and 'deceit' (*mirmâ*, 5:27) refer to their lifestyle which is so given over to cheating and trickery that there is no place for God. This is an intensification of v. 3 where the fact of their not having a true inner commitment to the LORD is stated. Now it is emphasised that this has come about because of an obstinate refusal on their part.

4. Divine Refining (9:7-9) [MT 9:6-8]

7. Refusal to acknowledge their king is not a course that can be adopted with impunity. It is therefore unsurprising that the divine response follows. Although introduced by **therefore** (*lākēn*, 2:9), which often functions to indicate that divine judgment follows on from misconduct, here **this is what the LORD Almighty says** (for the title see 2:19) sets out not so much punishment as the start of a process of trial in response to the affront given to his majesty. **See, I will refine and test them.** This is the language of the smelter seeking to refine (6:29) and remove the impurities of the ore, so that its true quality will be ascertained (for 'test' *bāḥan*, see 6:27b). It is a task involving effort and patience that the LORD now undertakes himself, rather than delegating it to the prophet as in 6:27-30. Refining does, however, suggest that there is at least a possibility of something being recovered as a result of the discipline to which the king will subject his people. It is not a picture of total abandonment of the nation, but of bringing difficulties and trying circumstances upon them, perhaps to remove those who promote falsehood from their midst, but more probably in view of the general condemnation of the people that is expressed in the context, the idea is that of refining them so as to convert them from impure and useless ore into what the LORD will consider valuable.

It is not going to be an easy process and will bring much suffering upon the people. There is more than a hint of divine reluctance to impose this on them, but their conduct has left no other way of effectively counteracting their alliance with sin. **For** (*kî*) **what else can I do because of the sin of my people?** 'Sin' is not in the Massoretic Text which simply reads 'because of the daughter of my people' (cf. 4:11). It is, however, present in the LXX and in the early Jewish Targum, though probably as an explanatory gloss on a difficult text rather than reflecting an omission in the Massoretic Text.

8. Once more the accusations focus on sins of speech (cf. vv. 3-5), which provide evidence of the inner heart disposition of the people.

Their tongue is a deadly[26] arrow (Pss. 57:4; 64:3; Prov. 25:18; 26:18). English translations generally suppose that this involves a change of the figure from v. 3 where the tongue is a bow. However Holladay's interpretation mentioned above is supported by this verse, which would imply that English versions have misunderstood v. 3. **It speaks with deceit.** The tongue utters deliberate distortion of the truth (*mirmâ*, v. 5), so totally is the behaviour of the people warped away from that conduct which the LORD requires of those who are in covenant with him. **With his mouth each speaks cordially to his neighbour**. 'Neighbour' (*rēaʿ*) is the same word as is translated 'friend' in vv. 4-5. There are four different bases for identifying a neighbour: by location; by tribal/ethnic identity; by companionship on a task or journey; by close friendship (*NIDOTTE* 3:1146). Here it is most probably the ethnic/tribal relationship that is in view. 'Speaks cordially'/'speaks peace' (*šālôm* 6:14) may indicate the use of the customary greeting of 'Shalom!' to invoke divine blessing on an individual. In doing so the neighbour would be representing himself as well-disposed and personally desirous of seeing the other prosper. **But in his heart he sets a trap for him.** 'Heart' is *qereb*, the 'inner being', viewed as setting the course of life. In Jeremiah it is seen as the source of evil (cf. 'within you', 4:14; 17:9; Pss. 5:9; 62:4; Prov. 26:24). Whenever someone of the same clan was encountered, there would be an outward mask of seeming friendship, but inwardly there would be the desire to gain an advantage over him by any means possible. 'Trap' is associated with setting an ambush so as to waylay and rob.

9. The two questions of v. 9 have been asked before (5:9, 29), but they are still appropriate, and their repetition is emphatic. The answers that are anticipated remain the same: Yes, of course. **Shall I not punish them for this?** Yes, of course, the LORD is entitled and expected to come and assess such behaviour so as to reward/penalise it as he judges appropriate. He is, after all, the ruler of the land and he has every right to ensure that his standards of conduct are maintained. **Should I** (<*nepeš*, 'self' cf. 6:8) **not avenge myself on such a nation as this?** Yes, of course, the Overlord will vindicate himself by enforcing his rights over against those who have despised his authority and

26. The kethibh is *šôḥēṭ*, an active participle <√*šāḥaṭ* I, 'to kill' or 'to slaughter' (usually of a sacrificial animal) and hence the translation 'deadly' (as in the LXX and Vulgate). The qere (and many manuscripts) reads *šāḥûṭ*, a passive participle (<√*šāḥaṭ* II, 'to hammer, beat down') which is elsewhere (1 Kgs. 10:16-17; 2 Chron. 9:15-16) used of gold beaten thin, and hence implying 'beaten, pointed, sharpened'. Both make good sense in this context.

ignored his requirements. For 'avenge myself' (and the rest of this verse) see on 5:9. However, Judah was not prepared to acknowledge that they were storing up trouble for themselves by the way they trampled on the requirements of their heavenly king.

5. Country and Town Ruined (9:10-11) [MT 9:9-10]

Neither v. 10 nor v. 11 has a speaker stated, but there can be no doubt that the one who brings destruction upon Jerusalem in v. 11 is the LORD. It is less clear who is the speaker in v. 10. It is probably Jeremiah describing his reaction to the situation that the LORD will impose on the land (so the punctuation of the NIV, NKJV, NLT), though it is possible to take it as a bold figure whereby the LORD himself is viewed not as weeping over the people but over what has happened to the land that is his (so NASB).[27]

10. I will weep and wail/'take up weeping and wailing' **for the mountains.** The verbs are true futures indicating that the calamity is anticipated but has not yet occurred. Although the preposition *ʿal* may also mean 'on' or 'upon', it is clear that the idea here is 'about' or 'concerning'. This is the language of a mourner bemoaning the disaster that has encompassed these places. 'Weeping' (<√*bākâ*, v. 1) denotes the cries the mourner makes; 'wailing' (*nəhî*, cf. v. 20) is the sound made by those who bemoan the dead. These responses are not occasioned by the inner social disintegration of the land, but rather reflect the dire consequences of the LORD's punishment coming on the people (v. 9). The mountains are the less fertile areas high on hillsides, which would be used for grazing. Even they will feel the impact of the destruction wreaked by the invaders. **And take up a lament concerning** (*ʿal*) **the desert pastures** expresses the same idea. The desert/wilderness pastures refers to areas of poor, rough ground, generally not close to fixed settlements, which afforded seasonal grazing for animals (2:2). 'Lament' (*qînâ*) is not the expression of a complaint for which perhaps some suitable remedy might be found, but a death song, a dirge, bewailing the hopelessness of a situation for which there is no earthly remedy.

The nation has been overrun and even the fringes of the land are devastated, and so it is envisaged that they will become the subject of

---

27. The NRSV follows the LXX which reads a plural imperative here. This is probably not original, but an early attempt to smooth out one of the abrupt transitions in this dialogue.

the melancholy song 'because' (*kî*) **they are desolate.**[28] This may depict land burned by a scorched earth policy, or burned up by the sun because it is no longer being cultivated (though this is less probable given that these areas were not normally subject to cultivation). Less probably, 'desolate' may indicate that they have been abandoned by those who fled before the invading army whose arrival Jeremiah had so long threatened. The parallel phrase **untravelled**, 'without one passing through', pictures an area without life, movement, or sound. **The lowing of cattle is not heard.** No one would be there to tend a herd if any had been left after the enemy had driven off all they could find as booty. 'Lowing' is simply 'sound', and 'cattle' refers to domestic animals in general. In place of what we might think of as farmyard sounds there is silence. The area has become so unattractive that **the birds of the air have fled and the animals are gone**/'from birds of the air even as far as the animals, they have fled, they are gone.' This is an emphatic, all-encompassing statement (4:25). There is nothing left to sustain the wildlife of the area. 'Fled' (<√*nādad*) is frequently used in connection with birds, and may suggest the fluttering of their wings.

11. There is then a switch from the rural areas to an urban environment. There is also a switch of speaker, but the thought of the two verses coheres in that they present contrasting scenarios under the same general rubric of the impact of the enemy invasion. **I will make Jerusalem a heap of ruins,**[29] **a haunt of jackals.** A similar description is given of the fate of Babylon (51:37). Earlier versions had difficulty in identifying the animal involved, and though the REB still offers 'wolves', there is general agreement on jackals (10:22; 14:6; 49:33; 51:37; cf. Zeph. 2:13-15 for an extended description of a city taken over by animals). These are scavenging animals, and their presence is a sign that only decaying ruins are left. 'Haunt of jackals' refers to a desolate and fearful place, where a previously populated area has reverted to a wild, uninhabited state (10:22; 49:22; 51:37). **I will lay waste the towns of Judah so that no one can live there.** 'Waste' (*šəmāmâ*, 4:7) implies the devastation is so complete that there is no possibility of rebuilding and living in the ruins. Such an outcome had long been threatened if the terms of the covenant were not observed (Lev. 26:33; Deut. 28:64).

---

28. *niṣṣətû* is a niphal and could be either from the root *yāṣat*, 'be burned up', or from a root *nāṣâ* (II), 'be destroyed, be devastated' (2:15; 9:12; 46:19). McKane (1986, 1:204) suggests it refers to the enemies' scorched earth policy.

29. *ləgallîm*: *lə* may be a *lamedh* of purpose or goal (*IBHS* § 11.2.10d). *gal* refers to the heaps of stones that were left after a city was razed to the ground.

C. WISDOM IN THE FACE OF CALAMITY (9:12-26) [MT 9:11-25]

There is no clear boundary marker to set this section off from what precedes, but the switch from the prophet's personal reaction to the impending judgment to a more general perspective seems to merit treating it separately. There is a measure of inclusion with the mention of the 'wise' in vv. 12 and 23 (cf. also v. 17). At first the question is posed and answered as to why such devastation will come on the land (vv. 12-16). This is followed by a divine call to get ready for what is imminent by assembling the mourners for the inevitable funeral (vv. 17-22). The two concluding sections, though brief, are significant. The first sets out the nature of true religion in terms of a correct perception of the character of the LORD (vv. 23-24), and the second exposes the inadequacy of relying only on religious privilege and ritual (vv. 25-26).

1. Explaining the Ruin (9:12-16) [MT 9:11-15]

This section is generally considered to be prose (though BHS prints the second part of v. 12 as two lines of poetry), and this has frequently raised the question of who is responsible for it. On the basis of critical presuppositions, it is felt that these verses have been added by the Deuteronomic editors of Jeremiah's sayings, and reflect a later understanding of what had already taken place with the fall of Jerusalem in 586 BC. There can be no doubt that what Jeremiah says here is influenced by the language and thought of Deuteronomy, but accepting the Mosaic origin of the Pentateuch, it is hardly surprising that both the prophet and the editors of the book of Kings (2 Kgs. 17:13-23, 34-41) drew on such a definitive source to explain what had happened to the people—and especially so in the light of the renewed interest in the Book of the Law under Josiah. There is therefore no need, apart from critical presuppositions, to deny these words to Jeremiah.

The fact that the section is prose may indicate that the original setting is that of an address in the Temple. If such prose, consciously modelled on the final addresses of Moses, was characteristic of the sermons that were given there, then Jeremiah not only echoes the language of Moses, he also reproduces his thought. This is no display of platitudes to win the favour of the people, but a critique of their conduct and an authoritative pronouncement of the doom awaiting them.

12. In the light of his presentation of the devastating judgment that will fall on Judah and Jerusalem (vv. 10-11) Jeremiah issues a challenge: **What man is wise enough to understand**[30] **this?** 'This' looks forward to the question he propounds at the end of the verse. The wise are those who by dint of natural sagacity and acute observation of what is going on around them are able to advance insights into the events that are taking place. The term is, however, probably used more narrowly of the wise as a class. McKane identifies them as the political advisers of the day. 'Who among the statesmen of Judah has real insight into the meaning of her ruin?' (1965:83). Though they prided themselves on their political skill and perspicacity, they did not really grasp why events were taking the course they did, and so the country lurched blindly into disaster.

But turning to the religious leaders of the community did not produce any better results. **Who has been instructed by the LORD and can explain it?** It is better to translate with the RSV, 'To whom has the mouth of the LORD spoken, that he may declare it?' This makes clear that we are dealing with the prophets of the Jerusalem Temple who claimed that they had been given divine revelation directly from the mouth of God. But they were so intent on prophesying security and prosperity to a nation on the brink of disaster that they would not acknowledge the accuracy of Jeremiah's prediction, and certainly would not be prepared to think or speak in terms such as sin and punishment which alone could explain it. 'Explain'/'declare' (<√*nāgad* hiphil, 'to announce, reveal') relates to the prophet as a divine messenger setting out what the LORD has revealed to him. The phenomenon that requires explanation is: **Why has the land been ruined** (<√*ʾābad*, 'be in a state of destruction) **and laid waste** (<√*nāṣâ* 'desolate' v. 10) **like a desert that no one can cross?** This is a description of the future situation already outlined in vv. 10-11. Jeremiah is treating its realisation as certain and asking if the leaders of the land really grasped why it would occur. The fact that he adds a divine oracle which does explain the disaster shows that Jeremiah is also implicitly claiming that as a true prophet of the LORD he can explain it.

13. No response would be forthcoming from the leaders of the land because from their point of view Jeremiah was asking hypothetical questions on the basis of a scenario they rejected out of hand. But Jeremiah had not raised the matter to hear the currently approved commentary on events, but rather to set out clearly the divine reason for the state of the nation. **The LORD said, 'It is because they have**

30. *wəyābēn*: ordinary *waw* plus a jussive, expressing facts that may be expected to be true (GKC §109i).

forsaken my law, which I set before them; they have not obeyed me or followed my law.' The LORD's answer does not introduce some startling new feature to explain what will come on the people. It does not call for a difficult or complicated exercise in logic or theology, but for spiritual awareness of well-known covenant obligations. They should have responded to the law that the LORD had given them as the basis of their living. Indeed they had so responded at one time, but now they have forsaken (<√*ʿāzab*, 1:16; 2:13) the LORD's rules for living (cf. 7:23-26). For 'followed my law'/'walked in it', compare 2:23.

14. The alternative lifestyle the nation had adopted was based on two principles. **Instead, they have followed**/'walked after' (2:2) **the stubbornness** (cf. 3:17) **of their hearts.** They had decided to stick by their own ways, and what they had decided was right for themselves. This was a symptom of the unteachability of people who were so sure of themselves and their own wisdom that they ignored any correction sent by the LORD. But it was not just a matter of what they found within themselves (for 'heart', see 4:14). Having turned from the way of the LORD they were open to whatever spiritual trends and pressures were around them, and to these they soon succumbed. **They have followed the Baals, as their fathers taught them.** They had become involved in the worship of the gods of Canaan of whom Baal was the most prominent (2:8). The plural indicates that in each site where he was worshipped there was thought to be a specific localised manifestation of his power (2:23). Baal was viewed as a fertility god, and the rituals associated with Baal worship involved sexual activity. It was not just Jeremiah's contemporaries who found this attractive. It was a legacy conveyed to them by previous generations (7:26; 16:12).

15. Therefore (*lākēn* of judgment)**, this is what the LORD Almighty, the God of Israel, says.** There can be no doubt but the LORD will act, and so they are given due warning yet again. The formal address (7:21) indicates his character, power and claim so that the people may be duly impressed, and some vestige of conscience and reasoning might be stirred up. **See, I will make this people**[31] **eat bitter food and drink poisoned water.** These describe experiences of considerable suffering and death (8:14; 23:15), and are the consequences that befall those who break their covenant obligations (Deut. 29:18). The same judgment will later be imposed on the false prophets (23:15).

31. Literally, 'I will make them eat, this people' where 'this people' is in apposition to 'them', to define the pronominal suffix more clearly (GKC §131m), and is not a second object.

'Bitter food'/'wormwood' is a small shrub with many branches and hairy leaves, found extensively in southern Palestine. It is not itself deadly, and its very bitter leaves were used extensively in folk medicine. It is often associated with 'poisoned water', which was possibly an infusion of a poisonous plant (8:14).

16. The curse of the broken covenant is further spelled out: **I will scatter them among the nations that neither they nor their fathers have known.** This involves the threat of dispersal in exile. 'Scatter' (<√*pûṣ*) is used of water running into the street (Prov. 5:16), or of the extension of a battle (2 Sam. 18:8), or of a farmer scattering seed (Isa. 28:25). Scattering was the punishment imposed after Babel (Gen. 10:18; 11:8-9), and is used here of the reversal of covenant blessing (Deut. 4:27; 28:64). Possibly the covenant curse of Lev. 26:33, 'I will scatter you among the nations and will draw out my sword and pursue you', provides the background to this passage, though there the synonym *zārâ*, 'to scatter' (cf. 31:10), is used. Other terms used to describe their expulsion from the land by God include 'to uproot' (*nātaš*, 12:14; 45:4), 'to sling out' (*qālaʿ*, 10:18) and 'to hurl away' (*ṭûl*, 16:13). **And I will pursue them with the sword until I have destroyed** (<√*kālâ* piel, 5:3) **them.** The LORD sends the armies of the nations to accomplish his purposes (cf. also 44:27; 49:37). It is improbable that this passage shows Jeremiah prophesying the total destruction of the people. Although the language used seems to be absolute, the curses of the Mosaic covenant always envisaged that there would be survivors (see for instance Lev. 26:36, 39, 44). There remained the possibility of repentance and restoration from the land of their enemies, but that in no way undermined the reality and horror of the LORD's judgment on his disobedient people.

There is evidence from second millennium BC Egyptian, Hittite and Mesopotamian documents of the use by a state of resettlement programmes to break the bond of a conquered people with its territory. Since deities were considered to be geographically limited in their ability to help their devotees, they would no longer be able to assist a deported people. Furthermore, a disoriented people in strange territory were less likely to be a source of rebellion. There was also the possibility of introducing tribes from elsewhere into the vacated or partly vacated land, further reducing local cohesion and producing a population obligated to the superpower for their possession of the land. The Assyrians developed the technique of deportation as an instrument for subjugating their empire, and used it extensively (2 Kgs. 17:24-40), and from them it was adopted by the Babylonians.

2. Death Coming through the Window (9:17-22) [MT 9:16-21]

The thematic unity of vv. 17-22, focusing as they do on death and mourning, is evident. The passage is also noteworthy because of the vivid imagery it employs. Who the speakers are in the first sequence (vv. 18-19) is a matter of some obscurity, but vv. 20-21 are advice given by the prophet and v. 22 is a divine oracle probably matching v. 17. The whole unit seeks to engage the imagination of Judah and Jerusalem with a scenario of their future that runs counter to the peace and prosperity ideology that was prevalent in the community. If they continued with their current obdurate conduct, it was death and mourning that awaited them.

17. The introductory formula, **This is what the LORD Almighty says**, is omitted from the LXX, and several commentators follow this (Holladay 1986, 1:309; McKane 1986, 1:208). It has the advantage of solving who the speaker in v. 18 is by having the prophet speak throughout vv. 17-22. However, there is no problem in taking v. 17 as divine address to the community. Disaster and tragedy are about to engulf their land, and so they had better prepare themselves for the situation. **Consider now!** is a plural exhortation to the group to reflect upon their situation so as to be able to take appropriate action (2:10). **Call for the wailing women** (<√*qānēn* polel, 'to chant a *qînâ*, a lament') **to come.** They were a professional group of mourners who would dishevel their hair, bare their breasts, flail their arms about, and above all utter piercing cries to mourn the dead. These are the mourners 'that go about the streets' (Eccl. 12:5), 'those who are skilled in lamentation' (Amos 5:16, NRSV). Although the disaster is still future, it is being presented as so certain that they had better make preparations for the funeral now. But the funeral is not that of an individual, but a state funeral for the nation; the occasion is public and the scale of mourning is to be massive. **Send for the most skilful of them.** Literally, 'to the wise women', those who have the practical know-how to do it well. This is the wisdom that will be needed to cope with the aftermath of coming events (cf. vv. 12, 23). The Massoretic Text adds 'so that they may come' (so NKJV, NRSV), but the NIV and the REB take it as the beginning of the next verse.

18. The main difficulty in v. 18 is to determine who is uttering these words. 'Over *us*', '*our* eyes' and '*our* eyelids' argue against punctuation which indicates no break in the speaker from v. 17. This problem is generally ignored in English translations, though NLT changes 'our eyes' to 'your eyes' (following the LXX). GNB, however, inserts 'The people said' at the beginning of the verse, and, unless we follow the LXX, it must surely be correct to take this verse as the people's anticipated response in the day of tragedy, 'Say' or 'You will say' being understood. **Let them come quickly and wail**/'take up a *nəhî*' (v. 20) **over us.** In the East funerals followed quickly upon death, but what is to be made of 'over us'? In that the speakers are not yet dead, presumably they are making their own funeral arrangements. But that will not do because they also number themselves among the mourners in the following words. This is part of the poetic imagery treating the people as a unity and where the figures of speech blend into one another. **Till**[32] **our eyes overflow with tears and water streams from our eyelids.** The dead nation is mourned over and the survivors join in the national funeral rites.

19. 'For' (*kî*) introduces v. 19 presumably indicating the reason that the speakers of v. 18 agree to call for the women who are specialists in public displays of mourning. It is because the sounds of grief have already started to go up from Jerusalem; only when events force themselves upon them will the community admit that Jeremiah was right and their view was wrong. **The sound of wailing is heard from Zion.** For 'wailing' (*nəhî*) see v. 20. Zion is here simply an alternative name for Jerusalem, and not a reference to the Temple area. The wailing on this occasion is articulate. The first cry, **How ruined we are!**, begins with *ʾêk*, a variant form of the word that is commonly used to begin a lament (Lam. 1:1; 2:1; 4:1). 'Ruined' (4:13) refers to the destruction caused by an invading army. **How great is our shame!** Their standing in the world of the day has been utterly lost because of the capture of their land, and they recognise that they are now a people without status (2:26).

The reason for their shame is given as 'for' (*kî*) **we must leave our land because** (*kî*) **our houses are in ruins.** 'Leave' is 'forsake'/'abandon', used earlier of their desertion of the LORD (2:13). Now they are forced to leave the inheritance he had bestowed on them. This is further explained by 'they have ruined (<√*šālak* hiphil, 'to throw out/away') our dwellings'. The reference is either completely indefinite, and hence the passive rendering in the NIV, or else the subject 'the enemy' is assumed to be obvious from the context. Both verbs are perfects and rather than rendering them as prophetic perfects with future reference (NIV), it is probably better to take them as true past tenses, 'because we have left the land, because they have cast

32. *wətēradnâ*: the conjunction is taken as indicating purpose or consequence.

down our dwellings' (NRSV, cf. NKJV). The cry might be that of country dwellers who have taken refuge in Jerusalem as the invasion swept through the land. Their despair would soon be taken up by the whole city as it also suffered at the hands of the enemy.

20. Jeremiah then elaborates on the previous scene by adding a message from God which he refers to rather than quotes. **Now** (*kî*, 'for', treated as an emphatic)**, O women, hear the word of the LORD.** There is no specific message unless v. 22 is to be taken as fulfilling that role. The following clause, **Open your**[33] **ears to the words of his mouth**, seems to indicate that it is a general exhortation to pay attention to the whole message that Jeremiah is bringing to them. The women addressed are presumably all the women of Zion. The slaughter will be so great that the number of trained wailing women will not suffice for the task and therefore the women are exhorted to get ready for that contingency and to **teach your daughters how to wail; teach one another a lament.** 'Wail' (*nəhî*) refers to the sounds made by those who bemoan the dead; 'lament' *(qînâ)* is often a more articulate expression of grief on such an occasion using either a standard form of words or something composed for the occasion. The catastrophe about to engulf the nation is so extensive that all must be trained to take part in the lamentation. Christ uttered similar words of warning as he anticipated the later fall of Jerusalem (Luke 23:28-29).

21. The verse begins with *kî* presumably indicating the reason why so many mourners will be needed. **Death has climbed in through our windows** is the first of two vivid portrayals of death. This is personification, because the Old Testament does not accord to death a discrete personality in the way in which Canaanite texts treat Mot, the god of death, more specifically death through pestilence. Death is pictured as a resourceful individual who can overcome any obstacle in his way. Though the door of the house may have been closed, that will not prevent the entry of death, any more than it would prevent the entry of a determined thief. The word 'window' is traditionally derived from a root meaning 'to pierce' and denotes a narrow slit in a wall, generally high up below the eaves, to permit the entry of light and air. It would not, of course, be glazed, and would only rarely have shutters. Usually in the Old Testament one goes down to the realms of death; so here death climbing in (literally, 'comes up') has an aggressive note. Death **has entered our fortresses.** 'Fortresses' (*ʾarmôn*, 6:5) suggests that

33. 'Your' is unexpectedly a masculine suffix (so also in 'your daughters'), but the reference is clear (GKC §135o).

the thought is that no matter how stout the defences erected death is easily able to overcome them. The alternative translation 'palaces' (NKJV, NRSV) presents a picture of death as the leveller; from the lowest to the highest in the land there will be no stopping of death. 'Our' points to the way in which the prophet associates himself with the people as he speaks.

Death does not just come to the aged. Its sweeping influence is felt even among the youngest (6:11) and healthiest. **It has cut off the children from the streets and the young men from the public squares.** As death takes its grim toll, the city becomes deserted, and those who would have been found playing or talking on the city streets are no longer there. That it is the young that have been snatched away points to this as the city with no future.

22. Jeremiah adds a second picture that had been revealed to him of the impact of death on the community. **Say, 'This is what the LORD declares.'**[34] The image of death is now that of a farmer who spreads corpses on his field as fertiliser. **The dead bodies of men will lie like refuse on the open field.** It is a picture of a shameful end, with perhaps the implication that there are so many that there is no one able to bury them all (8:2; 16:4; 20:6; 25:33). Then the picture changes to death as the reaper. **Like cut corn behind the reaper.** When the reaper put his sickle into the crop, he gathered it in his arm until there was too much to hold, when he put it down in a heap for another to come and gather them it up and tie it into a sheaf. But here what is envisaged is a scene **with no one to gather them.** The wheat lies wasting on the ground because there is no one left to bind the sheaves. It is a picture of a devastating disaster.

3. Delusion and Reality (9:23-24) [MT 9:22-23]

The previous sections have painted a dark picture of what awaits the people. Jeremiah now presents two brief oracles which deal with related aspects of their response to the doom that overshadows them. He first deals in vv. 23-24 with the matter of self-delusion. The people had thought that they would be able to survive come what may, because they were putting their trust in various false and insubstantial props, but these were going to be swept away. There is only one true

34. *dabbēr* might also be taken as an infinitive absolute functioning as an imperative, in which case the subject might be the women, so that what follows is the content of the dirge they are to teach their daughters. Notice also the unusual use here of *nəʾum Yhwh* in an initial position.

foundation for confidence, and that is the LORD himself, of whom a notable description is given in terms of Israel's covenant faith. This saying would encourage confidence in the LORD, and also stimulate further thought about God's purposes for his people.

23. This is what the LORD says, 'Let not the wise man boast of his wisdom or the strong man boast of his strength or the rich man boast of his riches.' Here are three sources of self-confidence by which people delude themselves that they will secure them immunity from the vicissitudes of life. 'Boast' (<√*hālal* II hithpael, 'to praise oneself', 'to express confidence in the qualities of someone/something'; 1 Kgs. 20:11) is an exercise in self-congratulation as one enumerates the plus points of whatever characteristic is being thought of. But the idea is conveyed that this self-praise is unjustified. Paul had learned to evaluate correctly the human standards of wealth, social position and power that the Corinthians based their judgments of worth on, and used these words to point them to a right understanding of the matter (1 Cor. 1:31). He also applied the same standards to what he himself had achieved (2 Cor. 10:17).

The individual who considers himself wise reckons that his intellectual understanding and skill will stand him in good stead when the time of testing comes, so that he will be able to survive. The man who is proud of his physical prowess reckons his stamina and physique give him a better than average chance of coping with life. The rich man places his trust in the material resources that are at his disposal. The reference may be particularly directed at those families who over the previous two centuries had built up substantial estates and formed a powerful landowning class in Judah. It is reckoned that at this time 3 to 5 per cent of the population owned 50 to 70 per cent of the land (*NIDOTTE* 3:559), and that was the main productive resource in the economy. But whether it was wisdom or personal strength or riches (or a Solomonic combination of all three), none of these would avail in the day of reckoning, and so none provided a proper basis for planning and living in this life. The people are being warned not to make these the basis for their confidence.

24. But there is also a positive aspect to the message. If anyone wishes to boast, **But let him who boasts boast about this, that he understands and knows me.** This is the only suitable basis for confidence (Pss. 34:2; 64:10; 105:3; Isa. 41:16). The ultimate ground of all human living is a right perspective on the divine, to have discrimination and knowledge of God. 'Understand' (<√*śākal*, 'to have insight') also refers to the prosperity that may flow from such insight. To 'know me' is not just to know about God, but to have a true commitment to him (8:7; 9:6). 'This is eternal life, that they may know you, the only true God, and Jesus Christ whom you have sent' (John 17:3).

Contrasting with the triad of the self-sufficient (v. 23), three aspects of the divine character are mentioned: **that I am the LORD, who exercises kindness, justice and righteousness on earth.** This knowledge of God is to be in terms of his covenant name, the LORD, Yahweh, which is indicative of his presence with his people to deliver and uphold (Exod. 3:14-15; 6:2-8). He is not to be thought of as a collection of abstract attributes, for the expression here brings out the LORD's divine activity: 'exercises'/'does' (<√*ʿāśâ*, 'to do, make'). It is knowledge of the active and involved God that is commended, not arid speculation.

This divine activity is described using three terms that are at the heart of Old Testament theology. 'Kindness' (*ḥesed*, 2:2) describes God's committed love towards his people. It has such a range of meaning that no single term can catch it in English: 'lovingkindness' (NKJV); 'steadfast love' (NRSV); 'unfailing love' (REB). The covenant king of Israel was one who had committed himself to the outworking of his relationship with the people he has chosen for himself, and there could be no doubt as to his good intentions towards them. Knowing his *ḥesed* should lead to wonder that it exists at all and to being mindful that it was made known to the people through the covenant, which in turn demands a response from them. 'Justice' (*mišpāṭ*, 5:4) covers the administration of God's kingdom as a realm characterised by standards of equity and truth that reflect what he himself is. 'Righteousness' (*ṣədāqâ*, 4:2) refers to conformity to a standard. He is the one who always matches up to the norms required by his own eternal being and by the covenant bond into which he has voluntarily entered. 'The LORD is righteous in all his ways and loving (*ḥāsîd* 3:12) towards all he has made' (Ps. 145:17). As he does not deviate from what he is in himself, he can be relied upon in all his dealings with mankind 'on earth'.

'For (*kî*[35]) **in these I delight,' declares the LORD** raises the possibility that not only does God delight in exercising these qualities, he delights in seeing them exercised by those who are his.

---

35. It is possible that *kî* does not function here to state the reason why the LORD acts in this way, that is, he displays these qualities because he delights in them. It may rather be in parallel with the *kî* that introduced the content of the knowledge that was to be valued, 'knows me that I am the LORD … ⌊and⌋ that I delight in these'.

In 1 Cor. 1:18-31 we find Paul developing an argument similar to that of Jeremiah. On the one hand he sets the wisdom and strength of mankind and on the other divine wisdom embodied in Jesus Christ, which appears to be mere foolishness and weakness from a worldly perspective. But this has been done to show the emptiness of all human boasting, and leads to the conclusion, 'Let him who boasts boast in the Lord' (1 Cor. 1:31; cf. also Rom. 3:27). This challenge remains pertinent still because the tension between what appeals to human thought and wisdom and what is enjoined by the word of God is as acute as ever.

4. Circumcision No Guarantee (9:25-26) [MT 9:24-25]

Jeremiah has dealt with the delusive qualities of human talents and achievements; now he turns to religious delusion. Though Judah were the surviving part of the covenant people, their religion had become corrupt because they were mistaking the outward embodiment of the covenant for its essence. This has already been seen as regards the ark (3:16), the Temple (7:4) and the Book of the Law (8:8). Now the same ritualistic notion is attacked as regards the rite of circumcision. This had been granted as a sign of covenant allegiance to Abraham (Gen. 17:9-14) and was an integral part of the arrangements for the people at Sinai (Lev. 12:3). But Moses had made clear from the beginning that circumcision in the flesh did not suffice on its own (Deut. 10:16; 30:6). The outward sacrament had to be accompanied by an inward heart circumcision before the true goal of the exercise was achieved (4:4; 6:10).

25. The section begins with the standard phrase indicating it refers to the impending, but as yet unspecified, future (7:32). **'The days are coming,' declares the LORD.** This is a vision of the LORD's judgment coming upon earth. **When I will punish all who are circumcised only in the flesh.** 'Punish' (<√*pāqad*) points to the inspection and, where necessary, punishment carried out by the overlord. 'Circumcised only in the flesh' (*kol-mûl bĕʿorlâ*) has been variously understood. The RSV took it as a paradox, 'circumcised but yet uncircumcised'; the traditional rendering is 'circumcised with the uncircumcised' (NKJV); but most modern translations are similar to the NIV. This seems probable as the following verse then lists those who practice circumcision.

26. Egypt, Judah, Edom, Ammon, Moab and all who live in the desert in distant places. These nations all practised circumcision. In Egypt it seems mainly to have been a priestly ritual. The other peoples mentioned, however, are recorded as having Abraham as a common ancestor (Edom, Gen. 36:1; Ammon, Gen. 19:36; Moab, Gen. 19:37; the desert dwellers, Gen. 25:13-18), but among them the rite seems to have been performed at puberty. The point here is that Judah, the covenant people, is lined up among these heathen nations. Their circumcision was an outward ceremonial which did them no good at all because it was not accompanied by inward consecration to the LORD. There is a suspicion that these nations are also listed as being involved in joint action against the Babylonians (Ellison 1962:26), but it is not the political dimension of the situation that is being focused on. Rather it is the attitude of the LORD's own people. He is telling them that though they regarded their circumcision as a mark of covenant privilege, they are really no different from all the other nations that practise it if there is not covenant obedience.

The phrase 'in distant places' (literally, 'those cut off at the edges'; 25:23; 49:32; cf. REB) has also been understood as 'who clip the hair by their foreheads' (NIV margin). This would refer to cropping the edges of the beard and sides of the head, a practice forbidden by the law (Lev. 19:27; Deut. 14:1). Among heathen nations hair cut off in this way was frequently dedicated to a deity. Most ancient versions understand the phrase as referring to hairstyle rather than to a geographical location.

For (*kî*) all these nations are really uncircumcised, and even the whole house of Israel is uncircumcised in heart. This is the basis of the LORD's judgment against them, their lack of inner dedication to him. 'Heart' refers to their inner life, which is unconsecrated. When the LORD inspects the house of Israel, the people with the outward privilege of having the covenant set before them, it will not be outward acts that will be the basis of his scrutiny, but inward allegiance. Because the LORD judges impartially, he will use the same standards for Israel and for the nations, 'Jew and Gentile alike' (Rom. 3:9).

This too is a theme that is taken up by Paul to the same effect. 'Circumcision has value if you observe the law, but if you break the law, you have become as though you had not been circumcised' (Rom. 2:25). The sign of covenant allegiance, be it circumcision or its new covenant equivalent of baptism, is no guarantee of covenant blessing unless it be accompanied by covenant obedience. The outward, physical sign on its own is a mark of privilege, but not proof of salvation. For that there needs to be inward change where 'circumcision is circumcision of the heart, by the Spirit' (Rom. 2:29), and that requirement carries forward into the new covenant also where the rite of water baptism, though a mark of spiritual privilege especially in terms of access to the word of God (Rom. 3:2), is ineffective on its own and needs to be accompanied by Spirit-wrought heart change for entry into the Kingdom of God.

D. THE FOUR CONTRASTS (10:1-16)

Although this passage has been the subject of much critical inquiry, that must not be allowed to obscure the fact that it is a scathing critique of idolatry, presented in a logical and compelling manner. The structure of the passage has been well analysed by Margaliot (1980), the main features of whose outline are followed here. There are four blocks of material, within each of which there is a contrast between the false and the true. In the first section (vv. 2-7) the people are exhorted not to be terrified by astrology because the gods that are presumed to lie behind it are simply impotent idols, whereas the LORD is the God of power. The contrast between the false gods and the true God is then explored further in terms of their lifelessness and the living and eternal nature of the LORD (vv. 8-10). Next there is set out the difference between the gods of the nations who did not create the universe and the LORD who created it and continues to control it (vv. 11-13). In the final section (vv. 14-16) the contrast focuses more on the worshippers of the idols, who will perish in the same way as the idols themselves, and Israel, whom the LORD has taken as his inheritance for which he will provide.

However, it must be recognised that several substantial issues have been raised regarding the authenticity of the passage.

(1) It is felt that there is a decided change of attitude towards Judah. Elsewhere the prophet is concerned with condemning the people, and charging them with covenant trespass and being totally taken up with idolatry, whereas the tone in this passage is irenic, quite dissimilar to that found in other addresses with the possible exception of 29:1-14.

(2) It is argued that many of the passages have parallels and similarities with Isaiah (Isa. 40:18-20; 41:7; 44:9-20; 46:5-7), and it is therefore felt that this polemic against idolatry should be located against a later exilic background.

(3) It is noted on textual grounds that the Septuagint preserves a significantly different shorter text of this passage (for instance, it omits vv. 6-8 and v. 10, and v. 9 is found after 'cannot speak' in v. 5), and that a Qumran scroll (4QJer[a]) indicates the existence of a Hebrew text similar to that of the LXX (see Introduction §2.6). So it is argued that the longer Massoretic Text arose because of later incorporations into the text. Similarly, the repetition of vv. 12-16 in 51:15-19 has been felt

to support the later, composite nature of what is found here.

(4) The most surprising aspect of the passage is that v. 11 is not in Hebrew at all, but in Aramaic, a feature often taken as marking it as a marginal gloss that was incorporated into the text. But this verse is also found in the LXX and in the Qumran text, and it is highly problematic that an Aramaic gloss would have been incorporated into a Hebrew text. Since the verse is integral to the structure of the passage as a whole, the fact that it is in Aramaic must be seen as a deliberate choice on the part of Jeremiah.

(5) Many have also remarked on the irregular nature of the passage, and of the changes in its grammar that are frequently smoothed out in English translations. Far from treating this as evidence of later insertions, Holladay (1986, 1:325) argues with some plausibility that it may be characteristic of such polemic passages against idols, finding similar features also in Isa. 44:9-20. For instance, switching from singular to plural in reference to the idols may well be a poetic means of expressing contempt for them.

By way of a positive approach it may be remarked that the passage does cohere in terms of its theme. It looks alternately at the idols and the LORD, most effectively contrasting them. Equally there is no need to assign the passage a late date. Part of the critical hypothesis rests on dating the passage as contemporary with deutero-Isaiah, but accepting the integrity of Isaiah leads one to see Jeremiah's thought being moulded by what had been said by the earlier prophet. Holladay supposes that Jeremiah (and if Jeremiah, how much more Isaiah, one might add) may have been stimulated to this by reflecting on what took place in 701 BC. 'It is possible that this passage, if authentic to Jeremiah, is a product of his meditation on the incident of the Assyrian siege of Jerusalem in the eighth century, when the officer of the Assyrian king, the Rabshakeh, made light of the city and its God (2 Kings 18-19)' (Holladay 1986, 1:329). There is no need to suppose that this comes out of an exilic background. Indeed in the years after that incident Mesopotamian religious influences were rampant in Judah. Jones argues that the tone of these chapters is at variance with the hopelessness of the situation and the certainty of judgment found in chapters 8–9 and that 'here it is assumed that Israel has the time and opportunity to learn the lesson (v. 1)' (1992:171), but does not all that fit precisely into the early years of Jeremiah's ministry during the optimism that must have been generated by Josiah's reforms?

The matter of the longer and shorter texts is generally supposed to be solvable by positing an original short text, though it must be noticed that this has to be different on critical presuppositions from any that has survived because what is taken as an Aramaic gloss (v. 11) is found in the LXX. But it is equally probable that longer and shorter versions of this passage originated with Jeremiah, particularly if we envisage him in the years after 597 BC as sending copies of his Scroll to those already in exile. It is probable that in writing it up, the version that has survived here represents his own later elaboration of the text, possibly with a view to the greater number exposed to such temptations at the time of the deportation. This may well explain the existence of more than one text. Jeremiah as a book was not written at one sitting. It developed over the years, and the author reworked and re-presented material in a number of ways. This is speculative, but it seems far more healthy speculation than that of considerable later editorial invention.

1. Weakness *v.* Power (10:1-7)

1. The prophet calls on the people to give attention to him because he is bringing the divine message. **Hear what the LORD says to**[36] **you, O house of Israel.** While the designation 'house of Israel' may refer to the northern kingdom, these words are addressed to Judah and Jerusalem as the remaining representatives of the covenant people as in 9:26. In this way there is a suitable link back to the preceding discussion of circumcision, the mark of the true covenant people. Previously Jeremiah had mentioned various surrounding peoples, and now he adds other material in which he had relayed warnings to the people about forgetting the primary demands of the covenant, losing their unique covenant identity, and becoming deluded and oppressed by idolatry. If some of the customs mentioned are identified as of Mesopotamian rather than Canaanite origin, this might well fit an early stage in Jeremiah's ministry and reflect foreign practices that were prevalent in Manasseh's time. Equally the absence in this passage of any reference to the fertility rites of Canaanite religion (as in 2:20-28; 3:1-3) or other practices such as child sacrifice (7:31) may also point to the introduction of Mesopotamian ideas (as in 7:17-18).

2. The focus is first of all on pagan practices (vv. 2-5) which the people are urged to avoid. They are also counselled not to be apprehensive about them. **This is what the LORD says: 'Do not learn the ways of the nations.'** The preposition used before 'ways' is 'to' (*'el*), which does not usually occur after this verb and suggests that the

---

36. The REB 'against you' is out of line with the context, which is warning rather than condemnatory. *'ălêkem* is probably a variant for *'ălêkem*, the prepositions often being interchanged in Jeremiah (see on 1:7).

thought is, 'Do not become accustomed to the ways of the nations' (Keil 1873, 1:196), or 'Do not resort to/become involved with learning' (Holladay 1986, 1:330). 'Ways' (2:23) refers to the lifestyle, particularly the ethical and religious practices, of the heathen nations. Given that Israel had very successfully learned the ways of the nations in Palestine, it is probable that this is said in connection with Mesopotamian practices which had become prevalent in the territory of the former northern kingdom (2 Kgs. 17:29-34), and which were also established in Judah during the reign of Manasseh. Indeed it had been one of the first acts of Josiah's reformation to purge Jerusalem of these foreign imports (2 Kgs. 23:5, 11, 12). Here the message that Jeremiah brings can be appropriately interpreted as showing that he was supportive of such reforms.

The people were also warned not to **be terrified by signs in the sky**. 'Terrified'/'dismayed' (<√*ḥātat*, 1:17) is a strong word denoting inability to act or think things through because of outside pressure. 'Signs in the sky' may be used of portents—eclipses, comets, conjunction of planets and the like—and also of the changes in the relative position of the sun, moon and stars, including changes in the seasons (cf. 'signs' in Gen. 1:14). Astral deities were significant in Near Eastern religions, and had affected Israel from early times (8:2; Amos 5:25-26). Those who worshipped the sun, moon and stars thought that movements of the heavenly bodies influenced and foretold what would happen on earth. **Though** (*kî* used concessively) **the nations are terrified** (<√*ḥātat*) **by them.** The nations believed that the stars were under the control of supernatural powers, and that interpreting their movements allowed forecasts to be made of the future. When such omens were unfavourable, they reacted with panic and dread, but that sort of response was quite inappropriate for those who were the people of the LORD and confessed that he had acted powerfully in the life of their nation.

This raises the problem of why, in defiance of what had been revealed to them, the covenant people were so often attracted to heathen worship. At one level it was a matter of not wishing to appear out of step with their neighbours, but here we also see that they could not free themselves from the notion that these supposed gods could and would act malevolently in their lives. That explains the emphasis in this polemic on the reality, originality and power of the LORD. It is an attempt to meet the needs of the people in their insecurity over against the dominant interpretation of events in the world as propagated by the pagan thinking of their culture and environment.

3. However, such terror at astrological predictions was, and remains, incongruous **for** (*kî*) **the customs**[37] **of the peoples are worthless.** 'Customs' (*ḥuqqôt*, 'statutes', cf. 5:24) are the prescribed ordinances of the religion of the heathen nations which are so embedded in their culture that they adopt them unthinkingly (Lev. 18:3; 20:23; 2 Kgs. 17:8). But the LORD's evaluation of them is that they are 'worthless' (*hebel,* 2:5). For all the physical presence of idols, the gods they represent were no more substantial than a puff of wind or smoke. This general statement is then followed by a more specific reason why heathen observances may be safely ignored: just think how they construct an idol. **They cut**[38] **a tree out of the forest.** The idol begins as timber in a forest—a Palestinian rather than a Mesopotamian scene. **And a craftsman shapes it with his chisel.** The word for 'craftsman' is quite general, and could apply to a skilled worker in wood, stone or metal (24:1); quite obviously here it is a carpenter. His tool is not so obvious. The word is found here and in Isa. 44:12 for an implement used in making idols, probably to shape the wood roughly. It may imply the crudeness of the idol-maker's product (*NIDOTTE* 2:1027). 'Shapes it' is an NIV addition. 'Axe' (NKJV, NRSV) suggests the reference is to an earlier stage of the work than 'chisel' (also in REB) would imply. 'Cutting tool' (NASB) leaves the matter undecided.

4. The description of the process of idol production continues. **They adorn it with silver and gold.** The metal was beaten thin and applied as a veneer to the wooden frame (Isa. 30:22; 40:19). Then there is the scathing climax to the description of this part of the production process. **They fasten it with hammer and nails so that it will not totter.**[39] The verb *pûl*, 'totter', is used only here and in Isa. 28:7, both in a context of shaking or trembling. That is what they have managed

---

37. It is the plural of the noun *ḥuqqâ* that is used here, which fits awkwardly with the singular *hû'* at the end of the clause. It may be singular through being attracted to the immediately foregoing predicate *hebel* (GKC §145uN³). Alternatively this may be part of the deliberate roughness of expression which brings out the sarcasm of the description. 'Carved images' (REB, cf. NJPS) follows the emendation suggested in BHS to *ḥittat*, 'terror, object of terror'.

38. *kərātô* is generic singular, 'one cuts it'; so too is 'one adorns it' at the beginning of v. 4. The generic singular then switches into generic plurals, 'they fasten them'. The mode of expression is smoothed out in the NIV by the addition of 'shapes it'. Literally, the lines read, 'A tree from ⌊the⌋ forest one cuts it, work of hands of a craftsman with the chisel'.

39. 'They fasten them and let it not totter': a jussive after simple imperfect to express intention (GKC §109g).

to produce: something that cannot even stand by itself, but has to be held in place by nails (Isa. 40:20; 41:7)! The idols are passive in their origin; they are created 'with' tools by human craftsmen.

5. The idols are also inert as regards their ongoing mode of existence. The first comparison in v. 5 is somewhat obscure. **Like a scarecrow in a melon patch, their idols**/'they' **cannot speak.** This is a derisive picture of the idols as bits of wood with rags attached to scare birds (an understanding reflected as early as the use of this passage in the apocryphal Epistle of Jeremiah 70, probably intertestamental; = Bar. 6:70). However effectively they may operate against birds, that should not be sufficient to terrify a human being. It also fits in with the inability of the idols to make a sound, even at the level of shooing birds away from cucumbers. Older translations give a rendering such as that in the NKJV, 'They are upright, like a palm tree, and they cannot speak.' The evidence is evenly weighed between the two renderings.[40] The palm tree with its leaves at the top may be intended to be a derisive reference to the way the idols look. 'Upright'/'straight' may refer to their inability to move. **They must be**[41] **carried**[42] **because** (*kî*) **they cannot walk** (Isa. 46:7). The root *ṣāʿad* is rather 'step, march' rather than 'walk'. There were many processions in Babylon involving the carrying of the images, and presumably in Canaan also. Even their sacred ceremonies gave evidence of the impotence of the idols for those who had eyes to see it. And so the section concludes, **Do not fear them;** 'for' (*kî*) **they can do no harm nor can they**[43] **do any good** (Isa. 41:23). 'Fear' is both terror and fright (1:8), and also reverential awe (5:22). The correlation of harm and good is merism, a figure of speech naming opposites to cover everything in between these extremes. Here it is in effect said that they cannot do anything at

40. *tāmār* means a 'palm tree' (Judg. 4:5), which is by extension sometimes assumed to mean a pillar-like object. The form found here is *tōmer* which may be taken to be another form of *tāmār*, 'palm tree' (Vulgate, Syriac, Targum; clause not in the LXX) or a form meaning 'scarecrow' (McKane 1986, 1:222-23). *miqšār* may be understood as 'hammered work', the product of a craftsman's activity, or as 'a garden of cucumbers' (Isa. 1:8 NKJV) or 'a field of melons' (NIV).

41. The qal infinitive absolute is often used with the niphal as here (*IBHS* §35.2.1d; GKC §113w).

42. *yinnāśûʾ* is an early scribal error for *yinnāśəʾû*, caused by the preceding infinitive absolute (GKC §§23i, 47n).

43. *ʾôtām* for *ʾittām* as often, cf. 1:16. Literally, 'and also doing-good it is not with them'.

all. This was what the people of Jerusalem thought about the LORD ('The LORD will do nothing, either good or bad', Zeph. 1:12), but that assessment really applied to these idol gods.

6. Over against this description of the inert and passive idols, Jeremiah sets out in the language of praise the incomparability of the LORD. Realising who he is gives a proper perspective on the emptiness of the claims made for the idols. **No one**[44] **is like you, O LORD.** Such a formula had been used on many occasions in Israel's history to indicate that one could not bring the LORD and the other gods into the same terms of reference to effect a comparison (e.g. Exod. 8:10; 9:14; 15:11; Deut. 33:26; 2 Sam. 7:22; Ps. 71:19; Isa. 40:18; 42:8; Mic. 7:18). **You are great** refers to every aspect of his being and character, and the same thought is continued. **And your name is mighty in power**/'great in might' (*gəbûrâ*, the might of a strong man, the ability of the warrior king to perform acts of surpassing power; cf. 16:21) is almost a technical term for divine omnipotence (Isa. 33:13; Pss. 21:13; 145:11). 'Name' refers to what the LORD has made known of himself, and his strength has been displayed as being such as to effect wonders whereas the idols and their gods can do no harm or good.

7. There should be an appropriate response from all mankind to the revelation that the LORD has given of himself. **Who should not revere you, O King of the nations?** 'Revere'/'fear' (<√*yārēʾ*, 5:22) points to the respect and honour that is due to such a sovereign. The kingship of the LORD played an important role in the theological thinking of Israel, being deeply embedded in the whole concept of covenant, but here the thought goes beyond that of being the covenant Overlord of the chosen people to the international sovereignty of the LORD (Pss. 22:28; 47:7-9; 96:10; Zech. 14:16). 'For' (*kî*) **this is your due.**[45] It is only appropriate that all mankind should acknowledge the status of the LORD in reverence and worship.

Another reason is added why the LORD should be adored. 'For' (*kî*) **among all the wise men of the nations** may introduce the class of wise men who acted as political advisers (8:9) or the reference may be

---

44. *mēʾên* which usually means 'without' or 'so that not' is not readily understood here. It may be a double negative of some sort, with the prefixed *min* seemingly redundant, or else emphatic, 'No one at all'. The REB (following BDB) points the consonants as *mēʾayin*, 'from where?' and translates, 'Where can one be found like you, LORD?' This does not affect the general understanding of the verse.

45. *yāʾātâ* from *yāʾâ* = *nāʾâ*, 'to be seemly'. For the use of the feminine in connection with an abstract, see GKC §§122q, 144b.

more general, 'among the wisest of the nations' (REB, treating 'all' as equivalent to a superlative). Take human wisdom at the highest level you can find anywhere, and it is not worthy to be compared to the wisdom that the LORD shows. As 'men' in 'wise men' is a translator's supplement, it is possible to take the phrase as 'the wise ones of the nations' (so NRSV, but probably not just as a feature of inclusive style because it is already in the RSV). These wise ones might well point to the gods whose wisdom they venerated (but note the possible link into v. 8). **And in all their kingdoms** extends the comparison probably to the kings of the nations who are advised by the wise ('among all their royalty', REB, taking the abstract term as used for the concrete, 'kings'). **There is no one like you.** This repeats the phrase of v. 6 to conclude this ascription of praise to the incomparable God whose wisdom is supreme in heaven and on earth.

2. Lifeless *v.* Living (10:8-10)

8. The focus reverts to idols and idol worshippers. It would seem that the reference in v. 8 is to all the wise men of v. 7. **They are all senseless and foolish.** 'All' (or 'at one and the same time' *HALOT* 30) who claim to be wise are 'senseless' (<√*bāʿar* III, repeated in vv. 14 and 21), that is, individuals who do not display the qualities that differentiate humans from animals (Pss. 73:22; 94:8). It is not that they lack intellectual ability, but exhibit moral and religious deficiency. They are unable to show truly human discrimination and learning because their thinking has been dominated by the dehumanising tenets of idolatry. **They are taught by worthless wooden idols.** This is a difficult clause, 'the instruction of worthless ones (<*hebel*, v. 5) is wood'. The thought seems to be that just as the idols themselves are basically pieces of wood, no matter how cleverly carved and decorated, so the teaching, instruction and moral correction that pervades those religions does not rise to any higher a level: it too is wood. On the significance of instruction, see 2:30; 5:3; cf. Prov. 8:10; 23:23.

9. The description of the idol manufacture continues, elaborating on the first stage mentioned in v. 4. Indeed many commentators would transfer v. 9 to that position, but that is to make Jeremiah conform to our ideas of logical development, and to depart from the contrasting pattern that is found throughout this material. **Hammered silver is brought from Tarshish and gold from Uphaz.** Silver was hammered into a thin sheet to be applied to the wooden idol (Isa. 40:19). Tarshish refers to a Phoenician settlement in the western Mediterranean, either Tartessus in Spain, or perhaps a site in Sardinia, where ore was mined before being transported to Tyre (Ezek. 27:12). The location of Uphaz (mentioned again in Dan. 10:5, NKJV, NRSV) is unknown, and the phrase may simply indicate 'finest gold' (Dan. 10:5 NIV). Following the Syriac version and the Targum, many emend Uphaz to Ophir (REB), situated in south-west Arabia and famous for its gold (1 Kgs. 9:28; Job 28:16). If Uphaz does refer to a geographical location, it may have been situated in the same area, so that the precious metals are described as being imported from the furthest west and east. Nothing was spared to get the best quality materials to produce these idols.

When the shaping of the human-like figures has been carried out by the craftsman and the idols have been covered in silver or gold, then they are dressed up in regal clothing. **What the craftsman and goldsmith have made is then dressed in blue and purple.** The vagaries of ancient production processes meant that there was little consistency in the colour of dyes; what mattered was the lustre and richness of the garment. 'Blue' (*təkēlet*) was a deep violet-purple colour with a variety of shades, principally occurring in the Old Testament in connection with the cloth used in the tabernacle and the garments of the priests. 'Purple' (*ʾargāmān*) is a deep red-purple, verging on black, also used for regal and priestly vestments. Both dyes were obtained from Mediterranean shellfish. These costly pigments were used to produce cloth that could be afforded only by the richest of the land. For the idols too no expense was spared and their garments were produced with great care. **All made by skilled workers.** 'Skilled' is 'wise', that is, endowed with practical skills. It is the same word as 'wise men' in v. 7. All that human ingenuity and prowess can produce is involved in the construction and adornment of the idols, but is it really 'wise'?

10. Over against the costly skills of idol production is set again the reality of the LORD. **But the LORD is the true God.** 'True God' is *ʾĕlōhîm ʾĕmet*, 'the God of truth', that is, the one whose existence is real and who can be depended upon ('faithfulness', Exod. 34:6). He is not *šeqer*, 'deception', a figment of human imagination and a product of skilful artifice. This statement is the language of confession of faith (Josh. 2:11; 2 Chron. 20:6; Ps. 100:3), and emphasises that the LORD is genuinely deity while dismissing the so-called gods. **He is the living**[46] **God.** It has been made clear that the idols are lifeless, without power or speech, but God is the one who has life in himself (23:36; Deut. 5:26; Josh. 3:10). It is encounter with that vital power of God that is at the heart of true religion. What is more, he is **the eternal King.**

46. For the plural of the adjective with *ʾĕlōhîm*, see GKC §132h.

'King' was a common title for a god in the ancient world, and this is true also of the Old Testament understanding of the LORD, particularly in a covenant context. But 'king' is used of the LORD not only as regards divine-human relationships, but also of his control of the heavenly realm (Pss. 95:3-5; 103:19-20) and over all the earth and its nations (cf. Mal. 1:14). The prophets were quite at home with the concept of the LORD as the universal sovereign and at the same time in a particular sense the God of Israel (Ps. 10:16; Isa. 43:15; 44:6). The epithet 'eternal' (*ʿôlām*) may possibly refer to the domain over which he rules, the full extent of time from beginning to end so that he is 'King of Eternity', but English translations prefer to take it as a divine attribute. His beginning is unknown, unlike that of the idols that have been made, and his dominion and sovereignty are of quite a different order from anything that idols can lay claim to (Exod. 15:18; Ps. 9:7; 10:16; 29:10; 66:7; 145:13; 146:10). This is a king whose reign does not come to an end. As the ever-living God he has all the time it needs to work out his purposes.

When he is angry/'at his wrath' (*qeṣep*) points to the expression of strong displeasure. At the LORD's anger, **the earth trembles.** 'Trembles' (<√*rāʿaš* I, 'to quake, shake') is applied to foreign nations, the heavens, the earth and various weapons of war (see Hag. 2:6-7). This brings out the fact of human accountability to the LORD. He is the one whose anger at sin and at the conduct of the nations is something that must be taken into account, because he has absolute power to enforce his decrees. **The nations cannot endure his wrath.** 'Endure' (<√*kûl* hiphil, 'to bear up under') points to the fact that the reality of divine wrath exposes the ineffectiveness of human resources just as clearly as the earthquake turns buildings into rubble. 'Wrath' (*zaʿam*) denotes extreme indignation, focusing more on its expression than on the inner emotion.

3. Doomed Impostors *v.* The Creator (10:11-13)

11. Surprisingly v. 11 is in Aramaic, the only Aramaic verse in Jeremiah, a fact that has often led to it being taken as a later insertion. But because it concerns the pagan gods and vv. 12-13 revert to the character of the LORD, it is needed to maintain the structure of the poem which alternately focuses on the idols and the LORD. Aramaic was a language which had existed for centuries and was widely used as the language of diplomacy and trade throughout the Near East in Jeremiah's day. It would have been known by many in Jerusalem (notice, for instance, the courtiers of Hezekiah, 2 Kgs. 18:26). The advice being given here is directed to the foreign people in their own language. The message is a carefully crafted one, which though not poetry (but see Holladay 1986, 1:325) has a symmetrical, chiastic structure, at whose centre there is a balance between the verbs 'make' (*ʿābad*, not used in this sense in Hebrew) and 'perish' (*ʾābad*), which involves a wordplay possible only in Aramaic. The NIV preserves the balance between 'heavens' and 'from under the heavens', and between 'the earth' and 'from the earth', but the first word 'these' is in fact last in the Hebrew, balancing 'gods' at the start of the verse.[47] It may be that the saying was a traditional proverb that had developed in interaction with the pagan religions of the area. **Tell them this.** The NIV punctuates in a way which indicates that these words are to be taken as a direct divine command to the people relayed by the prophet. It could equally be the prophet's own exhortation to the people as to what to say to their pagan neighbours.

The statement describes the heathen gods as being non-creative. This is central to the understanding of who the LORD is: he is the Creator. The false claims made on behalf of the heathen gods will be such as to ensure that they are removed from the universe. **These gods, who did not make the heavens and the earth, will perish from the earth and from under the heavens.** The verb may either declare their fate: 'they shall perish', or express a wish (or should one say curse?) 'let them perish'. Margaliot argues that the theology behind this verse points to a polemic against Babylonian influences. Anti-Canaanite texts rarely mention the role of the chief gods of Syria–Palestine as creating the universe (1980:301), but an important attribute of Babylonian high gods was to have created heaven and earth (1980:303). One of the epithets of Marduk, the main god of the neo-Babylonians, was 'lord of heaven and earth'. But it does not follow that this passage has then to be dated after the impact of Babylonian deportations on Judah. Assyrian religion shared many features with that of Babylon. In the light of the false claims made for Mesopotamian deities, the truth set out for Israel many centuries previously through Moses, took on a new significance: the LORD was the sole and true Creator of the universe, and he was its only ruler and judge. This re-presentation of old truths had already played a significant role in the polemic of Isaiah.

12. The focus switches back to the LORD; indeed it does so somewhat abruptly, without mentioning him by name ('But God' is a translator's

47. Others take 'these' as qualifying the heavens (NKJV, REB, NJPS), but that is probably not its function here.

supplement). Verses 12-16 are repeated in 51:15-19. This is a hymnic description of the power of the Creator. **But God made the earth by his power.** 'Power' is now *kōaḥ* (the vital energy inhering in a person or thing; the physical and mental capacity an individual can exert) rather than the synonym *gəbûrâ*, 'might' (v. 6). The verbs are in fact participles, expressing ongoing truths rather than relating past actions: 'It is he who made the earth by his power' (NRSV). The Creator (Pss. 96:5; 115:15; 136:5) is the one who is truly at the focus of Israel's religion. **He founded the world by his wisdom,** picking up the theme of human wisdom from v. 7b, and contrasting it with the multifaceted wisdom of the LORD. 'By wisdom the LORD laid the earth's foundations, by understanding he set the heavens in place' (Prov. 3:19). 'World' (*tēbēl*) is the whole earth or the world considered as a single entity, a poetic word often used in parallelism with 'earth' (*ʾereṣ*). **And stretched out the heavens by his understanding.** 'Stretching out' is a metaphor from erecting a tent. 'He stretches out the heavens like a tent' (Ps. 104:2; cf. also Isa. 40:22; 42:5).

13. When he thunders, the waters in the heavens roar.[48] The verse pictures the LORD as the one who controls meteorological phenomena. 'When he thunders' (*ləqôl tittô*, 'at the voice of his giving') is probably a deliberate inversion of the usual Hebrew phrase for a loud utterance, 'to give voice', drawing attention to the storm as the LORD's speaking. The tremendous forces unleashed in a thunderstorm are used to assert the completeness of the LORD's mastery of the elements—after all he created the thunder, and it has certainly not run out of his control. The following items of the description are drawn from Ps. 135:7. **He makes clouds rise**[49] **from the ends of the earth.**[50] 'Clouds' (*nāśîm*, 'lifted up ones') is a poetic term, which may also be taken as 'mists' (so REB; *HALOT*). 'The ends of the earth' may mean 'the horizon, the most distant visible land, from which the Hebrews believed the clouds arose (Ps. 135:7; Jer. 10:13)' (*NIDOTTE* 3:957). **He sends lightning with the rain and brings out the wind from his storehouses.** Lightning was frequently associated with divine judgment (Nah. 2:4; Hab. 3:11; Zech. 9:14). 'Rain' (*māṭār*) is the downpour which accompanied the storm. The 'storehouses' are the king's treasury from which he can

48. *hămôn*, 'roar', is also used of the sound of rain in 1 Kgs. 18:41. The noun may be associated with the noise made by a crowd or multitude, sometimes with overtones of confusion. It is translated as 'commotion' in 3:23.

49. A gnomic use of *waw*-consecutive imperfect after a participle (*IBHS* §33.3.5d).

50. The kethibh is *ʾereṣ*, 'earth'; the qere is *hāʾāreṣ*, 'the earth', cf. 51:16.

disperse largess as he sees fit (Deut. 28:12; Job 38:22; Ps. 33:7). All the realm the LORD has created remains under the sovereign control of its powerful ruler.

4. Man-made Frauds *v.* Israel's LORD (10:14-16)

14. For the final time the switch is made back to the idol-makers and their idols. **Everyone is senseless and without knowledge** picks up the theme of v. 8a, but now the focus seems to be more on the idol-makers than on the wise in the nations. 'Is senseless' (<√*bāʿar* niphal) is used in v. 8 (in the qal) to describe their condition of less than human perceptivity, but here (and in v. 21) the niphal of the verb is used, probably suggesting 'be overcome by senselessness' or 'display senseless by one's conduct'. It is not the technical skill of the craftsmen or their artistic finesse that is being criticised, but their religious sensitivity and awareness of the one true God. Indeed the word suggests that their conduct is totally lacking in truly human perceptivity; they have descended to the level of animal life ('brutish' AV, REB). **Every goldsmith is shamed by**[51] **his idols.** He has expended a great deal of time and effort to make them, and one would expect him to be proud of his artistry. It is not that he feels shame, but what he has produced does not match up to expectations. After all it is a god that he is making, and how can the lifeless be divine? He is therefore shown up by his workmanship 'for' (*kî*) **his images**[52] **are a fraud.** They are 'a lie' (*šeqer* 5:2), a delusion; they are not what they purport to be because they do not come to life. **They have no breath in them.** 'Breath' (*rûaḥ*) is what characterised both man and animals ('every creature that has the breath of life in it', Gen. 6:17; a different word is used for 'breath' in Gen. 2:7) and gave them the capacity to come to life. But the workmanship of the idol-craftsmen is inanimate, without life—and yet they worship these lifeless things, and say they are gods.

15. They are worthless uses *hebel* (vv. 2, 8) to describe the idols as a puff of smoke or a current of air in contrast to breath associated with life. Consequently they are **the objects of mockery**, or perhaps better, 'a work of delusion' (NRSV). Certainly 'objects' (<√*ʿāśâ*, 'to do/make') presents the idols as produced by labour, and 'mockery'

51. The preposition *min*, 'from', is used in two different idioms: first privatively, marking what is missing, 'without' knowledge; and then causally, 'because of, by'.

52. *niskô* is usually 'his drink-offering' (cf. 7:15), which comes from √*nāsak*, 'to pour', but this is also used of pouring molten metal into a mould; hence the translation 'image'.

(<√*tāʿaʿ*, 'to mock, trick, jeer at') may indicate the attitude that should be adopted towards them, or else refer to the mistaken beliefs of those who made them. **When their judgment comes** (<√*pāqad*, 6:15; 8:12), **they will perish.** At the time when the LORD comes to inspect and reward as appropriate what the nations are doing, they—probably both the idols and their makers—will be condemned and destroyed by him.

16. But that is not the fate awaiting those in Israel who worship the one true God. **He who is the Portion**[53] **of Jacob is not like these.** 'Jacob' refers to the covenant people as a whole (2:4). 'The portion of Jacob' is the one who has given himself to his people as their allotted inheritance. Though this particular title is found elsewhere only in 51:19, the idea of the LORD as the portion of his people is common (Pss. 16:5; 73:26; 119:57; 142:5; Lam. 3:24). It may be that the expression arose through awareness of the reciprocal nature of the covenant bond by inverting the expression of passages such as Deut. 32:9, 'the LORD's portion is his people'. When the Israelites took Canaan, each tribe received its portion, except the Levites whose portion was the LORD. As the others lived off the land, they were to live from the offerings brought to the LORD at the Tabernacle (Num. 18:20-24; Deut. 18:1-2). This title then refers to the LORD as the one who sustains and provides for Jacob. In this he is unlike the ineffectual non-entities associated with the idols, **for** (*kî*) **he is the Maker of all things.** 'Maker'/ 'Former' (<√*yāṣar*, 1:5) points not only to God's general creative skill, but also to the way he has been active in providing salvation. **Including Israel, the tribe of his inheritance** (12:7). This describes the relationship from the opposite point of view: the LORD has taken Israel as his possession (2:7). 'Tribe' (*šebeṭ*) originally referred to a part of a tree, a branch formed into a war-club or a sceptre of royal office. It then became transferred to the leaders who exercised that office and also the people over whom they had authority. Here Israel is not thought of as twelve tribes but as a single entity over which the LORD rules by right of deliverance.

The final description is **The LORD Almighty is his name.** 'LORD Almighty'/'The LORD of hosts' (2:19) indicated that all heavenly and earthly powers were under his control. Since every conceivable force and power was at his disposal, the hymnic ascription of dominance is a very fitting way to end this poem which contrasts the ineffectiveness and futility of idols with the reality of the power of the LORD.

In the ancient world the divinity of a god or goddess was recognised

53. The REB repoints to yield *ḥōlēq*, 'Jacob's chosen God'.

through their having associated with them characteristics such as incomparable power, eternity, the ability to control natural forces and the ability to create and restore life. This polemic shows that far from possessing such attributes (even to some limited extent) the lifeless idols and the gods which they represent, and which were assumed in some way to live in and through the image, were utterly impotent and incapable of doing anything. To worship them was to become something less than human because the worshippers were abasing themselves before the inanimate and the non-existent. Only in the LORD, the true and all powerful God, could true security and fulfilment be found. The many, varied titles and descriptions of the LORD recall the people to covenant loyalty to him and to faith commitment to his control and provision.

Polemic against idolatry seems remote from modern concerns, but that is a major misconception. The idol was the product of human craftsmanship, and the ideology associated with pagan worship was the precipitate of corrupt human thinking. The pursuit of wealth and economic prowess still sets up human achievement and physical production as the goal of social activity. If the qualities that a civilisation admires are ruthless exploitation and business success, it has created for itself a materialist culture where ultimate values are found in the world of things. This is the basis for an idolatrous society just as surely as the behaviour of the ancient world. It leads to a society denying the existence, let alone the significance, of the spiritual realm. It sets up a society trying to live estranged from God and not realising that its own downfall is inevitably entailed in the value system it has embraced, a system which promotes human self-sufficiency and which seeks to find the ultimate basis for existence in what mankind dictate. The only response to such futile and doomed thinking is that which is presented here: to point beyond terms of reference created by human skill to the reality of the God of creation and the provision of the Portion of Jacob.

E. THE COMING EXILE (10:17-25)

This section brings to a close the Second Scroll of Jeremiah. In it we leave the polemic against idolatry and resume the description of the invasion coming upon the land. It is often read against the circumstances of Nebuchadnezzar's first invasion of the land in 597 BC though there is nothing which absolutely establishes this.

The identity of the speakers in these verses is a feature that causes considerable problems. There are three possibilities: the prophet, the LORD, and the community, probably Jerusalem personified as a woman, which would resume the language of earlier sections. As regards allocating verses to the speakers, the only clear factors are that the LORD is the speaker in v. 18, and that he is not the speaker in v. 21 or vv. 23-25. The references in v. 20 to 'my tent' and particularly to 'my sons' connects this verse with Jerusalem. However, there are many who consider that the 'I' who speaks throughout these verses is in fact the prophet, who to a greater or lesser extent identifies with the people and gives voice not so much to what they *do* think as to what they *should* think. Though it is not totally certain, I have taken vv. 17-18 as a prophetic announcement of impending destruction, and vv. 19-25 as an instance of Jeremiah's prophetic intercession on behalf of the people.

1. Invasion and Destruction (10:17-18)

17. Jeremiah speaks to the people, personified as a woman. **Gather up your belongings to leave the land, you who live[54] under siege[55].** Both the imperative 'gather up' (*ʾispî* <√*ʾāsap,* 'to gather', also 'to remove', 16:5) and the participle 'you who live' *(yōšebet*) are feminine. 'Belongings' occurs only here and may well be 'bundle' (NRSV), such possessions as might be gathered in a large sheet, tied together and carried over one's shoulder. 'To leave the land' is simply 'from the land' (*mēʾereṣ*), but the expansion seems justified in the light of the following verse. Otherwise it is simply an injunction to pick them up from the ground. Jeremiah sees the city not only under siege, but on the point of capitulation, and advises that the inhabitants gather up their possessions into the small bundle that they will be allowed to take with them when they are marched off into exile by their captors.

18. The prophet justifies his exhortation to the people by stating the divine message on which it was based. **For** (*kî*) **this is what the LORD says: 'At this time I will hurl out those who live in this land.'** 'Those who live' (*yôšəbê*) echoes 'you who live' (*yôšebet*) in the previous verse. 'Hurl' (<√*qālaʿ*) is used for a slinger hurling the stone from the catapult (Isa. 22:17-18), of God's action against David's enemies in 1 Sam. 25:29, and is expressive of the decision and energy with which the LORD will expel his people from their land. 'At this time'/'on this occasion' indicates that the LORD's judgment on the

54. The kethibh reads *yšbty*, perhaps to be pointed as a 2nd person feminine perfect with the old style ending, *yāšabtî*, 'you live/dwell', but the qere fits in better, cf. GKC §90n.

55. 'O inhabitant of the fortress' (NKJV) takes *māṣôr*, 'siege', in its other sense, 'a fortified city, a stronghold' (Ps. 60:9).

people had not previously taken this form. **I will bring distress**[56] **on them so that they may be captured.** The final clause is not easy to understand as it is literally 'so that they will find' with neither subject nor object clearly defined. The NKJV supplies '⌞it so⌟', with the sense that the people will find it a time of distress (similarly NRSV). The NASB follows the LXX and Vulgate by repointing the verb as a passive (*yimmāṣĕʾû* niphal), 'they may be found', that is, 'captured' as in the NIV. Much less plausibly the REB relates the word to the root *māṣâ*, 'to squeeze' so that the phrase intensifies the previous verb, 'I shall press them and squeeze them dry'. Perhaps the NRSV 'so that they shall feel it' expresses the underlying idea as well as any. It is the LORD who is at work in the situation, pressing the people hard in the siege, and their enemies are surely going to get the upper hand, so the people may as well be prepared for disaster.

2. Prophetic Intercession (10:19-25)

Jeremiah sets out a series of impressions that capture the tension and despair of a land being invaded by enemy forces (vv. 19-22). Against this background he presents a case to the LORD, not for averting punishment but for moderating it so that there may be some hope left (vv. 23-25).

a. A Cry of Anguish (10:19-20)

19. The cry of grief, **Woe to me because of my injury!**, indicates a situation of intense personal danger and distress, often with the idea of impending death. 'Injury' (*šeber*) uses the word that Jeremiah is fond of to indicate the destruction of the land (8:21; 14:17; 30:12, 15). But who is uttering these words? It cannot be the prophet speaking of an injury he had personally sustained. Either the city/land as personified is speaking, or the prophet gives voice on her behalf regarding what she feels. (Similar interpretative problems occur in 4:19-20 and 8:18–9:1.) There is perhaps not much difference between these two representations, though if it is the land speaking then this is a prophecy of what the reaction of the people is going to be, but if it is the prophet speaking on behalf of the city/land the prophecy is rather one of what Jeremiah considers her reaction ought to be (without implying that it will in fact be so). 'He did not grieve on his own account; but, as I have said, he represents the grief which the whole people ought to have felt, which yet they did not feel at all. As then they were so stupid, and

56. 'Bring distress' is the hiphil form *wahăṣērôtî* <√*ṣārar*, which involves a play on and re-echoes 'siege' *māṣôr*, from the related root *ṣûr*.

proudly derided God and his threatenings, the Prophet shows to them, as it were in a mirror, what grievous and bitter lamentation awaited them' (Calvin 1850, 2:47).

The enemy has inflicted devastation on the city. **My wound is incurable!**[57] Her situation is 'severe' (NKJV, NRSV). **Yet I said to myself, 'This**[58] **is my sickness**[59]**, and I must endure it.'** Wound and sickness are also found together in 6:7. Perhaps 'sickness' contains the idea of a deteriorating but not fatal condition (*NIDOTTE* 2:142). The prophet is speaking on behalf of Jerusalem and setting out how she should feel when the enemy besiege her. The language is that of resignation arising out of recognition of the inevitability and justice of the judgment that has fallen on her. Alternatively, the prophet may be taken as speaking mockingly. Prior to the fall of the city, the people blindly continue to rely on the peace prophets and their view that Jerusalem will not be destroyed whatever happens. 'But this is just a sickness I have to put up with. No matter what, all will be well' (6:14; 8:11). The prophet describes such unfounded optimism to expose it for what it is.

20. Jeremiah then shows the people that they ought to acknowledge that the crisis they will face is extremely severe. The language used is that of a desert nomad whose tent has been destroyed (cf. 4:20). **My tent is destroyed; all its ropes are snapped.** It is not just a matter of it having fallen down, so that it could be easily and quickly re-erected. There had been major damage done. Its ropes are broken. Those in the city under siege recognise that the land has already been devastated. **My sons are gone from me and are no more; no one is left now to pitch my tent or to set up my shelter.** 'My sons' refers to citizens of the city who have already gone out of the city to battle, and have been captured or slain. Even should the enemy depart in a night, the population has been decimated and would be insufficient for the task of rebuilding the economy.

b. Folly and Its Consequences (10:21-22)

21. In words that reflect Jeremiah's thinking the cause of the city's downfall is traced back to the poor quality of leadership in the land. 'For' (*kî*) **the shepherds are senseless.** The shepherds are the rulers

57. The feminine niphal participle is pointed *naḥlâ* (<√*ḥālâ*, 'to be/become ill/weak') to distinguish it from *naḥălâ*, 'inheritance' (GKC §63c).

58. The direct speech begins with *ʾak*, which may be a particle of emphasis, 'indeed, surely', or of contrast, 'but, however'.

59. The form *ḥŏlî* may have arisen by contraction from *ḥolyiy* (GKC §126y).

(2:8; Ezek. 34:1-31), who should have been providing adequate guidance for the people, but who have failed. ‘Senseless’ (<√*bāʿar* III, vv. 8, 14) points not to lack of intelligence, but to lack of spiritual perception. They have not grasped the true dimensions of the situation facing the people. Consequently they **do not enquire** (<√*dāraš*) **of the LORD.** They have not sought true guidance from the LORD for the way they were to direct the affairs of state, presumably by going to a prophet like Jeremiah for help (21:2; 37:3; Exod. 18:15; 1 Sam. 9:9). **So** (‘on account of this’) **they do not prosper and all their flock is scattered.** ‘Scattered’ (<√*pûṣ*, 9:16) is used of scattering as divine chastisement. ‘Prosper’ (<√*śākal*, cf. 9:23) can also mean ‘have insight, have wisdom, deal wisely’. This imagery is developed more extensively in Ezekiel 34. Note that here it is ‘their flock’ (<*marʿît*, ‘pasturage’ as in 23:1, but by metonymy also denoting the flock they provide pasture and care for [Ps. 95:7]) rather than ‘my flock’.

22. This verse continues Jeremiah’s description of what he has been permitted to see in vision. He speaks in terms similar to those found in 4:19-20. **Listen! The report is coming.** *qôl* (‘voice’) is here used with exclamatory force (GKC §146b). News of what is happening elsewhere is in process of reaching the city. **A great commotion from the land of the north!** ‘Commotion’ (*raʿaš*, 8:16; 10:10) is a word used of the impact of an earthquake (Amos 1:1) which tosses everything down in ruins. But this commotion is brought about not by a natural phenomenon but by the armed might of the invading army as it rumbles along (47:3; Isa. 9:4). The reference is to the northern invaders so long prophesied by Jeremiah (‘land of the north’, 6:22). Their advance will not halt until it has wiped Judah out. **It will make the towns of Judah desolate, a haunt of jackals.** For first phrase, see 4:7; 6:8; 9:10. For ‘desolate’ (*səmāmâ*), see 4:27 and 9:11; and for ‘a haunt of jackals’, see 9:10. There will be nothing left.

c. Jeremiah’s Prayer (10:23-25)

Many feel that vv. 23-25 are secondary in the text because they seem to be a concatenation of other passages: v. 23 reflects Prov. 16:9 and 20:24; v. 24, Ps. 6:2; and v. 25 is obviously related to Ps. 79:6-7. It is also argued that these words are pious, whining, vengeful, self-excusing words of people confident of their own knowledge. Holladay views Ps. 79 as earlier than Jeremiah (but see on v. 25) and observes: ‘It is appalling to see traditional words used to justify irresponsibility, but there is no doubt that such words were used in Jeremiah’s day, and his weaving together of these texts is in an ironic way to give resonance to Yahweh's determination to punish' (1986, 1:344). However, it seems more reasonable to take these words as uttered by the prophet, drawing on the use of the language of Scripture, shared by the people and himself, in such a way as to plead on their behalf.

23. Jeremiah begins his petition on behalf of the people by acknowledging the LORD's sovereignty and human incapacity. **I know, O LORD, that a man's life is not his own.** Life is *derek*, 'way', probably in the sense of his whole lifestyle including its outcome (2:17). The direction mankind generally find their lives taking is influenced by factors outwith their control. **It is not for man to direct[60] his steps.** An individual travelling through this life does not ultimately determine what happens to him. 'Life'/'way' and 'steps' are expressions often found in wisdom literature (Ps. 37:23; Prov. 16:9; 20:24). Jeremiah is pleading for divine action because what has happened to the people has not been solely determined by them, but has come upon them because of external and uncontrollable factors. He is not presenting the people as guiltless in the situation, but rather helpless and in need of divine intervention from the one who really directs and controls the circumstances of life.

24. On behalf of the people Jeremiah recognises their need of correction and discipline. **Correct me, LORD, but only** (*'ak*) **with justice.** 'Correct' (2:19) is used of verbal and physical punishment, but asks that this be with restraint, according to the measure of what has gone wrong. **Not[61] in your anger** (*'ap*)**, lest you reduce me to nothing.** If the people had to bear the full force of God's wrath against their sin, they would be utterly consumed. Jeremiah does not plead for avoidance of punishment, but that there would be a remnant left who would experience the restoration of the LORD's favour.

25. This verse should not be read as an expression of vindictive nationalism, as if the heathen nations were only fit for experiencing God's wrath while Judah was exempt from divine scrutiny and judgment. It expresses acceptance of the LORD's rule and his right to punish those who rebel against his purposes. **Pour out your wrath** (*ḥēmâ*, 4:4) **on the nations that do not acknowledge you, on the peoples** (*mišpāḥâ*, 'clan', 1:15) **who do not call on your name.** 'Call

60. The Hebrew combination of participle plus infinitive 'walking and making firm' is unusual.

61. This is a less frequent use of *'al*, 'not', not before the verb but before another strongly emphasised word in the sentence (*IBHS* §34.2.1e; GKC §152h).

on your name' is a technical term (occurring only here in Jeremiah) for general prayer or address to the deity in worship (Gen. 4:26; Ps. 79:6). It is not a specifically Yahwistic term, being also applied to the invocation of the Baal prophets (1 Kgs. 18:24, 25, 26). It may indicate a confession of general faithfulness (Isa. 12:4; Ps. 80:19; 116:13, 17) or perhaps a call to worship (Ps. 105:1; Balentine 1984:166). The heathen do not acknowledge the LORD's sovereignty over them; Israel, as his covenant people, should. What the nations have been permitted to inflict on the LORD's people is incongruous. They have gone beyond what was remitted to them and their advance should be brought to a halt. **For (*kî*) they have devoured Jacob; they have devoured him completely and destroyed[62] his homeland.** For 'Jacob' see v. 15. 'Homeland' (*nāweh*) is used of the whole land of Canaan (23:3; Ps. 79:7) or of Zion (31:23; 2 Sam. 15:25; Isa. 27:10; Jer. 31:23). It embodies the idea of 'rest' often in a rural setting, and its meaning then developed to cover both settlement and pasture. The notion of military outposts (*NIDOTTE* 3:55) seems quite improbable. If the enemy are allowed to carry on with their plans, the chosen people will not be chastised, but exterminated. What has already occurred leads them to speak in absolute terms already, but there is more to come.

These words correspond to Ps. 79:6-7, though for *mišpāḥôt*, 'clans', 'families, peoples', Ps. 79 has *mamlākōt*, 'kingdoms', and 'devoured and consumed' is lacking in Ps. 79:7. The psalm begins with the destruction of Jerusalem and the Temple, and would seem to draw on what the prophet had already said. At this juncture in the development of the Second Scroll, Jeremiah puts these words into the mouths of the people to alert them to the intensity of the impending crisis. They should recognise that though people may decide on the course of action which they think appropriate, God can and will overrule it (Luke 12:20; Rom. 11:36; Phil. 2:13). When the course of action has been one of rebellion, then there should be repentance and a return to the LORD. If not, the stark alternative is spelled out for all to see.

62. *šāmam* most frequently occurs with the sense 'to suffer destruction', but when it has fientive force, it is regularly glossed as 'to lay waste, to cause desolation' (Num. 21:30; Hos. 2:12).

V. REJECTION OF THE COVENANT

(11:1–13:27)

OUTLINE

A. Rejection of the Covenant Message (11:1-17)
   1. Hear the Curse of the Covenant (11:1-5)
   2. Hear and Do (11:6-8)
   3. Refusal to Hear (11:9-13)
   4. I Will Not Hear (11:14)
   5. Lightning Will Strike (11:15-17)

B. Rejection of the Covenant Messenger (11:18–12:17)
   1. The Plot at Anathoth (11:18-23)
   2. The Prosperity of the Wicked (12:1-6)
   3. My Abandoned Inheritance (12:7-13)
   4. The Prospect for Other Peoples (12:14-17)

C. Rejection of the Covenant People (13:1-27)
   1. The Linen Belt (13:1-11)
   2. The Wineskin (13:12-14)
   3. Caught by Darkness (13:15-17)
   4. Royal Humiliation (13:18-19)
   5. The Threefold Impossibility (13:20-23)
   6. Scattered to the Winds (13:24-27)

Chapters 11–20

There are certain fixed points in the analysis of the structure of Jeremiah. One of these is to be located at the end of chapter 20, which brings a major block of material to a close. Less certain, but still plausible, is the view that chapter 11 marks the beginning of additional material which can be divided into four main sections, 11:1–13:37; 14:1–15:9; 15:10–17:27; and 18:1–20:18. The repetition of 'Cursed is/be the man who' (11:3; 20:15) may well be a compositional device to indicate that this material is to be taken as bracketed together. That the link is of this sort—the curse of the covenant—is also significant for the theme of this block in which (in comparison to, say, 7:7) it is conspicuous that there is no mention of the prospect of blessing if Judah were to change its behaviour for the better. Though Jeremiah continues to reiterate the need for repentance (13:15-17; 17:19-27; 18:12), it is no longer as prominent a feature of the prophet's message as it was previously.

The material in this part of the prophecy is also differentiated from the Second Scroll by having a greater proportion of prose relative to poetry. In this prose we have descriptions of symbolic actions that Jeremiah engaged in (chaps. 13, 18, 19) as well as narrative concerning his personal history (11:18-23; 20:1-6). Whereas in chapters 2–10 the person of Jeremiah remained fairly much in the shadows, he now becomes significant in himself. Especially we become aware of his inner suffering in the series of passages traditionally known as the Confessions (11:18-23; 12:1-6; 15:10-21; 17:14-18; 18:18-23; 20:7-18). However, it is not principally for biographical information that these are included, but because the prophet's fate anticipatively mirrors that of his people. By spurning Jeremiah as the LORD's prophet the community brings upon itself the suffering of the people rejected by the LORD, just as the prophet had already known suffering through their rejection of his mission.

The dating of this material is uncertain. In general one supposes that 11:1–20:18 pre-dates the material in the block from chapter 21 on, but this is not conclusively established. It is probable that 13:18-19 date from the brief reign of Jehoiachin in 597 BC, and that they and 14:17-18 are the latest material to be incorporated in this extension to Jeremiah's Scroll, which was probably brought together in its present form and sequence not long after Jehoiachin went into exile. Generally there is an absence of references to Babylon, which would indicate Jeremiah was drawing on earlier material from the reign of Jehoiakim, if not from that of Josiah. Though it is no longer possible to be certain when individual oracles were originally delivered, the selection has been made because of the dire circumstances that faced the nation in that the Babylonians have now made their presence felt.

Chapters 11–13
This division of the prophecy focuses on the covenant, and does so in three sections: the people's attitude towards the covenant (11:1-17), their attitude towards the covenant messenger (11:18–12:17), and then the LORD's attitude towards the covenant people, which is set out principally by means of two enacted parables (13:1-27).

A. REJECTION OF THE COVENANT MESSAGE (11:1-17)

This section contains the second major prose sermon of the prophecy, in which are employed language and style very similar to the early section, 7:1–8:3. Of particular interest is the fact that there are substantial echoes of material also found in Deuteronomy. For instance, 'the terms of this covenant' (vv. 2, 3, 6) also occurs in Deut. 29:1, 9; 'cursed is the man who …' (v. 3) occurs repeatedly in Deut. 27:15-26, along with 'Amen!' found here in v. 5; the phrase 'out of the iron-smelting furnace' (v. 4) parallels that found in Deut. 4:20; and the phrase 'a land flowing with milk and honey' (v. 5) recalls that found in Deut. 6:3; 11:9; 26:9, 15; 27:3; 31:20. The similarities extend from single words such as 'stubbornness' (v. 8; 'persist' in Deut. 29:19) through to standard expressions such as 'follow other gods'/'walk after other gods' (v. 10; Deut. 6:4; 8:19; 11:28; 13:2; 28:14).

The explanations advanced for these resemblances are determined by the reconstruction of the life and times of Jeremiah adopted by various writers. Those who find little or nothing of Jeremiah in the book called after him take the use of these phrases as indicating the common background of Deuteronomy and the prophecy in the work of the Deuteronomic editors who during the Exile produced both the book of Jeremiah we now have and who are also held to be responsible for producing the history of the book of Kings. The material of 11:1-17 is therefore interpreted as an attempt to explain to the exilic community what happened to Jerusalem in its last days. It is of course the case that accepting Deuteronomy as Mosaic in origin considerably diminishes the appeal of such an hypothesis. It may well be that Jeremiah and the editor(s) of Kings shared a style common to their day that reflected the impact of Josiah's reformation and the interest aroused at that time in Jerusalem in the material of the Pentateuch.

Those who are more favourably inclined towards the prophecy as preserving material that is to be substantially attributed to Jeremiah himself find two possible locations in his life for the original delivery of this sermon. One is at a point early in the reign of Josiah, not long after the scroll of the Law was found in the Temple. This date would explain the references to the prevalence of idolatrous worship in v. 13, a feature which is hardly consistent with the reforming moves made by Josiah. This section would then record some of the earliest of Jeremiah's preaching at a time when he was supportive of Josiah's reforms.

Another possibility, and the one adopted here, is to take this material as a recall to covenant faithfulness at a later stage in Jeremiah's ministry, possibly early in the reign of Jehoiakim, perhaps before the Temple Address of chapters 7 and 26. While this material bears many resemblances to passages in the Pentateuch, and especially Deuteronomy, the connection is of a very general sort and is not in itself conclusive regarding the setting of the sermon or its origin. It should also be noted that there is distinctive vocabulary in this section which is not found in Deuteronomy, e.g. 'conspiracy' (v. 9) and 'forefathers' (v. 10). The mention of a conspiracy and of 'returned' in vv. 9-10 further supports a later date for this material.

1. Hear the Curse of the Covenant (11:1-5)

In vv. 1-5 we have the presentation of the demands of the covenant, followed by a statement of the consequences both in blessing and cursing that will be determined by the people's reaction.

1-2. This is the word that came to Jeremiah from the LORD is an introductory formula that is found elsewhere in the book (7:1; 18:1; 30:1), marking the start of a distinct section of the prophecy. It leads to the expectation that Jeremiah is about to be addressed, but v. 2 begins with a plural command, **Listen to the terms of this covenant**. The simplest way of understanding this injunction is that it was addressed to Jeremiah's original audience, not necessarily at the time when they first renewed their covenant allegiance to the LORD under Josiah (2 Kgs. 23:3), but at some later date when their attention was again drawn to that pledge, possibly during the course of some ceremony at the Temple.

But problems arise because in the following clause, **Tell them to the people of Judah and to those who live in Jerusalem,**[1] where the

1. One notices that the preposition 'to' is first *ʾel* and then *ʿal* (also in 18:11). This is an instance of the interchangeability of these two prepositions.

verb is singular. Emending the form of the Hebrew verb to a plural form[2] is unsatisfactory because it requires further changes to be made, for instance, to the first verb in v. 3, which is also singular. The repetition of 'listen to/obey the words of this covenant' at the end of v. 3 has generated the suggestion that v. 2 and the first clause of v. 3 is an addition which should be deleted (e.g. McKane 1986, 1:236-37). Keil (1873, 1:211), following Kimchi, understands the plural to refer to the prophets in general, and their responsibility to proclaim the truths God had committed to them. This would then make for a natural transition to Jeremiah in the singular as one of the prophetic number. Ellison (1962:155) follows a suggestion of Weiser that 'Listen to the terms of this covenant' is a heading to the sermon in which 'covenant' is repeated as a key term, and that the second statement is the directive to Jeremiah to address a particular audience. Usually these items are in the reverse order, and recognition of this makes involved hypotheses unnecessary.

'Terms'/'words' refers to the stipulations of the covenant where the overlord sets out what he requires of his subject people (Exod. 20:1; Deut. 29:1, 9). 'This covenant' should not be taken simply as a reference to Josiah's covenant (or, with many modern scholars, to the recently composed Deuteronomy). As v. 4 makes clear, 'this' in v. 1 anticipates the later reference to the Sinai covenant established through the mediatorship of Moses. Indeed, it is a false dichotomy to distinguish between the Sinai covenant and Josiah's covenant because the latter was essentially viewed as a renewal and perpetuation of the former. Similarly it is an unfortunate feature of much scholarship to set the conception of the covenant in Deuteronomy over against that of the Sinai covenant rather than accepting the straightforward understanding of Deuteronomy as an hortatory reinforcement of the Sinai covenant as it was applied by Moses to the conditions expected to prevail among the people once they had entered the land—which they were shortly to do.

Apart from reference to the ark of the covenant in 3:16, this is the first use of the word 'covenant' in Jeremiah. Indeed, it is remarkable how infrequently the prophets do in fact use the word, but the absence of the term does not imply unfamiliarity with the concept. The

2. 'Tell them' in BHS is *wədibbartām*, 'you (sing.) speak them', with a plural pronominal suffix pointing back to the 'terms/words of this covenant'. BHS suggests that the form should be plural *wədibbartem*. This does not solve the problem of the switch to the singular, but delays it to the start of v. 3. The LXX reads a singular verb, which as the harder reading should be retained.

prophetic message was an elaboration of the implications and demands of the covenant. Jeremiah again refers to covenant explicitly in 14:21; 22:9; 31:31-34; 32:40; 33:20-26; 34:8-22; 50:5.

The injunction to 'listen' introduces the verb *šāmaʿ*, 'to hear', which is one of the key terms in these addresses. This is made possible by the Hebrew idiom 'listen to voice of' (*šāmaʿ bəqôl*) which has the sense 'to obey'. The full expression is found in vv. 4, 7, and the NIV considers an abbreviated form occurs in 'obey' (v. 3). Note also 'hear' (v. 6), 'listen' (vv. 8, 10, and used of God in vv. 11, 14). The repetition drives home the point that the covenant is all about listening to what is said and obeying. The older word 'heed' makes the point well. True self-knowledge does not arise through introspection alone but requires also a response to be given to the divine word. It is only as physical hearing is translated into obedient action that an individual or a nation finds satisfaction and self-fulfilment in living relationship with God himself. That is when self-knowledge is truly achieved.

3. Jeremiah is directed to **tell them that this is what the LORD, the God of Israel, says.** The reference is, of course, to Israel as the covenant people of God. **Cursed is the man who does not obey the terms of this covenant.** When kings of the ancient world imposed their treaty obligations on subject peoples, they accompanied them with a statement of the blessings that would be theirs if they obeyed and of the curses that would fall on them if they failed to keep what was required of them. These obligations were undertaken in the presence of the gods, who were supposed to bring the curses upon those who failed to live up to their obligations. The same structure is found in the Sinai covenant (Lev. 26:3-46; Deut. 28; 30:15-20). The reality of God's covenant involves enduring the penalty of God's curse if the covenant is disregarded. 'Cursed is the man who does not uphold the words of this law by carrying them out' (Deut. 27:26). Hence the importance of the people being informed about what those terms and conditions were. That the focus of the prophet's message is on the curse rather than the blessing is realistic, but ominous.

4. The requirements of the covenant have not changed since the days of the Exodus. **The terms I commanded your forefathers when I brought them out of Egypt** (cf. 7:22), **out of the iron-smelting furnace.** The covenant words were divinely imposed because the covenant had not been negotiated between equal parties; rather the LORD had laid claim to the people by rescuing them from their situation of extreme misery and determined the terms of the relationship between them. Iron smelting involved very high temperatures, and such a furnace is used as a picture of abject misery (Deut. 4:20; 7:8; 8:18; 26:8-9; 31:20; 1 Kgs. 8:51: developed further in Ezek. 22:18-22; notice also 'furnace of affliction', Isa. 48:10). There was an obligation of gratitude, and the covenant terms spelled out the form in which that gratitude and loyalty should shape itself.

The main condition of continuing to enjoy the positive provisions of the covenant could be summed up as obedience. **I said, 'Obey me and do everything I command you, and you will be my people, and I will be your God.'** 'Obey me' is literally 'hear my voice' (Deut. 28:1, 2). The formula of the covenant bond ('You will be my people and I will be your God', 7:23; Exod. 6:7; 19:5; Lev. 26:12; Deut. 29:13) brings out the bilateral nature of the covenant commitment. The king who had rescued them required complete obedience to his commands, but there is also the promise of his ongoing protection and provision.

5. The address of God to the generation of the Exodus continues: **Then I will fulfil the oath I swore to your forefathers, to give them a land flowing with milk and honey.** 'Then' is probably too weak a translation of *ləmaʿan*, 'so that, in order that' (7:18), which sets out the important link between covenant obedience and enjoyment of covenant blessing (Gen. 18:19). The LORD's oath is the solemn promise which he gave as the covenant king to their forefathers, the patriarchs. 'Fulfil'/'cause to stand' refers to his confirmation and bestowal of covenant blessing (Gen. 6:18; 17:7, 19; Exod. 6:4). What happened at Sinai was the realisation of the covenant promise made to them (Gen. 15:18; 17:8; 35:12; Exod. 3:17). This particularly involved their occupation of the land of promise. The description 'flowing with milk and honey' is a proverbial one for the bounty and fertility of the land, particularly as it would be viewed by a pastoral group of people rather than by settled farmers. It occurs repeatedly in the Pentateuch (e.g. Exod. 3:8, 17; Deut. 6:3; 11:9), but apart from that it is found only here and in 32:22, Josh. 5:6 and Ezek. 20:6, 15.

But from this historical résumé there was an important principle to be learned by the current generation. Then and now, if there is no obedience, the subjects of the king cannot expect to enjoy his favour; his blessing does not descend on rebels. That was precisely what the majority theology of Jeremiah's day had forgotten. Occupation of the land of promise was very much at the centre of the covenant blessing which the people were already enjoying, **the land you possess today**/'as at this day'. The phrase denotes the continuity of the blessing from the time of the Exodus down to the time of the delivery of this message (Deut. 2:30; 4:20). The LORD had been true to his covenant obligations, but if the people persist in reneging on their commitment, then the threat that hangs over them is obvious.

I answered, 'Amen, LORD.' Jeremiah indicates his acceptance of what has been stated (28:6). But there is more than just a personal pledge of loyalty. In the liturgy of the covenant renewal ceremony, 'Amen' was the response of the people to the curses of the covenant (Deut. 27:15-26). In entering into the covenant they had accepted that these penalties would be imposed on them if they were disobedient. Jeremiah is therefore expressing his acceptance of the continuing force of the curse for the people of God. They had recently renewed their acceptance of these very terms. Surely they had to recognise what they had committed themselves to?

2. Hear and Do (11:6-8)

In vv. 6-8, we have a second message on this theme of the covenant, but now the focus is on the people's response—or rather the lack of one—over the centuries from Sinai.

6. The LORD said to me, 'Proclaim all these words in the towns of Judah and in the streets of Jerusalem.' The significance of this command has been variously understood. Ellison argues strongly that Jeremiah's ministry took place mainly at the Temple. Apart from instances where the prophet rebuked an individual, the norm was for people to come to the prophet and not the other way round (1962:157). Further evidence for this view may be found at 28:1; 29:24; 36:5. Even though the phrase 'in the towns of Judah and in the streets of Jerusalem' may simply be equivalent to 'widely throughout the land', many have felt this to direct Jeremiah to engage in a peripatetic ministry throughout Judah. It is not possible to tie this directly to Josiah's attempts to get the whole nation to respond appropriately to his reforming activities (2 Kgs. 23: 15, 19), but it does support those who argue that the prophet's ministry was not confined to Jerusalem.

Listen to the terms of this covenant and follow them. 'This covenant' is again (as in v. 3) further identified in the words that follow as being the Sinai covenant, which had of course been ratified and renewed in Josiah's ceremony. But covenant blessing did not flow from the appropriate renewal ceremony or even from knowledge of their king's requirements. Covenant blessing depended on covenant obedience. 'Follow them'/'do them' (Deut. 29:9). Knowledge had to bear fruit in transformed lives. 'Now that you know these things, you will be blessed if you do them' (John 13:17).

7. In fact the history of the people over the centuries had been one of repeated disobedience, to which the LORD had responded by sending repeated warnings.[3] The people should have corrected any tendency to stray from the path of obedience, 'for' (*kî*) **from the time I brought your forefathers up from Egypt until today, I warned them again and again, saying, 'Obey me.'** For 'again and again', an idiom implying repeated and earnest activity (GKC §113 k), see on 7:13. 'Warn' (<√*ʿûd*, hiphil 'to warn, call to witness', 6:10) occurs three times in the Hebrew of this verse to emphasise the repeated and solemn nature of what was done. The verb is often used with covenantal overtones (Deut. 30:19; 32:46; Ps. 50:7), here alerting the people to the comprehensive and peremptory requirement of God for obedience. 'Until today' shows that the warnings have not stopped and the covenant requirements have not lapsed.

8. But though there were times when a measure of covenant faithfulness had prevailed in Israel, the overall record was not good. **But they did not listen or pay attention** (7:24); **instead, they followed the stubbornness of their evil hearts** (3:17). They did not respond as they should, but obdurately kept to their own plans and desires. This was not allowed to happen without divine reaction. 'They reaped what they sowed' (Gal. 6:7). **So I brought on them[4] all the curses of this covenant I had commanded them to follow but that they did keep.** 'The curses of this covenant' is simply 'words'/'terms', but because they had been rebellious, it was inevitably the curses that were activated. They had not followed/done what they had been ordered to. 'Brought' is not an exilic expression looking back to the fall of Jerusalem, but a historical resume of the disasters that had come upon the people of the covenant, including the exile of the northern kingdom Israel. Holladay (1986, 1:351) emphasises the similarity of the unusual phrase 'bring words on them' (the hiphil of *bôʾ* followed by *dəbārîm*, 'words') to the saying of Huldah in 2 Kgs. 22:16. Although this has been a history lesson, it ends with a reference to their own recent past and suggests that the lesson was not without continuing relevance.

---

3. The LXX omits vv. 7-8 apart from the concluding words of v. 8, 'but that they did not keep'. There may have been some confusion with the similar material in vv. 4-5, but the situations are quite different, and the words should be retained.

4. The NKJV translation, 'Therefore I will bring upon them', is an improbable rendering of the *waw*-consecutive imperfect.

3. Refusal to Hear (11:9-13)

In vv. 9-13 the focus falls on the contemporary generation in Judah who are resisting the requirements of the covenant just as much as any previous generation had done.

9. Then the LORD said to me, 'There is a conspiracy among the people of Judah and those who live in Jerusalem.' The significance of these words depends on what we read into the word 'conspiracy' (*qešer*, from a root indicating 'to tie' or 'to join'). Apart from the RSV which uses 'revolt', English translations retain the basic meaning of 'conspiracy', a political plot to overthrow constituted authority. The picture which springs to mind is that of a huddle of conspirators in some dark corner as they devise secret plans. If these words are early, then they point to an unexpressed determination to resist the policy of which Josiah was the representative. At a later stage, during Jehoiakim's reign, there was nothing secret about what was going on in Judah; there was no furtive plotting but rather there was a widespread meeting of minds. A consensus had emerged whereby the sovereignty of the LORD was rejected and also their obligation to respond to the demands his covenant had placed on them. It had not arisen suddenly from nowhere, but came out of the mind-set of the people. Although they do not seem to have given open voice to their attitudes and there was continuing observance of Temple rituals, the nation as a whole was effectively united in agreement over this, and the result in the realm of religion is like the anarchy and turmoil that is associated with a coup d'état.

10. The behaviour of the people was a reversion to what characterised former generations. **They have returned to the sins of their forefathers, who refused to listen to my words.** 'Returned' (<√*šûb*, 3:1) is yet another instance of the use of this root, but this time it is used ironically in the sense of backsliding, turning away from the LORD and reverting to evil practices. Still the fact that the people are viewed as having returned acknowledges that there had been a period when there was a measure of reformation in the land, presumably under Josiah. That would make it probable that these words were uttered during Jehoiakim's reign.

'Their forefathers' here is a rendering of *ʾăbôtām hāriʾšōnîm*, 'their fathers the former ones'. In vv. 4, 5, 7 'forefathers' translates *ʾābôt*, 'fathers', which may itself refer to more than the immediately preceding generation. The compound phrase used here makes clear that the reference is not to the evil conduct of the immediately preceding generations under Manasseh, but rather back to a much earlier period of the nation's history, to when it had first come into existence, to episodes of rebellion at the time of Moses or the judges (Exod. 32; Num. 14; 16; Judg. 2:10-23).

The current generation were walking in the steps of their ancestors. **They have followed**[5] **other gods** (1:16) **to serve them.** This is the main charge against them, and it is obviously not a peripheral matter but takes up the central demand of the covenant that there be total and undeviating loyalty to the LORD. There is then an ominous linking of the history of the northern and southern kingdoms. **Both the house of Israel and the house of Judah have broken the covenant I made with their forefathers.** 'Broken' (<√*pārar*) indicates the removal or withdrawal (whether directly or as an indirect consequence of one's actions) of ongoing support for, and maintenance of, an agreement (*NIDOTTE* 3:696). Both kingdoms had a common origin in one set of forefathers; they followed a common course of conduct in breaking the covenant of the LORD; and they will come to the same end.

11. The judgment that is going to come upon the covenant breakers of Judah is then set out. **Therefore** (*lākēn*) **this is what the LORD says: 'I will bring on them a disaster they cannot escape.'** For 'I am about to bring on them', see on 4:6; 5:15. The catastrophe that will overtake them will be no chance occurrence, but the direct consequence of divine action that has already been initiated. Consequently it will not simply be the case that they will not in fact escape. Rather the fact that the catastrophe is divinely determined means that it will be impossible to find any avenue of escape. It is then envisaged that in those dire circumstances they will either acknowledge their wrongdoing, or else will seek help from any quarter at all (the next verse makes the second more probable). But in turning to the LORD too late, they will find that they will not gain a hearing. **Although they cry out to me, I will not listen to them.** 'Cry out' (<√*zāʿaq*) is not an attempt to summon human help but an expression of distress, generally addressed to God and imploring his intervention. But his response is stated by means of an ironic use of 'listen' (*šāmaʿ*, v. 1). Despite all the appeals made to them to listen to the voice of the LORD, they had not; when they seek to be heard by him, they will find that no audience is granted to them.

12. Nor will they find solace through approaching the gods they have been worshipping in preference to the LORD. What awaits them is

---

5. *wəhēmmâ hāləkû*, 'but as for them, they walked', indicates a disjunction from 'forefathers', the subject of the previous clause. It is the behaviour of Jeremiah's contemporaries that is being described.

stated in terms similar to those found in 2:27-28 (cf. also 7:17). Though time has moved on from the reign of Josiah to that of Jehoiakim, conditions in Judah are still the same. Judah and Jerusalem are frequently linked, but the combination **the towns of Judah and the people of Jerusalem** is not found elsewhere. In their distress they **will go and cry out** (v. 11) **to the gods to whom they burn incense, but they will not help them at all**[6] **when disaster strikes.** 'Burn incense' (1:16) is a participial phrase indicating that this was their habitual practice. 'Help' (<√*yāšaʿ* hiphil, 4:14) is a general word for deliverance, translated as 'save' in 2:27-28. It is from the LORD alone that such effective intervention can come (14:8). 'When disaster strikes' is literally 'at time of their disaster', referring back to v. 11.

13. The reason for the LORD's attitude towards them is then stated in direct address to the people (a figure of speech known as apostrophe). 'For' (*kî*) **you** (masc. sing.) **have as many gods as you have towns, O Judah** (2:27). The multiplicity of idols arose because it was common practice for the god of each town to be viewed as a particular manifestation of Baal. **The altars you** (masc. pl.) **have set up to burn incense to that shameful god Baal are as many as the streets of Jerusalem.** The plural 'streets' comes before the verb 'set up' in Hebrew, and probably accounts for the change in number of 'you'. For 'shameful god', see on 3:24. Though the implication is that there is one for every street in the capital, that is probably a hyperbolic statement. Nor does it necessarily follow that the altars were openly on the streets. These circumstances may well have arisen after Josiah's reformation came to be ignored under Jehoiakim.

4. I Will Not Hear (11:14)

14. Because of the LORD's revulsion at this renewed apostasy on the part of his people, prayer for them is forbidden as being useless. The words of v. 14 are addressed to Jeremiah: 'but as for you' (*wəʾattâ*, focusing on the prophet) **do not pray for this people nor offer any plea or petition for them, because** (*kî*) **I will not listen when they call to me in the time of their distress.** 'Pray' (<√*pālal* hithpael + *bəʿad*, 7:16) is 'intercede' on their behalf, seeking mercy for them. The following expressions are also to be found in 7:16. The LORD will listen neither to the people nor to the prophet pleading on their behalf (7:16; 14:11; 15:1). 'In the time of their distress' adopts the reading of

6. 'At all' renders the infinitive absolute put before the finite verb for emphasis, 'helping they will not help' (GKC §113p).

many manuscripts (*bəʿēt*, 'at time of'), where the Massoretic Text reads *bəʿad*, 'on behalf of', and so 'because of' (NKJV, NASB). The Massoretic reading probably arose through confusion with the same prepositional phrase earlier in the verse.

This renewed prohibition may well indicate that Jeremiah continued to plead on behalf of the people despite what was said in 7:16 (though that may not be chronologically prior). However, if intercession for the well-being of the people was recognised as a prophetic task, it may well have been that announcement of a ban on prayer for them had the nature of a symbolic action. It was an attempt to make clear to the people how desperate their situation had become.

5. Lightning Will Strike (11:15-17)

The message of these verses is very similar to that of 7:21-26, except that perhaps the imminence of the doom awaiting the rebellious people is more evident. Jeremiah proclaims a message that is bold and unequivocal in its condemnation of the nation. It is no surprise that such a candid exposure of their conduct aroused bitter opposition.

15. The text of v. 15 has been very badly transmitted, and this has given rise to various scholarly hypotheses, of which some account is given in the footnotes. Surprisingly, despite the uncertainty regarding the details of the text, there is general agreement regarding the theme of the verse, and so it is possible to proceed on the basis of the NIV rendering, which is as plausible as any.

The LORD is speaking and talks of his people as 'my beloved' (12:7; Isa. 5:1; Ps. 78:68; 87:2). It is from within the covenant relationship that he approaches them, and as they are found 'in my house', that is, the Temple, it would seem that they were acknowledging the existence of that relationship. But the thrust of his question is to point out that they were not living true to their covenant confession. **What is my beloved[7] doing in my temple as she works out her evil schemes**

7. *yādîd*, 'beloved', is masculine, and does not fit in with the following feminines. In contrast to *dôd*, 'beloved' (found throughout the Song of Solomon), the noun *yādîd* does not carry a primarily erotic connotation. The LXX ignores the preposition *lə* before the noun and takes it as the subject of the following verb, 'Why has the beloved made an abominable ⌞idol⌟ in my house?' This smoother reading suggests that it is not original, and most English versions find a challenge in the first three words of the line, 'What to my beloved in my house?'—either 'What is she doing there?' (as in the NIV) or 'What right does she have to be there?' (NRSV).

with the many?[8] It is not clear what or who the 'many' are. Even though the word 'many' in v. 13 translates a different Hebrew idiom, it points to one way of understanding the phrase in terms of the many gods which Judah now worships. Alternatively the reference may be to the many nations with whom she is seeking political alliances rather than trusting in the LORD. 'Her schemes' (<*məzimmâ*, often used of divine purposes, 23:20; 30:24, but when used of human plans, generally with negative overtones, Ps. 10:2, 4; hence the supplement 'evil') may simply be the rationale she attributes to sacrifice which she thought effective in placating God and evoking his favour. The point is that her worship is compromised, but she still thinks that by going through the ritual she can satisfy the requirements of the LORD.

Can consecrated meat avert ⌞your punishment⌟?[9] 'Consecrated meat' also occurs in Hag. 2:12 in reference to the flesh of sacrificed animals. The offerings would be unable to turn away the punishment coming on an unrepentant people. **When** (*kî*) **you engage in your wickedness, then you rejoice.**[10] This is the true source of their

---

8. *hārabbîm*, 'the many', is masculine plural and cannot qualify the preceding 'schemes', which is a feminine noun, and in fact singular. The line divisions in BHS, which do not respect the Massoretic accents, take the word with the following line as part of a compound subject, as did the LXX which has *euchai*, 'votive offerings' (= *hannədārîm*). This is followed by the NRSV. If the MT is accurate, this is an improbable corruption of it, and the Old Latin *adipes*, 'fat' (= *ḥălābîm*) is more probable. But rather than representing the original text both are probably attempts to avoid its obscurity. The NIV retains 'many' as a second accusative though that is unnatural Hebrew.

9. The Massoretic Text reads 'flesh of holiness they pass over from upon you', but the verb *yaʿabrû* can be read either as a qal, 'pass over, through' (so NKJV), or as a hiphil without yodh, 'take away', the *î* being shortened to *ə* (GKC §53n), to yield 'flesh of holiness they make to pass from upon you', where there is a plural verb with no obvious subject. The NIV translation ignores this lack of concord. If 'they' refers to the 'many' in the previous clause, then it might mean 'And they [the gods/the nations] make holy flesh pass away from you,' that is, they do nothing more than use up your resources. The margin of NJPS suggests 'Can your treacheries be cancelled by sacred flesh?' repointing *mēʿālāyik*, 'from upon you', as *maʿălāyik*, 'your treacheries'.

10. Another difficult line: 'For/when your wickedness, then you rejoice'. The noun has an unusual second feminine singular suffix (GKC §91e; *IBHS* §16.4a). As regards *taʿălōzî* <√*ʿālaz*, 'to exult' (15:17; 50:11; 51:39), the BHS textual note changes the verb to *zākâ*, 'to be pure', with *ʾaz*, 'then', becoming the first part of the verb. 'Shall I declare you pure?' 'Will you escape these things?' (LXX) apparently read a third root here, *ʿûz*, 'to take refuge, be safe'.

satisfaction: not in pleasing the LORD, but in their own evil schemes.

16. Jeremiah recalls the LORD's former attitude to his people. **The LORD called you a thriving olive tree with fruit beautiful in form.**[11] The picture is of a flourishing olive tree that has a crop of excellent fruit. The imagery as applied to Israel is not found elsewhere, but is used of a righteous person (see especially Hos. 14:7; and also Ps. 52:8; 92:12-14). The focus is on the fruit that the LORD is looking for, that is, he is looking for obedient action, and at one time recognised them as living that way (cf. 2:2). 'Called you' is literally, 'called your name', where 'name' stands for the qualities they displayed. That time of obedience has, however, long since passed. **But with the roar of a mighty storm he will set it**[12] **on fire, and its branches will be broken.** 'Storm' (*hămullâ*) occurs elsewhere only in Ezek. 1:24 to describe the tumult of an army on the move (NKJV, NLT), but invasion does not seem present in this passage and the picture is that of a tremendous thunderstorm. The verbs are perfects, hence the past translations in the NKJV, REB and NASB. But it seems better (as in the NIV and NRSV) to take them as prophetic perfects, underscoring the certainty of the impending judgment. Instead of a fruitful olive tree we are left with the image of a lightning-struck tree, that still stands where it once did, but is now a shadow of its former self. This seems to anticipate the events of 597 BC rather than the destruction of the city in the following decade.

17. The poetry of vv. 15-16 is then complemented by a prose explanation. For the title, **the LORD Almighty**, see on 2:19; 10:16. Here the description is supplemented with **who planted you**, which links in with the previous imagery of the people as a tree (2:21; Isa. 5:2, 7). The God who has all power and who has bestowed on the tree all the conditions requisite for fruitfulness is justly able to condemn it for its failure. He therefore **has decreed disaster for you, because the house of Israel and the house of Judah have done evil and provoked me to anger by burning incense to Baal**. The theme of the intertwined destiny of the two kingdoms is picked up from v. 10. Judah should not think she is different from Israel and has immunity from divine judgment. If she breaks her covenant pledge, she too will experience the

---

11. The construct chain is *yəpēh pərî-tōʾar*, 'beautiful of fruit of form'. It is not two attributes as in NKJV, 'Lovely *and* of Good Fruit'; the beauty arises from the well-shaped fruit. The REB 'leafy and fair' omits the fruit entirely. Only here is *tōʾar* used of plants as distinct from humans or animals.

12. For *ʿālêhā*, 'upon it', several commentators suggest *bəʿālēhū*, 'in its leaves'.

curse of the covenant. The repetition of the same word in 'disaster' and 'evil' (*rāʿâ biglal rāʿat*, 'evil because of evil', 6:19) intensifies the cause-and-effect chain that has been set in motion by their sin. The phrasing of the NIV fails to bring out the fact that the people were responsible for this in that they had acted contrary to their own interests: 'for the evil of the house of Israel and of the house of Judah, which they have done against themselves' (NKJV). For 'provoke to anger', see on 7:18, and for 'burn incense', see 1:16; 7:9.

B. REJECTION OF THE COVENANT MESSENGER (11:18–12:17)

It was one thing for Jeremiah to have lived through the previous twenty years experiencing continual rejection of his message; it was a much more intense experience for him to find himself in peril of his life in Jerusalem (chap. 26) especially when that danger was seen to be real by the subsequent judicial murder of Uriah son of Shemaiah (26:20-23). But it would seem that arising out of that incident Jeremiah had to face an even greater personal challenge from family and close neighbours.

Over the years commentators have delighted in devising schemes for reordering the material in 11:18–12:6 to make it conform to their ideas of the sequence of events. There have been many proposals, but it is the form that we have in the text that is of concern to us. The reconstructions often tell us more about the thought patterns of western culture than about the text.

The Confessions of Jeremiah

One feature that recurs throughout the material of chapters 11–20 is the Confessions of Jeremiah. Though this term has become traditional, it is not the most apt because Jeremiah is neither admitting that he has sinned nor engaging in general praise of God's greatness and goodness. Other suggestions such as *complaints* seem nearer the mark in that the prophet expresses in first-person language his grief and anger at the task assigned to him of bringing such a hard message to an unresponsive, indeed actively hostile, people.

The Confessions are generally reckoned to be: 11:18-23; 12:1-6; 15:10-21; 17:14-18; 18:18-23; 20:7-18. They are characterised by unrestrained, candid language, and more than anywhere else in the Old Testament we have exposed to us the feelings of an individual before God. There is no holding back Jeremiah's speech towards God, and there is a corresponding openness about the LORD's responses to him.

It is common to distinguish the Confessions from passages such as 4:19-21; 8:18-23; 10:19-23; 13:17; 14:17-18; 23:9, where Jeremiah expresses his concern and grief over the fate awaiting the people. The Confessions are distinct in that they focus on the prophet's concern over his own status and well-being, on the rejection of his message and of himself as a divine messenger. There are of course connections between these two sets of material so that the Confessions are not totally erratic in the literature of Jeremiah. There are, however, very few similar insights into the subjective response of other prophets to the outworking of their commission, though mention might be made of Moses' complaints in Exod. 17:4 and Num. 11, and the attitude of Elijah in 1 Kgs. 19:10.

Scholarly opinion has expressed several views about the nature of the Confessions. The traditional view was that they were the highly personal utterances of a man acutely sensitive to the situation he was in. 'They lay bare the inmost secrets of the prophet's life, his fightings without and fears within, his mental conflict with adversity and doubt and temptation, and the reaction of his whole nature on a world that threatened to crush him and a task whose difficulty overwhelmed him' (Skinner 1922:202). More recent writers have expressed doubts regarding the extent to which the Confessions provide us with material for spiritual biography, so that some find in them not personal utterances of the prophet, but only stereotyped, cultic language. The prophet becomes a paradigm to illustrate a contemporary issue. He is used by the Deuteronomic preachers as a vehicle to explain the community's experience in the Exile. Indeed it does not matter if the prophet really existed; what is significant is the viewpoint being expressed through the character or 'persona' of the literary–theological rather than the historical Jeremiah.

However, the Confessions stoutly resist such reductionism. The prayers are direct and personal, but they also show themselves to be the speech of an individual who is saturated with already existing Scripture. In particular Jeremiah's mode of expression draws heavily on the forms and language of the book of Psalms, and especially the psalms of lament. The relationship between these two bodies of literature has been variously assessed. Again there are those who argue that the Jeremianic literature is not really personal at all, and regard Jeremiah as the holder of a cultic office in which he acts as a mediator for the community. What he says has no personal reference, and the 'I' of Jeremiah's speech is simply a conventional way of saying 'we' on behalf of the people. However, there are problems in such approaches in that the Confessions are about personal pain, grief and rage.

Treating them as a confession on behalf of the nation obscures and loses the individuality of the prophet.

The Confessions ought not to be depersonalised and have to be seen as originally an expression of Jeremiah's own position. But it would be misunderstanding matters to take them exclusively as an individual, personal expression. They are the words of a prophet, speaking as a prophet and speaking about his prophetic commission. As such they set out a view of the relationship between the divine word and its outworking in the processes of history. That is probably why Jeremiah was led to place them in the record of his ministry. Though anchored in his own experience, the Confessions go beyond personal grief and perplexity and address questions of wider, perennial significance regarding the sovereignty and purposes of the LORD.

1. The Plot at Anathoth (11:18-23)

The period at which this plot against Jeremiah's life took place is uncertain. As before (see introduction to 11:1-17) two possible scenarios have been suggested. One is set around 622 BC, at the time of Josiah's reformation. If Jeremiah was a supporter of this reform which involved the suppression of shrines throughout Judah, then this might have aroused strong feelings among his relatives and neighbours in Anathoth. If their responsibilities were mainly connected with ministry at a local shrine there rather than in Jerusalem, then it would have been their livelihoods that were under threat. But it is improbable that those who were plotting to assassinate Jeremiah would have expected to escape detection during Josiah's reign, and especially so if the prophet was a supporter of the royal reform movement. It is therefore highly likely that this plot is to be dated early in the reign of Jehoiakim. Ellison argues that if the record of the incident stood completely on its own, 'most expositors would refer it to the days of growing gloom under Jehoiakim, when the disappearance of an unwelcome voice like that of Jeremiah's would have been positively welcomed at the court' (1962:155).

a. Jeremiah's Complaint (11:18-19)

The first Confession is often analysed in terms of the pattern found in many of the psalms of individual complaint: complaint, setting out the difficult situation being faced (vv. 18-19); petition, imploring the LORD to act to relieve distress (v. 20); and then a divine response (vv. 21-23). Although there is a broad similarity of structure, it must be observed that Jeremiah here innovatively moulds the conventional categories to suit his personal purpose. Indeed, the resemblance does not so much lie at a literary level, but arises out of the situation of prayer in general.

18. At v. 18 the theme of the chapter seems suddenly to change. At first it is not at all clear what is being talked about because the 'they' being spoken of are as yet unspecified, and the Hebrew leaves unclear what they were doing. The NIV removes the element of suspense and mystery by introducing the words 'their plot', but Jeremiah's style here deliberately conveys the confusion and uncertainty he had experienced as events unfolded. **Because the LORD revealed their plot to me, I knew it**/literally, 'The LORD made me know and I knew'. As 'know' can refer to the intimate relationship that exists between the parties to the covenant, at first the statement seems to be a general statement about the privileged access the prophet had to the divine council. But then the storyline is focused on Jeremiah's personal circumstances. The second occurrence of 'know' conveys the notion of 'have understanding', which would fit in with a scenario where Jeremiah was aware of some of the things that were taking place but did not grasp their significance until the LORD revealed it to him. **For at that time he showed me what they were doing.** Up to that point Jeremiah had had no idea what the unspecified 'they' were about; he realised what was really happening solely through divine intervention and revelation.

19. Jeremiah continues to emphasise how unsuspecting he had been in the situation. **I had been like a gentle lamb led to the slaughter.** 'Gentle' may also suggest 'familiar' (*ʾallûp*, cf. 'friend' 3:4), a 'pet lamb' (REB; cf. also 2 Sam. 12:3), one which had got used to the family and so was not naturally on its guard against what was going on around it—suspecting nothing and no one. Comparisons have often been drawn with the description of the Servant who 'was led like a lamb to the slaughter and as a sheep before her shearers is silent' (Isa. 53:7), but these seem unlikely. The point of the comparison is different; there the focus is on lack of resistance, here the main thought is that of being unsuspecting; and also the language is different. Though the word used here for 'lamb' is ordinarily found in sacrificial contexts, the word for 'slaughter' (<√*ṭābaḥ*, 51:40) generally refers to domestic butchering of animals for food and not to ceremonial rituals. 'Slaughter' is the first hint that a threat against Jeremiah's life was involved. Ellison proposes as a possible scenario that after a period in which Jeremiah lived in Jerusalem estranged from family and friends, a change seemed to take place. 'As one and another of his relations met him in Jerusalem, there was a sudden new cordiality and appreciation of his message. For Jeremiah's wounded spirit this must have been balm' (1963:9-10). Then after this thawing of relationships, someone from Anathoth had gone to Jerusalem with an invitation to the prophet to come back to the village. Jeremiah, suspecting nothing, happily accepted. **I did not realise that** (*kî* introducing noun clause) **they had plotted against me**/'they schemed schemes' where the noun 'schemes' (plural of *maḥăšābâ*, 4:14) is found as a cognate accusative after *ḥāšab*, 'to devise, reckon, regard', perhaps conveying the ingenuity of the schemes involved (18:11, 18; 29:11; 49:20, 30; 50:45). The position of 'against me' at the beginning of its clause renders it emphatic. 'That it had been against *me* they had been plotting.' This leaves open the possibility that he had been aware that something had been going on, but had never realised it had anything to do with him personally.

Suddenly the LORD had revealed to him what it was they had been saying.[13] Had he started out for the village? Was it after he arrived there? **'Let us destroy the tree and its fruit.'** 'Destroy' (<√*šāḥat*) is used of destroying fruit trees in Deut. 20:19 (cf. 5:10). The comparison of Jeremiah to a tree has been brought forward as a reason for this passage being located after vv. 15-16, but the connection is very loose, and it seems more probable that what is being intended is the people's reaction against the messenger of the LORD. They had repudiated the LORD by their actions: this is what they did to his prophet who brought his message. 'Its fruit' is a difficult phrase,[14] but the saying is probably a traditional proverb for the destruction of a man and any remaining influence of what he has said or done. The implication would be that they would cut off Jeremiah and suppress his message ('all his words' NLT). He had no family, so 'fruit' cannot refer to offspring. The picture of total eradication and extermination is reinforced by, **Let us cut him off from the land of the living, that his name be remembered no more.** It was viewed as the ultimate ignominy if no one remembered your name (Isa. 56:5). 'The land of the living' is not

---

13. The NIV renders these words as poetry, as well as v. 20. It is difficult to distinguish poetry and prose here, and translations differ: the NKJV and REB take vv. 18-19 as prose, and only v. 20 as poetry. The NASB and NRSV take vv. 18-20 as poetry. The NJPS takes vv. 18-20 as poetry, which seems to fit the oblique, allusive nature of the language, and fits in with vv. 21-23 being a prose commentary on what has preceded.

14. *bəlaḥmô* means 'with its bread, or food', and hence may be taken by extension to refer to the edible part of the tree as distinct from its wood. The REB changes to *bəlēḥāmô*, 'with its sap' (perhaps = 'in its prime'), cf. the BHS critical apparatus which proposes *lēḥô* (< *lēaḥ*, 'moisture'), in which case lack of moisture would point to death. The change is unnecessary.

found elsewhere in Jeremiah, but in Ps. 52:5 it refers to this present world.

b. Jeremiah's Petition (11:20)

20. Jeremiah then records that he responded to this threat against his life by committing himself to the LORD (cf. 20:12). **But, O LORD Almighty, you who judge righteously and test the heart and mind.** The prophet acknowledges God's power and control as the ruler of all (for the divine title see 2:19; 10:16) and presents his petition before the king who has supreme authority in human affairs. Judging righteously (*ṣedeq*, ⌊with⌋ 'righteousness') refers to ensuring that there is a proper ordering of relationships in the community (12:1). Jeremiah is confident of his personal integrity, and even more confident of the equity of the judge who is scrupulously fair, and from whom no evidence can be withheld, for he has access to the deepest secrets of man. The phrase 'heart and mind' is literally 'kidneys and heart' (cf. 17:10; 20:12) where 'kidneys' refers to the inmost being, the seat of the conscience in which inner feelings and awareness of wrongdoing are localised, and where 'heart' is also used to refer to the inner life of an individual, particularly his thoughts. 'Test' (<√*bāḥan*, 6:27) refers to divine scrutiny and evaluation. The phrases and the description may suggest that Jeremiah had in mind here the words of Ps. 7:10, 12 as he brought both his own attitude and motives and those of his enemies before the LORD.

The prayer, **Let me see your vengeance upon them,**[15] must not be misunderstood. 'Vengeance' (<√*nāqam*, 5:9) does not refer to Jeremiah's own feelings of vindictiveness. His prayer moves beyond the plea of a righteous sufferer who, wronged by the schemes of the wicked, asserts his innocence before the LORD and claims entitlement to the intervention of the judge who will ensure that his people are treated fairly. Jeremiah is speaking as one who holds the king's commission as his messenger in respect of his prophetic office, and it is his prophetic commission that is at the centre of the dispute, as is clearly brought out in the following verse. So the prophet is seeking the king's vindication of his messenger. This is not an act of private vengeance, but rather a surrender to the power and wisdom of the God who acts righteously. It would be wrong to treat this petition as on a par with a request to satisfy the feelings of hatred nursed by those who are embittered against others. The prophet acknowledges the rule and

15. The unusual preposition *min* in *mēhem* seems to be the idiom with this root, cf. 20:10.

authority of God and requests that it be seen in the circumstances of his life. He calls on the LORD to acknowledge him, and to take due action against those who have been prepared to ill-treat him. **For** (*kî*) **to you I have committed my cause.**[16] The petition and the reason for it are repeated in 20:12. Jeremiah here uses *rîb*, 'dispute, complaint' (2:9). The grievance that Jeremiah has is against the men of Anathoth (and through them with the people as a whole) for the way they have treated him as the LORD's prophet. What is in view is a tripartite process in which the LORD as judge adjudicates between the prophet and the people.

c. The LORD's Response (11:21-23)

21. The remaining three verses are in prose, and provide the LORD's verdict as regards the prophet's complaint, while at the same time helping to clarify certain aspects of what has been referred to in the preceding verses. **Therefore** (*lākēn* of judgment) **this is what the LORD says about the men of Anathoth who are seeking your life** (*nepeš*, 2:34). For the first time the identity of Jeremiah's would-be killers is revealed. Anathoth was Jeremiah's own village (1:1). The phrase 'men of Anathoth' probably does not refer to all the male population of the village, but to the leaders of the community, probably those who owned land locally. This may well have been a group whose numbers had diminished during previous years in the changing economic climate of Judah, where those who had smallholdings increasingly found their land being incorporated into larger estates (Isa. 5:8-10; Mic. 2:2). The extent to which this took place in Anathoth is not known. Jeremiah's family were among the landowners in Anathoth (32:7). It is unlikely that the relatively small number involved in the village would have acted without the knowledge, implicit consent or even personal involvement of his own family (12:6).

We also are given here an indication of why they were opposed to Jeremiah. They were **saying, 'Do not prophesy in the name of the LORD or**[17] **you will die by our hands.'** Presumably they had at first tried to stop him delivering his message by threats, in much the same way that Amaziah, the priest of Bethel, had tried to silence Amos

16. The NIV repoints the Massoretic Text *gillîtî*, 'I have revealed', as *gallôtî*, 'I have rolled', and hence on the analogy of Ps. 22:8; 37:5, 'I have committed'. 'Revealed' is rejected here because there was nothing for Jeremiah to reveal. The matter had been made known to him by the LORD in the first instance.

17. For the construction of this negative final clause, see GKC §109g.

(Amos 7:12-13). Some have felt that the aspect of Jeremiah's prophecy that aroused them to indignation was the fact that he was speaking in favour of Josiah's reforms which involved centralisation of the cult at Jerusalem (Deut. 12), the closing down of local sanctuaries with the priests there being transferred to Jerusalem as minor officials. Since Anathoth was a priestly settlement (Josh. 21:18; 1 Kgs. 2:26), it was felt that this would have aroused considerable opposition that one of their own number was speaking in favour of such moves. These words do not, however, indicate what aspect of Jeremiah's message was involved. It may well have been his whole message criticising the way in which religion was going in his day. The men of Anathoth did not accept his criticisms, and what is more they felt in some way responsible for Jeremiah because he came from their community and his conduct was bringing shame on them by his unpopular and isolated stance (see further on 12:6). 'Do not prophesy'[18] indicates a permanent prohibition, not just silence about one aspect of his message. They were repudiating him and his claim to be the LORD's messenger.

22. There is then a resumption of the construction started at the beginning of v. 21. **Therefore** (*lākēn* of judgment) **this is what the LORD Almighty says: 'I will punish them. Their young men will die by the sword, their sons and daughters by famine.'** This represents judgment coming upon the whole community. It is not Jeremiah who will die (v. 21) but the community that has plotted against him.

23. Not even a remnant will be left to them is a severe punishment. Since Anathoth was close to Jerusalem, it would be exposed to the invading troops besieging that city. Ezra 2:23 (cf. Neh. 7:27) shows that 128 men did return from Anathoth, so presumably those in view here are those who were hostile to Jeremiah, and not the whole community. This decimation of the population will occur **because** (*kî*) **I will bring disaster on the men of Anathoth in the year of their punishment.** 'Punishment' (<√*pāqad*) is the overlord's determination of appropriate action after he has scrutinised the situation. 'Year' is not used in the sense of a specific period of twelve months, but as the indefinite (perhaps prolonged) period of the overlord's action (8:12; 10:15). It, of course, finally occurred when Nebuchadnezzar invaded the land, and took Jerusalem, destroying cities throughout Judah.

The men of Anathoth had rejected the prophetic warnings relayed by Jeremiah and in doing so they had revealed their hostility to the

18. The negative used is *lōʾ* and not *ʿal*, indicating that the speakers felt they had authority to put a permanent ban on all Jeremiah's speaking.

ultimate fact of human existence—that of accountability before God. The message presented to them was one which judged, and brought to an end, the religious and social consensus that prevailed at Jerusalem because it ran counter to the purposes of the LORD. When the LORD intervenes, it is more than a matter of extending protection and deliverance to his prophet. It is the vindication of the divine word that is his primary concern. The LORD's sovereign judgment on the beliefs and conduct of mankind cannot be frustrated. Those who mock the LORD's control (and his expression of that control through his prophet) will be called to account.

In this passage we are also brought face to face with the hostility Jeremiah had to endure to his ministry. Those in authority in church and state would later seek to take his life, but the first recorded challenge comes from his own relatives and townspeople. 'Only in his home town, among his relatives and in his own house is a prophet without honour' (Mark 6:4). In many respects what Jeremiah suffered was a preview of the furious reaction to the ministry of the final Prophet by his own countrymen. 'They got up, drove him out of the town, and took him to the brow of the hill on which the town was built, in order to throw him down the cliff' (Luke 4:29). Being the divine spokesman to a spiritually hostile generation involves immense personal cost which can only be endured if there is close fellowship and personal trust between the messenger and the one who has commissioned him.

2. The Prosperity of the Wicked (12:1-6)

The second Confession of Jeremiah is linked with the previous one in a number of ways, both literary and in terms of historical setting, so that several commentators treat them as one. Literary links include 'You are righteous, O LORD' (v. 1) and 'O LORD Almighty, you who judge righteously' (11:20); and 'you … test my thoughts about you' (v. 3) and 'you who … test the heart and mind' (11:20).

The situation that prevails in this section continues to be that of 11:18-23, as the references in v. 6 make clear. But it is not limited to Jeremiah's own circumstances. Arising out of the startling impact of the revelation of the plot against his life, Jeremiah has been led to meditate, as many others have before and since, about the fairness of life and the apparent anomalies in God's providential dealings (Ps. 37, 73; Hab. 1:12-13; Mal. 3:15). Although expressed as a complaint regarding the prosperity of the wicked, the underlying counter-motif is the treatment accorded the prophet. Jeremiah is particularly perplexed because he cannot see how to reconcile the success the wicked enjoy with his belief in the goodness of God. 'Why does this happen?' is the anguished plea that he sets out before the LORD. But we must notice that it is before God he brings it. His faith is such that he is not driven to despair, but to ask deep questions about the way God orders events in this life, in particular why he has not acted to vindicate the message he has given to his messenger.

a. Jeremiah's Complaint (12:1-4)

1. The language of v. 1 is forensic. As translated in the NIV, Jeremiah affirms his confidence in the integrity and competence of the judge: **You are always righteous, O LORD, when** (*kî*) **I bring a case before you.** 'Always' is a translator's supplement to indicate that 'righteous' refers to an abiding quality of the LORD and not just to what he does on one particular occasion. The significance of *kî* is problematic, but on this approach it is equivalent to 'whenever'. On every occasion on which the prophet brings a matter before the judge, his sentence is righteous, that is, in accordance with what is right. This is because of what the judge himself is; he is the one who is inherently righteous (Ps. 119:137), and whose verdicts manifest that (Ps. 51:4).

However, that is not the only reading of this verse. Modern commentators (for example, Holladay 1986, 1:375) take the LORD not as the judge in the case, but as the defendant. Jeremiah is considered to be challenging and condemning the way the LORD has acted. It is argued that 'bring a case' (*rîb*) denotes a process of argument between two parties, not bringing a case to court (cf. NRSV 'when I lay charges against you'); and that the use elsewhere in Jeremiah of the phrase *dibber mišpāṭîm*, 'speak about justice', is of sentencing ('pronounce judgments', 1:16; 4:12; 39:5). 'Righteous' is then to be understood in the sense of 'innocent' (2 Kgs. 10:9; Prov. 24:24), a bitterly ironic expression.

While such an approach does reflect the questions that were uppermost in Jeremiah's mind, it is an improbable reading of the first part of this verse, if only because Jeremiah says that he is bringing a case to the LORD (*ʾēleykā*, 'to you') and not against him. He recognises that the appropriate place to argue through his complaint against the treatment he has received from his fellow countrymen is in the presence of God.

God is the ultimate standard of righteousness, the one true norm for the behaviour of every moral being. That is a foundational postulate of Scripture. Furthermore God reveals what he is by what he does. His righteousness is not conformity to a standard other than himself.

Because we can determine from the LORD's patterns of behaviour something of the motives that inform his action, we can see that his righteousness is his being true to himself. It is therefore a cause of perturbation and mental consternation when God appears to act otherwise than by his own norms which he has disclosed. Faith often fails to reconcile present appearances and fundamental principles, and is found asking a perplexed 'Why?' (Hab. 1:2; Job 10; 21:7; Ps. 73). The only answer is often to acknowledge that all the facts and consequences are not known to us and to await the wider perspective that the day of divine intervention in justice will reveal, accepting by faith in the meatime that as God is the one who makes promises, he will intervene to ensure that his promises come true.

Yet (*ʾak*, used adversatively) despite all Jeremiah affirms to be true of God, the prophet cannot reconcile his personal experience with these truths. There is much that he feels is incompatible with God's rectitude and commitment, and so he says, **I would speak with you about your justice.** 'Justice' (*mišpāṭîm*) is a plural, referring to decisions in particular cases. The divine verdicts that are problematic for Jeremiah are stated in the questions at the end of v. 1 and in v. 4.

The first problem that Jeremiah raises is that of the prosperity of the wicked. **Why does the way of the wicked prosper** (<√*ṣālaḥ*, 'to be successful, prosperous, powerful')? 'The wicked' (<√*rāšāʿ*, 5:26) are those whose conduct violates appropriate standards and who ought therefore to be pronounced guilty. Consequently the wicked constitute a group whose actions and thinking are quite the opposite of the righteous, who are characterised by their trustful reliance on the LORD (Ps. 34:21; 68:2). As he thinks through this matter, Jeremiah uses general language drawn from Scripture. For instance, Ps. 1:1 promised, 'Blessed is the man who does not walk in the counsel of the wicked or stand in the way of sinners or sit in the seat of mockers'. It also concluded that 'the LORD watches over the way of the righteous, but the way of the wicked will perish' (Ps. 1:6). Did these truths no longer hold? Jeremiah is not engaging in abstract thinking, but raising questions because of the difficulty he has in reconciling these truths with his personal experience. As he is trying to grapple with matters that directly impinge on his own life, he starts from what he accepts as foundational and certain: the revealed truth of God.

The tension between his beliefs about God and his experience is further brought out in a second question: **Why do all the faithless live at ease?** 'Faithless' renders a phrase consisting of a qal participle followed by a cognate noun from the root *bāgad*, 'to betray, be treacherous, lack good faith' (3:7). It is used again in v. 6 ('betrayed') of those who have acted treacherously towards Jeremiah, but here it is betrayal of the LORD and his demands that is in view. They are 'those whose outward appearance masks inward reality' (Carroll 1986:285); whatever their seeming piety, it is not loyalty towards God that rules their hearts. Although the language is again general, Jeremiah's problem was distressingly immediate and personal, and we may take this description as framed with his opponents at Anathoth in view. We can detect something of the prophet's personal outlook at this time in that he attributes prosperity to *all* those who practise treachery. That is of course an exaggeration, but Jeremiah is so intensely aware of his own problem and suffering that he makes the situation absolute. As far as he is concerned, those who are against him have everything going for them; their projects and private life know no obstacles or restraints. Jeremiah is therefore petitioning God to act to correct the injustice he perceives and to show that there is moral coherence in the divine control of the history of the world.

2. It is at this point that Jeremiah voices his complaint against God. The prosperity of the wicked has not come about by chance. **You have planted them, and they took root; they grow and bear fruit.** The thoughts again remind one of Psalm 1 where it is the righteous man who is likened to a prosperous tree. Here it is the wicked. They have been deliberately set in the ground by God (the first two verbs are perfects relating to past facts), and now they enjoy a situation of continuing prosperity.[19] Jeremiah is certainly holding God responsible for the presence of the wicked, indeed, for the prosperity they enjoy despite the fact that their lives are a sham. **You are always on their lips but far from their hearts**/'kidneys' (11:20). What they are saying is outwardly pious, but it does not correspond to their inner thinking where God is not really recognised (9:8). The situation was one of which the LORD himself had previously complained: 'These people come near to me with their mouth and honour me with their lips, but their hearts are far from me. Their worship of me is made up only of rules taught by men' (Isa. 29:13). Here the thought goes beyond cultic practice to include their everyday living. All their talk about God has not impinged on their consciences; they live without being obviously aware of him. This is an unnatural and dishonest state of affairs because an outward profession of loyalty should reflect inner devotion. It is hypocrisy that prevails when that link is not present (Matt. 7:21).

---

19. *yēləkû* ('they grow', <√*hālak*, usually 'to go, walk', but the sense 'grow' is found in Hos. 14:7) is an imperfect of ongoing circumstances, looking at the process of their growth.

3. Jeremiah contrasts his own situation with that of the wicked. **Yet you know me, O LORD.** 'Know' here is not just a superficial, factual knowledge; it is the 'know' of covenant recognition and relationship (1:5). Jeremiah is the one whom the LORD designated as his chosen messenger. **You see me and test my thoughts**/'heart' **about you.** For 'test', see 6:27; 11:20. The prophet presents himself as one whose outward behaviour is loyal to the LORD, and who has also been inwardly scrutinised by him. He is protesting that there is no hypocrisy in his life.

Jeremiah then presents his petition. Because he is being unjustly attacked by the wicked and the faithless, the prophet has only one course of action to recommend to the LORD: **Drag them off** (<√*nātaq*, hiphil 'to separate, draw away') **like sheep to be butchered! Set them apart for the day of slaughter**! Jeremiah had been 'set apart' (<√*qādaš* hiphil, 1:5) for specific divine service, but 'set them apart to be sacrifices' may not be what is in mind here because 'butcher' (<√*ṭābaḥ*, 11:19) is used of profane slaughter of animals for food and 'slaughter' also is not a word specifically associated with the cult. They are then to be set apart in the divine purposes as those marked for punishment. Who are they? In its present location it is the men of Anathoth who must be assumed to be the primary reference, but they stand for all those who resist the prophetic word.

However, it is not the language of the metaphor that causes most concern, but the ethics of Jeremiah's requests here and in 11:20b. Surely these are unworthy sentiments for the prophet of the LORD to utter. Some explain them as being Old Testament language which cannot be justifiably used now. Nevertheless, such expressions are not confined to the Old Testament. The martyrs' prayer of Rev. 6:10, 'How long, Sovereign Lord, holy and true, until you judge the inhabitants of the earth and avenge our blood?', presents a similar request. The language is that of those who are so identified with the cause of the LORD that their enemies are the enemies of the LORD. The prophet was undoubtedly suffering because he was acting as the LORD's spokesman, and, echoing 11:19, Jeremiah proposes that this would be a clear way in which the unfairness of what he is having to suffer might be corrected.

4. This verse is often treated as highly intrusive and to be removed (despite all the versional evidence). But it is possible to relate it to the context, as detailing the consequences of the prosperity of the wicked and leading to a second matter of justice (v. 1) that Jeremiah wished to pose to the LORD. What was going wrong was not merely a matter of the prophet's personal injury, but the state of the land as a whole. **How long will the land lie parched and the grass in every field be withered?** 'How long?' was a question often asked in laments (e.g. Ps. 13:1-2). There seems to have been a number of droughts in Judah at this time (14:1). 'Grass' refers to vegetation in general. Such a calamity was viewed as divine chastisement (3:3; 5:24; 14:2; Amos 4:6-10). The LORD was using natural disaster to alert the people to the precariousness of their situation. Jeremiah is not questioning his right to do so, but asking if it would not be easier/more appropriate to remove the wicked than to take such general action. **Because those who live in it are wicked, the animals and birds have perished**[20]**.** 'Wicked' (<*ra‘*) now reflects moral misconduct; there was no doubt about that. 'Perish' (<√*sāpâ*) conveys the idea of gathering things together and then sweeping them away in a cloud of dust, perhaps chosen because it is a scene of drought that is being described. The impact of the drought is severe and all inclusive (4:25); all creation is contingent and suffers or rejoices because it is affected by human conduct/misconduct (Gen. 3:17; Rom. 8:19-27).

The last part of v. 4 is retained by commentators, but its reference has always been a matter of perplexity. **Moreover (*kî*), the people are saying, 'He will not see what happens to us.'** The simplest solution seems to be to take *kî* in its causal sense (note NRSV) and understand the clause as epexegetic of the wickedness of the inhabitants of the land. This drought—and other divine chastisements—had come about because of the evil of those who have spoken in this way. The 'he' referred to in their speech may be Jeremiah: in which case, either they are viewing him in the light of their plot against him, and saying that whatever happens, we are going to make sure he is not around to see it; or they are saying that his prophecies are false, and so there is no possibility that he will see his predicitons come true because the threatened disaster is not going to occur. But it is more probable that 'he' refers to God. The LXX has God in the text, and one Qumran manuscript seems to have the LORD, which may possibly have slipped out of the Massoretic Text. The LXX also reads the final Hebrew word differently, 'God will not see our ways' (reading *ʾorḥôtênû*, 'our ways', for *ʾaḥărîtēnû*, 'our future, final end'), an alteration adopted by the REB and NRSV. Either way the quotation reflects the mistaken assumption of the wicked that God is distant and unconcerned about

20. 'Animals' (*bəhēmôt*) may be taken as an inanimate plural with a fem. sing. verb (GKC §145k), but a few Hebrew manuscripts and the versions read the collective singular *bəhēmâ*.

their behaviour. 'God has forgotten; he covers his face and never sees' (Ps. 10:11; cf. also Ps. 73:11; 94:7; Ezek. 8:12). But the seeming inaction of God against the wicked should not be interpreted in this way. The LORD had long before shown how he would react against his people when they behaved in such ways. ' "I will hide my face from them," he said, "and see what their end will be; for they are a perverse generation, children who are unfaithful" ' (Deut. 32:20). It was the warning contained in these words that they refused to acknowledge.

b. The LORD's Response (12:5-6)

In vv. 5-6 we have the first part of the divine response to Jeremiah's complaint. God does not explain the workings of his providence; nor does he seek to cheer up the prophet by pointing to some set of good times to come. Instead his words are brusque and challenging. This perhaps permits us to gauge how Jeremiah's complaint ought to be read in this context. He has been speaking in a voice of self-pity at the hardship he has sustained and the trials he is having to undergo in the discharge of his divine commission. The LORD is warning him that he has not yet experienced anything very much at all.

5. If Jeremiah has questions for the LORD, the response he gets is in terms of two questions the LORD has for him. **If** (*kî*) **you have raced with men on foot and they have worn you out, how can you compete**[21] **with horses**? If what is relatively easy is too much for you, what are you going to do when things get worse? The metaphor is probably martial rather than athletic. It is not so much Jeremiah competing in a race against athletes or messengers, and having to retire exhausted, and so being unable to compete with the greater competition when running against mounted messengers; rather it is between fighting against infantry (*raglî*, 'on foot', frequently occurs with reference to soldiers fighting on foot), and then being faced with the challenge as a foot-soldier of engaging with cavalry. The battle he has had so far has been on equal terms; what is yet to come is much worse. It may be possible to detect in the background of this imagery the time when the invaders from the north come against the country as being the time of greater trial.

If you stumble in safe country, how will you manage in the thickets by the Jordan? The basic argument is similar, with 'if' being supplied from the beginning of the verse. 'Stumble' translates a participle (*bôṭēaḥ*) indicating ongoing action. The NIV (also the

21. *tətaḥăreh*, second imperfect tiphel (GKC §55h) of *ḥārâ*, 'to burn, glow with anger', and so 'to have a sense of zealous rivalry'.

NRSV) identifies it as from a root *bāṭaḥ* II whose meaning is adduced on the basis of a corresponding Arabic root, 'to fall on the ground' (*HALOT* 120). There are two passages where this root has been identified (here and Prov. 14:16), but its existence cannot be confirmed with certainty because both passages can be explained on the basis of the usual root 'to trust' (*NIDOTTE* 1:649). If it required that Jeremiah be in a 'safe country'/'a land of peace' (*šālôm*) for him to trust in the LORD, then his faith was going to be sorely tried when he was confronted with territory that was anything but safe. The thickets, or pride, of the Jordan (<√*gā'â*, 'to rise up, be exalted', may be used literally of plants rising and growing tall or thick, Job 8:11) were a strip of land near the river-bank, overgrown with shrubs, and a favourite haunt of lions and other wild animals (49:19; 50:44; Zech. 11:3). The older understanding, 'the floodplain of the Jordan' (NKJV), took the reference to be to the time when the river floods and conditions near it become treacherous. This is less probable in that travel along the banks of the river was not common. The comparison is between easy and dangerous circumstances, and it is the latter that are coming.

What are the two sorts of challenge to be faced by Jeremiah? Rashi identified the men on foot as Jeremiah's relatives at Anathoth and the horses as the priests in Jerusalem, though perhaps these should be reversed in the light of v. 6. More probably the argument is quite general, and applies not only to the personal experience of the prophet but also to that of the nation whose future is mirrored in his circumstances. The LORD is indicating that prophet and people have alike harsher times ahead of them.

6. There are two features of v. 6 that are not represented in the NIV: the verse begins with *kî*, 'for', and the particle *gam*, 'also/even', is repeated three times. To make clear to Jeremiah the intensity of the perils that he is going to have to face, the LORD mentions the situation in Anathoth. It is not just the men of Anathoth in general who are opposing him, but his own kinsmen. 'For' (*kî*) 'also/even' **your brothers, your own family.** The former might be a more general term for relatives, in which case 'your own family'/'the house of your father' refers to near blood relatives, and the first of the three occurrences of *gam*, 'even', 'what is more', serves to intensify the close origin of the threat against the prophet.

Jeremiah's was a priestly family, as were most of those that inhabited Anathoth. 'They must have felt the same way about Jeremiah's words as did the priests who were on duty in the Temple at the time. To make matters much worse he had brought shame on his family. A family council will have met and decided that the death penalty was called for. Any who know something of Near Eastern life with its fierce sense of honour and family pride will regard this as quite normal' (Ellison 1963:9).

Even (*gam*) **they have betrayed you** uses the root *bāgad* (3:7) to convey the treachery his family members had exhibited in plotting against him. 'Even' (*gam*) **they have raised a loud cry against you.** Literally the expression is something like 'called after you fully (*mālēʾ*)'. 'Called a multitude after you' (NKJV) reflects an older understanding of 'fully' as a group of people, but it seems better to take the adjective as used adverbially not just in the sense of loudly (4:5), but of raising a hue and cry in pursuit of a wrongdoer. The expression would be a metaphor for the intensity with which his own kith and kin had turned against him. **Do not trust them, though** (*kî*) **they speak well of you.** It would seem that part of their treachery was that they maintained an outward attitude of pleasantness towards Jeremiah, even while they were encouraging and conniving with those who were plotting to take his life away. 'Well' refers to 'good' words in keeping with covenant relationships and duties.

Ellison (1963:9) envisaged a situation where Jeremiah was induced to return to Anathoth for a time, perhaps for some family festival. While there, it was arranged that some of the men of Anathoth would accuse him of a capital offence such as blasphemy. 'While his relations held back "so as not to interfere with justice", he would be condemned and stoned to death by the men of Anathoth. Were the news gradually to leak out, Jehoiakim was not the man to ask awkward questions about those that had rid him of a turbulent prophet' (1963:9).

The response of vv. 5-6 does not directly address the question posed by the prophet regarding the good fortune of the wicked and the hard time endured by those who are loyal to the LORD. It would seem that the LORD is saying that loyalty to him is its own reward. Those who are granted the privilege of serving the king have to do so without having revealed to them all the counsel of the king. Often they have to live with perplexing problems and open opposition. What they are called on to do is to maintain their obedience to their God despite the puzzles that the circumstances of life frequently set for them. Notwithstanding their lack of comprehension they are to struggle to remain faithful and rely on the provision of the one who had promised his presence would be with them (1:19). The thought is not unlike that with which Paul exhorts the Corinthians (1 Cor. 10:13) or what we find in Heb. 12:4.

3. My Abandoned Inheritance (12:7-13)

The divine speech continues in this section, and seems to relate to Jeremiah's problem. God has spoken to stir him out of his self-pity, and there are two lines along which the thought may continue. God may be intimating that he is in fact going to punish the wicked persons about whom Jeremiah complains, and so Jeremiah need not worry about them getting their proper deserts. But it is more probable that the connection is at an altogether more fundamental level in which the LORD challenges the prophet to view his own difficulties in the light of those the LORD is facing. As Jeremiah had been treated by his family, so had God been treated by his people. The prophet's tragedy was a miniature of the divine (Isa. 1:2; Hos. 2:2-23; 11:1-4). The poem is written in *qinah* rhythm (3:2) usually associated with laments because God too had reason for grief.

7. The challenge to think about the divine situation is brought about poetically by the repetition of 'I' and 'my'. Each of the first three lines starts with a verb having the first singular ending *î* and concludes with a noun with the first singular pronominal ending *î*, 'my house', 'my inheritance', 'the one I love'. These nouns bringing out the special attachment between the LORD and his people, and render all the more poignant the fact that this passage is about the LORD's abandonment of them. How great their offence must have been to merit such punishment! There is a problem about the translation of the verbs, linked to the location and understanding of the whole passage. The verbs are perfects, which most English translations render as past tenses, referring to events that occurred before the fall of Jerusalem in 586 BC, that is, before Jeremiah wrote up this part of the prophecy. It is possible to find appropriate circumstances in the closing years of Jehoiakim's reign when marauding bands of Babylonians, Arameans, Moabites and Ammonites overran the land (cf. 35:11; 2 Kgs. 24:2). However, it is also the case that the verbs may be prophetic perfects (Introduction §7.2) where future events are viewed as so certain that they are thought of as being as good as done. This is reflected in the NIV translation which considers these events as prospective (cf. v. 9).

I will forsake my house is the first of three expressions of rejection that the LORD utters not in anger but in exhaustion. This is part of the answer to Jeremiah's question: they will be punished. 'House' is used in Jeremiah for the Temple (7:2) and also for the people viewed as a nation (3:18) and as descendants of Jacob (2:4). Here the parallel references may suggest that 'house' is equivalent to 'people', but it is more likely that the threefold pattern involves a build up of terms which look at the situation from different angles. Forsaking the Temple need not imply that this looks forward to 586 BC. Ezekiel saw the LORD's glory departing from the Temple in 592 BC (Ezek. 8:1; 10:4, 18; 11:23), and Jeremiah was given to understand that this was also shown in events up to and including those of 597 BC.

For a second time the LORD says, 'I will **abandon my inheritance**.' 'Abandon' (<√*nāṭaš*) is a less common term than *ʿāzab*, 'forsake', but with the same meaning. 'Inheritance'/'heritage' (*naḥălâ*) can refer to the people (10:16) or the land (2:7), possibly the latter in this verse because the people are identified in the third expression of rejection. The land rightfully belongs to the LORD but he will no longer protect it.

The thought is repeated for a third time. **I will give the one I love**[22] **into the hands of her enemies.** 'Give into the hand of' (*nātan bəyad*) occurs in military contexts (here the similar expression *bəkap* is used, cf. Judg. 6:13) for the delivery/abandonment of a person into the power of another. The LORD's people are called 'the love of my soul' (11:15; cf. Isa. 5:1), where 'soul' (*nepeš*) is used as a personal indicator, but his displeasure with them and their disobedience will be such that they will be subjected to foreign domination. Had they not already willingly adopted foreign gods and practices?

8. This is the outcome of a changed divine appraisal of the people. **My inheritance has become to me like a lion in the forest.** That translation may suggest that the change is only on the LORD's side. The fact is rather that the people have changed their behaviour with respect to the LORD so that they act with untamed ferocity against him. **She roars at me** ('gives against me with her voice' may pick up on 'give' in v. 7) describes a threatening action, born of defiance and animosity. The LORD then starkly states his reaction to this ungrateful and rebellious behaviour. **Therefore** ('on account of this') **I hate her.** This is strong language that wells up from the depths of holiness because of the persistent wrongdoing of the people. Their rebellious actions have alienated the LORD from his people, and he turns from them in loathing (<√*śānēʾ*, 'to hate'). Since they have renounced the bond of the covenant, there can no longer be the close attachment that once existed, and God no longer identifies with those who exhibit behaviour that is contrary to what he himself is and to what he requires from others (Ps. 5:5; 11:5; Hos. 9:15; Amos 5:21; 6:8).

---

22. 'The one I love'/'the loved one (*yədidût*, only occurring here) of my soul (*nepeš*, 6:8) expresses the strongest, most personal attachment.

9. The metaphor is changed from that of a lion to a bird of prey which is marked out by unusual plumage and which is therefore the object of attack by other birds. **Has not my inheritance become to me like a speckled bird of prey that other birds of prey surround and attack?** 'My inheritance' is the people rather than the land (cf. v. 7). The evidence for the translation 'speckled' is limited, with the LXX translating as 'hyena' (hence REB, NRSV). The rhetorical question indicates that this is indeed how the LORD views her. Though Israel was distinguished from the other nations as the chosen inheritance of God, in reality she too is just a bird of prey, a carrion eater like all the others. Calvin draws attention to the 'to me' found here and in v. 8 and argues that it points to the people as a wild bird of intractable disposition towards the LORD (1850, 2:140-41). This alienation between the LORD and his people makes it unsurprising to hear him address a masculine plural invitation to some unknown persons: **Go and gather all the wild beasts; bring them to devour.** The marked bird/nation is to be killed and eaten, that is, destroyed by enemy action. 'Wild beasts' are 'animals of the field', not domesticated but destructive carnivores (Lev. 26:22; Ezek. 34:5, 8). These commands invoking future action would support the view that the previous verbs should be taken as prophetic perfects (cf. v. 7).

10. The enemy action is then described in greater detail. **Many shepherds will ruin my vineyard.** The verbs are still perfects which may refer to past events or confidently expected future action. Though 'shepherds' coupled with a past translation may refer to Judah's rulers (2:8) who have wasted the land with their imprudent actions, it is more probable that the phrase points to the leaders of the invading armies (6:3; 25:34-36). It is a figure of more organised and concerted action against the land than that of Ps. 80:13, 'The boar out of the woods uproots it'. The 'vineyard' is here a figure for the people (5:10; 6:9). Throughout the East vineyards were associated with joy and abundance, and were a symbol for blessing, wealth and prosperity (2:20; Isa. 5:1-7). Once more there is the note of the LORD's attachment and loss in the situation, by the repeated *my*, which occurs three times at the end of the lines of Hebrew poetry. **And trample down my field**. 'Trample' refers to the action of an aggressor (Isa. 14:25; 63:6; Zech. 10:5). 'My field' is 'my portion', originally an area of land divided off from the larger tribal allotment, but then simply any tract of ground. **They will turn my pleasant field into a desolate wasteland.** 'Turn' (<√*nātan*) is literally 'to give'; 'field' is again 'portion'; and 'pleasant' (<√*ḥāmad*) signifies what is visually attractive. For 'desolate' (*šəmāmâ*), see 4:7. 'Wasteland' is 'desert'/'wilderness' (2:2). Because the land in which the LORD delighted no longer enjoys his protection as he guarded it 'day and night so that no one may harm it' (Isa. 27:3), it is ravaged by the enemy and becomes bleak and uninhabitable.

11. The desolation of v. 10 is set out starkly by using Hebrew words in which the assonance of 's'/'sh' and 'm' sounds evoke the whistling of the wind through the emptiness. These sounds are found in six words in these two verses: *šəmāmâ* (v. 10); *śāmāh, šəmāmmâ, šəmēmâ, nāšammâ, śām* (v. 11). **It will be made a wasteland, parched and desolate before me; the whole land will be laid waste.**[23] 'Parched (<√'*ābal*, 4:28) … before me' may also be translated 'it mourns to me' (NKJV, NRSV; cf. v. 4). There is great poignancy in the clause **because** (*kî*) **there is no one who cares**/'lays it on their heart'. The phrase implies that no one focuses on it and gives it the importance and attention it deserves. Its welfare obviously remains a matter of great concern to the LORD, but the people are heedless of the consequences of their actions.

12. The invading forces are pictured as they sweep or have swept (the verbs are still perfects, possibly prophetic perfects) through the land. **Over all the barren heights in the desert destroyers will swarm, for** (*kî*) **the sword of the LORD will devour from one end of the land to the other.** For 'barren heights', see on 3:2. These might well have had military outposts that are overwhelmed in the advance. It would perhaps be better to translate 'a sword of the LORD' (*ḥereb ləyhwh*), but it is no longer the case that this brings triumph to Israel (Judg. 7:20). Rather the enemy forces are an instrument in the LORD's hand for executing judgment upon the land. The devastation will be so complete that **no one will be safe**/'no flesh (*bāśār*, 17:5) has peace (*šālôm*, 6:14)' (RSV). It is possible that there is a commentary here on the proclamation of 'peace' that was the focus of the ministry of the false prophets (6:14). When the LORD's judgment falls on the land, it will be evident which message had a divine origin.

---

23. Literally, 'he has set her [i.e. the land] for/as a desolation, it mourns to me being desolate; all the land has been made desolate'. 'Wasteland' is an NIV addition repeated from the previous verse. The subject of the first verb is undetermined. It is unlikely to be the LORD, and may be either an impersonal usage (hence the NIV translation) or a reference to Nebuchadnezzar (Lundbom 1999:657). Many commentators emend to a plural form to agree with 'shepherds' in v. 10.

13. The devastation caused by the enemy invasion means that the people will be frustrated in their endeavours. **They will sow wheat but reap thorns.** Wheat was the principal grain crop in Israel; when it was scarce, there would be a time of great hardship in the land (Joel 1:11). The invading army has either destroyed or taken the crops; all that is left is the weeds. **They will wear themselves out but gain nothing.** 'Wear themselves out' (<√*ḥālâ* 'to be ill', niphal 'to be worn out to the point of being sick with tiredness') points to the people making an effort that results in exhaustion, but even so it will not profit them (*lōʾ yôʿilû*, cf. 'worthless', 2:8, 11).

The final words of v. 13 raise the problem of who is speaking in vv. 12-13. The third person references to the LORD when he is the speaker are possible, but 'your harvest' denotes a change, as does the imperative 'bear the shame';[24] in both of these the 'you' is masculine plural. Both verses may well be the prophet's own conclusion which he added when he made public the answer that had originally been given by the LORD in respect of his own complaint. **So bear the shame of your harvest because of the LORD's fierce anger.** For 'fierce anger' (*ḥărôn ʾap*), see on 4:8. This injunction fits better into a scenario of continued residence in the land (as happened in 597 BC) rather than one of exile, unless of course the harvests spoken about (it is a plural noun) are taken as entirely metaphorical—the outcome of their actions.

Though the LORD here abandons his inheritance, there is a remarkable feature of the covenant: this abandonment is not absolute. Throughout the Old Testament it is recognised that the LORD may absent himself from fellowship with an individual, from his people, their land and sanctuary.

> Even so it is remarkable that, although the covenant curses list a host of disastrous consequences for persistent rebellion against Yahweh, neither version hints at this eventuality. Leviticus 26 warns that Yahweh will set his face against, he will act with hostility toward, he will send a host of agents of destruction against, and his soul will loathe Israel, and he will expel them from the land, but there is no mention of abandoning them. On the contrary, Yahweh affirms that he will not reject (*māʾas*) or loathe (*gāʿal*) them to destroy them. Deuteronomy 28 is similar, emphasizing even more

24. The verb *ûbōšû* may be a third plural perfect qal as well as a masculine plural imperative. The former is preferred in the NRSV translation, 'they shall be ashamed of their harvests', but that requires emending 'your harvests' to 'their harvests'. The verb is more likely to be an imperative, and the whole expression a further instance of apostrophe (9:4; 11:13).

> strongly Yahweh's direct (even if destructive) involvement in the nation's fate from the onset of the curses to the people's expulsion to foreign lands to their return from exile. (Block 2000:136)

It is because of the divine commitment that lasts through the people rejecting him and his punishment of them that there is a future beyond the immediate gloom, and it is to that brighter prospect that Jeremiah now turns.

4. The Prospect for Other Peoples (12:14-17)

In the concluding section of the chapter Jeremiah is given a view of the longer term purposes of God in a way that anticipates later material found in chapters 30–33 and 46–51. By doing so, God is directing the prophet's thoughts away from himself and towards the final outworking of the divine purpose. In this way he is being told that much that puzzles him now will eventually become clear. This section contains an astonishing picture of the restoration that will be given to the nations, and the part that they will be given in God's purpose. There is also here conscious reflection of Jeremiah's commission especially in the repeated use of 'uproot' (twice in v. 14, and also in vv. 15, 17), and also 'be established/built' (v. 16), and 'destroy' (v. 17). The fact that the section is prose and that it presents a positive picture of the future has led to it being characterised as 'a late tidying up operation' (Jones 1992:193), but there is no substantive reason to doubt that it comes from Jeremiah in its entirety.

14. This is what the LORD says: 'As for all my wicked neighbours who seize the inheritance I gave to my people Israel.' 'Seize' (<*nāgaʿ bə*, 'touch on' as an enemy, Zech. 2:8) describes hostile action which reaches out and lays hands on something so as to harm it or to appropriate it. Because they act in this way, there can be no blurring of the status of these nations: they are 'wicked' (<*raʿ*). They are also the LORD's neighbours, because he is the king who is pleased to dwell in his land with his own people. Those peoples adjacent to 'his vineyard' are his neighbours (<*šākēn*) as much as they are those of his people. (See discussion on 'neighbour', *rēʿâ*, at 9:8; here the reference is to the geographically close.) Various considerations come into play in determining who those neighbours are. (1) They were those adjacent to Israel. (2) They were those who touch with hostile intent the inheritance the LORD has given his people (2:7; 3:19). This may refer to particular circumstances viewed as the background of previous section, or it may be a more general reference to the number of times over the centuries that Israel's territory had been encroached on by those about it, such as Edom, Moab, Ammon and the Philistines. (3) There is a further characterisation in v. 16, 'Even as they once taught my people to swear by Baal', which indicates Canaanite-influenced peoples are principally in view. Though this description may not be intended to be exhaustive, it probably does rule out Egypt, Assyria, or Babylon. (4) In that the people are going to be uprooted from their lands (v. 15), and this was done through the Babylonians, the description would exclude them. Also to be taken into consideration are the specific prophecies given later in the book (46:26 about Egypt; 48:47 about Moab; 49: 6, 39 about Ammon and Elam) where a return for other nations is also forecast. The description therefore seems to point to Ammon, Edom, Moab, the Philistines, and also Tyre and Sidon.

I will uproot them from their lands. For 'uproot' see 1:10. Deportation had become a common instrument of empire in the Near East, and so it would be inappropriate to say that this insight must be post-exilic. What had already happened to Israel was clearly remembered. The other nations are viewed as being deported, and this occurred during the various campaigns of Nebuchadnezzar.

And I will uproot the house of Judah from among them is of less easy interpretation. If we emphasise that 'uproot' is a reference to deportation, then it might seem to refer to the events of 586 BC. On the other hand in this prophecy, the nations are already viewed as having been deported, so how can moving Judah from its land after the others have gone qualify as uprooting 'from among them'? An alternative explanation notes that the clause in Hebrew does not follow on from the previous one as a consequence, but expresses a parallel set of circumstances. When the people were uprooted from the land, some were taken into exile along with other nations, while others sought refuge among surrounding nations, such as Egypt (24:8) or Moab, Ammon or Edom (40:11). The uprooting of Judah is then a positive use of the verb as the LORD's people are brought back from these places.

15. If Judah's uprooting is her return from exile and dispersion, then the reference at the beginning of v. 15, **but after I uproot them,** is clearly to the nations, of whom the LORD says: **I will again have compassion and will bring each of them back to his own inheritance and his own country.** The translation 'again' understands the root *šûb* as used in an auxiliary verb in the sense of doing something again (GKC §120d). The LORD had previously had compassion (<√*rāḥam*, 6:23) on the nations in his forbearance in not bringing judgment on them sooner. Alternatively the verb may be understood as 'relent' (Ps. 90:13; Joel 2:14). The LORD will change his policy towards them and restore them to their lands (48:47; 49:6). The REB seems to take the verse as referring to Judah: 'I shall have pity on them again and bring each man back to his holding and land'. But the connection into v. 16 strongly argues for these words being understood of the nations, and the restoration of Israel being described in the closing words of v. 14.

Calvin viewed this promise of pardon and salvation to the surrounding nations provided they repented as being an additional source of encouragement to his people. 'We indeed know that all nations were then excluded from the covenant of God: as, then, he would extend his mercy even to them, the Jews might with some confidence entertain hope, since they were already as it were near to God, he having adopted them as his peculiar people and heritage' (1850, 2:155). If there was a way for those who were outwith the covenant people to experience the compassion of the LORD, the door of hope might not be permanently barred against those who had rebelled against their covenant king.

16. But the restoration of the nations does not automatically ensure continuing blessing. What happens to them depends on their religious response. For vv. 16-17, compare 18:7-10. **And if they learn well the ways of my people and swear by my name, saying, 'As surely as the LORD lives'**. This does not point to a nominal response, but to a true acceptance of the standards of the covenant. 'Ways of my people' are those that they should espouse as the covenant nation, not those that they had in practice followed. This is the opposite situation to that warned against in 10:2. 'Swearing by my name' was not merely an outward pledge of allegiance, but complete acknowledgment of his supremacy as the one who is to be worshipped (3:17; Isa. 45:23). In the past the influence had gone the other way round. **Even as they once taught my people to swear by Baal.** Now Israel is to be the teacher of the nations in the ways of the LORD. If they accept this, **then they will be established among my people.** 'Be established' (<√*bānâ*, 'to build' 1:10) presents a picture of the nations being accepted among the Israelites (Isa. 2:3; 56:3-8). There was always in the Old Testament the wider picture of the divine purpose embracing all nations, and in that respect this prophecy is Messianic in its scope, awaiting the New Testament for the fulfilment of it in its ultimate extent.

17. But due warning is given that fulfilment of this prophecy is conditional on an appropriate response to the prophetic word. **'But if**

any nation does not listen, I will completely uproot and destroy it,'[25] **declares the LORD.** 'If' indicates that the future prospects are contingent on a fundamental and far-reaching change of lifestyle. It is only as they are transformed into obedient citizens of the heavenly king that they will enjoy blessing. There is nothing said in the text about grace, but in no other way can the sinful rebel give up his contrary ways. If he does not, then the devastating judgment of God will surely come upon him.

C. REJECTION OF THE COVENANT PEOPLE (13:1-27)

The chapter consists of six sections, each of which contains warnings about the conduct of the people. A number of times mention is made of their pride (vv. 9, 15), which will lead to their downfall. When the incidents took place and the sayings were first uttered is not clear. It is generally assumed that after Jehoiakim burned the Scroll (chap. 36) Jeremiah was no longer able to move about freely in Jerusalem and spent some time in hiding. There are several years in which we hear little or nothing of his activity. It may well be that these sayings date from his reappearance in public life during Jehoiachin's brief reign, as the reference in v. 18 suggests.

Symbolic Action

Prophetic communication involved more than verbal delivery of the divine message and, when appropriate, recording it in writing. The prophets also engaged in actions to attract attention to their message, to impress upon their hearers the essence of what they wish to convey, and to make their words more memorable. It is misleading to think of their symbolic actions as a form of street theatre. The objective was not entertainment, but to communicate an urgent divine message. Since what the LORD had to say to his people was paramount, the symbolism was also verbalised so that the audience were not left to guess the significance of the prophet's actions.

Symbolic actions may be classified in a number of categories: (a) one-off dramatic gestures, such as that of chapter 13 where Jeremiah hides the linen belt (see also 3:12; 19:1-15; 27:1-28:17; 32:6-44; 43:8-13); (b) ongoing practices, such as refusal to marry or attend

25. Literally, 'I will uproot that nation uprooting and destroying', where the double infinitive absolute, 'uprooting and destroying', qualifies the character of the main verb, 'I will uproot it in such a way that the uprooting will be complete and result in destruction' (*IBHS* §35.3.2d).

funerals and their accompanying banquets (16:1-13); and (c) actions carried out by others where the prophet as an observer points out the significance of what has taken place (13:12-14; 18:1-12; 35:1-19). In Jeremiah most symbolic actions pertain to the imminent destruction of Jerusalem. In terms of form they consist of (a) a divine directive; (b) a report of the prophet's compliance; and (c) an authoritative interpretation of the action.

These symbolic actions pointed beyond themselves to make more vivid to the prophet's hearers the message he had to convey. 'Such an action is a form of the divine word. It is *verbum visibile*, a visible word, and shares in all the qualities which distinguish the divine word' (Lindblom 1962:172). Unfortunately Lindblom goes on to suggest that prophetic symbolism was a developmental carry-over that was akin to the actions of sympathetic magic commonly practised in primitive cultures. He does, however, acknowledge that that was not how the prophets themselves thought about matters. What they did, as much as what they said, was a direct consequence of the LORD's command. Its intended impact on onlookers was 'to convince them that the events predicted by the prophet would really take place' (Lindblom 1962:172). O'Connor notes that the three invitations to repentance in chapters 11–20 occur in association with Jeremiah's symbolic activity. The plea for repentance in 13:15-17 follows closely on the account of the destruction of the linen sash (13:1-11), the appeal of 17:19-27 precedes the visit to the potter's house, and the summons to repent of 18:11 follows the account of that visit. 'It can be asserted confidently that this close association of the two types of material has the effect of increasing the urgency of the prophet's message' (O'Connor 1988:129). By this vivid mode of presentation Jeremiah aimed at persuading the people to abandon the prevalent delusive conception of their future and to replace it with the divine verdict on their conduct and their future.

1. The Linen Belt (13:1-11)

In this incident involving a linen belt Jeremiah engages in symbolic activity to draw the attention of the people to an urgent message from the LORD. There are two distinct questions to be answered about this symbolism: what was the nature of the action Jeremiah performed? and, what precisely was the message that he was conveying?

Regarding what it was Jeremiah did, the unresolved matter is whether or not he actually travelled to the Euphrates. In favour of this is the fact that the Hebrew text four times mentions the Euphrates

(vv. 4, 5, 6, 7; NKJV, NRSV). On each occasion the NIV renders the term as Perath with a footnote, 'Or possibly the Euphrates.' The normal Old Testament expression is 'the river Euphrates' (46: 2, 6, 10), but there are three texts in which the word which we have here is used alone in reference to the Euphrates (Gen. 2:14; Jer. 51:63; 2 Chron. 35:20), and so a case can be made out for this being a reference to the river.

However, if the Euphrates is intended, that would have involved the prophet in two extended journeys from Jerusalem to Mesopotamia and back. The evidence of Ezra (7:7-9) indicates four months for a journey from Persia to Jerusalem, though the numbers involved might have made that slower and of course the Euphrates is of some length, so that the actual distance varies from 250 miles (400 km) at its nearest to Jerusalem to 400 miles (640 km) at Babylon by the routes then used to travel. Even when allowance is made for Jeremiah travelling speedily to the nearest point on the Euphrates, the time taken to go and return twice would have been considerable, and this has been felt to militate against a literal journey. 'It is impossible to suppose that the narrative is a literal description of actual events. We cannot imagine that Jeremiah in his real life again and again went to the distant region of the Euphrates' (Lindblom 1962:131). Lindblom therefore argues that this was a visionary experience of the prophet (with symbolic significance). However, the typical indicators of a vision report, such as 'I saw' or 'the LORD revealed to me', are entirely absent. There is no reason to take this as anything other than historical narrative.

Carroll proposes that this is an enacted parable in which the prophet 'performs his strange drama before a mystified audience ... : marking out the ground to represent the mighty Euphrates, parading around in his splendid girdle, trudging off to the river to bury the girdle, returning and waiting, then off to the river again and ... lo and behold, the garment is ruined!' (1986:297). This is a 'dramatic enactment of exile in Babylon and good theatre at that!' Carroll does not tell us how the stage effects required, for instance, for the spoiling of the garment, were managed, and there is nothing in the text to support such an approach to this passage.

A third approach, which is that underlying the NIV rendering (see on v. 4), is that a place near Jerusalem was used as a proxy for the Euphrates and Babylon in the enactment of this prophetic symbol. The prophet probably gathered a group in Jerusalem to whom he announced his intention, possibly taking witnesses with him to and from Perath (in a manner similar to chap. 19), and he certainly reported to a public gathering the outcome of his visits there.

But that still leaves the significance of Jeremiah's actions to be determined. It is clear that the prophet represents the LORD and the linen belt represents the people (v. 11). Furthermore, the message is one about the LORD's judgment on the people. But does it predict the place where that judgment would be experienced—in the Exile in Babylon? Or does it give the reason for that judgment—the corruption of the people? Or is it rather the nature of the impending judgment that is the focus of the action—the ruin and spoiling of the people?

At first glance the symbolism invites interpretation in terms of the removal of the people to Babylonia and their remaining there for many days. But quite apart from whether this was conveyed through two long journeys to the Euphrates or not, it must be questioned if the details of the account can reasonably be taken to support this interpretation. If a soiled garment being buried at the Euphrates symbolised the impact of the Exile on Judah, then the implication is that the Exile was the cause of Judah's spiritual decay, whereas the prophet clearly indicates that Judah was spiritually corrupt long before the Exile. Indeed in chapter 24 it is the exiles in Babylon who are presented as 'the good figs', which would clash with the notion of the Exile as a corrupting influence. Furthermore there is nothing said about the return of the linen belt from Babylon.

Alternatively, what is pictured may be thought of as the extent to which corrupting Mesopotamian influences had penetrated the life of Judah. The worship of astral deities is mentioned as early as Amos 5:26-27, and it is well known that under Ahaz and again under Manasseh such worship had taken over in the Jerusalem Temple (2 Kgs. 16:10-16; 21:3-8). Jeremiah had to battle against the Queen of Heaven cult (7:16-19). However, while this was a significant feature in the decline of Judah before the Exile (2:18b), it does not correspond to the basic movement of the symbolism where the belt is taken to the river and not the other way round, which would have been consonant with this interpretation. To get round this Holladay proposes that Perath represents the Euphrates come to Palestine, and suggests that this would be indicated by the phrase 'crevice of the rock' found in prophecies such as Isa. 8:7-8 (1986, 1:398).

However, the first interpretation is probably along the right lines, provided it is emphasised that it is not the people who are going to be ruined by the Exile, but their pride (v. 9). The nation had despised the special status accorded to them by God and had become superior in their own esteem. They should have functioned as a linen belt, an ornament bringing renown to the LORD (cf. Deut. 4:5-8). However, their disobedience and spiritual impurity showed that they had failed in the mission assigned them, and they had become in God's sight like a cast-off garment. In many ways the Exile was a restorative influence for the people, but only after what blocked a right relationship with the LORD was removed. The message being conveyed was that what was going to come upon the nation would remove from them that outlook which was preventing them from giving due acknowledgment to their covenant Overlord.

a. Buy a Linen Belt. (13:1-2)

1. This what the LORD said to me is an autobiographical introduction that relates this section very clearly to Jeremiah. The 'I' cannot here be plausibly interpreted of the community or anyone other than the prophet.

The first direction given to Jeremiah is threefold: **Go and buy a linen belt and put it round your waist**/'loins', **but do not let it touch water.** The command to go and buy is similar to that given to the prophet in 19:1 in respect of a clay jar: it must have made life interesting when Jeremiah said he was going shopping! The garment referred to (*ʾēzôr*, eight times in this chapter, plus another six elsewhere, 2 Kgs. 1:8; Job 12:18; Isa. 5:27; 11:5, twice; Ezek. 23:15) has caused translators considerable problems: 'girdle' (AV, ASV), 'waistband' (NASB), 'waistcloth' (RSV), 'sash' (NKJV), 'belt' (NIV, NLT), 'loincloth' (NRSV, REB), and 'shorts' (GNB). It was a type of kilt, worn by most males, wrapped around the waist and extending to the middle of the thigh. In the stele of Sennacherib the soldiers of Lachish are shown wearing such a garment. Here the garment is specifically said to be made of linen. Because linen was especially worn by the priests (Exod. 28:39, 42; Lev. 16:4; Ezek. 44:17-18), this may point to Israel's calling as a kingdom of priests (Exod. 19:6). When it was worn by the prophet next to his skin, it would depict the close relationship between the LORD and his people (v. 11).

The fact that Jeremiah was never to put it in water (an enduring prohibition) might be to ensure that it was put on undamaged and that no rotting would occur while it was in contact with his body. There is also the fact that since it was not taken off to be washed, it became a garment worn not only close to the body but also constantly, to fit in with the indissoluble bond the LORD had with his people (v. 11). As a result the garment that is mentioned at the next stage of the symbolic action would have been soiled.

2. The prophet complied with the instructions he was given. **So I bought a belt, as the LORD directed, and put it round my waist.**

b. Hide the Linen Belt (13:3-5)

3-5. Then the word of the LORD came to me a second time. This second command comes after an unspecified lapse of time (cf. 1:13). Jeremiah is told to **take the belt you bought and are wearing round your waist, and go now**[26] **to Perath and hide it there in a crevice in the rocks**[27]. The word rendered Perath is elsewhere translated Euphrates. In Josh. 18:23 Parah is listed as a settlement in the eastern part of the tribal territory of Benjamin.[28] The site is generally identified with the modern Tell Fara some six miles (10 km) north of Jerusalem, and so three miles (5 km) north-east of Anathoth, where there is a substantial spring which still contributes to the water supply of Jerusalem. This place was probably chosen because of the similarity in sound to the Euphrates, and perhaps we are to envisage Jeremiah as accompanied when he went there just as he was on his visit to the Valley of Ben Hinnom (19:1-2). The mention of rocks does not fit in with the middle or lower reaches of the Euphrates, but they would be found in the upper stretches of the river. However, a problem then arises in that that region was hardly associated with Babylon or the Exile.

'Crevice' (*nāqîq*) implies inaccessibility. Southwood (1979:233-34) notes that the phrase 'crevices in the rocks' (*nəqîqê hassəlāʿîm*) occurs elsewhere only in Isa. 7:19 and Jer. 16:16 in reference to remote hiding places high on the hills where people try to find safety from their enemies (cf. also 4:29). He argues that the humbling of Judah takes place while she seeks refuge from the flood of invading forces (47:2; Isa. 8:6-8). But this introduces an element that is not mentioned in the symbolism: the movement of someone or something from Babylon to Palestine, and so seems less plausible than traditional interpretations.

The text does not say that the belt was put in the water, but it is generally assumed that the contrast with v. 1 means that the cleft in the rock was near the river's edge so that moisture could readily penetrate

26. 'Go now', literally 'arise, go', is an idiom employing the verb *qûm*, 'to arise', to urge immediate action, and hence the translation 'now'. The idiom recurs in v. 6.

27. Grammarians differ on the significance of the construct phrase here: GKC §127e argue that the noun in bound form appears to be used indefinitely notwithstanding the following determinate noun, while *IBHS* §13.4c consider that there is an exceptional use of the article in an indefinite construct phrase.

28. Identification of the site with Parah either requires repointing of the Massoretic *pərātâ*, 'to Perath' i.e. the Euphrates, to a form such as *pārātâ*, 'to Parah' or else it must be assumed that there were alternative pronunciations/ spellings of that place name.

the garment. Jeremiah's sign then expresses the threat that Israel, like the loincloth, will be carried away and left to rot in an inaccessible place by the Euphrates.

The prophet again reports his diligence. **So I went and hid it at Perath[29], as the LORD told me.**

c. Recover the Linen Belt (13:6-7)

6-7. Many days later the LORD said to me does not specify an exact length of time, but certainly a matter of months must be assumed (in which case it becomes difficult to fit it all into the brief reign of Jehoiachin). The prophet is enjoined: **Go now to Perath and get the belt I told you to hide there.** It had been hidden so that it would not be interfered with. Presumably this was not just a matter of placing it deep in a crack in the rock, but covering it with stones or earth. On this third occasion Jeremiah records his obedience to the divine command, and reports what he found. **So I went to Perath and dug up the belt and took it from the place where I had hidden it.** The sash had of course suffered in the interval **but now it was ruined and completely useless.** 'Ruined' (<√*šāḥat* niphal, 'become corrupt') can be used to describe spoiling and destruction in a variety of ways. The imperfect is used to denote a continuing condition in past time (GKC §107b). 'Completely useless'/'not useful for anything' (<√*ṣālaḥ*, 'to be successful, prosperous') refers to lack of success in various activities of life, the inability to accomplish effectively whatever is intended. The fabric had rotted due to the dampness of its location and could no longer be used as clothing or for anything else.

d. The Ruined Belt (13:8-11)

The question obviously arises as to what this all means. In accordance with the explanation offered in v. 8-11 it seems best to view the symbolic action as an allegory of the Exile, and its impact in one particular respect—the removal from the covenant community of the pride that had fatally distorted their relationship with the LORD. This would fit in with an understanding of the command in v. 1 not to put it in water as not to wash it, so that the people going to exile, brought there by the prophet acting on behalf of God, are presented as dirty and polluted. The linen belt is removed from the prophet's waist as a sign of the rending apart of God and his people as they are taken from the land of promise.

29. Possibly reading *bəpārātâ* with 4QJer[a] as noted by Holladay (1986, 1:393) instead of *biprāt* in the Massoretic Text.

8-9. The divine explanation of what he has been doing is given to Jeremiah only after he had dug up the belt. **Then the word of the LORD came to me: 'This is what the LORD says: "In the same way I will ruin the pride of Judah and the great pride of Jerusalem".'** 'In this way' is literally 'according to thus' (19:11; 51:64), pointing both back to the action and forwards to the explanation: the sash was ruined, and ruin is to come on the covenant community. 'Ruined' in v. 8 is *nišḥat*; 'I will ruin' in v. 9 is *'ašḥût*, both <√*šāḥat* niphal, 'to be marred/corrupt'. But the focus of the ruin is not simply the people, but the character flaw that had led to their downfall.

While 'pride' might be used in a positive sense to refer to their grandeur, their power and the excellence of their buildings (BDB 144; Ps. 47:4; Isa. 14:11; Amos 8:7; Zech. 10:11), this is unlikely in view of the following reference to 'these wicked people' (v. 10). More than their buildings will be brought low. Pride (*gā'ôn*, 12:5) describes their haughty conduct especially evident in their unwarranted assumption of superiority and independence from God (Lev. 26:19) . Possibly Jerusalem's pride is mentioned as being great because it was the capital, though from its position in the sentence 'great' could be taken with both occurrences of pride.

10. The imagery of the spoiled belt is extended to show why and how judgment is going to come on the people. **These wicked people**[30], **who refuse to listen to my words** (11:10), **who follow the stubbornness of their hearts** (3:17) **and go after other gods to serve and worship them** (11:10), **will be**[31] **like this belt—completely useless!** The verdict on them is identical with the words at the end of v. 7. This brings out one aspect of what was involved in the Exile. Because the people had rebelled against the LORD, preferring their own ways to his, they no longer were of use to him. Consequently they would be banished from the land which he had intended them to inhabit and where there should have been true fellowship with him.

11. The matter is then viewed in terms of the closeness of the relationship between linen belt and wearer, between the people and the LORD. In v. 1 the prophet had been told to wear the belt to illustrate how close God wanted his people to be to him. **'For as a belt is bound round a man's waist, so I bound the whole house of Israel and the whole house of Judah to me,' declares the LORD.** This looks back to the covenant bond the LORD had created between

30. The order in Hebrew *hā'ām hazzeh hārā'* is unusual, and perhaps indicates 'this people which is wicked', emphasising the quality of wickedness.

31. *wîhî* is ordinary *waw* followed by the jussive, 'Let them become like'.

himself and his people. Perhaps the use of the word 'cling' (<√*dābaq*), which is the same as that in Gen. 2:24, indicates that the relationship between the LORD and his people was to be as intimate as that between husband and wife. Certainly the word emphasises the closest of personal relationships and the faithfulness that should characterise them. In this way it was the LORD's intention that they would **be my people for my renown**/'name' **and praise and honour.** This phrase reflects that found in Deut. 26:19 where it describes the status of Israel as exalted over the nations (cf. also 34:9). 'Honour' is literally 'beauty, glory, boasting' (*tip'eret*), indicating adornment that leads to renown and dignity. Here the reference is ambiguous: is it the LORD who gains renown (as the NIV suggests by adding 'my'), or the people? It would seem to be the latter. The linen belt as originally worn pointed to the distinction that the people had through their close link with the LORD. The obedient life of the covenant people would have brought praise to them themselves and also to God who had called them and constituted them his own. **But they have not listened.** Their refusal to obey led to their downfall and the loss of the status they should rightfully have enjoyed.

There are thus two aspects to the symbolism of the linen belt. It is a picture of the Exile coming upon a people who had failed to realise the potential of the situation they had been blessed with. They would be cast off by the LORD as completely useless. But there is a more hopeful note also. Insofar as the belt represents the sinful pride of the nation which led them to putting their own wisdom and desires before that of God, it indicates the way in which through the Exile the LORD would take action to remove their arrogance. Nothing is said about the return of the belt from Perath, because it did not. But there is still left open the possibility of the return of the people after their faulty disposition has been corrected by the divine discipline of the Exile.

2. The Wineskin (13:12-14)

These verses contain another piece of prophetic symbolism, but there is nothing to suggest that there was any symbolic action. Jeremiah is not said to have taken two wine jars and smashed them together. At most he spoke these words with a full wineskin in his hands. More probably it is a matter of a graphic object lesson using a well-known article as a verbal illustration.

12. The impending judgment of the LORD is again brought graphically before the people under the guise of another figure—that of wine jars. **Say to them** is addressed to Jeremiah, telling him to pass on the message he is given.[32] There is probably a contrast between the solemn introduction, **This is what the LORD, the God of Israel says**, and the brief speech, **Every wineskin should be filled with wine.** This seems to be quoting a current proverb (as is done in 31:29 and Ezek. 18:2) with an optimistic tone, 'Everything has its use', or perhaps in the context of a drinking feast, something like 'The preparations are complete so that we can get on with it and enjoy ourselves'. The prophet, however, turns the optimistic saying into a warning.

Whether the translation ought to be 'wine jar' (REB, NRSV) or 'wineskin' (NIV) has long been a source of perplexity. The word itself (*nēbel*) may indicate an animal skin prepared to hold liquid (so LXX). The idea of a *wine*-skin is derived from the context. It could equally well contain water, and was often used for that purpose. Here, however, the use of 'smash' (v. 14) does not cohere with the idea of a skin container, and there are other passages also where it seems to be used of a pottery jar (48:12; Isa. 22:24; 30:14; Lam. 4:2). Perhaps the term was applied to the pottery vessel which was shaped like an animal-skin container (King 1993:175) or held a similar volume of liquid.

The formal introduction had prepared the people for a solemn divine message, so the quotation of a popular saying created such an anticlimax that it at least would provoke the people to make some sort of response. 'And if they say to you' is a dynamic rendering of 'And they will say to you' (NRSV).[33] This is the next stage in the sequence of events the LORD tells Jeremiah about. The people will be quite ready to dismiss the prophet as an irrelevance, which was their prevailing attitude in any event. **And if they say to you, 'Don't we know[34] that every wineskin should be filled with wine?'** The prophet had nothing profound to say, so why was he wasting their time?

---

32. 'Say to them this word' is followed by a paragraph marker in the Masoretic Text, indicating that the words were understood as concluding the previous section with a command to Jeremiah to make the interpretation of the symbolism known to the people who are not directly involved in the narrative of vv. 1-11. But the introduction of this divine command at the end of a section would be awkward and it is easier to take the words as part of v. 12.

33. The rendering 'if they say' is also found in the LXX. It does not function to introduce a note of uncertainty, but interprets the construction of two *waw*-consecutive perfects as contingent or consequential here, i.e., 'and when they say to you … then you will say to them' (GKC §159g).

34. The use of the infinitive absolute indicates an indignant or impassioned question (GKC §113q).

13. Then tell them, 'This is what the LORD says: "I am going to fill with drunkenness all who live in this land, including the kings who sit on David's throne, the priests, the prophets and all those living in Jerusalem".' In the Hebrew 'drunkenness' is delayed to the very end of the sentence. The original saying had been an optimistic one, and 'I am going to fill' leaves open the possibility of divine blessing, which the addition of 'drunkenness' converts into a speech of judgment. No level of society will be exempted, but special mention is made of those in positions of leadership (2:26; 4:9). 'Kings' probably refers to those who reigned after Josiah. For 'sit on David's throne', see 22:4. Drunkenness is a state of confusion, lack of co-ordination and loss of control. The land will not have well thought out policies and coherent direction. In terms of the picture of the wineskins, however, there is the added dimension of divine wrath. The people are compared to containers filled with the wine of God's wrath (25:15-16, 27; 48:26; 49:12; 51:57; Ps. 60:3; Isa. 51:22; Lam. 4:21), and his judgment on them will in part consist of internal disorder and instability.

14. 'I will smash them one against another/'a man against his brother' (perhaps the idiom is used here with extra edge)**, fathers and sons alike,' declares the LORD.** This is a picture of a society at odds with itself. The people are represented as drunk men bumping into each other, but being of pottery (the idea of wineskins does not really work here), the impact causes them to shatter. The LORD is bringing this upon them as part of the curse of the broken covenant. Internecine strife will be part of the scenario when Judah collapses before the enemy. There is then a threefold statement of the LORD's determination to bring his judgment upon the people. **I will allow no pity or mercy or compassion to keep me from destroying them.** 'Pity' (<√*ḥāmal*, 'to spare, have compassion') relates to holding back from an action that might reasonably be expected. It need not have the sense of pity (cf. 50:14), though that is present in this passage. 'Mercy' (<√*ḥûs*, 'to spare, look on with compassion') refers to not letting human emotion come in the way of the duty imposed (Deut. 7:16; 13:9; 19:13, 21; 25:12). 'Compassion' (<√*rāḥam*, 'to have mercy, 6:23;12:15) arises from a deep emotional bond with someone, showing itself in pity if they are in unfortunate circumstances. The three words are used to build up a picture of unrelenting judgment. 'Destroying' (<√*šāḥat*) picks up on the theme of the previous section (vv. 7, 9). This is what is involved in the ruin of a community.

3. Caught by Darkness (13:15-17)

This section contains another plea for Judah to turn before it is too late. The people are urged not to leave the word of the LORD out of their thinking and living.

15. The plural imperatives indicate a change of speaker from the LORD to Jeremiah. **Hear and pay attention, do not be arrogant.** The prophet urges the people to respond appropriately to the message he is bringing them. The figure behind arrogance is height (<√*gābâ*, 'to be high, haughty'). The attitude condemned is that of those who are so high up in their own esteem or that of contemporary society that they consider they need not pay attention to any warning. But the dissuasive against arrogance is justified **for** (*kî*) **the LORD has spoken.** The message the prophet is bringing is not his own; he is the messenger of the God of Israel.

16. The injunction in v. 16 is one that requires acknowledgment of the LORD's position by showing true repentance. **Give glory to the LORD your God**, the emphasis on 'your' is one that focuses on the relationship that should exist, which God has brought into existence. 'Give glory' is used to express the need to confess apostasy from God and to return to him in sincere repentance (Josh. 7:19; Mal. 2:2; John 9:24). It seems especially appropriate in these circumstances, where the proud nation was doing all it could to boost its self-image and was placing its confidence in the outward privileges it enjoyed.

Then a picture is drawn of travellers on a mountain track overtaken by night before they reach their destination. The mention of 'flock' in v. 17 is too remote to justify taking this as a picture of a flock of sheep marooned at night, deserted by their shepherds, and awaiting dawn before they can move safely (McKane 1986, 1:301). **Before he brings the darkness,**[35] **before your feet stumble**[36] **on the darkening hills.** The repeated 'before' emphasises that this is their last opportunity to do something before catastrophe engulfs them. 'Stumble' (<√*nāgap*, 'to strike, smite, injure, stumble against') evokes the picture of an accident that might easily occur on a rocky Palestinian path. The figure of stumbling is frequently used to express misfortune and divine judgment (Isa. 8:14; John 11:10; 12:35). 'Darkening hills'/'hills of twilight' (*nešep*). 'Twilight' is used of both early morning and evening, but it is

35. 'Before the darkness falls' (REB) treats *yaḥšik* as an impersonal expression (here masc., but may also be fem.) used to describe natural phenomena (GKC §144c).

36. For masculine verb with feminine subject see GKC §145p; *IBHS* §6.6c.

the latter, the gloaming, here. When the traveller finds himself caught in rough terrain in the darkness, all he can safely do is to wait for the light of day to come.

You hope for light, but he will turn it to thick darkness (see on 2:6) **and change**[37] **it to deep gloom.** 'Hope for' (<√*qāwâ* I, 'to wait, hope') becomes a pointless and frustrating exercise because the night does not turn into the light of day as might be expected. The LORD has intervened to reverse the order of nature and intensify the darkness. The people are described as those who are well aware that the dark circumstances of tragedy, invasion and defeat have entered their lives, but who are expecting it to be only a temporary phenomenon. If they just wait, matters are sure to improve. Hadn't that happened in the past in the days of Hezekiah? The Assyrians in the land had seemed to be invincible, but the LORD intervened miraculously and the enemy departed (2 Kgs. 19:35-36). Jeremiah too assures them that there is going to be a miraculous intervention—but it is not going to relieve the problem. Rather the LORD is going to bring on deep gloom (*ʿărāpel*, possibly the deep darkness of a storm cloud). The description fits what took place at the time of the fall of Jerusalem.

17. To make the people aware that he was not uttering threats he knew to be empty, Jeremiah tells them of his own reaction if they continue intransigent. **But if you do not listen, I**[38] **will weep in secret because of your pride.** Their pride (*gēwâ* a contracted form <√*gāʾâ*, 12:5; 13:9) had made them unwilling to respond to the LORD's message and the LORD's messenger. But the rebuffs he had received had not hardened him so that he would rejoice in their downfall. When they react with coldness and indifference to his message ('if you will not hear it' NKJV; contrast v. 15), even before their end comes, he will weep (<√*bākâ*, 9:1) over their misconceived attitude. Jeremiah indicates that he is not at first going to make a public spectacle of himself. Perhaps the 'secret places' refer to the depths of his own soul. His grief will be genuine, and well up from the depths of his being. Alternatively, Jeremiah may be viewing himself as weeping 'alone' (NLT), as being the only one in the hardened society who accepts the inevitability of their prophesied doom. **My eyes will weep bitterly, overflowing with tears.** 'Weep' (<√*dāmaʿ*, 'shed tears') is intensified by an infinitive

37. The kethibh is *yāšît*, an imperfect, without any conjunction. The conjunction plus infinitive offered by the qere *wəšît* is unnecessary.

38. *nepeš* is used here with an individual reference (2:34). Since *nepeš* is feminine, this explains the feminine *tibkeh*, 'she will weep'. The following verbs are also feminine because of the feminine noun *ʿayin*, 'eye'.

absolute which is rendered 'bitterly'. There is no doubt regarding the intensity of the prophet's reaction **because** (*kî*) **the LORD's flock will be taken captive.** The LORD's flock are his covenant people (*'ēder*, 31:10; Zech. 10:3). This is one of the relatively few clear predictions regarding the Exile (v. 19; 15:2; 20:4, 6). The perfect verb functions as a future perfect. After they shall have been taken captive, Jeremiah will weep as well as in anticipation of the tragedy.

Is this weeping a sign of weakness? Not if we take Christ as our example and think of the tears he shed over Jerusalem (Luke 19:41). There is also Paul's 'great sorrow and unceasing anguish' in his heart over the destiny of his fellow countrymen (Rom. 9:2). It was no small change that Jeremiah was asking the people to make. They had to recognise what they were doing and reverse their course of conduct. Though Jeremiah tells us of his tears, he does not simply make an emotional appeal. It is not a feeling of sorrow for himself that he seeks to induce, but an appropriate response to God's word. He is not speaking coldly—in a take it or leave it manner. His love and concern for the people are such that he cannot remain indifferent to their destiny.

4. Royal Humiliation (13:18-19)

Jeremiah repeatedly emphasises the role of those in positions of authority in the corruption of Judah, and the fact that they will not be exempt from the consequent judgment (v. 13). In this section he focuses on the royal family.

18. The command comes from the LORD to Jeremiah, **Say to the king and to the queen mother.** There is no hint given as to how Jeremiah was to do this, but if this passage is correctly located in Jehoiachin's reign, then this may well mark Jeremiah's resumption of a public ministry after his years of hiding during the later years of Jehoiakim's reign. 'Queen mother' (*gəbîrâ*) may also mean 'queen' (1 Kgs. 11:19), but the rendering 'queen mother' seems appropriate here. Although it does not seem to have been an officially recognised role, in Judah the queen mother had considerable status, and her name (unlike those of the mothers of kings in the Northern Kingdom) is regularly recorded in the Book of Kings. In the event of her son being a minor when his father died, the queen mother seems to have played a role in the conduct of public affairs. It is widely assumed that the individuals involved here are Jehoiachin and his mother Nehusta, daughter of Elnathan, from Jerusalem (2 Kgs. 24:8), presumably a member of an influential family in the capital. His reign lasted for only three months in 597 BC, and his youthfulness at eighteen[39] may perhaps have enhanced her position. They were both taken into exile in the second deportation under Nebuchadnezzar in 597 BC (2 Kgs. 24:15).

They are called upon to cast themselves down and sit. **Come down from your thrones.** 'Come down' (<√*šāpal*, 'to be/become low, be levelled, be humiliated') is a call for humility as much as physical movement. They will shortly lose their regal status, and they may as well accustom themselves to that right away by sitting, presumably on the ground—as slaves? That this is in prospect fits in with the translation of the following verbs as prophetic perfects so that the description is a prophecy of what will happen in the future (unlike NRSV), and when Jeremiah's message reaches them they are still on the throne. **For** (*kî*) **your glorious crowns will fall** (a prophetic perfect) **from your heads.**[40] The reference is to a 'crown' (singular), probably a golden diadem worn on the front of the king's turban, and applied by extension to the authority exercised by the queen mother because of her connection with her son. Nebuchadnezzar would deprive them of all authority.

19. There is general agreement that the divine prediction does not continue into this verse. Jeremiah himself adds this description of the circumstances that he has been shown will occur. The verbs are perfects and may be translated as past tenses, which would then be understood as a hyperbolic description of what happened in 597 BC if Nebuchadnezzar (like Sennacherib a century before him) first occupied these southern outposts before laying siege to Jerusalem. Treating the verbs as prophetic perfects permits the description to be a telescoped anticipation of what occurred in both 597 and 586 BC. **The cities in the Negev will be shut up, and there will be no one to open them.** The mention of the Negev, the desert area to the south of Judah (probably here it is the northern edge of that barren area that is meant, where towns like Beersheba were situated), indicates that the invasion will

39. This figure is taken from 2 Kgs. 24:8. In 2 Chron. 36:9 most Hebrew manuscripts give his age as eight years, which is obviously incorrect if 22:28 implies he already had children at the time of his deportation. Probably the Chronicles passage refers to his age on becoming co-regent with his father in 608 BC (McFall 1991:39).

40. *marʾăšôtêkem*, 'your head-support/pillow', scarcely fits the context. Following the LXX, many read as though *mērāʾšêkem*, 'from your head'. More recently, on the basis of Ugaritic, it has been suggested that this translation can be justified on the basis of repointing the consonants to read *mērāʾšōtêkem*, from the plural of a feminine noun for 'head', *rāšt* (Holladay 1986, 1:408).

sweep through the whole land from north to south. When the invaders lay siege to these towns, their gates will be closed, and there will be no one in a position to open the city gates and bring relief to their beleaguered inhabitants: they are doomed. **All Judah will be carried into exile, carried completely away.**[41] Neither in 597 nor 586 BC was there a total deportation. The language is hyperbolic to impress on the king and queen mother that there are no grounds for optimism.

5. The Threefold Impossibility (13:20-23)

The invasion is on the horizon. Perhaps this relates to the circumstances of Jehoiachin's reign which began after enemy forces had already set out for Judah. The threat is evident and those addressed are being challenged to respond before it is too late. But who is being spoken to? The vocative in v. 27 establishes the feminine 'you' of vv. 25-27 as being Jerusalem. The LXX added 'Jerusalem' to v. 20 to clarify the second-person feminine references in vv. 20-22, but not all commentators are convinced, and it is possible to argue that v. 20 continues to address the queen mother (Lundbom 1999:679-82). The language of v. 22 and its similarity to that of v. 26 fit in better with Jerusalem being addressed there. At some point there has to be a change in who is addressed, and it is suitable to follow the LXX and also the paragraph markings of the MT in taking this to occur at the start of v. 20.

20. Lift up your eyes and see[42] are feminine commands addressed to Jerusalem, which is not named until v. 27, but which is personified throughout and taken to represent the land of which it was the capital. She is called on to look at **those who are coming from the north,** resuming the theme of the invader from the north that had been so prominent earlier in Jeremiah's prophecy (1:14-15; 4:6; 6:1, 22;

---

41. The grammar is difficult. Judah here is feminine, and so gives rise to the feminine singular *hoglāt* (an older form of the third pers. fem. sing. perf. hophal; GKC §75m). *šəlômîm* is a masculine plural form derived from *šālôm*, 'peace', but perhaps functioning as an abstract term and used as a modal accusative with the sense of completeness (*HALOT* 1510).

42. The kethibh has two feminine singular imperatives *śəʾî* and *ûrəʾî*, doubtless referring to Jerusalem personified as daughter Zion. The qere has masculine plurals *śəʾû* and *ûrəʾû*, perhaps influenced by the masculine plural suffix on 'your eyes', which may been understood to refer to the king and queen-mother, still being addressed as in v. 18. The plural form may simply be part of an oscillation between Jerusalem/Zion as an entity and the many members of the community found in her.

10:22), but in the events of 597 BC there was no doubt about the identity of the invader. The question is then asked: **Where is the flock that was entrusted to you, the sheep of which you boasted?** The repetition of the noun *tipʾeret*, 'ornament, glory, splendour' (here translated as 'of which you boasted') from v. 18 ('glorious') links these two passages, but it is difficult to say that this argues for their unity as distinct from being a verbal association that caused the passages to be recorded together. The city as a shepherdess is asked to give an account of the sheep that had been put into her care by the LORD. The implication is that they are under threat, and the answer that they are safe and secure cannot be returned.

21. The various translations of this verse show how difficult it is to understand. Perhaps the initial question reflects their surprise at the situation they find themselves in. **What will you say when** (*kî*) **⌊the LORD⌋ sets over you those you cultivated as your special allies?** The underbrackets indicate that the LORD is a translator's supplement where the text is simply 'he appoints/punishes' (<√*pāqad*). The second clause is literally, 'and you yourself taught them over you, allies for a head'. Those whom Judah had looked to for help and whom she had accustomed to having a role in her affairs will be divinely set over her, no longer as friends, but as despots. 'Allies' (*ʾallupîm*) is used in Gen. 9:7 for leaders over groups of people, but elsewhere the word means 'friends', and that seems to be its meaning here.[43] What is being alluded to is the way in which Judah had been at pains to ally herself with Assyria, then Egypt, then Babylon, and then Egypt again. They would show how little they thought of her and how they were prepared to use her for their own ends (4:30). **Will not pain grip you like that of a woman in labour?**[44] This is a comparison that Jeremiah frequently uses (4:31; 6:24; 22:23). It is not the fact that this pain has an element of hope associated with it in the prospective birth that constitutes the point of the comparison, but that the onset of labour pains is sudden, severe and commanding. The rhetorical question emphasises that there will be a rapid and inescapable reversal of their fortunes.

22. At last Jerusalem will be aroused from her complacency and

---

43. The REB does, however, take *ʾallupîm* as 'leaders', makes the verb plural, and gives it a different meaning, so as to render, 'What will you say when your leaders are missing, though trained by you to be your head?', perhaps reflecting back on v. 18 because the REB takes vv. 18-22 as one section.

44. Literally, 'a woman of childbearing', the infinitive construct being used in a construct chain (*IBHS* §36.2.1c).

alerted to the depth and unremitting nature of her plight. **And if you ask yourself** refers to her inner thinking ('say in your heart', 5:24). **'Why has this happened to me?'** *'Me* of all people; surely I am not one to deserve this sort of treatment.' So completely was their thinking dominated by the consensus outlook of popular religion—that Jerusalem was immune from total disaster—the people of the city cannot grasp that that is precisely what is staring them in the face. There is an implicit recognition of divine sovereignty, with the LORD as the one who is controlling events. But that only serves to increase her surprise that one with whom she thought she had a good relationship has failed to honour his covenant commitments. This is the incredulous voice of a conscience that has been dulled by religious nominalism. The answer is bluntly given, **It is because of your many sins** (< *'āwōn*, 2:22), or 'the greatness of your iniquity' (NKJV; NRSV). Her behaviour and lifestyle with which she was so self-satisfied belied her true situation which she refused to recognise. The magnitude of her offence was proportionate to the dignity of the one she had offended.

The rest of the verse presents in euphemistic language a picture of a woman badly treated as a violent and shocking image of how the land will suffer under the enemy's outrages. **That your skirts have been torn off**/uncovered (Nah. 3:5; Isa. 47:3; Hos. 2:3) may refer to sexual assault, or to being subjected to the indignity of exposure as punishment for gross immoral behaviour, prostitution or adultery. **And your body ill-treated** is literally 'your heels suffered violence (<√*hāmas* niphal)'. 'Heels' may be a euphemism for the body, and violence may indicate action to make bare (*HALOT* 329). This shameful public disgrace associated with prostitutes was a final reminder by Jeremiah that punishment would be the inevitable consequence of wilful continuance in sin. It was not uncommon for those taken captive in war to be marched off naked into slavery (Isa. 20:4).

23. The change in this verse to 'you' as masculine plural suggests that a common proverb is quoted and applied to the situation of the people to emphasise the unremitting nature of their rebellion. **Can the Ethiopian change his skin or the leopard its spots?** The Cushite or Ethiopian came from the upper Nile region where the people were dark skinned. There was nothing they could do to change that. In the same way the leopard (cf. 5:6) cannot alter the markings on its coat. Leopards roamed in the wilderness area south and east of the Dead Sea. Their skins would have been familiar, being brought by traders to the city. These two impossibilities are matched by a third: Judah is unable to do anything about its behaviour. The nation had come to a point where it could not separate itself from its sin. **Neither can you** (masculine plural) **do good who are accustomed** (*limmûd*, 'learned, practised', <√*lāmad*, 'to learn') **to doing evil.** The contrast and mutual incompatibility of doing good and doing evil are made clear. By nature mankind has a propensity to do evil, but what Jeremiah focuses on is that evil conduct is learned and reinforced over the years by repetition. The good referred to is not merely a matter of social kindness or even of external support of the worship of God. It refers to the standards of the covenant they had entered into with the LORD. The nation had been for so long schooled in evil that it had lost the capacity to turn from it and so rescue itself from the impending catastrophe by returning to covenant allegiance. The only way in which deliverance could come was by the sovereign intervention of God, but that first of all involved a divine purging of the land by means of a total break from the customs and practices of their past. Calvin (1850, 2:192) compares the situation of Judah to those suffering from a chronic disease which has corrupted what is healthy in their body and has become incurable. Their life may be prolonged, but in continual weakness.

6. Scattered to the Winds (13:24-27)

In this final section Jerusalem is addressed by the LORD himself (the NIV and NKJV indicate divine speech begins here; the NASB starts it at v. 20). There is a succession of images to impress on Jerusalem that her conduct will inevitably lead to shameful punishment.

24. This verse shows the consequences of such dyed-in-the-wool degeneracy (the first verb is *waw*-consecutive imperfect, indicating that this is the next step in the story). **I will scatter** (9:15) **you like chaff driven by the desert wind**. 'You' is literally 'them', clearly a reference to the people of Judah. Since they are previously and in the following verses referred to in the feminine singular (masculine plural in v. 23), this may indicate that this verse was originally spoken on a different occasion. Alternatively the use of a plural may have been occasioned by the imagery of chaff.

The LORD says that there is no other solution to the problem of Judah's persistent sin than by disrupting their link with the land, that is, blowing them off into exile. 'The desert wind' came in from the east (4:11; 18:17). Holladay (1986, 1:415) insists that *qaš* ('drifting straw', NASB) should not be confused with 'chaff' (for which the Hebrew is *môṣ*). 'Chaff' refers to the husks that are winnowed from the grain whereas what is described here is the stubble that has been left in the field after the crop has been reaped. It has withered and been dried up by the sun and the searing east wind before being blown away. Stubble is a metaphor for what is worthless (Isa. 33:11), ready to be destroyed by the fire of divine judgment (Isa. 5:24). Ps. 83:13 combines the images.

25. This refers back to the judgments already described in vv. 20-22 and v. 24. **'This is your lot, the portion I have decreed for you,'**[45] **declares the LORD.** The lot (*gôrāl*, that which falls by lot) is their designated destiny (Isa. 17:14) which the LORD has decided must apply as the inevitable and due outcome of their disloyalty. 'Portion' (<√*mānâ*, 'to count, reckon, assign') here refers to the punishment the LORD has 'decreed'/'measured' out for them. The metaphor may be derived from the cutting of cloth, or from the apportionment of territory in the land (cf. Ps. 16:3). They would no longer dwell in property divinely allotted to them in the land of promise, but as displaced persons in the land of their captivity. **Because** (*'ăšer* here = 'inasmuch as', introducing the particular specification that follows) **you have forgotten me and trusted in false gods.** For 'forget' see 2:32; for 'false gods'/'falsehood' see 3:10; 16:19. The LORD's punishment is equitable: they have abandoned him, so he now abandons them. They did not recognise the jurisdiction of the king of the land, so now they will have to dwell elsewhere.

26. The verse begins 'But I also for my part' (*wəgam-'ănî*), which stresses that the LORD himself will act and that what he will do matches and responds to what they have already done. **I will pull up** (<√*ḥāśap*, 'to strip, make bare', a prophetic perfect) **your skirts over your face that your shame may be seen.** This verse (cf. Nah. 3:5) continues the language of v. 22. Jerusalem will be treated like the harlot/prostitute she had been (cf. Isa. 47:3). She will be publicly humiliated when she is openly confronted by her wrongdoing. This occurred through the agency of Babylon, but it was the LORD who was the one ultimately in control.

27. The degeneracy of their conduct is driven home by the cumulative impact of the terms that are now listed to describe it. **Your adulteries** (*ni'upîm*, only here and Ezek. 23:43) **and lustful neighings** (*miṣhālôt*, 5:8)**, your shameless**[46] (Ezek. 16:27; 22:9) **prostitution** (3:2, 9) all

45. For *middayik*, 'your decrees', BHS suggests reading on the basis of the LXX *meryēk*, 'your contentiousness, rebellion', which is reflected in the REB 'as a rebel'.

46. *zimmâ* may mean 'plan', but it is also a technical term for indecent conduct, especially sexual misconduct (Judg. 20:6), 'lewd harlotries' (RSV).

refer to the Baal cult and its associated ritual sexual behaviour. These are an abomination to the LORD. **I have seen your detestable acts on the hills and in the fields** (4:1; 7:30; Lev. 18:17). Hills and fields ('open country', or else the word also has the meaning 'highland', *NIDOTTE* 3:1218) are mentioned as the sites used for Baal worship and where they had indulged in immoral conduct. Nothing of what had gone on had escaped divine scrutiny (7:11), and there is no doubt about the LORD's revulsion at the popular religion of the day. **Woe**[47] **to you, O Jerusalem!** 'Woe' (*'ôy*) conveys the threat of coming judgment.

The final three words of v. 27 are obscure, possibly because they give utterance to strong emotion: 'after when? still.'[48] If they are read with the two preceding words, 'you will not be clean', then **How long will you be unclean?** expresses a plaintive wish that the people would appreciate their urgent need and take appropriate action to become clean. 'Unclean' is repeatedly used of ceremonial uncleanness in Leviticus. Here it is a matter of being so morally polluted as to be unfit to appear in the LORD's presence. It is, however, possible to take the words as, 'You are unclean. How long can this continue?' with a reluctant recognition of the inevitability of the impending judgment. The LORD cannot see himself as continuing to hold back in the face of their repeated provocations and uncleanness. Indeed, it may be that the final comment is the prophet's own plea to the people in the light of all that the LORD has said.

---

47. For the use of *'ôy*, 'woe!', see *IBHS* §40.2.4a.

48. REB rearranges and repoints to *'ad mātay tə'aḥērî*, 'How long will you delay?'

VI. INESCAPABLE DOOM

(14:1–17:27)

OUTLINE

A. Drought and Disaster (14:1–15:21)
   1. The Drought (14:1-6)
   2. Confession (14:7-9)
   3. Sword, Famine and Plague (14:10-12)
   4. Prophetic Lies (14:13-16)
   5. Disaster (14:17-18)
   6. Renewed Confession (14:19-22)
   7. Fourfold Destruction (15:1-4)
   8. No More Compassion (15:5-9)
   9. A Prophet's Agony (15:10-21)
B. Living Witness (16:1-21)
   1. Do Not Marry (16:1-4)
   2. Avoid Funerals and Weddings (16:5-9)
   3. Judgment on the Spiritually Blind (16:10-13)
   4. Restoration (16:14-15)
   5. Fishermen and Hunters (16:16-18)
   6. Idolatry Renounced (16:19-21)
C. Heart Condition (17:1-18)
   1. Judah's Sin (17:1-4)
   2. The Two Destinies (17:5-8)
   3. Deceitful above All Things (17:9-11)
   4. The Source of Hope and Life (17:12-13)
   5. When Nothing Happens (17:14-18)
D. The Significance of the Sabbath (17:19-27)
   1. Present Disobedience (17:19-23)
   2. Obedience Rewarded (17:24-27)

The structure of the prophecy between the headings at 14:1 and 18:1 has been variously analysed. In her examination of the Confessions, O'Connor (1988:130) provided a useful approach to this division. She identified two main blocks of material: chapters 14–16 which bring together material regarding the end of life in the land, with chapter 14 focusing on the end of physical life and chapters 15 and 16 the end of social life; and chapter 17 which comprises material on the heart which is subject to the scrutiny and verdict of the LORD. A case study in covenant obedience is presented in 17:19-27 regarding observance of the Sabbath.

It is difficult to ascertain the dates at which much of this material was originally proclaimed. Some sections are early (e.g. 16:1-4) and others (such as 14:18) are probably late. It would seem that they have been brought together in their present sequence at some point in the closing years of Jehoiakim or the early years of Zedekiah.

A. DROUGHT AND DISASTER (14:1–15:21)

The structure and extent of this division are not easy to determine. Perhaps the clearest internal marker is the resumption of Jeremiah's Confessions at 15:10, in which the prophet reflects on the lack of response to the message he had brought. Presumably this is to be read against the background of the preceding oracles concerning drought and disaster which exhibit a striking inversion of the normal complaint form. Both Holladay (1986, 1:422) and Craigie et al. (1991:194) call it a 'counter-liturgy'. Rather than the people setting before the LORD the circumstances that have given rise to their grievance, the direction of complaint is reversed so that it becomes a vehicle for announcing God's judgment in which he presents the people with a description of the disasters facing them (vv. 1-6, 17-18). Whereas many commentators view the material as a miscellaneous collection, Holladay calls 14:1–15:9 'a unity drafted at one time for a specific setting, a counter-liturgy as an expression of the judgment of Yahweh' (1986, 1:422). The specific setting he envisages is based on a number of detailed hypotheses which are largely unprovable (see Introduction §4.1), but the idea of a prophetic commentary and response regarding widespread emergencies in the nation seems cogent.

It is, however, difficult to date the original setting of the oracles. The fact that drought is mentioned as occurring during Jeremiah's early ministry (3:3) has suggested to some the possibility of a date during Josiah's reign. On the other hand, the description of v. 18 seems to indicate that the land has already suffered from the ravages of invasion, which would place that saying in the later part of Jehoiakim's reign. Since at that time Jeremiah is generally reckoned to have been debarred from public ministry, it may be that some of this material was originally written rather than delivered orally.

Another feature of this material that is possibly relevant to its date is the prohibition on intercession in v. 11, which repeats those already found in 7:15 and 11:14 from the early years of Jehoiakim. If these prohibitions were issued in the same general period, then this would indicate the period around 605 BC as the original setting. The reference to fasting in v. 12 might point to the fast of 36:9, but that is highly speculative.

1. The Drought (14:1-6)

1. This is the word of the LORD to Jeremiah renders an unusual formula, 'what came ⌞as⌟ the word of the LORD to Jeremiah', which also occurs in 46:1; 47:1; and 49:34, and to which 1:2 bears some resemblance. Calvin thought what follows was predictive prophecy. 'As then a drought was near at hand which would cause great scarcity, his [God's] purpose was to forewarn the Jews of it before the time, that they might know that the dryness did not happen by chance, but was an evidence of God's vengeance' (1850, 2:202). The notion of a 'counter-liturgy' (see above) takes this as a divine description of what the people are already suffering. But even so the drought functioned as a divine warning of greater judgments to come.

Concerning the drought/'concerning the words/matters of the droughts'. Similar thematic titles occur at v. 15, 'about the prophets'; 21:11, 'concerning the house of the king of Judah' (NKJV, NRSV); 23:9, 'concerning the prophets'; and 46:1 'concerning the nations'. The singular noun *baṣṣārâ* occurs in Pss. 9:9; 10:1, where it is usually translated as 'trouble' or 'distress', but the related form *baṣṣōret*, 'drought', is found in 17:8, which provides an appropriate contrast to this description. The plural 'droughts' may indicate a succession of droughts, of which there are other indications in 3:3; 12:4; and 23:10, but it is more probably a Hebrew idiom to bring out the intensity of one prolonged severe drought which may have occurred during the enemy harassment in Jehoiakim's reign and been intensified by it (v. 18). Droughts were not infrequent in Palestine, and had disastrous impact on the land and its inhabitants (Ruth 1:1; Hag. 1:10-11). Extreme droughts are recorded as happening in the time of Elijah (1 Kgs. 17:1) and again in the time of Elisha (2 Kgs. 8:1). Such droughts were never viewed as chance occurrences, but were rather recognised as being divinely controlled and sent as a rebuke for iniquity (Ps. 107:33-34; 1 Kgs. 8:35-36), to make the people reflect on the precariousness of their existence, and to bring them back to realise their dependence upon the LORD. The curses of the broken covenant included drought coming upon the land when the LORD would make the sky above the people become like iron and the ground beneath them like bronze (Lev. 26:19-20; Deut. 11:17; 28:22-24).

2. The carefully crafted poem of vv. 2-6 begins with a general statement of the extent of the drought, which is followed by four individual pictures, each of which highlights one feature of the intense suffering that has come upon the land.

Judah, her cities and Jerusalem are personified as mourners. **Judah mourns** (<√*ʾābal*, 4:28). Whether or not there are two homonyms meaning 'mourn' and 'be dried up', the word is obviously chosen here as a deliberate play on this double reference to the land crying out with sorrow because of the intensity of the drought. The REB attempts to convey this by using 'droops'. **Her cities languish** also involves a wordplay because the verb can denote both a physical effect on crops ('fails' Joel 1:10; 'is withered' Joel 1:12) and also human sorrow that is so severe as to lead to physical exhaustion and weakness ('grow faint', 15:9; 'pine away', 1 Sam. 2:5; Isa. 19:8). 'Cities' is literally 'gates' (NKJV, NRSV), which being the focus of the communal life of the city (1:15) is used by synecdoche for activity in the city as a whole: 'Her businesses have ground to a halt' (NLT). **They wail for the land** still has 'cities'/'gates' as its subject, a personification for those who are found in the gates. Rather than engaging in the business that was ordinarily transacted there, they are in mourning. 'Wail' is the third occurrence of the root *qādar* in Jeremiah. In 4:28 it was used to refer to the heavens growing dark, and in 8:21 to the prophet mourning over the fate of his people. It does not seem that mourners at this time dressed in black so that the reference is metaphorically to the lack of light, the gloom that settles on those who mourn; hence 'they lie in gloom on the ground' (NRSV). **And a cry goes up from Jerusalem** refers to a 'cry of lament' (*ṣəwāḥâ*). That it 'goes up' is possibly a reference to prayer to God.

3. The first scene depicting the distress concerns the impact of the drought on the upper classes. **The nobles send their servants for water.** 'Nobles' (<*ʾaddîr*, 'mighty, glorious') is a traditional term for those who are in authority (Judg. 5:13) and are distinguished in the community. Literally the expression is 'their nobles', referring to the civic dignitaries of the towns of Judah, possibly with overtones not dissimilar to ‘Their Excellencies’. It is a rare word that is used for servants[1] here, indicating those who are young and consequently of no great standing (‘little ones’, 48:4). Here it might perhaps be rendered ‘underlings/retainers’. The description is not the normal routine of these upper-class families, where matters such as procuring water would have been beneath the notice of the head of the household. This is a search of an irregular, unusual nature. What is more, it shows how serious the situation has become because the rich and influential would have been able to acquire water long after difficulties had arisen for ordinary folk. **They go to the cisterns but find no water.** ‘Cisterns’ (*gēbîm*) is not the normal word (which is *bôr*, 37:16), but is a term found only here and in 2 Kgs. 3:16 (‘ditches’). It denotes something dug, and hence the REB ‘pools’, perhaps in connection with irrigation works, but quite possibly the reference is to the bedouin technique of digging a hole, perhaps 2 feet deep, in a dry river bed. In a normal summer such a hole would fill with water in a matter of hours (Negev and Gibson 2001:529). But these circumstances are abnormal. There is nothing left in the normal storage cisterns in the city (cf. 2:13). Any and every other means of procuring water has being tried, but the drought is so severe that even these extraordinary measures no longer yield any supply so that **they return with their jars unfilled.**[2] In the desperation of drought it was not unknown for people to go searching in neighbouring towns for water (Amos 4:8). The two verbs **dismayed and despairing** reinforce each other. The first reaction (<√*bôš*, ‘to be ashamed’, 2:7) seems unusual, but catches their embarrassment and frustration at being unable to carry out such simple duties. The reaction of shame is further expressed by ‘despairing’ (<√*kālam*, ‘to be put to shame/confusion’); they have been publicly humiliated and see no hope as to how they might recover from the situation. Their disappointment and disillusionment is such that **they cover their heads**. This is a gesture of grief (2 Sam. 15:30; 19:5),[3] conveying both sorrow and humility, but not without an element of supplication towards God. Although the reference might seem to be only to the servants, it is probably the nobles themselves who are principally in view. No matter

1. The kethibh is *ṣəʿûrêhem*, an unusual form, while the qere gives the usual spelling with *î*, *ṣəʿîrêhem*. The same substitution is made in 48:4.

2. The Hebrew could equally be understood as ‘their vessels come back empty’.

3. Here and in the next verse (as elsewhere) the REB renders *ḥāpâ* as ‘uncover’, this being considered a gesture more appropriate as an expression of grief (McKane 1986, 1:318).

how they try, they are unable to meet their responsibilities to their households because the blessing of the LORD has been withheld.

4. The second illustrative example turns from an urban to a rural setting, and to the other end of the social scale, the small landholders. **The ground is cracked**[4] **because** (*kî*) **there is no rain in the land.** 'Ground' (*'ădāmâ*) is the cultivable land which needed moisture for a good harvest. But the shrivelling impact of the extended drought has led to the surface of the soil being baked by the sun until it is cracked (<*ḥātat*, 'to be dismayed' (1:17) or 'to be broken in pieces'). **The farmers are dismayed** (<√*bôš*, cf. v. 3) **and cover their heads** is a deliberate repetition of the similar clause at the end of the previous verse. Its force comes from the word 'farmers' which denotes not the smallholders themselves but hired labourers in the fields, who were employed by others to prepare the soil for crops and to care for oxen (but not as shepherds or vinedressers, which were more skilled tasks). Those of lowest social significance, who would be the first to experience any agricultural setback (Joel 1:11), are in fact suffering to the same extent as the highest in the land.

5. The next two pictures feature the impact of the drought on the animal world. **Even** (*kî gam*, with *kî* used as an intensive reinforcing *gam*, 'also, even') **the doe in the field deserts**[5] **her newborn fawn, because** (*kî*) **there is no grass.** It may be that there are two aspects to this comparison. If 'field' here denotes open ground (rather than the countryside in general), then this would not be the usual place for the retiring female deer to give birth. She would normally choose a quiet, probably wooded, spot (more easily found in ancient Palestine than today), but now the drought has forced her into open ground. However, the major emphasis is on the deer as tender and caring for her young. Circumstances are so extreme that she has been compelled to desert her fawn and go off to search for food to survive. Without its mother, the young animal will die.

6. Wild donkeys stand on the barren heights (3:2) **and pant like jackals.** These are animals used to harsh conditions and normally well able to fend for themselves. But here they are represented as sniffing

4. The Hebrew is difficult to render: *ba'ăbûr hā'ădāmâ ḥattâ*. The last word may on its own constitute a relative clause so that the two clauses could be understood as one, 'on account of the ground which is cracked … the farmers are dismayed'.

5. It is the infinitive absolute *'āzôb*, 'abandon', that is used in place of the finite verb (GKC §113z).

the wind (the same verb is used in 2:24 but with different overtones) to see if they can detect any trace of moisture that would lead them to a source of the water that they urgently need to survive. The comparison with jackals (9:11; 10:22) intensifies the note of desperation in the way they have their mouths open as they scavenge for anything to eat. **Their eyesight fails for lack of pasture** (literally, 'for (*kî*) there is no pasture'). The donkeys are worn out and emaciated; indeed they are at the point of death. Starvation has led to their eyes being glazed over in their weakness. 'Pasture' (*ʿēśeb*) may denote 'bushes' or 'vegetation in general' as distinct from *dešeʾ* ('grass', v. 5), or it may be virtually synonymous with the latter term, which seems to be the case here.

In vv. 4, 5 and 6 there are three clauses introduced by *kî*, 'for', which present the reason for the distress in ever more terse form: 'because/for there is no rain in the land' (five words in Hebrew); 'because/for there is no grass' (four words); and 'for lack of pasture'/ 'for there is no vegetation' (three words), the fading out of the refrain fitting in with a picture of increasing exhaustion.

2. Confession (14:7-9)

In vv. 7-9 (and also vv. 19-22) the 'we' who speak are the community. It is improbable that this is a report of what the people actually said, either in a genuine expression of contrition or in a standardised liturgical response (e.g. Skinner 1922:130-31). The mention in v. 11 (and also 15:1) of intercessory prayer points to Jeremiah as the speaker who identifies with the community and prays in their name and on their behalf. The people did not utter these words, but the prophet knows this is how they should have reacted to the lesson the LORD was teaching them in his providence. That they were not doing so is clear from the response of v. 10. Indeed, the record does not show the people as learning anything from their circumstances. However, Jeremiah's prayer remains a model from which his own and succeeding generations have much to learn.

7. The prayer begins with confession of sin, **although our sins testify against us.** 'Sins'/'iniquities' (<*ʿāwōn*, 2:22) indicates that their conduct has not conformed to the LORD's requirements. Their improper actions are personified as witnesses giving evidence in court against them (an idea already found in Isa. 59:12). But despite their acknowledged infringement of their Overlord's standards, the people approach him and ask that he intervene in their situation: **O LORD, do something for the sake of your name.** They do not presume to dictate the response of the LORD; they simply ask that he 'do something'/'act'.

The plea for divine intervention is based on what God is and not on what they are. 'For the sake of your name' points to all that God has revealed himself to be (cf. v. 21). At times it refers to the LORD's power and sovereignty, and so the action looked for would be such as would keep his name from being maligned among the heathen—but that does not seem to be the force of it here. Equally, divine action for his own name's sake may involve punishing wrongdoers, so that the LORD's justice be openly vindicated—but again that does not fit this context. Rather it seems to be a plea focused on the graciousness of God who has revealed himself as the one characterised by loving-kindness. Jeremiah is teaching the people to plead God's mercy and his covenant commitment as the ground for his action. It is only on the basis of grace that they can hope for relief from suffering the penalty that is justly their due.

For (*kî*) our backsliding is great;[6] we have sinned against you. 'For' does not at first sight seem to be the best translation of *kî*; a concessive rendering, 'although', or an intensive one, 'indeed', looks more probable. A very similar plea is found in Ps. 25:11 and there the NIV does in fact translate *kî* as 'though': 'For the sake of your name, O LORD, forgive my iniquity, though (*kî*) it is great.' However, in both texts realisation of the magnitude of guilt is presented as a reason for divine intervention and initiative: there is simply no other way in which the matter can be successfully dealt with (Ps. 25:11 NKJV, NRSV). This is the plea of the desperate who urge action on the basis of the LORD's character because they know their conduct has undermined any other argument with which they might approach him (such as, 'Help us because we are innocent'). Two more terms are employed to indicate their awareness (or rather Jeremiah's awareness on their behalf) of the sweeping nature of the charges against them. 'Backslidings' (<*məšûbâ*, 3:6) refers to their acts of wilful departure from the standards of the covenant. Rather than 'great' the plural noun suggests 'many' (NKJV; NRSV). It is not one offence that has caused the rupture of their relationship with the LORD but an accumulation of repeated breaches of the covenant. 'Sinned' (<√*ḥāṭā'*, 2:35) acknowledges that they have failed to comply with the norms of conduct laid down for them. What is more, this is not merely a technical infringement of an impersonal code, but 'against you', an affront to the lawmaker himself.

8. The vocative, **O Hope of Israel** (17:13; 50:7; Ps. 71:5; Joel 3:16), looks to the LORD as the one whose commitment to act is the basis on

---

6. *rābab* may indicate either 'be many' (NRSV, NKJV, REB) or 'be great' (NIV).

which the people may ground positive views regarding their future. 'Hope' (*miqweh* <√*qāwâ* 'to hope'[7]) refers to eager expectation that is able to endure adverse conditions because in faith it looks for the intervention of God. **Its Saviour** (<√*yāšaʿ*, 4:14) **in times of distress** recognises the LORD as the one who is able to act and rescue in situations of danger and oppression. Here the peril facing the people was the pressure they were under because of the drought and consequent famine. As they considered the state their land was in, the people were perplexed by the gap between what the LORD had committed himself to be to them and the reality they were facing. **Why are you like a stranger in the land?** 'Why?' was the typical question of the lament psalms (e.g. Ps. 10:1; 22:1). The LORD had said he would dwell among his people, but instead he is acting like a 'stranger'/'a resident alien' (7:6), one who might move back to his homeland and who could therefore not be expected to have the interests of the land at heart during his temporary stay there. **Like a traveller who stays only a night** suggests an even shorter stay of one who has turned off the road he was travelling on and pitched his tent just for one night. The LORD seemed to be one who lacked commitment and had at most only a temporary and passing interest in the circumstances of the land.

9. Further questions also use similes. **Why are you like a man taken by surprise?**[8] This describes someone who has suddenly been confronted by circumstances which have so overwhelmed him that he is confused and unable to act. **Like a warrior powerless to save?** A soldier is expected to be able to engage in successful combat and thus rid his nation of its enemies. But from what is happening to them the people are represented as expressing puzzlement as to whether the LORD, the warrior God of his people (20:11), has lost his ability to intervene on their behalf ('save' <√*yāšaʿ* hiphil, cf. v. 8).[9]

These possibilities are presented as questions, indeed as questions with an accusing edge to them. They reflect the way things seem to the

7. Holladay (1986, 1:433) points out that there is another noun *miqweh* (<√*qāwâ* II niphal, 'to assemble') which is used to refer to a 'pool of water' (Exod. 7:19) and considers that using this divine title at a time of drought plays on the thought of the LORD as the true pool of water for Israel.

8. The verb *dāham* is found only here in the Old Testament, but now also a 7th century BC Hebrew inscription confirms the sense 'be helpless'. The niphal seems to have the meaning 'be taken by surprise, be confused' (*HALOT* 214), and so be unable to act as a saviour.

9. The REB 'powerless to save himself' reads a niphal used reflexively instead of the hiphil *hôšîaʿ*.

people as they view the dire state they are in. But the prophet shows them that they are not to leave their petition with questions. As in the lament psalms, their approach to God is to end positively. They must affirm the LORD's presence in their midst. **You are among us, O LORD** may well refer to the Temple as being the symbol of God's dwelling as the covenant king in the midst of his people, and since he is there, surely he may be expected to act on their behalf. **And we bear your name**. They are recognised as the people of the LORD, who are owned by him (7:10). The people are pleading for the LORD's help on the basis of the covenant bond that already exists between them. **Do not forsake us!** is the final plea for help. 'Forsake' (<√*nûaḥ* hiphil, 'to set, lay aside, leave behind') conveys the idea of going from them and leaving them in the state they were in.

3. Sword, Famine and Plague (14:10-12)

The LORD now responds to the people/Jeremiah in two ways, neither of which provides any hope for the situation. In v. 10 he dismisses any plea on behalf of the people because their conduct has gone too far. Then in vv. 11-12 he again instructs the prophet not to intercede for the people. The LORD's mind is made up and he will not look on them favourably.

10. The first part of the LORD's response is expressed in poetic form, and this links it closely to the petition uttered on behalf of the people. **This is what the LORD says about this people.** 'This people' indicates that the LORD is alienated from them. This attitude influences the translation of the preposition *lə*, which after verbs of speech is usually rendered 'to', but here 'about'. The LORD does not address either the people or the prophet but describes the people in a distant manner, and in this formal verdict even refers to himself in the third person.

They greatly love to wander. 'Greatly' attempts to bring out the force of *kēn*, 'thus (NKJV), so', which usually refers back to what has preceded. It is not clear here which aspect of the previous context is being referred to, possibly the backsliding of v. 7 or perhaps it is a general comparison (*IBHS* §39.3.4e). The NRSV and NJPS try to convey this with 'truly'.

'Love' (5:31) reflects the inner attitude of the people. They do not want to have fixed allegiance to the LORD, but much prefer moving restlessly about between one idol shrine and another, or if understood in political terms, between one foreign alliance and another. They would do anything at all so long as it did not involve recognition of the LORD. **They do not restrain their feet.** They make no effort at all to keep themselves back from whatever takes their fancy. Does this reflect on the staggering course of a drunkard?

So the LORD does not accept them. This has the character of an official pronouncement. The verb used (<√*rāṣâ*, 'to be pleased, delight in') is the same as that for a priest giving an official pronouncement about the acceptability of a sacrifice (Lev. 1:4). Here and in v. 12 it is a word of authoritative rejection. **He will now remember their wickedness** (<*'āwōn*, 'sins' v. 7) **and punish them for their sins** (picking up the root of 'we have sinned' in v. 7). They have attempted to join together the worship of the LORD and that of idols, and have refused to give up their false ways. Therefore they are rejected. 'Punish' (<√*pāqad*, 5:9) conveys the idea of official inspection and consequent imposition of penalty. For the whole expression, compare Hos. 8:13.

11. The second aspect of the LORD's response is addressed to the prophet who is again forbidden to intercede on behalf of the people. The LORD has determined what their punishment is to be, and so it is inappropriate to plead for it to be averted. **Then the LORD said to me, 'Do not pray for the well-being of this people.'** This raises the question of whether Jeremiah had obeyed on previous occasions (7:15; 11:14). The construction used is not that for a permanent, binding prohibition, but may refer to a temporary injunction. Such conduct was therefore vetoed because it was inappropriate in the prevailing circumstances. That a limited ban was in view is further suggested here by the qualification 'for the well-being'/'for good'. The enjoyment of covenant blessing and deliverance could not be extended to those who had so flagrantly and repeatedly violated their covenant obligations.

12. Although (*kî*) **they fast, I will not listen to their cry** (cf. 11:14). The people were prepared to go through the rituals of repentance, and returning to the LORD. Fasting was a period of abstinence from food as a religious observance especially observed at a time of personal or national crisis (cf. 36:6, 9). It was often accompanied by other acts of humiliation, but to be approved of God it had to be accompanied by positive virtues (cf. Isa. 58:1-7). What was required to validate the people's religious exercises was true obedience (6:20; 7:21-28; 11:15). In their spiritual obduracy the nation was incapable of recognising this, and so their religious ceremonies were unacceptable to God, who did not respond to their shouts for help (*rinnâ*, 7:16). **Though** (*wəkî*, 'and though') **they offer burnt offerings and grain offerings, I will not accept them.** 'Them' could refer either to the people, or to their offerings. There was no doubt that they were prepared to sacrifice, that was not the problem. For 'burnt offerings', see 7:21. 'Grain offerings' may simply be offerings of any sort, or it may refer to cereal offerings as part of a more extensive sacrifice. The people were prepared to go through the rituals of the cult; indeed they were eager to do so. But ritual without heart commitment to the LORD was ineffective, and again we hear the authoritative word of refusal. For 'accept' (<√*rāṣâ*), see v. 10. Such conduct did not please God and was rejected (Mic. 6:7). **Instead** (*kî*, after the negative, 'but rather'), **I will destroy them with sword, famine and plague**. 'With sword, famine and plague' is brought forward for emphasis (cf. NRSV), and the repetition of 'with'/'by' before each element adds to the solemn comprehensiveness of the destruction ('destroy' <√*kālâ* piel, 'bring to an end', 5:3). 'Famine' here does not refer back to the 'natural' drought in the beginning verse of the chapter, but is the result of enemy invasion. The consequences of this are described in the deadly trio which is found fourteen other times in Jeremiah (21:7, 9; 24:10; 27:8, 13; 29:17, 18; 32:24, 36; 34:17; 38:2; 42:17, 22; 44:13) with two of the three items occurring together elsewhere (5:12; 14:15). They portray the devastation brought on the nation by the incursion of foreign forces. 'Sword' points to loss of life in battle; 'famine' to the lack of foodstuffs through enemy destruction of crops and particularly through siege; and 'plague' (*deber*) refers to an epidemic that causes multiple deaths. Though some specifically identify it as 'bubonic plague' (*HALOT* 212), it might refer to any disease that would decimate the weakened, starving population of a besieged city. Some insight into the suffering involved in siege warfare may be gained from the descriptions given in the book of Lamentations (Lam. 2:19-21; 4:6-10). This combination of divine inflictions is the curse that awaits the people because of their failure to obey the terms of the covenant (Lev. 26:25-26).

4. Prophetic Lies (14:13-16)

While not exactly interceding on behalf of the people, Jeremiah does bring before the LORD an additional factor in the situation: that the people have been deceived into adopting the attitude that they are exhibiting. The (false) prophets have presented them with assurances that all will be well (similar claims have already been mentioned in 5:12-17). To this the LORD replies in vv. 14-16, denouncing the prophets who said that the people would not see sword or famine, and imposing that fate on the prophets themselves (v. 15) as well as the people (v. 16).

13. But I said, 'Ah, Sovereign LORD.' 'Ah!' introduces a note of dismay as in 1:6; 4:10. For the divine name, see on 1:6 also. Jeremiah is indirectly raising with God a consideration that should be taken into account in assessing the situation. **The prophets keep telling them** renders a participle of ongoing action. The people have been exposed to an unremitting brain-washing exercise which has dimmed their perception. The phenomenon of false prophecy is mentioned in the early part of Jeremiah in 4:10; 5:12-13; 6:13-14; 8:10-11, and is discussed more fully in chapters 23; 27–29, though Jeremiah does not in fact use the term *false* prophets. These credible opponents of Jeremiah spoke as though they had received a message from the LORD (as the following 'I will give' clearly shows), but their perception of the requirements of the covenant was false. It was an optimistic picture they presented despite the abundant evidence of the people's sin. **'You will not see the sword or suffer famine.'** They rejected the warnings being given by such as Jeremiah, and posing as spokesmen of the LORD, they said on his behalf, **Indeed** (*kî*, 'for', probably introducing the reason why they would not see disaster), **I will give you lasting peace in this place.** 'Lasting peace' (*šəlôm ʾĕmet*, 'peace of truth, peace of faithfulness') was a condition of prosperity guaranteed by the reliable promise of God, and so 'assured' (NKJV, RSV). The prophets' message of absence of war and bestowal of material abundance was one which in the name of the LORD they urged the people to rely on (4:10; 5:12). It was very much associated with 'this place' (7:3, 7, 14) whether that be understood as the Temple, the chosen city of Jerusalem, or the land of promise. God had said he would dwell with his people, and therefore they proclaimed that come what may, their national well-being was assured with the ironclad promise of God. Now this Zion theology, as it is often termed, was not without some plausibility in that it could cite scriptural passages in its support. The false prophets had not devised a completely new religion. It was rather that they were presenting half the truth, and so had totally distorted the essence of the covenant. The LORD extended his guarantee of prosperity only to those who were obedient and faithful. Pictures of the inviolability of Zion could not be divorced from Zion's commitment to, and trust in, the LORD. As Moses had said long before, 'I command you today to love the LORD your God, to walk in his ways, and to keep his commands, decrees and laws; then you will live and increase, and the LORD your God will bless you in the land you are entering to possess' (Deut. 30:16).

14. In his reply to Jeremiah the LORD completely rejects the message of the prophets and denies that they are genuine. **Then the LORD said to me, 'The prophets are prophesying lies in my name.'** 'Lies'/

'falsehood' (*šeqer*) is fronted for emphasis. The REB brings this out: 'These are lies the prophets are prophesying in my name.' They were not hesitating to use the name of the LORD when they proclaimed the messages they had devised themselves. They were thus fraudulently claiming to be his spokesmen and what they declared had no divine authorisation. A threefold repudiation of their standing and message follows: **I have not sent them or appointed or spoken to them.** Their situation was unlike that of Jeremiah who had been sent (*šālaḥ*, 1:7), appointed (*ṣāwâ*, piel 'to command' 1:7; 26:2; contrast 23:32; 29:23; cf. Deut. 18:20) and spoken to (<√*dābar* piel, cf. 1:2, 9; 2:1 etc.). **They are prophesying**[10] **to you false visions, divinations, idolatries and the delusions of their own minds.** 'You' is plural, referring to the whole community and not just Jeremiah. There are three, possibly four, features of false prophecy listed here. 'False visions'/'a vision of falsehood' (*šeqer*) presented insubstantial dreams for the future. 'Divination' was forbidden to Israel (Deut. 18:10; 2 Kgs. 17:17; Ezek. 13:6). It attempted to foretell the future using magical manipulation of, for instance, the falling of arrows (Ezek. 21:21) or the pattern of liquid in a cup (Gen. 44:5). The word rendered 'idolatries' (*ʾĕlîl*) is used elsewhere to indicate heathen gods (Ps. 96:5), so that it might refer to the promotion of the false gods. However, its basic meaning is of what is weak, insignificant and worthless ('a worthless thing' NKJV). If it is used in hendiadys with 'divination', it would convey the thought of 'worthless divination' (NIV margin, REB, NRSV).[11] Finally, 'the delusions (cf. 8:5) of their own minds/hearts' refers to the counterfeit notions they fraudulently claimed as inspired so as to delude others. 'Day-dreams' (REB) conveys how their ideas lacked true substance and were merely wishful thinking.

15. Therefore (*lākēn* of judgment)**, this is what the LORD says**

---

10. Whereas the first occurrence of 'are prophesying' in this verse is the niphal participle of *nābāʾ*, here it is the hithpael participle that is used. By Jeremiah's day these stems were used interchangeably, but critical reconstructions of the early history of prophecy in Israel have often argued that the niphal originally meant 'to be in a prophetic trance, behave like a prophet', generally but not always in terms of speech, and the hithpael 'to exhibit the behaviour of a prophet', often 'to rage' (*HALOT* 659) or 'to rave'. The change here may be derogatory, but it is probably just stylistic variation.

11. The kethibh has twice uncommon forms in *û* (*weʾĕlûl* and *wətarmût*) for which the qere substitutes the more common forms in *î* (*weʾĕlîl* and *wətarmît*). This *û*/*î* change has occurred earlier and may be a spelling variation rather than a copying error.

about the prophets who are prophesying in my name: I (*wa'ănî*, 'but I', a decisive disjunction) **did not send them, yet they are saying, 'No sword or famine will touch this land.' Those same prophets will perish by sword and famine.** Having denied that these calamities would occur, they themselves will not escape that fate when it does come. The false prophets will be condemned to experience the reality they had unwarrantably said God would not impose. 'Perish' (<√*tāmam*, 'to be complete/perfect/at an end') points to the divine eradication of that style of prophet and prophecy.

16. However, the judgment on the false prophets will not exempt the people from punishment. The plea of having been misled would not be accepted, presumably because the community in general had allowed itself to be misled. They had the revealed truth of the LORD and should have judged the utterances of the false prophets by the standards of the covenant. They had the additional witness of the LORD's prophets such as Jeremiah, and that should at least have made them pause in their acceptance of what other prophets were saying. That they did not do so means that their condemnation still stands. **And the people they are prophesying to will be thrown out into the streets of Jerusalem because of the famine and sword**. The same catastrophic judgment is going to come on them also. They will be thrown as corpses into the streets, an expression of the utter degradation that will come on the people (22:19). **There will be no one to bury**[12] **them or their wives, their sons or their daughters** (8:2; 16:4; 36:30). Lack of burial was considered a great indignity (9:22), but since all had become involved in the idolatrous practices that polluted the land (7:18), they all share the same fate.

The final statement of the verse plays on the two meanings of the word *rā'â*, 'evil'. It can be either wickedness, moral evil committed by persons, and so 'I will pour their wickedness on them' (NKJV, NRSV), or else the catastrophe of judgment, **I will pour out on them the calamity they deserve** (cf. also the REB). What is going to come on them will match and be retribution for what they themselves have done. In this wordplay there is another expression of the connection between deed and consequence, not as arbitrarily linked but as imposed by divine justice (cf. Miller 1982:127)

12. The piel here probably refers to mass burial, as distinct from individual burial (qal).

5. Disaster (14:17-18)

17. The introductory rubric, **Speak this word**[13] **to them**, is again puzzling as one might have expected it to be followed by divine speech to be relayed to the people. Some argue that is indeed what does follow: a description of divine grief over the people's future because of their intransigence. But 'this word' is not explicitly identified as directly revealed by God, and it seems rather that Jeremiah is being commanded to relate his own feelings to the people so that where his warnings did not get through to them, his evident sorrow over their future might. It is not clear whether this is a reaction to the vision of the impending disaster just granted to him, or whether it refers to a situation that has already arisen, possibly in the years after 605 BC or even after Nebuchadnezzar's invasion in 597 BC (2 Kgs. 24:10-17).

The prophet gives voice to his own reaction in the face of the foretaste of catastrophe. **Let my eyes overflow**[14] **with tears night and day without ceasing** (<√*dāmâ* II, 'to come to an end, rest'; cf. 8:14).[15] For 'overflow' see on 9:18; 13:17. 'Night and day' may have become the more common idiom after the Exile (2 Chron. 6:20; Neh. 13:19) whereas 'day and night' was customary earlier (9:1; 1 Kgs. 8:29). The prophet envisages himself as engaging in unceasing sorrow on behalf of the people for the devastation that has affected her. **For** (*kî*) **the virgin daughter—my people**[16]**—has suffered a grievous wound, a crushing blow.** The people are again treated as a personified woman (8:11). Jeremiah expresses his close bond to them and his concern for

13. Holladay (1986, 1:436) in this passage and in 13:12 avoids the seeming incongruity by taking the words as the conclusion of the previous verse.

14. Treating the verb as a jussive (rather than a present 'My eyes overflow' [NLT] or a future, 'My eyes will overflow') arises from the following verb, translated by the NIV as 'without ceasing', but literally 'and let them not cease', where the negative *ʾal* is that usually associated with a third person prohibition. This negative form may, however, be used to express the conviction that something will not happen (GKC §107p) as in 46:6 or Ps. 121:3, and that may be the case here so that the clause may be rendered, 'My eyes will overflow with tears night and day so that they do not cease'.

15. The NKJV and NASB line division whereby 'night and day' goes with what precedes follows the Massoretic accentuation. This, however, may be wrong as it gives a very short colon in 'and let them not cease'.

16. The NIV takes the phrase *bətulat bat-ʿammî* as composed of a two-part construct chain *bətulat bat*, 'virgin of daughter' and a noun in apposition *ʿammî*, 'my people' (cf. NRSV) rather than a three-part construct chain, 'the virgin daughter of my people' (NKJV).

their welfare with the phrase 'daughter, my people' (4:11). Possibly the term 'virgin' is used to refer to the fact that Jerusalem had remained inviolable up to that time (597 BC), but now the people are said to have 'been broken with a great break' (the verb and the cognate noun <√*šābar*, 4:6). The prophet also describes it as a 'very crushing blow'. For 'blow', see 'wound' (10:19). 'Crushing' (<√*ḥālâ*, niphal 'to cause illness') with the addition of 'very' probably points to a fatal wound.

18. These words must be those of the prophet as he describes what he sees wherever he goes in the land. 'Country' and 'city' are used to describe all of the land as in the first of the covenant curses of Deut. 28: 'You will be cursed in the city and cursed in the country' (Deut. 28:16). **If I go**[17] **into the country, I see those slain by the sword.** In the open fields, those who have been caught by the invaders have been put to death by the sword. **If I go into the city, I see the ravages of famine.**[18] The term 'ravages'/'sicknesses' is not specific; it is used of diseases in general. The famine may be caused by the presence of enemy armies, or by natural catastrophe, or both. These calamities have occurred in the land which the prophets had said would not experience sword or famine and are representative of all the disasters that will afflict them.

The final words of v. 18 are difficult to understand. 'For' (*kî*) **both prophet and priest have gone to a land they know not.** The verb of motion (<√*sāḥar*) generally means to 'go around in a circuit', and is, for instance, used of traders going about selling their wares. The problem is whether this refers to exile or to movement within the land. The NIV opts for exile, and shows the false religious leaders of the community being taken away by the invaders, but this seems less likely in that the MT reads 'to a land and they did not know' (though BHS notes that many manuscripts and the LXX omit the 'and'). The alternative 'go about' (NKJV) or 'ply their trade' (NRSV) points to activity within Judah, but it is described as fatally flawed because the religious leaders of the community lack true knowledge of the LORD and allegiance to him (2:8; 5:5; 9:3, 24). This is preferable in that it also makes sense of 'for' at the beginning of the clause. These calamities have come on the land because its teachers did not really know the LORD, and so their instruction was deficient in substance and wisdom.

---

17. The perfect is used of action completed before the main verb, 'if I have gone … then I see'.

18. The NIV 'the ravages of famine' retains the abstract conception of the Hebrew, 'diseases'/'illnesses', which is used in place of a concrete expression such as 'those sick from famine' (NKJV), or 'the victims of famine' (REB).

6. Renewed Confession (14:19-22)

The major problem in understanding these closing four verses is to decide the tone in which they were uttered. Is this the people pleading on their own behalf using sound religious vocabulary but without heart commitment, or is this the prophet uttering on their behalf what they should have been saying for themselves? On the one reading, the words are false; on the other, the sentiments are true but unable to lead to reconciliation in that they were not endorsed by the people. It seems best to adopt the same interpretation as in vv. 7-9 that here Jeremiah again utters words that the people should, but do not, adopt for themselves.

19. The prophet seems to have taken a measure of encouragement from the command to speak to the people (v. 17), and therefore he questions the extent to which the LORD has reacted against the people. **Have you rejected Judah completely?** The emphasis in the question is on 'completely' (Lam. 5:22), expressed by an infinitive absolute. Obviously the LORD had turned away from Zion, but was there no hope at all in the situation? Is his rejection simply the opposite of his originally having chosen them? Was that choice now reversed, or was there more to it? Compare 2:14, where the first question sets out a state of affairs that is regarded as incredible, and the second one adds a note of wonder and inability to accept it. **Do you despise Zion?** 'You' renders *nepeš*, 'your soul' (NKJV; for the use of *nepeš* in relation to God, see on 6:8 and compare 15:1), but the emphasis on the emotional and volitional is better expressed by 'your heart' (NRSV). 'Despise' (<√*gāʿal*, 'to loathe, cast from one') describes the disdain and rejection with which someone puts something away. This was the attitude the people had shown in turning from the covenant stipulations (Lev. 26:11), and is also that displayed by the LORD in his righteous response to their rejection (Lev. 26:30). However, even in the covenant curse there was held out the possibility of a return (see also on 12:13). 'They will pay for their sins because they rejected my laws and abhorred my decrees. Yet in spite of this, when they are in the land of their enemies, I will not reject them or abhor them so as to destroy them completely, breaking my covenant with them. I am the LORD their God' (Lev. 26:43b-44). It is this aspect of the covenant that Jeremiah is probing as v. 21 makes explicit. What more is there on the dark side of the covenant beyond the imposition of the curse on covenant violators?

Why have you afflicted us so that we cannot be healed? 'Afflicted' (<√*nākâ*, 'to strike') is from the same root as 'blow' (v. 17; cf. 2:30; 5:3). Such violence frequently turns out to be fatal, and it seems that there was no obvious route for recovery from what had come on the land. It is not clear what sort of healing is envisaged: spiritual? or economic after the ravages of drought and invasion? Probably both aspects of the situation are intended. **We hoped[19] for peace but no good has come, for a time of healing but there is only terror.** This repeats 8:15, and portrays the people as finally realising that they had entertained delusive hopes regarding the future. The only true hope was that provided by the LORD himself (v. 8, 22).

20. Again there is an acknowledgment of sin (cf. v. 7) in words that echo those of Ps. 79:8-9. **O LORD, we acknowledge our wickedness, and the guilt of our fathers.** 'Acknowledge'/'know' is used here in the sense of 'confess' (3:13). 'Wickedness' is *rešaʿ* (cf. 12:1), evil deeds that violate legal requirements, and 'guilt' is *ʿāwôn* (2:22), possibly 'iniquity' (NKJV, NRSV). They see themselves as part of the same covenant community as their forefathers (2:5; 3:25; 7:15) and realise that their national alienation from the LORD has not arisen overnight. This is not presented as exonerating the current generation, but as a basic spiritual reality. Their acknowledgment arises from the facts of the matter, 'for' (*kî*, translated as an intensive 'indeed' by the NIV, but as causal by the NKJV and NRSV) **we have indeed sinned against you.** 'Have sinned' (<√*ḥāṭāʾ*) picks up the theme of v. 7. In presenting the people with the need for confession, Jeremiah is faithfully reflecting the covenant instruction given through Moses as to what was required from those experiencing the curse of the broken covenant (Lev. 26:40-41; Deut. 30:1-3) and repeated by Solomon in his inaugural prayer in the Temple (1 Kgs. 8:46-50).

21. The people are then given three reasons to present to the LORD as to why he should act to alleviate their distress. They do not bring forward any good inherent in the people but point to the character of God himself. (1) **For the sake of your name do not despise us.** 'Despise' (<√*nāʾaṣ*) in the qal with God as subject means not 'to show contempt' but 'to reject, spurn' (Deut. 32:19). Again the mention of the name of the LORD sets up a parallel with v. 7. It may well be that 'us' is the wrong supplement, though one that is generally employed by translators. It is possible that 'the throne of your glory' in the next line is doing double duty and should be understood here also. (2) **Do not dishonour your glorious throne.** 'Dishonour' (<√*nābal*, piel 'treat as a fool', cf. Deut. 32:15, 'treat contemptibly') urges the LORD to show due regard for what he himself has set up in Judah. This could

19. An infinitive absolute is used for an historic tense (GKC §113ff).

be identified as the ark or the Temple, or indeed the city of Jerusalem itself (3:17; 17:12). It is the place where God has been pleased to reveal his splendour ('glory', *kābôd*), the unapproachable luminous glory-cloud that was the visible accompaniment of his presence (Exod. 40:34; 1 Kgs. 8:11). If the land and city are captured, then his Temple will be desecrated and destroyed. Surely God cannot let that happen to the place which he has so highly honoured. (3) **Remember your covenant with us and do not break it.** This is an astonishing plea in view of the fact that the people had broken the covenant so completely. However, it proceeds from the passages of the covenant where the possibility of restoration is mentioned (Lev. 26:40-45; Deut. 30:1-10), particularly the words, 'I will remember the covenant' (Lev. 26:45). 'Break' (<√*pārar*, 'annul' NJPS, 'make void' REB), does not refer to divine breach of the covenant terms in the way in which the people had broken what was stipulated for them. When one party to the covenant broke its terms, the whole future of the relationship depended on the attitude of the offended party. The people are pleading that the LORD would not utterly repudiate the covenant bond between them, but rather that his punishment of them be so limited that there may be a subsequent resumption of good relationships. This hope for the future is later given greater clarity in terms of the new covenant of chapter 31. It is significant that about this time Ezekiel was presenting the same message to the early exilic community. 'This is what the Sovereign LORD says: I will deal with you as you deserve, because you have despised my oath by breaking the covenant. Yet I will remember the covenant I made with you in the days of your youth, and I will establish an everlasting covenant with you' (Ezek. 16:59-60).

22. The final argument that is presented is that the LORD should hear because there is no one else to whom they may turn. The two rhetorical questions expect the answer 'No'. **Do any of the worthless idols of the nations** (8:19) **bring rain?** The hardships of drought soon ensued if the seasonal rains failed. The Canaanites explained such meteorological phenomena as being within the control of their deities, but the people (through the prophet) here decisively reject such a pagan theology, reversing their previous attitude and endorsing the description Jeremiah had given of God alone as the one in control of the natural world (10:13). This is an argument that Paul also used in New Testament times: 'Yet he [God] has not left himself without testimony: He has shown you kindness by giving you rain from heaven and crops in their seasons' (Acts 14:17). **Do the skies themselves send down showers?** (3:3) 'Showers' (*rəbibîm*) refers to light rain or drizzle, presumably at the time of the early or late rains (cf. 5:24). They were not fortuitous events, of an impersonal sort, but rather the direct gift of the LORD alone. **No, it is you, O LORD our God.** In Hebrew it is a third rhetorical question, 'Is it not you, O LORD our God?' (NRSV). This is the acknowledgment of the reality, power, and obligation of the covenant relationship. There may be an implied appeal to the history of Elijah (1 Kgs. 18:41) or to a passage such as Joel 2:23. **Therefore** ('and') **our hope is in you, for** (*kî*) **you are the one who does all this.** 'Our hope is in you'/'We have set our hope on you' refers back to the title given earlier to God, 'Hope of Israel' (v. 8).

Breach of covenant is no light thing and results in disaster. There are two alternating ideas in the passage: the hope that the false prophets had encouraged the people to have, namely that everything will turn out well in the end, and the divine negative. The prophet's plea and the pleas he puts on the lips of the people are of no avail in averting the impending catastrophe, for after all the people remain impenitent. How can God extend the blessings of the covenant to those who are so resolute in wandering off from him and entertaining all manner of unjustified expectations? It is not God who must be asked not to reject his people (v. 21), but the people who must be asked why they rejected their God (15:6). And yet, throughout it all, there is in the words that the prophet utters on behalf of the people something more, a glimpse that after the darkness there might be repentance and restoration.

7. Fourfold Destruction (15:1-4)

In 14:19-22 Jeremiah had uttered a complaint/lament on behalf of the people as he had already done in 14:7-9. Then the LORD had responded not with words of acceptance and deliverance but of rejection (14:10-12), and it is same reaction that is recorded in this section. Indeed the divine refusal to heed the entreaties made is again couched in terms of the intercessory ministry of Jeremiah. It would be of no avail for the prophet to plead on behalf of the people because their conduct had not changed from the days of Manasseh.

1. In this section the LORD addresses Jeremiah. **Then the LORD said to me: 'Even if Moses and Samuel were to stand**[20] **before me, my**

---

20. The verb is singular possibly suggesting that *wə* has the force of 'or' (Holladay 1986, 1:439), in which case the two are viewed as interceding separately. But a singular verb may be found with such a double subject (GKC §146f), and then it is the stronger hypothesis of joint intercession that is presented as ineffective.

heart would not go out to[21] this people.' Moses and Samuel were noted figures from the past who had acted as intercessors on behalf of the people, and been instrumental in averting the LORD's judgment from coming upon them. Moses is twice specifically described as praying to God on behalf of others (Num. 21:7; Deut. 9:20), and in other passages intercession is clearly implied (Exod. 32:11-14, 31-34; Num. 14:13-19). So too Samuel is three times described as praying to the LORD for others (1 Sam. 7:5; 12:19, 23). Moses and Samuel are also mentioned together in Ps. 99:6 as individuals whom the LORD had answered when they called on his name, and they are linked in a similar way in Ezek. 14:14. But even if such persons whose intercessory ministry had been availing in the past were to do so again, they would be unsuccessful. It is obviously a hypothetical set of circumstances that is being considered, but it effectively rules out any mediation as being able to gain a reprieve for the people whose wickedness was such that they were beyond the reach of any intercessor's plea.

The petition of the previous chapter had been based on the covenant, and Moses and Samuel are probably mentioned because of their role as covenant mediators. 'Stand' is virtually a technical term here, equivalent to appearing in the sovereign's court as his attendant (Gen. 19:27, Deut. 4:10). It is more frequently used of the priests who 'stand to minister' to the people on behalf of the LORD (Num. 16:9; Deut. 10:8; 17:12; 18:5, 7). But the pleas of covenant relationship are ineffective when the people have rejected the covenant. 'My heart' (*nepeš*, 6:8) refers to 'myself', possibly in the sense of 'my desire', and hence the rendering 'heart'. The LORD says that 'his heart was not towards this people', again an expression of dissociation (14:10). Their behaviour had so disrupted the relationship that he could no longer be favourably disposed towards them.

Send them away from my presence! Let them go! 'Send away' (<√*šālaḥ* piel) reuses the language of the Exodus when Pharaoh was urged to let the people go (Exod. 8:1). 'Let them go'/'that they may go out' (<√*yāṣaʾ*, 'go out', hiphil 'bring out') also looks back to the same period (Exod. 3:10; 6:6). Now, however, these words do not convey the promise of the LORD's deliverance. The covenant had been broken, and there is a reversal of the Exodus. No longer is Pharaoh urged through Moses to let the people of the LORD go so that they might

21. Literally, 'Not myself/my soul to this people' where *ʾel*, 'to/towards', is used here to express an ethic dative, of advantage or disadvantage (*IBHS* §11.2.2a).

serve him. Rather the LORD is commanding the prophet to convey the word of dismissal to the people, sending away from his presence those who no longer serve him. The movement is from the Temple or, more probably, from the land of covenant promise. Those who have rejected the covenant may no longer reside in it and enjoy the privileges it bestows.

2. The LORD anticipates that the people will not hear the prophetic word without asking further questions. The answer given to their expected inquiry spells out the grim future that awaited them. **And if** (*kî*) **they ask you, 'Where shall we go/**'go out'**?' tell them, 'This is what the LORD says: "Those destined for death, to death; those for the sword, to the sword; those for starvation, to starvation; those for captivity, to captivity".'** The Jeremianic triplet of 'sword, famine and plague' (14:12) is here expanded by the addition of a fourth scenario. 'Death' as distinct from 'the sword' may refer to death from other causes, principally 'plague'. 'Starvation' is a translation variant for 'famine' (14:12). But even some of those who survive the horrors of invasion and siege will not be exempt from catastrophe because they will be taken into captivity (*šəbî*, capture by the enemy and deportation into a foreign land). The four options tersely spelled out the possibilities facing a country about to be conquered. None of these stark outcomes corresponded to the future the people were envisaging for themselves.

3. However, further gruesome detail is added to the scene of death, using phraseology reminiscent of Deut. 28:26. **'I will send four kinds of destroyers against them,' says the LORD.** 'Send' (<√*pāqad*, 1:10; 13:21) often describes the action of a superior who examines the conduct of a subordinate and responds appropriately, but here the reference is rather to the appointment of officers of state (cf. 1:10). 'Ordain' (REB) or 'appoint' (NKJV) catches the note of sovereign determination as regards those who are set 'over'/'against' the people—the idea that punishment is involved cannot be excluded. 'Kinds'/'families' (<*mišpāḥâ*, 'clan, family division') is used metaphorically in the plural to express type or class without any sense of blood kinship. It is not at first made clear what these four kinds consist of; 'of destroyers' is a translator's clarification.

Four aspects to the slaughter of the people are set out. First, **the sword to kill** as the enemy massacre the army and population of the land. Then the work of the sword is completed by three sets of scavengers which dispose of those left fallen. **The dogs to drag**

away[22] (22:19; 49:20 = 50:45) builds on the earlier prediction that there would be no burial possible because of the numbers involved (14:16). Dogs were unclean animals, and that they are able to abuse the corpses of the dead shows a community helpless before the calamity that has engulfed it. Indeed their shameful destiny is worse than that: **the birds of the air and the beasts of the earth to devour and destroy** (<√*šāḥat*, 5:10), these two groups completing the process that the dogs had begun (7:33). It is a picture of horrific and unmitigated slaughter.

4. I will make them abhorrent[23] **to all the kingdoms of the earth.** 'Abhorrent' (*zawăʿâ*, 'a source of horror') again recalls the curses of the covenant, 'you will become a thing of horror (*zaʿăwâ*, see footnote) to all the kingdoms on earth' (Deut. 28:25). As other nations look at them, they will shudder at the gruesome fate which has come on Judah. This judgment is then traced back to its root cause. **Because of what Manasseh the son of Hezekiah king of Judah did in Jerusalem.** Here we are reminded of a feature of the history of the southern kingdom, that its godly kings often had ne'er-do-well sons. Manasseh's long reign marked the beginning of the process of irreversible decline for the nation (2 Kgs. 23:26; 24:3; see Introduction §3.4). Not that matters were totally perfect before that, but his reign tainted and twisted the conscience of the people in a way that it could not be shaken off. Although the Book of Kings makes much of the impact of Manasseh's reign on the nation, this is the only place that he is mentioned by Jeremiah. The prophet did not address his own generation as though they were inevitably doomed by their past. Undoubtedly the history of their nation did not bequeath to them a promising start, but Jeremiah's ministry calling for repentance pointed out how they should react to escape the impending judgment on them. It was only when they in turn rejected the LORD's gracious overtures

22. *sāḥab* is translated 'to tear' (AV, RSV) from the LXX and Vulgate renderings.

23. The noun in the kethibh is spelled *zəwāʿâ*, 'an object of horror or terror' (<√*zāwaʿ*, 'to toss hither and thither'). Here and in 24:9; 29:18; 34:17 the term is closely associated with other sufferings inflicted by divine judgment on Israel. The qere is an alternative spelling *zaʿăwâ* (Ezek. 23:46; 2 Chron. 29:8) with transposed letters, which is usually identified as a later orthographic variation though it is found in BHS (i.e. Codex Leningradensis) in Deut. 28:25. The NKJV 'I will hand them over to trouble, to all the kingdoms of the earth' takes *zawăʿâ* in the sense of being subject to persecution and ill-treatment at the hands of the nations.

through the prophet that they identified with previous generations and brought themselves under the same condemnation as had been expressed against them.

8. No More Compassion (15:5-9)

The rejection of the people is further described in divine speech, addressed first of all to the personified city (vv. 5-6) and then to the prophet (vv. 7-9).

5. This divine utterance is linked to what precedes by 'for' (*kî*). The thought may be that this end will come upon Jerusalem because there will be no one prepared to help her. Absence of assistance is expressed in three plaintive questions, each expecting the answer 'No one'. **Who will have pity** (<√*ḥāmal*, 'to spare' and also 'to have compassion, pity'; 13:14) **on you, Jerusalem?** The city is again personified as a woman, for whom none will feel sympathy. 'There is none to comfort her' (Lam. 1:2, 17). **Who will mourn for you?** The verb (<√*nûd*, cf. 4:1) denotes a backwards and forwards motion, either of the head, or of the whole body, and was obviously associated with behaviour expressive of grief. **Who will stop to ask how you are?** The picture is that of someone turning aside (<√*sûr*, 17:5) either from their normal tasks or from their journey to inquire after the peace or well-being (*šālōm*) of Jerusalem. 'Is it nothing to you, all you who pass by?' (Lam. 1:12). There is probably a conscious contrast with the scene in Ps. 122:6-9 which focuses on prayers for the peace (*šālôm*) of Jerusalem. Here there is so little concern for her that people cannot be bothered to spare a moment to ask how she fares.

6. The reason for Jerusalem's rejection is then restated, picking up the theme of 14:19 where the LORD had been asked why he had rejected Judah. That was not the right question to ask, because it did not start at the beginning of the story of the disintegrating relationship between the LORD and his people. **'You have rejected me,' declares the LORD.** 'You' (*'att*, feminine singular in reference to Jerusalem) is fronted for emphasis, and is the verbal equivalent of pointing the finger at them. The REB renders, 'You yourselves cast me off.' The covenant relationship had been decisively broken by their action (for *nāṭaš* ,'reject', see 12:7, 'abandon'), not by the LORD's breach of promise. **You keep on backsliding** (imperfect of repeated action), literally 'you go backwards', is reminiscent of the expression 'were with respect to backwards' (7:24). After they had rejected the LORD, they had shown no signs of changing direction, but were keeping their faces turned away from him and so their situation constantly deteriorated.

The LORD's sentence on them follows. The problem that arises is whether the verbs[24] are to be translated as pasts (REB, NRSV, RSV) or prophetic perfects, that is emphatic futures (NIV, NKJV, NASB, NJPS). If past tenses are used, the description could be viewed against a background such as what had already happened in 597 BC since the suddenness described in v. 8 would not be applicable in the protracted events of 586 BC. But a future reference adopted by the NIV is equally likely.

So I will lay hands on you and destroy you. 'I will stretch out my hand' can be an action signifying either doom or salvation (6:12; Exod. 6:6; 24:11; Isa. 5:25; 30:30; 31:3; Deut. 4:34; 5:15). **I can no longer show compassion,** or 'I am weary of relenting!' (NKJV, REB). 'Can no longer' (<√*lā'â*, 'to be weary') often relates to emotional tiredness (9:5; 20:9), perhaps responding with impatience, at other times being incapable of responding at all (6:11). The form here is niphal, which may describe a subject coming to be in a particular state (*IBHS* §23.3c). 'Show compassion' (<√*nāḥam*, 'to regret', 'to change one's course') points to the fact that the LORD had repeatedly warned them of the consequences of their behaviour and had time and again exercised gracious compassion towards the people in averting the judgment that should have fallen on them. This was how the LORD had responded to those who had interceded with him on behalf of Israel. 'Then the LORD relented and did not bring on his people the disaster he had threatened' (Exod. 32:14; see also Num. 14:20; 1 Sam. 7:10). However, the people repeatedly abused the mercy shown to them, and now God can no longer continue in this way (4:28; Isa. 1:14; 7:13).

7. Although the theme of the destruction to come on the people continues, in v. 7 the address changes from the feminine singular with reference to the city to a third-person masculine plural, perhaps because of the nature of the metaphor employed: **I will winnow them with a winnowing fork at the city gates of the land.** The comparison is similar to that of 4:11. When the grain had been harvested, it was first chopped up with the threshing sled and then the mixture of ear and chaff was tossed in the air using a long, wooden fork. Generally this would be done on an open site where there was a current of air to blow the lighter chaff away and let the grain fall back to the ground. But this would no ordinary winnowing because at 'the ⌞city⌟ gates of the land'

24. 'Lay' and 'destroy' are imperfect consecutives. This is true of the first two verbs in v. 7, with perfects thereafter and in vv. 8 and 9, until 'I will put' which is imperfect. Notice the REB after a series of past tenses has 'I shall give' in v. 9c.

people, not grain, would be found. The metaphor describes close scrutiny and separation as their foreign conquerors determine their fate (1:15): who will be slain, who will be permitted to stay, who will be taken away. **I will bring bereavement and destruction on my people.** 'Bereave' is more specifically 'cause to be childless'. 'Bring ... destruction'/'destroy' as in 1:10. These are the inevitable consequences of their sin and rebellion. **For**[25] **they have not changed their ways** adds to their sin their rejection of the repeated offers of restoration if they repent, but they had not 'changed'/'gone back' (*šûb*). 'Their ways' are the ones they have chosen for themselves, not the path the LORD had set before them (2:17).

8. More detail is graphically given of the impact of the LORD's judgment: **I will make their widows**[26] **more numerous**[27] **than the sand of the sea.** 'The sand of the sea' was a common simile for what cannot be counted (here a plural 'seas' is used, which intensifies the comparison), but the expression is usually found in contexts of blessing and increase, and in particular the blessing of the covenant promises to Abraham and Jacob: 'I will … make your descendants as numerous … as the sand on the seashore' (Gen. 22:17; 32:13). That is about to be reversed. The next few words are obscure: **At midday I will bring a destroyer against the mothers of their young men,** where both 'mother' and 'young man' are taken as collective terms. For 'destroyer', see 6:26. Midday (cf. 6:4) would be a time when attack was unexpected (as expressed by 'suddenly' in the next line), but the destroyer is so certain of victory and the people are so unprepared to defend themselves that the destroyer need not delay. But the full impact of this action does not fall on the young men, in their prime for military service, but rather on their mothers who are left to feel the loss. Possibly the figure of Jerusalem is at the back of this expression; the whole community feels the impact of the invasion. **Suddenly I will bring down on them anguish and terror.** 'Anguish' (<√*ʿîr* II) refers to the perturbation caused by the shock of the sudden occurrence.

---

25. The NIV begins this clause with 'for'; the NLT with 'because'. Both are translator's supplements to bring out the unexpressed (and therefore startlingly abrupt) connection of thought. If the verbs are being treated as prophetic perfects, then perhaps it ought to be, 'They will not change their ways.'

26. The kethibh *ʾalmənōtāw* lacks the *yodh* in the suffix which the qere supplies.

27. Literally it is, 'Their widows will be numerous for me', where *lî*, 'for me', is a dative of interest, in respect of my judgment or action, and hence 'I will make' (NIV, cf. REB).

'Terror' (<√*bāhal*) involves the idea of alarm and horror and that of making haste. It seems to indicate the fright that is caused by something that has happened swiftly.

9. Again it is emphasised that the horrors of the invasion will not affect only those fighting in the field, but will bring sorrow and death throughout the community. **The mother of seven will grow faint and breathe her last** (cf. 50:12). A mother of seven is one who has been given by the LORD a full complement of sons (Ruth 4:15; 1 Sam. 2:5), so that she should have been able to look forward to a secure and well-provided-for old age. She now grows faint (14:2) at what has happened. The phrase 'breathe her last'[28] may also be understood as 'her breathing is laboured' (NASB), and this may be preferable if the thought in the following colon is of her still alive and experiencing disgrace (McKane 1986, 1:341; Bright 1965:109). **Her sun will set[29] while it is still day** may refer to the sun of her life, what gave it light and warmth, or this may be a metaphor for death, the light of her life will end prematurely (Amos 8:4). **She will be disgraced and humiliated.** For 'disgraced' (<√*bôš*), see on 2:26. She will have no standing left in the community because she no longer has any children. The thought is amplified by the addition of 'humiliated', which also refers to loss of status and reputation. **'I will put the survivors to the sword before their enemies,' declares the LORD.** 'Their' presumably refers to the community as a whole. 'Survivors' (6:9) from the invasion will not find conditions becoming any easier because the enemy will be relentless in pursuing and killing them.

9. A Prophet's Agony (15:10-21)

In this section we have the second complex of Jeremiah's Confessions in which the prophet initiates a dialogue by announcing his complaint (v. 10) to which the LORD then responds (vv. 11-14). Jeremiah approaches God a second time in vv. 15-18, after which the LORD recalls him to his duty and repeats the promises given to him at his original installation into office (vv. 19-21).

The question may properly be asked as to why this section is included at this point. Three different varieties of answer have been

28. 'Breathe her last' (*napəḥâ napšāh*, 'breathe out her life/soul'; for *nepeš*, see on 2:34): is the noun the subject or the object of the verb? Both the LXX and Vulgate understood 'life/soul' not as the object but as the subject, the idea being one of fainting under despair.

29. The kethibh *bāʾâ* is feminine; the qere has the masculine *bāʾ*. The qere is not needed as *šemeš*, 'sun', can be either masculine or feminine.

proposed. (1) The arrangement is arbitrary and arose by chance in the process of compilation. This is basically unsatisfactory. (2) The arrangement is literary, and there are thematic links which made it appropriate to insert this material at this juncture. For instance, 'my mother' (v. 10) picks up 'the mothers' of v. 8, and in the same way the use of the root *yālad* in 'that you gave me birth' (v. 10) echoes its use in 'mother of'/'she who bore' in v. 9. (3) The arrangement is historical. This need not rule out (2), and seems the most probable. As a result of his obedience in delivering the preceding messages about famine and repeating his warnings about the fate awaiting the country, Jeremiah again came under pressure from his fellow countrymen. No doubt tempers were more than a little frayed by the hardships caused by the drought, and the last thing people wanted was to be recalled to covenant faithfulness, especially when they thought that they were already being faithful.

a. Rejected and Cursed (15:10)

Jeremiah was no automaton when he delivered the LORD's message to the people. He recognised the seriousness of what he had to say, and he personally felt the bitterness of rejection when the people failed to respond adequately to what he declared to them. Here he gives way to his feelings of dejection and misery. His words seem to be a soliloquy, but though he does not directly address God, the prophet knew he was speaking to himself in the divine presence. He wanted something to happen to end the perplexity he was in.

10. Alas, my mother, that (*kî*) **you gave me birth.** We do not know if Jeremiah's mother was still alive. If she was, she too probably felt the sword piercing her own soul (Luke 2:35) at the opposition her son had to face. But it is sufficient to take this as a poetic form of expression in which Jeremiah imagines himself as speaking to his mother. 'Alas' (*'ôy* followed by *lî,* 'to me') expresses an intense personal reaction to trouble and hardship, traditionally rendered, 'Woe is me!' (NKJV, NRSV). Jeremiah is trying to work out just what purpose his life is serving in bringing God's word to a people who are not prepared to respond to it, and for whom he is not allowed to intercede. His lament is equivalent to, 'Why ever was I born?' However, Jeremiah's problems do not really lie at his birth, but in his subsequent life. Furthermore, since he knows that the LORD had chosen him even before his birth, this complaint is tantamount to questioning the divine purpose in his life.

But it is particularly the reaction to his ministry that causes him bewilderment. He characterises himself as **a man with whom the whole land strives and contends**/'a man of strife and a man of contention' (NKJV). 'Strife' (*rîb*, 2:9) and 'contention' (*mādôn* <√*dîn*, 'to plead one's cause, execute judgment') are both legal words for formal or informal process, calling up the image of someone who is constantly been taken to charge for what he has said or done. Though the construct chains may be either subjective or objective, that is, either Jeremiah is the one who brings the nation to trial or he is the one against whom others fight, it is more probable that Jeremiah sees himself as one who is opposed by the whole land—which in itself is hardly surprising! As the messenger of the LORD's covenant he was giving them no peace with his message regarding their sin. But Jeremiah is not thinking logically here. He has become depressed and considers himself hard done by. **I have neither lent nor borrowed, yet everyone curses me.**[30] Lending and borrowing are frequent sources of strife (for examples of the way in which the law on debt worked, see Exod. 22:25; 2 Kgs. 4:1; Pss. 15:5; 109:11; Prov. 6:1-5; Isa. 24:2), but Jeremiah presents himself as not having engaged in activity that gave rise to this ordinary sort of trouble. (As regards borrowing, this would indicate that Jeremiah had sufficient personal means to survive without depending on others; see also 32:9-10.) 'Curses' (<√*qālal*) means to treat as light or insignificant ('abuses' REB). No one speaks well of him, a fact that was intensely galling to someone who had done them no harm, and had their best interests at heart.

b. Vindication Assured (15:11-14)

11. For 'said' at the beginning of this verse the LXX reads 'Amen' (changing *ʾāmar* to *ʾāmēn*) and assumes Jeremiah continues to speak. This is reflected in the RSV rendering: 'So let it be, O LORD, if I have not entreated thee for their good, if I have not pleaded with thee on behalf of the enemy in the time of trouble and in the time of distress!' But there is no Hebrew manuscript evidence to support the alteration, and so the words must be understood as divine speech in which God promises Jeremiah that he will intervene to deal with his enemies. The

30. The kethibh is *kullōh məqaləlûnî*, a participle with a perfect plural ending and pronominal suffix. The qere, *kullô məqaləlanî*, 'all of him [i.e. the people] is cursing me', as is found in many manuscripts, is impossible. It is generally accepted that the *mem* has been wrongly moved to the second word, and that what should be read is *kulləhem qillûnî*, 'all of them have cursed me' (GKC §61h).

LORD's answer seems almost to interrupt Jeremiah's complaint before it got too far. **The LORD said,**[31] **'Surely I will deliver you for a good purpose.'**

However, difficulties remain with the word translated 'deliver'.[32] Traditionally this has been interpreted as a noun, 'your remnant',[33] and so the NKJV rendering, 'Surely it will be well with your remnant' (cf. NJPS). This can only refer to the remnant of the nation who are promised divine protection. But it is difficult to see how the second part of the verse applies to Judah's enemies who showed no mercy when the land was captured.

Taking the words as referring to the prophet seems the best option. The verbs are then prophetic perfects introduced by the emphatic asseveration *ʾim-loʾ* (GKC §149a). The LORD assures Jeremiah of help to resolve his difficulties and provide him with vindication. 'For good' is not specific. It might refer to the outworking of God's overall purpose as much to Jeremiah's personal comfort. Certainly it assures the prophet that what is happening in his life is not without meaning. The LORD is in control and working out his purposes.

There is a second affirmation. **Surely I will make your enemies plead with you**[34] **in times of disaster and times of distress.** 'Disaster' (*rāʿâ*) is intensified by the addition of 'distress' (*ṣārâ*) to describe traumatic conditions which result in loss of energy and vitality and from which divine intervention alone can effectively deliver. Jeremiah is told that there will be a time when those who were hostile towards him in the community will experience a change of attitude, but it will take the arrival of the calamity he had been predicting to make them do so. Then they will come and plead with him for advice and help, and this in fact happened (21:1; 37:3, 17; 38:14; 42:1-7).

---

31. The clause begins without any conjunction, and unusually it lacks *kōh*, 'thus' (which is also missing in 46:25).

32. The word that is the crux is *šrwtk* in the kethibh, and *šrytyk* in the qere. There is no agreement as to how these forms should be pointed. The qere and some manuscripts may be read as *šērîtîkā*, a piel form from *šārâ*, understood as 'I have loosed you/set you free'. Others take it as a piel form from *šārat*, 'to serve'.

33. This assumes the noun is a contracted form with an *aleph* missing, *šērûtəkā* for *šəʾērûtəkā*.

34. The REB rendering, 'Shall I not bring the enemy against you in a time of trouble and distress?', alerts us to the difficulties involved in translating *hipgaʿtî*, and also in determining the tone of this verse, whether it is reassuring or threatening (cf. also NRSV). The verb *pāgaʿ*, 'to meet, encounter, reach', can be used of hostile action and also of intercession.

12. Verse 12 is also terse and obscure. Indeed many commentators eliminate vv. 12-14 in whole or part. **Can a man break iron—iron from the north—or bronze?**[35] This is a question which is to be answered 'No'. At a physical level iron and bronze (an alloy of copper and tin) are too hard to be snapped by man. This would certainly have been true of iron from the north, which may particularly refer to the Black Sea area, from Chalybes in Pontus. It was renowned in later Greek and Roman sources as having the best quality iron which was rather like steel in its properties.

The fact that a cryptic answer is given to the prophet calls him to reflect further on the word the LORD has given him. However, the tone of the response shows it conveys reassurance from the LORD to Jeremiah, and this seems to focus on the fulfilment of his prophecies. He need not fear that they will prove false. Human opposition cannot break iron; the hostility of his opponents is incapable of frustrating the judgment of God which has been announced through Jeremiah.

Another interpretation is to find in the mention of 'from the north' a reference to the foe from the north which was one of the main themes of the prophet's ministry (1:14; 4:6; 6:1; 13:20). This leads to a translation such as that of the NRSV, 'Can iron and bronze break iron from the north?' The military might that the people of Judah are able to muster ('iron and bronze') will not be able to break the forces that will come upon them ('iron from the north'). When the LORD acts in judgment against his people, they will surely be powerless and fall before the invaders. Then Jeremiah's prophecy of impending trouble and distress will come to pass. Alternatively the iron and bronze might refer to Jeremiah's enemies among the people. Though they appear strong, they will be unable to resist the armies the LORD will bring from the north as his agents (O'Connor 1988:36).

13. The fact that Jeremiah's ministry will be vindicated by events leads into vv. 13-14 where the LORD again speaks about the judgment he will bring on the people, who are addressed in the masculine singular. **Your wealth and your treasures I will give as plunder, without charge.** These verses are very similar to 17:3-4. 'Wealth' refers to the resources at the disposal of an individual or nation. 'Treasure' refers to valuables that are kept securely locked up. Both are divinely bestowed on the enemy as plunder/booty when they ransack the land. 'To the ancient mindset, the shame of being pillaged was as

35. It is uncertain whether the verb is impersonal or has 'iron' as its subject. Equally the relationship of 'and bronze' to the other words in the sentence is unclear.

great as, if not greater than, the actual physical loss and abuse' (*NIDOTTE* 1:632). This was because such a tragedy was interpreted as proving the ineffectiveness of one's gods to intervene, or else that those affected has been rejected by their gods. It was the latter in the case of Judah whom the LORD gave away 'without charge' (Ps. 44:12), either without the enemy having to pay a heavy price in loss of life or without making any payment to the former owners.

The reason for such an outcome was not hard to find: **because of all your sins** (<√*ḥāṭā'*, 2:35) **throughout your country.** 'Country'/ 'borders' refers to the land as a geographical and administrative entity. Wherever one went in the land, the same offences were being committed.

14. I will enslave you to your enemies in a land you do not know, for (*kî*) my anger will kindle a fire that will burn against you (masc. pl.). The Massoretic Text reads *wəhaʿăbartî*, 'and I will make/ bring over', a reading retained by the NASB which suggests 'it', referring to the treasure, as a supplement rather than 'you'. NJPS also retains the text and renders, 'And I will bring your enemies by way of a land you have not known', though it is more difficult to see what is referred to by that. However, *daleth* and *resh* could easily be confused, and many Hebrew manuscripts read *wəhaʿăbadtî*, 'and I will enslave', which is adopted by the NIV, REB and NRSV. Not only is the land plundered (v. 13), the people are taken as slaves to work for their conquerors in a foreign land with which they were previously unacquainted. This will occur because the LORD's anger (*'ap*, 4:8) will lead to punishment for their sins.

c. Renewed Complaint (15:15-18)

The LORD's replies have given no hint of vindication to the prophet; they have provided no comfort for him in his immediate distress. So Jeremiah takes up his complaint again, and he does so in very personal terms. He accepts that the LORD's word of judgment will come upon the impenitent nation, but in the meantime what about his own situation?

15. Jeremiah is so oppressed by his present circumstances that knowing his message is divinely guaranteed to come true in the future does not satisfy him. He wants something now, and he addresses God abruptly with a boldness that characterises one who lives close to him. **You understand, O LORD.** Literally, 'You know'; indeed the emphasis on the initial pronoun 'you' is such that it is, 'You are the one who knows' (compare 12:3; 17:16; 18:23). What is known is not stated, but it seems to cover both Jeremiah and his circumstances. The Hebrew does not readily lend itself to being interpreted as an ascription of omniscience. What matters to Jeremiah is that he is living for, and living before, the God who has chosen him ('I knew you', 1:5). So he asks, **Remember me.** 'Remember' is not simply recall what you know about me, but do so with a view to action. In Hebrew the exercise of memory in remembrance always has this overtone. McComiskey (1993:95) argues that here the verb describes a complex act of mental apprehension and implicit response on the part of God that precedes or accompanies the bestowal of divine blessing. The verb does not describe the positive action it signals. It is a picture of God giving his attention to the situation without prescribing the extent of the action that will follow.

Care for me again uses the verb *pāqad* which here requests God to come as his superior to scrutinise his situation and deal with it appropriately. 'Visit' (NRSV, NKJV) may convey the wrong impression. Here when Jeremiah is sure that he is being wrongfully treated, it is a plea for action against those who are troubling him. **Avenge** (<√*nāqam* niphal, 5:9) **me on my persecutors.** He has stood as the LORD's spokesman, and he asks that his standing (which is in effect the LORD's status) be vindicated over against those who had systematically harassed and harried him. **You are long-suffering**[36]**—do not take me away.** 'Long-suffering' is literally 'length of anger', pointing to how long it takes before the LORD gets angry. The patience and forbearance that he displays towards his people is one of the attributes that the LORD included in his self-disclosure to Moses (Exod. 34:6). Is Jeremiah afraid that the LORD's long-suffering towards the people will be extended to such an extent that he may well be dead before the judgment that has been threatened will come? Is the LORD going to resolve the situation by translating ('taking him') as he did Enoch (Gen. 5:24) or Elijah (2 Kgs. 2:1)? Jeremiah, however, wants immediate action to rectify matters here and now, and gives reasons why the LORD should do so. First, his suffering has arisen because of his connection with the LORD. **Think of** ('know') **how I suffer reproach for your sake.** 'Reproach' (*ḥerpâ*, cf. 'offensive' 6:10) is the scorn and contempt displayed towards Jeremiah as a result of his fulfilling the commission the LORD has given him (Ps. 69:7). The insults hurled at him have got through to the prophet, and he urges that God act now.

16. Jeremiah then gives details of two further aspects of his life that

36. Preceded by the negative *ʾal*, which is unusually positioned away from the verb for emphasis (GKC §152h; *IBHS* §34.2.1e).

reveal his willingness to be the LORD's servant. There is the fact that as a prophet he had acted in accordance with his commission. He was no Jonah who had to be forced to go to Nineveh to deliver a message he was unhappy about. Instead Jeremiah can testify, **When your words came, I ate them.** 'Came'/'were found' implies no activity on the part of the recipient; he had not gone looking for them. This may look back to the finding of the word of the LORD in the Temple in the middle of Josiah's reformation (2 Kgs. 22:13), but more probably it refers to the time of his call and the visions that were associated with it. Jeremiah devoured them, totally accepting their message and pondering them deeply to ascertain their full significance. In connection with his prophetic call Ezekiel ate the word (Ezek. 2:9; 3:3) in a way that symbolised prophetic inspiration whereby the divine words became so much a part of the prophet that he had no doubt that what he was saying was inspired by God. **They** (literally 'your word'[37]) **were my joy and my heart's delight.** 'Joy' (*śāśôn*) when used on its own indicates the joy that accompanies the experience of salvation (31:13; 33:9). It arises out of a healthy covenant relationship. The LORD's word was a source of pleasure to his entire inner being (cf. Ps. 119:103). This is the positive side of Jeremiah's theology of the heart (cf. chap. 17). **For** (*kî*) **I bear your name, O LORD God Almighty.** 'Bear your name'/'Your name is called upon me' indicates a formal, legal mark of ownership (7:10-11; 14:9), and Jeremiah acknowledges himself to be completely the servant of the LORD whose authority and majesty he gladly recognises. For the ascription 'Almighty', see on 2:19; 5:14.

17. What was more Jeremiah argued that his life had been shaped by the LORD's message to him. Whereas in Ps. 26:4-5 David had refused to associate with those he described as deceitful and wicked, Jeremiah had shunned company that need not in itself have been sinful. **I never sat in the company of revellers, never made merry with them.** 'Revellers' (<√*śāḥaq*, 'to laugh, make merry, scoff') may be used negatively ('mockers' NKJV) or positively. This is the loneliness of the prophet cut off from the ordinary social activities of his day (cf. 16:8). **I sat alone because your hand was on me.** For 'hand' compare Ezek. 1:3; 3:14, 22 in the sense of an overpowering experience of divine self-disclosure. It may also indicate the constraint Jeremiah felt because of his prophetic commission (1:9). This was not his personal choice, but what the LORD required of him. 'Alone' (*bādād*) is used

37. The kethibh is *dəbārẹ̄kā*, 'your words'; the qere is *dəbārəkā*, 'your word', a correction to agree with the verb which is singular.

with *yāšab*, 'to dwell', to indicate that a leper must live alone outside the camp (Lev. 13:46). Jeremiah considered himself a social leper because of the LORD's claim upon him as a prophet (Holladay 1986, 1:460). The phrase can also denote the separation of Israel in judgment (Lam. 1:1). He knew the compulsion and power of the LORD which gave him the message he had to proclaim. **And** (lit. *kî*, 'for, because') **you had filled me with indignation** refers either to the message of the LORD's indignation (*zaʿam*, 10:10) at the moral and spiritual corruption in Judah, or else the personal reaction of Jeremiah to the content of the message that the LORD had given him (6:11). How then could he joke?

18. Given that Jeremiah had conducted himself in this way which distinguished his reaction from that of the people as a whole, he then asks, **Why is my pain unending and my wound grievous and incurable?** 'Pain' more generally refers to mental anguish as may 'wound'/'blow' (6:7). It is unnecessary to think of the prophet as physically ill, but no remedy seems to avail for his inner condition which he views as 'grievous'/'incurable' (*ʾānûš*, 17:9, 16; 30:12, 15) and 'incurable'/'that refuses to be healed'. He is perplexed by having to endure agony and rejection because of the task that the LORD has assigned him. He has been obedient and yet he is suffering. So he is looking for some token of things coming true, some relief from the taunts of the people.

The extent of his feelings is revealed by the question he asks next, which verges on blasphemy. **Will you** 'really' (an infinitive absolute) **be to me like a deceptive brook, like a spring that fails?** There is no explicit interrogative. The NIV continues the questioning from the initial 'why?', but note the stronger rendering in the REB, 'You are to me like a brook that fails, whose waters are not to be relied on' (cf. NRSV). Everyone in Palestine was familiar with the wadi which would be full of water during the rainy season, but soon dried up and had no flow of water in hot weather. Jeremiah, however, was the one who had been sure that the LORD was a fountain of living water (2:13), not like the heathen gods who could not be relied upon. Now in his depression and self-pity Jeremiah is wondering if in his own personal crisis the LORD was no better than the gods of the nations he had so often denounced. Would the LORD be no more to him than a wadi (cf. Job 6:15-20) or 'a spring that fails'/'waters that are unreliable, unfaithful'? Quite an accusation to pose, even if couched as a question, regarding the God who had revealed himself as 'abounding in faithfulness' (Exod. 34:16).

d. Repentance and Recommissioning (15:19-21)

19. The LORD reacts to his prophet's complaint not with compassion and the assurance of his presence as might be expected in response to a lament, but with a word of judgment. **Therefore** (*lākēn*, used judgmentally) **this is what the LORD says** does not spare Jeremiah. Although God does not question the accuracy of the prophet's claims about his response to the divine word (vv. 16-17), he does challenge the attitude he is currently displaying. Jeremiah was in the wrong as regards his accusations and questioning of God's faithfulness just as much as the people were in the wrong as regards their attitude to the LORD, and so he, like them, is called on to repent. This is a further instance where the prophet's experience mirrors that of the people.

In this verse there is another extensive play on the various meanings of the root *šûb*: 'repent' (*tāšûb*, qal), 'restore you' (*wa'ăšîbəkā*, hiphil), 'let … turn' (*yāšubû*, qal) and 'not turn' (*lō'-tāšûb*, qal) (4:1; 8:4). **If you repent, I will restore you.** His ability to fulfil his prophetic office has been compromised by his attitude, and the LORD promises to restore him ('bring him back') if he mends his ways. **That you may serve me**/'stand before me' is a common idiom to indicate the attitude of a servant before his master, human or divine, ready to do his bidding (15:1). An alternative understanding of the construction used in this verse notes the lack of a conjunction before 'serve', so that there may be two conditions expressed, and if both are fulfilled then Jeremiah will be able to continue his prophetic office: 'If you repent and I restore you, you may stand before me' (Laetsch 1952:149; Holladay 1986, 1:462-63). In that case there would be both a human recognition of wrong and turning from it, and a divine act of grace involved in restoring the erring prophet to his former role. He would then have access to the divine council and would therefore become once more a reliable source of information regarding the purpose of God.

The second part of v. 19 also reflects on Jeremiah's prophetic task. **And if you utter worthy, not worthless, words**. 'Utter' is literally 'cause to come out' and may well reflect on Jeremiah's task as an assayer: 'If you take out the precious from the vile' (NKJV). More commonly the reference is taken simply to be to the content of Jeremiah's speech ('bring out' as in Job 15:13; Eccl. 5:1). His words are to be 'worthy' (<*yāqār*, 'precious, costly, excellent') and not 'worthless' (<√*zālal* I, 'be frivolous', cf. 2:36). There is no wordplay in the Hebrew. Jeremiah's own speech had been rebellious, and as such not the utterance of one able to act as the spokesman of God because uttering his own rebellious thoughts was a mark of a false prophet. **You**

will be my spokesman/'as my mouth' (Exod. 4:16), the one capable and qualified to act as the LORD's spokesman, relaying accurately to the people what reflected the determination of the LORD.

> There is a widespread belief in certain circles that anything that comes welling up from the depths of my being with almost irresistible force must be from the Holy Spirit. Some such feeling was probably shared by Jeremiah, and it explains how he ventured to go as far as he did in his complaint against God. In answer to this feeling God told him that a true prophet must be able to discriminate between the precious and the vile. He is not a mere channel only, but remains in conscious control of his emotions and words (cf. 1 Cor. 14:32). (Ellison 1963:14)

The third part of the verse reminds the prophet of his task of bringing the people over to thinking in the LORD's way. **Let this people turn to you.** 'This people' is the NIV rendering (also the REB) of an emphatic *hēmmâ*, 'they', contrasting with *'attâ*, 'you', in the next clause. The change the LORD wants to see is one on the part of the people, coming back in repentance to him as his word is ministered to them by the prophet. **But you must not turn to them** reflects the insidious compulsion that the majority can exert on one who does not fall in with their lifestyle. Jeremiah is not to 'turn', that is, 'turn away, apostatise', by adopting their thinking and culture (Isa. 8:11). The pressure to do so would be all the more intense for someone as sensitive as Jeremiah was to his social isolation and loneliness. But their ways are wrong, and to be allured by their arguments or their company would be to compromise his God-given role.

20-21. To strengthen Jeremiah for his task the LORD reminds him of his original commission in what is virtually a recommissioning of Jeremiah. **I will make you a wall to this people, a fortified wall of bronze** reflects on 1:18. A wall of bronze would not have gaps between the stones into which a crowbar could be inserted to undermine it. **'They will fight against you but will not overcome you, for** (*kî*) **I am with you to rescue and save you,' declares the LORD** takes up the promise of 1:19. There is no relief from the task of standing steadfast and obdurate against the sinfulness of the people. Opposition is guaranteed, but so also is the LORD's presence as deliverer. Indeed salvation is elaborated on in v. 21, **I will save you from the hands of the wicked and redeem you from the grasp of the cruel.** Notice the way in which the vocabulary of salvation is used to assure Jeremiah of divine assistance. 'Rescue' (<√*yāšaʿ*, hiphil 'to save'; 4:14) is the most general term for extricating someone from a situation of peril and granting them safety. 'Save', occurring twice,

(<√*nāṣal*, hiphil 'to snatch away'; 'to rescue' 1:8) is used of removing prey from the grasp of a powerful predator, as can be seen in v. 21. 'Wicked' ('evil ones') are those acting contrary to God's law. 'Redeem' (<√*pādâ*, 'to buy back') refers to obtaining the liberty of an individual, sometimes with the thought of paying a ransom price, at other times being equivalent just to rescue. This promise seems to envisage Jeremiah actually in their grasp (*kap*, 'hollow of the hand'), but the LORD has committed himself to act on his behalf and, if not to provide vindication, at least to take him out of the situation of powerlessness under the control of the cruel (<*ʿārîṣ*, one who acts harshly and forcibly towards others, causing them to be terror stricken).

Surrounded as he was by strife and contention, the pressure had become too much for Jeremiah, and he gave way to dejection and spoke in a manner that was out of line with his commission and office. But challenged by God, he turned back, and knew renewed protection and blessing; indeed he was recommissioned for the ministry the LORD had allotted him. In many respects this period of his life parallels that of Peter when he was restored by the risen Lord and strengthened to sustain even greater hardships in divine service in the days that lay ahead (John 21:15-19). Like Paul, Jeremiah reaffirmed that his life's goal was to please God, not men (Gal. 1:10). What greater challenge and encouragement could be given to the people of Judah and Jerusalem than the utterance of a prophet who has returned and been restored to divine favour as he urges them to follow the same path?

B. LIVING WITNESS (16:1-21)

The theme of the predicted end of life in the land is continued in this chapter, where the first two sections (vv. 1-4 and vv. 5-9) focus on how Jeremiah's own lifestyle was a living embodiment of what is going to happen to the people because of the disaster the LORD was going to bring on them.[38] The LORD's messenger was to impress the reality of

38. Jones (1992:228-29) gives an effective rebuttal of the views of those who treat prose passages of this sort as the work of Deuteronomistic preachers during the Exile. 'What does it signify to tell the community not to marry and have children, when everyone knows they will do this, even in time of crisis? It does however make sense to accept the text as it is and to understand the command as delivered to Jeremiah himself, who then becomes in himself a sign to the community, whether they believe him or not.' Jones is, however, unwilling to take the further step of attributing the passage itself to the prophet, believing it to be the work of various scribes.

impending judgment on the nation using every means possible, even to the extent of making himself seem ridiculous and open to charges not merely of unsociability, but one would suppose even of insanity. In vv. 10-13 the anticipated questions of the people regarding Jeremiah's unconventional behaviour are answered with a further word of judgment. Surprisingly this is then followed by a vision of restoration (vv. 14-15), but that does not bring hope for the immediate future because it looks forward to events that will only take place after the people have been banished. The next section (vv. 16-18) focuses on how thoroughly the invading forces will devastate the land and its people. Finally, in vv. 19-21 a confession of idolatry is accompanied by a divine resolution to rid the people utterly of this perversion.

1. Do Not Marry (16:1-4)

In this section and the one following Jeremiah is divinely prohibited from getting married, and also from engaging in the normal social activities of his day. These were not arbitrary restraints placed on the prophet's life, but were prophetic symbols designed to teach the nation regarding what awaited them as those who had abandoned their loyalty to the one true God. The prophet did not just proclaim his message; he lived it. He had always known that it was part of his calling to be 'an iron pillar and a bronze wall to stand against the whole land' (1:18; cf. 15:20), but here there is an intensification of the cost of standing out in condemnation and rebuke of the people. The prophet's feelings of isolation and loneliness no doubt sprang in part from being unmarried. In making his life totally subservient to his ministry in these respects, what was required of Jeremiah was not unlike the command to Hosea to marry an adulterous wife (Hos. 1:2), or the way Ezekiel was forbidden to mourn his wife's death (Ezek. 24:15-18). By accepting that his life had to reflect the tenor of his message, Jeremiah showed himself a prophet approved by the LORD and thus in terms of 15:19-21 a prophet who would be divinely protected. This message must have originated shortly after Jeremiah's call to be a prophet (cf. v. 2).

1. Then the word of the LORD came to me (as in 1:4) is an indication of the autobiographical nature of this narrative. Though the introductory 'then' of the NIV might seem to indicate a close link with the previous chapter, the Hebrew is simply 'and', which is inconclusive as to what time elapsed, if any. It is also necessary to distinguish between the time at which this command was given to Jeremiah (see on v. 2), and the time of composition of this section of his prophecy. If, as seems likely, the present form of this material dates from around 597 BC, then the original message might well have come to the prophet thirty years earlier. Throughout that period he had been a living symbol of his message that divine judgment was going to tear apart the social fabric of the community.

2. Jeremiah is not to get married because the doom looming over Judah is so overwhelming that the land will be no fit place to marry and bring up a family. **You must not marry and have sons or daughters in this place.** Marriage was considered the norm in ancient society. It was God's provision for mankind (Gen. 2:24), and to have numerous offspring was the sign of divine blessing (Gen. 22:17; Pss. 127:3-5; 128:3-4). Marriage was not something that Jeremiah was to avoid as imprudent 'because of the present crisis' (1 Cor. 7:26); he was forbidden to get married so that his life would be a symbol of his message. But at what stage of his life was this command given? Normally marriage would have been undertaken early in adult life. Unless Jeremiah had been married and was now a childless widower, this command must be set not long after his call and so in the years before the discovery of the Book of the Law in 622 BC (2 Kgs. 22:3). It therefore sets the background for his whole ministry, contributing both to the prophet's perception of what the future held for the nation and to the people's perception of him as one who by his very person challenged their conduct and presumption of security. That Jeremiah accepted this prohibition indicates how much he was prepared to undergo in submission to the LORD's will. 'In this place' probably indicates the land as a whole (notice the expression in v. 3), thought of as the place where God made his presence known and which he had given to his people as their covenant inheritance. The prophet's symbolic lifestyle indicated the withdrawal of the blessings of the covenant, especially the right to enjoy occupation of the land and divine protection in it.

3. Following the pattern that prevails when the LORD directs that a prophet engage in symbolic behaviour, the command is followed by the reason for the prohibition so that the symbol may be interpreted correctly. **For (*kî*) this is what the LORD says about the sons and daughters born in this land and about the women who are their mothers and the men who are their fathers.** Four groups are solemnly enumerated to bring out the sweeping nature of what is to happen. Though most English translations render it only twice (but see AV), *ʿal*, 'about', is repeated before each group. Its omission in English between 'sons' and 'daughters' is needed to make clear that the masculine adjective 'born' which follows 'daughters' qualifies both the two preceding groups. They are said to be born 'in this place', repeating the phrase found in v. 2. Confusingly the NIV here translates it as 'in this land' and then omits 'in this land' when it does occur at the end of the verse (contrast NKJV, NRSV). It is being emphasised that what is being said and done focuses on conditions that prevail in the land of covenant promise. Three times the root *yālad*, 'to bear, bring forth, beget', is used: in 'born', in 'who are their mothers'/'who give them birth', and in 'who are their fathers'/'who beget them'. This is the association that ought to have prevailed: the land of promise should have been a place of life and birth.

4. But this makes the LORD's pronouncement all the more stark. **They will die of deadly diseases.** 'From deaths of sufferings' (*taḥălu'îm*, cf. 'ravages', 14:18) is fronted for emphasis. The picture is one of widespread trouble and catastrophe coming on the land (8:2; 9:22), with parents and children alike being wiped out. If this divine word came to the prophet early in his ministry, then here we have the first occurrence of a number of phrases and thoughts which were to recur later. In **they will not be mourned** the verb (<√*sāpad*, 'to mourn') refers to taking part in the rites associated with funerals and interment. These will not occur because those who die will not be **buried** (cf. v. 6; 8:2; 25:33), which was a sign of shame. **But will be like refuse lying on the ground** (8:2; 25:33), probably because the survivors would be so few that they would be unable to bury the dead. **They will perish by sword and famine** are the two most commonly cited members (5:12; 14:13, 15, 16) of the Jeremianic trio of 'sword, famine and plague' (14:12). 'Perish' (<√*kālâ*, 5:3) emphasises the finality of what happens to them. **And their dead bodies will become food for the birds of the air and the beasts of the earth** (7:33; 15:3; 19:7; 34:20) is again a picture of a community overwhelmed by the extent of the disaster that has come on them, and unable to perform the customary funeral rites for its dead. Anticipating these circumstances of widespread bereavement, Jeremiah is without wife or children. That is the fate awaiting the nation; so many will die that those who remain will become like him. The prophet lives out the tragedy that he predicts will come as God's judgment on his people.

2. Avoid Funerals and Weddings (16:5-9)

Jeremiah's enactment of the social devastation that would come on the land also involved not participating in funerals (vv. 5-7) or weddings (vv. 8-9). There was no place for consolation or rejoicing in the judgment God was bringing on his disobedient people.

5. The second symbolic action is connected with death, not in connection with the final destruction of the land set out in v. 4, but as regards deaths that occurred during the course of Jeremiah's ministry. The prophet is not to participate in funeral rites because the doom looming over Judah is so overwhelming that no comfort will be derived from mourning. **For (*kî*) this is what the LORD says: 'Do not enter a house where there is a funeral meal.'** This prohibition is expressed somewhat differently from that of v. 2 where the negative used was *lōʾ*, generally associated with a permanent ban. Here the negative employed is *ʾal*, which may be used for a specific prohibition, and so perhaps indicating that there had been or would yet be times when Jeremiah could do this, whereas he was to remain unmarried all his life (but note v. 8). A house where there is a funeral meal[39] reflects the practice of gathering to comfort those who mourn and sharing in a meal. But Jeremiah is told, **Do not go to mourn** (<√*sāpad*, v. 4) **or show sympathy**. 'Show sympathy' (<√*nûd*, 'to sway, move back and forth', 15:5) refers to an expression of sympathy and condolence carried out by shaking the head. The same gesture was used in other circumstances also (18:16; 48:27).

The reason why Jeremiah was to dissociate himself from such collective expressions of grief is then stated: **'Because (*kî*) I have withdrawn** (<√*ʾāsap*, 'to gather' in the sense of 'bring together and remove'; cf. 10:17) **my blessing, my love and my pity[40] from this people,' declares the LORD.** Attending a funeral meal was an expression of sympathy, but the devastating consequence of Israel's

39. Though the only other time *marzēaḥ* is found in Old Testament is Amos 6:7 where the meaning seems to reflect a banquet of rejoicing in which things were taken to excess, Ugaritic and Aramaic evidence establish the possibility of a mourning feast. Ugaritic evidence relates *mrzḥ* to a feast among the wealthy, though only once in connection with death (*NIDOTTE* 2:1102). It appears that such feasts were associated with religious guilds or brotherhoods, and there may have been pagan overtones to the practice. However, there is no condemnation of the *marzēaḥ* as such here. The idea that it involved a meal goes back to the LXX, *thiasos*, 'feasting'. (For further information, see King 1993:140-41.) It is not clear how this was connected to the practice of fasting at the time of a death (2 Sam. 1:12; 3:35), but it may be that the time of fasting was followed by a banquet of some sort where all the mourners gathered.

40. It is possible to argue with the NIV that the suffix 'my' on *šəlômî*, 'my peace', also serves to qualify *haḥesed* and *hāraḥămîm*, but their position in the clause and the presence of the article with the additional two nouns makes it more probable that they function epexegetically, rather than as the second two parts of a triplet: i.e. 'my peace which consists of love and pity'.

disobedience is that the LORD no longer has any sympathy for the people, and the prophet is to give a living warning to that effect by his behaviour. ‘Blessing’/‘peace’ (*šālôm*) points to the total well-being which is provided for the people by the LORD. It is not the false peace offered by the establishment prophets on a spurious basis (6:14), but ‘*my* peace’, which originates with God alone. What this true prosperity consists of is further clarified by the addition of ‘love’ (*ḥesed*, 2:2) and ‘pity’ (*raḥămîm*, ‘deep compassion’), which characterise the LORD’s covenant engagement with his people. But the covenant has been broken, and the people are going to suffer the curse of the broken covenant, for the LORD will no longer forgive their misconduct.

6. In the absence of covenant blessing **both high and low will die in this land**, linking back to ‘in this land’ at the end of v. 3 (not translated in the NIV). The disintegration of society in Judah will be so extensive that social standing will not exempt from the catastrophe. **They will not be buried or mourned** repeats in reverse order the words of v. 4, but the Hebrew is now ‘they (i.e. others) shall not mourn for them’. **And no one will cut himself or shave his head for them.** These were pagan practices, possibly originally associated with the cult of the Canaanite god of death, Mot, and they had been forbidden in Israel (Lev. 19:28; 21:5; Deut. 14:1). Nevertheless, they continued to be widespread (41:5; 47:5; 48:37; Isa. 15:2-3; 22:12; Ezek. 7:18; Amos 8:10; Mic. 1:16). The emphasis here is not on their illicit nature. Mourning of any sort—whether in approved fashion or otherwise—is not going to take place. Rather the catastrophe will be of such a magnitude and death will become so common that the people’s capacity for mourning will be exhausted and all mourning customs will cease.

7. No one will offer (<√*pāras*, ‘to break’, that is to measure and distribute food in the course of a meal) **food**[41] **to comfort those who mourn**[42] (<√*ʾābal*, 14:2) **for the dead.** The subject of the verb ‘offer’ is an unspecified ‘they’ (cf. NKJV), which the NIV renders by ‘no one’. It is uncertain whether this refers to the need for clean food being brought to a house where a corpse was (2 Sam. 3:35; Ezek. 24:17; Hos. 9:4), or whether in the light of the practice of fasting during the day this represents a gesture of sympathy in providing food for the

41. The Massoretic Text is *lāhem*, ‘to them’, but the LXX and a few Hebrew manuscripts offer *leḥem*, ‘bread, food’, which in view of the following mention of ‘a drink’/‘cup’ has considerable plausibility.

42. The Massoretic Text has *ʾēbel*, ‘[the act of] mourning’, rather than *ʾābēl*, ‘one mourning’, which seems to be read by the NIV, NRSV and REB.

mourners at evening when they broke their fast (Deut. 26:14; Ezek. 24:17, 22; Hos. 9:4). The NIV takes **not even for a father or mother** with the first clause of the verse, even though the phrase stands last in the verse, and certainly qualifies the second clause, though perhaps both. Not even when the loss is of intimate family will mourning rites be observed. **Nor will anyone give them a drink to console them**/'a cup of consolations'. In later Judaism the cup of consolation was offered to the chief mourner at a funeral as an act of sympathy. This was not going to be offered here because of the vast scale of the disaster.

Jeremiah's dissociation from mourning rites would have attracted attention as being unsociable and unnatural behaviour. When he gave the divine explanation for his action, it should have served to impress on the people the grievous nature of the impending calamity.

8. Next a different situation[43] is described because it is not only from places of mourning that Jeremiah is to stand apart, but also from places of joy. The prophet is not to participate in celebrations because the doom looming over Judah is so overwhelming that rejoicing and festivities are macabre and grotesque. **And do not enter[44] a house where there is feasting and sit down to eat and drink.** In view of the following verse it is probable that the feasting being envisaged is specifically that of a wedding. This too shall come to an end in the shattered community, and Jeremiah's non-involvement is an indication of what is going to befall them all. This command gives the background to Jeremiah's protestation in 15:17.

9. The reason for avoiding feasts is then specified: **For** (*kî*) **this is what the LORD Almighty, the God of Israel, says: 'Before your eyes and in your days I will bring an end to the sounds of joy and gladness and to the voices of bride and bridegroom in this place.'** In 'your eyes' and 'your days' the pronominal references are masculine plural. The explanation is one that God (for the divine titles see 7:3) intended for the whole community. Within the lifetime of the current generation the sounds of happiness would be banished from the land. The thought is similar to that of 7:34, but this verse also picks up themes from v. 2, notably Jeremiah's not being married, and the phrase 'in this place' (perhaps Jerusalem, possibly the land as a whole), and serves to bring the section to a conclusion with a picture of a society no

---

43. The verse begins *ûbêt-mišteh*, 'but [*waw*-disjunctive] as for a house of feasting'. In Eccl. 7:2 there is a contrast with a house of mourning, *bêt-ʾēbel.*

44. This command is expressed in the absolute form *lōʾ-tābôʾ*, which in line with v. 2 may be translated, 'You must not enter'.

longer able to function even at the basic level of perpetuating itself. The life of the community—marriage, children, and even death—has been terminated.

3. Judgment on the Spiritually Blind (16:10-13)

Jeremiah's behaviour functioned as signs to the people, and unusual ones at that. But they were signs with accompanying interpretations which the prophet passed on to the people. It is anticipated that when they are told, they would in effect reply, 'What? Us?' Their spiritual blindness was such that they could not comprehend how his message could be intended for them. Similar envisaged questions and the answers provided are found at 5:19; 9:12-16; 22:8-9.

10. When (*kî*) **you tell**[45] **these people all this and they ask you.** After the prophet has delivered his message to 'this people' (again a note of estrangement), it is envisaged that they will begin to quiz him about the propriety of how he was living and and what he was saying. They ask three questions. **Why has the LORD decreed** (<√*dābar* piel, 'to speak'; 'pronounced' NKJV, NRSV) **such a great disaster** (*rāʿâ*, 1:16) **against us? What wrong** (*ʿāwōn*, 2:22) **have we done? What sin** (*ḥaṭṭāʾt*, 2:35) **have we committed against the LORD our God?** The questions build on one another, using the same interrogative *meh*, 'what?' The puzzlement of the people tells its own story of religious insensitivity and total satisfaction with what they were doing (compare the repeated questions in Mal. 1–2). They could not relate the prophet's words of condemnation to themselves, so warped had their self-perception become. Though this had been fostered by the message of the false prophets, the people were probably also suffering from a misguided standard of comparison. Looking back to conditions as they had been under Manasseh, they readily assumed that the improvements made by Josiah meant that all was now well. They failed to appreciate that the true standard was what the LORD required in his covenant, not the situation in an earlier regime. They did not understand how far short they fell of what was required, and that this would ensure their doom.

11. There are three parts to the response that the prophet is charged to give when accosted by his audience: the behaviour of former generations (v. 11), their own behaviour (v. 12), and the LORD's verdict on them (v. 13). **Then say to them, 'It is because your fathers forsook**

---

45. *nāgad* hiphil is a verb of speech, and so NKJV 'show' is to be avoided. Note that 'all this' is *kol-haddəbārîm hāʾēleh*, 'all these words/things'.

me,' declares the LORD, 'and followed other gods and served and worshipped them.' There is a clear allusion here to the opening commandments of the Decalogue, and possibly also to Huldah's prophecy (2 Kgs. 22:17). The language employed is found frequently elsewhere in Jeremiah: 'forsake' 1:16; 'follow other gods' 7:6; 'serve and worship' (13:10; 25:6). If indeed the people had fallen into the mistake of comparing themselves with former generations, then it was appropriate to begin by making clear not only that past generations had strayed from the requirements of the covenant, but that their behaviour had left a legacy of disloyalty to their offspring. **They forsook me and did not keep my law.** Both 'me' and 'my law' are brought forward for emphasis. The law was the expression of the sovereign's will for his people, and abandoning it was an act of ungrateful defiance against him (6:19; 8:8; 9:13).

12. However, it had not only been in the past that there had been such rebellion. Though the present generation might pride themselves in being better, they were in fact worse. **But you** (*wəʾattem*) **have behaved more wickedly than your fathers** (2:7; 3:11; 7:24, 26; 9:13; 1 Kgs. 14:9). The precise ways in which their behaviour represented a deterioration are not specifically identified here. **See how each of you is following the stubbornness of his evil heart instead of obeying me.** This substantially reflects the same charge as that levelled against the former generations (3:17; 7:24). Perhaps the intensification of their guilt is to be found in the idea of the increased and repeated warnings they had been given (7:25; 25:3-4; 26:4-5; 35:14-15; 44:4-5), or it may have been a matter of regressing from such improvements as Josiah's reforms had effected.

13. The LORD's verdict is then set out once more. **So I will throw you out of this land.** 'Hurl' (NASB) or 'fling' (REB) catch the degree of effort involved in 'throw' (<√*ṭûl*), which can be used of hurling a javelin (1 Sam. 18:11; 20:33). It is the LORD's decisive and violent judgment against those who have rebelled that they can no longer be permitted to stay in the land of promise. Whether their departure is by death or by exile matters little, for exile from the land of divine presence is a living death as much as banishment from Eden ever was (Gen. 3:24). They will be expelled **into a land neither you nor your fathers have known**. This does not mean that they had never heard of Babylon. 'Know' is used here in the sense of having had personal experience of it. Indeed the Hebrew is actually 'into *the* land', the specific one about which I am talking. **And there you will serve other gods day and night** is an ironic observation on their idolatry

(Deut. 28:64). Once they were quit of the LORD's land, they find themselves in a pagan environment where they will experience no difficulty as regards serving/worshipping other gods, though it will occur with overtones of the other sense of serve in that their condition will be one of servitude. **For** (*'ăšer* used causally) **I will show you no favour.** In being sent to the land of deportation they will not experience any mercy from the LORD. 'Showing favour' (the noun occurs only here, but comes from the root *ḥānan*, 'to be gracious, pity') referred to the LORD's gracious activity in terms of extending and deepening the covenant relationship. Here the phrase is of similar significance to the withdrawal of blessing in v. 5. 'No favour' is the LORD's final word on his disobedient people.

However, we must remember that though the curses that fell on disobedience to the covenant were clearly set out right from the beginning, yet there had also always been stated provision for coping with the reality of disobedience. It was not that the people's disobedience abrogated the covenant. It loosed the overlord from any obligation to bless, and so the future destiny of the people depended simply and solely on the disposition of their overlord. Before ever the Israelites had set out from the encampment at the base of Sinai they had fallen into grievous rebellion—sin for which judgment and destruction was the due penalty. Yet it did not fall on them then, or on many subsequent occasions. Why? Because of the sovereign good pleasure of God. It is not that the sin at Sinai was treated as having no consequences. There was punishment: there was the threat of withdrawn fellowship. But there was also the fundamental fact of divine grace as set out in the revealed name of God (Exod. 34:6-7) that let the relationship be renewed in response to Moses' plea. So too here, there would be divine punishment. Yet as Deuteronomy pointed out there was still the opening provided by divine grace that when the people returned to the LORD even in the land of exile, then there could and would be restoration to favour (Deut. 30:1-10).

4. Restoration (16:14-15)

Surprisingly it is restoration to divine favour that is taken up in vv. 14-15. The change of theme seems so sudden, and the message seems so incongruent with what has gone before that these words are generally reckoned to reflect exilic hope and to be a later insertion into the current text from 23:7-8 where the same words are to be found. But it must be remembered that God has a twofold purpose that reflects the alternative outcomes of the covenant relationship: life or death, blessing or curse. That was not a discovery of the Exile, but had been inherent in the covenant from the beginning. Nor is it the case that messages of blessing were of no significance in the ministry of Jeremiah prior to 586 BC. The reality of the suffering, shame and trauma that awaited the disobedient people was in no way mitigated by the knowledge that restoration awaited subsequent repentance. Indeed that knowledge intensified the current crisis in that it unequivocally presented the impending tragedy as needless, if only repentance came sooner. Glimpsing what through divine goodness the future may hold shows up even more clearly what the people now lack.

14. The verse begins with *lākēn*, 'therefore, so', which introduces a consequence, often the judgment that comes on sinful behaviour. Keil tried to explain the connection here by saying, 'Because the Lord will, for their idolatry, cast forth his people into the lands of the heathen, just for that very reason will their redemption from exile not fail to follow' (1873, 1:271). But this seems to be artificial and does not really fit the present context. Those who assume that these verses have been secondarily inserted here from another context understand the cause–result sequence to be disrupted by the relocation. Others note, however, that there are a number of occasions in Jeremiah where the phrase 'days are coming' is preceded by *lākēn* where it does not seem to indicate consequence, but contrast ('but' in 30:16; 48:12; 49:2; 51:52). It cannot be said that the matter has been totally clarified, and it may be that another translation is appropriate: 'however' (NIV), 'assuredly' (NJPS; *HALOT* 530), 'hereafter' (Lundbom 1999:768).

'However, the days are coming,' declares the LORD is a phrase often used by Jeremiah to denote a future whose date is not clearly known, but whose reality is seen as emerging out of what already is (7:32). This time that is envisaged is one **when men will no longer say** (an impersonal idiom, 'it will no longer be said'), **'As surely as the LORD lives, who brought the Israelites up out of Egypt.'** The formula is one that would be used in oath-taking as a preface to the commitment being undertaken or the assurances being given. The LORD was invoked as the guarantor of the fulfilment of the oath, and designated in terms of his supreme act of self-revelation in the Exodus. This was the fundamental tenet of Israel's faith. It was what had brought them into existence as a nation when in the dejection and hopelessness of their enslavement in Egypt they had experienced the transforming power and graciousness of the LORD. The faithful recognised the LORD as the one who could subvert the inevitability of historical processes. What more massive and secure empire had there been than that of Egypt? Despite that, its power was incapable of withstanding the purpose of the LORD when he had come to save his people.

15. However, there is going to be a more amazing display of the LORD's sovereign power in redemption. **But** (*kî 'im*, 'but rather') **they will say, 'As surely as the LORD lives, who brought the Israelites up out of the land of the north and out of all the countries where he had banished them.'** The verb 'bring up', which was the characteristic description of the LORD's redemptive action from Egypt, is now transferred to a second exodus in which he gathers his people not only from the land of the north, which has been presented as the major threat against them, but from everywhere they had been driven by his judgment ('banish' <√*nādâ*, 8:3). It is a complete ingathering of the people that will be remembered. This foretold that, beyond the harshness and completeness of the LORD's chastisement, there was still the prospect of renewed favour.

There is a further dimension to this transforming power and grace of the LORD. In Egypt the redeemed people had been believing (Exod. 4:31), but cowed and discouraged (Exod. 6:9). Now it is not only the power of Babylon that has to be overthrown; there has also to be the transformation of the hearts of those who have departed from the LORD. **For** ('and') **I will restore them to the land I gave to their forefathers.** The covenant promise (Gen. 12:1-3, 7) will again be realised. In the light of the use of the root elsewhere in the book 'restore' (<√*šûb*) hints at the spiritual processes that are required to bring this about (cf. 15:19; 31:18). Because of divine graciousness, after the horror of the Exile there will be renewed grace.

This message is not simply one of hope. There is implicit in it the threat that there is impending a time that will rival the oppression of Egypt in its harshness. 'As then they knew how cruelly their fathers had been treated by the Egyptians, the comparison he states more fully showed what a dreadful punishment awaited them, for their redemption would be much more incredible' (Calvin 1850, 2:321).

5. Fishermen and Hunters (16:16-18)

This divine speech is remarkable in that it does not directly identify who the hunted are. This has led Brueggemann (following an early interpretation in the Targum) to suggest that the reference may be to the judgment of the nations, though he continues to prefer the traditional understanding that these verses assert the coming devastation of Judah (1998:155). The principal thought in the passage is the thoroughness of the search that the enemy will make.

16. To indicate the contrast which the Hebrew achieves by passing on to v. 16 without any connecting word at all, the NIV adds 'But now'. The LORD indicates he is in process of bringing judgment upon the land. **'But now I will send for many fishermen[46],' declares the LORD, 'and they will catch them.'** It is not merely 'fish for them' (NASB), though this preserves the play in the Hebrew between 'fishermen' and 'fish', but fish successfully, that is 'catch them'. This probably pictures the people being trapped by fishermen's drag-nets (rather than by hooks) as the enemy sweeps through the land (Ezek. 12:13; 29:4-5; Amos 4:2; Hab. 1:15). Another metaphor is added: **After that I will send for many hunters,[47] and they will hunt them down on every mountain and hill and from the crevices of the rocks** (4:29; Amos 9:1-4). 'Afterwards' has been interpreted in terms of 586 BC, whereas the fishermen are taken as descriptive of the previous judgment of 597 BC. It may also be understood as an amplification of the totality of the judgment which will come without a particular date being in view. The fishermen represent the general invasion which captures the vast majority of the inhabitants of the land. Afterwards, perhaps when the cities are captured, there are some who manage to flee, but even these fugitives are allowed no hiding place though they seek it in the barren country and in the caves and slits in the rocks/'crevices', all seemingly inaccessible spots (13:4). It is a picture of judgment that is carried out efficiently and thoroughly from which none can expect to escape because the enemy armies will ruthlessly pursue them and round them up for extermination or for exile (Amos 4:2; Hab. 1:14-17).

17. The reason for this thorough action is not merely enemy hostility but divine vigilance, 'for' (*kî*) **my eyes are on all their ways; they are not hidden from me, nor is their sin** (*'āwōn*, 2:22) **concealed from my eyes.** The LORD shows himself as the one who watches and sees all. 'Ways' probably refers first of all to the paths taken by those trying to escape, but its ethical significance, 'the lifestyle they have adopted', leads into the following observation about their sinful behaviour. The LORD has not been unaware of their religious proclivities, and so with

---

46. The kethibh is *dawwāgîm*, a form also found in Ezek. 47:10; the qere is *dayyāgîm*, found in Isa. 19:8. Presumably they are to be taken as alternative spellings, with the qere being the one approved by the Massoretes.

47. The order is inverted to adjective plus noun, probably because *rabbîm* is being placed before the substantive on the analogy of a numeral (GKC §132b; *IBHS* §14.3.1b).

the evidence openly before him his justice will ensure that their sin is duly punished (23:24; 32:19).

18. The NIV translation of v. 18 omits the word 'first', which is rendered in the REB by 'I shall first make them pay'. This has often been thought to be a later addition (it is not found in the LXX), perhaps to indicate that this will occur before the picture of restoration in v. 15. There is going to be no escape from the LORD's judgment. How can he lead them back, if they have not first been led away? **I will repay them double for their wickedness** (*ʿāwōn*, 2:22) **and their sin** (*ḥaṭṭāʾt*, 2:35). The combination of these two nouns is found elsewhere (v. 10; 5:25; 18:23; 30:14-15; 31:34; 36:3; 50:20), and would seem to be a stereotyped expression where the terms reinforce each other rather than call for precise discrimination. The translation 'repay double' has increasingly been felt to be misleading, as if the punishment they had to undergo was twice as severe as their offences required. Some have taken it as a figure for a severe, thorough judgment ('a just and complete measure', Calvin 1850, 2:326). However, there is evidence, including the use of a cognate term in related languages, that *mišneh*, 'double', may also be translated as 'equivalent' (Kline 1989:176-77). They will be forced to repay what is a carbon-copy of what they have done wrong (17:18; Deut. 15:18; Isa. 40:2).

That offence is defined in terms of idolatry. **Because they have defiled my land** is similar to the expression found in 2:7 and 3:2, but in this passage the verb is from the root *ḥālal* I, 'to profane', which is particularly associated with objects and institutions that were especially associated with the LORD (e.g. his name in 34:16) and which were polluted by being brought into forbidden contact with that which he had vetoed. So here the land which he has specially designated as his own is viewed as contaminated by idolatry, by being brought into contact **with the lifeless forms of their vile images and have filled my inheritance with their detestable idols.**[48] 'Detestable idols' (<*tōʿēbâ*, 2:7) is a general term for something offensive to a person's values, culture or religion while 'vile images'(<*šiqqûṣ*, 4:1) is a technical term for those forbidden pagan practices that violate the worship of the LORD. 'Lifeless forms'/'carcasses' views the idols as so many

48. The accentuation of the Massoretic Text divides the verse differently: 'they have defiled my land; with the lifeless forms of their vile images and ⌊with⌋ their detestable idols they have filled my inheritance.' However, elsewhere the verb *mālēʾ*, 'to fill', is not found with an object preceded by the preposition *bə*, and English versions generally ignore the Massoretic punctuation here.

corpses which were defiling the land (Lev. 26:30, though a different word is used for corpse), and making it necessary for the LORD to purge it clean. 'Inheritance' may point to the land that the LORD has given to his people on trust (12:14), but the double reference here to '*my* land' and '*my* inheritance' shows that both terms refer to the LORD as the owner of the land (2:7), 'the land which belongs to me ... my possession' (REB). By getting involved with idolatry the people have given direct offence to the sovereign whose land it ultimately was.

6. Idolatry Renounced (16:19-21)

The last section of the chapter is generally recognised as included at this point because of a thematic association between the idols of the Israelites mentioned in v. 18 and the false gods of the heathen in v. 19. It is, however, also possible to trace a reason for its placement here in terms of Judah being reminded of the hope that was theirs, namely that all the nations would come to recognise the LORD. That future awakening constituted a rebuke to Judah's present defection in the opposite direction to idolatry.

19. The prophet begins by addressing the LORD as the one who gives support and protection in difficult circumstances. **O LORD, my strength and my fortress,** or better, 'my strength and my stronghold' (NRSV) to bring out the play in the Hebrew expression *'uzzî ûmā'uzzî*. The idea of God as the fortress/stronghold of his people is frequently found in the Psalms and prophets (e.g., Ps. 27:1; Isa. 25:4). There is also added, **my refuge in time of distress**. 'Refuge' (<√*nûs*, 'to flee') refers to the LORD as a shelter to which the faithful may safely entrust their destiny (Ps. 59:16; 142:5), something which is not available to those trying to escape divine judgment (25:35; 46:5). This too is language often found in the Psalms (Ps. 18:2-3; 28:1, 7-8; 59:10, 17-18). One can well understand how Jeremiah in his loneliness and isolation in the community would have strengthened himself by appropriating these terms and giving emphasis to the threefold *my*.

The description of the LORD also serves as a contrast to the character of the heathen gods. **To you the nations will come from the ends of the earth and say, 'Our fathers possessed nothing but false gods, worthless idols that did them no good.'** It was always part of Israel's faith that there was a dimension that incorporated future blessing for the nations (Gen. 12:3). In this passage the nations whom they looked down on are presented as recognising that they had not profited from their heathen worship. This is an element of the larger picture of the coming of the nations to acknowledge the LORD that is often found in the Old Testament (4:1-2; Isa. 2:1-4; 45:14; Zech. 8:20-23). It could undoubtedly serve as a goad to cause the people of Judah to think about their own behaviour. If the nations (*gôyīm*, those outwith the covenant) will in the future confess that their traditional gods were false (*šeqer*, 3:23), worthless (*hebel*, 2:5), and ineffective (2:8; 14:22), what should Judah be saying right now?

20. This verse is probably to be understood as the NIV takes it, that is, as part of the speech Jeremiah places on the lips of the nations as they come to their senses. **Do men make their own gods? Yes, but they are not gods!** This in measure reflects on Gen. 1:26, where it is God who makes man/mankind, and does so with a view to mankind serving as his image and likeness on earth. For man to make God is to turn the universe upside down. Of course, they can make something, but it is not worthy of the designation God. The nations are envisaged as coming to the true God in the realisation that what they previously called 'gods' were really nothing of the sort at all.

21. In this verse it is clear that the prophet cites a saying of the LORD. But who are the 'them' of whom he speaks: the nations, or his own people? If it is the former, then the saying develops further the prospect of future blessing on the nations (Isa. 2:3) brought about by divine enlightenment and mentioned here to provoke a response from Judah (Rom. 11:11-12). However, 'therefore' and 'this time' probably swing the balance in favour of the reference being directly to Judah. **Therefore** (*lākēn*) **I will teach them—this time**[49] **I will teach them my power and might.** 'Therefore' can be explained as a word of judgment that draws together the conduct of Judah in v. 18 and the future confession of the nations in vv. 19-20 as constituting the grounds on which the LORD will act. The forefathers of Judah had been privileged with more than lifeless gods and worthless idols, and so there was no excuse for their conduct in defiling the land with image worship. They need to learn this lesson, and the LORD is going to act as his people's teacher. 'This time' implies that he had previously sought to convey this to them (7:25; 11:7), but now in exasperation he will act so that there will be no way that his power and might remain unacknowledged. 'Power' (literally 'hand') is often used to convey the idea of strength in action, but here serves the additional purpose of reminding them of the nation's deliverance from Egypt by the mighty hand of the LORD (Exod. 3:20; 6:1; 7:4-5; 15:6). 'Might' ('strength' 9:23) is the

49. In 10:18 *bappaʿam hazzōʾt* has the meaning 'at this time', but perhaps here a case can be made out for the REB rendering 'once for all'.

ability of the strong that enables them to accomplish what they want.

The Exodus overtones continue ironically in **then they will know**[50] **that** (*kî*) **my name is the LORD**, that is, they will truly recognise his reality and his attributes. Once this had come about in the context of deliverance from oppression (Exod. 3:14), but now they will have to recognise it in the chastisement he will bring on them for their rebellion.

C. HEART CONDITION (17:1-18)

Chapter 17 gathers together a number of sayings which do not seem to have any specific development of thought running through them, but are generally related to the sin of Judah and its inevitable consequences. Bright (1965:119) called it Jeremiah's 'miscellaneous file'. But there is a certain measure of continuity. One key term linking the various sections is the word 'heart' (vv. 1, 5, 9).

'Heart' (*lēb*, *lēbāb*) is used frequently in the Old Testament as a metaphor for the inaccessible region of an individual's inner life where thought occurs, longings arise, and decisions are made. It is thus more comprehensive than the English use of 'heart' which refers principally to the emotions. Here Jeremiah points to the deep-seated, incorrigible wickedness of the human heart (vv. 1, 9) that leads to divine condemnation and judgment (vv. 5-6). Though the inner recesses of the heart are hidden from public scrutiny, they are not concealed from the LORD (v. 10). Those who inwardly trust in him, he blesses (vv. 7-8), but those who disobey him incur his displeasure and will be punished. From these general considerations Jeremiah is led to ponder his own situation before the true and exalted God (vv. 12-13). He knows he requires divine assistance to continue his prophetic ministry, and so he prays for inner healing and strength (vv. 14-18).

1. Judah's Sin (17:1-4)

Verses 1-4 pick up the idea of the contrast between the rejection of idolatry that the nations will display in the future (16:19-20) and the

50. In Hebrew the saying is constructed round a threefold repetition of the root, *yādaʿ*, 'to know'. 'I will teach them'/'I am about to make them know' renders the hiphil participle, *môdîʿām*, denoting a characteristic ongoing process, 'causing them to know' and so 'teaching them'. The second 'I will teach them' is an imperfect hiphil, *ʾôdîʿēm*, probably pointing to a repeated action which leads to their acquiring knowledge. 'They will know', *wəyādəʿû*, is a *waw*-consecutive perfect of the result that will be achieved.

current preoccupation of Judah with such idolatry (16:18). The focus of these verses is on the Canaanite fertility worship which re-emerged during Jehoiakim's reign and again took hold of the people. The text of the verses is not always easily understood, and hence translations vary somewhat.[51] There is no formal textual indication that a new speech of the LORD begins here, and so it is possible to see this as a continuation of the end of the previous chapter.

1. It is v. 3 before the speaker is clearly identified as the LORD. Here the divine speech focuses on the indelibility of Judah's sinful practices. **Judah's sin** (*ḥaṭṭāʾt*, 2:35) **is engraved with an iron tool.** Her knowledge of, and tendency towards, sin was not a superficial or passing trait, but something deeply embedded in her national character. 'Iron tool'/'pen of iron' refers to a stylus or perhaps even a chisel, forged from iron and capable of marking rock (cf. Job 19:24), though in 8:8 and Ps. 45:1 it probably refers to a reed used for writing on papyrus. In a society where information was generally spread by word of mouth, written documentation was employed for what was important and permanent. It is the implication of permanence that is developed here. **Inscribed with a flint point** refers to a very hard substance (*šāmîr*, also mentioned in Ezek. 3:9; Zech. 7:12), identified as 'diamond' in the NRSV and REB. The Massoretic accents divide the verse differently: 'engraved with an iron tool, with a flint point, inscribed on the tablets of their hearts' (cf. AV). In that case there is only one implement involved, a metal stylus tipped with a harder substance. There may be some archaeological evidence to support the existence of such a tool (King 1993:100), and contrary to previous opinions that diamonds were unknown at this early period such a reference is increasingly favoured. 'Inscribed' (<√*ḥāraš* I, 'to plough') points to the creation of a furrow of sorts, not on some stone monument, but **on the tablets of their hearts.** Tablets were normally reusable wooden boards covered with wax on which letters were scratched out. The most famous tablets in Scripture are, however, those of stone on which the Decalogue was engraved (Exod. 24:12). The tablets of their hearts conveys the idea of what is deep within them (Prov. 3:3; 7:3), and it is now no longer God's requirements that are found there governing their lives. The implements used to mark them indicates that *stone* tablets are in view here, and this suggests that the people would be impervious

51. Verses 1-4 are omitted in the LXX, probably by accident. Archer argues, 'It might be possible to see this omission as a matter of editorial choice, with a view to avoiding any unnecessary exacerbation of the desperation felt by the Jewish remnant taking refuge in Egypt' (1991:144).

to pleas to change their ways. Their corruption was deep seated and ineradicable (2:22; 13:23).

It is also written **on the horns of their**[52] **altars.** The horns of the altar were stone projections, one at each of the top corners of the altar. They performed the utilitarian role of stabilising the sacrifice being burned on the altar, but more significantly when sacrifices for atonement were presented, blood was smeared on these horns to indicate the propitiatory nature of the sacrifice (Exod. 27:2; 29:12; 30:1-3; Lev. 4:7, 30, 34; 8:15; 16:18). The record of their sin as an indictment against them is recorded in the blood on the horns of the altars—it should have spoken of forgiveness, but because of their rebellion it now testifies not of sin forgiven, but of sin perpetuated. However, although the Jerusalem sanctuary had in fact two altars (the bronze altar in the court, and the altar of incense in the holy place), both of which were ritually smeared with blood, the plural 'altars' suggests that the reference is to pagan altars, which we know from archaeological excavations also had horns at the corners. This fits in with the reference to altars in v. 2. The sacrifices of pagan worship also testify to the sin of the people, presumably in the period when Josiah's reforms had broken down.

2. The following three verses all have textual problems connected with them to such an extent that, while their general import is clear, details cannot be completely decided. There are two interpretations of v. 2, according as 'their children'/'sons' is taken as the subject or the object of the verb.[53] The NASB represents the latter approach. 'As they remember their children, so they *remember* their altars and their Asherim.' That presents a picture of the intensity of their attachment to the pagan fertility cults, as great as to their children. It does, however, suffer from the problem that the second word of comparison 'so' is not found in the text nor is there a second verb. The other approach is to take 'their sons' as the subject: **Even their children remember their altars and Asherah poles.** The problem with this is whether 'even' attaches a valid meaning to *kə*, 'like, as', or 'when'. It would indicate the extent to which the children of the Judahites were indoctrinated from their youth in pagan practices so that they 'remembered'

52. The Massoretic Text has *mizbəḥôtêkem*, 'your altars', but English translations, along with many Hebrew manuscripts, read 'their'.

53. The verb itself is an infinitive with a prefixed *kə*. The awkwardness of this expression has led to a rearrangement from *kizkōr bənêhem* to *kəzikrôn bāhem*, 'as a memorial against them', which is then attached to the previous verse as in the REB, 'on the horns of their altars to witness against them'.

(possibly = 'kept thinking about') their altars. It was not just an adult pursuit, but had permeated the whole community, so reinforcing the allegations of v. 1. The altars here would be those of the fertility cults as is made clear by the reference to the Asherah poles (2:27). These were originally trees, later just wooden poles, which symbolised the Canaanite goddess of fertility and were found at the shrines which were typically located **beside the spreading trees and on the high hills**[54] (2:20). Such poles had been interdicted in Israel (Exod. 34:13; Deut. 12:3).

3. The first words of the verse are obscure, and the rest of the verse and v. 4 bear substantial similarities to 15:13-14. The NIV footnote, NRSV and the REB take the first phrase with the previous verse, 'on the high hills and mountains of the land'.[55] Keeping the phrase as part of v. 3 involves choosing between a vocative rendering such as 'O my mountain in the field' (NKJV) and an accusative one such as that of the NIV, **My mountain in the land and your wealth and all your treasures I will give away as plunder.** The first approach explains the masculine singular second person references that follow, but does not fit in easily with the development in v. 4. In the second, 'my mountain' would be used by metonymy for the sacred buildings and possessions to be found on it, which will be plundered along with the possessions of the people (addressed in the masculine singular). The reference to mountain 'in the land' (literally 'field, countryside', but also 'land, territory' as in Gen. 14:7; 32:4; Ezek. 21:2; for another possible meaning see on 13:27) is agreed to be to Zion. By divine decree it is going to be stripped of its wealth and treasures. **Together with your high places**[56] points to sites of pagan worship (7:31) which will be despoiled as well as the Temple. NJPS follows an earlier suggestion of Kimchi that there is here a reverse construct chain and translates 'because of the sin of your shrines'. The NIV follows the traditional understanding that this states the reason for the devastation as **because of sin** (*ḥaṭṭā't*, 2:35) **throughout your country**. 'Sin' lacks 'your' found in 15:13, but the phrase 'throughout your country' is the same.

---

54. Note the unusual article on the last word. GKC takes this as probably an error (§126x).

55. 'Mountains of the land' involves repointing *hărārî*, 'my mountain', to a construct plural form *harərê*, 'mountains of'.

56. This phrase is often felt to be awkward, and by changing *bāmōtệkā* to *bimḥîr*, on the analogy of the parallel passage in 15:13, it and the following word may be rendered 'as the price of your sin' (NRSV); the REB goes further and inserts a negative (as in 15:13) and reads 'for no payment'.

4. The description of the impending judgment and penalty for covenant disobedience continues with a sentence not found in 15:14. **Through your own fault you will lose the inheritance I gave you.** Though early Jewish exegesis noted the connection between the sabbatical year and the verb used here (*šāmat*, 'to let fall'; used in Exod. 23:11, 'to leave unploughed', and Deut. 15:2-3, 'to cancel', in connection with the sabbatical year), and suggested that the punishment was coming because of non-observance of it, this seems to be too particular an interpretation of the words. The people would be deprived of residence in the land because of the idolatrous worship that had become part of their national life. 'Through your own fault' renders an awkward word *ûbəkā*, 'and in/by you', which may emphasise the pronoun, 'You, even yourself' (NKJV), or indicate the instrumentality through which the loss will occur, 'by your own act' (NRSV).[57]

I will enslave you to your enemies in a land you do not know is similar to 15:14. The inheritance of the covenant is lost and then the freedom from Egyptian domination granted to them as a people at the time of the Exodus is also reversed. **For** (*kî*) **you have kindled**[58] **my anger, and it will burn for ever.** The continuing response of divine anger is due to their rebellion.

2. The Two Destinies (17:5-8)

Commentators have tried to date this section by identifying the man who is cursed with a particular king of Judah: Josiah, Jehoiakim or Zedekiah. To take it as Zedekiah would treat the passage as exilic in origin, looking back on the fate of a king whose vacillating character makes it somewhat inappropriate to designate him as 'man' (*geber*, v. 5). Jehoiakim trusted in Egyptian promises of help when he withdrew his allegiance from Nebuchadnezzar. Or it might reflect the circumstances of Josiah if he is understood to have turned away from the LORD (v. 5) in mounting his attack against Neco in 609 BC. On the whole it seems best to hear these words at a more general level as Jeremiah reflects on his own situation.

5. The language of this section resembles that of wisdom literature and also that of Ps. 1. It does not seem to be connected with vv. 1-4, and

57. The RSV rendering, 'You shall loosen your hand from your heritage', follows an old emendation of the text to *yādəkā*, 'your hand', which it is felt is more appropriate to the verb *šāmaṭ*.

58. The switch from the second masculine singular to a plural in this verb has been felt to be awkward, and by changing it to *qādəḥâ* (cf. 15:14) the REB renders 'the fire of my anger is kindled by you'.

looks not at the life of the nation but at the life of the individual. Holladay (1974:98-9) argued that this section is to be taken as one of the series of Jeremiah's Confessions, being in fact his response to God's call to repentance in 15:19-21. This would be supported by the fact that God is referred to throughout in the third person. Thompson too (1980:419) inclines to accept that interpretation. What, however, is to be done with the introductory, **This is what the LORD says**? Thompson dismisses it as an editorial transition, lacking in the LXX, and Lundbom calls it 'inappropriate' (1999:780). But there is no Hebrew manuscript evidence for its deletion. Taking it as an editorial link introduced by Jeremiah himself indicates his awareness that these words were more than a human reflection on life. Just as much as when the LORD spoke directly to him, Jeremiah was aware that in composing this material he had been subject to spiritual influences and enlightenment that had been divinely mediated to him. These were worthy, and not worthless, words (15:19) even though they step beyond the boundaries of usual prophetic message bearing.

The relationship with Ps. 1 is obvious, though in which direction dependence is to be traced depends on the dating of the psalm, which has no indication of authorship. Unlike many commentators, Holladay (1986, 1:489-90) argues that Jeremiah drew on the model of Ps. 1 (which he also reflected on, but in a different way, in 12:1-2) and also Ps. 40:4-5—which is marked 'Of David'. (For the significance of the titles to psalms, see Kidner 1973:32-5.)

Though it shares a common structure with Ps. 1 in contrasting the destinies of the wicked and the righteous, a structure derived from the covenant alternatives of curse and blessing, Jeremiah's psalm reverses the order in which they are considered. **Cursed is the one who trusts in man** involves a contrast between two Hebrew words for man, the first rendered 'the one' is man in his prime and strength (*geber*; cf. 30:6), though in such formulae as 'Cursed is …' and 'Blessed is …' its force may be weakened. Even such a one is cursed if he puts his trust in 'man'/'mankind' (*'ādām*), man from the dust, characterised by creaturely weakness ('mortal' REB, NRSV). **Who depends on flesh for his strength**/'sets flesh as his arm', where *zərōaʿ*, 'arm', often denoting 'strength' or 'might', amplifies the previous thought. 'Flesh' (*bāśār*) is the Old Testament term for mankind viewed as weak and mortal, and so incapable of mastering in his own strength the situations with which he is confronted. 'Flesh' is the antithesis of spirit (Isa. 31:3; Job 10:4; Ps. 56:5). Such an attitude of reliance on 'flesh'/human resources (whether military, technological or economic) arises because man is the one **whose heart turns away** (<√*sûr*, 'to turn aside', 'to stand aloof from') **from the LORD.** This describes an individual who ought to have been in covenant with the LORD and trusting in him. 'It is better to take refuge in the LORD than to trust in man' (Ps. 118:8). But now his inner inclination has turned away from the LORD. He no longer trusts in him but, intent on finding human substitutes to provide the wisdom and strength he needs to survive, all he has achieved is to sentence himself to living in the wilderness.

6. He will be like a bush in the wastelands. 'Bush' (*ʿarʿār* <√*ʿārar*, 'to be naked/bare', cf. 48:6), may, as in Ps. 102:18, not indicate a plant at all, but an individual lacking proper means of subsistence in a desert region (so McKane 1986, 1:390). However, the context makes a reference to a plant of some sort more likely. Most translations prefer a general term such as 'shrub' or 'bush', but the REB opts, probably correctly, for 'juniper', a low-growing evergreen shrub with scale-like leaves. Another possibility is 'tamarisk' (LXX, NJPS margin), a hardy bush found in semi-arid areas around the Mediterranean. There is a pleasing assonance between 'bush' and 'wastelands' (*ʿărābâ*, 5:6), and possibly also with 'cursed' (*ʾārûr*, v. 5; Carroll 1986:350). It is not totally clear whether **he will not see prosperity** (*ṭôb*, 'good') **when** (*kî*) **it comes** refers to the bush enjoying heavy rainfall (Deut. 28:12) or the man experiencing a time of affluence. There is probably a neat merging of the two pictures. The bush in the wilderness gets passed by when the rainy season comes, and similarly the individual who has placed his confidence in human endeavour and foresight will miss out on the blessing the LORD will provide. **He will dwell in the parched places**[59] **of the desert** (*midbār*, 'wilderness' 2:2)**, in a salt land where no one lives** (Deut. 29:23). Again there is oscillation between the bush and the man. Although scattering salt over the fields of a defeated enemy to lower their productivity was a recognised military procedure (Judg. 9:45), the reference here is to an area such as that near the Dead Sea where the naturally occurring presence of salt has adversely affected fertility (Job 39:6).

7. But, which does not correspond to any word in Hebrew, is used by the NIV at the beginning of v. 7 to express the contrast which is effected in the text by asyndeton. **Blessed is the man** (*geber*, v. 5) **who trusts in the LORD.** Unlike Ps. 1:1 where 'Blessed is the man ...' renders the Hebrew *ʾašrê*, a term of congratulation on the state of

59. *ḥărērîm* (<√*ḥārar*, 'to burn') probably means 'burned up/scorched places', but others on the basis of Arabic suggest 'lava flows' (hence 'rocks', or 'stony deserts', REB).

happiness he enjoys, here the word *bārûk* is used for 'blessed', which looks more to the divine origin of the blessing and the favour that is enjoyed. 'Trusts (<√*bāṭaḥ*) in the LORD' is a standard expression for the life of faith, relying on the LORD (Ps. 40:4). This is emphatically expressed by the virtual repetition of the thought in the second line, **whose confidence** (*mibṭāḥ*) **is in him**, where there is assonance between 'trusts' (*yibṭaḥ*) and the cognate term 'confidence'.

8. The man who trusts in the LORD is also compared to a tree in a manner that builds on the picture of Ps. 1:3: 'He is like a tree planted by streams of water, which yields its fruit in season and whose leaf does not wither. Whatever he does prospers.' The man who trusts is not to be thought of as a bush in the wasteland, but **he will be like a tree planted by the water that sends out its roots by the stream.** Comparisons of those favoured by God to trees are also found in Pss. 52:8; 92:14, and Ezekiel uses similar images to tell the story of Israel (Ezek. 19:10-13). 'Planted' refers to placing cuttings in the ground so that they may grow. It might possibly convey the idea 'transplanted', and definitely points to the tree having been deliberately set there, rather than a bush which just happens to grow in the wasteland. The sending out of the roots denotes an active and vigorous growth. 'Stream' is also an unusual word (<√*yābal*, 'to conduct, bear along') and describes an irrigation channel (*HALOT* 398), the point being that it is not a wadi that dries up in summer, but a place where water will be found all the year round. This tree is therefore in a good situation. **It does not fear**[60] **when** (*kî*) **heat comes; its leaves are always green** (*ra'ănān*, 2:20). 'Whoever trusts in his riches will fall, but the righteous will thrive like a green leaf' (Prov. 11:28). This is a picture of the normal course of events when the midday heat even in summer time does not cause it to wilt. Furthermore, even in abnormal times of testing it survives. **It has no worries in a year of drought**[61] (14:1) **and never fails to bear fruit.** 'Worries' (<√*dā'ag*, 'to be anxious/ concerned') is a synonym of *yārē'*, 'to fear', though it is not used as a religious concept. This tree/man has no anxiety because of its situation in which it has become deeply rooted. Unlike the desert scrub which dies off in drought, this tree survives; indeed it is more than survival. It is productive and able to be a means of blessing to others.

These statements are true at a general level, but here they also

60. The kethibh *yr'* is an imperfect form *yirā'*, from *yārē'*, 'to fear', paralleling 'not worry' (so LXX). The qere takes the form as *yir'eh*, from *rā'â*, 'he will (not) see', reflecting back on v. 6.

61. 'Drought' is a hapax *baṣṣōret* <√*bāṣar* II, 'to reduce, humble', cf. 14:1.

reflect on Jeremiah's own experience. Verses 5-6 may show something of how he felt during a time of despondency, when he was depending on man for his sustenance and desiring popular approval. He was turned away from the LORD and incapable of enjoying his blessing. But now he has been restored to a right relationship with God and transplanted to a source of never-failing revitalisation, he has no occasion to fear because he has put down deep roots in a favourable environment. It is not that he will be exempt from times of testing. The tree near the water is not exempt from the heat or the year of drought, but the provision made for it will enable it not only to survive but to bear fruit through it. So too Jeremiah is assured that though his present circumstances constitute a very real time of testing, good will still come through his ministry.

3. Deceitful above All Things (17:9-11)

The sequence of thought seems to try to elucidate how it is that individuals choose to be like the bush in the wilderness when the two destinies of blessing and cursing are so clearly set before them. The answer is found to lie in the perverse self-deceit of human nature, which warps accurate perception of good and evil.

9. There is no textual evidence of a change of speaker at this point and so, accepting the NIV punctuation, we may take v. 9 as embodying Jeremiah's own reflection rather than being the LORD's assessment of the human heart. 'For me it is almost certain that … 17:9 is Jeremiah's verdict, not primarily on his contemporaries, but on himself. Like Paul in Romans 7, he found a conflict in himself he could not fathom' (Ellison 1963:162). Though the sentiment is expressed in a very general fashion, it was probably a reflection prompted by the prophet's own increasing self-understanding, or rather realisation of how little he knew himself. **The heart is deceitful above all things,** or 'most deceitful of all ⌊things⌋' (*IBHS* §14.5d). 'Heart' here refers to the interior life of an individual. It is not just, or even primarily, the emotional life, but includes the thoughts and will of the individual. It is said to be 'deceitful' (*ʿāqōb*, a word that comes from the same root as Jacob, the supplanter; cf. 9:4). *ʿāqōb* in Isa. 40:4 signifies a rough place as distinct from a level ground, and it may be that the unevenness of such areas led to them being viewed as deceitful and liable to cause stumbling. The thought here is that in his inner life a person constantly tries to supplant the place that should be given to the LORD, and he accords priority to other objectives than pleasing the LORD in determining his conduct. Certainly Jeremiah is affirming out of his own experience that if you want to see deceit then the place to find it is deep within oneself. **And beyond cure** (*ʾānuš*, 15:18; 30:12; <√*ʾānaš*, to be sick/weak) may convey the thought 'desperately sick' (NASB, REB), or terminally ill. 'Desperately wicked' (NKJV) or 'perverse' (NRSV) interpret rather than translate the term. Jeremiah's question **Who can understand it?** is a musing, rhetorical question which expresses the thought that no one can really 'understand'/'know' his own inner nature and corruption.

10. But over against this there is set a word from the LORD, which in effect answers the question of the previous verse by saying, 'I do. I understand the heart of man. Furthermore, on the basis of my accurate and insightful observation, I will judge it with perfect righteousness.' The deep recesses of one's inner life may not be fully known to the individual himself, but they are not hidden from God (11:20; 12:3). **I the LORD search the heart and examine the mind.** 'Heart' refers, as in v. 9 to the inner life of an individual, principally the thoughts and will. 'Mind' here renders 'kidneys' (11:20), used to refer the ethical and emotional responses that well up from deep within an individual's psyche. *ḥāqar*, 'to search', occurs relatively infrequently but denotes a thorough search, and so is suited to conveying the intensity of divine scrutiny to expose the motives behind a person's actions (Pss. 44:21; 139:1, 23). 'Search' and 'examine' are here participles describing what the LORD characteristically does. The LORD examines/tests (*bāḥan*, 6:27; 11:20; 12:2; cf. Ps. 26:2) with an end in view[62]: **to reward a man according to his conduct,**[63] **according to what his deeds deserve** (cf. 32:19; Isa. 3:10-11; 11:3^{b},4). The latter phrase (literally 'according to the fruit of his deeds') picks up the thought of bearing fruit from the end of v. 8. The truth expressed here corresponds to the New Testament teaching of judgment according to works. 'He will reward each person according to what he has done' (Matt. 16:27). 'I will give to everyone according to what he has done' (Rev. 22:12). The outer actions are the incontrovertible evidence of the inner allegiance. The LORD knows what is within a person, and acts appropriately on the basis of that knowledge. Jeremiah is therefore able to go on with confidence knowing that his reward will be from the LORD.

11. This section is brought to a conclusion by reverting to consideration of the fate of the wicked. **Like a partridge that hatches eggs it did not lay** is variously understood. 'Hatch' (<√*dāgar*, elsewhere only

62. *wəlātēt*, *waw* explicativum, GKC §154a.

63. The kethibh is *kədarkô*, 'according to his way', whereas the qere has *kidrākāw*, 'according to his ways'.

in Isa. 34:15) may also mean 'to gather' (BDB, RSV). 'Lay' (<√*yālad*, the common word for 'to give birth') may here mean 'to lay' or perhaps 'to hatch'. Furthermore the sets of facts are just set side by side and no explicit comparison is made (GKC §161a): 'A partridge hatches/gathers but does not lay/hatch, one making rich but not by justice.'[64] This was possibly a proverbial saying (hence its concision) which may be explained on the basis of a prevalent belief that the partridge gathered eggs from other nests and hatched them, but that the young then flew away from it. This may have arisen from observing that partridges (very common in Palestine) lay considerable numbers of eggs and that the male bird often incubates a second nest. The focus of the comparison would then be the fact that the male bird takes care of eggs he did not lay just as **the man who gains riches** (again paranomasia, *ʿōśeh ʿōśer*) **by unjust means** has stolen from and defrauded others to acquire the riches he so carefully looks after.

The NKJV rendering, '*As* a partridge that broods but does not hatch, *so is* he who gets riches, but not by right', finds the point of the comparison in another aspect of the situation: the precarious hold the partridge has over its eggs. The partridge's nest is close to the ground, and is easily attacked by predators; indeed, the nests are often robbed by humans. The bird may have a large number of eggs, but it cannot be sure that it will bring them all through to life. The idea is then the folly of the rich, who amass wealth unjustly, but who are liable to lose everything that they have worked so hard for.

The second half of the verse brings out further the lesson to be learned. **When his life is half gone**[65]**, they will desert him.** He will find that his wealth can vanish, taken away by others, just as predators steal the partridge's eggs. Those who look for historical application of these proverbial sayings apply this to Jehoiakim who died when he was thirty-six years old and left his treasures, which were shortly thereafter taken to Babylon. The impermanence of human possessions is a frequent theme in Scripture (Ps. 39:6; Prov. 28:8; Luke 12:20). **And in the end he will prove to be a fool.** 'The end'/'his end' refers to the end of his life. 'A fool' (*nābāl*) is one lacking in religious perceptivity, rather than in intellectual powers. At the end of the day it will be shown that he has pursued a course that has no true reward, because his heart has turned away from the LORD (v. 5).

---

64. The parallelism with the second half of the verse seems to require that *wəlōʾ yālād* should be circumstantial to the preceding: the partridge hatches an egg which she has not laid.

65. The kethibh is *yōmô*, 'his day', whereas the qere is *yāmāw*, 'his days'.

This too would encourage Jeremiah who was very much affected by the comparison between his own lot and that of the rich and seemingly successful, but wicked, around him (12:1-2).

4. The Source of Hope and Life (17:12-13)

This unit has caused problems because it is not clear if it is the start of Jeremiah's Confession (vv. 14-18) or is a separate unit that has been placed here. Though many interpreters have found vv. 12 and 13 troublesome, they do seem to arise out of what has preceded.

12. The speaker is Jeremiah. There are three noun phrases to which a verb has to be added in English to give sense, though the NRSV has three isolated vocatives. **A glorious throne, exalted from the beginning, is the place of our sanctuary.** Thrones are seats associated with superiority and honour, mostly royal or divine. 'Glorious throne'/'throne of glory' refers to the ark, above which the LORD sat enthroned (14:21; Ps. 80:2), and hence the expression may be extended to describe the whole Temple in which the ark was subsequently placed. This is sometimes felt to be incongruous in that in chapter 7 Jeremiah had scathingly attacked the confidence that the people put in the Temple. But it was not the Temple as such that he had criticised, but the use of it as a talisman quite apart from the obedience that the covenant king demanded. It is therefore unnecessary to suppose that the reference here is to a heavenly temple. It is the LORD's presence with this people at the place where his majesty is revealed that is the focus of Jeremiah's thought. 'Exalted' (<√*rûm*, 'to be high, raised up') may be employed of heaven (Isa. 57:15; Ps. 7:8) or of Zion (Ezek. 17:23; 20:40). While 'from the beginning' may be used absolutely (Isa. 40:21; 41:4), and so the thought would be 'exalted in intention' before ever the shrine was there (cf. Exod. 15:17), it is more probable that the phrase is used for a relative beginning (Isa. 41:26; 48:16), and so points to the duration of the period under consideration, either from Sinai or the construction of the Temple. **The place of our sanctuary** refers to the site that was consecrated as the divine dwelling to be found in the midst of the covenant people. 'Our' points to the community as a whole who have such a king and judge in their midst at the Temple.

13. Having in this way recalled the privileges extended to the covenant people, Jeremiah turns to the LORD, and confesses, **O LORD, the hope of Israel, all who forsake** (<√*ʿāzab*, 2:13) **you will be put to shame.** 'Hope of Israel' was used as a divine title in 14:8 (cf. 50:7), referring to the future the LORD provides for his people. This is not what will be experienced by those who abandon the LORD and his ways as set out for them in the covenant. They no longer have access to what the Temple is really about, and so they have no proper ground on which to look forward positively. Their future is one of shame (<√*bôš*, 2:26), when their hopes are confounded and they are brought to judgment because they are not in a right relationship with the LORD. They will then know the misery of abandonment. **Those who turn away from you**[66] **will be written in the dust**. 'Turn away' (<√*sûr*) echoes v. 5b. Writing here refers to the secular practice of keeping citizen lists (22:30), from which the notion of a divine book of life probably derived (Pss. 69:28; 87:6; 139:16). Such records were part of the polity of the covenant king, and those whose names were on his list enjoyed his fellowship and protection (Exod. 32:32-33). But those who desert the LORD have their names written in the 'dust'/'land' (*ʾereṣ*, an unusual term to use for dust), where their names and memory will be easily brushed away—a decided contrast with names engraved in the rock for ever (Job 19:24; cf. v. 1). Writing in the dust seems to have been a common practice (attested in John 8:6) for a record that was soon to be erased (similar to the use of scrap paper). The NRSV 'recorded in the underworld' takes *ʾereṣ* in a different sense (*HALOT* 91) which is by no means established. It has been argued for by comparing the way the word is used in some psalms with similar expressions in pagan literature. Whatever the translation, the thought is, however, similar: 'Rebels and sinners will both be broken, and those who forsake the LORD will perish' (Isa. 1:28). The reason such people will have no enduring possession or memorial is **because** (*kî*) **they have forsaken the LORD, the spring of living water** (2:13). The LORD is presented as the source of water that is fresh, and also sustains life. Those who depart from him can only expect to wither away.

66. The kethibh has *yswry*, for which the qere reads *wəsûray*, 'and those turning away from me', which would suggest that this line is the speech of the LORD. English versions substitute 'from you' to keep the sense, though Lundbom argues 'me' should be retained and v. 13^{b} taken as divine speech (1999:798). If, however, it is pointed as *wəsûrê* it might be taken as a construct before a prepositional phrase, 'those turning away in the land', but that would leave the problem of knowing what to do with 'they will be written'. Jones (1992:246) suggests, 'The names of those in the land who turn away shall be written down' in a permanent record of the decision given against them.

5. When Nothing Happens (17:14-18)

This is the briefest of Jeremiah's Confessions, consisting of a single petition addressed to God. It is also remarkable in that there is no recorded reply. Jeremiah presents himself as one who truly worships the LORD and trusts in him. As one who is innocent but suffering, the prophet implores the LORD to provide him with relief and justice.

14. Heal me, O LORD, and I shall be healed[67] does not refer to a physical malady but harks back to Jeremiah's perception of himself as the one who is spiritually wounded and distressed (15:18). The prophet is sure that the only healing that will be effective for his condition is that which comes from the LORD (Pss. 6:3; 30:3). The words were obviously spoken at a time of dejection and depression, but even so Jeremiah has not given up looking to the LORD alone as the one who can help. Though he is still in spiritual perplexity and despair, there remains (unlike 15:18) an underlying note of confidence in the LORD. **Save me, and I shall be saved**[68] repeats the root *yāšaʿ* (hiphil and niphal; cf. 4:14), which is used of rescue from circumstances of danger. He urges as the reason why the LORD should intervene, **for** (*kî*) **you are the one I praise**/'you ⌊are⌋ my praise' (<√*hālal* II, 4:2). For the thought compare Deut. 10:21; Ps. 71:6. Jeremiah professes his allegiance to, and worship of, the LORD not in a spirit of fear but of joyful adoration and thanksgiving.

15. The reason for the prophet's perplexity was the popular reaction to his ministry. **They keep saying to me.** 'They' may be the people in general, or more specifically those who were actively opposed to him. They taunt the prophet that what he had proclaimed had not come true nor was it likely to (cf. Isa. 5:18-19; Ezek. 12:22). The implication is that he is a false prophet, deserving death. **Where is the word of the LORD? Let it now be fulfilled!**[69] One of the tests of a true prophet was that what he said in the name of the LORD came to pass (Deut. 18:22). Jeremiah had been prophesying disaster, and this had not come. At first sight this might seem to locate this Confession prior to 597 BC when the city was captured and its treasures removed (2 Kgs. 24:13).

---

67. Possibly this is a cohortative form, which is not usually formally marked for final-aleph verbs (note the following cohortative); in that case the translation would be 'that I may be healed'.

68. This is a cohortative form *wəʾiwwāšēʿâ* and so may be rendered 'that I may be saved' (cf. preceding note).

69. The precative particle *nāʾ* probably here has its full significance 'please', though of course the whole request is ironic.

But it is evident that even that disaster was insufficient to make the false prophets stop and reflect. The city itself had not been destroyed and so they believed its fortunes would be speedily restored (28:2-4). Jeremiah's doom-laden predictions had simply not happened. At the last moment the LORD had intervened (and always would); Jerusalem would not be forsaken. Therefore they derided Jeremiah because his message foretold a calamity far more overwhelming than anything that had taken place, a calamity they believed was inconceivable.

16. In the face of such opposition Jeremiah protests his faithfulness to the commission the LORD had given him. He begins 'but as for me' (*wa'ănî*). Three times in this unit the personal pronoun 'I' occurs for emphasis (here and twice in v. 18), and three times 'you' occurs in reference to God (vv. 14, 16, 17), though the first and last of these are in non-verbal clauses and therefore not emphatic. This does not detract significantly from Brueggemann's observation, 'The repeated use of such strong pronouns indicates that this relationship is one of intense communion' (1998:164). **I have not run away from being your shepherd.**[70] 'Run away' is from the root *'ûṣ*, 'to urge' or 'to be in haste' (*HALOT* 23), which is not quite the same as 'run away' (NIV, NRSV). Unusually he employs the word 'shepherd' to refer to himself as a prophet who had the care of the people entrusted to him by the LORD. He had continued to exercise this remit in terms and after the example that the LORD had given ('shepherd after you', that is, following the LORD) and had not shirked the task. **You** (with the pronoun expressed for emphasis) **know**[71] **I have not desired the day of despair.** 'Day of despair' (*'ānûš* 'beyond cure', v. 9) describes the ultimate disaster that would irrevocably spell the end of their nationhood. Jeremiah had not carried out his mission because he wished ill on the people and wanted such judgment to come upon the country.

70. 'It is not the prospect of disaster that makes me press after you' (REB) points *mērō'eh*, 'from being a shepherd' as *mērā'â*, 'from evil, on account of disaster', and takes *lō'*, 'not', with it, following two Greek versions (Aquila and Symmachus) and the Syriac. This may also be argued for on the basis that a prophet being called a shepherd is not otherwise attested, that 'after you' is an unusual locution to follow 'shepherd', and that 'day of despair' is in parallelism with 'prospect of disaster'.

71. 'You know' is taken with the preceding words 'I have not desired the day of despair' by the NIV. This is in accordance with the Massoretic accentuation. But most English versions take 'I have not desired the day of despair' as an independent statement, and read 'you know' with the following words.

What passes my lips is open before you. There was nothing Jeremiah had been saying that the LORD had not known, and so his integrity as he fulfilled his commission could be vouched for by the LORD himself.

17. However, in fulfilling this commission and especially since the word that had been given to him had not come to pass, Jeremiah felt himself to be in an intolerable situation. If the LORD did not act in one way or another to resolve the situation, he felt he was on the point of collapse. **Do not be**[72] **a terror to me.** 'Terror' (<√*ḥātat*, 'to be shattered, dismayed, terrified', 1:17) is better taken as 'a cause of dismay' (NJPS), viewing God as one whose action/inaction leads Jeremiah to collapse through a nervous breakdown. That was what the LORD had threatened him with if he did not carry out his commission (1:17), but surely it was not what should happen when he is acting in accordance with the directions given to him. **You are my refuge in the day of disaster.** 'Refuge' (*maḥseh*, Ps. 46:2) is the defensive or external aspect of salvation, corresponding to human insecurity and inability to fend for oneself in the face of hostility. Unlike 'day of despair' in v. 16, 'the day of disaster'/'the evil day' is not referring to the judgment that would come upon the nation, but to the desperate circumstances Jeremiah found himself in, his personal experience of disaster.

18. Rather he wishes his own situation and that of his opponents to be reversed. **Let my persecutors be put to shame, but keep me** (*'ănî*, emphatic) **from shame.** For 'persecutors' see 15:15. The reference here is to those parties who were taunting him (v. 15). They are the ones who should be shamed (<√*bôš*, 2:26) when the word from the LORD that they reject comes to pass (cf. Pss. 35:4; 40:14), but Jeremiah knows he has already been embarrassed and perplexed, and is afraid that will continue to occur. He pleads that the LORD act to preserve him from this. **Let them**[73] **be terrified, but keep me from terror.** 'Terrified' and 'terror' are both from the root *ḥātat* (v. 17). Jeremiah is looking back to the message he received when he was called (1:17), and is asking that his opponents know the loss of morale that comes from a devastating blow. **Bring on them the day of disaster.** Again this phrase 'day of disaster'/'evil day' (v. 17) probably does not refer to the destruction that is to come on the city, but rather to the judgment that will vindicate Jeremiah as opposed to his persecutors. **Destroy**

72. The form *tihyēh* rather than *tihyeh* may be through Aramaic influence (GKC §75hh).

73. The pronouns 'them' and 'me' are expressed to intensify the explicit antithesis (*IBHS* §16.3.2d).

them with double destruction, or better 'with a full (*mišneh*, 16:18) destruction'. 'Destruction' (<√*šābar*) denotes a 'collapse' or 'breakdown'.

D. THE SIGNIFICANCE OF THE SABBATH (17:19-27)

This section is often dismissed as a later insertion into Jeremiah because Sabbath-keeping is regarded as a concern of the post-exilic community, reflected for instance in Neh. 13:15-22. While the problem of Sabbath observance was undoubtedly acute then, it would be idle to suppose that it only emerged at that time, as indeed the passage in Nehemiah attests: 'Didn't your forefathers do the same things, so that our God brought all this calamity upon us and upon this city?' (Neh. 13:18). Pre-exilic concern for Sabbath observance is also expressed in Amos 8:5 where the people are seen eagerly awaiting the end of the Sabbath so that they can get on with their business ('observed but disliked', Ellison 1962:25), and Isa. 58:13-14, where there is an expression of the blessings that would attend keeping the Sabbath, not dissimilar to that found here. Jeremiah is urging the people not to squander wilfully the privileges and benefits conferred on them by their covenant king.

'Remember the Sabbath day by keeping it holy' (Exod. 20:8) is the fourth word of the Decalogue, and the divine origins of this practice are set out in Gen. 2:2-3 and Exod. 20:11. Even more significant is the fact that in the arrangements set up under Moses at Sinai the Sabbath is given the status of a sign of the covenant (Exod. 31:13, 17). Because of this it was a key index of the nation's spiritual commitment to the LORD, challenging them as to whether God or their own economic and personal interests were to be the ultimate determinant of their lifestyle.

It was therefore in accordance with the demands of the covenant that the Sabbath should be used as a test of the community's attitude towards the LORD. It is probably significant that this material is added as an appendix to a chapter that has involved repeated references to the heart. Salvation is not a matter of legalistic observance of the Sabbath, and judgment does not ensue merely because details of the Sabbath law were breached. However, desecration of the Sabbath was an obvious and reliable indicator of the deep inner malaise affecting the people, namely, that they had no real regard for the requirements of the covenant and respect for their covenant Overlord. A similar focus on a related sabbatic command is found in 34:8-22. This prose passage reflects the style of other addresses elsewhere throughout the book, again probably because of its sermonic origin (v. 19).

1. Present Disobedience (17:19-23)

19. Since Jeremiah is required to stand at prominent parts of the city where he could be sure of getting an audience, it is more probable that this address was originally delivered during the reign of Josiah (or at the latest during the early years of Jehoiakim). During the earlier reign of Manasseh Sabbath observance had virtually died out in the land, and the people had to be reacquainted with the behaviour that should characterise true worshippers of the LORD. It is an appeal to be loyal to the covenant relationship and is shaped by covenant structures and concerns. **This is what the LORD said to me: 'Go and stand at the gate of the people[74], through which the kings of Judah go in and out.'** The 'gate of the people/sons of the people' ('common people' 26:23) is not otherwise identified in the Old Testament. It has been supposed that its use here by the kings of Judah, and also the phrase 'go in and out' (rather than 'out and in' as might be expected of a city gate), suggest a Temple gate used by the king and the people in general as opposed to the priests. The details of the courtyards surrounding Solomon's Temple are obscure. The 'great courtyard' (1 Kgs. 7:12) contained the palace and the Temple, with an inner courtyard that enclosed the sacred area with the Temple (1 Kgs. 6:36), which may be the same as the 'middle court' (2 Kgs. 20:4) and also equivalent to the 'large court' in the Chronicler's description (2 Chron. 4:9). The inner/middle courtyard had in turn within it, and adjacent to the Temple itself, the 'courtyard of the priests' (2 Chron. 4:9), which together with the middle courtyard constituted 'both courts of the temple of the LORD' (2 Kgs. 21:5; 23:12). Various gates (Pss. 24:7; 100:4; 118:19-20) permitted passage between the courtyards. The gate of the people probably gave access from the royal compound and the city in general into the middle courtyard. Only the priests would have been permitted to venture further. Though this courtyard would have been a place where many would gather, Jeremiah was to take further measures to publicise his message. **Stand also at all the other gates of Jerusalem.** Here the reference is to the gates into the city, and in particular to the areas of public activity just inside them. There too Jeremiah has to issue his challenge repeatedly, probably at the very sites where people engaged in much of the trading banned by the Sabbath commandment.

---

74. The kethibh lacks the article which the qere provides in *bənê-hāʿām*. The RSV and REB follow an emendation which lacks versional support to *binyāmîn*, 'Benjamin Gate', which although an otherwise known location (37:13; 38:7) would on that account be less likely to be confused.

20. The spiritual significance of Jeremiah's address is summed up in the word 'Hear'/'obey' (also in vv. 24 and 27). The focus is not on legalistic observance, but on willing acceptance of what the LORD requires. **Say to them, 'Hear the word of the LORD, O kings of Judah and all people of Judah and everyone living in Jerusalem who come through these gates.'** This command to the prophet is unusual in that it involves the 'kings of Judah', the plural perhaps being explained in terms of sons of the king being involved (see also 19:3; 20:5). This is an occasion when Jeremiah felt he had to address the king as well as the people. Kimchi suggested that this might be because the king had a special role in promoting Sabbath observance. The phrase 'everyone living in Jerusalem who come through these gates' suggests that the focus is more on the Temple gates, and the people are characterised as those who enter its precincts claiming to be worshipping the LORD. Ellison suggests that here we are dealing with a situation where 'those that came up for the Temple worship saw no reason for not combining business with their worship' (1962:25)—an attempt to have the best of both worlds as they saw it.

21. They are all solemnly warned. **This is what the LORD says: 'Be careful not to carry a load on the Sabbath day or bring it through the gates of Jerusalem.'** These are cited as two specific and blatant breaches of the commandment, probably in connection with the carrying out of business (Neh. 13:15-18). They were therefore also public breaches of the command. It is a matter of considerable significance. 'Be careful' probably requires a stronger translation. It is not merely, 'Take heed to yourselves' (NKJV), but because this unique expression uses the preposition *bə*, 'at' (rather than *lə*, 'with respect to') it is rather, 'Do not put your lives (<*nepeš*, 2:34) at risk' (REB), or 'For the sake of your lives, take care' (NRSV) (9:3; Deut. 4:15; Josh. 23:11). What they were doing revealed their attitude to the LORD. Infringing his rights and prerogatives was not something that should be done lightly or with the thought that it can occur with impunity. Mere profession of loyalty was insufficient. What was required was heart change that willingly conformed every aspect of an individual's life to the LORD's requirements.

22. The negatives used in this verse are emphatic, indicating permanent prohibitions. **Do not bring out a load out of your houses.** Part of the houses of craftsmen would be given over to their workshop. They would bring out into the street, or carry to the local market, items they wished to sell. 'Do not' **do any work on the Sabbath** is a citation from the Decalogue (Exod. 20:10; Deut. 5:14), as also is the following:

But keep the Sabbath day holy. By keeping it holy (<√*qādaš*, 1:5; 6:4) was meant setting it apart for the service of the LORD as a day sacred to him (Exod. 20:10; 31:5; 35:2; Lev. 24:8). This had been clearly set out at Sinai **as I commanded your forefathers** (cf. 11:4), and so the practice was one of longstanding and basic to the covenant constitution. As such, the people ought to have been careful to give attention to it. The reference to the LORD 'commanding' Sabbath observance may indicate that it is the form of the commandments found in Deuteronomy that lies behind this statement. Unlike Exodus, Deut. 5:12 has the phrase 'as the LORD your God has commanded you' and Deut. 5:15 ends, 'Therefore the LORD your God has commanded you to observe the Sabbath day.' The use of 'command' may relate to the need for direct revelation before the nature of this observance is obvious to fallen mankind.

23. While it is possible to take the divine speech as finishing with v. 22 and to read this verse as reporting the disobedience of Jeremiah's generation (= 'they') so that there then follows a second divine speech in vv. 24-27 (Lundbom 1999:804), the absence of a formal introduction in a prose passage indictates it is better to take vv. 20-27 as one address ('they' = Jeremiah's contemporaries). This verse is then part of the LORD's review of the history of Israel and Judah showing that former generations had had difficulty in obeying the command. **Yet they did not listen or pay attention; they were stiff-necked** (7:26) **and would not listen**[75] **or respond to discipline** (7:28). These phrases are frequently used in Jeremiah to indicate the spiritual insensitivity and rebellion of the people. The prevalence of such attitudes meant that this specific command was also treated lightly.

2. Obedience Rewarded (17:24-27)

The people are then reminded of the basic structure of the covenant: that obedience would be rewarded (vv. 24-26) but that disobedience would bring on them the curse of the broken covenant (v. 27).

24. The failure of their forefathers was one thing, but what was the present generation going to do? Covenant living is based on obedience to the requirements of the covenant Overlord. **But if you are careful to obey me**/'hearing you hear to me'**, declares the LORD, and bring no load through the gates of this city on the Sabbath, but keep the**

75. The kethibh *šwmʿ* cannot be intended to be a participle here. It seems to be a scribal error (for similar ones see 2:25; 8:6) for *šəmôaʿ*, the infinitive construct written plene.

Sabbath day holy by not doing any work on it.[76] The key to this statement is the need to obey the LORD. Sabbath keeping is not to be viewed as an impersonal, ritualistic observance. It may well convey general blessing in that it accords with the way in which humanity have been created, but as a source of spiritual blessing it is a matter of obeying 'me', a tribute paid out of personal loyalty and attachment to the LORD.

25. This is then followed by a description of threefold blessing, firstly involving the king, his officials and the people in general. **Then kings who sit on David's throne will come through the gates of this city with their officials.**[77] **They and their officials will come riding in chariots and on horses, accompanied by the men of Judah and those living in Jerusalem.** The picture is one of a prosperous, if not triumphant, procession involving all in the land. Jeremiah foresaw a role for the line of David if they kept the requirements of the covenant (23:5-6; 30:9; 33:15; cf. 2 Sam. 7). 'Kings' here (unlike v. 20) probably refers to a number of different kings who will repeat this scene on a variety of future occasions. The officials played a significant role in the administration of the land and became a key group during Zedekiah's reign, when they demanded Jeremiah's death (38:4). 'Chariots and horses' depicts a people not lacking in military resources. They were also symbols of royal pomp (1 Kgs. 4:26; Isa. 36:8). The whole scene contrasts with the arrival of the Messianic king (Zech. 9:9-10).

Secondly there is a promise of the continued existence of the capital city of Jerusalem itself. **And this city will be inhabited for ever.** Jeremiah genuinely wanted to see Jerusalem blessed. His struggle was with those who detached that blessing from covenant obedience and thought that it would be automatically provided by God, no matter how the city and its inhabitants conducted themselves. Here the people are being directed towards true loyalty to the LORD as the only route by which their desires for the future could be realised. See the similar promise made in 7:7.

26. The third picture is that of the population coming bringing

---

76. The kethibh *bh* could be either *bōh*, an old masculine form written with *he* rather than *waw*, or *bāh*, a feminine form. Either is possible as *šabbat* can be masculine or feminine. The qere has the masculine form *bô*.

77. The Hebrew text is 'kings and officials sitting', where 'officials' has often felt to be a dittography from later in the verse. But the NIV gives a rendering which is quite appropriate, where the main emphasis is on 'kings' and 'officials' are viewed as merely accompanying them. The REB and NRSV omit 'officials'.

sacrifices to the Temple. **People will come from the towns of Judah and the villages around Jerusalem, from the territory of Benjamin and the western foothills, from the hill country and the Negev.** From every part of the kingdom the people will voluntarily and wholeheartedly come to the Temple to worship. It is a scene of a general response, which is also found elsewhere (32:44; 33:13) in descriptions of restoration. What is being anticipated here is continued preservation of the nation in the land. Benjamin lay to the north of Jerusalem; the 'western foothills'/'Shephelah' were lower territory situated between the central mountainous region and the coastal plain; the hill country was the central part of the land to the south of Jerusalem; and the Negev was the bleaker region further south still. It is not just as an act of political allegiance, or for economic purposes that they go to the capital. It is specifically for worship that they come **bringing burnt offerings and sacrifices, grain offerings, incense and thank-offerings to the house of the LORD.** The terms are multiplied to convey the abundance and generosity of their offerings. For 'burnt offerings and sacrifices' see on 6:20. For 'grain offerings' see on 14:12: *minḥâ* which may elsewhere mean sacrifices in general is here used in its more specific sense alongside these other terms for sacrifice. 'Incense' is not the incense offering but the frankincense which was added to the cereal offering (Lev. 2:1, 2, 15, 16). For the thank-offering, see on Lev. 7:12-15. It is added as a final category, 'and bringing thank offerings' (NRSV), probably indicating personal offerings for blessings bestowed. Again there is no tension here with passages in which Jeremiah critiques current sacrificial worship (6:20; 7:21; 14:12). What is being envisaged is not a hypocritical offering of those whose lives testify to their rebellion against God, but the sincere worship of those whose desire is to 'obey me'.

27. But times of blessing and revival are not the only potential scenario. There is the distinct possibility of doom and disaster, and that will come about if there is continued disobedience to the LORD. Again it is a matter of fundamental heart loyalty, and the desire to please the LORD. **But if you do not obey me**/'hear to me' **to keep the Sabbath day holy by not carrying any load as you come through the gates of Jerusalem on the Sabbath day, then I will kindle an unquenchable fire** (7:20; 11:16) **in the gates of Jerusalem that will consume her fortresses** (6:5). A few short years and this warning came to pass. The behaviour of those who enter the gates of the city will determine the destiny of those very gates because the LORD will not permit his rights to be trampled on. It is significant that the passage assumes that there was still knowledge of, and some regard for, Sabbath observance.

The people knew what Jeremiah was talking about, but sadly they had no real respect for it. If they continued to focus on self and act in a spirit of self-reliance and self-promotion, then they would be disregarding the rights of God in their lives and would bring about the destruction of their community. The LORD and his covenant demand obedience.

VII. JEREMIAH AND THE POTTER

(18:1–20:18)

OUTLINE

A. Visiting the Potter's House (18:1-12)
   1. Reworking the Clay (18:1-4)
   2. The Divine Potter (18:5-12)

B. The Scattering of the Forgetful (18:13-17)

C. Responding to Attacks (18:18-23)
   1. Conspiracy against the Prophet (18:18)
   2. Awaiting Divine Intervention (18:19-23)

D. The Shattered Jar (19:1–20:6)
   1. Indictment in the Valley (19:1-5)
   2. Sentence Pronounced (19:6-9)
   3. The Smashed Nation (19:10-13)
   4. The Temple Sermon (19:14-15)
   5. Terror on Every Side (20:1-6)

E. The Shattered Prophet (20:7-18)
   1. From the Depths (20:7-13)
   2. An Accursed Day (20:14-18)

The material found in chapters 18–20 is tightly knit and thematically linked by the visit to the potter's workshop in chapter 18 and the breaking of the potter's jar in chapter 19. These two incidents may well have been separated by a number of years. Certainly the breaking of the jar and the consequences of that action fall in the early part of the reign of Jehoiakim, probably in the tense period around the battle of Carchemish (605 BC). By that period the official policy of the regime was no longer that of Josiah, and various religious corruptions had been permitted to re-emerge. Jeremiah's opposition to the consensus viewpoint brought physical persecution upon him, and this block of material, probably written up in the 'silent' years of the latter part of Jehoiakim's reign ends with Jeremiah's bleak reflections on his life and ministry (20:7-18). The date of the earlier incident in chapter 18 is much less certain. It is possible that 18:1-12 may have occurred as early as the closing years of Josiah's reign. The choice of which way to go was still before the people (as it was also at the time of the Temple Sermon of chaps. 7 and 26 which are to be located in the early part of Jehoiakim's reign), but as the remainder of the chapter records, this choice gradually vanished as the inner attitude of the people became ever more evident and official policy hardened against the prophet. It is thus possible to see 18:13-23 as a record of the deteriorating situation over a number of years in the initial period of Jehoiakim's reign.

A. VISITING THE POTTER'S HOUSE (18:1-12)

In this section we have an illustration from everyday life used by God to teach an important truth. It is not strictly a symbolic action carried out by Jeremiah himself, but a symbolic event (see the introduction to chap. 13) in which the prophet observes actions carried out by others, and which are given divine significance through the revelation he receives. Verses 1-4 set up the incident, and vv. 5-12 set out the divine explanation.

1. Reworking the Clay (18:1-4)

1. This is the word that came to Jeremiah from the LORD forms a title to the section 18:1–20:18, and is one that is common in Jeremiah (7:1; 11:1). Though it is in the third person, it precedes a clearly autobiographical section (note vv. 3, 5).

2. The first command to Jeremiah is 'Arise' (not translated in the NIV), indicating the urgency with which Jeremiah was to carry it out, rather than his posture when the LORD spoke to him. He is to obey straightaway (13:4): 'Go down now' (REB). **Go down to the potter's house.** 'Potter' (<√*yāṣar*, 'to shape, form', v. 6) renders a term which may also be used for craftsmen who make objects from wood or metal ('carved' Hab. 2:18; 'shapes' Isa. 44:12), but it is most often denotes those working in clay. 'Go down' raises questions as to where Jeremiah was when the command came. Probably, the word does not indicate that the prophet was at the highest part of Jerusalem when he received the message (i.e. at the Temple), but rather the fact that potters were to be found living in a lower section of the city, probably on the southern slopes down to the valley of Ben-Hinnom, where there would be an adequate water supply for their work, perhaps coming from the pool of Siloam or the Gihon Spring. The direction to go to the potter's *house* is not primarily concerned with visiting him at home but at his workshop, which would ordinarily be situated next to where he lived. **And there**[1] **I will give you my message**/'cause you to hear my words'. It is the divine word that will reveal the significance of what Jeremiah will see at the potter's.

3. Jeremiah records that he complied with the instructions the LORD gave him. **So I went down to the potter's house, and I saw him**[2] **working at the wheel.** Pottery was one of the major crafts of the ancient world. Clay was formed into vessels of many sorts which were used for carrying liquids and cooking, and the various techniques required to produce the finished article meant that being a potter was reckoned to be a highly skilled occupation. The wheel, literally 'the two stones' (*hā'obnāyim*, a dual form), was in earlier times formed by a horizontal upper stone with a protrusion on its lower surface which fitted into a socket on the top surface of a static lower stone. The traditional term 'stones' was retained even after the wheels were made of wood. By Jeremiah's time a revolving lower wheel of much larger circumference was used, attached to the upper platform by a wooden shaft. As the potter turned the lower wheel by foot, the upper stone at arm level spun much faster allowing the potter to shape the rotating clay into whatever type of vessel was required (King 1993:166-67). A second-century BC description of a potter's work was given by Ben Sira: 'So it is with the potter, sitting at his work, turning the wheel with his feet, always engrossed in the task of making up his tally of vessels; he moulds the clay with his arm, crouching forward to exert his

1. 'There' is *šāmmâ*, 'to there', but the ending lost its directional significance (GKC §90d).

2. The qere *wəhinnē' hû'* means the same as the kethibh *wəhinnēhû*, a form with a pronominal suffix not found elsewhere.

strength. He concentrates on finishing the glazing, and stays up to clean out the furnace' (Ecclus. 38:29-30, REB). Thomson described an eastern potter he encountered whose technique was virtually unchanged from biblical times. 'He had a heap of the prepared clay near him, and a pan of water by his side. Taking a lump in his hand, he placed it on top of the wheel (which revolves horizontally), and smoothed it into a low cone, like the upper end of a sugar loaf; then thrusting his thumb into the top of it, he opened a hole down through the centre, and this he constantly widened by pressing the edges of the revolving cone between his hands. As it enlarged and became thinner, he gave it whatever shape he pleased with the utmost ease and expedition' (1872:520).

4. But the pot he was shaping from the clay[3] **was marred** (13:7) **in his hands; so the potter formed it into another pot.** Although the NIV translation suggests Jeremiah saw just one pot being made, the verbs used indicate that he made quite a number of observations.[4] 'When the vessel which he was making was marred … he would make it again …' (cf. NJPS). As the potter worked, no matter that he was a craftsman of the highest skill, the lump of clay he was shaping under his hands would sometimes display an imperfection or inconsistency of material that would necessitate it being turned into a lump again and the work started afresh. It is not a picture of total rejection. The material is worked and reworked until what is there conforms to what the potter wants, **shaping it as seemed best to him.** 'Seemed best' usually refers to what is legally or ethically right, but here the expression denotes conformity to the standard that the potter wanted (Num. 23:27; 27:5). The potter was serious about the task he was engaged in; the clay was totally under his control; and only what matched up to his standards was approved.

2. The Divine Potter (18:5-12)

The lesson to be learned from the potter's actions is now spelled out. Verses 5-6 set out the basis for the comparison between the LORD and the potter; vv. 7-10 give the two-sided implications of the situation; v. 11 contains an exhortation from the LORD to the people; and v. 12

3. Literally, 'in clay' (*baḥōmer*). Some Hebrew manuscripts read *kaḥōmer*, 'like clay'; 'as clay sometimes will' (Bright 1965:121); 'now and then' (REB); 'as happens to clay' (NJPS). The phrase is omitted in the LXX.

4. *wənišḥat*, 'was marred', and *wəšāb*, 'did again', are *waw*-consecutive perfects, presumably with a frequentative force after the participle 'working'/ 'making' (GKC §112e).

indicates that no matter how vividly the possibilities are presented, the outcome to be anticipated is that the people will reject the divine word and wilfully determine to carry on with their own plans.

5-6. As Jeremiah watched the potter working and reworking his material, he came to perceive the significance of the scene through divine revelation. **Then the word of the LORD came to me.** It was a word not primarily directed to the prophet, but through him to the people of the LORD. **'O house of Israel, can I not do with you as this potter does?' declares the LORD** is an address to the covenant community of Israel, at this time represented by the people of the southern kingdom of Judah. This rhetorical question emphasises that the LORD (the potter) has the power and determination to work out his purposes for the people (the clay) whom he has chosen. **Like clay in the hand of the potter, so are you in my hand, O house of Israel** asserts his sovereign control over them. 'Potter' recalls the use of the root *yāṣar* to indicate the creative power and activity of God, the one who 'formed'/moulded man and the animals when he first gave them existence (Gen. 2:7-8, 19; Isa. 29:16; 45:9; 64:8). It is also used in 1:5 of the way God controlled Jeremiah's formation in his mother's womb. God was saying to his people, 'I am in control; and what is more if you do not match up to what I want, I have the right and the power to sweep away all that I have given to you so far and to start again from scratch.'

Thompson seems unnecessarily restrictive in his application of the illustration. 'The particular clay that lay on the wheel at the time was not suitable for the vessel the potter had designed, that is, the quality of the clay determined what the potter could do with it. He could make something else from the same clay, but not the particular vessel he had hoped for. The clay could thus frustrate the potter's original intention and cause him to change it. Yahweh the potter was dealing with a clay that was resistant to his purpose. The quality of the people in some way determined what God might do with them' (1980:433). But this is to confuse illustration with reality. The clay the LORD uses is not some chance find, but his own creation. The parable of the potter does not present a picture of divine frustration and compromise. It is an uncompromising assertion of the sovereign, authoritative control of God. He is in charge: not just theoretically in charge, but actually, really governing what goes on here on earth, and what he produces matches exactly what he intends. Furthermore he is completely in control of the processes he employs in achieving his purpose.

7-8. There is no getting away from the divine sovereignty and control portrayed here, but it is important to recognise that it is a sovereignty that is exercised in a situation that God himself has set up. Divine sovereignty is not heavenly tyranny. God has created mankind so that there may be an intelligent and rational interaction between heaven and earth, and so he uses suasion, pleading with his people even though they are in rebellion against him. The illustration of the potter cannot say it all, for what potter ever went on to explain to the clay what he was doing and to call for a reply (v. 11b)? But God does that in seeking a reasoned and discerning response to what he presents to mankind. Though they act contrary to his stated will, God is prepared in long-suffering to lead them to repentance so that his people will willingly conform to what he desires (Rom. 9:21; 11:26).

Two hypothetical sets of circumstances bring out the divine scope for shaping as seems best to him the nations with whom he deals. Verses 7-8 and vv. 9-10 obviously present a balancing pair. Both statements are introduced by the word *regaʿ*, which is frequently used in the Old Testament to mean 'instantly, immediately, or suddenly' (cf. 4:20) and hence the translations found in the AV and NKJV. But it is not easy to relate that meaning to the context here, and it is better to take them as used correlatively, 'at one time … at another time'. The first situation that is envisaged is one of divine warning of impending disaster. **If at any time I announce that a nation or kingdom is to be uprooted, torn down and destroyed.** These verbs are those found in the initial statement of Jeremiah's ministry (1:10). They depict divine judgment on a nation, not as some arbitrary imposition, but as the consequence of their behaviour. Although phrased in general terms, what is in view is primarily the LORD's covenant relationship with Israel, in which enjoyment of covenant blessing is conditioned on covenant obedience. Here the threat is the removal of blessing in the light of disobedience, but as v. 8 continues **and if that nation I warned repents** (<√*šûb*) **of its evil** (*rāʿâ*) it reveals the divine word as a genuine warning. The outcome depends on the response given to the message by its hearers. They are being called to abandon their wicked rebellion against their covenant king. **Then I will relent** uses the verb *nāḥam* (niphal; 4:28), which in human terms denotes that change of mind associated with repentance, but in the divine sphere it relates to that changed attitude of God which occurs when the behaviour of mankind changes. The penalty he had said he would impose is revoked because those who were cautioned have heeded the warning given to them and turned away from their evil. **And not inflict the disaster I had planned.** Again we find the play on the word *rāʿâ*, covering both the moral evil of their rebellion and the disaster that is the consequence of that evil (1:16). 'Planned' (<√*ḥāšab*, 'to consider, devise, reckon'; cf. vv. 11 and 18) relates to the action that the LORD had reckoned matched the course of conduct they were following. If it is appropriate to continue the analogy of the potter, then the clay on the wheel which had not been turning out as the potter wished and which he therefore decided to discard and turn back into a lump has at last yielded to the potter's touch (divine warnings) and will not be subject to the reshaping judgment he was going to impose on it but instead experience divine blessing. This is an anticipation of what is spelled out more fully in the New Covenant promise (31:31-34).

9-10. On the other hand, the divine word of blessing does not unconditionally guarantee good. The recipients of the promise must exhibit an appropriate response. **And if at another time I announce that a nation or kingdom is to be built up and planted** (again notice the vocabulary is that of 1:10), still that nation cannot go on its way heedless. **And if it does evil**[5] **in my sight and does not obey me, then I will reconsider** (<√*nāḥam* niphal, 'to relent', v. 8) **the good I had intended** (<√*ʾāmar*, 'to say', or 'to say within oneself', 'to think') **to do for it.** God will revoke what he announced regarding blessing for that nation since it has now renounced its loyalty to him. The people had to grasp that there is no guaranteed connection between previous enjoyment of divine blessing, or awareness of divine promises, and future blessing unless there is ongoing obedience. If the people are recalcitrant, then the divine potter will be responsive to the way they are shaping up and, if need be, will undo the good he has already bestowed on the nation and leave aside the blessing, starting out all over again until what is found conforms to what he wants.

11. The application for Jeremiah's contemporaries was obvious. In *wəʿattâ*, **now therefore**, *ʿattâ*, 'now', can indicate either time or consequence: here it is used to indicate the conclusion of the argument. **Say**/'please say' **to the people of Judah and those living in Jerusalem** asks in polite but definite tones that this message be conveyed by Jeremiah to warn the citizens of the southern kingdom regarding what the LORD has in store for them. **This is what the LORD says: 'Look! I am preparing a disaster for you.'** 'Preparing'/'moulding' (<√*yāṣar*)

5. The qere *hāraʿ*, 'the evil', and the kethibh *hārāʿâ* are respectively the masculine and feminine of the same word. Perhaps the qere is to be followed here as being the usual form with *ʿāśâ*, and the less usual in this context (note *rāʿâ* occurs in v. 8 and v. 11). The feminine *haṭṭôbâ*, 'the good', is used in apposition in this verse and this may have led to an original masculine form being changed to a feminine as in the kethibh.

renders the same root as has been used in 'potter' (v. 2). The LORD creates judgments in history that are consonant with the evil that people have done so that they reap what they have sown (Gal. 6:7-8); disaster is again the response to their disastrous conduct. **And devising a plan against you** with its double use of the root *ḥāšab*, 'to devise', picks up the idea of what the LORD had planned in v. 8. The noun, *maḥăšābâ*, 'plan', which often stands as a cognate accusative after the verb, may be used to express the ingenuity of one's plans (11:19). The injunction is then to turn in repentance. **So turn** (<√*šûb*, followed by the precative particle indicating a polite but definite request) **from your evil ways, each one of you, and reform your ways and your actions.** They are again called on to 'reform'/'make good' (7:3) their paths, that is, their actions and lifestyle. This was to apply not just to national policy and the rituals of the Temple, but at the level of their individual personal conduct which had to conform to the requirements of their covenant king.

12. However, there is added a sorry appendix: **But they will reply**[6], **'It is no use!'** Their reply begins with the same word as is found in 2:25. This might indicate the self-despair of the people as they hear the message of the prophet, but that seems to involve too great a degree of spiritual responsiveness on the part of Jeremiah's audience. The LORD is alerting his prophet that no matter how vividly he sets before the people the disastrous implications of their behaviour, he is not to expect much by way of response. Over against the LORD's statement of intent, they have their own plans and will not be prepared to abandon them because in their spiritual obstinacy they have become inured to doing evil. So they defiantly tell Jeremiah that it is no use for him to speak to them in the way he has, and they dismiss him and his warnings, preferring their own ideas about how they are going to live. **We will continue**/'walk' **with our own plans; each of us will follow the stubbornness of his evil heart.** The words put on their lips as they write off the LORD's plans as irrelevant reflect the LORD's assessment of their attitude, not their own, unless they are presented as sarcastically mocking what the prophet had said to them. For 'stubbornness of his evil heart' see on 3:17; the phrase is used in connection with inclinations/plans in 7:24. 'Each' (rendering *'îš*, 'man', used distributively) shows that their response was as inclusive as the invitation had

---

6. The verb *wə'āmərû* is *waw*-consecutive perfect, and this seems to rule out the past tense rendering 'They said' (NKJV), unless following the LXX one inserts a yodh to read *wayy'ōmərû*, 'and they said'. The NRSV understands the verb as the report of an actual, not an anticipated, response.

been (v. 11). What then can be expected as the divine reaction? There comes a time when there will be no more appeals to repent.

Mankind is here compared to clay that has some fault in it, and it is easy to see that that flaw is the evil which taints all our desires and actions. Those who refuse to respond to the divine potter's touch (his message to repent) will repeat the downward spiral that Judah here displays. In v. 12 they tell the prophet to go away and not bother them any more. By v. 18 they are making plans against him. They are not just going to ignore him; they are going to malign him and undermine his credibility. By v. 23 we are being told of all their plots to kill the prophet. The outworking of the plans of the evil heart leads to individuals and nations becoming more and more enmeshed in sin.

This presentation also has a hopeful aspect in that it is still not too late to change. Once the clay has been fired in the oven, the situation is irreversible since then the only way to change its shape and destiny is to smash it. That is portrayed in chapter 19 when Jeremiah buys a clay jar and breaks it, but that is not the picture here. The rejected clay is still pliable, and by the potter's skill may be recycled and reworked. The people were being urged to submit to the touch of the potter. Uncomfortable though it would be, they should give up their own ways and accept his, so that he might take the marred vessel and start all over again with it to make something suitable.

The metaphor of the potter and the clay is one that is employed on a number of occasions in Scripture. Isaiah used it in countering the complaints of Israel over the way in which God was bringing them salvation. He presented the argument that just as the clay has no right to demand an explanation from the potter of what he is doing, so too Israel must let God sovereignly work out his plans for them as he sees best (Isa. 45:9-10). Paul uses the analogy of the people of God as jars of clay in a more positive way, to show that their achievements are the result of divine power not human resources (2 Cor. 4:7).

B. THE SCATTERING OF THE FORGETFUL (18:13-17)

After the prose narrative of vv. 1-12 there follows a section in poetry which functions as a judgment speech against the attitudes displayed in v. 12. The prophet's announcement had been one of proposed disaster on the nation if they did not amend their ways. The matter was still open, though it was anticipated that the response would be negative. Probably after some time elapsed, it became clear that the people had reacted as predicted and had again rejected the prophet's warning.

13. Therefore (*lākēn*) **this is what the LORD says** introduces a message of judgment, which is not fully spelled out until v. 16. First, in a manner reminiscent of 2:10-13, there is further reflection regarding the startling intransigence of Israel in not responding to the LORD's entreaties with them. The invitation given, **Enquire among the nations**, is a plural request, addressed to any among the people who cared to respond to the challenge. **Who has ever heard anything like this?** The rhetorical question implies that no matter where the search is made the answer that is returned will be negative because the situation is without parallel. Even among the heathen nations there were none who had so abused the privileges granted them and remained obdurate when entreated by their god in such a way as this.

A most horrible thing has been done by Virgin Israel. 'A most horrible thing' (*šaʿărûrit*, another form of the word found in 5:30 and 23:14) describes conduct that is morally defiled (Hos. 6:10) and repulsive. The identity of the perpetrator is dramatically delayed. 'Virgin' (*bətûlâ*, cf. 14:17) describes a 'girl under the guardianship of her father' (*NIDOTTE* 1:781), so she is still living as part of her father's household and of good repute. 'Virgin Israel'[7] pictures the covenant people as still living in the LORD's land, but what is said of them means that they have lost their good reputation by their shockingly unfaithful conduct (14:17; Isa. 1:8). Inevitably then their breaches of the covenant bond have imposed severe strains on their relationship with the LORD, and they have forfeited their right to remain in the land he had provided for them. The situation they are in is not one that the LORD will permit to continue indefinitely.

14. Two rhetorical questions are asked to emphasise the constancy of natural phenomena. **Does the snow of Lebanon ever vanish from its rocky slopes?**[8] 'Vanish' translates a form of the verb *ʿāzab*, 'to forsake' (2:13), which is used to make clear a pointed comparison with Israel. Perhaps the addition of 'ever' is unfortunate, in that it raises questions as to whether or not there is any period during the year when the snow melts on the high mountains of Lebanon. To this different answers have been given. The illustration is, however, just as valid if it

---

7. The translation 'virgin of Israel' (NKJV) misunderstands the nature of the construct chain. It is a 'genitive of association', indicating that Israel viewed as an individual belongs to the class 'virgin' (*IBHS* §9.5.3h).

8. The MT has *śāday*, 'my fields', but many now associate the word with an Akkadian root *šadu*, 'mountains', and so come to a translation such as 'mountain crags' or 'rocky slopes'. Others take *śāday* as a scribal error for *śiryôn*, the ancient name of Hermon, thus the NRSV.

is taken as indicating the constancy of the annual snowfall on Lebanon's heights. Indeed, the name Lebanon describes it as the white or snowy one. The people's conduct should match the snow of Lebanon in its predictability.

As regards the second question the NIV footnote admits, 'The meaning of the Hebrew for this sentence is uncertain.' **Do its cool waters from distant sources ever cease[9] to flow?** takes the reference to be to the same area. 'From distant sources' (<√*zûr*, 'to be a stranger') is rendered 'strange waters' in NKJV, but there does not seem to be any reference to the waters as being foreign or pagan (2:25). The melting of the snow of Lebanon causes the perennial flowing of its streams, which, being refreshingly 'cool' (<√*qārar*, hiphil 'to be cold'), readily slake one's thirst (Song of S. 4:15). In the same way God's gracious provision for Israel was dependable and invigorating, quite different from what was supplied by inconstant and unpredictable false gods (2:28; cf. also 2:13).

15. Over against the reliability of the phenomena of nature has to be set the unreliability and inexplicability of Israel's response. **Yet** (*kî*, 'for', probably 'No, but' because the preceding questions expect a strong negative response) **my people have forgotten me.** 'My people' picks up the theme of the covenant bond from v. 13, and also stresses that they were the very ones who should not have forgotten the LORD (2:32). **They burn incense** (1:16) **to a worthless idols** (*šāwʾ*), literally 'to a vain thing', perhaps here a reference to Baal (2:30), **which made them stumble[10] in their ways and in the ancient paths.** The people are led astray by the influence of idol worship so that they are no longer able to walk properly in the ancient paths[11] (6:16) which the LORD had appointed for his people. Instead, their lives are now

9. The niphal form *yinnātəšû* comes from the root *ntš*, 'to root up, pluck up', so a literal translation would be, 'foreign waters are plucked up'. This is generally reckoned to be corrupt. Transposing the final two consonants yields the root *nāšat*, 'to dry up', as in the NIV. Alternatively changing the second root letter yields *nāṭaš*, 'to abandon, forsake' (NJPS).

10. For the hiphil *wayyakšilûm*, the NRSV, following the LXX, reads a qal verb without the suffix *wayyikšəlû*, 'and they [that is, the people] stumbled'. It is better to retain the hiphil 'cause to stumble' and explain the plural subject as arising from the multitude of idols collectively referred to as *šāwʾ*, 'worthless [thing]'.

11. Thompson (1980:438) suggests that the translation should be 'the way of wisdom', taking the noun *ʿôlām*, 'long time, duration', from a root *ʿlm* found in Arabic and Ugaritic with the meaning 'knowledge, wisdom'.

characterised by moral and spiritual stumbling (6:21). The same imagery is pursued further: it is not just a matter of difficulty in the right way; it is being off the proper road entirely. **They made them walk in bypaths** (*nətîbâ*, a path not constructed as a proper roadway), **and on roads not built up.** They are no longer on the highway of covenant blessing which had been clearly set out in the law. Having substituted pagan lifestyles for that of the covenant, they have made the going hard for themselves, and they will not reach the destination they hoped for. This pictures a society that is unable to function properly because it has rejected the moral and spiritual norms set out by the LORD in the covenant.

16. Further consequences of their deluded association with idolatry are then spelled out (in terms similar to 19:8). Religious apostasy is not just a matter of personal choice, but of national disaster. **Their land will be laid waste, an object of lasting scorn.**[12] Or rather, 'to make their land a desolation, an object of lasting scorn'. This is the outcome the people bring on themselves when they depart from the right road through their involvement in idolatrous cults. 'Waste'/'desolation' (*šammâ*, 2:15) here clearly focuses on the horrified reaction of those who see the ruin of the land. 'An object of lasting scorn'/'a thing to be hissed at for ever' (NRSV) points to the derision that will be heaped on it by those who pass through it. The noise made in such situations differs between cultures, and the precise sound or gesture indicated by the Hebrew word is uncertain, possibly a jeering whistle or else a sharp intake of breath with hissing through the teeth (McKane 1986, 1:434), but there is no doubt that it denotes contempt and disparagement. A notable feature of the verse in the original is the repetition of s-sounds to emphasise the gesture being described. **All who pass by will be appalled and will shake**[13] **their heads.**[14] 'Be appalled' (<√*šāmam*, 2:12) points to inner numbness at the tragedy before them, which is accompanied by a gesture of profound agitation. 'Shake the head' (<√*nûd*, 15:5) can be used in situations of mourning, but here it

12. *šərîqōt*, 'object of scorn' indicates 'hissing, whistling' (Judg. 5:16). The qere would be an intensive plural; the kethibh is *šərûqat*, a singular form of similar meaning (cf. 19:8).

13. The verb *wəyānîd*, 'and will shake', has an ordinary *waw* before an imperfect. Either the two ideas are co-ordinated as two aspects of the one phenomenon, or else the second is represented as the consequence of the first, 'they are so appalled that they shake their heads'.

14. *bərōʾšô*, 'with his head', *beth* of instrument, an idiomatic use (GKC §119q).

denotes a reaction of wonder and horror at the destruction they are witnessing.

17. Like a wind from the east describes the sirocco, a dry, scorching wind that comes off the desert and wreaks havoc with the crops and vegetation of the land (cf. 4:11; 13:24). The Babylonian invaders are described in similar terms because their coming will devastate the land. But in this they would be the instruments of the LORD's judgment, for he is the one who says, **I will scatter them before their enemies.** Because of the offence the LORD's people have given to him by their embroilment in idolatry, he announces, **I will show them**[15] **my back and not my face.** The attitude of turning one's back on someone was a gesture of displeasure with their conduct, and of estrangement from them, no longer having a desire to associate with them or be in their company. Elsewhere Israel's apostasy is described as turning the back or neck (2:27; 32:33), but here it is used ironically to describe the LORD's reaction to them. This will take place **in the day of their disaster.** 'Day of disaster' (46:21; 48:16; 49:8, 32) is an old phrase (Deut. 32:35) for the time when the LORD's devastating judgment is experienced.

C. RESPONDING TO ATTACKS (18:18-23)

Jeremiah then relates the developing reaction of the people to his message recorded in vv. 1-12 and in vv. 13-17. Their response was quite the reverse of what the prophet had hoped for (v. 18), and this again drove him to set the situation before the LORD (vv. 19-23) in another of his Confessions (see on 11:18). As in 17:14-18, there is no record of any direct reply to Jeremiah's petition, though it may be that chapter 19 is intended to function as the LORD's response.

1. Conspiracy against the Prophet (18:18)

18. They said, 'Come, let's make plans (a cohortative expressing self-encouragement, GKC §108b) **against Jeremiah'** picks up the idea of Yahweh's plan ('I had planned' [<*ḥāšab*, v. 8] and 'devising a plan' [<*ḥāšab*, v. 11] and the counter-resolution of v. 12, 'we will continue with our own plans', again using the root *ḥāšab*. The speakers are not identified but would seem not to be the people as a whole (contrast

15. The Massoretic Text is *ʾerʾēm*, the qal, 'I will look at them'. But the Oriental text tradition, as well as the LXX, Syriac, and Vulgate, have renderings corresponding to the hiphil *ʾarʾem*, 'I will cause them to see'.

v. 12) but an influential group seeking to sway the community against the prophet. There are parallels in the way in which those opposed to Christ plotted against him (Matt. 12:14; 27:1; Mark 3:6; Luke 6:11). Jeremiah records what his enemies were saying, but we do not know how he got this information. The reason they give for their action is **for** (*kî*) **the teaching of the law by the priest will not be lost, nor will counsel from the wise, nor the word from the prophets.** Three groups in society are named from whom advice and counsel could be expected (8:8-10; Ezek. 7:26). In connection with each group the characteristic substance of their speech is mentioned. In many respects this division is reflected in the threefold canonical division of the Hebrew Old Testament, but the holders of these offices in Jeremiah's day were engaged in flawed ministries.

(1) The priestly office was focused on the law (*tôrâ*). This was not limited merely to the details of the ceremonial law. Priests were charged with a responsibility for communicating the whole covenant teaching of God (Lev. 10:9-11; Deut. 33:8-10; Mal. 2:1-9). As we have seen, the priests were largely a failed group in Jerusalem, being more concerned with propping up the existing political power structure so as to ensure continuing maintenance for themselves than with promoting the whole counsel of God. (2) Although *NIDOTTE* 2:491 claims that the root *yāʿaṣ* (from which the word 'counsel' is derived) does not have special connections with a well-defined wisdom tradition or with a particular social group but is simply a word for 'advice', 'counsellor' is a word associated with court circles, and the king would call on 'wise men'/'experts' to give practical advice in particular circumstances. 'The wise' were the administrative elite of the kingdom (9:23), and the speakers here are sure of their political sagacity. But whether theirs was true wisdom or not depended on the extent to which they were in a right relationship with the LORD. To offer the king counsel was in effect a claim to be able to discern God's providential purpose in events (Jones 1992:262). But all too often royal counsellors disregarded the vertical dimension in the life of the covenant people and relied on political and military alliances rather than faithfulness to the LORD. (3) Of the third group mentioned, the prophets, we shall hear much more before the book is finished (23:9-40; chaps. 27–29). 'Prophets' were those whose task was to receive and relay the message of the LORD for the particular circumstances, but the peace prophets courted popularity, and proclaimed their own message not one they had received from the LORD.

In Jerusalem in Jeremiah's day these three groups were united in supporting the royal establishment and, promoting a flawed theology, were intent on declaring the inviolable security and God-given prosperity of David's throne and David's city. The message of Jeremiah cut across their presuppositions and challenged the consensus they had established. The opinion formers of the day, confident of the wisdom and sagacity of the leaders of the community, turned on Jeremiah and sought to undermine him. In itself this testifies to the intolerant tyranny a majority often imposes, but it may also point to troubled consciences. Why all this fuss over one man if his words did not ring true? Why the desire to suppress the testimony of one individual if the majority themselves did not harbour unexpressed doubts about the prevailing ideology?

It is to be noted that killing Jeremiah is not directly stated as a policy option in v. 18. The first ploy is, **So come, let's attack him with our tongues.** 'Striking with the tongue' denotes slanderous and malicious speech (9:2, 4, 7; Pss. 59:7; 64:3-6). This seems to be the thinking of a group within society rather than the society as a whole because they are going to conduct a propaganda campaign against Jeremiah so that he is discredited in public esteem ('Ought we really to trust someone like that? Surely there's no smoke without a fire.') and his message does not spread gloom and disaffection among the people in general. Perhaps the 'spin' they would put on the situation was just a matter of starting rumours about him. Possibly their strategy involved proceedings against Jeremiah on the basis of false charges; 'Let us invent some charges against him' (REB; cf. NRSV). It may be that the outcome of this sort of thinking is to be found in 20:1-3 where Pashhur takes action against Jeremiah. The conspirators' resolution, **And pay no attention** (*qāšab* hiphil) **to anything he says**, shows that rather than enter into frank discussion with Jeremiah—that might further unsettle the equilibrium of the community and expose flaws in the establishment facade—they felt it more politically expedient to malign the prophet and to treat him dismissively.

2. Awaiting Divine Intervention (18:19-23)

Jeremiah then sets out before the LORD his petition in these circumstances. He asks for a hearing (v. 19), indicates the inequity of what his opponents are doing (v. 20a), recalls his own actions (v. 20b), and then requests divine intervention (vv. 21-23). The prophet does not here engage in angry complaint against the LORD, but waits with patience for the intervention of his divine Overlord.

19. The plea Jeremiah utters, **Listen to me, O LORD,** repeats the same root (*qāšab* hiphil) as was used in 'pay ... attention' (v. 18). Since his adversaries were adopting a policy of ignoring him, Jeremiah turns in confidence to the LORD who had commissioned him, knowing that he would be ready to listen to his servant. He presents the attitudes and speech of his opponents as a reason why the LORD should act on his behalf. **Hear what my accusers are saying!**[16] 'Accusers' (<√*rîb*, 2:9) presents them as quarrelling with Jeremiah and acting out of a sense of grievance against him. Possibly they were seeking to build up a case against him. But Jeremiah is eager that the matter be heard by the judge who is in control of all.

20. Jeremiah pleads with the LORD, **Should good be repaid with evil?** This was a frequent complaint in the Psalms (Pss. 35:12; 38:20; 109:5). 'Repay' (<√*šālēm* pual, 'to requite, make restitution') shows Jeremiah had no doubt that his own conduct had been motivated by a right attitude. Later in the verse he spells out how he had acted on their behalf. But though he had spoken with the desire to benefit them, **yet they have dug a pit for me**/'myself' (<*nepeš*, 2:34)**.** This is a common metaphor for plotting to do someone harm, drawing on the actions of a hunter as he digs a hole in the ground and covers it so that an animal may be trapped and slain (Ps. 7:16). Their attitude towards Jeremiah was one of such hostility that they were determined to get rid of him by taking action against him as if he were a dangerous beast. There is no information to enable us to be more specific about what this trap consisted of, though later Jeremiah would be incarcerated in such a hole in the ground (37:16; 38:6).

Remember that I stood before you and spoke on their behalf to turn your wrath away from them. This recalls earlier incidents in Jeremiah's career such as 14:7-9, 13, 19-22, when he had interceded with the LORD on behalf of the people. Note the use of 'stand' here and in 15:1 to denote being in attendance on a king and waiting to do his will. One who stood had access at court, and was thus able to act as an intercessor with the king. Jeremiah did not wish to see the wrath of the LORD's judgment poured out on his people, and so he had spoken to try to avert this. Against that background 'they' is naturally taken as a reference to the people as a whole, but it is possible that in this context the focus is principally on those leading the opposition to the prophet. One might compare the way the unidentified 'they' of 6:11-12 comprises both a core group of community leaders (6:13) as well as the people as a whole. It is significant that this was what Jeremiah was remembered for in later Judaism, where he is described as 'a man who

---

16. The RSV (cf. NJPS footnote) emends *yərîbāy* 'my accusers' to *rîbî*, 'my plea', 'my case', following the LXX. The change is unnecessary.

loves the family of Israel and prays much for the people and the holy city' (2 Macc. 15:14 NRSV).

21. Earlier Jeremiah had interceded for the people, but now his outlook has changed. Their persistent rejection of his message has brought him to realise that there is no point in pleading with them, and he asks the LORD to pour out on them the judgment he has already said he would bring on the land. These are the words of a man recording his very human emotions. Unlike the imprecatory psalms which were part of the divinely given liturgy of ancient Israel, this is a record of the prophet's own thinking, and is not necessarily presented as normative. The interpreter is called on to evaluate Jeremiah's statements in the light of the total testimony of Scripture, and many have felt it would have been better had these words not been uttered.

> The prophet seems here to have been driven through indignation to utter imprecations which are not consistent with a right feeling; for even if Christ had not said with his own mouth, that we are to pray for those who curse us, the very law of God, ever known to the holy fathers, was sufficient. Jeremiah then ought not to have uttered these curses, and to have imprecated final destruction on his enemies, though they fully deserved it. (Calvin 1850, 2:423)

Even so, it would be wrong to treat this as a mere fit of pique and spite on the part of the prophet. Jeremiah, like Jonah before him, thought that he did well to be angry (Jon. 4:9)—and perhaps with more reason. Having personally engaged in such a ministry for many years, Jeremiah realised that all that could be said or done to induce the people to change had been said and done. So he is not speaking rashly or impatiently, but as the LORD's spokesman he did not doubt that the LORD's judgment was just, and no longer could he find any grounds for asking for it to be withheld. What the prophet did was to request that God's own words be fulfilled. 'It is therefore misleading to contrast the "forgive not" of v. 23 with the "Father, forgive them" of the crucifixion, without a serious attempt to understand the context and the motive' (Jones 1992:264).

The disasters that are envisaged are distributed over four groups which take in the whole community. **So** (*lākēn*, 'therefore' of judgment) **give their children over to famine; hand them over** (<√*nāgar* hiphil, 'to pour out/down'; used several times in the context of judgment, 2 Sam. 14:14; Job 20:28; Ps. 75:8; Mic. 1:4) **to the power of the sword** (cf. Ezek. 35:5; Ps. 63:10). The 'sword' refers to the armies of their enemies who will have it within their control to put them to death. **Let their wives be made childless and widows.** This particularly envisages the death of males in war, leaving families without fathers and mothers without children or husbands. **Let their men be put to death.** 'Be put to death' (<√*hārag*, 'to slay') generally refers to a violent death. In 'death' the REB and NRSV find a reference specifically to the impact of pestilence as in 15:2. **Their young men slain by the sword in battle.** In saying this, Jeremiah is appealing to a higher authority to obtain redress and justice.

22. Their fate is then more particularly described in terms of invasion. **Let a cry** (<√*zāʿaq*, 11:11; here a cry of distress) **be heard from their houses when** (*kî*, quite possibly 'for') **you suddenly bring invaders against them.** The invasion is seen as principally directed against those who have derided and threatened the LORD's servant. **For** (*kî*) **they have dug a pit**[17] **to capture me and have hidden snares for my feet.** 'Snares' often refers to a fowler's net for trapping birds (Pss. 140:5; 142:3), but the term is used here of something more substantial to capture an unsuspecting animal.

23. In his threatened situation the prophet finds comfort in the realisation that these matters have not been concealed from God. **But you** (emphatic) **know, O LORD, all their plots to kill me**/'for death'. He already had had experience of the LORD's knowledge of plots against him (11:18). Indeed the reference might be to the events recorded there and also in chapter 26, which are to be dated around this time. 'Plots'/'counsel'/'plotting' is a different word from 'plans' (v. 18), being the same as 'counsel' of the wise in that verse. This is what worldly wisdom eventually aimed at—the death of the prophet. It is not clear how often Jeremiah was their target, but 'know' points to God's familiarity with all that they were doing, and Jeremiah draws encouragement from the fact of divine awareness (12:3; 15:15).

Even so it is often argued that Jeremiah's final prayer is an unworthy response to this situation. **Do not forgive their crimes** (*ʿāwōn*, 2:22) **or blot out**[18] **their sins from your sight.** 'Forgive' (<√*kāpar* piel, 'to make atonement, remove guilt') introduces a concept that lay at the heart of the sacrificial worship of Israel. Various views have been put forward as to the fundamental significance of the root *kpr*, including a covering over of sin, or a ransoming from the consequences of sin by paying an appropriate price. A third view that *kpr* signifies a wiping clean, a purging of the effects of sin, receives

17. The qere is *šûḥâ*, 'pit' (used literally in 2:6), which is also found in many manuscripts, and is the same form as in v. 20. The kethibh would be *šîḥâ*, which may have the same meaning.

18. The form *temḥî* is unusual. It may reflect an Aramaic-style alternative for *temaḥ* (GKC §75ii).

significant support from this verse where *kpr* is found in parallelism with *māḥah*, 'to wipe'; NIV 'to blot out'. This root is used for making erasures in leather scrolls which would be done by washing or sponging off the ink rather than blotting (TWOT #1178). Jeremiah does not wish the LORD to provide them with any escape from the consequences of their sin. Such a prayer is found elsewhere in the Old Testament, though it is not common (Neh. 4:5; Ps. 109:14). **Let them be**[19] **overthrown before you; deal with them in the time of your anger.** 'Be overthrown'/'made to stumble' (6:15, 21) points to their ruin.

There would come a point when the time of gracious pleading with the intransigent would come to an end. Jeremiah confidently expects his adversaries to be dealt with in the ensuing time of the outpouring of divine anger. It may be that Jeremiah is here calling into effect the curses of the covenant. He sees himself as one who is loyal to the LORD and therefore deserving of his protection against those who unjustly oppose him. He has exposed the inequity of their action, and from a position of personal helplessness commits his cause to the LORD to intervene and rectify the situation.

D. THE SHATTERED JAR (19:1-20:6)

The pottery theme of chapter 18 is continued in 19:1–20:6 which constitute a continuous prose narrative concerning an incident with a shattered clay jar. In that v. 1 envisages no difficulties in Jeremiah being able to gather a group of influential people from Jerusalem this indicates the incident occurred before the hostility of the upper classes was visible, or at any rate entrenched. Equally Jeremiah has access to the Temple, which he does not in 36:5, a passage to be dated in 605/604 BC. On the other hand the incident of 20:1-6 is obviously later than Josiah's reign, because he would not have countenanced such mistreatment of the prophet. Further, the mention of the king of Babylon in 20:4 indicates a time after Nebuchadnezzar's victory at Carchemish. Whereas Pashhur is here the chief officer of the Temple (20:1), in 29:26 another person, Zephaniah the son of Masseiah, holds that post. As chapter 29 is to be dated after the 597 BC invasion by Nebuchadnezzar, the prophecy against Pashhur (20:6) had come true and he had been deported. It thus is reasonable to place this incident in the middle of Jehoiakim's reign, probably after the battle of

19. The kethibh *wəhāyû* is a *waw*-consecutive perfect, continuing the preceding jussives. The qere *wəyihyû* may indicate consequence: 'Do not blot out … so that they may be overthrown'.

Carchemish and prior to the reading of the Scroll. Indeed, the treatment accorded Jeremiah in 20:2 may well be the precursor of a formal ban on his entering the Temple precincts (36:5).

However, another factor has been noted as of significance in the dating of Jeremiah's prophecies, and that is the nature of his message. Holladay argues that up to the destruction of the First Scroll in 604 BC there was always the possibility of repentance held out to the people, but thereafter Jeremiah's message was one of impending judgment. The message of the shattered jar is one that holds out no hope, and Jeremiah's proclamation here is exclusively that of judgment (unlike chaps. 7 and 26, or even the First Scroll itself [36:3, 7]). Holladay therefore concludes that the incident falls after 604 BC and suggests 601-600 BC as a likely period, with whatever had prevented Jeremiah from entering the Temple in 36:5 no longer being operative (1986, 1:539). While Holladay is undoubtedly correct in identifying the burning of the Scroll as a watershed in Jeremiah's ministry, it is unlikely that it was accompanied by such a sudden alteration in his preaching as he suggests. It is more probable that over a number of years during Jehoiakim's reign there was a change in the balance of Jeremiah's ministry with messages urging repentance gradually diminishing and the inevitability of judgment coming to play a dominant role, corresponding to the deteriorating attitude of the community and its rulers. On that basis a date around 605/604 BC may be allowed to stand.

The thematic link with the previous chapter is obvious in terms of the potter. But there is now one major difference: previously the clay had been still pliable and capable of being reshaped by the potter according to his plan. Now the vessel has been finished and has been baked hard in an oven. So when it is dropped, it shatters into pieces and cannot be restored (v. 10).

The use made in this section of visual symbolism is to be differentiated from magic. It does not proceed as some sort of enacted curse by which human participants seek to exert leverage over divine powers to compel them to do their bidding against their enemies. This is a vivid portrayal of what the LORD intends to do. The form chosen is selected because of the impact it would make on those present. Furthermore the action is accompanied by a spoken message which explains the symbolism.

1. Indictment in the Valley (19:1-5)

1. This is what the LORD says: 'Go[20] and buy' suggests that we do not have a straight follow-on from the visit to the potter's house in the previous chapter. However, this incident in many ways constitutes the LORD's answer to Jeremiah's plea that he intervene in judgment (18:23). Although some Hebrew manuscripts and some of the versions have 'to me', the Massoretic Text does not specify to whom the LORD spoke, though obviously it was to Jeremiah. As in 26:1 the absence of a personal reference to the prophet strongly suggests that this narrative never existed separately from what precedes it in chapter 18, so that the identity of the prophet was immediately obvious.

Jeremiah is to go again to the Hinnom valley where potters' workshops were located and buy **a clay jar from a potter** (literally 'a jar of one who forms clay', see 18:2). The fact that the jar was made of earthenware is emphasised to allow for its subsequently being broken. Perhaps there were similar containers made of metal, that could not have been smashed. 'Jar' is a specific word, denoting an expensive vessel of four to ten inches in height (10–25 cm), with a narrow neck, a heavy bulbous base, and a handle attached to neck and rim (King 1993:171-2). Such decanters were well decorated and valuable items. The Hebrew word *baqbuq* (found only here, v. 10, and 1 Kgs. 14:3) probably derives from the gurgling sound made as the contents of the vessel were poured out. Unlike chapter 18 where the clay was still soft and pliable, it has now been fired. The jar can be broken quite easily, and if anything happens to it, the fragments have to be discarded.

Unlike the incident in chapter 18, Jeremiah was also to take witnesses with him. **Take[21] along some of the elders of the people and of the priests.** The Massoretic Text repeats 'elders of' before priests so that there are clearly two groups. The first is undoubtedly the same group as 'the elders of the land' (26:17). The 'elders of the priests' are mentioned elsewhere in 2 Kgs. 19:2 and Isa. 37:2, and were the most influential and senior of the priests, who would have access to the king and be part of the controlling group in Jerusalem. We have already seen that the presence of such men has implications for the dating of this incident in terms of Jeremiah's ability to gain a hearing. That both laity and priests were in the group accompanying Jeremiah provides him not only with witnesses but with a representative assembly of the

20. An infinitive absolute, possibly functioning as an emphatic imperative (GKC §113bb).

21. 'Take' is not in the MT, but is found in the LXX. Some such supplement is undoubtedly needed to complete the sense. The Syriac has 'take with you'.

people whose fate is going to be graphically set before them.

2. He is instructed, **Go out to the Valley of Ben Hinnom.** This valley was to the south of Jerusalem, just outside the city walls, and had been the scene of pagan worship (7:31). It also was the area where the city's rubbish was dumped, and this perhaps explains the added instruction **near the entrance of the Potsherd Gate.** This gate is otherwise unknown, although the Targum identifies it with the Dung Gate, itself of uncertain location, but mentioned in Neh. 2:13; 3:13-14; 12:31. If this was the exit through which the city's rubbish was taken for dumping, then it might have had another name. Potsherds are the broken fragments of pottery vessels, and have been found on archaeological sites all over the Near East. The choice of this gate is evidently motivated here by the task that will be assigned to the prophet, that of adding to the potsherds (v. 10).

But Jeremiah has not only to perform an action; he is first commissioned to deliver a message from the LORD. **There proclaim the words which I tell you.**

3. The address is, **Say, 'Hear the word of the LORD, O kings of Judah and people of Jerusalem.'** The valley of Ben Hinnom (cf. 7:27-34) had seen many sights over the years, and it was quite natural for the prophet to remind his audience of what had gone on there in the past. Perhaps the use of the plural 'kings' arises from the fact that various kings of Judah, such as Manasseh and Ahaz, had encouraged what occurred there. Alternatively, the plural may reflect that from very early in the reign of Jehoiakim, his son, Jehoiachin, was co-regent with him (see Volume 2, Appendix §2). The elders and priests are of course there as witnesses on behalf of the nation, and there is no need to assume that the king and/or his sons were being addressed directly.

In speaking the LORD uses his full title, **This what the LORD Almighty, the God of Israel, says**. For these divine titles see on 7:3. This is what constitutes his claim on their attention and obedience; he was their covenant king. And now, through his prophet, he warns them of the judgment that will shortly ensue. **Listen! I am going to bring a disaster** (for this phrase see 11:11) **on this place that will make the ears of everyone who hears of it tingle.** The last phrase indicates an involuntary reaction of astonishment and dismay at a catastrophe of unprecedented severity (1 Sam. 3:11; 2 Kgs. 21:12). Again, 'this place' (*māqôm*, 7:3) is of ambiguous reference. While the word is sometimes used of sacred precincts and could possibly be a reference to the Temple, or even the city as a whole, the following verses (vv. 4, 6) make it clear that it is the valley that is in view.

4. The reasons for the judgment that is going to be inflicted on them are again stated so that there might be no doubt that the people had been adequately warned and that the LORD was acting with due cause. **For** (*yaʿan ʾăšer*, 'because') **they have forsaken me.** This refers to the fundamental breach of the covenant bond by refusing to show the loyalty and attachment to the LORD that was expected of them (2:13). 'They' are presumably the people of Jerusalem and not just their kings, though they gave their subjects the lead in many of their rebellious acts. There then follows a unique phrase; they have **made this a place of foreign gods**/'made this an alien place' (NKJV). The verb is the piel of the root *nākar*, 'to act or treat as foreign' (and by implication 'to profane'). The root is also found in the context of heathen worship in 5:19, 'foreign gods', and in 8:19, 'worthless foreign idols'. Their actions had effectively alienated this part of the land of promise because their worship there had made it over to other gods. The multiple possible references in 'this place' extend the condemnation to the city as a whole. It is no longer able to function as the abode of the LORD because it has been transferred to foreign ownership. They have **burned sacrifices in it to gods that neither they nor their fathers nor the kings of Judah ever knew.** For 'burned sacrifices' (*qāṭar* piel) see on 1:16; for 'gods they did not know' see on 7:9.

When Jeremiah goes on to record that **they have filled**[22] **this place with the blood of the innocent**, our understanding of the reference is partly determined by the identification of 'this place'. If in the light of the description of Manasseh's reign (2 Kgs. 21:16; 24:4) or of Jehoiakim's (22:17; cf. also 2:34; 7:6) 'this place' is taken to be the city as a whole, then acts of oppression and injustice are being condemned, with child sacrifice not being mentioned until the next verse. More probably, however, the verb form used indicates that this is explanatory of the worship just mentioned. 'This place' continues to be the valley, 'they' refers to the populace and their rulers, and the final phrase anticipates the description given in the next verse.

5. They have built[23] **the high places of Baal to burn their sons in the fire as offerings to Baal.** The 'high places' were the sacred sites used in worship of the Canaanite gods (7:31). What is said in vv. 5-6

22. *ûmālǝʾû*, 'and they filled', is an example of *waw* plus the perfect signifying a situation that is subordinate or epexegetical to that represented in the previous clause (*IBHS* §32.2.3e).

23. Again the verb, *ûbānû*, is *waw* plus perfect, further explaining the content of the preceding clause. 'Gone on building' (NRSV) takes the perfect as having an imperfective (frequentative) meaning. Again see *IBHS* §32.2.3e.

closely resembles 7:31-32a, where the practice of child sacrifice is discussed. 'Offerings' here is specifically 'burnt offerings', sacrifices that were totally consumed in the fire. 'Baal' is omitted in the LXX and some consider it textually dubious in that elsewhere such sacrifices are said to be part of the cult of Molech (32:35; Lev. 18:21; 20:2-5; 2 Kgs. 23:10). Such child sacrifice is again presented as totally outwith the intention of the LORD. **Something I did not command or mention, nor did it**[24] **enter my mind.** It is not saying that this possibility did not occur to the LORD; it obviously had, as the prohibitions of the Law attest (Lev. 18:21; Deut. 12:30; 18:10). But this was not something that the LORD had in any way desired should happen (cf. 7:31). It is possible that this emphatic dissociation from these sacrifices by the LORD indicates that the people were engaging in syncretistic worship in which they connected these offerings in some way with both Yahweh and Baal.

2. Sentence Pronounced (19:6-9)

6. Having set out the indictment to be faced by the people, the LORD proceeds to intimate the sentence that is passed on them as a consequence on their misdeeds. **So** (*lākēn*, 'therefore' of judgment) **beware, the days are coming, declares the LORD, when people will no longer call this place Topheth or the Valley of Ben Hinnom, but** (*kî 'im*, 'but rather') **the Valley of Slaughter.** 'Days are coming' looks to the certain, but as yet indefinite, future (see 7:32 which is similar to this verse) when conditions will change, generally for the better (16:14) but not here. 'This place' (not in 7:32) is specifically identified as the Valley, whose change of name will accompany its change of fortune. Topheth may have originally come from a word meaning 'hearth' or 'fireplace', but the vowels accompanying it seem to have been deliberately changed to those of the word *bošet*, 'shame', in a disparaging, contemptuous reference. The slaughter is going to come about due to enemy action, but behind that is the condemnation of the LORD.

7. The focus remains on the valley. **In this place I will ruin the plans of Judah and Jerusalem.** As the NIV footnote points out, the Hebrew word for 'ruin' (<√*bāqaq* I, 'to lay waste' a land, as in 51:2; 'to devastate') was chosen because of the resemblance in sound to the word for 'jar' (*baqbuq*) used in vv. 1 and 10. This emphasises the interconnection between the LORD's announced purpose and the action

24. The verb *ʿālətâ* has an impersonal feminine subject (see 7:31).

the prophet is ordered to carry out. 'Plans' (*'ēṣâ*, 'counsel' 18:18, 23) refers to the policy measures dictated by human wisdom. They will prove worthless because they have been formulated by those who refused to hear the LORD's word and whose advice consequently ran counter to his counsel. Some have suggested that at this point Jeremiah poured out liquid that was in the jar he had bought (Craigie et al. 1991:260). Such an enacted prophecy would have vividly shown that the plans/counsel of Jerusalem were only fit to be tipped out on the city dump. Those who have trusted such foolish counsel will then experience the consequences of their rebellion. **I will make them fall by the sword before their enemies, at the hands of those who seek their lives** (<*nepeš*, 2:34)**, and I will give their carcasses as food to the birds of the air and the beasts of the earth.** They will die in the enemy assault on them and their remains will be subject to the ultimate indignity of lying unburied as carrion for scavengers to eat (7:33).

8. I will devastate this city and make it an object of scorn; all who pass by will be appalled and will scoff because of all its wounds. For 'devastate' ('set … as devastation', *šammâ*) and 'object of scorn', see 18:16. There is a double wordplay in the verse: 'devastate' and 'be appalled' both come from the root *šāmam* (2:12), and 'object of scorn' and 'scoff' both come from the root *šāraq*, 'to whistle, hiss', perhaps even 'to shriek'. 'All her wounds', literally 'all her smitings' (in this context not 'plagues', NKJV), are the blows that she suffered at the hands of her enemies. Those who see the ruins of the land will shudder at the destruction but also mock the city because of its downfall (Lam. 2:15-16; Zeph. 2:15).

9. I will make them eat the flesh of their sons and daughters, and they will eat one another's flesh during the stress of the siege imposed on them by the enemies who seek their lives (cf. v. 7). Cannibalism was often one of the horrors of ancient sieges (2 Kgs. 6:23-31) and it had been threatened as one aspect of the curse of the broken covenant (Deut. 28:53). Lam. 2:20; 4:10 show that this did really occur in the final siege of Jerusalem. 'During the stress of the siege' is literally 'in siege and in distress', involving a wordplay between *māṣôr*, 'siege' (<√*ṣûr* I, 'to tie up, collect; enclose, besiege'), and *māṣôq*, 'hardship, suffering' (<√*ṣûq* I, hiphil, 'to bring into straits, harass, vex'), describing severe physical and psychological hardship suffered because of external force which is 'imposed' (again from √*ṣûq*).

3. The Shattered Nation (19:10-13)

10. After he had delivered the message, Jeremiah was told that he must **then break the jar while those who go with you**[25] **are watching.** The symbolic act is very much part of the message God wanted delivered. Shattering a pottery vessel to symbolise the destruction of a nation or of a person was a common piece of symbolism throughout the ancient Near East, for instance in Ps. 2:9, 'You will rule them with an iron sceptre; you will dash them to pieces like pottery.' In Egypt the practice was widespread of writing the names of persons who were considered enemies of the state (but who were not under Egyptian control—their fate would have been quite different otherwise) on pottery vessels, pronouncing a curse, and then shattering the bowls, thus seeking to induce the gods to bring a similar fate on those who had been named. When those present saw Jeremiah deliberately fragment the jar, they would have been in no doubt about the ominous significance of the act.

11. But the symbolic act is explicitly interpreted. The significant point of the symbolism is the irreparable nature of the action taken with respect to the jar, and the irreparable nature of the LORD's action against his people. **Say to them, 'This is what the LORD Almighty says: I**[26] **smash this nation and this city just as this potter's jar is smashed and cannot be repaired.'** 'By the mind of the day such an action was not understood merely as the dramatic illustration of a point, or play acting, but as the actual setting in motion of Yahweh's destroying word' (Bright 1965:133), but this ought not to be taken too far. It is the divine sentence that is significant, and the prophetic action only serves to express it vividly. However the witnesses may have mistakenly understood the action, the smashed jar was intended as a striking illustration of the great *šeber* (4:6) which it had already been determined would come upon the city. 'Cannot be repaired' uses a phrase also found in the covenant curses regarding the irreversibility of divine judgments (Deut. 28:27, 35). 'Your wound (*šeber*) is as deep as the sea. Who can heal you?' (Lam. 2:13). 'Repaired' (<√*rāpāʾ*, 'to heal') points to the desperately needed treatment that the city required after the blow of the LORD's punishment came upon her. Brown (1995:193) remarks on how illuminating the semantic ranges of the

---

25. *ʾôtāk* is the pausal form of the object marker which the MT has here through a copyist's mistake for *ʾittāk*, 'with you'.

26. 'I' is preceded by 'thus, so', not translated in the NIV. *IBHS* §39.3.4e notes that *kōh*, 'thus', points forward, 'in the following way', whereas *kākâ*, 'so' (as here), points back to what precedes, 'in the foregoing way'.

roots *šābar* ('to break') and *rāpā'/rāpâ* ('to heal') are in Jeremiah: with reference to a clay jar, smashed and repaired respectively; with reference to bone, fractured and treated; with reference to a body, sick and healed; with reference to a city, collapsed and restored.

Because the presence of corpses within the city would render it unclean (Num. 5:2-3), burials would take place outwith the city walls. But there will not be enough room even there. **They will bury the dead in Topheth until there is no more room** reflects 7:32b. Topheth will become a cemetery that is overflowing because of the massive disaster that will engulf the city.

12-13. In **'This what I will do to this place and to those who live here,' declares the LORD,** 'this' (*kēn*, 'thus, so', usually with reference to what has preceded) looks back to Jeremiah's dramatic action in v. 10, and 'this place' now clearly refers to the city. **I will make this city like Topheth** is further explained in v. 13 in terms of defilement and abandonment because of the conduct they had displayed. **The houses in Jerusalem and those of the kings of Judah will be defiled** (<√*ṭāmē'*, 3:1) **like this place, Topheth—all the houses where they burned incense on the roofs to all the starry hosts and poured out drink offerings to other gods.** The flat roofs of the houses were used for various activities (32:29; 2 Kgs. 23:12; Zeph. 1:5). King (1993:xxv) records that excavations at the Philistine city of Ashkelon destroyed by the Babylonians in 604 BC found the remains of incense burners that had been located on the roofs of houses. For 'burning incense', see on 1:16; for 'starry hosts', see on 8:2; and for 'pouring out drink offerings to other gods', see on 7:19. The scene of their rebellious practices will witness the divine judgment on them.

4. The Temple Sermon (19:14-15)

14. There is no explicit statement that Jeremiah carried out all that the LORD had commanded him to do in Topheth, but that is certainly the implication when we are told **Jeremiah then returned from Topheth, where the LORD had sent him to prophesy.** 'Returned'/'entered, came in' to the city itself, having been outside the walls. This is the first use of 'prophesy' or 'prophet' in connection with Jeremiah since chapter 1. It is used against the background of the conflict that will take place in Jerusalem between the recognised religious officials of the land and the one who has been appointed by the LORD himself, between Jeremiah and Pashhur who also claimed to prophesy (20:6).

Jeremiah boldly takes his message back to the city. He does not just deliver it to a select few outside the Potsherd Gate. We are told that he

stood in the court of the LORD's temple, the area where the people met (26:2), **and said to all the people.**

15. We are given a summary of the message Jeremiah delivered (or else what is recorded is as much as he could say before Pashhur intervened; but see 20:1). The full designation of the God in whose name he speaks (cf. v. 3) makes it clear that this is a solemn, official pronouncement: **This is what the LORD Almighty, the God of Israel, says.** The message is one of impending disaster. **Listen! I am going to bring**[27] **on this city and the villages around it** ... disaster. The phrase 'I am going to bring disaster' (v. 3; 11:11) is frequent in Jeremiah for the judgment the LORD intends to impose on the people. 'On this city and the villages around it'/'on this city and on her cities' is a puzzling phrase, which has led to various conjectures. The rendering 'villages', denoting small subsidiary settlements in the immediate environs of Jerusalem, goes back to the LXX. Alternatively, retaining *ʿîr* ('city') in its proper sense of 'fortified town', this may be seen as a natural extension of the much more common phrase 'Judah and her cities', implying here the cities that were controlled from and by Jerusalem (cf. 34:1). **Every disaster I pronounced against them** presumably refers not only to the words recorded as being spoken outside the city on this occasion, but also to what Jeremiah had been saying throughout his earlier ministry.

The reason advanced for the judgment is the continued unwillingness of the people to respond. **Because** (*kî*) **they were stiff-necked and would not listen**/'so as not to listen' **to my words** (7:26; 17:23). The people had decided to pay no attention to what was said to them, and so their spiritual intransigence in the face of the warnings of the LORD became the ultimate cause of their downfall.

5. Terror on Every Side (20:1-6)

The dismissal of Jeremiah's message and the physical abuse of the LORD's messenger by one of the top officials of the Temple hierarchy is as significant a development in the ministry of Jeremiah as King Jehoiakim's burning of the Scroll in chapter 36. The one encapsulates the rejection of the LORD and his warnings by the religious authorities of Jerusalem just as the other dramatically sums up the rejection by the political authorities. The Temple, the place of the LORD's presence,

27. The kethibh *mēbî* lacks a final *aleph*, which is supplied in the qere. The loss was perhaps due to haplography with the following *ʾel*, though the omission of the silent *aleph* is attested elsewhere (e.g. 39:16) (GKC §74k).

has become the scene of defiant repudiation of the LORD, and there can be no doubt that Jerusalem is doomed.

Pashhur's opposition to Jeremiah can be seen as an attempt by the Jerusalem establishment to silence an unwelcome, critical voice. Pashhur embodies and expresses the viewpoint of the ecclesiastical authorities who were satisfied on theological and political grounds that existing conditions in Judah should, and would, be preserved. Jeremiah was claiming that he had a divine warrant not merely to challenge the complacency of the consensus, but also to predict the overthrow of the status quo. The official point of view was that such a revolutionary voice upset the equilibrium of the nation and introduced a note of divisiveness just when internal unity was most needed in the face of massive changes and uncertainty on the international scene. Now was the time to deal with Jeremiah. He had been uttering similar predictions for years and nothing had ever come of them. In the face of a national crisis nothing must deflect the nation from supporting the powers that be.

1. The narrative of this chapter follows on from chapter 19: note 'these words' at the end of v. 1. **The priest Pashhur** had a name that was common in Jeremiah's day. A different individual is referred to in 38:1, and seals and ostraca from this period have been found with this name (King 1993:58). It is possible that the name is of Egyptian origin, meaning, 'son of Horus', an Egyptian god. He is described here as **son of Immer**, probably referring to his father, though Immer was also one of the classes of priests (1 Chron. 24:14). He held the post of **the chief officer in the temple of the LORD**. 'Chief' (*nāgîd*, a term of leadership) 'officer'/'overseer'[28] (<√*pāqad*) denotes the official whose duty it was to maintain order in the Temple precincts. Several men held this rank (2 Chron. 35:8 mentions three who served under Josiah), and Pashhur is here called the 'chief'. This made him an important figure in Jerusalem, someone who would have access to royal circles. Zephaniah, one of his successors in the post (29:26), is represented as being next in rank to the high priest (52:24, 26; see also 2 Kgs. 25:18). Pashhur **heard Jeremiah prophesying these things**, and took offence at what he was saying. Alternatively, because the verb form is ambiguous,[29] it may be that 'he heard that Jeremiah prophesied these

28. In Hebrew the nouns are in reverse order 'overseer chief' with the second noun in apposition, and particularising the designation overseer (GKC §130b).

29. Because the root *nābāʾ* is final *aleph*, the form *nibbāʾ* may be a niphal participle, 'prophesying', or else the niphal perfect, 'he prophesied'.

things' (NKJV) and having received a report of his behaviour reacted in the way he considered appropriate.

2. Pashhur had authority over conduct in the Temple. **He had Jeremiah the prophet beaten.** The hiphil verb *wayyakkeh*, 'and he beat/struck' (<√*nākâ*, a violent blow, often leading to death, v. 4), would ordinarily imply that he personally struck Jeremiah (so NKJV), and it may be that Pashhur was so overcome with anger at what he heard that he did lose control of himself. More probably the verb indicates that 'he caused him to be struck' by others, presumably 'beaten' or flogged as in Deut. 25:3. That he had legitimate authority to do so is implied by 29:26. We have here the first use of the phrase 'Jeremiah the prophet'—the title does not occur in 1–19, but is used 31 times in the book as a whole (cf. 19:14). This is often taken by critics as evidence of a later hand at work, probably trying to establish the official standing of the prophet. But we note that in terms of the narrative there is a clash here—the priest against the prophet; the priest who turns out to be himself a false prophet (v. 6) against the true prophet who might have been a priest; the officer/overseer (*pāqîd*) of the Temple of the LORD over against the one whom the LORD had appointed as overseer (<√*pāqad*, 1:10) over nations and kingdoms.

Pashhur took further action also, but it is not clear quite what is implied by **put in the stocks.** *hāpak*, the root of the Hebrew word 'stocks', conveys the notion 'to twist', and it is generally held that this was a framework that held the hands, feet, and neck so that the body was twisted and contorted into an unnatural position, causing pain. This was also done in an exposed public place to humiliate the victim. Another possibility is that it refers to a small cell ('put in the cell' NJPS) in which the offender was forced to adopt a cramped and uncomfortable posture (compare 2 Chron. 16:10 where the expression used is 'house of stocks' suggesting confinement). Whatever it was, Jeremiah was not allowed to go free but was confined **at the Upper Gate of Benjamin at the LORD's temple.** This Benjamin Gate is to be distinguished from the one in the city wall (37:13; 38:7), though both got their names because they faced north or north-west to the territory of Benjamin. This Upper Gate, so called presumably because the Temple precincts were on higher ground than the lower gate in the city wall, or alternatively because it was on higher ground above the gate in the outer court of the Temple, had been built by Jotham (2 Kgs. 15:35; 2 Chron. 20:5) between the old and new courts of the Temple. A gateway would have been an obvious place to have a guardhouse of some sort, or a place of public punishment. If this occurred early in

605 BC, Pashhur's action on this occasion might explain Jeremiah's subsequent ban from the Temple precincts (36:5).

3. The next day, when Pashhur released him from the stocks, probably because a night's detention was considered sufficient punishment, he found out that his action had not caused Jeremiah to become apologetic or to modify the message he proclaimed. Instead, speaking not out of personal spite at the injury done to him, but as the LORD's representative who had been commissioned to deliver precisely the message that he had, Jeremiah applies that message to Pashhur personally, giving him a new name. **Jeremiah said to him, 'The LORD's name for you is not Pashhur, but** (*kî 'im*, 'but rather') **Magor-Missabib.'** Giving a new name was a significant event, denoting a change of status or purpose. When it is divinely bestowed, it incorporates a prophecy of what the LORD will ensure will happen. The precise significance of this change of name has been variously understood. Holladay (1986, 1:543-4) points out that it is to be expected that the new name to be effective will be a deformation of the old one, not necessarily based on what the old one actually meant, but on the possibilities afforded by what it sounded like. Given that component 'Missabib' of the new name means 'from every side', Holladay identifies the play as based on hearing in Pashhur the Aramaic word *səḥôr*, 'surrounding' preceded by the Aramaic word *pāš*, 'fruitful'. His name will no longer sound like 'Fruitful all around', but Magor on every side. What then does *māgôr* signify? Unfortunately there are three homonymous roots *gûr* from which the noun may be derived: 'to be a resident alien', 'to attack', and 'to be afraid'. The LXX and Syriac opted for the first, presumably finding an anticipation of the Exile. The most generally accepted idea is that of an object of horror, causing others on all sides to be afraid, though Holladay suggests that all three might be involved, for, after all, Jeremiah delighted in plays on the multiple meanings of words. However, three levels of multiple association and even Aramaic word plays are stretching things too far. The context makes clear that it is the new name that is significant and that 'terror' is the dominant motif, with v. 4 opening up the possibility of a secondary reference to exile. Pashhur, epitomising the Temple establishment, is going to be a reminder to others of terror to come, and will be one surrounded by horror on all sides. The theme of 'terror round about' is found a number of times in Jeremiah (6:25; 20:3, 10; 46:5; 49:29; cf. also Ps. 31:13; Lam. 2:22). Pashhur is no longer to be fruitful on all sides, nor the one imposing pain on others, but to be its victim and the one in association with whom suffering comes to others. As his post is filled by someone else after 597 BC, and if, as his name may suggest, he came from a family which looked favourably towards Egypt, then he and those associated with him might have been singled out for deportation by the Babylonians.

4. The reason for this change of name is then explained. **For** (*kî*) **this is what the LORD says: 'I will make you a terror to yourself and to all your friends.'** 'Terror' (*māgôr*) refers to a source of terror: whenever they saw him they would remember this name and the prophecy associated with it, and, no matter what outward face they would put on the situation, they would inwardly shudder as they contemplated what it foretold. Who were these friends? 'Friends'/'those who love you' is not found elsewhere in the sense of personal friends. 'To love' (*'āhab*, 2:25; 8:2) is probably used in its covenantal sense, perhaps to indicate the priests of whom he was a leader, his colleagues who espoused the same viewpoint as him. Perhaps it even verges into 'allies' as the word can be used to denote political alliances as well.

But Pashhur is not going to witness the success of the policy he promoted. Instead he is told, **with your own eyes you will see them fall by the sword of their enemies**/'they will fall by the sword of their enemies while (*waw*-disjunctive of accompanying circumstances) your eyes are seeing ⌞it⌟' (compare Zedekiah's fate in 39:5-6). His colleagues/allies will die in battle, and he will witness it and experience the trauma. Mention is then made of Babylon for the first time in the text of the book (though not in commentaries on it!), as the foe from the north (1:13) is specifically identified. Indeed, Babylon is named four times in vv. 4-6 to emphasise that all that Jeremiah had repeated over the years was coming true. Judah is not going to enjoy peace; rather the LORD's devastating judgment is going to fall on it through the instrumentality of the king of Babylon. **I will hand all Judah over to the king of Babylon, who will carry them away** (<√*gālâ* hiphil, 'to deport, exile') **to Babylon or put them** (<√*nākâ*, 'to smite', cf. v. 2) **to the sword.** We are to read this against the background of the events of 605 BC. The presence of the victorious Babylonian army in Syria–Palestine meant that the future in view for Judah was one of deportation or death, not simply because of the success of the powerful Babylonian forces, but because of the LORD's determination to punish his rebellious people.

5. The possessions of the people will be subject to enemy depredation just as much as their persons. **I will hand over to their enemies all the wealth of this city—all its products, all its valuables and all the**

treasures of the kings of Judah. They will take it away as plunder and carry it off to Babylon. 'Wealth' (*ḥōsen*) refers to material possessions which are stored up and constitute the strength or reserves of a country. The accumulation of terms emphasises the inclusiveness of the spoil that will be taken away.

6. The focus then reverts to Pashhur personally. **And you, Pashhur, and all who live in your house will go into exile to Babylon**[30]**. There you will die and be buried, you and all your friends.** He, his family and his servants will be involved in the exile, and will die in a foreign land. This fate will also extend to include all his friends. In v. 4 his friends are said to die by the sword of their enemies, but a contradiction obviously exists only at one level of speech. A twofold fate is anticipated for them: some slaughtered; some deported. This occurred when Jerusalem under Jehoiachin was captured by the Babylonians in 597 BC, and shortly thereafter we find Zephaniah is addressed as the person in charge of the Temple (29:25-26).

To whom you have prophesied lies/'in falsehood' or 'by the Lie' (*šeqer*, 14:13) describes Pashhur, so that he must have claimed to be a prophet, one of those who had fair words to speak to Jerusalem concerning her destiny, that no harm would befall the nation. But his words had not been given him by the LORD. Rather they had originated in the deceptive belief that the LORD was irrevocably committed to the city where he had his Temple (7:4, 8).

The suffering of Jeremiah, beaten and then incarcerated, in many respects foreshadowed what was to come upon Judah and Jerusalem. The prophet's word to Pashhur is a word that embraces the community the priest represents. Though it is not brought out explicitly in the narrative, there was perhaps an element of hope that might have been discerned in the situation. Jeremiah was released from the stocks. Perhaps after the impending trauma of divine judgment there will be release for the community also. But Jeremiah's proclamation focuses on the harrowing future that awaits the disobedient city.

E. THE SHATTERED PROPHET (20:7-18)

It has been traditionally recognised that the section 20:7-18 comprises a unit within the prophecy as a whole, and that it provides biographical (if not autobiographical) insight into the inner spiritual struggles of the prophet. However, there remains no agreement as to what constitute its

30. The accusative of place is preposed for emphasis (GKC §118f).

components. In particular, there are those who argue that there are three sections in this unit expressing quite different emotions: vv. 7-10 conveying the prophet's helplessness; vv. 11-13 setting out his trust and confidence in the LORD; and vv. 14-18 again reverting to despair (see, for instance, Lundbom 1999:851-52). However, O'Connor has argued on form critical grounds that vv. 7-13 constitute a literary unit incorporating the conventional components of a psalm of individual lament (1988:66-69), and this argument is accepted below. Moreover it is reinforced if we see the prophet at a time of personal perplexity reverting to the patterns of piety in which he had been brought up. This is a man struggling in the face of intense disquiet to maintain his faith and seeking to use the spiritual remedies at his disposal to do so. It then seems appropriate to treat this Confession of Jeremiah as following the same structure as earlier ones by having two parts, vv. 7-13 and vv. 14-18 (compare 11:18–12:6 and 15:10-21).

1. From the Depths (20:7-13)

In this section Jeremiah gives voice to his perplexity using the approach of a psalm of complaint, with an introductory address to God in v. 7a, a description of the troubles in which the prophet finds himself (vv. 7b-10), a confession of confidence (v. 11), a petition for redress (v. 12), and a final expression of praise, not here the anticipated praise of the speaker but as an invocation to others to do so (v. 13). As well as this modification of the psalm of complaint, Jeremiah omits a direct expression of assurance of being heard (O'Connor 1988:67), perhaps because of the intensity of his doubt.

7. The initial address to God that is characteristic of the psalms of complaint is here simply, **O LORD.** The following words, however, present us with difficulties of translation and interpretation. **You deceived me, and I was deceived** repeats the root *pātâ* in different conjugations of the verb (first as a piel and then as a niphal). Perhaps the root originally conveyed the idea 'to be spacious, wide', and then 'to be open-minded or naive' and so it came to indicate 'to be deceived or beguiled' (BDB 834). However, it is very difficult to pin down its precise meaning in this passage, particularly taking into account the pual of the root which occurs in v. 10. The translation 'deceived' is found in the NIV text and the NASB; 'enticed' is offered by the NJPS and the NRSV, and 'duped' by the REB; and the NKJV has first 'induced' and then 'persuaded', the latter also being offered in the NIV margin in both instances.[31] It is unlikely that 'deceive' (that is, to mislead in a belief or action through the provision of false information) is the correct interpretation here because the LORD had never withheld from the prophet the sort of reception he would encounter (1:8, 17-18). 'Persuade' seems to catch the idea best. Jeremiah expressed strong reservations about his suitability and capacity (1:6), but the LORD persuaded him, that is, 'overcame his initial reluctance'. Looking back, Jeremiah is saying that if he had known what he now knew about what being the LORD's prophet entailed, he would have protested more strongly, he might even have said 'No'. It was one thing to have been warned—which he was; it was another to grasp the full extent of the experiences those warnings conveyed. In the depths of his discouragement he bemoans the fact that he permitted himself to be talked into acceptance.[32] But what else could he have done? **You overpowered me and prevailed.** 'Overpower' (<√*ḥāzaq*, 'to be strong/powerful') may be used here in a comparative sense, 'You were/are stronger than I' (cf. NKJV). It was therefore inevitable that divine force would accomplish its objective. There was no other option for Jeremiah but to submit to the command of the powerful LORD who demanded that he be his prophet. This compulsion would be similar to that which Paul described in 1 Cor. 9:16, or that which Isaiah knew when 'the LORD spoke to me with his strong hand upon me' (Isa. 8:11).

But it is the consequence of having to live with that call that is proving intolerable for the prophet. He had been told by the LORD from the beginning that it would involve facing opposition and hardening himself for what he would have to endure, but the reality had nonetheless cut deeply into him. **I am ridiculed all day long; everyone**[33] **mocks me.** 'Ridiculed' (<√*śāḥaq*, 15:17) denotes speech that makes another an object of fun. 'Mocks' (<√*lāʿag*, 'to mock, deride') refers to

31. The word is found in Exod. 22:16 with reference to sexual seduction (possibly also Judg. 14:15; 16:5). Some commentators (e.g. Bright 1965:132) find here the notion that Jeremiah has likened himself to a woman who has been assaulted and raped. But this is reading far too much into the passage. For once one can agree with Carroll, 'A disgruntled prophet complaining about divine rape … is an image too grotesque and modern to be the likeliest reading of the text' (1986:398).

32. The niphal *wāʾeppāt* may have this sense ('niphal tolerativum') of permitting an action to take place. In this construction the subject is 'half-willing' that the action occur (*IBHS* §23.4.f).

33. 'Everyone' renders Hebrew *kullōh*, where the masculine suffix would most naturally relate back to the immediately preceding noun 'day', but is generally taken by English versions to refer to some word such as *hāʿām*, 'the people', understood. For the form of the suffix, see GKC §91e.

hostile, contemptuous speech. It is in fact a participial expression which points to the prophet as having ridicule continually cast upon him (GKC §116b). This raises the problem of the connection between this passage and what preceded. It has been objected that Jeremiah does not complain about the physical violence done to his person, but rather about the verbal abuse he had suffered, and that this does not connect with Pashhur's treatment of him. But presumably putting him in the stocks (or in the cells for a night) was to expose him to the taunts of public ridicule. This was not the first time he had been mocked, but it was the culminating experience. It was something that he had been continually exposed to, and something that came from throughout the community—and it hurt!

8. The reason for the general mockery of the prophet is then stated. That it has to do with his fulfilment of his prophetic commission is brought out by the threefold use of the root *dābar*, in 'speak' and 'word' (v. 8) and 'speak' (v. 9). 'For' (*kî*) **whenever I speak, I cry out proclaiming violence and destruction.** *ḥāmās*, 'violence', may refer to destructive speech (Prov. 10:6; 16:29), but usually it refers to physical violence against an individual or to acts of destruction and pillaging against a nation. It has been suggested that if *ḥāmās* generally points to assault on life, then *šōd*, 'destruction', points to assaults on property (*NIDOTTE* 2:178). Various views have been taken of the significance of this pair here. 'Proclaim' (<√*qārā'*, 'to call out') may denote Jeremiah's preaching (2:2) or it may simply be a shout. In the latter case the words used in the shout would be 'Violence and destruction' (or it might be twofold, ' "Violence!" and "Assault!" ', as in the REB) as the cry raised by one who is suffering and calling for help (6:7; Ezek. 45:9; Isa. 59:6-7; 60:18; Amos 3:10; Hab. 1:3; 2:17). It has been suggested that this is what Jeremiah himself has to say because of the violence done to him by the people.[34] But it is more probable, as the NIV rendering suggests, that this phrase encapsulates the message of Jeremiah. God had given him only one message to proclaim: impending catastrophe as the punishment for sin. Not only does Jeremiah proclaim this message, he does so by 'crying out' (<√*zā'aq*), normally a cry for help in view of anticipated calamity, but here a cry of horror at what awaits the people.

So the word of the LORD has brought me insult and reproach all day long. Jeremiah begins this statement with 'for' (*kî*) rather than

34. Another suggestion has been that it is because of the violence done to him by the LORD, but that generally depends on the rendering of v. 7 as being 'seduced' which is alien to the context.

'so'. If the previous words are taken as his personal cry at the response given to him, then this introduces the reason why he had to cry in this way; it was because of the LORD's message which he proclaimed. Taking the previous words as the substance of his message, the 'for' is parallel to the one at the beginning of the verse and links back to v. 7, explaining what carrying out his mission meant for Jeremiah. The prophet had to face non-stop mockery because the message he proclaimed has not come true. Rather than the LORD vindicating his prophet by acting in accordance with the message he had commissioned him to deliver, nothing has happened, and Jeremiah has to face insult (*ḥerpâ*, 6:10) and reproach (*qeles*, 'scornful belittling that goes beyond conventional standards of behaviour'). For years he had been proclaiming that the land would be invaded because of its rebellion against the LORD, but nothing had happened. Little wonder that he felt the edge of their taunts. 'They keep saying to me, "Where is the word of the LORD? let it now be fulfilled"' (17:15).

9. One possible reaction to the abuse that was constantly hurled at him was to stop speaking, and he had contemplated this; indeed it would seem he had tried to carry it out for a while, but had to give up. **But if[35] I say, 'I will not mention him[36] or speak any more in his name.'** 'Say' can cover internal thought as well as external speech (3:19). 'Speak in his name' indicates Jeremiah's prophetic task as the LORD's authorised spokesman (14:14; Exod. 5:23; Deut. 18:19). The natural reaction to the intense hostility towards the prophet was for him to give up in despair at the contrary reaction to his proclamation, but that did not reckon with the power of the word that had been revealed to him. **His word[37] is in my heart like a fire, a fire shut up[38] in my bones.** 'In my heart' and 'in my bones' are both ways of saying 'within me' (23:9; Ps. 6:2), 'bones' being used in Hebrew in a figurative sense for

35. There is no word corresponding to 'if' in the Hebrew.

36. The suffix on the verb may refer to God, hence 'him' (NIV, NKJV, NASB), or to the 'word' which is mentioned in the previous and next clause, so 'it' (REB). The verb *zākar* probably only secondarily acquired its common meaning 'to remember', and here has its original force of 'to mention'.

37. For construction, cf GKC § 112kk, 159g; the perfects may also be taken as past frequentatives.

38. Literally, 'like fire burning, shut up in my bones' where 'fire' occurs only once in the Hebrew as a feminine noun qualified by the feminine form of participle 'burning'. However, 'shut up' is a masculine form. This may be an instance of the remoter adjective reverting to a masculine form (GKC §132d, *IBHS* §14.2d), or it may be 'the word' that is to be thought of as shut up.

the whole person (Ps. 35:10), and especially for the emotional aspect of one's being (*TWOT* #1673c). Jeremiah is the only Old Testament writer to compare God's word to fire (5:14; 23:29), although the metaphor is frequently used of the LORD himself. It indicates a power that is awesome and cannot be contained, a force that cannot be stopped, presumably related to a message of judgment. The prophet is so aware of the crucial nature of the message that has been given to him and its vital significance for the community to whom he is designated to bring it that this inner knowledge of God's word exerts irresistible pressure on him so that he cannot refrain from speaking. He experiences a burning inner compulsion to speak (Ps. 39:3), which leaves keeping quiet not an option that will bring relief to him in his situation. This experience clearly shows the prophet as being aware that the word he proclaimed was not something he had thought up for himself, but a reality that had been revealed to him by the LORD.

I am weary of holding it in; indeed, I cannot. Trying to resign his commission and to suppress the message he had been given to deliver was not something he was able to do. Again to give expression to his feelings he draws on his knowledge of psalms such as 'I will put a muzzle on my mouth as long as the wicked are in my presence. But when I was silent and still, not even saying anything good, my anguish increased' (Ps. 39:1-2). The fire could not be contained. 'Cannot' repeats the root found earlier in 'prevail' (v. 7). If there is a contest of wills between Jeremiah and the LORD, then it is inevitable that the LORD will prevail. Jeremiah is left exhausted and with no alternative.

10. As well as inner tension the prophet had also to contend with a campaign against him. The 'for' (*kî*) with which the verse begins may link back to vv. 7-8. This is another reason why he has to endure ridicule and mockery all the time. Alternatively, the thought may be that the prophet cannot hold the message in because he hears the whisperings of many as they mock him. **I hear many whispering, 'Terror on every side! Report him! Let's report him!'** 'Whispering' is the usual rendering of *dibbâ*, which denotes speech, whether quiet or loud, intended to defame. 'Terror on every side' is drawn from the words of Ps. 31 to describe a harassed condition, a hopeless state of terror and tension. 'For I hear the slander (*dibbâ*) of many; there is terror on every side; they conspire against me and plot to take my life' (Ps. 31:13). Jeremiah had used the same phrase earlier (6:25), but it would seem that particularly after he employed it as a name for Pashhur, it was turned on him himself to upbraid him for the non-fulfilment of his prophecies. 'Where's the truth of your prophecies then? Terror on every side, indeed: where is it?' This would seem to indicate that these words come from the period when the presence of Babylon was less obvious. (Might it be after Nebuchadnezzar's sudden departure to Babylon in August 605 BC? See Volume 2, Appendix §5.) The cry to report him to the authorities presumably means something more than to the Temple overseer. No doubt an allegation of treason was one they intended to bring before the king.

Some similar scheme also seems to be the thrust of the following words: **All my friends are waiting for me to slip, saying, 'Perhaps he will be deceived.'** 'Friends'/'every man of my peace' (Ps. 41:9) is an ironic reference to those who would greet him saying, 'Shalom! Peace!' and who might have been thought to have had his best interests at heart. O'Connor additionally suggests (1988:74) that 'man of my peace' may be Jeremiah's mocking description of the false prophets who were for ever promising everyone peace (6:14). Certainly this term does not refer to the small group of men who are known to have supported Jeremiah, but might well have pointed to his relatives and fellow villagers who were watching him[39] (Pss. 66:7; 71:10), waiting for him to make 'a false step' (REB) (*ṣelaʿ*, a move that makes one unstable and liable to fall, Pss. 35:15; 38:17). Presumably they were hoping he would say something that would allow action to be taken before the king. (One is reminded of the similar attitude of the scribes and Pharisees against Jesus, Matt. 12:10; 22:15; Mark 12:13.) 'Deceived' is the same word as v. 7, and perhaps indicates that he might be induced into saying or doing something so blatantly treacherous that he can be charged. **Then we will prevail**[40] (1:19; 15:20) **over him and take our revenge on him.** 'Prevail' is the same word as is found in v. 7. Jeremiah feels himself caught between two parties, his opponents and the LORD, both of whom want to have the final say on his life. 'Revenge' (<√*nāqam*, 5:9; 11:20) in the case of human beings can refer to the destructive and hate-filled attitude that leads to vengeful acts (Pss. 8:2; 44:16; Lam. 3:60). This sort of revenge was prohibited in Lev. 19:18.

11. Jeremiah now expresses his confidence in the LORD. The prophet is aware of his depression and dejection. He is perplexed but not yet in despair (2 Cor. 4:8), and seeks to apply the effective spiritual remedy for his condition by not being drawn into introspection but rather

39. *šōmərê*, 'waiting/watching ones', a participle denoting ongoing action; not just vigilance on one occasion, but constant scrutiny.

40. *wenûkəlâ* is a cohortative form, probably with the notion of intended purpose (GKC §108f; *IBHS* §34.5.2b).

meditating on the LORD and what he has promised to be to the man who trusts in him (17:7-8). **But** (*waw*-disjunctive) **the LORD is with me**[41] **like a mighty warrior.** 'With me' recalls the promises of 1:8, 19; 15:20 where the LORD assured him of his presence with him in times of difficulty and opposition (see also v. 13). 'Mighty'/'formidable' (*'ārîṣ*, 15:21) elsewhere refers to the wicked. It is used here to contrast those who have displayed violence against the prophet with the LORD, the divine warrior (quite a change from Jeremiah's attitude in 14:9!) who has granted the prophet his protection and whose power will show up just how puny his opponents are and who really is the dread warrior in this contest of wills.

So (*'al-kēn*, on account of the preceding) **my persecutors will stumble** (6:21) **and not prevail** (vv. 7, 10). He argues from what the LORD is and his commitment to himself so as to give himself confidence. **They will fail and be thoroughly disgraced**/'they will be thoroughly disgraced for (*kî*) they will not succeed/prosper' (<√*śākal*, 9:21). In a religious sense 'shame' refers to the painful experience of guilt because of perceived sinful conduct. **Their dishonour** (<√*kālam*, 'to be shamed, humiliated', 3:3) **will never** (*'ôlām*, 'eternity', 'perpetuity'; cf. 23:40 where a similar expression is translated 'everlasting shame that will not be forgotten') **be forgotten.** When the LORD acts to vindicate the word he has sent through Jeremiah, then he will remember what the prophet's persecutors had done and he will permanently show them up for what they are. They will experience 'disgrace of perpetuity' which would last throughout their lives (*NIDOTTE* 3:347) and beyond.

12. Again Jeremiah begins with a *waw*-disjunctive, 'but', as he turns to present his petition before God. **O LORD Almighty, you who examine the righteous and probe the heart and mind, let me see your vengeance upon them, for to you I have committed my cause.** The terms of Jeremiah's request mirror those of his first confession (11:20) except that there 'judge righteously' is found rather than 'examine (*bāḥan*, 6:27) the righteous', and 'test heart and mind' rather than 'probe (<√*rā'â*, 'to see') heart and mind'. Again 'vengeance' is not arbitrary, but a request for the LORD's rule and word to be vindicated.

13. This verse is often thought to be incongruous here in that it is an expression of praise. But this was the way that individual laments were often brought to a close in the book of Psalms, and here we have a

41. The object marker *'ôtî* is found instead of the preposition *'ittî*, cf. 19:10.

record of the experience of a man who is undergoing intense strain and is attempting to bolster his spirits. The psalmists frequently vowed that they would give praise to the LORD when he had delivered them. Perhaps it is significant, deriving from his prophetic calling and outlook, that Jeremiah addresses others. He knows he will be heard by God so that his situation will be remedied, and in the light of that he urges those who hear him: **Sing to the LORD! Give praise to the LORD!** 'For' (*kî*) **he rescues the life** (*nepeš*, 2:34) **of the needy from the hands of the wicked.** 'Rescue' (<√*nāṣal* hiphil, 1:8, 19) looks back to the LORD's initial promises to Jeremiah.

But at what stage did Jeremiah make public his inward anguish and these reflections on it? It need not be thought that this awaited the final fall of the city. It would seem that in the closing years of Jehoiakim Jeremiah was excluded from public ministry and kept a low profile in the face of royal threats. It was a time of dejection and personal turmoil. However, in these verses he does not speak as one who is still in the depths of despair, but as one who has been there. When he resumed his ministry, this was part of his presentation of himself, and of his rebuke of the people for their rejection of his message. He was in effect saying to his audience, 'You insulted and assaulted me, but you are not reckoning with the LORD being on my side'. He then urged them to rejoice in the rescue that the LORD extends to the needy (*'ebyôn*, Pss. 22:23-24; 31:8; 35:9-10, 28; 140:12-13). Although the word at one level refers to those in physical need, it has more often reference to spiritual poverty (2:34; 5:28; 22:16). The needy person is the one who is so aware of his own lack of inner resources that he waits on the LORD to provide for him. His piety and reliance on the LORD arouse the opposition of the wicked (<√*rā'a'* hiphil, 'to mistreat, act corruptly'), but that opposition is vanquished when the LORD intervenes on his behalf. The expressions used here are general, but there is no doubt that Jeremiah is identifying himself as one of the class of those who are needy. It is another matter, however, whether his opponents were prepared to identify themselves as 'the wicked'.

2. An Accursed Day (20:14-18)

Again there is a sudden switch of mood. Although Jeremiah can assuage his doubts, they do not go away. He is still plagued with the thought of the fruitlessness of his ministry. Quite apart from the problem occasioned by the change of mood (How long are we to think elapses between the verses? Is this a presentation of Jeremiah's stream of consciousness, or is it merely a literary juxtaposition?), there are problems connected with the propriety of the thought expressed. It should be noticed that Jeremiah does not address God directly, nor is there any degree of argument. It is an expression of black gloom, reminiscent in many ways of Heman's sentiment, 'the darkness is my closest friend' (Ps. 88:18). Those who have never been through an experience like that of the prophet are best advised to stand in silent sympathy rather than to act as armchair critics of the sorely tested.

14. Jeremiah wishes he had never been born. This is a stronger expression that in 15:10, but the thought is not dissimilar. He speaks ironically: the news that was brought of his birth should have been good news, but he sees it as quite the reverse. **Cursed be the day I was born!**[42] **May the day my mother bore me not be blessed!** The words remind one of Job 3:3-12, but Job is more violent and passionate. His speech is directly against God, whereas Jeremiah does not directly blame God for it, nor does he curse his parents. His thinking is too turned in on himself. One might think of the changes in Elijah's mood (1 Kgs. 19:1-3), where, having steeled himself for great effort, he subsequently relapses.

It is difficult to see how a day that has already passed may be retrospectively cursed, and it is to be noted that the verbs have to be supplied in English. The proposal that the supplement be indicative rather than optative is therefore attractive: 'Cursed ⌊was⌋ the day on which I was born, the day on which my mother gave birth to me it could never be blessed' (Craigie et al. 1991:277-279).[43] A similar declaration of the blackness and bleakness that really was involved in his birth (and therefore in his prophetic calling) may then also be found in the retrospective evaluation of them which Jeremiah sets out in the following verses.

15. In continuing to look back to the circumstances of his birth, Jeremiah gives vent to his present grief and despair by blackening that day and all connected with it. He especially thinks of the role of the messenger who conveyed the news about his birth. **Cursed be the man who brought my father the news, who made him very glad,**[44]

---

42. 'Born' and 'bore' are both forms of the root *yālad*, which occurs also in the following verse in 'is born'.

43. However, the *waw* plus perfect with which v. 16 begins expresses a wish 'May he be …', and that weakens the force of this argument.

44. This asyndetic clause falls at the end of the Hebrew sentence, and is a circumstantial verbal clause (GKC §156d). An infinitive absolute intensifies the verb *śimmŏḥāhû* (for this form see GKC §59f).

saying, 'A child[45] has been born to you—a son!' It should not be thought that there was any personal animus against whoever it was that brought his father the news. Jeremiah is saying, 'O that there had never been such a day! O that there had never been such grotesque circumstances that any should have been glad over the birth of one like me!' The stress in the verse is on how the joy over the birth of a child (cf. John 16:21), especially a son to continue the family name, was ill-founded and misconceived in the case of the Jeremiah.

16. The prophet further elaborates the scene found in the previous verses, focusing his expression on the messenger, but in reality bemoaning the facts that gave rise to the message. **May that man be like the towns the LORD overthrew without pity** (<√*nāḥam* niphal, 4:28; 18:8). **May he hear wailing in the morning, a battle cry at noon.** The reference is to the overthrow of the cities of the plain which were completely destroyed (Gen. 19:25). They had become proverbial for their wickedness and for the destruction that the LORD brought on them because of it (23:14; 49:18; Isa. 1:9-10; 13:19). Jeremiah in his despair wishes the same to be true of all connected with his birth. 'Wailing' (*zəʿāqâ*, a 'cry' of distress, 18:22) would accompany death, here probably arising from battle. But it is not a minor skirmish that Jeremiah has in mind, because what he described as having caused distress at daybreak is still going on at noon. 'Battle cry' (*terûʿâ*, 'a signal', 'a shout of defeat/victory'; 4:19) conveys one of the sounds of an army engaging in conflict (1 Sam. 4:5-6; Amos 1:14; 2:2), perhaps a signal (instrumental or vocal) for further fighting (Num. 31:6; Josh. 6:5, 20).

17. The picture then becomes even more extreme, echoing the tone of Job 3:11, 'Why did I not perish at birth, and die as I came from the womb?' **For** (*ʾăšer* used causally) **he did not kill me in the womb[46], with my mother[47] as my grave, her womb[48] enlarged for ever.**

45. The NIV rendering shows that *bēn* could indicate 'child', rather than specifically 'son' for which the word *zākār*, 'a male', had to be added.

46. *mērāḥem* 'from the womb' is in tension with the next line if it is taken to imply Jeremiah wished he had been killed after birth, but *min* may be used in the sense 'from the time that [I was in] the womb'. Alternatively, Ugaritic sources may support the meaning 'in' for *min* (*HALOT* 597).

47. The imperfect consecutive expresses facts that occur only contingently, 'My mother would be my grave' (GKC §111 l, x; *IBHS* §33.2.1a).

48. GKC §122n² notes 'womb' is here unusually a feminine noun. Note the raphe in the BHS text over the final *he*, suggesting that the ending *â* stands for *āh* before the following *he* (GKC §91e).

Jeremiah is not thinking about how this could happen, or the rightness of it. He is consumed by his own dejection as he thinks about what the messenger of v. 15 did not do. 'Enlarged for ever' is literally 'conception of everlastingness', but his life would have got no further than that because he would never have been born.

18. Job's expressions in Job 3:20-23 continue to provide a background for these utterances of profound grief. 'Days' echoes 'day' (v. 14) to form an inclusion: whether it is his birth or the rest of his life Jeremiah can only look on it in with gloom and misery. **Why did I ever[49] come out of the womb to see trouble and sorrow and to end my days in shame?** 'Trouble' (*ʿāmāl*) comes from a root that denotes 'work' or 'labour'. Though generally work is viewed positively in Scripture as part of man's privileged endowment from God (Gen. 2:15), in an environment polluted by sin it now involves toil and drudgery (Gen. 3:17-19). It is these negative overtones of misery and adversity which are emphasised in this word (Ps. 90:10; Eccl. 1:3; 2:11, 20-22). It may also be the product of wickedness (Job 3:10; 7:3; 11:16; Pss. 7:14; 10:7; Hab. 1:3). 'Sorrow' (8:18; 31:13; 45:3) refers to the inward turmoil accompanying external hardship. The prophet does not discern any signs of the prophecies he has uttered coming true. The LORD had given him a message to proclaim, but there has been no action to effectuate the word of warning. If this continues, Jeremiah sees no prospect before him other than coming to the end of his life as the prophet whose prophecies did not come true. This is his shame.

The anguished cries of Jeremiah (and of Job before him) uttered in the face of the perplexities of life are not to be condemned as unworthy. Tension, stress and frustration are part of the inevitable consequences of living in this warped and sinful world. Situations have to be faced that pose problems of severe agony, intensified in the experience of the righteous sufferer by the fact that the face of God is often hidden at such times. Some perspective on Jeremiah's experience may again be derived by considering the parallels between him and Christ. 'During the days of Jesus' life on earth, he offered up prayers and petitions with loud cries and tears to the one who could save him from death, and he was heard because of his reverent submission' (Heb. 5:7). The Gethsemane experience of Christ cuts across attempts to view and experience the suffering and horrors of this life with tranquillity. A protest and a cry for relief may properly be uttered. But the defiance of Job's spirit and the gloom of Jeremiah's despair fall short of the

49. *zeh*, 'this', 'ever', adds emphasis and urgency to the question (cf. 6:20).

reverent submission of Christ. 'My Father, if it is not possible for this cup to be taken away unless I drink it, may your will be done' (Matt. 26:42). Those who are not living near the abyss of despair are called on to be thankful; those who have been engulfed are pointed to the 'one who has been tempted in every way, just as we are—yet was without sin' and are thus encouraged to approach him for the help they need (Heb. 4:15-16).

The prophet is faced with the difficulty of seeing any way through the situation that is inherent in his office. There is no way forward that he can discern. But the book does not stop here, because the prophet did not do so either. Despite his perplexity and desperation he did not give up. The echo of the rescue provided by the LORD (v. 13) continued to resound even in the darkness of his soul.